Readings in African Popular Fiction

Reviews of
Readings in African Popular Culture
Edited by Karin Barber

'Despite the overwhelming reality of economic decline, despite unimaginable poverty, despite wars, malnutrition, disease and political instability, African cultural productivity grows apace. popular literature, oral narrative and poetry. dance, drama, music and visual art all thrive.' – Kwame Anthony Appiah, *In My Father's House*

'...likely to become the main source book for African culture studies during the next decade ... the enormous value of Readings in African Popular Culture *in bringing together such a heterogeneous selection of nuanced, well-researched, thought-provoking articles from the emerging field of African Cultural Studies.'* - David Kerr in *African Theatre in Development*

'... extraordinarily rich collection full of informative detail and excellent interpretative analysis. There is not a single piece that fails to fascinate, my own favourites include Olatande Bayo Lawuyi on 'The World of the Yoruba Taxi Driver', Achille Mbembe on Cameroonian cartoons, and Alec J. C. Pongweni on 'The Chimurenga Songs of the Zimbabwean War of Revolution'. Broader contextualising essays include Barber's own scholarly Introduction and Johannes Fabian's 1978 essay 'Popular Culture in Africa'. The volume both reprints pieces that have previously been published (mainly in journals) and offers pieces specially commissioned for this publication. The bibliographical information bronght together is worth the price of the volume alone.' – Martin Banham, Emeritus Professor of Drama and Theatre Studies in the University of Leeds, in *Leeds African Studies Bulletin*

'... a critical testament of African popular culture. I strongly recommend it to readers and libraries.' – Tanure Ojaide in *African Studies Review*

'... (one of) a rich diet of delicious scholarship on contemporary African culture...' – Graham Furniss, Reader in Hausa Cultural Studies and former Director of the Centre of African Studies, School of Oriental and African Studies, in *African Affairs*

'Readings in African Popular Culture *is an important and welcome contribution to a field where standard textbooks are hard to find... Much in the volume points to the fact that although popular culture studies may still be in its formative stage as a field, it has already over the years, generated work of great insight and mature scholarship.* Readings in African Popular Culture *is an impressive collection of inspiring and thought-provoking essays.'* – Francis B. Nyamnjoh in *Media Development*

General Editors

Karin Barber is Professor of African Cultural Anthropology and Director of the Centre of West African Studies at the University of Birmingham. She has published widely in the field of Yoruba, oral literature and popular culture. Her book *I Could Speak until Tomorrow: Oriki, Women and the Past in a Yoruba Town* has been hailed as truly innovative. She also edited the first and widely acclaimed book in this series *Readings in African Popular Culture.*

Tom Young is Head of the Department of Politics at the School of Oriental and African Studies. His special areas of interest are Mozambique and Southern Africa. He is Reviews Editor of the IAI journal *Africa* and guest-edited a special issue of *Africa* entitled 'Understanding Elections in Africa' (vol. 63/3).

Readings in ...

This series makes available to students a representative selection of the best and most exciting work in fields where standard textbooks have hitherto been lacking. Such fields may be located anywhere across the full range of Africanist humanities and social sciences, but the emphasis will be on newly emerging fields or fields that cross older disciplinary or subject boundaries. It is in these areas that the task of accessing materials is most difficult or students, because relevant works may be scattered across a wide range of periodicals in different disciplines. The aim is to bring together central, key works – classics that helped to define the field – with other significant pieces that cut across established or conventional positions from different angles. Within reasonable limits all the sub-regions of Africa will be covered in each volume.

Each Reader will include materials from journals and books, condensed or edited where appropriate. Work published or produced in Africa which, because of the widening economic divide, may otherwise be unavailable in Europe and the US, will be included wherever possible. Readers may also include new work invited and hitherto unpublished where there are significant gaps in the field or where the editors know of exciting developments that have not yet been represented in the literature.

The significance of the readings and the overall nature of the field they contribute to, will be discussed in an introductory essay in each volume. In some cases these introductory essays may be significant contributions to the development of the field in their own right; in all cases, they will provide a 'reading map' to help students explore the materials presented.

The material included will obviously vary in complexity and difficulty, but the overall level will be appropriate for second- and third-year undergraduate courses and for postgraduate courses.

Edited by STEPHANIE NEWELL

Readings in African Popular Fiction

The International African Institute in association with

INDIANA UNIVERSITY PRESS
BLOOMINGTON & INDIANAPOLIS

JAMES CURREY
OXFORD

First published in the United Kingdom by
The International African Institute
School of Oriental & African Studies
Thornhaugh Street
London WClH 0XG

in association with
James Currey Ltd
73 Botley Rd
Oxford
OX2 0BS

and in North America by
Indiana University Press
601 North Morton Street
Bloomington
Indiana 47404-3797
Tel: 1 800 842 6796
http://iupress.indiana.edu

First published 2002
1 2 3 4 5 06 05 04 03 02

British Library Cataloguing in Publication Data
Readings in African popular fiction
1. African fiction – History and criticism
I. Newell, Stephanie II. International African Institute
III. University of London. School of Oriental and African Studies
896

ISBN 0-85255-564-4 (James Currey paper)

Library of Congress Cataloging-in-Publication Data
Readings in African popular fiction / edited by Stephanie Newell
p. cm. — (Readings in ...)
Includes bibliographical references and index
ISBN 0-253-34051-9 (cloth : alk. paper)—ISBN 0-253-21510-2 (paper : alk. paper)
1. African fiction—20th century—History and criticism. 2. Popular literature—Africa—History and criticism. I. Newell, Stephanie, date
PL8010.6 .R43 2002
896—dc21

2001039665

1 2 3 4 5 07 06 05 04 03 02

Typeset in 9.5 pt Bembo by Long House Publishing Services
Printed and bound in Britain by Woolnough, Irthlingborough

Contents

3. Perspectives on Southern African Popular Fiction

Permissions

The publishers and editor are grateful to the following authors and publishers for permission to republish articles: Graham Fumiss for 'Hausa Creative Writing in the 1930s: an exploration in post-colonial theory', *Research in African Literatures* 29 (l), pp. 87–102, 1998; Brian Larkin for 'lndian Films and Nigerian Lovers: media and the creation of parallel modernities', *Africa* 67 (3), pp. 406–40; 1997; Balaraba Ramat Yakubu and her publishers for extracts from *Alhaki Kwikwiyo*, Kano: Ramat General Enterprises [1990] 1992; Pat Nwoga on behalf of the late Donatus Nwoga for 'Onitsha Market Literature', *Transition* 19, pp. 26–33, 1965; Don Dodson for 'The Role of the Publisher in Onitsha Market Literature', *Research in African Literatures* 4 (2), pp. 172–88, 1973; the University of Umea Press and Raoul Granqvist on behalf of the late Richard Bjornson for 'Writing and Popular Culture in Cameroon', in R. Granqvist (ed.), *Signs and Signals: Popular Culture in Africa*. Umea, Sweden: Acta Universitatis Umensis, pp. 19–33, 1990; Ime Ikiddeh and Heinemann Educational Publishers, a division of Reed Educational and Professional Publishing, for 'The Character of Popular Fiction in Ghana', in C. Heywood (ed.), *Perspectives on African Literature*, London: Heinemann, pp. 106–16, 1971; Raoul Granqvist for 'Storylines, Spellbinders and Heartbeats: decentring the African oral–popular discourse', in R. Granqvist (ed.), *Major Minorities: English Literatures in Transit*, Amsterdam: Rodopi, pp. 55–70, 1992; Bernth Lindfors for 'Romances for the Office Worker: Aubrey Kalitera and Malawi's white-collar reading public', in *Loaded Vehicles: Studies in African Literary Media*. Trenton, N.J.: Africa World Press, pp. 73–90, 1996; Bodil Folke Frederiksen, for '*Joe*, the Sweetest Reading in Africa: documentation and discussion of a popular magazine in Kenya', *African Languages and Cultures* 4 (2), pp. 135–55, 1991; Terry Hirst for facsimiles of cartoons, stories and covers from *Joe* magazine, 1974–76; Nici Nelson for 'Representations of Men and Women, City and Town in Kenyan Novels of the 1970s and 1980s', *African Languages and Cultures* 9 (2), pp. 145–68, 1996; Henry Chakava and East African Eduacational Publishers for excerpts from Charles Mangua, *Son of Woman*. Nairobi: East African Educational Publishers, pp.7–32, [1971] 1994; J. Roger Kurtz and Robert M. Kurtz for 'Language and Ideology in Postcolonial Kenyan Literature: the case of David Maillu's macaronic fiction', *Journal of Commonwealth Literature* 33 (1), pp. 63–73, 1998; Heko Publishers for excerpts from Ben R. Mtobwa's *Dar es Salaam Usiku* (*Dar es Salaam by Night*). Dar es Salaam: Heko Publishers, pp.16–27, [1990] 1994; Njabulo Ndebele for 'Rediscovery of the Ordinary', in *Essays on South African Literatures and Culture: Rediscovery of the Ordinary*, Manchester: Manchester University Press, pp. 41–59, [1991] 1994; Michael Chapman for 'African Popular Fiction: consideration of a category', adapted from 'Matshoba: the storyteller as teacher', in M. Chapman, *Southern African Literatures*, London and New York: Longman, pp. 372–6, 1996; Paul Gready for 'The Sophiatown Writers of the Fifties: the unreal reality of their world', *Journal of Southern African Studies* 16 (1), pp. 139–64, 1990; Dorothy Driver for '*Drum* Magazine (1951–9) and the Spatial Configurations of Gender', in K. Darian-Smith, L. Gunner and S. Nuttall (eds.), *Text, Theory, Space: Land, Literature and History in South Africa and Australia*, London: Routledge, pp. 231–42, 1996; Marie Human of the Jim Bailey Archive for permission to use facsimiles of front covers, stories, letters and advertisements from *Drum* magazine, 1952–5; Roger Field for 'La Guma's *Little Libby: the Adventures of Liberation Chabalala*', rewritten for this volume from 'Art and the Man: La Guma's Comics and Paintings', in *Critical Survey* 11 (2), pp. 45–63,1999; Blanche La Guma on behalf of the late Alex La Guma for 'Little Libby' comic strips appearing in New Age, March–November 1959; Sarah Nuttall for 'Reading Lives', adapted from 'Reading in the Lives and Writing of Black South African Women', *Journal of Southern African Studies* 20 (1), pp. 85– 98, 1994; Vivlia publishers for extracts from Gomolemo Mokae, *The Secret in my Bosom*, Florida Hills, SA: Vivlia, pp. 81–98, 1996.

Despite repeated attempts, it has not been possible to contact J. C. Anorue, author and publisher of *How to Become Rich and Avoid Poverty*, Onitsha: J. C. Brothers Bookshop (1962). Information as to his whereabouts should be sent to the editor, care of the International African Institute.

Notes on Contributors

J. C. Anorue wrote and published numerous works of 'Onitsha market literature' in the 1960s and 1970s under his various pseudonyms. His bookselling business, J. C. Brothers, remains operational to this day, reprinting classic, bestselling pamphlets from the 1960s for distribution in and around Onitsha market.

Misty Bastian is a Professor of Anthopology at Franklin and Marshall College in Lancaster, Pennsylvania, USA. She is the author of numerous articles on popular media and society in Nigeria and its diaspora as well as the co-editor with Jane L. Parpart of *Great Ideas for Teaching about Africa* (1999).

Felicitas Becker completed her Masters in Area Studies (Africa) at SOAS, University of London before embarking on her doctoral research at the University of Cambridge. Her PhD topic is the social history of southeast Tanzania, 1890–1940, and her research interests include the negotiation of gender, 'moral economies' and the ways in which villagers survive technocratic interference by the state

Richard Bjornson was Professor of Comparative Literature at Ohio State University and author of *The African Quest for Freedom and Identity: Cameroonian Writing and the National Experience* (1991), *The Picaresque Hero in European Fiction* (1977), and numerous essays and reviews on African and world literatures. At the time of his death in 1992 he was editor of *Research in African Literatures.*

William Burgess was editor of the Hausa language programmes of the BBC World Service for more than 20 years and, known more widely as Barry, or Barau Cedi, has often been heard at the microphone.

Michael Chapman is Professor of English and Dean of Human Sciences at the University of Natal, Durban. His numerous publications include *Soweto Poetry* (1982), *South African English Poetry: A Modern Perspective* (1984), *The Drum Decade: Short Stories of the 1950s* (1989) and, most recently, *Southern African Literatures* (1996).

Don Dodson is Professor of Communication and Vice Provost for Academic Affairs and University Planning at Santa Clara University in California, USA. He has published in the areas of mass communication, popular culture and African studies.

Dorothy Driver is a Professor in the English Department at the University of Cape Town, South Africa. She has published widely in the area of Southern African literature and gender studies, and her work includes studies of Olive Schreiner, Nadine Gordimer, Pauline Smith, Bessie Head and Zoë Wicomb. For 20 years she was the Bibliographer for the South African region for the *Journal of Commonwealth Literature.*

Roger Field teaches in the English Department of the University of the Westem Cape, South Africa. He is the co-editor of *Liberation Chabalala: The World of Alex La Guma* (1993). He has published articles on La Guma's travel writing, journalism, early fiction and painting. His PhD thesis takes the form of a biographical study of La Guma's South African years (1925–66).

Bodil Folke Frederiksen is Associate Professor, International Development Studies at Roskilde University in Denmark. Her background is in literature and cultural studies. She has published articles on literature, urban leisure and popular culture in East Africa.

Graham Furniss is Professor of African Literature at the School of Oriental and African Studies, University of London, and is the author of *Poetry, Prose and Popular Culture in Hausa* (1996) and *Ideology in Practice: Hausa Poetry as Exposition of Values and Viewpoints* (1994). He has also co-edited books on radio in Africa, on oral literature in Africa, and on African languages, development and the state.

Raoul Granqvist is Professor of English Literature in the Department of Modern Languages, Umeå University, Sweden. He is currently writing a book on the cultural scene in Nairobi.

Paul Gready is a lecturer in human rights at the Institute of Commonwealth Studies, University of London. His research is mainly in the fields of cultural studies and human rights in the context of political oppression, political transition and democratisation.

Ime Ikiddeh is Professor and Dean in the Faculty of Arts at the University of Uyo, Akwa Ibom State, Nigeria. His work on West African popular fiction has been widely anthologised.

J. Roger Kurtz is an associate professor of English at the State University of New York, Brockport. He is the author of *Urban Obsessions, Urban Fears: The Postcolonial Kenyan Novel* (1998).

Robert Kurtz gained his Masters degree in Linguistics from the University of Hawaii in 1994. He is currently a doctoral student in speech-language pathology at Purdue University in the United States.

Alex La Guma worked as a journalist and cartoonist on *New Age* newspaper in the 1950s and early 1960s until he was banned and placed under 24-hour house arrest. His early novels A *Walk in the Night* and *Threefold Cord* won international acclaim for their vivid descriptions of life in the South African ghettos. His political activities led to his arrest and trial along with 155 others in the infamous Treason Trial. In 1966 he went into exile in London with his family. At the time of his death in 1985, he was Chief Representative of the ANC in Cuba.

Brian Larkin is an assistant professor of Anthropology at Barnard College, Columbia University. He is the editor of 'Media and the Design for Modem Living', a symposium in *Visual Anthropology Review* and has published on cinema, technology and society in Northern Nigeria. Currently he is completing a manuscript on these topics.

Bernth Lindfors is Professor of English and African Literatures at the University of Texas at Austin, USA. He founded the journal

Research in African Literatures in 1970 and has written numerous articles on African popular literatures since then. His recent books on African verbal art forms include *Loaded Vehicles: Studies in African Literary Media* (1996), *African Textualities: Texts, Pre-texts and Contexts of African Literature* (1997) and the edited collection, *Africans on Stage* (1999).

Charles Mangua is the author of the immensely popular novel, *Son of Woman* (1971), as well as two other thrillers, *Son of Woman in Mombasa* (1986) and *A Tail in the Mouth*, both issued under the Spear Books imprint in Nairobi.

Gomolemo Mokae is a medical doctor, writer and political activist. He writes in Setswana and English, and his works have been short-listed for the M-Net Book Prize and Amstel Playwright of the Year Award. Amongst other literary honours, he has won the National Arts Coalition Prize and the African Heritage Literary Award.

Ben R. Mtobwa was born in Tanzania in 1958. He is author of a number of popular Swahili novels, including *Dar es Salaam Usiku* (1990), translated into English for the first time here.

Njabulo Ndebele has recently been appointed Vice Chancellor and Principal of the University of Cape Town. He has published poetry, fiction and critical essays on literature and culture in South Africa. He is the author of the award-winning *Fools and Other Stories* (1983), a children's book *Bonolo and the Peach Tree* (1992) and a highly influential collection of essays, *South African Literature and Culture: Rediscovery of the Ordinary* (1991). Currently he is writing a novel.

Nici Nelson is an anthropologist who worked for 25 years in Nairobi. She now lectures in the Anthropology Department of Goldsmiths College, University of London. Her research interests include African urbanisation, gender and development, gender power relations, female rural-urban migration, HIV/AIDS, the informal sector and the changing urban family in Kenya.

Stephanie Newell has recently taken up a lectureship in post-colonial literature at Trinity College, Dublin. Her research interests include West African popular literatures and the social history of literacy in Ghana. She has published several articles on these topics and her book, *Ghanaian Popular Fiction: 'Thrilling Discoveries in Conjugal Life' and Other Tales* was published in 2000.

Sarah Nuttall is a senior research fellow at the Wits Institute for Social and Economic Research (WISER), South Africa. She is the co-editor of *Text, Theory, Space: Land, Literature and History in South Africa and Australia* (1996), *Negotiating the Past: The Making of Memory in South Africa* (1998) and *Senses of Culture* (2000).

Donatus Nwoga was born in Ekwerazu, Owerri, in Eastern Nigeria. He studied English Literature at Queen's University, Belfast, and at the University College, London. He gained his PhD in West African Literature from the University of London and, until his death in 1992, was Professor of English and African Literature at the University of Nigeria, Nsukka.

Alain Ricard is a research professor with the French National Centre for Scientific Research (CNRS) of the African Studies Centre, University of Bordeaux. His field is African languages and literatures, including drama and popular literatures. He has spent many years researching and teaching in West and East Africa. Amongst his numerous publications, his most recent books include *Naissance du roman africain, Félix Couchoro* (1987), *Wole Soyinka, l'invention démocratique* (1988), *West African Popular Theatre* (1997) co-edited with Karin Barber and John Collins, and his latest book, *Ebrahim Hussein, Swahili Drama and Tanzanian Nationalism* (1998), appeared in English in Autumn 2000.

Lindy Stiebel is a senior lecturer at the University of Durban-Westville, South Africa. She has long had an interest in South African popular fiction, teaching courses on various genres to undergraduate and postgraduate students. She has published articles on gender and political struggle and her recent essay, 'Popular Literature: South Africa', appeared in *The Companion to African Literatures in English* (1999). Her PhD thesis on land and space in Rider Haggard's African romances is to be published shortly by Greenwood Press.

Balaraba Ramat Yakubu was born in the city of Kano, northern Nigeria. She trained as an adult literacy teacher working with women. Until 1984, when she left government service, she was involved with adult education, community and rural development. Her novellas are immensely popular with Hausa readers.

Acknowledgements

The editor wishes to thank Elizabeth Dunstan of the International African Institute for her immense patience and hard work in obtaining translators and securing copyright permissions for this volume. Help in tracing authors and academics also came from John Lonsdale, Roger Field, Isabel Hofmeyr, Mary Jay and Bernth Lindfors.

With great sadness we learnt of the death of Jacqueline Bardolph in 1999: she had intended to contribute an essay on East African popular literature to this volume. Richard Bjornson, whose article on Cameroonian popular literature is included here, died in 1992, as did Donatus Nwoga. It is our hope that their work will inspire future generations of African popular literature scholars.

Especial thanks go to the contributors themselves, whose enthusiasm energised this project over the three-year period of its completion.

STEPHANIE NEWELL

Introduction

The main questions are, 'Is the African going to read books and papers?' 'What kind of books does he read?' 'Who is going to write them for him?'
(Ida C. Ward, 1941: 49)

'Writing is one of the most powerful private media you can use to carry vital information across the horizons', commented one young man recently in Accra as he browsed the display of second-hand fiction and Ghanaian pamphlets laid out on the pavement before him (interview, 1999). Picking up a locally produced novelette entitled *The Price of Jealousy*, he continued, 'This book is tailored to Africans and can be used to educate one about some unavoidable circumstance. This book will open my mind on the issue of jealousy.' At this point, the bookseller intervened. Without causing any apparent annoyance to his customer, the bookseller proceeded to give away the entire plot before extracting a suitable moral from the narrative. Holding *The Price of Jealousy* before the young man, he pointed to each of the protagonists portrayed on the front cover and summarised the contents, laying particular emphasis upon the male characters. 'This writer will advise the up-and-coming youths to be of good character,' he said, perfectly tailoring his resumé to suit the young man's needs. 'Through this writer you can achieve your goals and dreams in life', he concluded, and the popular pamphlet changed hands.

Such book-selling scenes vividly display the issues to be explored in this anthology, which is concerned with local literary production and the dissemination of popular fiction within Africa, as well as with the expectations and responses of African readers to specific printed narratives.[1] The types of text being sold on West African bookstalls reveal some central features of popular literary consumption on the continent. Firstly, cost is the most significant element governing a book's 'bestselling' status in Africa, for most people cannot afford to buy full-length new texts on a regular basis; secondly, the relevance of a book to the reader's life is an important factor, for as many contributors to this volume reveal, what a popular novel teaches is considered by many African readers to be of equal importance to its entertainment value; finally, the bookseller's marketing ability is a significant factor in the success of a particular text, for fiction throughout Africa often is published on local printing presses and distributed within the locality, a process sometimes paid for and overseen by the authors themselves.

In Europe and North America, the 'African Literature' sections of bookshops are stocked with novels by Chinua Achebe, Ama Ata Aidoo, Ngugi wa Thiong'o and other authors published by international companies such as Heinemann and Macmillan. By contrast, bookshops and market book-stalls within Africa are filled to the brim with locally published and less internationally renowned authors, whose publications can be found side-by-side with the 'big names' of African literature. *Readings in African Popular Fiction* revolves around these lesser-known but locally significant writers, for Western-trained literary scholars have for too long neglected creative activity – including publishing and reading practices – *within* Africa. Lengthy extracts from primary texts, translated into English where not composed originally in English, have been reproduced in each section, and extensive quotations from comic strips and novels have been included in many of the essays. This primary material is ephemeral and difficult to obtain internationally, and the texts are included here as general 'appetisers' for students and researchers, aimed at encouraging further detailed research into particular regional literatures.[2]

In addition, this volume brings together a selection of critical perspectives on locally published fiction. Classics such as Donatus Nwoga's (1965) article on Onitsha market literature, and polemical pieces such as Njabulo Ndebele's (1991) critique of 'spectacular' literature in South Africa, are reprinted alongside newly commissioned articles on popular fiction.

Until recently, studies of African popular fiction have tended to be scattered through regional publications and international journals. Only a small sample from the enormous range of research can be included here, with discussions of printed fiction taking precedence over research into other immensely popular narrative forms such as video, song and theatre. *Readings in African Popular Fiction* aims to give readers a sense of the diversity of perspectives in the field and a sense of the shifting terms of the academic debates about popular literatures in Africa. The anglophone orientation of the book is intended to give readers a sense of 'the peculiar legacy of English literature to the post-colonial writer' in Africa (White and Couzens, 1984: 4): as we shall see, this legacy includes black American authors alongside popular novelists such as James Hadley Chase and Danielle Steel. By paying attention to this vast field of literature and including reprints of selected texts, the objective of this volume is to introduce readers to some of the rich and historically specific plots, themes and narrative styles that can be found in 'non-elite' and local language African fiction. It is only through a study of *locally published* literatures that we can begin to answer the educationist's perturbed questions, posed in the epigraph: 'Is the African going to read books and papers?' 'What kind of books does he read?' 'Who is going to write them for him?' (*op.cit.*).

I. The marketing of popular fiction

The organisation of this book according to sub-Saharan regions is designed to encourage an appreciation of the different 'zones of culture' in which African popular fiction is produced, and also to encourage inter-local comparisons between different regional literatures. The economic and infrastructural breakdown in many African countries means that newly published books tend to circulate within a relatively small regional radius.[3] New fiction often reaches only as far as local bookshops and market stalls. As a result, popular literature on the continent must be regarded from the outset as more individualistic and heterogeneous than the mass-produced titles available in Europe and North America. Circulating within the narrow geographical radius determined by the publisher's or author's mobility and marketing ability, most of these narratives occupy a *tangential* position in relation to the generic classifications applied to popular literature in the West.

In order to define what is 'popular' about local publishers' output in modern-day Africa, Western preconceptions about popular publishing therefore need to be displaced in favour of production models that are not bound to late-capitalist industrial societies. Western popular publishing is characterised by mass-production, mass-marketing and mass-consumption, and titles are sold to readers as cheap, disposable commodities, available alongside confectionary and tobacco in supermarkets and newsagents. Local publishing in Africa, on the other hand, is intricately intertwined with specific economic conditions in the various regions.

Operating in a highly competitive sector, individuals in the African 'literature industry' have to be *entrepreneurs* above all: the most successful of these book-entrepreneurs will understand the function of fiction and the ways in which local readers seek to organise their lives through popular narratives. To take the example explored by Bernth Lindfors in his essay, in the 1970s the Malawian novelist Aubrey Kalitera became frustrated at the low financial returns from his international publisher and acquired a second-hand duplicating machine, bought stencils, ran off copies of his novels and took to the streets of Blantyre, selling the publications by hand. Eager customers queued for Kalitera's didactic and 'romantic melodramas', which contained 'themes of great interest' and were designed 'solely for fellow Africans' (Lindfors, below).

Kalitera's high sales figures demonstrate a hunger for printed fiction among those East Africans who, not possessing the resources to enter bookshops and purchase 'heavy' literature, nevertheless respond positively to authors' direct sales techniques in the informal sector of the economy. As the Ghanaian author Asare Konadu says of his own popular fiction, which has sold in similar quantities to Kalitera's publications, the cardinal rule for an autonomous local publisher is that the price must be 'within reach of any person who wants to read' (Konadu, 1974). Since the mid-1960s, Konadu's 'romances and problematic stories' have undergone numerous reprints, remaining affordable to Ghanaians despite the rising price of imported paper and printing materials (*ibid.*).

Nigerian 'market literature' commands the most impressive sales figures to date. As Don Dodson and Donatus Nwoga describe in great detail in this book, market literature was produced in bulk by small printer-publishers who, in the 1950s and 1960s, bought disused newspaper presses and also imported reconditioned letterhead presses from Europe. This pamphlet literature fed the voracious book-hunger of young urban Nigerians who had recently left school having acquired a basic primary education. As in Malawi and Ghana, pamphlets were sold to newly literate locals in the markets and on the streets as well as in local bookshops. Ogali A. Ogali's *Veronica My Daughter* (1956) sold 60,000 copies within a few years of its release and remains available today on the bookstalls in Onitsha market; amongst others, *How to Speak to a Girl about Marriage* (Abiakam, 1964?) can still be purchased, as can *How to Make Friends with Girls* (Abiakam, 1971a). The pamphlet reproduced in this anthology, *How to Become Rich and Avoid Poverty* (Anorue, 1962?), was very popular with readers until the late 1980s and can be regarded as an exemplary instance of Nigerian popular literature, containing many of the major themes and formal innovations which recur in other anglophone pamphlets from West Africa in the 1960s.

Since 1990, as Brian Larkin reveals in his essay, a new and strikingly similar brand of 'market literature' has emerged in northern Nigeria. Cheap, privately published *soyayya* books circulate in large numbers around Kano and an excellent example of *soyayya* literature has been translated in Part One of this book. Like their Onitsha forebears, *soyayya* authors write about romantic love, parental interference in marriage plans and young people's relationship problems. The vital difference in northern Nigeria is that authors write in Hausa, and this choice of language clearly affects their themes, narrative style and orientation (see Larkin, below). Hausa authors liberate popular fiction from the English-language stronghold which – with the exception of the Swahili language zone in East Africa[4] – still prevails in numerous ex-British colonies.

It should be emphasised at this point that African authors' choice to write in English is not necessarily a sign of their metropolitan leanings or desire for accommodation in the Western academy. The rapid rate at which 'global' cultural forms are indigenised and imbued with specific local meanings prevents us from applying a simple centre-periphery model to popular art forms in Africa (see Furniss, below). The great question – 'For whom do I write?' – which led Ngugi (1986) to abandon the English language is problematised when one considers African popular fiction. The *Drum* writers in South Africa, for example, selected English as their medium as a gesture of defiance against the language and educational policies of the Afrikaner state (see Gready, below). In other cases, the slang-speaking gangsters of Hollywood movies provide authors with resources from which they can create new types of African cultural hero and new imaginary worlds for their readers (see Frederiksen and Mangua, below).

The impressive sales figures for locally produced African fiction contrast with the prevailing belief amongst scholars that literate school-leavers on the continent have not developed a 'reading habit' for fiction. Since the first days of the missionary journal *Books for Africa* in the early 1930s, numerous articles on indigenous publishing industries in Africa contain the lament that there is no local interest in leisure-reading. According to commentators, the problem lies in Africans' pragmatic attitudes towards the printed word: 'Africans read for utilitarian purposes, in virtual exclusion of all else', writes S. Kotei (1987: 180); rather than choosing to read fiction, 'the less educated take to textbooks to improve themselves occupationally' (Djoleto, 1985: 31). Reading for personal achievement rather than for fantasy or pleasure, Africans have what T. Gyedu terms a 'textbook mentality', selecting educational texts in the hope of acquiring knowledge for social or professional advancement (1976: 69–75). 'Less than one per cent of those who read, do so for reasons other than formal preparation for an examination, or a career', Solomon Unoh says of Nigerian readers (1993: 108). Likewise, the Ghanaian author Isaac Ephson dismisses 'the average Ghanaian' as being 'interested in beer, dances, frivolous life; they are not interested so much in reading, except those at school, to whom certain textbooks have been recommended' (1974). Even if there were a willing readership, these commentators continue, in all corners of the continent high production costs have created a 'book famine' in all but the African textbook sector (Crowder, 1986; Walsh, 1991).

The commercial success of popular magazines such as *Joe* in Kenya and *Drum* in South Africa and the prosperity achieved by local author-publishers such as Aubrey Kalitera in Malawi and Asare Konadu in Ghana, undermines the belief that Africans are unwilling and unable to buy fiction. Many of the scholars cited above have ignored the submerged but vibrant 'informal' sector of the market. In addition, commentators' laments seem to derive from a belief, firstly, that local publications should be *non-didactic* and at one remove from the ethical debates taking place in African societies; secondly, that leisure-reading should be produced by *national* publishing houses; and thirdly, that fiction should create for the reader a wholly *imaginary* world, set apart from reality. According to these preconceptions, creative writing is not 'fiction' if it presents scenarios that are edifying and educational. As many of the essays included in this book will reveal, however, locally published African novels and magazines are marketed very often in a way that emphasises their status as 'problem-solving' texts, as quasi-fictions which are relevant and didactic and thoroughly located in socio-political contexts.

Swahili novels in Kenya often end with a proverb or maxim, and Tanzanian Swahili novels often 'carry their culprits to Ujamaa Villages or National Service Camps' (Kezilahabi, 1980). Sales figures can soar when the covers of texts promise that 'this booklet ... is very useful to husbands and wives because it contains almost every advice necessary to help them not to misunderstand themselves after marriage' (Abiakam, 1971a: preface); or, 'this story will excite any couple involved in the endless search for harmony in marriage' (Nwoye, 1993: back cover.). The back cover of David Maillu's self-published *Kadosa* (1975) declares, 'Maillu tells a scaring but meaningfully loaded story: a philosophical-cum-social comment'. Charles Mangua's *A Tail in the Mouth* (1974) is described on the back cover as being full of 'slapstick farce and sex' alongside 'an altogether deeper dimension': upon reaching the end of the narrative, readers will find that they 'have been not only highly entertained but also given a tantalizing glimpse of the limits of the new morality which governs behaviour and values in Africa today'. In this manner, authors and publishers alike appeal to readers' personal interests, emphasising the moral knowledge to be gleaned from reading and, as several contributors to this book reveal, large numbers of African readers expect fiction to fulfil precisely this didactic function.

Critics are not necessarily wrong in their belief that African readers are utilitarian in their attitude towards reading material; however, given the above examples from popular novels across the continent, critics are perhaps misguided in presuming that African readers will not purchase fiction because fiction is not 'educational'. As many novelists declare in their books and as many local readers agree, African popular fiction must be included among the range of 'educational' texts that a reader will purchase.

Not all commentators on the publishing industry in Africa support the idea that there is a 'book famine'. A separate strand of research into indigenous literature acknowledges that large quantities of popular fiction – including vernacular novels – can be purchased locally from 'author-cum-publisher-cum-printer-cum-bookseller pioneers' (Ike, 1993: 137). Often this local production is disparaged or condemned, as Felicitas Becker suggests in the introduction to her translation of the popular Swahili novel, *Dar es Salaam Usiku* (see below). The distinction between 'serious' literature and 'trash' is upheld by many Swahili-speaking scholars who are keen to protect the high quality (and commitment to political conscientisation) of literature produced within their language-zone.

Popular Hausa literature in northern Nigeria has elicited similar responses from literary scholars. Concerned about the 'recent upsurge' in *soyayya* books, Sani Abba and Jibril Ibrahim complain that:

> The writing is conceived and executed in a rush. The author is usually the printer/publisher ... these young authors, equipped with relatively low educational standards, are putting to shame the serious Hausa literary establishment. (Abba and Ibrahim, 1995: 3, 5)[5]

Rather than putting 'serious' literature to shame, however, these popular vernacular novelists from East and West Africa can be seen to be 'filling a vacuum that conventional publishers have allowed to grow' (Dekutsey, 1993: 72). Many local author-publishers operate outside conventional book-selling networks, complementing rather than competing with their national and multinational rivals. Employing street-vendors and office workers, or visiting head teachers personally with copies of their novels and textbooks, these authors have adopted unofficial channels to promote their publications. Often, their 'agents' take the product directly to the customer rather than trusting the customer to visit a bookshop: 'we take the books to them', Asare Konadu commented in an interview (1974). Starting from nothing and entering a fragile leisure-reading market, many of these local author-publishers have had nerves of steel, for their survival or failure has depended upon their own marketing skills.

The marketing of African popular fiction remains easier for multinational companies and their subsidiaries than for autonomous sub-national publishers. Macmillan, Heinemann and Longman operate on economies of scale and have the advantage of established, extensive book distribution channels in Africa. In the last twenty years, Macmillan has re-styled its approach to the African non-textbook market, developing collaborative projects that are coordinated from its headquarters in Britain. Perceiving a gap in the literary market-place in the late 1970s, the company commissioned local authors to write thrillers, detective stories and romances for the new *Pacesetters* series. Not to be outdone, Longman followed swiftly with its *Drumbeat* series and Heinemann with its *Heartbeats* series. The *Pacesetters* are heavily edited, written in compliance with the publisher's generic specifications, printed and bound in Hong Kong, exported to African bookshops and advertised in Macmillan Education's glossy catalogues which are produced in Oxford, Britain. The company has utilised its distribution networks in Africa to promote the series on a large scale and the titles are immensely popular with young readers. Such a commissioning, editing and mass-marketing style makes the *Pacesetters* series thoroughly 'popular', but only in the Western sense of the term.

Few contemporary indigenous publishers have the capital to commission or mass-market series of generic novels and few African readers have the resources to purchase popular literature on a regular basis. Small print-runs of romances, detective stories and marriage guidance pamphlets often are payed for by authors-turned-publishers, or published by small companies with no in-house stylesheets to specify the content or structure of particular genres (see Ricard and Bjornson, below). In fact, unlike Macmillan's *Pacesetters*, the locally published 'popular' text in Africa can be defined as that which circulates *outside* the very structures that characterise popular literary production in late-capitalist economies. Operating outside official publishing channels, local creative writers and publishers have adopted the role of artisans, as in pre-capitalist Europe, crafting books for a limited market and relying upon external support rather than producing potentially profitable commodities for mass-circulation to pre-arranged outlets (see Radway, 1987: 20–45).

The absence of editorial input into locally published literature has caused concern about the diminishing moral and grammatical quality of books entering people's homes and schools. Euphrase Kezilahabi expresses concerns about the effect of violent Swahili literature on the 'common man', defined as a new class 'armed with the most dangerous weapon of half-education' and 'now looming threateningly across the continent', rejecting agricultural work and aspiring towards material wealth (1980: 78). In a similar vein, Jibril Aminu complains that:

> There is no shortage, and there never was, of junk books and magazines, some of which are probably better banned from the shelves of booksellers and libraries since they are motivated solely and simply by financial reasons ... The authors of these books, if they can be so called, do not bother to check the grammar, let alone the facts and the logic. (1993: xxxvi)

This absence of official intervention can be viewed in a positive light, however, for it has lent a certain freedom of creative movement to those authors and publishers who possess sufficient finances and marketing skills to release non-textbooks into the African literary market-place. Locally published literature represents, as Per Gedin says, 'a quite different kind of new African writing, which shows an independence of the ... European-oriented writing and which may become much more of a starting point for an autonomous literary development' (Gedin, 1984: 104). The 'starting-point' anticipated by Gedin can be located many decades ago. Local authorship has been stimulated by the keen local readership, by the book-vendors who touted (and continue to tout) texts in the informal sector, by the literary competitions set up in the 1930s (see Furniss, below), and by the multitudes of small publishing houses that have sprung up and vanished throughout the continent since Independence.

II. 'Popular' fiction: a category for Africa?

Book production and consumption patterns in Africa differ greatly from those of late capitalist economies: the term 'popular' therefore requires re-settling if it is to retain validity in modern African contexts. As we have seen, novels tend to be treated as luxury items in Africa, perhaps purchased regularly by the salaried elite but regarded as scarce commodities by most clerical and informal sector workers. At most, literate low-income workers might buy novelettes, newspapers, religious pamphlets, or weekly popular magazines, and some readers are loathe to enter the formal space of bookshops. These factors have to be taken into consideration in discussions of popular printed fiction in Africa and account for the large number of articles in this volume which focus upon 'small texts' – fiction and cartoons found in magazines and pamphlets – from diverse African countries.

In the West, popular genres are intimately connected with the development of large publishing conglomerates, which have an 'entrepreneurial vision of the book as an endlessly replicable commodity' (Radway, 1987: 23). Cultural commentators in the West tend to take for granted mass-production and mass-consumption when analysing popular genres: indeed, discussions of 'fan culture' depend upon the concept of mass audiences who view the popular artefact as a commodity to be purchased on a regular basis (see de Certeau, 1984). The vast majority of African readers, on the other hand, are excluded from definitions of 'popular fiction' which depend upon the idea of mass-consumption, for most printed literature costs too much for the non-elite reading public to buy regularly. Given these fundamental structural and economic differences, popular publications in Africa cannot be seen to inherit and 'mimic' the genres marketed by Western publishers. Frequently produced *outside* the genre-determining relationships that characterise Western popular fiction, African texts are less rigid in their adherence to literary formulas and in consequence, as many contributors to this book reveal, local authors remain receptive to wider varieties of intertextual currents (see e.g., Bastian and Stiebel, below).

Considering the lack of mass-marketing and the dynamic nature of literary genres on the continent, in what sense is the word 'popular' appropriate to describe locally published fiction in Africa? 'Popular' is a widely used but ill-defined term in studies of African fiction, but it is also immensely useful in demarcating a field of African creativity which is non-elite, unofficial and urban. Specifically 'popular' elements cannot, however, be quarried and quantified from local publications. As Karin Barber has argued in her seminal essay, 'Popular Arts in Africa' (1987) and in her introduction to the first of this series, *Readings in African Popular Culture* (1997), the definitive feature of African popular art forms is their lack of formal and stylistic regulation from 'outside'. This is an important point, explaining the problems that arise when one tries to pin down and label popular literary production on the continent.

Any effort to define popular fiction in Africa must account for the manner in which local practitioners constantly absorb new cultural currents, poach upon so-called 'traditional' and 'elite' discourses, adapt and innovate and operate outside of 'official' art forms. Many African popular art forms are evasive and difficult to classify. Recognising this, Barber deliberately postpones a final definition of the term 'popular' until she has allowed it to accrue a number of competing, cross-cutting meanings deriving from sociological, historical, aesthetic, anthropological and economic debates (1997: 3–5). In Africa at least, she suggests, 'popular' can never designate a clearly bounded category; in order to survive in the face of appropriation by official discourses, popular culture must be open-ended and slippery (*ibid.*).

Barber's argument encompasses African popular culture generally. We can usefully apply her framework to popular printed fiction on the continent. Her emphasis upon innovation allows us to appreciate local authors' experiments with global genres such as the romance. Additionally, her emphasis upon fluidity helps us to perceive the manner in which non-elite Africans participate in art forms that are forever changing and cannot, for that reason, easily be appropriated by existing power elites. When dominant Western genres such as the romance and thriller are put into operation by writers who are situated geographically and economically *outside* the centres of mass-production, then the ideologies commonly associated with the genres are detached. Thus, as several contributors to this volume demonstrate, when writers who are neither mainstream nor canonical take on popular genres such as the romance, the genre becomes an 'uprising' form, capable of conveying messages about gender and society which are saturated with new local meanings (see Larkin and Bastian, below).

It is not easy to catalogue the 'popular' qualities of fiction in Africa. Specific readerships are not necessarily implied by particular genres, as they are in the West: for example, men read *Harlequin* and *Mills and Boon* romances in West Africa in order to learn about women's behaviour, and Ghana boasts a long tradition of male romance writers dating back to the mid-1940s (see Newell, 2000). In addition, supposedly 'elite' novels such as Chinua Achebe's *Things Fall Apart* produce responses amongst African readers which are rooted in 'popular' local conceptions of gender roles, the self and society (*ibid.*). As these examples imply, it is necessary to focus upon African *readerships* just as much as upon texts if we wish to describe the 'popular' qualities of African fiction.

Bernth Lindfors (1991) makes the broad proposal that 'Any work that seeks to communicate an African perspective to a large audience in a style that can be readily apprehended and appreciated could legitimately be called a piece of African popular literature'

(p. 2). What can be stated at this stage, then, is that 'popular fiction' in Africa describes those types of narrative which never fail to generate debate amongst readers on moral and behavioural issues. In terms of their appeal, such narratives are popular in the sense of being in demand by African *readers*; in terms of their *content*, these texts are popular in the sense of containing ubiquitous character types and plots, reworked with each re-usage by authors.

III. Popular plots and character types

In the quest for original, realistic material, Western-trained literary critics have tended to neglect or disparage those African novels containing 'soapy romances and gruesome thrillers' and references to American popular culture (Ehling, 1990: 151).[6] In one typical discussion of lingering plots and 'derivative' character types, Rose Umelo (1983), the then commissioning editor for Macmillan in Nigeria, catalogues the 'stock situations and cardboard characters' which she encounters repeatedly in manuscripts submitted by Nigerian authors (p. 4). Her list includes the most resilient West African templates, many of which are discussed in this volume in the essays by Ime Ikiddeh, Donatus Nwoga and Brian Larkin: stories of young beauties forced by greedy parents into arranged marriages with abusive old men; barren women who give birth miraculously, only to pamper and spoil the child, who becomes a gun-wielding gangster or a whore in Lagos; pregnant schoolgirls whose lives end in prostitution or destitution (p. 2). Frustrated by the gender stereotypes and the frequent but 'inappropriate' use of motifs from foreign popular novels, Umelo leaves her audience in no doubt as to which types of narrative will result in the rejection of a manuscript (p. 2).

In a similar though more politically sensitive vein, Njabulo Ndebele's essay (reproduced below) on 'spectacular' literature in apartheid South Africa expresses profound concerns about the way in which popular authors set up simple binary oppositions between 'good' and 'bad' characters. Ndebele makes a close reading of Alex la Guma's short story, 'Coffee for the Road' and develops from it a catalogue of the 'spectacular' representations which typified South African political narratives in the late 1950s and early 1960s. At this time, Ndebele argues, black authors started to operate according to an aesthetic of 'recognition, understanding, historical documentation and indictment'. The latter term in particular dictated the glaring morality which popular authors instilled into their fictional characters, and in Ndebele's view this type of writing inhibited the development of stories about ordinary people's feelings and experiences.

An important question not asked by Umelo and the many other critics who are disappointed with typecasting in African popular fiction relates to the *function* of these character types and plots, and the ways in which they are designed to inspire particular modes of moral commentary amongst readers. Characters such as the good-time girl, the barren woman and the gangster surface recurrently in African popular fiction and comic strips throughout the continent. These characters take the form of 'old familiars', being ethical figures which readers will recognise and judge using existing repertoires of knowledge. A far more productive and culturally entrenched process is underway than the parrot-like 'imitation' of admired foreign models which Umelo and others criticise. As Richard Bjornson argues for Cameroon in this volume, and as Michael Chapman argues for South Africa, many African readers 'expect to extract a moral from such writing, and these authors give them every opportunity to do so, although the principal attraction of their work is its promise of a vicarious escape from everyday reality' (Bjornson, below).

Recent cross-cultural studies of popular fiction in non-Western locations contain refreshing alternatives to the anxious dismissals that have characterised studies of African popular literatures. Brian Larkin, whose essay appears in this book, compares the Indian romantic movies showing in northern Nigeria with the Hausa language *soyayya* books produced by local youths: he concludes that local romance writers occupy *different positions* from metropolitan romance writers in relation to the dominant 'global' genre. As with the gangsters of Sophiatown who forged their identities from Hollywood references (see Gready, below), Larkin finds that romantic narratives from India are used as 'a mode of social enquiry' in Hausa areas of Nigeria, borrowed in order to explore 'the limits of accepted Hausa attitudes to love and sexuality'. Local authors thus adapt their chosen genres to suit their own purposes.

Love stories published in diverse African locations convey young people's fights for their chosen marriage partners, as youths protest in the name of Love against betrothals arranged by their parents. Many plots revolve around this formula and common character types emerge from it (see Nwoga and Ricard, below). The common denominator linking these different regional literatures is that the romance formula serves to license attitudes and opinions which are challenging to established social practices such as bride price, arranged marriage and polygyny (see also Bastian, below). Through the romance's intense, personalised commitment to individuals, as well as its promotion of young female characters and their right to marry self-selected partners, authors can express criticisms and protests that might otherwise have been censored by their societies. As Nwoga and Larkin reveal in relation to Nigerian popular literature, in fiction published since the 1950s African writers with diverse political interests and agendas employ the language of romantic love to voice ideals about the social rights and duties of individuals. These ideals may be egalitarian or conservative in their gender perspective: often relating to domesticity and to women's status within marriage, these ideals are of course personal to the authors, but they are also deeply collective, promoting alternative social models for the community at large.

Just as many proverbs and folktales are incomprehensible to those without detailed contextual knowledge and experience of the society in which they are produced, so too the 'deep' meanings that attach to African popular plots, genres and character types require a great deal of contextualisation in order to be understood. Graham Furniss points out in this volume that written narratives which appear to be inconclusive and unstructured may in fact belong to a world governed by nuanced conventions of its own, a world remote from European aesthetic standards but structured by established local literary models. Michael Chapman offers a similar argument for South Africa in this volume, as does Raoul Granqvist in his general discussion of African popular fiction. These scholars agree that locally produced African novels should not be assessed as if they were realist texts within the European literary tradition. When local novelists use spectacular storylines, hyperbolic language and instantly recognisable character types, they set up affective devices, designed to create ethical debates among their readers (Chapman, below). In the manner of oral storytellers, Chapman suggests, South African popular authors such as Mtutuzeli Matshoba will 'pad' their narratives with episodes, 'digressions and exemplary incidents', deploying narrative strategies and residual plots drawn from an established, non-realist folktale tradition. Supporting this position with East African examples, Granqvist adds that 'the popular story tends to be oral by origin'. African popular fiction should therefore be labelled 'oral-popular discourse' in order to accentuate its differences from mass-produced popular genres in the West (Granqvist, below). In refusing the conventional divide between oral and written discourses, traditional and popular genres, Furniss, Chapman and Granqvist remain sensitive to the complex borrowings and negotiations with established forms that take place at a local level in Africa.

Not all contributors to this book agree that African folktales provide models for popular fiction: for instance, in South Africa during the Apartheid era, racy slang and foreign popular fiction provided African authors and readers with non-local models and escape-routes from the gruelling reality of political oppression (see Nuttall, below). Despite these areas of divergence, all of the contributors are attentive to cultural and contextual issues, remaining attuned to the *embeddedness* of fictional characters in Africa's diverse cultural and social histories: the prostitutes in Kenyan fiction described here by Nici Nelson diverge from the prostitutes who parade through male-authored fiction in Cameroon (see Bjornson and Ricard, below); the heroic gangster figures appearing in South Africa's *Drum* magazine in the 1950s symbolise vastly different sets of political and economic concerns to the gangsters that have surfaced recently in Nigerian popular fiction (see Gready and Driver, below); many of the cartoon characters in South African comic strips of the late 1950s are inspired by North American models but refer to Treason Trialists and political campaigns of the period (Field, below).

What is shared between all of the essays collected here is the sense that popular fiction is an *urban* phenomenon, conveying urban aspirations and fantasies, and assisting readers in their efforts to come to terms with crime and poverty and urban living conditions generally. Contributors agree that African popular fiction expresses, mediates and symbolically resolves 'common' people's experiences of post-colonial class society and urbanisation. In her essay on popular magazine fiction in Kenya, Bodil Folke Frederiksen comments that, to the average urban East African 'an ordinary, comfortable everyday life, free of misery and harassment is the adventure': such comfortable lives, she argues, are transferred to popular narratives in the form of 'realistic fantasies, meticulously describing the lives of the fabulously rich'. Positioned *without*, readers get a glimpse of the world of richly furnished houses filled with imported consumer goods. Concurring with Frederiksen, many other contributors assume the 'common' urban African to be the primary reader of popular literature, and in much of the fiction discussed in this book, explanations and solutions are proposed to the problem of ordinary people's exclusion from elite society.

IV. Good-time girls and sugar-daddies

Throughout the continent, popular novelists seem to be responding to Africa's pervasive economic crises through their protagonists and plots. Authors are engaged in the construction of symbolic economies, converting and transforming real economic relationships into symbolic ones and helping to generate explanations of (mis)fortune that will touch the experiences of their readers. Through such narratives, readers can start to rationalise their own poverty, for in a large number of novels wealthy characters are morally punished for their misappropriation of wealth. Plots thus offer symbolic resolutions to the everyday problems of non-elite readers.

One particular trajectory of this symbolic economy can be found in the stories of good-time girls and their sugar-daddies which proliferate in popular fiction across the continent. Gender seems to be an essential, primary lens through which popular novelists filter their interpretations of urban society at large. As local economies were hit in the late 1970s and early 1980s by successive oil crises and the global recession, so popular perceptions of economic inequalities found expression through new sexual stereotypes. In Kenyan literature in the 1970s, for example, 'it seemed that the novelists who were not writing about the Emergency and "Mau Mau" were all concerned with prostitutes' (Bardolph, 1989).[7] In Nigeria in the early 1980s, negative public feeling about young women's sexuality led to the production of the image of the sugar-daddy with his young, educated girlfriend. A 'syndrome' was diagnosed at this time, finding ample expression in local fiction: 'sugar-daddy syndrome' was a popular term, wielded in the media to criticise unmarried women's apparent greed for material rewards from workplace managers and corrupt officials (Ekekwe, 1983–4: 24). Women were assumed at this time to be using their 'bottom power' in order to operate as 'import smugglers' and 'fashion pace-setters in the urban areas' (p. 25).

Authors' criticisms of corruption and inequality in postcolonial Africa are frequently mediated by the female character types constructed within texts, and popular novels are fascinating for their nuanced, detailed revelations of popular attitudes towards women. The socially real figure of the good-time girl is greatly embellished in the process of her fictionalisation by African popular novelists. Recurring in local novels, she gives voice to the consumer imperative that, as one Nigerian heroine states, 'Our country is now flowing with petrol-naira and we must spend it' (Adebanjo, 1987: 14). The 'we' invoked by this particular good-time girl refers to a group of individualists, each competing with the other for access, by whatever means, to what is popularly labelled a 'slice of the national cake'.

A hoarder and private accumulator *par excellence*, the good-time girl is an *explanatory* figure in African popular fiction: particularly in male-authored fiction, this character is presented as a terrifyingly impressive 'shebeen queen' or 'highlife queen' (see Driver, below). In numerous narratives written since the 1970s, the story of a beautiful young woman's misuse of her sexuality forms the focal point for the author's condemnation of 'the craze for material wealth' in the wider polity. Authors return repeatedly to the character of the sexually self-determining woman who moves freely around the city, and writers rehearse similar ideological scripts in which materialistic good-time girls grab men's money before being punished (see Nelson, below). Writing in and about sprawling urban environments where strangers interact daily, contemporary novelists offer more than the symptoms of urban anxiety. They also teach *interpretive strategies* to readers, ways of reading the bodily signals emitted by others.

Many authors – the majority of whom live and work in African cities – focus upon the differences between rural and urban moralities, and so-called 'elite' authors often appear to be just as concerned with this theme as their 'popular' colleagues (see e.g., Ngugi, 1977). Their narratives reveal the moral contrasts between the village and the city, and the intriguing feature of *both* locations is that they are symbolised through female characters. In contemporary East African novels, as Nici Nelson shows in this volume, the rural mother-figure epitomises an alternative, morally pure order, containing many of the ideals that cannot be realised in fictional cities; by contrast, the urban good-time girl and prostitute symbolise the corruption of the postcolonial nation state (see also Stratton, 1994). Again and again, contemporary male authors displace good-time girls from the cities, returning them to idealised village locations in which the evil effects of urban life upon women can be purged.

Attitudes towards the city have changed across time and also differ according to the region in which popular fiction is produced. For example, unlike the Kenyan fiction produced in the 1950s and 1960s, in which rural areas are represented as 'tribal', backward places while the cities are filled with the excitements of modernity, Nici Nelson shows in her chapter how, in contemporary East African narratives, authors reinstate the village with its structures of vertical, patriarchal authority. City women are being sent back to their villages by narrators, to be controlled by fathers and elders (for West African examples, see Fresco, 1982). In much contemporary African writing the village is redeemed as a utopian setting in which local debates about community values, paternal authority, honest labour and female submission are staged.

What economic and political factors have induced this ideological shift away from the city in African popular fiction? Detailed attention to different countries will of course yield different explanations, and contextual, historical studies of popular fiction in the various regions of the continent will yield interesting explanations for the contrasts. The manner in which the city, the cash economy, land and marriage are thematised in early Kenyan fiction is unlikely to overlap with early Nigerian fiction, given the vastly different experience of colonisation in settler colonies and in commercial trading colonies.

What these shifting representations of the city and the village do make visible are the changing popular interpretations of socioeconomic trends in different parts of Africa. In particular, the village to which so many fictional good-time girls are returned can be read as a symbolic space in which authors are attempting to *resolve* the socioeconomic problems and contradictions encountered by young men in urban areas. It might be argued that male authors' representations stem from the threat of women's increasing financial autonomy as they move around African towns without male supervision. A kind of balancing act is in operation: rural settings have been idealised in many contemporary local novels to the same degree that economic conditions for the ordinary worker have degenerated in the cities. Such an argument is worth considering, especially in South Africa where Apartheid and the banning of market activities have until recently limited women's room for economic manoeuvre. In the urban popular imagination, then, as violence and competition for resources increase in the city, so village settings become more utopian, providing readers with ideological refuges from the pressures of urban life.

As both Nici Nelson and Dorothy Driver make clear in their essays, it is over-simplistic to suggest that the negative representations of unmarried urban women in printed fiction stem solely from the 'economic threat' posed by independent women in the non-fictional urban world. Any direct connection between the 'fictional' and the 'real' might be persuasive to readers – numerous West African readers praise the 'true-to-life' quality of novels depicting promiscuous women who use their bodies to enrich themselves – but it has to be moderated by the fact that women's economic independence from men is considered to be normal in many parts of Africa. A woman's ability to be financially self-determining and thus capable of contributing to the family pot is, in many instances, a central consideration in judgements of her suitability as a marriage partner. Indeed, in West Africa where there is a centuries-old tradition of women's 'own account' activities, women engage in trade even in Islamic areas where *purdah* tends to restrict their physical mobility (see Coles and Mack, 1991). In many areas of Africa, successful female entrepreneurs acquire property and titles; and poorer women throughout the continent can maximise their incomes by utilising established child-fostering networks, creating more time for their trading activities by redistributing the burden of child-care among their female relatives (see Adepoju and Oppong, 1994).

The negative representations of emancipated women in much popular fiction cannot easily be linked with 'real' women's economic independence. The vital factor giving rise to authors' increasingly negative representations of women seems to relate to women's marital status. It is *unmarried* women who inspire the fiercest criticism within male-authored popular fiction, for they are productive but not reproductive, self-centred rather than giving up their wombs – the centre of the self – to the continuation of the lineage. As Nici Nelson argues for popular Kenyan novels, 'sometimes the vilification of urban women as wicked and corrupt reaches such a pitch that it almost seems as if a magical power to destroy men is attributed to urban women'. This comment reveals that sociological factors alone cannot serve to explain local novelists' potent imagery of unmarried young women as socially destructive forces who cause havoc to the best-laid marriage plans.

By invoking the character of the good-time girl or the ideal wife in their narratives, African popular novelists are employing an *ideological device* to reinforce their value judgements about appropriate female behaviour at particular historical moments. Dense networks of local, culturally specific ideological concerns are instilled into the figure of the young, urban woman who has removed herself from the household sphere. Novels often contain moral warnings against such women's deceitful behaviour and solutions are offered to young readers to help them 'deal with the chronic societal ill [of] female waywardness and the love for transient values' (Adewoye, 1993: n.p.). This continent-wide representation of femininity might be interpreted as indicating the rise to power of a solid, 'hegemonic masculine ideology' (see Connell, 1987: 184–5). It could equally be argued, however, that the effort to enclose femininities again and again in the *same* character type indicates the failure of this masculinity: popular narratives could be seen to express men's deep sense of uncontrol in reaction to the rise of financially independent, successful and, crucially, *unmarried* women in society at large.[8]

Perhaps the repetition of certain female character types occurs because female morality is more manageable than political corruption in Africa, and narrators can criticise women's behaviour more readily (and safely) than that of the national political class. Having transposed their country's complex political and economic problems into a moral arena in which women are the primary participants, authors can then set about creating plots that attempt to resolve the problems for which their heroines are responsible. In this way, contemporary authors generate a masculine ideological model which can be used to contain female sexuality and also to express and symbolically resolve the broader problem of political corruption (or personal disempowerment) in the nation.

An analysis of the language and form of popular narratives is just as important as an analysis of their economic and political contexts, helping to reveal the *ideologies* which give rise to particular plots and character types. In their essay on David Maillu's *Without Kiinua Mgongo*, J. Roger Kurtz and Robert M. Kurtz offer detailed insights into the ideological sub-text of the novella, arguing that through a close linguistic analysis of the mixed Swahili-English sentences, the author's yearning to restore rural pre-colonial 'wholeness' to Kenyan culture can be revealed. Similarly, Dorothy Driver's close reading of *Drum* magazine reveals the manner in which, in the 1950s, many of its stories 'blandly reproduced European and American constructions of gender' and worked within 'an ideology of domesticity aiming for the establishment of a consumer-oriented nuclear family'.

V. African women writers: incurable romantics or popular novelists with a critical tongue?

In their essays on Kenyan and South African fiction, both Nici Nelson and Dorothy Driver expose the areas of incompatibility between popular representations of femininity and the empirical world, where women's daily lives run counter to sensational fictions about money-mongering women. Important challenges also come from African women writers themselves. In many cases their narratives manifest a 'feminine positionality' which transforms, embellishes and amplifies the plots and character types to be found in popular, male-authored novels (see Newell, 2000).

As Brian Larkin explores in his essay on Hausa *soyayya* books, when women writers use the language of romantic love, they sometimes redefine popular gender ideologies. Similarly, Misty Bastian shows how the Nigerian writer Gracy Osifo has redeployed sensational local '*ogbaanje*' narratives and developed from them a 'born again romance' in which the heroine's freedom to choose is prioritised. Very often it is the romance which provides women readers and writers with a potentially radical form, giving them the opportunity to imagine utopian marriage models: Sarah Nuttall demonstrates in her essay how these models can be viewed as idealised responses to women's experiences of marriage in the 'off-page' world. Perhaps it is the central status of the heroine in the conventional Western romance which allows writers to find in the genre a tool to critique gender relations in their societies. The romance is not a static genre in Africa: if one compares Larkin's and Nuttall's essays, one can see how this genre is put to different uses in different countries and contexts, as women utilise and rewrite what has, in Western societies, long been labelled a stultifying, 'dead' form.

All of these contributors reveal that, very often, what one finds in popular fiction by African women is a shift in emphasis, a distinct set of discursive manoeuvres carried out from their positions *within* popular constructions of gender roles. Rather than overthrowing existing gender ideologies, these writers work *within* them and rewrite the most rigid beliefs about the moral qualities that make women into good wives, spiritual mentors or good-time girls. Positioned thus, they might problematise the figures of the ideal wife, the rural mother or the good-time girl, but they do not necessarily reject these popular constructions of femininity.

VI. Local printed fiction and the African literary canon

Local African novels are anchored within particular social formations in a far more explicit manner than internationally available African texts. Using 'paratextual' spaces such as front covers, back covers and prefaces, local novelists aim their fictions at specific constituencies of readers, promising to teach essential moral truths about marriage or gender. By contrast, the Western publishing houses responsible for disseminating the best-known African authors have tended to disavow precisely these aspects of creativity. The promotional material on the back cover of Tsitsi Dangarembga's *Nervous Conditions* (1988) describes the novel as 'exploring human conditions that have a general echo for us all'; one early reviewer of Flora Nwapa's *Efuru* (1966) insisted, in a comment included on the back cover, that, 'The persons in Miss Nwapa's story have an *objective* complexity and sophistication' (emphasis retained); similarly, Ngugi wa Thiong'o's *Petals of Blood* (1977) is praised for the author's universal 'hatred of exploitation, cruelty and injustice'.

Rarely, if ever, are African popular novels marketed or read in terms of their timeless, cross-cultural, 'complex' or experimental qualities. 'This booklet contains good advice and interesting stories', declares J. Abiakam in his introduction to a new edition of *The Game of Love* (1971b); 'it is such a useful booklet', he continues, and 'every Nigerian both bachelors and married people should get a copy' (n.p.). As Ikiddeh points out in his essay on Ghanaian fiction, local publishers make no effort to stem the preaching tone of prefaces. Nor do they seek to suppress localised references to specific sets of readers. Even when we turn to foreign popular novels such as those by Ian Fleming and Jackie Collins, many African readers find in them points of self-recognition and empowerment. Sarah Nuttall's fascinating interviews with black women readers in South Africa reveal the process whereby readers seek 'inspiration' in foreign fiction, finding there 'a heightened register of ordinary life, a picture of what life could be like' (below).

Given the energy of local literary activity in Africa, it is necessary to reassess the centrality that has been conferred upon 'elite' authors such as Chinua Achebe, Wole Soyinka and Ngugi wa Thiong'o. While they are far more readily available to Western readers than the authors that are discussed in this volume, they nevertheless amount to a relatively small proportion of the continent's literary output, and they need to be contextualised in order to be understood. Africa's international authors represent a particular and partial trajectory of the continent's literary culture, and our understanding of their work can benefit from comparisons with local popular fiction. 'Global' and 'local' texts are not divorced from one another, for local popular novelists include references to canonical African texts in their work, and one can find 'good-time girls' with painted lips and miniskirts causing havoc to young men within Ngugi's and Ben Okri's publications.

Local and urban popular discourses about marriage, women, the city, wealth and good fortune are, in many cases, precisely where the plots and characters of 'elite' African literature are fertilised and raised. Where would Ama Ata Aidoo be without the Ghanaian 'good-time girl', a figure she appropriates from popular, male-authored narratives on numerous occasions and instils with new, politicised messages for readers? Where would Ngugi wa Thiong'o be without the East African manifestation of the same character type? Where would Ben Okri be without the sensational, popular *ogbaanje* stories which circulate around southern and eastern Nigeria (see Bastian, below)? These persistent character types and templates generate new social commentaries with each appearance in pamphlets, stage shows, videos, magazines and novels. Whether published internationally or within the locality, African novelists continually work with and re-create these familiar forms.

In addition, it is necessary to compare popular novels from different regions of the continent in order to highlight their shared features and differences. As we journey through the various regional literatures described in this book, it soon becomes clear that despite the pan-African – indeed, global – sweep of genres such as the romance, detective novel and thriller, local authors have instilled distinctive concerns into these forms. Such differences are fascinating for what they reveal about attitudes towards literature in the locality. 'Stories with the East African setting and theme do not interest me', one Ghanaian reader explained in a recent discussion (interview, 1999). Requiring relevance, the young woman continued, 'I do not buy these stories because they are not close to my heart'. Responding to such sentiments, popular novelists innovate from within their chosen genres to suit the aesthetic tastes and expectations of situated reading publics (see Stiebel and Larkin). In Kenyan thrillers and romances in the 1970s, for example, narratives revolve around the themes of poverty and the accumulation of wealth, alcoholism, prostitution, slum-living, crime, domestic violence and the nature of the city. In the romances and thrillers written by Onitsha authors in post-Independence Nigeria, authors express similar concerns about poverty and wealth, but they also voice distinctive views about suburban life in the 1960s, including complaints about high Igbo bride prices, arranged marriage practices and parental interference in the love-choices of educated young women.

At a thematic level and in spite of the various languages chosen for narratives, popular novelists across the continent are preoccupied with many similar issues concerning land, love, wealth, social class and the city; but often upon close analysis, apparently common tropes and character types are realised in vastly different ways. Such heterogeneity in popular fiction is only to be expected given the range of historical and political experiences across Africa. Indeed, fictional character types such as the good-time girl and the gangster are valuable precisely because they open up rare opportunities for latter-day readers to glimpse the kinds of didactic, historically specific commentaries that have been composed by Africans in the distant and more recent past. While sharing many qualities with their pan-African or North American counterparts – sexual promiscuity, for example, or membership of the criminal underworld – such characters symbolise different things at different times and in different contexts.

The aim of this volume is to highlight these contrasts but also to cluster the texts together beneath the shared umbrella of popular fiction. Africa boasts a profusion of literary genres and styles which, once-upon-a-time, might have been imported from Europe and North America but, over the decades, have been exceeded and indigenised by local authors to such an extent that all 'sources' have become blurred. Romances written in English for local consumption are just as inventive in their use of the genre as those composed originally in Swahili or Hausa. Pamphlets such as *How to Become Rich and Avoid Poverty* reveal this literature to be linguistically and generically ebullient, to such an extent that it nearly always *exceeds* the Western languages and models from which it may have emerged.

Whatever the language of particular narratives, the essays in this book reveal the inadequacy of centre-periphery models of cultural transmission: popular fiction on the continent illustrates the immense creative agency of 'the local', who can put the most hegemonic of international art forms to diverse new uses. In writing thrillers or detective stories, African popular novelists might buy into recognisable global art forms, but the *content* of their texts is reserved for the expression and resolution of local concerns. In this manner, popular novelists exemplify the much-theorised 'globalisation' process whereby particular commodities or art forms are managed, transformed, succumbed to or resisted by the new communities around which they circulate (see Appadurai, 1990).

Popular narratives are both fictional and cultural artefacts, produced within (and assisting our understanding of) complex socio-cultural formations. Through them we can overhear many of the hopes and fears of social classes excluded from the narration of nationalist histories. Caution should be exercised, however, to ensure that texts are not viewed as mirrors held up to society, reflecting the 'real' world in an unmediated form. The retrieval of past attitudes from fiction is not a simple process. As Wendy Griswold (1989) suggests, whether or not a narrative is composed in a 'realist' style, the whole field of textuality is erased when texts are regarded as objective reflections of 'real' societies. It is important to remember that locally published novels in Africa relate tangentially to readers' everyday lives; they provide an ideological arena in which old character types can be rejuvenated and resolutions can be imagined to economic and personal dilemmas. With each new publication readers are provided with new variants of old characters through whom they can participate in gender debates and through whom they can reinterpret their own social and emotional rights and roles. Filled with compressed meanings, containing warnings, advice, judgements and guidance, the popular character types to be found in African popular fiction need to be *applied* by readers in order to fulfil their potential meanings.

African popular fiction is of great ethnographic and historical interest to scholars, especially given its primary concern with 'ordinary' people and its steady growth over the fifty-year period spanning decolonisation and the emergence of postcolonial states. The essays in this volume reveal the extent to which each popular text is an authored, mediated, historically situated version of the world which deserves our detailed attention.

Notes

1 This introduction draws upon, broadens and develops ideas presented in chapter six and the conclusion of my book, *Ghanaian Popular Fiction: 'Thrilling Discoveries in Conjugal Life' and Other Tales*. Oxford and Athens, OH: James Currey and Ohio University Press, 2000.

2 The following libraries hold major collections of African popular literature: British Library, London; the School of Oriental and African Studies, London; the Herskovits Library of African Studies, Northwestern University, Illinois; Library of Congress, Washington DC. An excellent selection of locally published popular fiction can be obtained, at very reasonable prices, from the African Books Collective. For their African Literature and Languages catalogue, write to the African Books Collective, The Jam Factory, 27 Park End Street, Oxford OX1 1HU, UK. Email: abc@dial.pipex.com Web site: www.africanbookscollective.com

3 Sadly, little research has been undertaken into local lusophone literature and popular literatures in African languages. The lack of secondary material accounts for the gap in this anthology.

4 For major research into locally published and popular Swahili novels, see Richard Lepine (1987) and Elena Bertoncini (1989).

5 More recently, university academics in northern Nigeria have demonstrated their support for Kano market literature by writing prefaces to pamphlets as well as proof-reading and editing manuscripts on behalf of authors (Furniss, 2000).

6 There are, of course, significant exceptions to this trend, one of the most important being Bernth Lindfors, whose ground-breaking work on

African popular literature has generated interest and subsequent scholarship since his first articles on Nigerian 'market literature' appeared in the 1960s.

[7] Tragically, Jacqueline Bardolph died before she had completed her essay on East African popular fiction for inclusion in this volume. Her enormous contributions to the field of African literary studies include extensive bibliographies, books in French on anglophone literatures, and essays in English on francophone literatures.

[8] The ambiguous endings to many narratives testify to the gaps and anxieties in these hegemonic ideologies. Certainly, women are punished endlessly in male-authored African popular fiction, but many texts finish with a hiatus or a mass of unresolved questions. The confident manner in which the certain character types are punished or domesticated is thus destabilised by the structures of these texts, whose 'resolutions' often fail fully to resolve the familiar didactic templates.

Bibliography

Abba, Sani and Ibrahim, Jibril. (1995) 'Creative Writing, Writers and Publishing in Northern Nigeria', Unpublished research paper, Ibadan: IFRAA.

Abiakam, J. (1964?) *How to Speak to a Girl about Marriage*. Onitsha: J. C. Brothers Bookshop.

—— (1971a) *How to Make Friends with Girls*. Onitsha: J. C. Brothers Bookshop.

—— (1971b) *The Game of Love (a Classical Drama from West Africa)*. Onitsha: J. C. Brothers Bookshop.

Adebanjo, S. (1987) *The Birthday Party*. Ibadan: Paperback Publishers.

Adepoju, Aderanti and Oppong, Christine. (1994) *Gender, Work and Population in Sub-Saharan Africa*. London and Portsmouth, NH: James Currey and Heinemann.

Adewoye, S. A. (1993) *Glittering Fragments*. Ilorin: C.D. Books.

Aminu, Jibril. (1993) 'Books into Peoples', in *Culture and the Book Industry in Nigeria*, eds S. Bello and A. R. Augi, op. cit. (xxxvi).

Anorue, J. C. (1962?) *How to Become Rich and Avoid Poverty*. Onitsha: J. C. Brothers Bookshop.

Appadurai, Arjun. (1990) 'Disjuncture and Difference in the Global Cultural Economy', *Public Culture* 2, 2: 1–24.

Barber, Karin. (1987) 'Popular Arts in Africa', *The African Studies Review* 30, 3: 1–78.

—— (1997) 'Introduction', in *Readings in African Popular Culture* ed. Karin Barber, Bloomington and Oxford: Indiana University Press and James Currey (1–12) for the International African Institute.

Bardolph, Jacqueline. (1989) 'The Novel in East Africa, from *Petals of Blood* (1977) to *The Hills are Falling* (1989)', Unpublished conference paper. *ACLALS Conference*.

Bello, S. and A. R. Augi. eds. (1993) *Culture and the Book Industry in Nigeria*. Lagos: National Council for Arts and Culture.

Bertoncini, Elena Z. (1989) *Outline of Swahili Literature: Prose Fiction and Drama*. Leiden and NY: E. J. Brill.

de Certeau, Michel. (1984) *The Practice of Everyday Life*. Berkeley: University of California Press.

Coles, Catherine and Mack, Beverly. eds (1991) *Hausa Women in the Twentieth Century*. Madison: Wisconsin University Press.

Connell, R. W. (1987) *Gender and Power: Society, the Person and Sexual Politics*. Cambridge: Polity Press.

Crowder, M. (1986) 'The Book Crisis: Africa's Other Famine', *African Research and Documentation*, 41: 1–6.

Dangarembga, Tsitsi. (1988) *Nervous Conditions*. London: Women's Press.

Djoleto, S. A. (1985) *Books and Reading in Ghana*. France: Unesco.

Dekutsey, W. A. (1993) 'Ghana: A Case Study in Publishing Development', *Logos* 4, 2: 66–72.

Ehling, H. (1990) 'The Biafran War and Recent English-Language "Popular" Writing in Nigeria: Kalu Okpi's *Crossfire!* And Kalu Uka's *Colonel Ben Brim*', in *Signs and Signals: Popular Culture in Africa*, ed. Raoul Granqvist, Umea: Acta Universitatis Umensis (151–71).

Ekekwe, E. N. (1983) 'Notes on Oil and Contemporary Urban Culture in Nigeria', *African Urban Studies* 17: 19–29.

Ephson, Isaac. (1974) Interview with Richard Priebe, 4 June, Accra.

Fresco, Alain. (1982) '*Les Vies Africaines*: a Series of Popular Literature', in *African Literature Today 12: New Writing, New Approaches*, London: Heinemann (174–80).

Furniss, Graham (2000) 'Clubs, Commodities and Video Companies: making Hausa culture against all the odds', conference paper, University of Cambridge: Social Histories of Reading in Africa, 8–9 July.

Gedin, Per. (1984) 'Publishing in Africa – Autonomous and Transnational: a View from the Outside', *Development Dialogue* 1, 2: 98–112.

Griswold, Wendy. (1989) 'Formulaic Fiction: the Author as Agent of Elective Affinity', *Comparative Social Research* 11: 75–130.

Gyedu, T. (1976) 'Constraints on Book Development in Ghana', *Greenhill Journal of Administration* 2, 3: 68–78.

Ike, V. C. (1993) 'Problems of Book Industry in Nigeria', in *Culture and the Book Industry in Nigeria*, eds S. Bello and A. R. Augi, *op. cit.* (129–47).

Kezilahabi, E. (1980) 'The Swahili Novel and the Common Man in East Africa', in *The East African Experience: Essays on English nd Swahili Literature*, ed. U. Schild, Berlin: Dietrich Reimer Verlag (75-83).

Konadu, Asare. (1974) Interview with Richard Priebe, 29 May, Accra.

Kotei, S. I. A. (1987) *The Book Today in Africa*. France: Unesco.

Lepine, Richard. (1987) 'A Swahili Fiction Serial from the Kenyan Newspaper *Baraza*', *Ba Shiru* 13, 1: 61–74.

Lindfors, Bernth. (1991) *Popular Literatures in Africa*. Trenton, NJ: Africa World Press.

Maillu, David G. (1975) *Kadosa*. Nairobi: David Maillu Publishers Ltd.

Mangua, Charles. (1974) *A Tail in the Mouth*. Nairobi: East African Publishing House.

Newell, Stephanie. (2000) *Ghanaian Popular Fiction: 'Thrilling Discoveries in Conjugal Life' and Other Tales*. Oxford and Athens, OH: James Currey and Ohio University Press.

Ngugi wa Thiong'o. (1977) *Petals of Blood*. Oxford: Heinemann.

—— (1986) *Decolonising the Mind: the Politics of Language in African Literature*. London, Nairobi and Portsmouth, NH: James Currey, E.A.E.P and Heinemann.

Nwapa, Flora. (1966) *Efuru*. Oxford: Heinemann.

Nwoye, M. I. (1993) *Endless Search*. Ibadan: Kraft Books Ltd.

Ogali, Ogali A. (1956) *Veronica My Daughter*. Onitsha: Appolos Brothers Press.

Radway, Janice. (1987) *Reading the Romance: Women, Patriarchy and Popular Literature*. London: Verso.

Stratton, Florence. (1994) *Contemporary African Literature and the Politics of Gender*. London and NY: Routledge.

Umelo, Rose. (1983) 'Applying the Formula: a Preliminary Survey of Recurring Plots, Situations and Characters in Unsolicited Fiction Manuscripts', Conference paper, University of Calabar: Third International Conference on African Literature, 2–6 May.

Unoh, Solomon. (1993). 'The Promotion of Good Reading Habits in Nigeria for Leisure and Life-Long Education: Problems and Prospects', *Culture and the Book Industry in Nigeria*, eds S. Bello and A. R. Augi, *op. cit.* (97–116).

Walsh, G. (1991) *Publishing in Africa: a Neglected Component of Development*. African Studies Center Working Papers No. 156, Boston: Boston University.

Ward, Ida C. (1941) 'African Languages and Literature', *Books for Africa* 11, 4: 49–52.

White, Landeg and Couzens, Tim. (1984) 'Introduction', in *Literature and Society in South Africa*, eds Landeg White and Tim Couzens, Harlow: Longman.

1 Perspectives on West African Popular Fiction

GRAHAM FURNISS

Hausa Creative Writing in the 1930s

An Exploration in Postcolonial Theory

Reference
Research in African Literatures 29 (1), 1998: 87–102

Imaginative prose writing in Hausa dates very specifically from the early 1930s. Thirty years after Lugard's declaration of the Protectorate of Northern Nigeria, a group of five novellas was elicited from younger members of the northern elite who had gone, or were going, through the one or two Western educational institutions in Northern Nigeria at the time. The books were *Shaihu Umar* by Abubakar Tafawa Balewa, *Jiki Magayi* (Body language) by John Tafida and Rupert East, *Idon Matambayi* (The eye of the enquirer) by Muhammadu Gwarzo, *Ruwan Bagaja* (The water of cure) by Abubakar Imam, and *Gandoki* (Mr. Inquisitive) by Bello Kagara, Abubakar Imam's elder brother. The only one of these books that has been fully translated into English is *Shaihu Umar*; two of the others were abridged in English to provide English school readers for Nigerian schools.[1]

Of the five writers in that first batch, the eldest, Bello Kagara, had been about eleven at the time of the military campaigns against Kano and Sokoto, in the first years of the century, which resulted in the establishment of British rule. Fluent in English and Hausa, these writers were close enough to the experience of conquest to have confronted colonial society in its infancy and had come into close contact with the mores and attitudes of colonial officers through their experience at Katsina College[2] and in the schools where they taught or in the bureaucracies where they worked. For these writers a particular focus of confrontation between the colonial state and the societies out of which they came lay in their own personal transition into Western education. As Bello Kagara said on his retirement from government service as an Islamic Studies teacher in 1945:

> Indeed today I cannot but remember the year 1910, when Mr G. L. Monk, the then District Officer of Kagara, took me away from my father, Alkalin Kagara Malam Shehu Usman, and sent me to school. My father was unwilling to release me for one reason and that is, that he was very suspicious of European schools. He thought that the idea behind them was to convert boys to Christianity. He reluctantly agreed only when he heard that almost all the Moslem emirs in Northern Nigeria had already sent their sons to the school, and that the teaching of Arabic and Islamic Studies as well as moral training on the divine basis of Islam were among the subjects taught in the school... Turning to me he said, 'As for you, Muhammadu Bello, wherever these Europeans take you, whatever those Europeans do to you, know that Islam is your religion and learning is your tradition. God be with you.' (Mora 9-10)

The meld of Islamic knowledge and aspects of the Western curriculum that was being put together in Katsina College kept Bello Kagara's allegiance throughout his career as a teacher in that school. The act of imaginative prose writing itself was the product of an aspect of colonial educational logic. Rupert East, a colonial official, had been appointed Superintendent of the Translation Bureau in Zaria, and his brief was to supervise the translation of a wide variety of colonial government documents, both government regulations and public information on health, on agriculture, and other areas, into Hausa and other northern languages. This activity was closely linked with the work of the Education Department, whose immediate problem was the production of school primers in reading and writing in the roman script, along with textbooks covering the primary curriculum. Along with the small but growing school population in the 1920s and early 1930s was the larger issue of education in the roman script for the adult population, many of whom were already familiar with the Arabic script, whether as adapted for *ajami* Hausa or for Arabic itself. As East himself wrote, he quickly came up against the need to provide materials in roman-script Hausa that people could enjoy and therefore wish to read. Government information booklets were hardly going to engender an avid, expanding, reading public.[3] It was with that in mind that East went, in 1933, to the only Western secondary educational institution in the north of Nigeria, Katsina College, and suggested to pupils and Hausa staff that they write novels/novellas of around 20,000 words that he would then publish through the renamed Literature Bureau. Presented as a competition, East in fact published all five novellas that he received, one of which he himself co-wrote with John Tafida, who was working at the Literature Bureau at the time.[4] Cradled within a colonial logic, and elicited from northern Nigerians who were from an elite which had, by turns, resisted and accommodated itself to the colonial presence, and who were, as individuals, now closely enmeshed in colonial society as clerks, teachers, and students, these novellas would seem to be prime material for an examination of an indigenous perspective on the colonial encounter. Furthermore, there was no pre-existing tradition of imaginative prose writing within Hausa culture. The form itself would seem to bear examination as a colonial creation. The precolonial panorama of oral and literary genres in Hausa elite and popular culture included prose writing in the form of Islamic religious tracts, in chronicles and treatises upon administration, jurisprudence, and many other branches of Islamic knowledge. The frivolity of imagination was available in the Arabic literature of the stories of Shahr Zad, and in the knockabout world of Hausa oral tales in which pomposity was deflated, the powerful outwitted, and stereotypes reinforced through repeated clash and encounter. The narrative line of the oral tale moved seamlessly in and out of the human, animal, and supernatural worlds. Within the architecture of Hausa culture, the dominant cultural form of literary expression in precolonial times and, to a great extent, up to the present day has been poetry (see, for example, Hiskett). Complex relations of cross-referencing, imitation, borrowing, parody, and distancing characterize the construction of genres in Hausa,[5] but at the heart of one particular view of Hausa culture lies the voice of the poet whose legitimacy and authority to speak derive from the founders of the jihadist Sokoto caliphate in the early years of the nineteenth century. It was against this background that East proceeded with his proposal to elicit works of imaginative prose writing and so it was not surprising that there were ambivalent reactions to an unfamiliar category of self-expression and one which impinged upon notions of what was appropriate for the written form. East, with his usual forthrightness, put it as follows:

> With the object, therefore, of first finding authors, [I] visited the chief towns of Hausaland, and, having assembled as many as possible of the intelligentzia [sic], endeavoured to explain the scheme, and invite any who felt so gifted to try their hand at writing fiction. The first difficulty was to persuade these Malamai that the thing was worth doing. The influence of Islam, superimposed on the Hamitic strain in the blood of the Northern Nigerian, produces an extremely serious-minded type of person. The art of writing, moreover, being intimately connected in his mind with his religion, is not to be treated lightly. (351–52)

Undeterred, East continued to push his conception of the kind of book he needed:

> To these people, therefore, the idea of writing a book which was frankly intended neither for the edification of the mind, nor the good of the soul, a 'story' book which, however, followed none of the prescribed forms of story-telling, seemed very strange. The historical novel, which presented itself as a possible link between history, which they understood, and fiction writing, which they did not – in other words, the practice of deliberately mixing truth with falsehood under the same cover – appeared to some to be definitely immoral. In short, it was necessary to explain to a very conservative audience a conception which was entirely new, and of doubtful value, if not morality. (352)

The degree to which East provided positive guidelines is unclear; however, he had mixed reactions to the manuscripts. On the one hand, he was favorably impressed by the writing style of Bello Kagara and his younger brother, Abubakar Imam, but he bemoaned the lack of what he saw as structure: 'in the majority of manuscripts which have been sent in the chief fault lies in the failure to bring the tale to a fitting conclusion' (356). In terms of the immediate experience of the people involved in writing these novellas, clearly they were working in close conjunction with a man whose own vision of the colonial endeavor entailed a belief that a creative arena was there to be opened up – '[the manuscripts are] a hopeful sign that we may one day confound the sceptics by producing a really first-class indigenous literature' (352–53) – and in that endeavor, the plural subject 'we' provides the key to the combined agency involved.

Before turning to the nature of the product of this literary activity, I would like to spend a few moments reflecting upon current representations of postcolonial discourse. Following Ashcroft et al., I refer by the latter term to 'the culture affected by the imperial process from the moment of colonization to the present day,' rather than a periodization that takes 'national independence' as its starting point (2). Postcolonial writing is usually taken to refer to literary creativity in metropolitan languages off which feeds 'postcolonial criticism/theory' – more specifically the recent strands of thought relating either to Western discourse about other cultures (see Said) and its interlocking relationship with non-Western discourse (see Bhabha) or to 'Third-World' discourse about the colonial encounter. One strand of thought is represented by Fredric Jameson's proposition that

> [a]ll third-world texts are necessarily ... allegorical, and in a very special way: they are to be read as what I will call national allegories... Third-world texts, even those which are seemingly private and invested with a properly libidinal dynamic – necessarily project a political dimension in the form of national allegory: *the story of the private individual destiny is always an allegory of the embattled situation of the public third-world culture and society.* (Jameson 60; emphasis in original)

Aijaz Ahmad takes Jameson to task over the sweeping 'otherness' of the catch-all phrase 'third-world' and the indefensible reduction of infinite variety to 'national allegory' where 'nation' is the erroneously supposed subject of all debate (Ahmad 97–98), pointing, for example, to the existence of much literature in Urdu, which has its own priorities and preoccupations entirely separate from the framework presented by Jameson. Jameson's use of the phrase 'embattled situation' adds a further dimension to this particular construct; not only are 'third world' writers engaged in a struggle to inform the idea of nation, they are involved with a struggle against Western culture, against the metropolis from the periphery – the 'empire writes back,' to use the phrase borrowed from Rushdie by Ashcroft, Griffiths, and Tiffin in the title of their influential book. The commonality that underlies Jameson's notion of 'third-world' literature is the experience of colonialism and imperialism, and this view is articulated again by Ashcroft et al.:

> What each of these literatures has in common beyond their special and distinctive regional characteristics is that they emerged in their present form out of the experience of colonization and asserted themselves by foregrounding the tension with the imperial power and by emphasizing their differences from the assumptions of the imperial centre. (2)

However, not only does the 'colonial encounter' form the focus of what such literatures are supposedly talking about, their products are seen to be the result of years of arduous struggle to obtain the ability to speak. On the one hand, there is the 'colonizer's deafness' (Barber 5), as characterized by Edward Said:

> Without significant exception the universalising discourses of modern Europe and the United States assume the silence, willing or otherwise, of the non-European world. There is incorporation; there is inclusion; there is direct rule; there is coercion. But there is only infrequently an acknowledgment that the colonized people should be heard from, their ideas known. (*Culture and Imperialism* 58)

On the other hand, there is the 'native's muteness' (Barber 5), a silence in the presence of an overwhelming imposition of English. Ashcroft et al. make the point in relation to Gayatri Spivak's discussion of subaltern consciousness ('Can the Sulbaltern Speak?'):

> By implication the silencing of the subaltern woman extends to the whole of the colonial world, and to the silencing and muting of all natives, male or female. (177-78)

However, according to this particular train of thought within postcolonial criticism, out of that initial silence have come not only contributions to the metropolitan culture but a radical reappraisal of the center and the periphery:

> Having taken linguistic dispossession as its starting point, this style of post-colonial criticism goes on from there to celebrate a

vigorous come-back by the colonised. The early stage of self-denigration and espousal of British values is succeeded by a phase of rejection of colonial culture and then its radical re-appropriation. The periphery now takes on the culture and language of the centre and transforms it, breaking it, infusing it with local registers, and refashioning it so that it speaks with the voice of the marginalised. Instead of one hegemonic English we get a plurality of local englishes ... Thus in post-colonial criticism of African literature, the flowering of African literature in English, which occurred in the late 1950s and early 1960s, is interpreted as the colonial subject finally 'finding a voice.' It is more or less implied that until this flowering took place – showing that the colonised had mastered and subverted the colonial codes – the stunned natives literally could not articulate their responses to colonial rule. (Barber 6)

Karin Barber's cogent and trenchant critique goes on to examine the way in which such postcolonial criticism has sometimes effaced and sometimes genuflected to the presence of discourses in languages other than the metropolitan and local varieties of English, French, and Portuguese. Beyond statements, like that of Said above, to the effect that 'other' peoples should be listened to, the predominant framework within which references to other forms of discourse are set consists of a Manichean paradigm in which metropolitan language is 'modern,' written, contemporary, international, heterogeneous, obtains a wide audience, and is the object of 'criticism,' whereas African languages are seen as predominantly 'traditional,' oral, past-oriented, local, homogeneous, with a restricted audience, and constitute the embodiment of value (see Barber). Barber's reflections, consonant with some of Ahmad's reactions to Jameson, produce the contention that the general silence within postcolonial criticism, at least as far as Africa is concerned, on the subject of discourse within nonmetropolitan languages has produced most grievous distortions:

> This model [of postcolonial criticism] blocks a properly historical, localised understanding of any scene of colonial and post-Independence literary production in Africa. Instead it selects and overemphasizes one sliver of literary and cultural production – written literature in the English language – and treats this as all there is, representative of a whole culture or even a whole global 'colonial experience.' It thus negligently or deliberately erases all other forms of expression – written literature in African languages, oral literature in African languages, and a whole domain of cultural forms which cross the boundaries between 'written' and 'oral,' between 'foreign' and 'indigenous' – making way for the 'postcolonial Other' to emerge, defiant yet accessible, conveniently articulate in English and consolingly preoccupied with his or her relations to the center – 'writing back' in a language the ex-colonizers can understand because it is a modified register of their own. Thus decontextualized, inflated, and made to bear an excessive metonymic burden, the role and significance of African literature in English can not be properly appreciated. (3)

The first five Hausa novellas produced directly within a colonial context, as outlined above, constitute part of a pre-existing and subsequent multigeneric dialogue about the nature of a wide variety of West African societies, and the notion that such a dialogue (in *any* of Nigeria's 400 languages) fell silent in the face of English is, to anyone who knows Nigeria, quite laughable. The following discussion examines the degree to which these early examples of creative writing were 'preoccupied with the colonial experience' or were even aware of English and the colonial presence. Emerging from the discussion will be a picture of what the preoccupations of these stories actually are and what they say about the 'Hausa world' as constructed in the imagination of the 1930s.

The colonial experience can, of course, be approached at a number of levels. At a direct level there is the actual presence in the stories of British colonial officers, white men and women, or indeed their representatives in terms either of people – southern 'clerks,' army personnel, school teachers – or of 'colonial artefacts' – radios, telephones, cars, trains, planes, and the like. At another level, there is the representation of the social and political effects of the establishment of British overrule and commercial activity upon pre-existing society and administrations. And at another level again, there is, to use Jameson's phrase, the 'libidinal dynamic' whereby, within the individual presence, the stresses and strains, contradictions, and problematics of social dislocation are played out within the individual psyche.

Overwhelmingly these stories are situated in a world where the British, their representatives, and colonial artefacts are absent. The exception is the early and late narrative within the story *Gandoki*, to which we shall come shortly. Among the other stories, *Jiki Magayi*, despite (or perhaps because of) being coauthored by Rupert East, is entirely set in a world of premodern Hausa towns and intervening liminal space; *Shaihu Umar* ranges from Hausaland to the North African littoral, including reference to the historical figure of Rabeh in Borno, but is locked into the dynamics of being an ordinary person in a nineteenth-century world of slave-raiding, and thus vulnerable to sudden dislocation, grief, caprice, and suffering. *Idon Matambayi* is, like *Jiki Magayi*, set in a world of Hausa towns and intervening bush, and presents a picture of the relations between society in towns and social outsiders represented by thieves, in their bush hideouts. A momentary, but telling, reference to an aspect of the 'colonial experience' lies in the remark that one of the rich traders in town, targeted by the thieves, is an agent of the Niger Company, a trader in hides and groundnuts. The identification of the merchant class, an indigenous formation of precolonial origin, with the Royal Niger Company is neither foregrounded nor later relevant to the story as it unfolds. The fifth story, *Ruwan Bagaja*, a humorous story of slapstick and trickery within an episodic quest frame, sets the appearance of two Europeans alongside a series of other stereotypes interacting with the central character. The first appearance is a chance encounter where a passing European is, by a ruse, maneuvered into handing over cash in exchange for a parrot. On the second occasion, the central character, Alhaji Imam, in the course of a fantastical series of adventures, encounters a 'European in charge of boats' whom he has to ask for transportation back to the Western Sudan. In this encounter, the European says that Alhaji Imam should go away because he is dirty and smells. This very direct and revealing representation of racist attitudes is, however, explained by the narrator as demonstrating laughable European ignorance: the Englishman has simply mistaken a dark skin for dirt![6] These two occurrences are but the most minor of moments within a story that is dominated by the central character's picaresque adventures from Hausaland to Timbuctoo to India and back again. It is in the story *Gandoki* that we see presented a narrative that incorporates the British military campaign in northern Nigeria and its consequences.

Gandoki, the eponymous central character, along with his son

Garba Gagare, represent the Hausa military tradition in its confrontation with the British. He joins the forces defending Bida, then Kontagora, and many other skirmishes culminating in the defeat of the forces of Sultan Attahiru at Burmi in July 1903. He comes from a world of individual mounted warriors, champions whose prowess in hand-to-hand combat is such that their presence is sufficient to strike fear into the hearts of the enemy. Tactics and technology are not a part of Gandoki's world. It is the clash of lines of infantry and the sudden appearance of cavalry that makes for battle; valor and success are marked by the number of heads that roll. In the teeth of defeat before the machine guns of the British, Gandoki's response is always to cry, 'No surrender.' In this early section of the narrative, the only appearance of an individual European, rather than of the collective notion of the British forces, is when Gandoki kills a European who has entered a chief's house unannounced, leading to the chief's hurried departure for Lafiya, Keffi, and then Zaria.[7] The narrative does, however, give a strong sense of the effects of the British military campaign upon the body politic. On the one hand, there are those who compromise with the British and return to their homes to rebuild after the initial passage of conquest. On the other, defeated forces falling back produce ripples of mayhem in local communities, old enemies gloat at discomfort, and discord and confusion are spread everywhere. Groups of fighting men owing allegiance to one chief link up with others while refugees from Kontagora scatter through Kano and Katsina as a smallpox epidemic rages. The rallying cry of the resistance is to flee east, away from the power of infidel forces and towards Mecca, where the community can be reconstructed. These general trends are reflected in the events that befall Gandoki and his family. His wife, Inda Gana, a retainer, and Garba Gagare suffer thirst and danger as they make their way through the bush. Gandoki and Garba Gagare decide to head east to join the Sultan and Inda Gana refuses to go with them, saying he is off to Zaria to join the British military forces; Gandoki's wife decides to stay put and eke out a living. The three options facing northerners – subservience, accommodation, and departure – are personified within Gandoki's immediate entourage. The historical reality of defeat is then transformed into victory in the remainder of the book by a projection of the same military qualities in which Gandoki's personality was founded onto a world of repeated victorious conquest.

Up until the point when Gandoki and Garba Gagare fight in the battle of Bima Hill,[8] the narrative has been firmly anchored in the real geography and history of northern Nigeria in the early years of this century. The only passage into the miraculous earlier in the text is in the description of the Sarkin Sudan, the chief of Kontagora, Ibrahim Nagwamatse, who is reported to have displayed wondrous powers (miraculously crossing a river, talking to the birds) after his capture and incarceration by the British. The British, impressed by these powers, finally return him to Kontagora.[9] The transition, overnight, from the real Bima Hill to the fantastical island of Ceylon, occurs through the reassertion of the old-style military prowess with the sword. Being the only two surviving fighters after the battle of Bima Hill, Gandoki and Garba Gagare retreat into a cave to rest, carrying nothing but their weapons. The next morning, Garba is set upon by armed men dressed in black. His prowess with the sword, combined with his protective charms, beats them off, but they turn out to have been jinns who carry them through the air into a new world. Here in this new world, defeat becomes victory. Gandoki brings enemy after enemy, individual chief and associated community, by persuasion or by force, into the community of Islam. The social geography of this imagined world[10] is one in which a chief and his people inhabit a town which they defend or from which they move out to attack across undefined, indeterminate space; our hero is constantly traveling out in pursuit or returning home victorious, or occasionally lost and wandering in dangerous and featureless bush, prey to chance encounters with the fearsome supernatural. The specificity of time and space is immediately circumvented by the participation of both friendly and malevolent jinns who can transport themselves and our heroes instantly from place to place, seen or unseen. Two threads run through the episodic frame. Gandoki builds a network of allies and family – a new wife, a child – whose fates are followed and tied eventually back into that of Gandoki and his son. Gandoki's role as warrior is to set apart the wheat from the chaff, to do away with those who will not convert to Islam, and to bring together under one overarching allegiance the various disparate groups and individuals, both human and jinn, who now must weld together to form the *umma*. He sends them physically to go and live together, and to come to each other's aid in times of threat. The ideals of the *hijira* of Attahiru come true in the imagined world of India and the East. Finally Gandoki comes back to the real world of northern Nigeria, traveling via Egypt where he sees that the people are living in peace and that there are benefits to peace. This change of heart is then strengthened on his return to Katsina, where he sees justice prevailing under a British administration. When Garba says he refuses to give up the fight, Gandoki responds that it is very difficult to make war upon just rulers. The alternative is to pursue religious learning and make the pilgrimage. Implied in Gandoki's new position is that the advancement and protection of the faith is best served through learning and teaching rather than the sword. The malam is the peacetime equivalent of the warrior, the forcible converter to Islam. Garba goes to school in Katsina, and Gandoki makes a living as a trader. The position of the author, Bello Kagara, as an Arabic and Islamic studies teacher in the only Western secondary school in the north of Nigeria at the time, Katsina College, chimes with this final position taken by Gandoki. Accommodation at the heart of the British education system on condition that the faith is protected was at the heart of the deal made by Lugard with the northern emirs at the beginning of the century. The narrative concludes with Gandoki making a visit to the military barracks in Zaria where he marvels at the technology of modern war – artillery, semaphore, telescopic sights, anti-aircraft guns – a whole world away from the notions of battle, bravery, and triumph that have dominated the preceding pages. Finding his old retainer, Inda Gana, as gunner-sergeant, Gandoki makes a final remark acknowledging the ascendancy of the new over the old: 'Leave off, Inda Gana, it is lack of understanding that causes people to fight the Europeans.'

Rather than simply trying to please Rupert East, which has been suggested, the ending would appear to represent a coming to terms between the schisms within the northern response to the arrival of the British. Reconciliation is not between the 'no surrender' forces and the British in the form of individual Europeans (there was no settler presence to form an identifiable separate community), but rather between those who had resisted and those who had thrown in their lot with the British administration like Inda Gana. The pen being mightier than the sword, the appropriate role for the exwarrior within the now peaceful community is as teacher and scholar. Technological knowledge would appear to have superseded magical knowledge and power, at least as far as this ending is concerned.

The bulk of this narrative, however, does not address the 'colonial encounter'; it talks of the constitution of the Islamic community, an issue that long predates the colonial presence. Within that concern the narrative is structured around the passage of a hero and his son/companion from place to place, from encounter to encounter, sometimes befriended, sometimes confronted, moving from vicissitude to triumph, from reality to fantasy, and from human or jinn communities to liminal dangerous space and back again. The fixed point in all these episodes is the concluding discrimination between converts and persistent infidels. Yet this 'precolonial' discourse is also linked to the early part of the book. Not only is there the reversal of defeat into victory in the transition from real Nigeria to imaginary Ceylon, the ripples of discord, fighting, confusion, and suffering that radiate out from the first colonial encounters in Bida and Kontagora[11] are equivalent in descriptive terms to the ripples that radiate out in the fantastical world of India, Ceylon, and the jinns. Where fleeing enemies of the British sought refuge within the communities of sympathetic chiefs, so the sworn enemies of Gandoki, such as Koringo Karon Yaki, seek refuge with distant chiefs who then turn against Gandoki and have to be defeated; roles are reversed. Communities are under attack and battle is joined again and again.

The presence of the discussion of the British conquest of northern Nigeria within *Gandoki* has meant that I have concentrated my discussion so far upon it. The other books are directed at issues that would seem to have little if anything to do with the 'colonial encounter' or 'national allegory.' The issues are predominantly those of Hausa society and of the Western Sudan more generally. Hausa society itself contained many different kinds of outsiders and many understandings of things beyond its own geographical and social borders. *Shaihu Umar* and *Ruwan Bagaja*, like *Gandoki* are framed as a story within a story; the central character, upon request, narrates his life story leading up to his current position as a successful figure back in his home community after years of travel and hardship. Where *Shaihu Umar* is a serious and moral tale about suffering and enslavement in the Western Sudan and across the desert in North Africa, *Ruwan Bagaja* is a ribald story of jokes and slapstick as our hero and his companion/ protagonist trick and counter-trick each other while all the time engaged upon a quest.

Shaihu Umar is a story in which a network of family ties binds the narrative together. The primary relationship is between our hero and his mother, yet the story is one in which estrangement, loss and chance encounter dominate the plot. A real geography is laid out by the book whereby real towns in Hausaland provide the home from which *Shaihu Umar* is taken in slavery as a child to Tripoli, from where he returns through Borno eventually to Bauchi. This real itinerary is paralleled by his searching mother whose enslavement in the desert town of Muzuk leads to her eventual redemption in Tripoli and a reunion with her son before her death. Nevertheless, within this real landscape, the liminal spaces between habitations are, as in *Gandoki*, dangerous and capricious. Being on a bush path is being vulnerable to slave-raiders, being in a bush shelter is being vulnerable to attack from hyenas, traveling in the desert is to be vulnerable to sandstorms and heat. Chance encounters in liminal space can be fortuitous or disastrous: behind the next tree may be a helping hand or a slaver. The qualities inherent in the character of Shaihu Umar are the ability to bear with fortitude all the vicissitudes that come his way. Throughout, he remains a model of patience and forbearance.[12]

It is within the context of his growth to adulthood in North Africa, a process that is not described in any detail, that these aspects of his character combine with access to religious education to transform his situation. Islam and Islamic knowledge provide Shaihu Umar with the social mobility to go from slave to imam, within the context of the *umma*. It is this transformation that leads to his ability to return to his native land a free and famous man at the end of the story. Where *Gandoki* had placed at the center the process of conversion by sword and eventually by pen, *Shaihu Umar* focuses upon personal achievement and transformation afforded by Islam. The transition from reality to fantasy and back again, the intervention of jinns, and the occurrence of miraculous events are generally absent from *Shaihu Umar*. Fortuitous occurrences, reflecting the will of God, are an integral part of the story, but the intervention of other supernatural forces is not. In *Ruwan Bagaja*, however, we see a transition from a real world into a fantastical world of jinns very much in the same manner as in *Gandoki*.

The movement of *Ruwan Bagaja* into a fantastical world takes the central character, Alhaji Imam, east, this time to a land called Iram, to 'Hindu,' and on journeys in which he travels upon the Red Sea. The geography of the story is a fanciful one in which Alhaji Imam hops from one community to another, embezzling here and outwitting there until things become too hot for him so he moves on. From towns in the Western Sudan he travels in boats to desert islands and then is finally transported through the air by jinns to far-off lands, from where he eventually returns to appear out of a well in Kano that he concludes is linked underground to the waters of the Red Sea. The story is framed by a quest in search of magical water and to avenge the murder of his father by a stepbrother. In both of these he succeeds in his aims. But the overall framework is a rather insignificant part of the narrative. The feeling of the book is dominated by the series of laughing encounters along the way. Whether in the spaces between communities (where Imam and his companion/protagonist Malam Zurke are attacked by a crazed camel or Imam outwits a passing villager), or in the towns and communities where Imam appears, it is the confrontation between Imam and a kaleidoscope of characters that is the focus of attention. This kaleidoscope of stereotypes covers some of the stock figures of so much popular culture: the country bumpkin, the Syrian trader, the cuckold, the corrupt judge, the chief's bodyguard, the hot-tempered Fulani youth, the European, the cheeky girl. At the same time, Imam himself disguises himself in the persona of a variety of other stock characters: the learned scholar who is really a charlatan, the rich merchant, the raving madman, among others. Like the trickster in the oral tales, Imam gets away repeatedly with the most outrageous contraventions of social norms, often landing his partner, Zurke, in the trouble that was destined for him. Where Shaihu Umar sets out a serious exposition of moral qualities, Imam represents the laughing underbelly of Hausa popular culture, and the narrative derives its point from these representations of aspects of contemporary Hausa society to itself. In this context, the presence of a white man is but one among a series of encounters in which Imam continues to get the better.

The two remaining stories *Jiki Magayi* and *Idon Matambayi*, concentrate upon problematic confrontations within Hausa society. As such they are interesting as a first representation in this new form of the nature of society. In the first case, an older, richer man alienates a girl's affections from the young man who loves her. The story is the playing out of the consequences of the youth's desire for revenge. The tension between love and duty is the topic of many recent novels in Hausa but in the case of this first story it is not duty to obey parents that brings about Zainabu's estrangement from Abubakar, it is the use of magical charms by the older man, Malam Shaihu. Consequently, Abubakar sets out to find an equivalent charm with which to take his revenge. The application of such a charm to the child of Zainabu and Malam Shaihu produces a change in the child such that the child, Kyauta, turns criminal and eventually, unwittingly, effects his own father's death. Before Kyauta can wreak his own revenge on Abubakar, Abubakar dies. The power of an older and richer man to break up a love match is clearly a point of tension reflected in the many modern stories about rich alhajis and their corruption of school-age girls. The issue was clearly not much different in the 1930s.

The issue of the use of supernatural powers is also a central one within the story. While the story is not framed entirely within a quest model, the middle section of the book, where Abubakar seeks the means to take revenge, is set out in the familiar quest way. Abubakar sets out to find a charm. As with the previous books, the liminal space between towns is an ambivalent, dangerous one. He is attacked by robbers, who cut off half his ear, only to then be helped by some passing traders. In that space, he encounters a community of robbers, bori practitioners, and prostitutes whose chief offers to help him if he will complete a particular task. The task involves wandering in the bush, a directionless, featureless place, waiting to discover the gum of the *kalgo* tree. His discovery of it comes as a result of the intervention of jinns and miraculous occurrences. The chief of the robbers provides him with the poisonous charm in exchange for the magic gum. In this story, human outcomes are affected by medicine; medicine is power and that power is obtained from the bush, the same bush that can bring good luck or ill luck, help or hindrance to the traveler. The power is brokered by the chief of outcast forces – theft, bori spirit-possession, and prostitution.

In *Jiki Magayi* then, we see a representation of internal societal tensions surrounding marriage and the power to control others through wealth and seniority, combined with the issue of the cooption of supernatural powers, either by the powerful in the pursuit of their own aims, or by the weak in taking revenge against or resisting the powerful for acts of injustice. Struggle and the balance of forces can be constituted through both worldly and unworldly powers.

Where *Shaihu Umar* focused upon a 'good man,' *Ruwan Bagaja* presented our hero as rogue, and *Gandoki* conjured up the old-style warrior, *Idon Matambayi* features as central characters a group of social outcasts, three treacherous, conniving thieves, Idon Matambayi and two others. They work together but do not trust each other. Lest the reader think they might be Robin Hoods of their age, their cry is 'God grant that we pillage the wealthy and drive the ordinary man into poverty!' After meeting mixed success with their attempts at highway robbery, they decide to spy out the prospects in a local town with a view to burglary. It is here that they attempt to steal from Musa, a rich merchant and agent for the Royal Niger Company. Now in league with a fourth thief, they disguise themselves as merchants to effect an introduction to Musa's house. During the night the three steal from Musa and slip away, leaving the fourth to carry the can. The fourth manages to convince a court of his innocence and is released. Returning to the hideout in the bush, the fourth man tricks two of them into returning with him to Musa's house, saying there is a great deal more loot to obtain. During that night's attempts to steal, the fourth thief calls the town's security men and the two others are arrested and imprisoned for seven years. Idon Matambayi has by this time left for his home town, but God's retribution falls upon him when a fire destroys all his property and he is made destitute.

The story concentrates upon a theme familiar from oral tales, the lack of honor among thieves and the demise of the wrong-doer. Focused originally upon encounters between thieves in the bush, during which they demonstrate the effectiveness of protective charms and aggressive valor in combat, before finally agreeing to work together, the narrative presents, as with the other stories, a contrast between the dangerous bush and the organized society of the town. The perspectives are, however, reversed. Safety, for the thieves, against pursuit or capture lies in the bush. Danger lies in the town where they risk challenge and capture. Between the thieves, relations revolve around issues of trust and treachery. Their downfall lies more in their own betrayal of each other than in the efforts of the forces of law and order to capture them in their hideout. The final conclusion in which each thief gets his just desserts, unlike the trickster narratives where more often than not the trickster gets away with antisocial behavior, provides the moral framework for the narrative. *Idon Matambayi* may be an allegory for the politics of the time, who knows, but it certainly does not constitute in any sense a 'national allegory,' as the application of Jameson's notion would lead us to consider. The narrative would seem to link most directly with the discussion of the moral codes that are articulated through the notion of the 'good man' as we saw in the case of Shaihu Umar. In contrast to the *Shaihu Umar* story, we see the negative counterparts to positive traits: distrust, betrayal, dishonesty, greed, theft, murder. It is to these moral constructs that this narrative is directed, part of a broad discussion of ethics and religion that stretches way beyond *Shaihu Umar* into the history of religious verse writing and into modern poetry and song.

Of the five Hausa novellas that came out of the colonial creative writing competition held in 1933 in northern Nigeria, only one, *Gandoki*, addresses the issue of the 'colonial encounter' to any extent. And that is phrased not in terms of the internalization of the colonial presence but in terms of the options to resist or accommodate this external force.

Postcolonial criticism has foregrounded the 'colonial experience' as far as literary expression is concerned. Such literary expression is conceived in terms of writing in English. But to suggest that because people did not express themselves in English they did not express themselves at all is clearly absurd. On the evidence of these early Hausa novellas of the 1930s, the 'colonial encounter' is one rather insignificant component of experience during the colonial period. The writers of these novellas were deeply involved with the colonial education system and the formation of a Western-educated elite within northern Nigeria. Clearly their daily experience was intimately bound up with aspects of a 'colonial encounter.' Yet at the level of imagination, as expressed in these narratives, it was the nature of their own notions of Hausa society which concerned them. Coming to terms with the 'defeat' of that society is achieved in *Gandoki* through victory in fantasy and through survival and success in spite of suffering. Overall, the frameworks of these novellas are not of colonialism, they are made up of issues and concerns indigenous to the societies of the Western Sudan and Hausaland in particular – of slavery within the Western Sudan and North Africa, of forcible and voluntary conversion to Islam, of the constitution of the Islamic community, of relations of power in relation to marriage and family, of the community and outcast forces, of reality and the supernatural, of family ties, of the rich and powerful versus the poor and weak, of honesty and trickery, of suffering and salvation, of organized society symbolized in towns and the chaos and danger represented in the liminal spaces of the 'bush.'

These stories are not facing West; if they face anywhere they face East, to India, Ceylon, Egypt, the Red Sea, and the lands where famous warriors travel on elephants into battle. It is there that the popular imagination goes, transported by these stories, not as allegories of 'nation,' but as extensions of and challenges to the notion of community. And as for the idea that the presence of English led to the 'silencing ... of the whole of the colonial world' (Ashcroft et al. 177–78), I will simply quote the one piece of English language that appears in any of these five books, the line from page thirty-four of *Ruwan Bagaja*, uttered by the Englishman on being offered a talking parrot at a highly inflated price: 'Go away, you poor fool!'

Notes

[1] One of the stories, *Idon Matambayi*, was believed lost: '[*Idon Matamoayi*] has unfortunately been lost to posterity, a fate not unusual in the history of African language literature' (Westley 73). However, I have a photocopy that I have used for the current discussion.

[2] Bello Kagara, for example, was one of the African teachers on the Katsina College staff when it was established in 1921. He was a product of the Pioneer Primary School started by Hanns Vischer in 1908. He went on to become a judge in the Katsina Native Authority and died in 1971 (Mora 3, fn. 1).

[3] The problematic commercial question of how you make a success of selling books when there is no established reading public, and how you build a reading public if there are few books, was an issue that bedeviled publishing right up into the late 1950s (see Skinner, *NORLA*). In 1936, East put the enlightened colonial view succinctly: 'In the Northern Provinces of Nigeria ... there is a moderate, and rapidly growing number of literates in the vernacular, particularly Hausa, written in roman script. But until recently there has been no literature, and very little "reading matter," for them to make use of their ability when they have got it. We have taught them to ride, but we have given them no horses' (351).

[4] For further detailed discussion of this competition, see Cosentino; East; Pweddon and Westley.

[5] For a discussion of the genres of Hausa literature and their interrelations, see my *Poetry, Prose.*

[6] The laughing undercurrent that runs through popular representations of colonial officials, and Europeans more generally, extends through nicknames given to particular people such as Mai Wandon Karfe ('old iron pants') for Sir Bryan Sharwood Smith, to popular jokes about defiance and obedience such as the one where an Englishman is buying eggs in the market and asks a passing youth to carry them for him. The youth places the basket of eggs on his head and asks the Englishman if he is carrying out his instructions correctly. When the Englishman replies, in English, 'yes,' the youth mistakenly understands him to be saying the Hausa word 'yas,' which means to throw away. Disconcerted, the youth asks in Hausa whether the Englishman really wants him to throw the eggs away. Without having understood the question, the Englishman says 'yes' and is appalled at the defiance of the boy as he carries out his instructions! A laughing underculture, reminiscent of Bakhtin's representation of medieval European popular culture, that plays with the styles of ubiquitous but 'other' languages is discussed in relation to Hausa burlesque market entertainers in my 'Burlesque in Hausa.'

[7] The reference is probably to the killing of Captain Moloney by the Magajin Keffi, which provided Lugard with the basis upon which he was to pursue 'the criminal' and those who harbored him right on to Kano and beyond.

[8] Probably an engagement at a place called Gwoni on 17 May 1903, before the final battle at Burmi in July of that year.

[9] The discussion of these miraculous powers is missing from the earliest editions; it would appear to be an addition in either the 1955 or the 1965 edition.

[10] The fluidities between real worlds and the fantastical in Hausa imaginative writing is perceptively discussed in Skinner, 'Realism and Fantasy.'

[11] Some British officials were of the view that some of the Hausa states were corrupt, plagued by internecine fighting and on the verge of collapse. Kagara's representation sees any such disruption and mayhem as the indirect result of the British presence.

[12] A. H. M. Kirk-Greene uses the character of Shaihu Umar from this story in his perceptive discussion of the ideological construct of the 'good man' in Hausa, an idea that plays an important part in many aspects of the construction of self and identity in Hausa.

Works cited

Ahmad, Aijaz. *In Theory: Classes, Nations, Theories*. London: Verso, 1992.

Ashcroft, Bill, Gareth Griffiths, and Helen Tiffin. *The Empire Writes Back: Theory and Practice in Post-Colonial Literatures*. London: Routledge, 1989.

Bakhtin, M. M. *Rabelais and His World*. Trans. Helene Iswolsky. Cambridge: MIT P, 1966.

Barber, Karin. 'African-language literatures and postcolonial criticism.' *Research in African Literatures* 26.4 (1995): 3–30.

Bhabha, Homi K. *The Location of Culture*. London: Routledge, 1994.

Cosentino, Donald J. 'An Experiment in Inducing the Novel among the Hausa.' *Research in African Literatures* 9.1 (1978): 19–30.

East, Rupert M. 'A First Essay in Imaginative African Literature.' *Africa* 9.3 (1936): 350–57.

Furniss, Graham. 'Burlesque in Hausa: "And my text for today is food" said Mr Matches.' *Voice, Genre, Text: Anthropological Essays in Africa and Beyond*. Ed. Paul Baxter and Richard Fardon. *Bulletin of the John Rylands University Library of Manchester*. 73.3 (1991): 37–62.

—— *Poetry, Prose and Popular Culture in Hausa*. Edinburgh: Edinburgh University Press and Smithsonian Institution Press for the International African Institute, 1996.

Hiskett, Mervyn. *A History of Hausa Islamic Verse*. London: SOAS, 1975.

Jameson, Fredric. 'Third World Literature in the Era of Multinational Capitalism.' *Social Text* 15 (1986): 65–88.

Kirk-Greene, A. H. M. *Mutumin Kirkii: the Concept of the Good Man in Hausa* (Hans Wolff Memorial Lecture). Bloomington: Indiana University African Studies Program, 1974.

Mora, Abdurrahman, ed. *The Abubakar Imam Memoirs*. Zaria: Northern Nigerian Publishing Company, 1989.

Pweddon, Nicholas. 'Thematic Conflict and Narrative Technique in Abubakar Imam's "Ruwan Bagaja".' Diss. University of Wisconsin-Madison, 1977.

Said, Edward. *Orientalism*. London: Routledge, 1978.

—— *Culture and Imperialism*. London: Chatto and Windus, 1993.

Skinner, A. Neil. 'NORLA: An Experiment in the Production of Vernacular Literature 1954–1959.' *Revue des Langues Vivantes* 36.2 (1970): 166–75.

—— 'Realism and Fantasy in Hausa literature.' *Review of National Literatures* 2.2 (1971): 67–87.

Spivak, Gayatri Chakravorty. 'Can the Subaltern Speak?' *Marxism and the Interpretation of Culture*. Ed. Cary Nelson and Lawrence Grossberg. Basingstoke: Macmillan, 1988. 271–313.

Westley, David. 'The Oral Tradition and the Beginnings of Hausa Fiction.' Diss. University of Wisconsin Madison, 1986.

BRIAN LARKIN

Indian Films & Nigerian Lovers

Media & the Creation of Parallel Modernities

Reference
Africa 67(3), 1997: 406–40

> God make him rich so he can go to India.
> *Mallam Sidi, husband of Hotiho.*
> Sidi's ambition is for God to make him rich so he can go to India.
> *Mallam Sidi, husband of Hotiho.*
> His ambition is to see Hotiho ...
> *Mallam Sidi, husband of Hotiho.*
> He swears if he sees Hotiho then no problems can move him.
> *Mallam Sidi, husband of Hotiho.*
> Mamman Shata, '*Mallam Sidi, mijin Hotiho*'
> 'Mallam Sidi is the husband of Hotiho'[1]

The sight of a 15-foot image of Sridevi, dancing erotically on the screens of the open-air cinemas of northern Nigeria, or the tall, angular figure of Amitabh Bachchan radiating charisma through the snowy, crackly reception of domestic television have become powerful, resonant images in Hausa popular culture. To this day, stickers of Indian films and stars decorate the taxis and buses of the north, posters of Indian films adorn the walls of tailors' shops and mechanics' garages, and love songs from Indian film songs are borrowed by religious singers who change the words to sing praises to the Prophet Mohammed. For over thirty years Indian films, their stars and fashions, music and stories have been a dominant part of everyday popular culture in northern Nigeria. If, as Bakhtin (1981) writes, communication is fundamental to human life, that self and society emerge in dialogue with others surrounding them, then Indian films have entered into the dialogic construction of Hausa popular culture by offering Hausa men and women an alternative world, similar to their own, from which they may imagine other forms of fashion, beauty, love and romance, coloniality and post-coloniality.

Before I began my research I read all I could find by Nigerian and Western scholars on media and film in Nigeria. For the most part, this scholarship dealt with the complex and continuing problem of cultural imperialism – the dominance of Western media and most especially Hollywood films. When I first visited Kano, the major city in northern Nigeria, it came as a surprise, then, that Indian films are shown five nights a week at the cinemas (compared with one night for Hollywood films and one night for Chinese films); that the most popular programme on television was the Sunday morning Indian film on City Television Kano (CTV); and that most video shops reserved the bulk of their space for Indian films (followed by Western and Chinese films, Nigerian dramas and religious videos). The question of why Indian films are so popular among Hausa viewers has occupied much of my research since that time.[2] What pleasures do Hausa viewers take from films portraying a culture and religion that seem so dissimilar and are watched usually in a language they cannot understand? Why has such a prominent part of the popular culture of many African societies received so little attention from academics?[3] This chapter attempts to answer these questions by taking seriously the significance of Indian films in Hausa culture. It explores the influence of Indian cinema on Hausa social life through the medium of Hausa *littatafan soyayya* (love stories). This pamphlet-type market literature, which began as recently as 1989, has created a popular reading public for wilful, passionate heroes and heroines who mimic a style of love and sexual interaction found in Indian films. *Soyayya* books, and videos based on their plots, produce a world where the imagined alternative of Indian romance is incorporated within local Hausa reality.

The popularity of Indian film in Nigeria highlights the circulation of media within and between non-Western countries, an aspect of transnational cultural flows that has been largely ignored in recent theories of globalisation. Indian films offer Hausa viewers a way of imaginatively engaging with forms of tradition different from their own at the same time as conceiving of a modernity that comes without the political and ideological significance of that of the West. After discussing reasons for the popularity of Indian films in a Hausa context, I account for this imaginative investment of viewers by looking at narrative as a mode of social enquiry. Hausa youth explore the limits of accepted Hausa attitudes to love and sexuality through the narratives of Indian film and Hausa love stories. This exploration has occasioned intense public debate, as *soyayya* authors are accused of corrupting Hausa youth by borrowing from Indian films foreign modes of love and sexual relations. I argue that this controversy indexes wider concerns about the shape and direction of contemporary Nigerian culture. Analysing *soyayya* books and Indian films gives insight into the local reworking and indigenising of transnational media flows that take place within and between Third World countries, disrupting the dichotomies between West and non-West, coloniser and colonised, modernity and tradition, foregrounding instead the ability of media to create parallel modernities.

Parallel modernities

I use the term 'parallel modernities' to refer to the coexistence in space and time of multiple economic, religious and cultural flows that are often subsumed within the term 'modernity'. This formulation resonates with the term 'alternative modernities' used by Appadurai (1991),[4] but with a key difference. Appadurai links the emergence of alternative modernities with the increased deterritorialisation of the globe and the movement of people, capital and political movements across cultural and national boundaries. While deterritorialisation is important, the experience of parallel modernities is not necessarily linked with the needs of relocated populations for contact with their homelands (Appadurai, 1991: 192). My concern, by contrast, is with an Indian film-watching Hausa populace who are not involved in nostalgic imaginings of a partly invented native land but who participate in the imagined realities of other cultures as part of their daily lives.

By stressing the importance of modernities that run parallel to the classical paradigm of the West I want to criticise recent work in African studies and media studies that has been dominated by the focus on local 'resistance' to various forms of 'dominant culture'. Abu-Lughod has warned that the 'romance of resistance' tends to focus on the creativity of resistors and fails to explore fully the effectiveness of systems of power (1990). My concern is different, arguing that concepts of resistance in African studies and elsewhere often depend on a reductive binary distinction between oppression and resistance. The effect of this is that phenomena that cannot be neatly organised within that binary distinction then fall out of view. In a recent review essay on African historiography Frederick Cooper addresses some of these concerns:

> The difficulty [in contemporary Africanist historiography] is to confront the power behind European expansion without assuming it was all-determining and to probe the clash of different forms of social organisation without treating them as self-contained and autonomous. The binaries of coloniser/colonised, Western/non-Western and domination/resistance begin as useful devices for opening up questions of power but end up constraining the search for precise ways in which power is deployed and the ways in which power is engaged, contested, deflected, and appropriated. [Cooper, 1994: 1517]

Cooper wishes to move away from what he sees as monolithic constructions of civilised coloniser and primitive colonised (and the related labels of modernity and tradition) by asserting the heterogeneity of both colonial rule and African resistances. While complicating the picture, he nevertheless remains wedded to a structural binarism that looks at the organisation of African experience in terms of its response to Western rule and its consequences.

Recent theories of postcolonialism have also unintentionally tended to reify this distinction in that the term 'postcolonial', despite a variety of different definitions, connotes a historical periodisation based on the core period of colonialism.[5] Northern Nigeria, for example, was colonised by the British in 1903, and achieved independence in 1960. A history of over a thousand years is divided into the period pre-colonial, colonial and postcolonial which centres less than sixty years of British rule at the heart of Hausa experience. Even while criticising the role of the West in postcolonial Nigerian life, theorists of cultural imperialism and postcolonialism often view Nigerian reality largely in terms of its relation to the West, with the resulting irony of reaffirming cultural imperialism at the same moment as critiquing it. It is as if the periphery could not have an experience independent of its relation to metropolitan centres. Shohat and Stam criticise this contemporary insistence on resistance for producing an 'inverted European narcissism' positing a monolithic West as the source of all evil in the world, and which 'reduces non-Western life to a pathological response to Western domination' (Shohat and Stam, 1994: 3). The widespread popularity of Indian films in Nigeria necessitates a revision of conceptions of global cultural flows that privilege the centrality of the West and refuse to recognise the common historical process of centres and peripheries engaged in contemporary cultural production.

The narrow conception of cultural imperialism has left little place for the study of phenomena such as Hong Kong or Indian film which cannot be as easily tied to a wider economic hegemony as is the case with Hollywood film.[6] This myopia has also been the result of the disciplinary boundaries of contemporary scholarship, which has little ethnographic understanding of cross-cultural media environments. Recent groundbreaking works in African cinema, such as Diawara (1992) and Ukadike (1994; see also Ekwuazi, 1987; Ekwuazi and Nasidi, 1992), deal largely with production by African film makers and are less concerned with what African film audiences are actually watching. Until recently anthropologists, with their disciplinary focus on indigenous cultural production, have been

Fig. 1. Almanac displayed in Northern Nigeria showing the popularity of Hindi film stars.

Fig. 2. Still from Hindi movie (title unknown) available in Kano.

suspicious of foreign mass-mediated cultural forms, no matter how popular they may be (cf. Abu-Lughod, 1993b; Ginsburg, 1991; Hannerz, 1992). Karin Barber, for instance, in her seminal definition of African popular arts (1987) argues that 'imported commercial entertainments ... symbolize Western culture (though they include Chinese Kung Fu movies and Indian romantic melodramas)' (1987: 25; her parenthesis). As well as reducing foreign media to a subset of Hollywood, Barber is reluctant to admit any real engagement by African audiences with these texts. Because they do not originate from an African reality she suggests they have little meaning in African life. '[E]ntertainment films that are least mediated by African culture ... [she concludes] are also the most easily replaced' (*ibid.*). Barber's observations are probably influenced by her experience among Yoruba, where indigenous videos have provided a popular alternative to imported cinema in recent years. She fails, however, to appreciate the complicated identifications that allow audiences to engage with media forms no matter how superficially 'foreign'. The popularity of Indian films in Africa has fallen into the interstices of academic analysis, as the *Indian* texts do not fit with studies of *African* cinema; the *African* audience is ignored in the growing work on Indian film; the films are too non-Western for Euro-American dominated media studies, and anthropologists are only beginning to theorise the social importance of media.

My intent is not to downplay the importance of the cultural struggle of Nigerians against foreign media, or to minimise the hegemony of Western culture, but to stress that this is only part of the cultural reality of many African nations. It is necessary to move toward a more ethnographic understanding of the range of the media environments that offer Hausa youth the choice between watching Hausa or Yoruba videos, Indian, Hong Kong or American films, or videos of Qur'anic *tafsir* (exegesis) by local preachers. In this my work has been influenced heavily by participation in the Program in Culture and Media and its affiliates within the department of anthropology at New York University. Borrowing from media and cultural studies as well as from traditional anthropological theory the Program is developing a variety of critical anthropological perspectives that examine the social relations within which media are embedded and enacted (Abu-Lughod, 1993b, 1995; Ginsburg, 1991, 1993, 1994; McLagan, 1996; Sullivan 1993). Examining the significance of Indian films in an African context, and the processes of identification by which the ideas, values and aesthetics of another culture are incorporated within an African quotidian, is a step further in this developing field. With other approaches to transnational cultural studies such as that emerging from the journal *Public Culture*, this work is building a sophisticated and supple theoretical frame to deal with what Appadurai terms a 'new cosmopolitanism' that unites the cultural, financial and political flows within and between Western and non-Western countries into a single conceptual whole. 'Modernity,' Appadurai and Breckenridge assert, 'is now everywhere, it is simultaneously everywhere, it is interactively everywhere' (1995: 2).

Appadurai argues that the new cosmopolitanism brought about by movements of people and capital in the contemporary era has created a deterritorialised world that has new significance for the understanding of media and of imagination (1990, 1991). Media figure prominently in creating interconnections between different peoples who can now consider alternative lives based not on experiences in their own locality but on a range of experiences brought to them through international mass media. As more people throughout the world see their reality 'through the prisms of possible lives offered by the mass media', Appadurai argues that contemporary ethnography must now expand to find ways of understanding the social reality of imagination: 'fantasy is now a social practice; it enters, in a host of ways, into the fabrication of social lives' (Appadurai, 1991: 198).

The concept of imagination as outlined by Appadurai is helpful in gaining insight into the pleasures that Indian films offer Hausa viewers. (I shall discuss this further below.) It also provides a theoretical way to understand the complicated identifications of audiences and cultural forms that cross expected racial, cultural and national lines. For Hausa viewers, Indian films offer images of a parallel modernity to the West, one intimately concerned with the changing basis of social life, but rooted in conservative cultural values. Characters in Indian films struggle over whether they should speak Hindi or borrow from English, whether they should marry the person they love or wed the person their parents choose. In these and many other decisions like them the narrative tensions of Indian films raise, consider and resolve minor and major anxieties within contemporary Indian society, anxieties that are relevant to Hausa viewers. Moreover, when Hausa youth rework Indian films within their own culture by adopting Indian fashions (such as the headscarves or jewellery of Indian actresses), by copying the music styles for religious purposes, or by using the filmic world of Indian sexual relations to probe the limitations within their own cultural world they can do so without engaging with the heavy ideological load of 'becoming Western'. The popularity of Indian films rests on this delicate balance of being situated between Nigerian 'tradition' and Western 'modernity', offering a mediating space for post-colonial Hausa viewers from which they may reflect on and consider the nature of contemporary social change.

Indian films and Hausa viewers

One result of the myopia regarding the presence of Indian films in West Africa is that hard data regarding their distribution and exhibition are extremely difficult to come by. Ekwuazi, for instance, borrows from UN statistics to write that in 1978-79, 86 per cent of all films imported into Nigeria were of American origin (1987: 121). Yet earlier in the same book he acknowledges that many films come in through a grey market that escapes official notice, and unofficially 'the all-time favourite is the Indian, not the American film' (1987: 44).[7] Whereas all American films were imported through the American Motion Picture Exporters and Cinema Association (AMPECA), later the Nigerian Film Distribution Company (NFDC), Indian films were imported by a host of entrepreneurs in different countries, including the Middle East, England and India. British censorship records reveal that Indian films were first introduced by Lebanese exhibitors in the 1950s who were eager to see whether the diet of American and English films could be supplemented by the odd Arab or Indian one.[8] These exhibitors speculated that Arabic films would be popular in the north because of the many religious links between northern Nigeria and the Islamic world. As the language of religious practice and debate Arabic carried immense authority, but despite these links the films never became popular on northern Nigerian screens while Indian films came to dominate them.[9]

The lack of information on the political economy of Indian film obscures the relation between the economic and symbolic reasons for its popularity (but see Pendakur and Subramanyam 1996). It seems likely that the disappearing presence of American films is related to the increasing cost of American film prints, which makes the cheaper Indian films more attractive. However, Hausa, Lebanese and Indian film and video entrepreneurs I interviewed all accounted for the dominance of Indian film in symbolic and cultural, rather than economic, terms. In an interview with Michel Issa, manager of the Cinema Distribution Circuit, which owns cinemas throughout northern Nigeria, Issa argued that Indian films were popular because 'their culture is the same' as Hausa culture.'[10] One Indian video entrepreneur posited that it was the (allegedly) common linguistic roots of Hindi and Hausa that accounted for the sense of cultural familiarity (an argument supported by Muhammad 1992).[11] Uninterested in my questions about why Indian films were more popular, Issa finally said he had no idea why Arab films had not been accepted. All he knew was that from the beginning Indian films gained a massive popular following in the north. Even before American films stopped being distributed in Nigeria, he pointed out, they had been largely replaced by Indian films on northern screens.

Indian film fans and theorists refer to contemporary Hindi films as *masala* films. Referring to the blend of spices used in Indian cooking, popular Indian cinema often mixes the genres of romance, melodrama, action, musical and comedy within the same film. For a considerable time this eclectic mix was seen by both Western and Indian academics as evidence of the inability of Indian film makers to make 'proper' American-style films. More recently, Indian film scholars have come to view Bombay films not as poor imitations of American films but as based on a distinct narrative style and structure (see Chakravarty, 1993; the special issue of *India International Centre Quarterly,* 1980; Mishray, 1985; Thomas, 1985, 1995). Rosie Thomas argues that:

> A form has developed in which narrative is comparatively loose and fragmented, realism irrelevant, psychological characterization disregarded, elaborate dialogues prized, music essential and both the emotional involvement of the audience and the pleasures of sheer spectacle privileged throughout the three hour long duration of the entertainment. [Thomas, 1995: 162; see also Thomas, 1985]

Indian films, or at least the Hindi ones that are imported into Nigeria, are made for a pan-Indian audience and the makers of the films are aware of the necessity of constructing a filmic style that crosses both linguistic and cultural boundaries. Even so, these films are embedded in a cultural specificity that presupposes familiarity with Indian cultural values, Hindu religion, and a strong sense of Indian nationalism. They are also playfully intertextual, making constant reference to classical Indian mythology, folk drama and literature and Hindu religious practice. Chakravarty (1993) argues that Indian films have created a 'communal' mode of address, a 'weness' of common cultural and national concerns that accounts for their appeal but which is largely a fiction in a country as large and diverse as India. Indian films are subtitled in English at Hausa cinemas, but the majority of those on television (which has the largest audience) are broadcast in Hindi only. This means that most Hausa viewers are watching Indian films in a language of which they have little understanding. After thirty years of watching Indian films Hausa audiences are, of course, sophisticated at understanding the narrative style of the films, and many families have several members who claim they can 'speak' Hindi, but inevitably there is a considerable cultural gap between the intertextual references to local cultural and religious values by Indian films and a Hausa viewing audience.

Despite the cultural gap between the Hindu Indian audience to which the filmic text is being addressed and the Muslim Hausa one watching in northern Nigeria, what is remarkable is how well the main messages of the films are communicated. This problem is made easier by the narrative structure of Indian films, which is borrowed from the Indian religious epics the *Mahabarata* and *Ramayana* (Mishray, 1985). The dependence upon the epics means that there is usually a fixed range of plots with clear moral contrasts that make the outlines of Indian films familiar to their viewers. The regularity of character types whose actions fall within a limited range of behaviour such as the hero, the mother, the comedic friend or the evil boss, with many of the lesser roles (such as boss or the mother) played by the same people in film after film, further aids the fixed parameters of plot structure within which the spectacle unfolds. This dependence on religious epics for narrative structure provides an easily comprehended moral guide for characters' actions and creates a limited set of narrative possibilities facilitating the easy 'translation' of Indian films across cultural, linguistic and national boundaries.[12]

Talking to many friends about their love of Indian films, I was struck by the common refrain that Indian culture was 'just like' Hausa culture. I found it surprising that staunchly Muslim Hausa should identify so strongly with Hindu Indian culture, but over time different cultural similarities became clearer. Most obvious are the many visual affinities between Indian and Hausa culture. Men in Indian films, for instance, often dress in long kaftans, similar to the Hausa *dogon riga*, over which they wear long waistcoats, much like the Hausa *palmaran*. Women are also dressed in long saris and scarves which veil their heads and accord with Hausa ideas of feminine decorum. The iconography of Indian 'tradition', such as marriage celebrations, food, village life and so on, even when different from Hausa culture, provides a similar cultural background that is frequently in opposition to the spread of 'westernisation'. Indian films place family and kinship at the centre of narrative tension as a key stimulus for characters' motivations to a degree that rarely occurs in Western films. They are based on a strict division between the sexes, and love songs and sexual relations, while sensuous, are kept within firm boundaries. Kissing is rare and nudity absent. These generic conventions provide a marked difference from Hollywood films, and many Hausa viewers argue that Indian films 'have culture' in a way that American films seem to lack.

More complexly, Indian films are based upon negotiating the tension of preserving traditional moral values in a time of profound change. Ashis Nandy argues, in terms as relevant for Nigerians as they are for Indians, that Indian films are successful with Indian masses because despite their spectacle and rich settings they are based in a moral universe of action that is grounded in a traditional world view.

> The basic principles of commercial cinema derive from the needs of Indians caught in the hinges of social change who are trying to understand their predicament in terms familiar to them. [Nandy, 1995: 205]

Nandy argues that commercial cinema tends to

> reaffirm the values that are being increasingly marginalized in public life by the language of the modernizing middle classes, values such as community ties, primacy of maternity over conjugality, priority of the mythic over the historical. [*ibid.*: 202]

Characters in Indian films have to negotiate the tension between traditional life and modernity in ways that Hausa, in a similar post-colonial situation, can sympathise with. The choice of wearing Indian or Western-style clothes; the use of English by arrogant upper-class characters or by imperious bureaucrats; even the endemic corruption of the postcolonial state, are all familiar situations with which Hausa viewers can engage.

The familiarity that Hausa viewers experience when watching Indian films is reinforced by changes over time in the style and themes of Indian film. Contemporary films are more sexually explicit and violent, and borrow heavily from the styles of Western film genres. Nigerian viewers comment on this when they compare older Indian films of the 1950s and 1960s that 'had culture' with newer ones which are more westernised. Older films were more often set among the rural poor than contemporary films. Characters, for instance, were more likely to wear traditional clothes, to keep animals or to travel by oxen. Not only did visual iconography change but musical styles, once based mainly on Indian classical forrns, began to incorporate disco beats and Western instrumentation. This perceived shift toward a growing materialism in Indian film echoed a similar shift in Nigerian society brought about by the radical dislocations of the oil boom of the mid-1970s. For Nigerian audiences the evolution of Indian film style thus corresponded with developments within their own society that brought home the similarities between the two. This has been a contentious process, and as difficult for Hausa viewers to accept in Indian films as to accept in their own culture. One young friend, who was a fan of Indian film, complained to me about this shift:

> When I was young and watching films, the Indian films we used to see were based on their tradition. You wouldn't see something like disco, going out to clubs, making gangs. Before, they didn't do it like that. But now Indian films are just like American films. They go to discos, make gangs, go out for picnics.[13] They'll do anything in a hotel and they play rough in romantic scenes where before you could never see things like that.

The perceived rise in violence, in sexual immorality and in materialism are all represented in my friend's complaint. Clubs, hotels and discos are symbols in Indian film and in Hausa popular culture of corrupt immoral spaces frequented by the rich. They are emblems of Western life and stand in moral contrast to the Indian or Hausa social spaces such as the temple, mosque or village. Indian films depict an ambivalent attitude to such spaces, exploiting their use as spectacle while at the same time ensuring that the heroes and heroines are at some moral distance from them. Nandy argues that Indian films stand against the vicissitudes of the postcolonial state by grounding the shifts in materialism, urbanisation and apparent westernisation within a moral universe that is structured around familiar religious values. This is why, despite apparent westernisation, Indian films depict moral dilemmas strikingly different from Hollywood or other Western films.

The reasons why Hausa viewers recognise commonalities between their culture and Indian culture are many and varied. In an Islamic African society the films are popular because they engage with the disjunctures of social change elaborated in terms that are familiar to Hausa society yet also distinct from it. This coexistence between likeness and dissimilarity is important because it is in the gap that the narratives of Indian film allow the exploration of social relations. I now discuss in greater detail this aspect of narrative and offer suggestions why it has become so controversial in *soyayya* books.

Imagination, narrative and social change

The narratives of Indian films allow the exploration of attitudes and social possibilities that are still controversial in everyday Hausa social life. The psychoanalyst Sudhir Kakar has discussed this phenomenon in India, arguing that Hindi films are successful because they engage everyday fantasy. 'The power of fantasy ...,' he argues, 'comes to our rescue by extending or withdrawing the desires beyond what is possible or reasonable' in the social order (1989: 27). He defines fantasy as 'that world of imagination which is fuelled by desire and which provides us with an alternative world where we can continue with our longstanding quarrel with reality' (*ibid.*). My concern in this article is with the narrative tension between love marriages and arranged marriages which is a dominant theme of both Hindi cinema and Hausa *soyayya* books. There is much more to Hindi films than this – the spectacle of beauty and wealth, the difficulty of reconciling responsibility to kin in a rapidly urbanising bureaucratic world or the problem of operating with honesty and honour in a corrupt postcolonial world – but this one genre of Indian film gives insight into broader conflict between desire and responsibility to a wider social order.

The romantic insistence on the potentially subversive power of imagination has been explored in two recent works on African oral literature and social structure. Beidelman (1993) argues that imagination has both an individual and a group importance. On the one hand, 'it relates to the ways that people construct images of the world in which they live ... a cosmology that ... presents a picture in which they measure, assess and reflect upon the reality of their experiences' (1993: 1). On the other hand, imagination offers a space from which to reflect upon the social order: 'In this sense imaginative exercise constitutes means for criticism, for distortion, even subversion of the moral social order' (*ibid.*). Michael Jackson, in his study of Kuranko oral literature, puts forward a similar picture of the power of narrative to explore ambiguities in social life. 'Kuranko narratives,' he argues, 'initiate a dialectic of doubt and uncertainty ... [that] promote ambivalence and exploit ambiguity as a way of stimulating listeners to resolve problems of choice' (Jackson, 1982: 2). Jackson stipulates that narratives are a secure way to bring up ambiguous situations, allowing readers the imaginative space to explore multiple resolutions of narrative tensions, before resolving them (in the case of oral literature) safely within the limits of accepted norms.

What Jackson and Beidelman see as a function of oral literature Kakar views as part of the collective fantasy provided by the mass culture of Indian films. I argue that the engagement with themes of romantic love revealed in *soyayya* books and Indian films exemplifies precisely this desire to explore the limits of social norms during a period of rapid change. The tension between arranged marriages and love marriages is not new to Hausa society, nor is the idea that romantic love may be subversive of the moral order, as many Hausa folk tales exemplify. What is new, however, is the speed of contemporary social change that has placed the issues of love, marriage and sexuality squarely at the forefront of social concern. The increase in conflicts over the style and nature of courtship, the appropriate age and conditions of marriage and over what is seen as the increased materialism of marriage partners condenses fears about the pace of social change. As Indian films and *soyayya* books are the main mass cultural forms that provide a sustained engagement with these issues over a long period of time, it is unsurprising that they have become a topic of public controversy. To account for the intensity of this controversy it is first necessary to outline the boundaries of social transformation in contemporary Hausa society.

Youth and marriage in contemporary Kano

The oil boom of the 1970s thrust Nigeria into the fast capitalism of an oil economy, transforming not only the economic basis of the country but the pace of urbanisation, consumption habits and the political system. Watts and Pred (1992) have borrowed from Benjamin to label this revolutionary change the 'shock of modernity'. As well as making the country dependent upon imports of basic foodstuffs, the boom internationalised the consumption habits of the middle classes, creating the easy assumption that fast capitalism meant fast westernisation. The economic crash which followed the oil boom exacerbated these transformations and contributed to a growing self-consciousness about the changing nature of Nigerian society, marked by Islamic revitalisation and criticism of secular westernisation. The transformative impact of the boom and bust of the oil economy continues to affect all classes of Nigerian society, but the position of youth has become an issue of considerable concern (Barkindo, 1993; 'Dan Asabe, n.d.; Said and Last, 1991).

The 'problems' of contemporary youth are evidenced in different realms, from the perceived rise in violence to theft, drug-taking, disrespect for elders and materialism. Even the rise in Islamic participation of youth has been a key moral discourse by which youths have challenged the authority of government and elders.[14] Important religious scholars such as Sheikh Isa Waziri in Kano preached regularly against the changing attitudes and behaviour of Hausa youth, and it is these social tensions that are indexed by the debate about *soyayya* books. At the forefront of this concern is the problem of changing marriage patterns in northern Nigeria, and more especially the concern over regulating female sexuality.

The collapse in the Nigerian economy has made the cost of the *lefe*, the gifts each man must give his wife before marriage, economically difficult for many young men. The *lefe* forms only part of the rising cost of marriage, and this inflation has been vehemently attacked as one of the most visible markers of the growing materialism of Hausa society. Religious leaders have complained regularly against the practice and there have even been attempts by state governments to regulate the costs involved, but to little avail. The result is that young men are delaying marriage until a later age when they have the income to afford the expense. Meanwhile the marrying age of women has also been moving upward. The introduction of compulsory primary-school education in 1976 affected the traditional practice of arranging marriages for girls before the onset of puberty, at around 13 years of age (Callaway, 1987). Nowadays it is more common for parents to wait until a child has finished school, around the age of 16 or 17, before choosing a marriage partner. Callaway, in her study of Hausa women in Kano, sees the rise in both Western and Islamic education as the source of potential change in the status of women (*ibid.*). As women are more enlightened as to their rights as women under Islamic law, she asserts there may be more room to resist Hausa cultural practices from the point of view of Islamic orthodoxy. One consequence is that increased education and the rise in marriage age mean that women may be more prepared to assert some measure of control over the choice of their marriage partners.

For parents and religious leaders the increase in the number of sexually mature young people outside the bounds of marriage is not only contrary to a proper Islamic social order but has become an issue demanding public regulation. In 1987 the Kano state government set up state committees to find solutions to contemporary social problems. Along with the rise in crime, hooliganism and begging, the 'problem' of unmarried women was the subject of state examination. Two years later, in his Ramadan sermon, Sheikh Isa Waziri, one of the prominent Islamic leaders in Kano, addressed the same issue when he sent out a call for rich men to marry more wives in order to solve what he termed the 'calamity' of unmarried women (Barkindo, 1993: 96). A perceived rise in sexual activity before marriage, as well as in the growing number of prostitutes (seen as a moral rather than an economic problem), has neatly conflated the issues of westernisation, materialism, the need to regulate sexuality, and the immorality of the secular Nigerian state, for northern political and religious leaders.

In her discussion of Hausa female marriage and sexuality Callaway points out that there is no acceptable space within Islamic society to be of childbearing age and unmarried. As more women occupy this 'unacceptable' space, relations between the sexes are evolving. Callaway, for instance, describes traditional Hausa interaction between the sexes as extremely limited. Compared with the West, she argues, Hausa men live separate physical and emotional lives. She concludes,

> Thus, men and women live in two separate worlds, normally do not share their thoughts or their lives, and function fairly independently of each other in their different spheres. Even husbands and wives do not normally socialize together or with each other; in order to show respect in the home, they do not eat together, seldom interact and avoid addressing each other by name. [Callaway, 1987: 44]

As a result of this sexual segregation, Callaway argues, 'The experience of romantic love is not normally part of an Islamic marriage'; '"Love" and "Romance" are Western concepts and have little real meaning in this [Hausa] culture' (1987: 36, 40). Callaway's comments caricature and devalue the complex emotions of Muslim marriages,[15] but she does represent problems that many Hausa experience. Many *soyayya* authors discussed the issue with me as they talked of the massive changes in the way young men and women interact with each other in contemporary Hausa society. Ideally, both women and men in Hausa society are expected to exhibit *kunya*, a sense of modesty and shame. Adamu Mohammed,[16] author of the novel *Garnak'ak'i* ('Uncompromising') explained what this meant in terms of sexual interaction. Traditionally, he said, all meetings between boys and girls would be chaperoned by older relatives. Frequently the couple involved might be too embarrassed even to speak to each other, and women especially, would communicate reluctantly, if at all. Another author, 'Dan Azumi 'Yan Gurasa,[17] confirmed this. 'When I was young,' he said, 'and came across the girl I loved I couldn't face her and tell her. Instead I would send someone who could talk to her about it.' Nowadays, both authors agreed, this sense of shyness has been transformed, and both men and women act in a manner that would have been unacceptable twenty years previously.

In their plots, *soyayya* authors examine some of the issues made contentious by the shift in gender interaction. The common narrative conflict between youth wishing to marry for love and parents who wish to organise marriage partners reveals how romance narratives allow a form of moral enquiry for Hausa youth.

The fantasy encoded in fictional narratives succeeds, as Beidelman points out, 'by presenting a version of experience and things that is both less and more than what we ordinarily encounter', allowing, in part, 'a luxuriation of qualities and possibilities not encountered in reality' (1993: 5). For over thirty years Indian films provided a dominant forum for the creation of an imaginary space where real social tensions over love and responsibility, individual desire and social control, appeared and various resolutions of these tensions were considered. Indian films could do this successfully only by engaging with issues that were meaningful to Hausa viewers yet at the same time providing enough of a difference for alternative resolutions to be possible. This engagement with the conflict of love and courtship in contemporary society is what has defined the plots of *soyayya* books for both their admirers and their critics. Examining these stories reveals the intertextual presence of Indian films and its appropriation within Hausa popular culture.

Figs 3 and 4. Soyayya *books on sale at Gidan Dabino, bookseller and publisher, Kano*

Market literature in the vernacular: the rise of *soyayya* books

In the last six years there has been a near-revolution in the publishing of Hausa literature. A whole new genre of *littatafan soyayya*, love stories, has emerged, published by authors themselves and sold through markets and small shops all over the northern region. During the time of the Structural Adjustment Programme (SAP), when the cost of imported goods (such as paper) has been soaring and the purchasing power of incomes has been collapsing, *soyayya* authors have published over 200 books, and created a system of publishing and distribution that keeps book prices within the range of ordinary people. Earlier books have achieved the status of 'best-seller', giving their authors a great deal of fame. Many of them are read out on the radio, on the extremely popular programme *Shafa Labari Shuni* (meaning 'a person exaggerates what he hears'), and adaptations of successful books form a significant proportion of the vibrant new market in Hausa videos. While the debate rages over whether *soyayya* books are a beneficial addition to Hausa culture, their great achievement has been to create a popular Hausa reading public for fiction.

In his major survey of Hausa literature Furniss (1996: 54–5) argues that *soyayya* writers 'appear to owe more to the English language publishing of Mills and Boon, and James Hadley Chase ... than to any Hausa precedent'. Furniss is correct in assessing the innovativeness of this new style of literature but mistaken in seeing it as based solely on Western precedents. *Soyayya* authors and their critics cite many sources for their books, including English romances and Hollywood 'best-sellers', but they also admit the important influence of Arabian tales, Nigerian romance magazines and Indian films. I concentrate on the influence of Indian films, not to ignore these other media, but as part of my larger point in analysing the flow of media within and between non-Western countries. The great appeal of Indian films across class, education and gender, along with the recognised similarities in culture, make them a significant precedent for contemporary writers and readers.

Soyayya books are pamphlets little more than fifty pages in length. Many run to two or three parts in order to keep costs down. They are badly typeset, badly printed and, from the point of view of critics, badly edited and written. Furniss argues that authors adopted the practice of publishing their own work, using offset litho printers, following the example of religious *ajami*[18] poets. Print runs are typically small, running from 2,000 to 5,000, but successful books will go into multiple printings. Originally, *soyayya* books were sold from shops and vendors selling school books. As they have become more established it is not uncommon to see market stalls devoted solely to *soyayya* books, or to see hawkers wandering round markets and business districts balancing books on their heads. The authors, unlike earlier generations of Hausa writers, come from neither an elite nor even a well educated background. Some have never received Western education and most of those who have, left after primary level, remaining only in Islamic schools, and consequently their knowledge of English, and with it their integration into existing literary culture, is often poor. Women make up a significant proportion of *soyayya* authors and some, like Hajiya Balaraba Ramat Yakubu (*Alhaki Kwikwiyo*, meaning 'Retribution is like a puppy, it follows its owner', 1990a, and *Budurwar Zuciya*, 'The heart's desire', 1990b), are among the most famous *soyayya* authors. Secondary-school leavers make up a significant proportion of the readers (though perhaps not as great a proportion as people claim) and there is a strong association in the public mind between *soyayya* books and women readers. Despite this, many young men I knew were avid readers of the literature, and the high percentage of men who write fan letters to the authors suggests that there is a significant male relationship.

Soyayya books first emerged from Kano, the metropolitan centre of northern Nigeria. Originally authors came together to organise writers' clubs modelled on the famous drama clubs organised by heroes of independence in the north, Mallam Aminu Kano, Sa'adu Zungur and Maitama Sule. The first and most famous clubs were Raina Kama ('Deceptive Appearances')[19] and Kukan Kurciya ('The Cry of a Dove'), created in order to exchange mutual aid and advice among neophyte authors. Since that time new writers' clubs have appeared in many major cities and contemporary *soyayya* authors come from all northern urban centres. Many authors began by basing their first novel on an experience that had happened to them or their friends, often an affair of love. In *da so da K'auna* I, II (meaning 'Where there's love and desire') by Ado Ahmad (1989) or *Garnak'ak'i* I, II by Adamu Mohammed (1991) are both examples of this. Many authors go on to write about other issues, whether it be politics in Bala Anas Babinlata's *Tsuntsu Mai Wayo* I, II ('The Clever Bird', 1993) or *'yan daba* [thugs] and crime in 'Dan Azumi Baba's *Rikicin Duniya* I, II, III ('This Deceptive World', 1990). The dominant theme with which most books are identified remains the conflict over love.

Soyayya books dramatise the problems of contemporary sexual relations, criticising forced marriages and the increasing material demands of both lovers and parents. Many authors claim a didactic purpose for their writing, arguing that they are educating young people and their parents against the problems that beset contemporary youth. The fact that many authors begin writing as a direct result of a personal experience underscores the close relation between the stories and perceived social problems. Adamu Mohammed explained to me that he began writing books when the parents of the girl he loved married her off, against the wishes of both the lovers, to a wealthier man. As a poor man, Mohammed argued, he had no means of fighting the decision except by writing his book *Garnak'ak'i* – 'Uncompromising'. The sense of outrage and vindication is common to many of the early *soyayya* writers. A similar event sparked off the career of Ado Ahmad. As Maigari Ahmed Bichi (1992) reports, the arrangements for Ahmad's first marriage were broken off despite the fact that he and his fiancee were in love and her parents were happy about the marriage: 'a misunderstanding between their two families . . . was caused by the grandmother of the girl, who . . . had arranged for the girl to be given to one Alhaji[20] for marriage' (1992: 7). Bichi continues that as a result Ahmad intended his first novel to 'show how love is played in Hausa society and the role of parents in marriage affairs' (*ibid.*). One fledgling author from Kaduna, Adamu Ciroma, who also began writing after a personal experience, argues that many if not most *soyayya* authors begin writing this way:

> Our writers today we share experiences which makes us start writing... An experience happens to me and so I decide to write about it in order to enlighten people on what has happened... Nine out of ten writers begin writing *soyayya* because they have experienced it.

For *soyayya* authors there is a didactic and moral purpose to their discourse on love that gives their novels a sense of social responsibility. They argue that incompatibility in the choice of marriage partner leads daughters to run away from their parents to become 'independent women' (and hence prostitutes), or to attempt suicide, or to go through an unhappy marriage and an early divorce – even if the partner chosen is wealthy. But as the author 'Dan Azumi Baba argues, 'now everything has changed [and] because of reading such books [*soyayya* books] no girl agrees with forced marriage and parents understand that if they force their daughter to marry somebody she will eventually go and become a prostitute' (interview, 28 June 1995). He continued, 'the main problem of marriage is lack of love' adding that most women now are wise to the fact that 'if there is love, they will not mind about any problems'. The concerns aired by 'Dan Azumi and others over the increasing commodification of contemporary love and the iniquities of forced marriage are not just the province of *soyayya* books but have formed staple themes of Indian films. For over thirty years Indian films have provided an extended narration of the problems of arranged marriages and of the place of materialism in a 'traditional' society that mimics real events in everyday Hausa lives. Before discussing *soyayya* books themselves it is worth returning briefly to the concept of fantasy and imagination to give an example of the investment of viewers in Indian narratives.

The possibility of imaginative investment was brought home to me one day when I was talking to an older Hausa friend in his 40s. Knowing he liked Indian films, I was surprised to hear him say that they had a negative influence on Hausa culture. He cited the example of his own marriage. He said that when he was young, in the 1970s, he went to see lots of Indian films. He, like many other men, liked the commitment of Indian films to the family, the importance of marriage and children, and many other cultural values in the films. The problem, he said, was that in Indian films women are very supportive of their husbands. He explained that what he meant was that when an Indian man sees his love they talk about their problems. He declares his love for her, she declares hers for him, and they embrace. In the 1970s men who went to the cinema were expecting or wanting similar behaviour from their wives. It was what he had wanted when he got married. But when he returned home and tried to talk to his wife she would turn away, answer as briefly as possible and try to leave the room. He told me women in Hausa society were taught that their husband is everything and they should be in awe of him. His wife was acting with the modesty that a good Hausa wife should have, whereas he wanted the sort of relationship he had seen in Indian films. As a result he had encountered many problems early in his marriage and that was why, he argued, the films could be harmful. Indian films, he said conveyed ideas about marriage and relationships that local culture could not support.

My friend's anecdote is a striking example of the complicated ways in which transnational media flows become incorporated into individual experience and affect larger social constructions such as gender. It is even more fascinating as it is so clearly dated. In the early 1970s the exhibition of Indian films was largely restricted to the cinema. The practice of female seclusion (*kulle*) meant that women were absent (for the most part) from the male arena of cinema and it was not until the growth of domestic technologies such as television and video that women gained access to the popular culture of Indian films. Since that time Indian films have become identified as 'women's films' because of their huge popularity. The stereotype now is that it is women who demand that their partners act more like lovers in Indian films and men who

Fig. 5. A cover of a soyayya *book.*

complain that Indian films create demands that cannot be met. This complaint has become all the more controversial as people accuse *soyayya* authors of dramatising the Bombay melodrama style of love within a Hausa context.

All you need is love...

To give some sense of the tone and structure of the texts I am dealing with I briefly outline the plots of two *soyayya* books. The books I discuss are *Inda so da K'auna* I, II by Ado Ahmad (1989) and *Kishi Kumallon Mata* (meaning 'Jealousy is the nausea of women') by Maryam Sahabi Liman (1993). *Inda* is a two-part volume that was abridged and translated into English as *The Soul of my Heart* in 1993. Its author, Ado Ahmad, says it is the best-selling of all *soyayya* books, selling over 50,000 copies, and has since been adapted into a three-part Hausa video and remains one of the few *soyayya* books to have been translated into English. (I cite from this text.)[21] *Inda*, as one of the earliest and most popular books, has been the subject of great attention and discussion, and exemplifies many of the major themes associated with *soyayya* books. *Kishi* is a more recent novel, published after *soyayya* books had received a great deal of public criticism. Because of this, Liman is careful to avoid many of the themes that have led to *soyayya* books being dismissed as a form of *iskanci* (immorality, loose living) and provides a good counterpoint to *Inda*.

Inda tells the story of Sumayya, a rich girl who falls in love with a much poorer boy, Mohammed. Unfortunately Sumayya herself is the object of the affections of Abdulkadir, a wealthy young businessman. When Abdulkadir is rejected by Sumayya he visits her grandmother, taking gifts and money, and persuades her to intervene on his behalf with Sumayya's parents. Accordingly she threatens to withdraw her blessing from her son if Sumayya is not wed to Abdulkadir. Abdulkadir, meanwhile, arranges to have Mohammed beaten up by thugs to warn him off Sumayya. Sumayya and Mohammed are crushed by the news of the arranged marriage. As the wedding nears, Sumayya throws herself down a well in a desperate attempt at suicide. She survives and is taken to hospital, where her life is saved by a timely blood transfusion from Mohammed. Her parents, seeing this, feel that now the couple should be united and agree to the marriage. They are wed and Mohammed goes into business, becoming rich, while Abdulkadir, returning from a business deal in Abuja, is pursued by armed robbers who force his Mercedes off the road and rob him of all his money, leaving him a pauper.

Kishi describes the problems that derive from jealous co-wives. It tells the story of a rich man, Usman, who falls in love and marries Ruk'ayya. They live happily together until it is found out that Ruk'ayya cannot conceive. After consulting both Western doctors and religious teachers, Ruk'ayya selflessly advises her husband that he should take a second wife. Ruk'ayya persuades her good friend Saratu to attract the attentions of her husband so that he will marry her, arguing that if she has to have a co-wife it should be someone she is friends with. Usman and Saratu marry and Saratu becomes pregnant. Immediately, though, she accuses Ruk'ayya of trying to poison her from jealousy. Usman comes to side with Saratu's accusations of poison and witchcraft against Ruk'ayya. He moves Saratu to a different house and later, when he travels to America on business, he leaves his affairs in the hands of Saratu's grasping father. After his departure, Ruk'ayya discovers she is two months pregnant. Months later, while Usman is still away, she gives birth and while she is in hospital Saratu is admitted because of a miscarriage. Usman returns home to discover that his and Saratu's baby has died, that Saratu orchestrated the accusations of poison and witchcraft against Ruktayya and that her father has been ruining his business. Usman divorces Saratu and returns to Ruk'ayya, who accepts him lovingly and without recrimination.

Soyayya books create a utopian world where the norms of sexual relations are inverted and transformed. *Inda* and *Kishi* recount the love stories of young people of equal age. Unlike usual Hausa sexual relations, men and women not only share social space with each other, but they spend recreational time together and lead a shared emotional life. The traditional sense of shyness that regulates social interaction is transformed. Men openly declare their love for women, and women, more shockingly, are equally vocal in expressing their love in return. In *Inda*, for instance, Sumayya is the first to look at Mohammed: She initiates contact with him through letters and when they finally meet:

> 'Mohammed,' she said shyly, 'I must confess that you are always on my mind. I love you very much.' [Ahmad, 1993a: 10]

Similarly, in *Kishi*, Usman and Ruk'ayya address each other in phrases that are new to Hausa love-making: in one scene Ruk'ayya approaches a worried Usman and asks, 'O my lover, the milk that cools my heart, what is worrying you?' (Liman, 1993: 20). Usman replies, 'There is nothing, light of my heart' (*ibid.*).

Soyayya books portray a field of sexual interaction very different from 'traditional' Hausa ideals. Open declarations of love, expressed in an elaborate and highly formalised way, are one of the most visible markers of the shift in styles of love among Hausa youth. In fact *Inda* represents a reversal of the norms of Hausa sexual hierarchy, with Sumayya, by virtue of her money and status, narratively more active and passionate than Mohammed. This subversive link between materialism and sexuality is another common theme of *soyayya* books, and reiterates the fears of many Hausa young about the difficulties of marriage. At the beginning of *Inda*, when his friends notice that Sumayya is eyeing Mohammed, it sets off an exchange among his friends, who dismiss Mohammed's concern that Sumayya is too rich for him. They make the familiar claim among male Hausa youth that there are too many unmarried women and lament the fact that they cannot afford to marry:

> 'Husbands are hard to come by now, anyway.'
> 'Exactly,' Garba agreed. 'The table has now turned. It is the girls that now court. Men are extremely scarce you know.' [Ahmad, 1993a: 3]

Garba discusses the reason for this unnatural state of affairs:

> 'The fault lies squarely on the parents. They try to commercialise marriages. It goes to the highest bidder.... [A]ll of us here crave marriage but it is the demands that scare us away.' [*ibid.*: 4]

The commodification of religious affairs such as marriage that Garba refers to is represented by the figure of the grandmother. Her age should represent the accrual of wisdom and authority but she loses the respect she is due when she commodifies her authority by accepting bribes from Abdulkadir. Instead of representing what is best about tradition she comes to stand for what is worst about the corruption of contemporary times. It is this illegitimate act that allows Sumayya's rebellion against parental authority to remain within the bounds of an ideal moral universe.

The tension between tradition and modernity that materialism represents in the story is mimicked in the conflict over individual desire and social responsibility. Early in the book, Mohammed points out to Sumayya that her parents are likely to view the possibility of their marriage negatively, owing to their unequal social status. Sumayya reveals her commitment to modern social values as she dismisses his argument:

> Please do understand that nothing is permanent, riches or otherwise. Are we the ones who determine our destinies? I assume that our creator has that singular quality. He gives to whomever he wishes and refuses whomever he wishes. Besides, talking about parental interference, I think that has by now been one of the bygones. They now accept what the boy and girl want. The evils of forced marriages are too clear for all to see. [*ibid.*: 1–11]

Sumayya is overconfident in believing forced marriage a thing of the past, and that parents will readily cede autonomy to their children. She makes the religiously acceptable argument that is Allah who determines destiny, but she does so as she sloughs off concern for parental authority and asserts the right to control her own destiny.

Fig. 6. Cover of a soyayya *book. Note the Indian features of Sumayya in this picture.*

While overt rebellion against parental authority is missing, this sense of individual control also marks the storyline of *Kishi*. *Kishi* was intended overtly to avoid the criticism that surrounded early *soyayya* books such as *Inda*. The suicide attempt by Sumayya, for instance, was alleged to have inspired other young girls to follow her example, and critics accused Ahmad of teaching girls to rebel against their parents (Giginyu, 1992). Liman is careful not to advocate rebellion and attempts to articulate the new subjectivity of youth, and the fascination of romantic love, within an accepted Hausa framework. Kishi is full of platitudinous statements about ideal behaviour which are immediately contradicted by the logic and tension of narrative development. Unlike *Inda*, all the youths in Kishi respect and obey their parents and never contemplate rebelling against their decisions. But Liman never puts them in a position where they have to. Usman and Ruktayya meet and court by themselves. When they fall in love *they* decide to tell their parents, who are delighted and form no embarrassing obstacles. Significantly, though, control over the decision as to marriage partner is left to the young people themselves. This is the case even with Usman's second marriage, to the devious but beautiful Saratu.

Liman creates a utopian world of rich and beautiful youth who fly to Europe for medical treatment, who act selflessly and love passionately, but always in the context of proper Hausa behaviour. It may be that the characters drive fancy cars, go to Western-style hotels for their honeymoon and live in large houses filled with the latest in electronic consumer goods, but Liman accompanies this spectacle of material wealth with moral homilies referencing key Hausa virtues. When Alhaji Lawal, Usman's grandfather, instructs him that now is the time to be thinking of marriage and to begin looking for a bride, he tells him, 'Even though I won't prevent you from looking for beauty, you should make sure it's religion that leads you to marriage and not your heart' (Liman, 1993: 2). Usman agrees to this obvious insertion of 'ideal' Hausa values, but in the next paragraph he sees a girl, their eyes meet and he falls in love, asking himself if she will agree to marry him before he has ever said a word to her, let alone found out about her religious values. Similarly, Usman announces his wedding to his grandfather with:

> 'Grandfather, today something wonderful has happened to us.' Then he told him the story from the beginning to the end. Fortunately Alhaji Lawal knew Mallarn Haruna [Ruk'ayya's father] and knew him for an upright character who doesn't care about worldly things. [Liman, 1993: 9-10]

Liman protects Usman's desire for control over his own life and Alhaji's concern for proper Hausa values, as individual desire and parental will coincide in a perfect world.

The dominant melodramatic tension in *Kishi* revolves around the moral of sacrifice. This theme constitutes part of the basic genre of Indian film and depends for its significance on the tension between modernity and tradition in postcolonial societies. Sacrifice, as it is mobilised in *Kishi* and many Indian films, depends upon a moral choice between individual desire and social responsibility, taking on a cultural as well as an individual resonance. Rukayya, in *Kishi*, is the supreme example of the self-sacrificing wife. Not only does she accept the unjust accusations of her co-wife uncomplainingly, the very fact that as a wife she insists on her husband marrying a second wife reveals how willing she is to sacrifice her individual happiness for the good of the family. In Hausa the name for co-wife, *kishiya*, derives from *kishi*, the Hausa word for jealousy, and is particularly identified with women (as the proverb and title of the book, 'Jealousy is the nausea of women', implies). Most Hausa readers I spoke to thought it highly unlikely that any husband and grandfather would not look for a second wife if the first were barren (again reiterating the utopian nature of the book), but this device is necessary to highlight the individual nature of Ruk'ayya's sacrifice.

Jackson argues that narratives function by raising 'ethical dissonance' (1982: 2), situations of doubt and uncertainty through which the audience can reflect upon the nature of the social order. He argues that this is especially true in folk tales about love. In many societies the choice of marriage partner is an important decision affecting the entire family and so is rarely left to the individuals directly concerned. Love affairs, Jackson points out, are based on individual choices. 'Love,' he states, 'like all strong emotions, is difficult to control, and its course is unpredictable' (ibid.: 202). In consequence love can be wild and a potential threat to the social order. To make sure the passing fancies of men and women are regulated for the common good, love has to be reined in and controlled by authorities, usually elder kin. Abu-Lughod makes a similar point in her discussion of the poetry of love and emotions among Bedouin. 'Succumbing to sexual desire, or merely to romantic love,' she asserts, 'can lead individuals to disregard social convention and social obligations' and threaten social values of honour and the authority of elders (1986: 147–8). Stories of romantic love raise questions about the importance of individual action versus familial obligation, but precisely how these stories are resolved varies. When, in *Kishi*, Ruk'ayya decides to regulate her emotions and sacrifice her desires for the good of the family she makes a choice in favour of the social order. Conversely, when Sumayya decides to reject what she sees as the illegitimate decision of her parents, she refuses their authority in an attempted suicide.

By presenting two radically different solutions to comparable problems these books bear out Jackson's argument that narratives promote ambivalence and ambiguity as a way of allowing readers to imaginately explore social tensions in their multiple connotations. Jackson argues that this process occurs in the development of a single narrative, but it is my point that the mass culture of *soyayya* books and Indian films develops the process of ambiguity by presenting vatious resolutions of similar predicaments in thousands of narratives extending over many years. By engaging both with individual stories and with the genre as a whole, narratives provide the ability for social inquiry. Sacrifice is significant to postcolonial societies negotiating the rapidity and direction of social change because it is for their readers and viewers that the conflict between parental authority and individual desire is most keenly felt. This is one reason why the theme of sacrifice is so prevalent in Indian films and *soyayya* books and relatively absent from Western genres such as Hollywood films. Precisely because this theme has such relevance to Hausa society, the success of *soyayya* books has occasioned a powerful backlash against them, and even, by proxy, against Indian films, which previously were a relatively unremarked part of the Hausa cultural landscape. To finish my discussion of transnational media and social change I now outline the contours of the public debate that surrounds the success of *soyayya* books. This controversy reveals how conflict over the direction of social change is condensed around issues of changing sexual relations among youth, and the place of Indian films as a cultural third space situated between Hausa tradition and Western modernity.[22]

Soyayya books, youth and social change: the controversy

> Right from your book cover the design is sinful... Similarly when somebody reads your books he will see that inside consists of sin and forbidden things. And when it comes to letters in the books to believe in them will make somebody deviate from the teachings of his religion. Quotations like 'my better half' [*rabin raina*], 'the light of my heart' [*hasken zuciyata*] and other lies makes you wonder whether the writer should not be lashed. [*Zuwa ga marabutan Soyayya*, 'An open letter to *soyayya* authors', from the editor, *Gwagwarmaya* ('Struggle') 2: 19]

The strong moral lessons embedded in *soyayya* books have gained enormous popularity with a young Hausa audience. Yet it is often youth who are the bitterest opponents of this new form of fiction. The success of *soyayya* books has created a public discourse that includes a profusion of articles in Hausa language magazines and newspapers, letters to the authors themselves, and the everyday conversation of fans and critics. The tone and passion of the public discourse indicate the volatility of response to the popular culture of romance. One letter to the editor of the Hausa-language newspaper *Nasiha* 'Advice') is typical of the debate:

> Dear Sir,
> I wish to take space in your widely read newspaper to appeal to the Federal Government and the State Government. In truth, it would be better if the Government took steps regarding the books that certain notorious elements are writing everywhere in Nigeria, especially in the north. [19 May 1995: 8]

The letter writer continues, 'These books only succeed in corrupting our youth, especially girls,' and adds that it has become necessary for the government to take action.

When I was in Nigeria the idea that the state government was about to take radical action 'against' *soyayya* books was widely believed by young men who were opposed to their continued distribution. Such youths had two main complaints against the books. The first was that the material world of fine clothes, expensive cars and generous lovers that the books presented encouraged girls to demand presents from their boyfriends and lovers that they could not afford. In consequence boys who may court a girl for years, giving her small presents and supporting her education, lose out to a rich Alhaji who meets and marries the girl within just a few months. The second complaint is that girls demand a different style of behaviour from their lovers. In a reverse of the complaints made against Indian films cited earlier, girls both demonstrate and demand greater sophistication in the language and behaviour of love. One friend of mine who attacked *soyayya* books vehemently said that in the past if you tried to kiss a girl before you were married she would scream and call for her brothers. Now, he said, if you don't kiss her by the second time you meet she will think you are 'bush' (backward) and this is the result of reading *soyayya* books. As well as calls for the government to intervene, some secondary school headmasters are said to have embarked on a campaign to expel any girls found with *soyayya* books in their possession. The discourse around the books then, has touched on an issue of considerable public passion.

The press debate was sparked by the efforts of two journalists (both fiction writers themselves) working at the newspaper *Nasiha*: Ibrahim Sheme and Ibrahim Malumfashi. Sheme initiated a regular literary page in the newspaper which, soon after *soyayya* books began to appear in northern markets, published an interview with one author, Hauwa Ibrahim Shariff (6 September 1991). Thus began the public debate over the pros and cons of *soyayya* books, including a seminal exchange of articles between Ibrahim Malumfashi (then at Usman Dan Fodio University in Sokoto) and Ado Ahmad. Malumfashi opened the debate with an attack on *soyayya* writers, 'On the need to change the style of Hausa literature' (November 1991: 7). In this article he charged *soyayya* writers with dwelling on themes of escapism that had little or no relevance to the problems of poverty and deteriorating life style that dominated everyday existence. He argued that the books shamelessly borrowed from other cultures, creating situations that could never possibly exist in Hausa society. Later, Malumfashi extended his critique of cultural borrowing in an article entitled 'Between second-hand and original' (*Nasiha*, 7 August 1992: 4; 14 August 1992: 4) where he argued that *soyayya* books were 'second-hand' and that if Ado Ahmad 'watches Indian films he will realise that it is these films that are being translated into Hausa and claimed to have happened in Kano, Kaduna, Katsina or Sokoto. Most of these books are filled with rubbish' (14 August 1992: 4).

Ahmad responded to Malumfashi as chairman of the main *soyayya* writing group, Raina Kama. His article 'Let's go with modern times! (*Nasiha* 24, 31 July 1992) makes the powerful point that for the first time Hausa markets are filled with books written in Hausa that, far from copying foreign cultures, represent an efflorescence of Hausa culture. Times have changed, Ahmad argues, and *soyayya* books call for the betterment of society rather than corrupting it. Ahmad's argument stems from the fact that many *soyayya* writers who create stories from personal experience are writing about issues that are important to contemporary culture and should not be ignored for the sake of more 'relevant' issues. It is a point of view echoed by Yusuf Adamu Mohammed when he asks why contemporary authors write love stories:

> The contemporary generation of readers are more interested in what concerns them: stories of ancient empires and jinns [spirits] are no longer appealing to them.[23] Second, many of these young authors are young and unmarried ... [and they suffer] from the misdeeds of autocratic rich men in society ... Since the young novelists are also among the downtrodden, in real life they are virtually helpless. Yet they can use their pens to fight for their rights and the rights of the oppressed. [*Association of Nigerian Authors Review*, October 1994: 9, 10]

The debate between Ahmad, Malumfashi and others sparked an outpouring in the pages of *Nasiha* and other Hausa-language magazines and newspapers. Sheme, who had initiated the debate, finally had to ask for no more submissions because the paper was inundated (*Nasiha*, 28 August 1992), though the debate still continues regularly. The debate in the press was supplemented by letters to the authors themselves. Many *soyayya* authors include a postal address on all books published, and popular authors such as Ahmad, 'Dan Azumi Baba and Adamu Mohhammed get an enormous response. Ahmad has received more than 2,000 letters covering a range of topics from requests for free copies, to expressions of love, to requests for advice on how to manage relationships, and compliments and criticism. One such letter from a recent (male) school graduate stated:

> Among all the writers of Hausa *soyayya* books you [Ado Ahmad] are the best of them. This is because you are aware of what is going on nowadays. And you are more devoted Islamically and culturally than all of them. ... [Your popularity is] because of your struggle to educate youth on marriage and not only children but parents too. The books stop parents making arranged marriages for their children and give freedom of choice to each and everybody irrespective of tribe or culture. This is of course the major aspect of your books that impresses and encourages people to read more *soyayya* books. [3 November 1993]

It is interesting and unsurprising that the writer registers Ahmad's devotion to religion and to culture, as these are the grounds on which *soyayya* authors are attacked most strongly. Many other letter writers have praised Ahmad for his stand against materialistic parents. One said that contemporary youth were sick of the greed of money mongers (*mai idon cin naira*) like Sumayya's grandmother and grateful for the 'educative' nature of *soyayya* books. Another said that the books showed him the wrongs of forced marriage (*auren dole*) and the importance of individual choice. The books, he continued, 'teach us how to live successfully in the world . . . how parents should take care of their children and be careful in letting their daughters choose the person they love and admire' (no date).

The insistence on individual choice curbing parental authority is cited by many critics as the prime reason for the pernicious effect of *soyayya* books. 'I swear, Mallam Ado,' wrote one youth in response to reading *Inda*, 'most of the crises that are occurring nowadays are caused by your writings. Our youths are spoiled by reading your books.' He continued:

> [Ado Ahmad] you are among those who mobilise our youth, especially our girls, to start feeling freedom of choice by force, and that they should start doing everything according to their own interest and to forget about their parents' interest, and that they should only marry the person they love. For example, mostly in your books you write about a girl running away from her parents, because of someone she loves and chooses to be with. And, as you see, this is a great deviation from the teachings of Islam and culture, as you forget that girls are under the thumb of their parents religiously and culturally. [29 January 1994]

The response of letter writers to Ahmad and other authors indicates how closely people view the relation between *soyayya* books and everyday life. One writer to Ahmad said he became a fan of his books when his girlfriend insisted he read them because there were so many things he could learn from them. Similarly, Baba and Ahmad receive many letters asking for advice in matters of love. It is unsurprising, then, that these books generate such passion, as fans of *soyayya* writers and their critics are both responding to the mundane concern about contemporary social change. *Soyayya* books effectively dramatise this change within the realm of romance and sexuality. The profusion of articles both for and against *soyayya* books in the press has taken what was mainly a controversy among young people (reading *soyayya* books would be considered too demanding for older men) into a wider public arena.

Conclusion

One Friday night I went with a friend to see the classic Indian film *Mother India* (1957, directed by Mehboob Khan) at the Marhaba. A Lebanese distributor had explained to me how despite the fact that he had been screening the film for decades it could still sell out any cinema in the north, and he made me curious to see whether it was true. Sure enough, on Friday night at the Marhaba, the busiest night (usually reserved for new films) at the newest and largest cinema in Kano, all the seats were full. As the film started the friend I went with turned to me and said, 'Besides you, everyone in the cinema has seen this film at least fifteen times.' I relate this anecdote to give some sense not just of the pervasiveness of Indian film but of the fan culture that surrounds it. This comes across strongly when you watch a film where everyone knows the songs, when people laugh at the comedy routines almost before they are finished, and where the dialogue, the narrative and the emotions invoked carry the familiarity and comfort of a well known and well loved film.[24] When I returned home that night another friend in his late 20s asked me where I had been. I told him and asked if he knew when the film was made. He laughed, saying, 'I don't know, but as soon as I knew film I knew *Mother India*.' Just as I, growing up in London in a cinematic world dominated by American stars, incorporated American media as part of English popular culture, so it is for Hausa audiences. Indian films have been reworked and incorporated to form an integral part of contemporary Hausa social life.

The long struggle against cultural imperialism has not so much criticised the influence of Indian films as ignored it. While the politics of representation, and the effects of cultural imperialism, are highly politicised topics in Nigeria, Indian films, by virtue of their traditions and 'culture', have created a space which largely sidesteps criticism. This is because for Hausa viewers Indian films have been situated in cultural space that stands outside the binary distinctions between tradition and modernity, Africa and the West, resistance and domination. The images of modernity they offer are mediated through a concern for maintaining traditional social relations and so they run parallel to, similar yet different from, the modernity offered by westernisation. Hausa viewers managed to engage with texts that showed a culture that was 'just like' Hausa culture as long as it was also irreducibly different. It is no surprise that, when the difference collapsed through the rise of *soyayya* books, Indian films became controversial in a way they never were before. As one writer to Ado Ahmad put it, 'In truth, Ado, you are among those who spread this modern love to our young people, not the films they watch, because in those films they don't usually understand what they are about. But now you are telling us in our own language' (letter of Ahmad, 29 January 1994).

The tendency of many Africanists to see resistance as the underlying cause of a vast range of social and cultural phenomena led, in its reductionism, to the elision of other cultural flows that did not fit neatly into the pattern. How else do we account for the absence of Indian films from analyses of African popular culture? The understandable tendency for anthropologists and others to concentrate on the vibrancy of popular arts produced by the people, though laudable, has elided some forms of mass-mediated culture from academic purview. Barber, for instance, asks, 'What exactly an African audience gets out of, say, a film in a foreign language, about culturally remote people who perform a series of actions almost invisible to the naked eye on a dim and flickering screen. Do these shows perhaps represent novelty itself in its most concentrated form?' (Barber, 1987: 25). What audiences take from these films is considerable. Indian film has been a popular form of entertainment in urban West Africa for well over forty years and commands viewers because it engages with real desires and conflicts in African societies. Instead of indulging in a blanket dismissal of these forms it is necessary to take them seriously in their textual, cultural and historical specificities. The task that remains is to theorise adequately the complexity and heterogeneity of contemporary national and transnational cultural flows. Why are Indian films more popular in northern than in southern Nigeria? Are the reasons for their popularity the same elsewhere in West Africa? Why have influential film genres such as Egyptian films had so little impact in Nigeria? These are questions that need to be answered, for, as Appadurai and Breckenridge (1988) observe, transnational cultural flows emerge from many centres and flow into many peripheries. In this article I have been concerned to articulate why one media form – Indian film – has resonance in the very different cultural environment of northern Nigeria. Indian films are popular because they provide a parallel modernity, a way of imaginatively engaging with the changing social basis of contemporary life that is an alternative to the pervasive influence of a secular West. Through spectacle and fantasy, romance and sexuality, Indian films provide arenas to consider what it means to be modern and what may be the place of Hausa society within that modernity. For northern Nigerians, who respond to a number of different centres, whether politically to the Nigerian state, religiously to the Middle East and North Africa, economically to the West, or culturally to the cinematic dominance of India, Indian films are just one part of the heterogeneity of everyday life.

Acknowledgements

Funding for this research was provided by the Wenner-Gren Foundation and a Dean's Research Grant from New York University. I am grateful to Faye Ginsburg, T. O. Beidelman, Lila Abu-Lughod and Meg McLagan, who all commented on drafts of this article. I also thank Karin Barber and Murray Last for their editorial comments. The article relies heavily on the generous help given by the *soyayya* authors 'Dan Azumi Baba, Yusuf Lawan and Adamu Mohammed. I especially thank Ado Ahmad and Yusuf Mohammad Adamu, who initiated me into the world of *soyayya* literature. This article could not have been written without them. Ibrahim Sheme and Ibrahim Malumfasrii added their critical view of *soyayya* books to the picture. Finally, I thank Usman Aliyu Abdulmalik and Abdullahi Kafin-Hausa for help with translation.

Notes

[1] Mamman Shata is one of the most famous Hausa singers. This song was written as a satire on his friend, Mallam Sidi, who 'fell in love' with an Indian film actress.

[2] I use the term 'Indian film' throughout as it is how Hausa viewers describe what is, in actuality, Bombay Hindi film. 'Indian film' should properly refer to the variety of Indian language films.

[3] To my knowledge, the only Nigerian film critics to discuss Indian films are Ekwuazi (1987), who criticises them, and Muhammad (1992), who praises them. For a journalist's view see Sheme (1995a, b). Fugelsang (1994) discusses viewing of Indian videos by Lamu youth.

[4] Abu-Lughod (1993a) also argues for increased attention to global flows that do not originate in Euro-American centres.

[5] My use of the term 'postcolonial' in this article is historical rather than theoretical, referring to the aftermath of the experience of colonialism for ex-colonised nations.

[6] The success of Brazilian *telenovelas* in China, the Soviet Union and elsewhere, and the regional dominance of Egyptian film and soap operas among Arabic-speaking countries, are other examples of the phenomenon. See McNeely and Soysal (1989) for a discussion of this trend. See Sreberny-Mohammadi (1991) for a critique.

[7] Ekwuazi, while admitting the widespread popularity of Indian film, argues that 'its impact on the cultural landscape is relatively minimal' (1987: 44). In almost direct contrast to this article, he argues that the reason is that Indian films are unable to offer a 'feasible model for (teenage) dreams' (*ibid.*). That Ekwuazi comes to what I see as a mistaken conclusion is a marker of the devalued position that popular Indian cinema has among scholars. (See Thomas 1985 for a discussion of this phenomenon.) Ekwuazi views Indian film as a cheap copy of American film and, rather than considering Indian narratives, stars or spectacles as governed by an alternative filmic style he judges them by their failure to live up to Westem standards: 'To anyone who has seen the real thing, the Indian imitation film is an aesthetic offense; it makes even the worst American film a sight for sore eyes' (*ibid.*).

[8] History and Culture Bureau, Kano (HCB): Edu/14, Cinematograph and Censorship of Films, Exhibition of Films.

[9] The reason why this is so is unclear. Arab films have long been successful internationally, and popular Egyptian films have a wide audience outside their own country. Perhaps it was precisely because Arabic is a religious language that its association with such a profane domain as cinema (as it is seen in northern Nigeria) made it impossible to attract an early viewing public. The recent introduction of satellite television in Nigeria has made channels from Saudi Arabia and Egypt available. As this comes at the same time as a revival in Arabic-language learning it may give Arab media a new popularity.

[10] Interview, Michel G. Issa, Manager, Cinema Distribution Circuit, May 1995.

[11] Many Arabic loan words are common to both Hindi and Hausa, which creates an oft-remarked sense of linguistic similarity.

[12] It is no accident that the two other popular genres of film in Nigeria are Chinese Kung-fu and gangster films, and American action films. Action films depend more heavily on visual sequences than on complex narrative development, which makes them easier to understand across linguistic barriers.

[13] Going for picnics is a disreputable activity because it refers to increased mixing between unrelated men and women. This goes against the traditional norm of sexual segregation and is widely seen (and criticised) as an index of growing immorality.

[14] The participation of youth in Islamic religious movements has been part of the history of northern Nigeria. Contemporary challenges, revealed in movements as diverse as the '*yan tatsine*' (see Lubeck, 1987; Watts and Pred, 1992) and the Muslim Brothers illustrate how oppositional contemporary religious movements can be for the *status quo*.

[15] Consider, for instance, that, during the time Callaway was researching and writing, Indian films were already established as a common part of everyday female popular culture. Often referred to as 'women's films', the concentration of romance and melodrama was and is seen as the prime reason for female identification. Only two years after Callaway's book was published, the efflorescence of a Hausa romance literature identified primarily with women readers (and with a significant number of women writers) makes her assertion that romance cannot exist in Islamic marriages untenable. Abu-Lughod (1986) provides a much more nuanced analysis of the romance, the poetry of love and emotional attachments among an equally sexually segregated Bedouin society.

[16] Interview, December 1994.

[17] Interview, June 1995.

[18] Hausa can be written in either Arabic or Latin script. *Ajami* refers to Hausa written in Arabic script, *boko* to Hausa written in Latin script.

[19] For the sake of consistency, wherever possible I follow (as here) the translation of *soyayya* clubs and books in Furniss (1996).

[20] *Alhaji* strictly means a man who has made the pilgrimage (*hajj*) to Mecca. In common Hausa usage it refers to any person of wealth or status.

[21] Ahmad abridged and translated his book into English in order to tap into a wider Nigerian English-speaking audience (interview, May 1995). Following its publication he did begin to receive letters in English from fans from many other Nigerian ethnic groups, indicating its success. In 1995 he abridged and published *Masoyan Zamani* I, II ('Modern Lovers', 1993) as *Nemesis*. The only other English-language *soyayya* book is *The Sign of the Times* (1994) by Tijani Usman Adamu. Adamu's book was written in English and no Hausa version exists.

[22] Indian films present an alternative to both Hausa tradition and Western modernity in that while they depict a culture 'just like' Hausa culture. Their popularity resides in the fact that Indian culture is also precisely *unlike* Hausa culture. Indian films portray an alternative world where actions that would not be tolerated within Hausa social norms are raised without attracting widespread condemnation. A comparison with Hausa reception of Yoruba or Igbo films is helpful here. Onitsha market literature, Yoruba and Igbo videos, and popular romance magazines such as *Hints*, all suggest how popular the theme of love remains in southern Nigeria. Clearly many of the Yoruba and Igbo films are set in locations with cultural references that are familiar to and have similarities with Hausa audiences. Yoruba and Igbo films, however, are often sexually more explicit in their themes than either Hausa videos or Indian films. While many Hausa viewers watch and enjoy these videos, for others their themes are too explicit for comfort. The attitude of one Hausa video shop owner I talked to, who sold Igbo and Yoruba films but was reluctant to let members of his family watch them, is not exceptional.

[23] Mohammed is here referring to the subject matter of stories which make up classic Hausa fiction such as Abubakar Imam's *Ruwan Bagaja* (1934) or *Gand'oki* by Bello Kagara (1934). For further discussion of these works see Furniss (1996); Rahim (1990); Sani (1990); Yahaya (1988).

[24] This familiarity is one reason why *bandiri* singers have drawn on popular Indian film songs for religious music. These sufi adepts will take the songs from a popular film, such as *Mother India*, or *Kabhi, Kabhie* (1976, directed by Yash Chopra), and change the words to sing praises to the Prophet Mohammed.

References

Abu-Lughod, Lila. 1986. *Veiled Sentiments: honor and poetry in a Bedouin society*. Berkeley, Cal.: University of California Press.

—— 1990. 'The romance of resistance: tracing transformations through Bedouin women', *American Ethnologist* 17 (1), 41–55.

—— 1993a. 'Editorial comment: screening politics in a world of nations', *Public Culture* 5 (3), 465–7.

—— 1993b. 'Finding a place for Islam: Egyptian television serials and the national interest', *Public Culture* 5 (3), 493–514.

—— 1995. 'The objects of soap opera: Egyptian television and the cultural politics of modernity', in Daniel Miller (ed.), *Worlds Apart: modernity through the prism of the local*, pp. 190–210. London: Routledge.

Adamu, Tijani Usman. 1994. *The Sign of the Times*. Kano: Gidan Dabino.

Ahmad, Ado. 1989. *In da so da K'auna*. Kano.

—— 1993a. *The Soul of my Heart*. Kano.

—— 1993b. *Masoyan Zamani*. Kano.

—— 1995. *Nemesis*. Kano.

Appadurai, Arjun. 1990. 'Disjuncture and difference in the global cultural economy', *Public Culture* 2 (2), 1–24.

—— 1991. 'Global ethnoscapes: notes and queries for a transnational anthropology', in Richard Fox (ed.), *Recapturing Anthropology: working in the present*, pp. 191–210. Santa Fe, Cal.: SAR Press.

Appadurai, Arjun, and Breckenridge, Carol A. 1988. 'Why public culture?' *Public Culture* 1 (1), 5–9.

—— 1995. 'Public modernity in India', in Carol A. Breckenridge (ed.), *Consuming Modernity: public culture in a South Asian world*, pp. 1–20. Minneapolis: University of Minnesota Press.

Baba, 'Dan Azumi. 1990. *Rikicin Duniya*. Kano.

Babinlata, Bala Anas. 1991. *Tsuntsu Mai Wayo*. Kano.

Bakhtin, Mikhail. 1981. *The Dialogic Imagination*. Austin: University of Texas Press.

Barber, Karin. 1987. 'Popular arts in Africa', *African Studies Review* 30 (3), 1-78.

Barkindo, Bawuro M. 1993. 'Growing Islamism in Kano City since 1970', in Louis Brenner (ed.), *Muslim Identity and Social Change in sub-Saharan Africa*, pp. 91–105. Bloomington: Indiana University Press.

Beidelman, T. O. 1986. *Moral Imagination among Kaguru Modes of Thought*, Bloomington, Ind.: Indiana University Press. New Edition, 1993, Washington, D.C.: Smithsonian Institution Press.

Bichi, Maigari Ahmed. 1992. 'The author's imagination' II, *The Triumph*, 17 March, p. 7.

Callaway, Barbara. 1987. *Muslim Hausa Women in Nigeria: tradition and change*. New York: Syracuse University Press.

Chakravarty, Sunita. 1993. *National Ideology in Indian Popular Cinema, 1947–87*. Austin: University of Texas Press.

Cooper, Frederick. 1994. 'Conflict and connection: rethinking African colonial history', *American Historical Review* 99 (5), 1516–45.

Dan Asabe, Abdul Karim. n.d. 'The Way Youth Organise Themselves: a study of clubs in Kano metropolis, Nigeria'. Kano (unpublished).

Diawara, Manthia. 1992. *African Cinema: politics and culture*. Bloomington: Indiana University Press.

Ekwuazi, Hyginus. 1987. *Film in Nigeria*. Jos: Nigerian Film Corporation.

—— and Nasidi Yakubu, (eds). 1992. *Operative Principles of the Film Industry: towards a film policy for Nigeria*. Jos: Nigerian Film Corporation.

Fugelsang, Minou. 1994. *Veils and Videos: female youth culture on the Kenyan coast*. Studies in Social Anthropology, Stockholm: Gotab.

Furniss, Graham. 1996. *Poetry, Prose and Popular Culture in Hausa*. Edinburgh: Edinburgh University Press; Washington, D.C.: Smithsonian Institution Press, for the International African Institute.

Giginyu, Nasiru Mudi. 1992. 'A little knowledge is a dangerous thing: a reply to Ado Ahmad Gidan Dabino', *Nasiha*, 28 August.

Ginsburg, Faye. 1991. 'Indigenous media: Faustian contract or global village?' *Cultural Anthropology* 6 (1), 92–112.

—— 1993. 'Aboriginal media and the aboriginal imaginary', *Public Culture* 5 (3), 557–78.

—— 1994. 'Embedded aesthetics: creating a discursive place for indigenous media', *Cultural Anthropology* 9 (3), 365–82.

Hannerz, Ulf. 1992. *Cultural Complexity: studies in the social organization of meaning*. New York: Columbia University Press.

Imam, Abubakar. 1934. *Ruwan Bagaja*. Zaria: NNPC.

India International Centre Quarterly. 1980. Special issue, 8 (1).

Jackson, Michael. 1982. *Allegories of the Wilderness: ethics and ambiguity in Kuranko narratives*. Bloomington: Indiana University Press.

Kagara, Bello. 1934. *Gand'oki*. Zaria: Literature Bureau.

Kakar, Sudhir. 1989. *Intimate Relations: exploring Indian sexuality*. Chicago: University of Chicago Press.

Lawan, Yusuf. 1993. *Komai Wahalar So*. Kano.

—— 1995. *Mai Hakuri* ... Kano.

Liman, Maryam Sahabi. 1993. *Kishi Kumallon Mata*. Gusau: Bushara Publishing House.

Lubeck, Paul. 1987. 'Islamic protest under semi-industrial capitalism: Yan Tatsine explained', in J.D.Y. Peel and C.C. Stewart (eds), *Popular Islam South of the Sahara*. pp. 369–89. Manchester: Manchester University Press, for the International African Institute.

McLagan, Meg. 1996. 'Computing for Tibet: virtual politics in the Cold War era', in G. Marcus (ed.) *Connected: engagements with media at century's end*. Late Editions 3. Chicago: University of Chicago Press.

McNeely, Connie and Soysal, Yasemin Muhoglu. 1989. 'International flows of television programming: a revisionist research orientation', *Public Culture* 2 (1), 136–45.

Mishray, Vijay. 1985. 'Toward a theoretical critique of Bombay cinema', *Screen* 26 (3–4), 133–46.

Mohammed, Adamu. 1991. *Garnak'ak'i*. Kano: Kamfanin Kwabon Masoyi.

Muhammad, Bala. 1992. 'The Hausa film: a study of slow growth, problems and prospects', in Hyginus Ekwuazi and Yakubu Nasidi (eds), *Operative Principles of the Film Industry: towards a film policy for Nigeria*, pp. 179–204. Jos: Nigerian Film Corporation.

Nandy, Ashis. 1995. *The Savage Freud and other Essays on Possible and Retrievable Selves*. Princeton; N.J.: Princeton University Press.

Pendakur, Manjunath and Subramanyam, Radha. 1996. 'Indian cinema beyond national borders', in John Sinclair, Elizabeth Jacka and Stuart Cunningham (eds), *New Patterns in Global Television: peripheral vision*, pp. 67–82. Oxford: Oxford University Press.

Rahim, Oba Abdul (ed.). 1990. *Essays on Northern Nigerian Literature* 1. Zaria: Hamdan Express Printers.

Said, H. I., and Last, Murray. 1991. *Youth and Health in Kano Today*. Special issue of Kano Studies.

Sani, Abba Aliyu. 1990. 'The place of Rupert East in the culture and literature of northern Nigeria', in Oba Abdul Raheem (ed.), *Essays on Northern Nigerian Literature* pp. 12–21. Zaria: Hamdan Express Printers.

Sheme, Ibrahim. 1995a. 'Indian films and our culture', *New Nigerian*, 13 May: 7.

—— 1995b. '*Zagon ktasar da finafinan Indiya ke yi wa al'adanmu*' ('The danger of Indian films to our culture'), *Gaskiya ta fi kwabo*, 15 May: 5.

Shohat, Ella and Stam, Robert. 1994. *Unthinking Eurocentrism*. New York: Routledge.

Sreberny-Mohammadi, Annabelle. 1991. 'The global and the local in international communications', in James Curran and Michael Gurevitch (eds), *Mass Media and Society*. London: Edward Arnold.

Sullivan, Nancy. 1993. 'Film and television production in New Guinea: how the media become the message', *Public Culture* 5 (3), 533–55.

Thomas, Rosie. 1985. 'Indian cinema: pleasures and popularity', *Screen* 26 (3–4), 116–31.

—— 1995. 'Melodrama and the negotiation of morality in mainstream Indian film', in *Consuming Modernity: public culture in a South Asian world*, pp. 157–82. Minneapolis: University of Minnesota Press.

Ukadike, Nwachukwu Frank. 1994. *Black African Cinema*. Berkeley, Cal.: University of California Press.

Watts, Michael and Pred, Allan, 1992. *The Shock of Modernity: capitalisms and symbolic discontent*. New Brunswick, N. J.: Rutgers University Press.

Yahaya, Ibrahim Yaro. 1988. *Hausa a Rubuce: tarihin rubuce rubuce cikin Hausa*. Zaria: NNPC.

Yakubu, Hajiya Balaraba Ramat. 1990a. *Alhaki Kwikwiyo*. Kano.

—— 1990b. *Budurwar Zuciya*. Kano.

Primary Text 1
Excerpts from Balaraba Ramat Yakubu *Alhaki Kwikwiyo*

translated from Hausa by William Burgess

Reference
Balaraba Ramat Yakubu, *Alhaki Kwikwiyo*
Kano: Ramat General Enterprises [1990] 1992: 7-9, 18-27

Rabi was having a bath so Alhaji Abdu had to wait for her to come out. He sat there and began to reflect on what sort of a husband and father he had been. He knew that people were talking about him and that they were saying he didn't do enough for his family. But he didn't think he was treating Rabi and her children badly. He put it down to her discussing his private family matters with strangers. He knew that there was no other way that anybody could be aware of whether he was contributing what he should or not to his wife and children. But now that he was going to take a new wife, things would be better. He would even be able to relax more at home. He had found it impossible before. Whenever he came home, the kids would start bothering him. His new bride-to-be had never had children and she was no longer young. She was over thirty-eight years old.

This new wife that Alhaji Abdu was now so keen to marry was in fact a former prostitute who had been married twice before. For her first marriage, after she had given up the unseemly life she had been leading on the streets, she had been hennaed and married off to an old man. But, within a year, she had run away from him. She then wandered around aimlessly for a while until one of the men that she used to hang out with during her days of intemperance turned up again and they decided to get married. She stayed with him for five years which, in her case, you might say was a long time. They used to get on quite well but he discovered eventually that this apparent harmony was a cover. She was in the habit of going out and meeting up with other men. At first he wouldn't listen to what people told him about her. Then his senior wife revealed to him that his own younger brother was having a relationship with her. She promised that she would make him see with his own eyes and catch them at it.

As luck would have it, two days after this conversation, this younger brother returned from the village where he worked. He didn't normally live in town but, every two or three weeks, he would come and spend Saturday and Sunday night, then go back to the village where he lived with his wife and children. Whenever he came to town, he and Delu would manage to find an opportunity for their wickedness. It was a big house with the husband's older and younger brothers and sisters all living together, as well as his parents who were still alive. The door to this younger brother's room was outside on the entry alley to the house. You had to pass it on your way into the main central yard. The people Delu lived with had already begun to notice how much trouble she was going to for her husband's younger brother. Whenever he arrived, she would prepare a fresh bowl of food for him. They all thought this was simply family loyalty, because it was her husband's brother. But the senior wife wasn't so sure and she decided to keep a close watch on how things developed. One night she pushed her door to but didn't go to sleep. Then some time later, when the whole house was silent, she heard Delu unlock her door, open it and then close it. The senior wife lifted her curtain and saw Delu head for the main entrance door into the courtyard. She decided to follow her, even though the husband was in her room with her when this was happening – he was sound asleep at the time.

As they approached the husband's younger brother's room, she saw Delu push the door open and enter. The door was then closed behind her and locked. The following day, the senior wife told her husband what had happened. That night both of them stayed awake and listened out for Delu. He heard her unlock the door to her room and he watched her as she made her way towards the front door. He became angry and made to go out but the senior wife stopped him. Instead they first went and woke up everybody in the house. Then they all headed for his younger brother's room. The husband broke down the door with a kick, switched on the light and there before him were his younger brother and Delu, at it like a mortar and pestle. It was disgusting.

That was the end of Delu's second marriage. The shame and the displeasure at what had happened meant that Delu had to get out of Kano. So she set off for Lagos. She then spent sixteen years wandering around as a prostitute from one town to another until, no more than six months ago, she had come back to her birthplace, Kano.

Alhaji Abdu had first met Delu at his stall in the market where she had gone to buy some cloth. Her body still had something of the buxom shape of a prostitute and her purse still had a few Naira left in it. Her aim was to make a purchase, a transaction. But what transpired was that an attraction grew between her and the stallholder. In fact, on that first encounter, Alhaji wouldn't allow her to pay for the cloth that she had chosen to buy. She had to take it as a gift from him. And he insisted on her waiting at his stall until after the late afternoon *la'asar* prayers so that he could take her home in his car and find out where she lived. Less than a week passed before he had started visiting her with more gifts and they had started talking about marriage. She made out that she had no dowry at all since her former husband in Lagos had refused to allow her to take away what was hers. And this lie wasn't enough for her. She went on to say that the reason why he had kept all her belongings was that he didn't want her to leave him. She said she knew what she had to do to get her things back from Lagos but Alhaji Abdu would have to be patient with her. Her only fear was that if she went back there now, her former husband wouldn't let her return here. The old whore was only up to her usual guile. In the end, she only agreed to marry Alhaji Abdu after he had promised to buy her everything she wanted for her own room. So he bought her a bed, a mattress, a wardrobe and a dressing table with drawers. Alhaji also had to give her some lino for her room, two armchairs and then three rolls of cloth, one of lace and one of silk, as well as a headdress and a long scarf. Sparing no expense, he also gave her one hundred Naira in cash to buy anything else she wanted.

The bed and all its accoutrements cost Alhaji Abdu four hundred and fifty Naira, no less. That was in addition to those two armchairs. Allah alone knows how much Alhaji Abdu spent on his marriage to this trollop. They arranged the date for the wedding and that very same day she would move into his house.

The day before the ceremonies, Alhaji Abdu was now about to inform Rabi that she was going to have a co-wife. As was the custom on this sort of occasion, he had brought with him some special gifts for her.

* * *

Rabi had finished her bath and was now out of the bathroom, oiling her skin. Bilki came and told her mother that her father was waiting for her in his room. Rabi quickly finished oiling herself, wrapped her skirt around her and went out into the courtyard. She went over to Alhaji's room and went in. She greeted him with '*Salamu alaikum*' and then continued, 'Here I am. The children said you wanted to see me.'

'Yes, hello there, senior wife,' replied Alhaji Abdu cheerfully. 'I've called you over to tell you the news. I'm going to get a younger sister for you today, I'm marrying another wife. So here, I've brought these special gifts for you as my senior wife.'

Rabi froze and was overcome with despair. She didn't know what to say to her husband. There were enough things to be dealt with, without this! Their young daughter at school was old enough to be married and yet he hadn't even bought anything for her dowry yet. And here he was now, about to take another wife himself. When Rabi didn't reply, Alhaji Abdu thought it was jealousy that had caught her tongue. So he went on, 'If you think these gifts I've brought you are not enough, just say and you'll get more. There's no need for you to go all sad as if you have learnt of a death in the family.'

Rabi raised her head and just looked at him. Then she said, 'Even if you marry ten more women, Alhaji, I couldn't care less about any presents you might give me to placate me.' She picked up some of the gifts, turned them over in her hand and then set them down again. 'If you had bought some bedclothes to keep for Saudatu's dowry, that would have been better than bringing me ten rolls of cloth.'

'So that means you don't like these things then? Or what exactly do you mean?' said Alhaji Abdu.

Rabi replied, 'It's not that I don't like these things. I'm grateful. May Allah repay your kindness. But I think that before you get married again yourself, you should marry off your young daughter who is still here at home with you.'

Alhaji Abdu said, 'Well, I've already arranged my marriage. It's going to take place this evening and tomorrow she will move in here. This doesn't mean that, if Saudatu does find a husband, her marriage can't take place.'

'So this new wife of yours,' said Rabi, 'is she a virgin or has she been married before?' Before he replied, she had continued, 'Of course! All those repairs to the house and those stocks of food you brought in are to impress your new bride, aren't they? To make her think that you feed your family well, eh?'

'You're talking nonsense,' he said. 'Do you mean to say I don't feed my own family?'

Rabi continued, 'You know you don't feed us. When was the last time you brought a sack of rice into this house for us? How much do you contribute towards buying the minor ingredients, let alone the cost of the actual food?'

Alhaji Abdu said, 'Are you going to start telling people all these lies about me because you know I'm going to get a new wife? You just want to use those deceitful ways of yours against me, don't you, so that when my bride comes to this house she won't stay long?'

'Allah is my witness,' said Rabi. 'And He will avenge all that you have done to me. May Allah bring you good fortune in marriage. But you'll soon be up to your old tricks.'

As Rabi finished what she was saying, she stood up to go out of the room, without taking the gifts he had offered her. But before she got to the door, Alhaji Abdu called her back. 'I haven't finished yet. Come, there's something else I want to say to you.'

Rabi turned back, sat down in front of Alhaji Abdu, lowered her head and was silent.

'I want you to listen to me,' he said, raising his finger at her. 'When my new bride comes, there's no way you're going to talk to me like this in front of her. And secondly, people keep giving you ideas and saying that since you and I have had several children together, I could never divorce you. Well, if you think that, you're deceiving yourself. If it gets to the point where there's going to be a divorce, even right now, then a divorce there will be. So I'm warning you. Things have changed now and you had better get some sense into that head of yours.'

Rabi simply lifted her head, looked at her husband for a few moments, then rose and left the room. Tears filled her eyes. She stayed in her own room for a while, weeping. She couldn't imagine what Alhaji Abdu meant when he said that things had now changed. Was he saying this because her mother had died or because he was going to get married again? Rabi had no time now to contact all the people she should have got in touch with about her husband's new marriage. She had to drop all idea of that and the only people she sent messages to were her own younger sister, her elder brother's wife and her close friend Salamatu. So these three were the only people keeping guard at the door to Rabi's room when her husband's new bride moved into the house and during the partying.

It turned out to be a lavish occasion and, as the new bride made her way into the house, she had about her the sort of haughty air that prominent, affluent women have. She spent the first seven nights in Alhaji Abdu's room and cooked every meal for him, morning, noon and night. Even for some time afterwards, on those days when it was Rabi's turn to cook for him, Alhaji Abdu wouldn't eat her food, taking Delu's instead. He said that Delu could cook the sort of food he liked. Although Rabi accepted the situation at first and kept quiet, she eventually started letting it be known elsewhere. But however much she had right on her side, there was nothing she could do to get from them what was due to her.

Even Alhaji Abdu's mother tried to intervene, but after several attempts she had had enough and gave up. Alhaji Abdu and Delu carried on blatantly in their sinful ways, while the world just looked on. And what is meant by their sinful ways in this marriage? Well, they left Rabi out of everything and she spent neither daytime nor nighttime with Alhaji Abdu. Whenever he wanted anything, Delu would do it for him, even when it was Rabi's day to do the cooking. Another source of discontentment was the young girl, Ladidi, Alhaji Abdu's daughter from a former wife who had left him. When Ladidi had been weaned, her mother had given her to Rabi to look after and she was the same age as Rabi's own daughter, Bilki. Whenever Rabi bought even just some earrings for Bilki, she had to buy some for Ladidi as well. If you saw them together, you would think they were twins. Through thick and thin, Rabi had always been a mother to them both and treated them the same from when Ladidi was just two years old. And now she was eleven.

Then one day, out of the blue, Delu goes to Alhaji Abdu and, with no shame or fear of Allah, manages to persuade him to take Ladidi, together with all her belongings, from Rabi and hand her over to Delu to look after. His mother asked him why he should do such an evil thing and he replied, 'Mother, she stays at home sitting by herself, with no-one looking after her. Honestly, just look at what's going on, you can see the difficult time she has with...'

'*La'ilaha Illallahu*,' said Alhaji Abdu's mother. 'There is no god but Allah. I can't believe what you're saying to me! You've really become so mean, haven't you? Just you be careful what you do with that young girl. Don't go making a big mistake—and I mean it. Are you telling me that all this time you didn't realise she was unhappy, only now? Mind you don't get yourself caught up in some serious quarrel.'

'Honestly, mother,' said Alhaji Abdu, 'she will be much happier being looked after by Delu, and...'

'Just leave me alone,' his mother said. 'Get out of here. You don't want to do what's right, so just go away and get on with your business. The day will come when Allah will make amends for what has happened to her and you'll be in trouble then. Get out!'

This warning from Alhaji Abdu's mother had no effect. As the wise say, 'The man who goes far away will not hear when he is being called.' Life just carried on in this awful way. Then, totally unexpectedly, Allah removed another of Rabi's defences. Alhaji Abdu's mother, Inna, had an attack of nausea in the middle of the night and by dawn she had passed away. During her final throes, she spoke again to Alhaji Abdu about Rabi and made her last wishes known to him. 'Abdu, that Rabi of yours, she's not simply a wife. She's a sister to you. I beg you in the name of Allah and the Prophet, take care of her, even if it's just for the sake of your children.'

These words of Inna were her last attempt at bringing reconciliation between Alhaji Abdu and Rabi. But only a few days would pass before Alhaji Abdu was back to his usual ways. This time, it was even worse than before. Now that his mother was dead and buried, there was no-one to keep him in check.

Saudatu had been away at school when her father took his new wife and when her grandmother died. But nobody had let her know. So when she returned home for the holidays, it was only then that she discovered what had happened. At the entrance to the house, Bilki and the others, keen as always to pass on all the tittle-tattle, were there to tell Saudatu that her father had got married again. And as she went through into the courtyard, she came face to face with Delu. From the moment their eyes met, Saudatu felt instinctively that she didn't like this woman, her father's new wife. And Delu felt that of all Alhaji Abdu's children there was none she hated more than Saudatu. This was the first time she had seen her and, apart from remembering her name, she had never bothered much about her. Delu gave Saudatu one of her dirty looks and carried on preparing some salad. Alhaji Abdu had salad with almost every meal now. No matter what type of meal was cooked for him, everything had to come with some salad and a groundnut dressing and little savoury cakes. Saudatu went through into her mother's room and found her trimming chillies. Her mother looked different, Saudatu noticed as soon as she saw her. There was no doubt about it. The children were by now making so much noise that Rabi looked up. She saw Saudatu followed by the children who were helping her carry her metal suitcase and the rest of her luggage. Rabi said, 'Saudatu! So your school holidays have started then, have they? Welcome home.'

'Have you been ill, Mummy? You look as if you've lost a lot of weight.'

'I'm fine, Saudatu. It's just my heart, it's giving me a bit of trouble.'

'How's Granny? Is she in her room?' asked Saudatu. Rabi didn't know what to say. She realised that Saudatu wasn't aware that her grandmother had died. But Mustapha just blurted it out at Saudatu, 'Granny's dead.'

Saudatu put her hands on her head and began to wail. The realisation of the loss of her grandmother made her cry out loud and then all her brothers and sisters started to sob as well. Rabi made no attempt to console them as she too was in tears. In the midst of all this weeping, Alhaji Abdu came home. He heard the crying coming from Rabi's room as soon as he entered the house and he asked Delu, 'Is everything alright? What's happened? What's all this crying for, Delu?'

'Don't ask me, Alhaji,' replied Delu. 'Ask that sheep of a wife of yours. Only an animal like her would gather the children together in her room and deafen us all with their wailing.'

Alhaji Abdu heard what Delu said and took her side. Rather than asking Rabi why she was crying, he simply barged into her room angrily. 'What is all this stupid nonsense? Are you out of your wits? Why on earth are you and these children crying like this? Will you never manage to pull yourself together and come to your senses?'

'That old trollop has called me an animal,' said Rabi. 'So now you want to have a go at me as well, do you? Is that what you want?'

'She was right when she called you an animal,' said Alhaji Abdu. 'Just look at this senseless stupidity you're up to now.'

Then Delu joined in. She had taken exception to being called an old trollop and wanted to give Rabi a piece of her mind. 'You bitch. If you're not an old trollop yourself, just tell me what you've managed to make of your life. Look at you, sitting there with nothing to do and no good for anyone.'

'Me with nothing to do and no good for anyone?' said Rabi. 'That's what you may think.' She stood up and continued, 'You hussy, you're no more than a scumbag off the garbage heap. You managed to get him to marry you and so your secret is safe. You're a twisted, useless bitch. He's helped you to get what you want and now you're treating people with contempt. I swear to Allah, I've had enough of you. If you say one more thing to me, damn you, your life is not going to be worth living here in this house.'

'A scumbag off the garbage heap, you call me,' said Delu. 'Just you wait. I'm going to make your life a misery in this house, starting today.'

Before Alhaji Abdu realised what was happening, the two of them had begun wrestling each other in front of him. He struggled to separate them. But then, as soon as Rabi's children realised what was happening, they came rushing from their room to join in and give Delu a beating. There was nothing Alhaji Abdu could do. As he pushed one child away, another would rush in and land Delu a punch. When Delu hit out at one of the children, then Rabi would hit her back. Eventually, by the grace of Allah, luck came Rabi's way and she managed to knock Delu over. She landed flat on the floor and, seeing her lying there, Saudatu quickly climbed on top of her and continued beating her. At the same time, Rabi carried on landing heavy punches on Delu as well. Alhaji Abdu tried to lift Saudatu off Delu so that Delu could at least stand up. But Rabi said, 'Make sure she doesn't get up, Saudatu, until you've beaten the daylights out of her first. Today you are going to see just how valuable motherhood is. You tricked your way into taking Ladidi but she's not your daughter, you bitch.'

'Are you out of your mind?' Alhaji Abdu said to Rabi.

'Are you lot just going to kill her? You useless idiots. Saudatu, I told you to help Delu up.'

Alhaji Abdu managed to drag Saudatu off and at that point Delu started ranting her woes. 'Allah, what a fine mess I've got myself into here! You lot think I've got nothing to my name, that's why you gang up on me as if you're killing a worthless nobody. I swear to Allah, Alhaji, I'm not going to stay here in this house with you. You just stand there and watch while she and her children try to kill me. As if you couldn't care less whatever happens! Allah, what have I got myself into here!'

Alhaji Abdu realised for sure that if he did nothing to stop Delu leaving the house now, there was no way he would be able to get her back. He did love her and, if he had to choose between Rabi and Delu, he would rather split up with Rabi. At that moment, Rabi was telling Delu, 'It's always a mistake for a man to marry a prostitute. Now you've got what you wanted it's time to move on. You'll soon find someone else who'll try his luck with you.'

Alhaji Abdu became even angrier when he heard Rabi say this. He raised his hand to her and slapped her. As he struck her, Kabiru was just coming in. No-one noticed his arrival but he saw his mother fall to the ground from the force of his father's blow. Alhaji Abdu took hold of Rabi's hand and pulled her up. He then went to strike her again but felt someone catch hold of his arm. He turned around to see Kabiru standing there. 'Is something wrong, father?' said Kabiru. 'What's happened? What has she done to you?'

Alhaji Abdu said, 'I didn't realise that this mother of yours was mad all along, the hussy. For no reason, she and her children will just gang up on another woman, and beat the daylights out of her.' Then he spoke to Rabi, 'I swear to Allah, I'm going to divorce you.'

'No, father,' said Kabiru. 'There's no need to start talking of divorce. Just calm down.' But then Rabi said, 'If you want to divorce me over that wretched old hag, just carry on. That's fine with me! She could see that you would be a good catch, so she married you. But don't be surprised if she just runs off and leaves you.'

'You're nothing but a wretched hag yourself,' said Delu. 'For Allah's sake, just look at her!'

'Well, there's nothing more wretched than marrying a whore,' said Rabi. Hardly had she finished saying this when Delu rushed at her and gave a fierce slap. When Kabiru saw that his father just stood there and did nothing, he became very angry. He lashed out at Delu with the palm of his hand, striking her violently and sending her to the ground.

'You scoundrel,' said Alhaji Abdu. 'What did you hit her for? Get out of my house. I never want to see you again. I'll have nothing to do with you any more, ever.'

Rabi said, 'If he goes, then all of us leave this house of yours with him. No way is he going alone.'

'You can get out too,' said Alhaji Abdu. 'I divorce you. You are no longer my wife. And take all of those kids of yours with you. Just get out of my house, all of you. I don't want any of you.'

Rabi said, 'I suppose you think something awful is going to happen to us if we leave, don't you? And I suppose you think the children are going to die, simply because you have turned your back on them. Well, remember, Allah enriches the slave. And He will enrich these children too. You get on with enjoying your own riches.'

'Yes, yes. Come on, get out of here!' said Alhaji Abdu. 'Take all your things with you. Hurry!' He looked over at Delu standing there wiping away her tears, 'You go and sit down in your room.'

Rabi spoke to Delu. 'You can rejoice now, can't you? You've got what you wanted. Because of you, he's sent me packing, me and all his children. You'll have to go and pay your sorcerer's fee now.'

'*Alhamdu lillahi*, I thank Allah,' said Delu. 'And I hope you have a weary journey back to your family home! You won't be coming back here, that's for sure. All you'll have are the memories.'

Rabi went into her room but her eyes couldn't see properly because she was so sad and upset. The first thing she did was to send Kabiru to her family home to see her younger sister Tasidi. Then herself and Saudatu went to her elder brother's house to let him know what was going on. She had to leave the other children at home as they had already come back from the Koranic school before she set out. By the time of the early afternoon azahar prayers, all Rabi's relatives and Alhaji Abdu's had heard of the sad events.

Rabi's elder brother rushed over to Alhaji Abdu's younger brother to tell him. Alhaji Bello said they should wait until evening, then go together to Alhaji Abdu to hear how things were and attempt a reconciliation so that Rabi could go back home to her husband. With that agreed, Rabi's elder brother, Malam Shehu, then went to Tasidi's house, only to find that she had already set off for his house. But luckily Tasidi's husband was at home and the two of them talked about what was going on. Tasidi's husband said that he would like to come along that evening as well. Both of them could join Alhaji Bello to see Alhaji Abdu. With all these arrangements made, Rabi's elder brother went back home.

So later that day, just after the evening *magariba* prayers, all of them turned up outside Alhaji Abdu's house. Alhaji Abdu's younger brother shouted a greeting in through the doorway and Rabi's son came out. He was told to go back inside and let his father know that he had visitors. So he went in and told his father that Alhaji Bello and Malam Shehu had sent in their greetings to him and were waiting for him outside. Alhaji Abdu knew for sure that they had come about Rabi.

And Delu realised what she was being confronted with too. They had come to try and have Rabi brought back. So she made one last attempt at making sure that Rabi had left the house for good. As Alhaji Abdu rose to come out of his room, she said to him, 'I know they have come about Rabi. But, I swear to Allah, if you bring her back, you'll have to give me a divorce because, I swear to Allah, I'm not going to live in the same house as her with her calling me names like that.'

Alhaji Abdu said, 'Have I said that I'm going to bring her back? Just take no notice of them!'

Delu said, 'But look, here they all are, they've got together and come to see you now, haven't they? It looks as if I've got no-one to stand up for me.'

'I'll stand up for you,' said Alhaji Abdu. 'I really have divorced her. If one of them thinks that I am under a special obligation to him because he married Rabi off to me by way of some special favour, well he had better let me know.'

It was more than fifteen minutes before Alhaji Abdu emerged to meet his visitors. He came out frowning and looking ruffled, as if he was going to listen to them apologise for something. But they were undeterred and decided to take no notice. They exchanged greetings and then Alhaji Bello addressed Alhaji Abdu. 'Just now, Malam Shehu went to my house and told me some news which I found disturbing. Wives arguing among themselves: that's not something that should lead to divorce.'

Alhaji Abdu said, 'If Allah means something to happen, there's no way of avoiding it. This breakup was meant by Allah.'

Tasidi's husband, Alhaji Sule, said, 'But come on, Alhaji. You should overlook things like this. When does one pay any attention to women these days? Forgive her and let her be brought back. Even if it's for the sake of her children, forgive her.'

Alhaji Abdu said, 'You just don't realise! There is no way I am going to be disobeyed in my own house. She and her children set about beating this woman up, for no reason. Then when I started scolding her, she simply took no notice of me. What was the point of my speaking to her?'

Malam Shehu had to wait a moment for Alhaji Abdu to regain his composure, then said, 'She went to my house just now but I wasn't in. So someone had to be sent to fetch me. When I did get home, she told me what had happened. But from the way she presented it to me, I didn't think there was reason enough to divorce her.'

Alhaji Abdu got himself settled again, then began to recount everything that had happened, skipping nothing. When he had finished, Alhaji Bello said to him, 'If that's the truth, then Kabiru did no wrong. You struck his mother because of something to do with her co-wife. Then that co-wife struck his mother as well and you just stood there and said nothing. I don't think it's wrong that he hit her. It's his mother we are talking about, you realise.'

'Well, you may think he's done no wrong,' Alhaji Abdu said.

'As I see it, the best thing now is that we let the matter rest,' said Alhaji Sule. 'There's no point in going over it again. Forgive her and let her be brought back. And may Allah make things easier in future.'

But Alhaji Abdu said, 'I have already divorced her and that means I'm rid of her for good.'

'Come on, Alhaji. Don't talk like that,' said Alhaji Bello. 'We're all asking you to forgive her. You can't just say no. It's not right to rebuff us all like that.'

Alhaji Abdu said, 'Am I under a special obligation to any of you over this marriage? Did one of you give me Rabi in marriage by way of some special favour? Well, it's no business of yours then. I'm not going to have her back. She and those children of hers should go, I don't want them.'

'You're not being very sensible,' said Alhaji Bello. 'How long are you going to carry on like this? What's the matter with you? Even if it's just for the sake of our dead mother, you should forgive her. And remember, this whole matter arose because of her death. That young girl came home from school for the holidays to discover that her grandmother had passed away. So everyone started weeping. Surely anyone who sheds a tear when they recall your mother's passing is someone who loves you. Isn't that so, Alhaji Sule?'

Alhaji Sule said, 'I can't think of anything more to say, Alhaji Bello. He may listen to you because you're his brother. But me, I'm going to go now. Malam Shehu, will you be along later?'

Malam Shehu stood up as well and said to Alhaji Abdu, 'I heard what you said. You've sent her and her children packing. Well, we've never turned our backs on her or her children. We were looking after them even when she was living with you. Now you say that you don't want her or the children. Well, we want them and may Allah give them long life and bring them wealth. In any settlement that there may be between the two of you, may Allah give her what is her due recompense. Good bye to you.'

Alhaji Sule and Malam Shehu went out, leaving Alhaji Abdu with his younger brother. Alhaji Bello just sat there with his head in his hands, not knowing what to say. Some time after the others had left, he said to Alhaji Abdu, 'So what you did was a good thing to do, was it? A good thing to do, was it, Alhaji Abdu?'

'What have I done?' said Alhaji Abdu. 'We're talking about marriage here and I'm not the first man to divorce a wife. What's so strange about that?'

DONATUS NWOGA
Onitsha Market Literature

Reference
Transition (4) 19, 1965: 26–33

A vast reading public exists in Nigeria and a large body of literature is addressed to this public that has not been much acknowledged in serious discussions on African literature. Sociological and economic factors have concentrated in certain centres a big collection of people who have left school after the minimum period of six to eight years with enough knowledge to be interested in reading novels, but not enough interest, or time, or even reading ability, to tackle the major novelists who were, in any case, in most of the novels available in the markets, talking of an environment that was most unfamiliar to the people under consideration.

Tutuola was published in 1952 and was acclaimed in Europe and America but was not known in Nigeria. Ekwensi's *People of the City* came out in 1954. A few more novels have been published, Tutuola, Ekwensi, Achebe, Nzekwu, Aluko etc. But the people have had their reading matter from the 1940s. It started with cheap, popular Indian novelettes. These came in large quantities, with flashy 'romantic' pictures of glamorous women being kissed by he-men on the covers, and large scale advertisements for talismen for all occasions – love, examinations – at the back. Then Nigerians started to supply their own material. One of the first titles to appear was Ekwensi's *When Love Whispers* which came out about 1947 with three others, published by Tabansi Bookshop in Onitsha. By 1963 there were more than 250 titles extant. And this, I am sure, is not the total. These books go quickly out of print. As with much popular art, there is no sense of preservation or continuity. Books are often not reprinted because they would be 'out of date'. One of the authors, Momoh Aroye of Aba, showed me 26 titles that he had had published. Only five of these were available in the markets. The others had had their run and disappeared. When the readers finished with a book they used it for toilet paper or rolled their tobacco in it to make cigarettes or just threw it away.

This lack of a sense of continuity has led the publishers not to put dates of publication on their books. One of them explained to me that if the date indicated that a book was up to a year old nobody would buy it. This lack of dating presents a problem to an interested person who wants to trace the development of theme – but I suppose that is not the concern of the people engaged in the business of publishing and selling. The point here is that many of the titles are lost. But there are about 250 current titles, which gives an impression of the prolific output of the authors and the volume of the audience.

Figs 1 and 2.

The bulk of this production is concentrated in Onitsha. Onitsha has always had the largest number of students in secondary and commercial schools, approved and unapproved, of any town in Nigeria, if not in West Africa. The Onitsha Market is also one of the biggest in Africa. Students and market traders make up the largest audience for this type of literature, and that is one reason for the concentration. Another is that Onitsha has a vast number of printing presses, and they are ready to print anything.

Unfortunately, many of these printing firms are staffed with compositors so poorly educated that they produce spellings so extraordinary that a reader has to work to extract the writer's words. Within three pages of a novel like Rosemary and the Taxi Driver, for example, we are told that Rosemary 'had packed all her suitcases like sardines and noisted (hoisted?) her headtie on her onboards shaving (a hair-style)', that 'her voilet (violet? violent?) gown with vibrant colours and heavenly colours vested (rested?) below her knees', that she 'gestriculated' (gesticulated) and that she said that 'Lagos is a neautiful (beautiful) town'. Sometimes, of course, the mistakes are the author's. Printers also present another problem. It appears that an established printer, for a price, will help to popularise a new enterprise by sending out his own products in the name of the new. It takes a lot of searching, and one is suspected for doing this, to discover who actually did print some of the books.

One thing that has to be realised from the start is that the authors of these pamphlets are serious in their intentions and with their art. In May 1962, the authors, through their Union, launched a magazine called *The Nigerian Author Magazine*. Unfortunately, this was a failure, especially a financial disaster for the editor Momoh Aroye. Only the first issue ever came out. But what is important here is the moral purpose expressed in the editorial column:

> In the verdict of a prolific writer, literature is supposed to reflect the time we live in – and that kind of literature being more prevalent than anything else, we are compelled and study it as 'The Mirror of the Age'.
>
> In spite of harassing difficulties which are often inevitable at the initial stage of any set-up, the fact remains clear that we obviously have explored new educational grounds by digging the well of knowledge with a needle, and by offering sacrificial efforts to launch this magazine to serve as a desirable asset to the community. That in theory and practice is indubitable. That too, as is here evident, is a colourful exhibition of latent powers unpurchaseable in the literary field; and a material contribution to the national progress of this country. In the main, let's call it a bold venture of a significant educational value – that which exceeds much expectation.
>
> 'Author' is, in our own candid opinion, and in the opinion of those who matter in the literary field, a prouder title than 'king'… (p. 3)

The emphasis is on educating the people. Education in the limited sense has produced pamphlets like *How to Write Good English and Compositions*, *How to Write Better Letters*, *Applications and Business Letters*, *How to Succeed in Life*, *How to Conduct Meetings*, *How to Write Love Letters*, and there are five different pamphlets on *How to Know Hausa, Ibo, Yoruba and English Languages*.

Mostly, however, education is taken in its broader sense and these authors are trying to teach people to live a more moral life. One of the more serious concerns of the Union of Authors was to eradicate what they called 'immoral, immaterial, aching, unartistic and flowery manuscripts' and they claimed that 'all literary productions bearing our "certificate of suitability for publishing" are censored and polished.' And in the prefaces to many of the pamphlets we read, 'It is to satisfy the romantic, offend the callous lover, redress the selfish principles of the monopolistic admirer that the novel is written'; 'This is a story about a married couple who had spent most part of their time in playing "High Life". This afterwards brought trouble into their domestic set-up,' and again, 'This is a way through which the public can learn good and bad.'

More than three quarters of the extant titles aim at the education of the readers, and more than half of these have to do with the relationship between men and women, boys and girls. This, in a was, is inevitable because when there is a break-up of established moral conscience, sex is the most common direction of expression of the new freedom. And so we have titles like *Beware of Harlots and Many Friends: The World is Hard* by Okenwa Olisah; *About Boys and Girls* by R. Okonkwo; *Rose Only Loved My Money* by H. O. Ogu; *Our Modern Ladies' Characters towards Boys* by Highbred Maxwell,(?)[1] *Why Men Never Trust Women, The Sorrows of Love, Money Hard But Some Women Don't Know* by Okenwa Olisah, *Why Harlots Hate Married Men and Love Bachelors* by Money-Hard, and most explicitly *Beware of Women* by Nathan Njoku. One of the authors declares in his preface:

> I have declared a wordy war with girls and ladies of nowadays and warn them to stop deceiving and telling lies to boys and also stop demanding much money from their boy friends.

There are many titles in this vein, warning men against the pitfalls they could fall into in their dealings with women, the dangers of bankruptcy in trade due to overspending on extravagant girls, the possibilities of students failing their exams because of chasing girls.

On the other hand, there are novels warning girls of what they let themselves into when they go with certain men. There are pamphlets like *The Broken Heart* by E. Uba, *How a Passenger Collector Posed and Got a LadyTeacher in Love* by H. Ogu, *The Sorrows of Love* or *Why Maria Killed Her Husband* and *John in the Romance of True Love* both by Thomas O. Igu. The danger expressed here is that girls are the ones that get pregnant and ruined. They might be going with boys who will leave them anytime, especially when there is trouble, and who will even go sometimes with the girls' own friends. One of the Prefaces reinforces the point:

> This drama … will serve as a warning to some of our girls who are often carried away by some fantastic never-to-come promises made to them by men.

In spite of these titles, there is really no balance and the greater bulk of the pamphlets is addressed to the masculine section of the population. The writers are men and most of their readers, after all, are men. And women, since the time of Eve, have caused most of the troubles in life. It appears they haven't yet paid for it in the volume of derogatory literature addressed against them. In most places, and Africa is no exception, the man is always right.

These writers produce an image of a new type of African girl. The girls are no longer the traditional quiet, modest, playthings of their parents. They write love letters. They are coy. They demand presents from their boy friends and victims. They even deceive men. They are no longer the dumb creatures to be won through their parents – *Miss Comfort's Heart Cries for Tommy's Love* by C. N. Aririguzo (?). They are sometimes too proud for the suitors that come to them either because they consider themselves too educated to accept the common suitor – *Miss Appolonia's Pride Leads Her To Be Unmarried* by C. N. Aririguzo (?) or they think themselves too beautiful – *Beauty is a Trouble* by R. I. M. Obioha. The beautiful ones are the most dangerous. A popular record in Nigeria was a song by 'Lord' Kitchener of the West Indies – 'Never marry a woman prettier than you'. The novelists make a point of this in *Stella at a Beauty and Fashion Parade*, *Nancy in Blooming Beauty* by Momoh Aroye, *Susanna 'The One in Town'* by G. H. Obi Nwala and *Jonny the Most Worried Husband* by H. O. Ogu.

The girls have changed and the boys need a new technique to tackle the new situation. Many authors have offered their prescriptions: Felix N. Stephen has supplied many means in his novels and plays – *The School of Love and How To Attend It*, *A Journey Into Love*, *How to Play Love*, *How To Make Love*, *How To Get a Lady in Love*, and he also offers a warning in one of his titles *Be Careful! Salution Is Not Love*.

Others prefer to approach the problem through letters and so we have titles like *How to Write Love Letters* by N. Njoku, *Our Modern Love Letters* by R. I. M. Obioha. A lot of guides have been produced to help the young men – *How to Make Friends With Girls* by R. Okonkwo, *A Guide to Marriage* by N. Okonkwo (?), *Guide for Engagement* by Highbred Maxwell (?), *How to Fall in Love With Girls* by H. O. Ogu. To some, love is a game – *The Game of Love* by R. Okonkwo. To others it is an art – *The Art of Love in Real Sense* by Speedy Eric. All are agreed that it is something to be approached with technique and caution. Many point out that the boys have to pretend that they are poorer than they really are in order to test the girl's love and find out whether it is for the person or for his money. All are agreed that the moment the girl starts making demands for presents is the time for the boy to draw back. They recommend however that the boy should make presents within his ability to his girl friend.

I mentioned earlier that these novelists present the image of change among the girls. Many times they do not disapprove of a certain type of change. One of the most serious problems that young men encounter is that of finding enough money to afford the bride price. Sometimes fantastic sums like £300 are asked from

Figs 3 and 4.

young men who are struggling to make £100 a year in the lower ranks of teaching or in trade. A law was passed sometime ago in Eastern Nigeria (and most of the writers are from Eastern Nigeria) limiting the bride price £30. This law is practically impossible to enforce as the father of the bride can refuse to allow his daughter to marry. Normally private agreements are arrived at and a receipt for £30 is given though more than £150 could have gone into fulfilling a variety of customs. This concerns the young writers intimately and they take their opportunity to raise to heroic proportions the girl who stands against her father in favour of the young man she has chosen to marry.

Ogali A. Ogali was one of the first to use this theme and he established the pattern that has become typical of the treatment of this topic. His play *Veronica, My Daughter* achieved immense popularity and sold up to 60,000 copies. The dramatis personae include a girl and her confidante: Veronica and Alice here, Alice and Caroline in *Alice in the Romance of Love*, Agnes and Beatrice in *Agnes the Faithful Lover*, Maria and Teresa in *Beautiful Maria in the Act of True Love*. Then there are the parents: the father, wicked and half-illiterate, the mother more educated and on her daughter's side; then there are the two men, the suitor approved by the father – usually old, rich and half-illiterate, and the unapproved suitor – young, handsome, educated, but above all poor and unable to pay anything beyond the government sanctioned price of £30.

The story usually starts with a discussion between the heroine and her confidante in the parlour of the wicked father's house. It is soon disclosed that the heroine is unhappy because she is in love with a young man and her father has provided her with a rich old friend of his own. But the girl is determined to marry her young man even if she should die for it. Agnes declares in *Agnes the Faithful Lover* that she will die and 'Then my name will go into history as having died like Julliet (sic) for the cause of true love'. Then comes the ogre of a father shouting for his "Mi-si-si-o" and talking in pidgin English as evidence of his half-illiteracy. The wife arrives and her support for the daughter leads to a beating that brings the neighbours in. These neighbours normally support the husband who has a right to dispose of his daughter without interference from a wife who thinks herself superior. But a meeting is called of the relations and the father is normally terrified by the threat of law into submitting.

Ogali created an exciting dialogue situation out of the discrepancies in the standard of spoken English. In *Veronica, My Daughter*, Chief Jombo, feeling that Veronica, his daughter, and Pauline, his wife, were trying to brow-beat him with their superior knowledge of the English language, sent for Bomber Billy, reputed for the word bombs he could throw. The following dialogue then ensued when Bomber Billy arrived:

CHIEF JOMBO: My pikin, you hear how my Misisi and Veronica my daughter dey talk grammarian for me?
BOMBER BILLY: Madam, what's the meaning of all the hullabaloo that disturbed my capillary and tonsorial artist from discharging his duty efficiently, thus compelling me to have a pedestrian excursion to this place'?
PAULINA: (?) [sic] My husband does not want Vero to marry the man of her choice and I feel he is making a sad mistake.
BOMBER BILLY: You are the person labouring under a delusion and not your husband.
VERO: What are you after? Are you hired to disturb us now?
BOMBER BILLY: If you talk to me again, I simply order your father to put you in a coffin of ostracism.
CHIEF JOMBO: Yes, make una talk grammarian. My pikin, talkam I dey hear.
PAULINA: You must know, Billy that I am at least older than you and (you) MUST stop talking nonsense now.
VERO: Don't mind him. Does he know more than Mike (the man of her choice) who has his Inter B.A.
BOMBER BILLY: Look here! Are you promulgating your exorditation or articulating superficial sentimentality and amicable philosophical observation, beware of platitudeness and ponderosity and learn to respect my integrity.
CHIEF JOMBO: Here! Here! [sic] (he claps and laughs) I hear you! Talkam, my pikin, for dem moth don closs.
VERO: My Mike will answer you well when he meets you.
PAULINA: Never mind that hopeless boy who is rather irresponsible.
BOMBER BILLY: Your statement, Veronica, indicates nothing but a psychological defeatism because you do not take into account the spirit of dynamism in my cerebrium and cerebellum.
PAULINA: I assure you that you are rather miscocopic [microscopic?] to be noticed. A negligible pocket radio that utters useless words.
BOMBER BILLY: I must advice [sic] you madam, to let your conversational communications possess a cherified [clarified?] consciousness and cogency, let your entamporaneous discernment and unpermitted expectectation have intangibility, veroness and versity. Avoid pomposity, proticity, verbocity and rapacity.
CHIEF JOMBO: Talk now misiss! My pikin, go your way and when they talk too much again, I go callam you.
BOMBER BILLY: Thank you. Chief. Before I go, I must make your wife know that she, as a woman, is expected to maintain perfect tranquility whenever you talk to her. Well, goodbye all. I'll see you again.
CHIEF JOMBO: Salute your papa for me – O!
(EXIT BOMBER BILLY)

There are various things of interest in this passage. There are Pauline's appeal to the traditional respect due to older people, Veronica's equation of Mike's Inter B.A. to the peak of academic prowess (it used to be!), and Bomber Billy's appeal to the traditional place of woman in the society, and his choice of words. This concatenation of bombasts would be greatly effective on stage in Nigeria where big words do make an impact. One shares Chief Jombo's enthusiastic asides. Achebe points at this love for big words in the speech of the President of the Umuofa Progressive Union at the reception for Obi Okonkwo in *No Longer at Ease*; Bambulu, in Henshaw's *This is Our Choice*, says of himself and his medicine:

> This is the child of my brain, the product of my endeavour I and the materialization of my inventive genius. It is an anti-snakebite vaccine. Western science has not succeeded in producing anything so potent, but I, Bambulu, have, without any laboratories, without any help, produced this medicine from the herbs of this village. I am a Scientist, I am an Analyst, I am a Catalyst. You may one day find this anti-snakebite vaccine very useful. It is a remedy not only for snakebites and various insect stings, but also for various canine and reptilian contingencies.

And Wole Soyinka's teacher, Lakunle, talks of the custom of paying bride price in *The Lion and the Jewel* as

> A savage custom, barbaric, out-dated
> Rejected, denounced, accursed
> Ex-communicated, archaic, degrading
> Humiliating, unspeakable, redundant,
> Retrogressive, remarkable, unpalatable.

He only stopped because he had only the Shorter Companion Dictionary – the longer edition which he had ordered hadn't arrived.

Many of the words of Bomber Bill are nonsense words, coined on the spur of the moment. Others appeal to various groups. 'Capillary and tonsorial artist' for barber is common among students of Latin; 'a coffin of ostracism' was popular among the early politicians who also would not 'fraternise' with the imperialist, 'integrity' is used frequently to mean ability and 'cerebrum' and 'cerebellum' were very popular terms in biology classes.

Okenwa Olisah, using the same theme in *My Wife, About Husband and Wife Who Hate Themselves*, concentrates the attention on the father's inability to understand why, after he had spent so much to bring up his daughter, he should accept £30 as compensation. He increases the immediacy of the speech by using pidgin English. Victoria breaks up her marriage with the rich Mark to whom she has been forcibly married by her father and falls in love with young but poor Bontus. When her father, Chief Monger[2] asks Bontus to pay a bride price of £180 and Bontus explains that the law puts the limit at £30, Chief Monger exclaims to his gathered relations:

> Israel, Rufus, Mrs. Una,[3] hear the law this boy de quote for me I no go givam my daughter again. Bontus go, go now, now.

When his relatives try to pacify him he continues:

> Law makers, I de hear you people. I go go prison because my daughter marry. How much I take train my daughter for school and the cost of other maintainance? The other man paid me £120. I go prison for that?

At a certain stage, his wife interjects a remark and he turns on her: 'Mrs. I no want your mouth again'.[4] Chief Monger tries to make a private arrangement:

> If Bontus pay me £180 for my daughter, who go tell Government that I received above £30?

When this fails, he reluctantly yields his consent:

> You see trouble, man takes all his money train his daughter, after any man come pack those training and pay only £30. Wetin I go do. Nobi this my daughter takes my foot out.[5] If she agree stay with the former husband, who and me go de talk with. Now if I receive £30 from Bontus I will add it £90 to settle the former husband. Wetin I will do. Bontus alright bring the smallest sum of £30.

The success of many of these authors lies in their closeness to their subject and their audience. They know what their audience wants. They too are part of that audience and they share the same problems, and in the mode of expression, they also know how to put things to catch the interest of that audience – bombastic words, pidgin English and the point of view. In supporting Victoria in the above play, Olisah also does manage to preserve some sympathy for Chief Monger. After all, he belonged to a tradition in which parents decided who their daughters married, and he had spent more than £30 on his daughter and, if he was to get compensation, £30 was a ridiculous sum. Justice demands that he be given some sympathy.

A certain sense of justice appears in the organisation of many of the pamphlets. *My Wives Are in Love With My Servants* by Okenwa Olisah is a bold attack on one of the more popular sins of the new affluent society of Nigeria—that husbands who, with even two wives of their own, go around with other women and harlots. Okenwa Olisah, like others, is interested in the processes of law administration. He has written a pamphlet on *Ibo Native Law and Custom*. In *My Wives Are in Love With My Servants*, old relatives, called in by Obiakaja to settle a dispute between him and his wives over extramarital love making, follow the established processes of examination and cross-examination and use expressions like: 'Your wives will make statements one by one before we ask questions …' This is time for judgement. Naturally, when there is dispute, the parties concerned would be asked to go out after giving 'evidence' so that their judges will be at every liberty to review their 'evidence' and then give judgement: '… I am directed by my co-judges to deliver this most impartial judgement.'

The play itself suggests a cure for the evil of the 'womanizing' husband – expressing a feminist egalitarian attitude that not many men will find appealing. Ubiakaja comes home one afternoon to find his wives half naked and playing with his servants. To his angry outburst one of the wives replies:

> We must continue to please ourselves with Joe and Emma [the servants]. We warned you time without number to abandon your love making with other females but you did nor heed the warning. We know many of your lovers some of them used to visit you here without being afraid of us. It is because you told them that your wives are nothing and this is why they are not afraid of us.
>
> If you know how you felt when you met us with Joe and Emma playing, it was the same feeling when we see you playing and making love with other women. If you are annoyed, then imagine what might have been our feelings long ago you started to mess up with other women. Human beings have similar feelings no matter the sex. Therefore we will never stop being in friendship with other men until we are satisfied that you have stopped to love other women.

I found this a rather alarming statement. It does something to the traditional male prerogative of infidelity – but it is justice. And that was what the judges called by Ubiakaja, all men, thought. Their 'impartial judgement' was:

> We are satisfied that Ubiakaja is a womanizer. He messed up very much and we appreciate the resentment which you his wives showed to him. You are human beings with feelings. You are not beasts. You are not blamed at all.

The case of the unfaithful husband also produced the poetic justice in *Why Some Rich Men Have No Trust in Some Girls* by H. O. Ogu. Again this is an attack on a rather common social practice – rich men having young girls whom they maintain in greater luxury than their wives. I might mention here that this play-novel gives an inkling of an answer to the problem of a kind of African (?) sense of humour that has cropped up over a few occasions. A group of Nigerian students watching a production of Antigone laughed in the last scene when the grief stricken Cleon came on stage weeping over his dear son. Joyce Cary, in *The African Witch*, describes the laughter of the crowd watching Akande Tom, who had denied the power of Elizabeth, the witch, creeping back to her on his knees to receive his punishment. I thought when I read this that Cary's explanation of the laughter with the proposition that the crowd was hysterical with fear was wrong. I would suggest that laughter in such situations has to do with the irony of fate, with the sense of relief at the re-establishment of order, with the bringing to line of the one that had dared to claim a new morality to himself. The comedy, with a purpose, of *Why Some Rich Men Have No Trust in Some Girls* is based on the irony of the situation produced, with poetic justice.

Nwankwo, a rich Lagos trader, is returning from a visit to Eastern Nigeria, and picks up a young girl, Rose, who had run away from home because she did not want to go through the fattening ceremony. He is going to keep Rose as his mistress but is not afraid to take her to his house when they arrive in Lagos. When his first wife asks 'Master, who is this lady with you? Have you married another wife without our information?' He replies with a burst of laughter:

> Oko-ko ko-kono! This my wife go kill me. How I go go marry a third wife put for house, when you two wey I get at present no allow me rest. This lady na Rose, him father be my tight, tight friend. Him father ben see me for home and giam me say make sendam to him brother wey de work for N.B.C. for this Lagos. Make una prepare chop foram. We don hungry tire for lorry.

So the wives entertain Rose generously. Later Nwankwo finds a house for Rose, keeps her lavishly and spends most of his nights with her. But then Rose tires of doing nothing and when Nwankwo has bought her a job, she promptly falls in love with Eddie, one of her young co-workers. One evening Nwankwo catches them walking hand in hand and is enraged and explodes.

> NWANKWO: Rose! you again? you again for this Lagos ? Who bi this man wey you and him dey walk like husband and wife? Eh?
> ROSE: Please try to control your temper whenever you are annoyed.
> NWANKWO: Control my temper! how, when I don see this with my eyes ?
> ROSE: What? See what with your eyes? What you should have done is to ask me whom the man whom I am walking with is.

> NWANKWO: O.K, who bi na man now?
> ROSE: Yes, this what I expect from you. You see this man here, his name is Eddy, he is from the same family with me. His father and my father are from the same parents. He is my first cousin. I met him here today in Lagos and he was so surprised to see me. I am just coming home with him so as to introduce him to you. I have already told him all about you – your kindness and your love to me.

And so Nwankwo is deceived just as he had deceived his wives, and he not only entertains Eddy but gives him money. Later, Eddy gives him a thrashing and pays the court fine with only a minor part of the money he and Rose had saved from Nwankwo's lavish generosity.

Another aspect of justice is exhibited in Ogali A. Ogali's *Caroline the One Guinea Girl*.[6] This has to do with what one might call the graph of African justice. One of the objections raised against Cyprian Ekwensi's *Jagua Nana* is that Jagua has too easy a relief from the consequences of her evil life. Ogali's explanation might help to create a calmer atmosphere for its discussion. Ogali's story is about a girl who chooses to lead what may be euphemistically called an irregular life. She leaves her family and rises from the lower rank of prostitution to become a high-class 'society lady'; she commits a series of abortions, something abhorred by a people that value children rather highly. She reaches an apex of vice and wealth. Then things begin to happen to her. She comes back from a night of revelry to discover all her property stolen. In her poverty she is rejected by all erstwhile admirers. Then she is struck down by a foul disease and is jeered at. Her parents take her back home and for a time she is village gossip. But she begins to mend, becomes religious, and is finally married by a prosperous lawyer whom she makes happy and gives two sons and a daughter.

It was suggested to Ogali that if he had any intentions of advising girls not to follow his heroine's way of life he had spoilt it by giving her a happily married life. His reply was that the girl had suffered for her evil ways and that at the end of punishment and disgrace comes salvation and forgiveness. It appears that many of the women who read the pamphlet, though they seriously disapproved of the girl's behaviour, pitied her enough in her sufferings to feel quite happy at her good fortune at the end. This rather clashes with the Christian notion of an eternal hell for the evil doer. The graph that goes down should go up again or balance is overthrown.

I am tempted to throw in Senghor's theory of rhythm as an element of the African consciousness – but it is probably too high-sounding for the present discussion. I have been trying to establish that the best of the pamphleteers take their sense of mission as educationists seriously. I also suggested that they take their art seriously. There are a few writers centred in Port Harcourt and they complain of the way in which their art is being degraded by some of the pamphlets published in Onitsha. One of the contributors to *The Nigerian Author Magazine* expresses concern over the existence of 'fake' authors of whom he writes:

> Fake authors do themselves great disservice when they refuse to stoop down to learn. This class of authors, from point of experience, often take special delight in copying the works of others, since it is obvious that they cannot rely on their own individual literary efforts. Such offence, if proved in a court of law means 'PLAGIARISM'. Apt quotations used with the names of such authors are permissible however ...[7]

There is something perhaps naive in the way the statement is made but it shows the author's serious concern with the dignity and the nature of his art. In the Introduction to his novelette, *Surprise Packet*, Sigis Kamalu comments on the poor quality of some of the literature on the market and attempts a critical analysis of his own novel. Most of these writers end their prefaces by inviting serious criticism of their works and express ready willingness to accept correction.

Grey Ikpoto starts the above-mentioned essay with the assertion that 'The "born" or "fair" authors are naturally thirsty for reading, hungry for learning ...' There is no doubt that the better writers of the group do read whatever is available to them and try to bring their reading into their writing – sometimes to show off their learning (one remembers many school-boy debates where the most applauded speakers were those who could roll out a string of quotations), at other times in a serious effort to improve their writing.

A dictum among the Ibos is to the effect that to make a speech without using proverbs is like trying to climb a palm tree without the climbing rope. I suggest that the tendency towards supporting one's statements with proverbs might have carried over into this market literature in the form of using quotations. In *Veronica, My Daughter*, between pages 20 and 23, there are quotations from Richard Whately, William Shakespeare G. A. Gallock, Rudyard Kipling, Benjamin Harrison, William Ernest Henley and Henry Longfellow; and before the end of the story there are further quotations from Johann Wolfgang Von Goethe and some unknown poet. Momoh Aroye's *Nancy in Blooming Beauty* opens with a quotation 'culled from GOOD WIVES, edited by Louisa M. Alcott.'

Incidentally, the mania for quotations is not determined by the standard of education. Onuorah Nzekwu's *Wand of Noble Wood*, for example, contains its fair share of quotations. Snatches of poems and songs keep running through the mind of Peter Obesie, the hero, and in one conversation in the story there are quotations from Sir Walter Scott, Southey, Reynold's *The Will*, and from Shakespeare. And on the day on which I first thought of this issue I glanced through one Nigerian newspaper and the leader article started its second paragraph with a quotation from Edmund Burke. This is impressive where breadth of knowledge of English is not only a prestige factor but also a guide to social and employment status. In *Veronica, My Daughter*, Veronica looks down on her father's intelligence and wisdom because he had not attended 'even infant school as to be able to read and write simple English.' But one has to admit that sometimes quotations are used for the genuine purpose of giving to the opinion of the speaker or writer an extra and higher authority.

Nancy in Blooming Beauty reveals another kind of influence from reading. Momoh Aroye's English in this novel is stilted and so is the framework in which he puts his story. Nancy says that she 'was born and bred in the little Cottage of Funland along the shores of the Rio de La Plata on the Ist day of April.' The setting gets all mixed up, some fantastic situations mingling with the customs of that part of Nigeria where Momoh Aroye was brought up. The author appears to be so intent on reproducing the tone and style of the romances he has read that he comes out with affected and pompous impossibilities and flourishes of style that may impress the semi-illiterate but sound rather ridiculous to the enlightened reader, even admitting the robustness of the experiment with words. And this is a pity because he has a story that supports his theme that 'Contentment can't be got by seeking.'

Another type of influence is interestingly portrayed in Thomas 0. Iguh's *Agnes the Faithful Lover*. Agnes declares that she is ready to die for her love and 'then my name will go into history as having died like Julliet [sic] for the cause of true love.' At the end of the play Agnes and her lover commit suicide in true Romeo and Juliet fashion and are mourned by all those who had opposed them. *Romeo and Juliet* also provides the inspiration for Igu's other play *Alice in the Romance of Love*. Alice's confidante warns her against being in love with Fidelis, the boy 'with whose family yours have been engaged in a series of court actions over a piece of land.' The feud had to be about a piece of land in Nigerian terms. Later in the 'drama' there is the following scene obviously influenced by *Romeo and Juliet* Act II, Scene ii.

ALICE: It is alright: good night.
(FIDELIS LEAVES).
ALICE: Come back darling for I can't afford to let you go without a kiss (She kisses him again).
FIDELIS: Sweet heart I shall be here again to see you tomorrow.
ALICE: Is tomorrow not too far? O! don't you know I find it difficult to control my sentimental emotions when I don't see you for a single hour.
FIDELIS: Alright darling, but for the memory of this great night, have this ring and wear it always on your fingers.
ALICE: In fact I have now agreed you love me and that being the case, always count me first among those that love you dearly for I don't think anybody loves you more than myself. Oh sweet heart hurry out for my dad is coming.
FIDELIS: Alright good night; (he leaves).
ALICE: Don't go please without a kiss for it is one of the pleasures of being in love with some one of the opposite sex. (They kiss themselves again).
FIDELIS: Alright I shall continue to remember you till we see again.
(EXIT FIDELIS)
ALICE: Oh this boy is really sweet. I don't know why I have within a short space of time loved him so much. He is my morning star and has ultimately stolen my heart away. No I must call him back. (She goes to the window)
ALICE: Fidelis! Fidelis! Fidelis, sweet heart! (she shouts for him). Oh! you're gone far, but how do I stay alone without you. Can't you listen and answer my call? I am Alice calling you. (At this stage she turns back). He has gone far. Oh! he doesn't hear me (she cries).

Reading, learning, taking expressions from here and there, sometimes borrowing settings, at others borrowing scenes, always interested in improving their vocabulary and technique, these writers are providing literature for the audience ready to take their works. They are read by traders and students, and I have seen some of these pamphlets in the hands of village children. Many of these writers are serious with their work. Their interests vary from love to politics. (There is a large body of political writing which, for purposes of brevity, I have not discussed.) They are interested in social problems – prostitution, drunkenness, bribery, bride price, the taking of brain pills by students; they are interested in the customs of the land.

Some, of course, are interested in nothing but catching the market. Miller O. Albert, for example, has produced an extravaganza called *Rosemary and the Taxi Driver* all fantasy and word exuberance. To illustrate, this pamphlet opens with:

> If there was a prize to be awarded for falling in love at first blush, Rosemary should be given the richest golden medal. She has been chasing around the romantic sea port of Lagos, with her flareful glush of romance. Her violet gown with vibrant colours and heavenly patterns vested below her knees. She wore a dazzling gold necklace, shiny ear rings and a botanical veil, stained all over with jet colours.

Occasionally there is an interesting word play resulting from the extravagance of the imagination, as when Rosemary muses: 'I know I'm Rosemary. Mary, is the last tail of it, Yes! But I will one day, add an "R" after a letter, from the last spelling, to make it a vital gut that's Yes the much sought after treasure "Marry".' But most of the book is in the vein of the following extraordinary passage, describing the sensation caused by Rosemary on entering the train:

> Soon she entered into the train rolling the sleeves of her gown, getting ready for any strange eventuality. All the mask faced odd boys were soaring on the air, for her cheerful romance because of her saucy red lips. The character they presented, became very thicky to happiness and some, were savouring insubordination, mostly the odd concomitant type, of immoral stimulation, which provoked the impetus of glaring at sexual menace, below the belt, leading to excessive giving back of daily toping and night time tipples of dry gin and whiskey.

There is much Onitsha market literature that is below the standard of even its own audience. The best of its examples do not attain a high literary standard. The English is rather poor though sometimes exciting, and is made worse by printing. Most of the characters are undeveloped types. Themes are treated much too superficially. Some of the authors know this and explain the handicaps under which they work. The publishers dictate to them about subject matter and number of pages. Some of the writers have no other source of income and since they do not receive much for a manuscript they have to produce rather fast.

The audience dictates to them. For example Love is the most popular theme and sometimes titles are distorted to attract interest. Okenwa Olisah's *My Seven Daughters Are After Young Boys*, for example, has a deceptive title. The play deals with the attempts being made on a king's life by his three wives whom he had 'sacked' following the evidence of his servant Godwin that they had tried to make love to him. The title only comes in at the end when the king, in rewarding Godwin for his services, says to him:

> My servant, Godwin, you are a very faithful servant, you serve me very well. You gives me informations. I trust you more than my wives and children. My wives want me to die. My children are stupid things.
>
> MY DAUGHTERS ARE AFTER YOUNG BOYS! They only know

how to play love and nothing more again. But Selinah will make a good wife. She is not after young boys as others, she is different from my daughters. Selinah will be your wife as from Thursday next week.

And Thursday, the following week Selinah became Godwin's wife. But this is not enough to justify the title and one must accept the existence of some outside pressure that led to the choice of that title.

The audience also demands vigorous action in love or crime or politics. It also demands big words. There is a middle group of better educated writers who try to psychologise in good but simple English and they are finding it difficult to make any impact or money.

With these handicaps it is surprising that so many books of definite interest are produced. And these books are significant both as literary efforts and in their revelation of the popular attitudes to sociocultural phenomena. We have a new life and a new language. In the unassuming simplicity and directness of Onitsha Market literature we find authentic evidence of what these new elements mean to the common man and what are his reactions to them.

Notes

[1] Where I put a question mark after the author's name, the author has denied authorship. I found that there are many authors who sell their manuscripts outright for £20 to £30 and the publisher then brings out the book under his own name.

[2] Those who are considered to follow money too eagerly are called money mongers.

[3] The plural for 'you' in Ibo is Unu.

[4] This is a translation from Ibo and is something equivalent to 'I don't want your cheek'.

[5] Again a translation from Ibo. Traditionally corpses are carried out feet first. To have one's feet taken out has come to mean to be exposed or disgraced, or generally to be a cause of public gathering and concern. Chief Jumbo is saying therefore that it is his daughter that has made him cause of public commotion. This is the power of pidgin English that, because it has no standard form, the speaker has the freedom to adopt whatever he chooses into it.

[6] Unfortunately this is out of print. The information that follows about the novel is the outcome of an interview with the author.

[7] Grey Ikpoto, 'The field of authorship', *The Nigerian Author Magazine* (May 1962), p. 7.

DON DODSON

The Role of the Publisher in Onitsha Market Literature

Reference
Research in African Literatures (4) 2, 1973: 172–88

Onitsha market literature – a proliferation of chapbooks with such titles as *How to Speak to Girls and Win Their Love*, *Mabel the Sweet Honey That Poured Away*, *No Condition Is Permanent*, *How to Write All Kinds of Letters and Compositions*, and *Money Hard to Get But Easy to Spend* – is usually portrayed as a true popular art written by the common man for the common man.[1] The chapbook writer is the mouthpiece of his readers: he voices their own concerns in their own English vernacular with little regard for monetary reward.[2] As Donatus Nwoga has written:

> The success of many of these authors lies in their closeness to their subject and their audience. They know what their audience wants. They too are part of that audience and they share the same problems, and in the mode of expression, they also know how to put things to catch the interest of the audience.[3]

The relationship between author and audience, however, is not as close as most of the research on Onitsha pamphlets implies. Field research conducted in 1971 points to more attenuated links.[4]

Pamphlet writers generally have more schooling than their readers. Out of sixty-one readers who answered a questionnaire sent to eighty-three mail order customers throughout Nigeria, forty-four had completed Primary VI or VII. Eight had less schooling and nine had some secondary education. Between ages twelve and thirty, their average age was eighteen. Twenty were students, eleven were traders, six were soldiers or policemen, seven were unemployed, and seventeen had occupations ranging from fisherman to houseboy. Twenty-four earned no money. The twenty-three who specified their monthly earnings said they made between £I and about £28 with an average of £8. These findings are supported by a second nonprobability sample of 141 Onitsha residents.

Most writers are more advanced students or provincial journalists with secondary schooling. Wilfred Onwuka, one of the most prolific pamphleteers, wrote his first pamphlet in 1963 after he had completed one year of secondary school as well as a battery of courses at a stenographic institute and evening adult classes on the British constitution, economics, and English. Ogali A. Ogali had completed Form V eight years before his first pamphlet, the immensely popular *Veronica My Daughter*, was published in 1957. He used his profits to attend the Ghana School of Journalism and the London School of Cinematography. Thomas Iguh was in secondary school when his first pamphlet, *Alice in the Romance of Love*, was published. He later studied law at the University of Lagos and he still writes pamphlets. Other pamphleteers, including E. U. Anya, Okwudili Orizu and J. N. C. Egemonye, also went on to attend universities.

Thus it is debatable that the authors are part of their audience. It might be more accurate to say that they have grown out of their audience to a higher level of education and social status.

Nor are the pamphlets a direct link between authors and audience. Authors usually surrender control over content to get their pamphlets into print. Lacking the capital to pay printing expenses, the typical author sells his manuscript to a publisher who pays for printing, handles distribution, and reaps all the profit. One of the few authors to rebel against this system is Chude Graham-Akus Jr., who grumbles that 'If I have to sell my works to them, I think they will have to make money out of my sweat... If I sell my works to them, I'm cheated. I wouldn't mind if the work is out and doesn't sell well. I wouldn't care.' His second pamphlet, *International Knowledge*, gathered dust at the City Press for weeks after it was printed because Akus could not complete payment. Other authors are not so dogged. Forsaking any further control over their manuscripts, they sell them outright.

Although the publishers play a pivotal role in pamphleteering, they are shadowy figures in most research on Onitsha chapbooks. Emmanuel Obiechina, whose *Literature for the Masses* is the most ambitious study of the pamphlets, writes that

> the publishers band themselves into a kind of guild with regulations and rules of conduct. They have common practices for commissioning works to would-be authors and they have evolved entrepreneurial techniques for regulating the pamphlet business and making money out of it.[5]

Who are these publishers? What kind of 'guild' do they have? What are their common practices? The answers to these questions have been sketchy because scholars have studied Onitsha pamphleteering more as a cultural phenomenon than as an entrepreneurial one.

The cultural aspect – however significant – is inseparable from the entrepreneurial. Pamphleteering is a major business in Onitsha. Hundreds of titles were published in the decade before the Nigerian civil war. More than seventy-five titles, many of them new, are available in the market today. Pamphlets usually go through several printings. *Veronica My Daughter*, the greatest best seller, has been reprinted so many times since 1957 that publisher Appolos Oguwike says he cannot keep track of the number. He states that he sold more than 80,000 copies in one year alone and that he printed another 10,000 shortly after the war. C. C. Obiaga, the owner of All Star Printers, estimates that he used to print about eight pamphlets a month with an average run of 6,000 copies – a total of well over three million copies in the six years before the war. Although All Star was probably the biggest pamphlet printer before the war, it had to compete with more than a dozen other presses.

The roots of this proliferous pamphleteering go back to the late 1940s, but it was not until it flourished in the 1960s that its commercial structure stiffened. The reconstruction of the Onitsha market, the rapid growth of literacy, the availability of printing equipment, and the vitality of a new 'democratic' spirit all fostered the feeling that any man could make a name and money by writing a story. This creative anarchy crystallized into an organized business as bookselling in Onitsha became highly competitive. With as many as forty separate booksellers on New Market Road and many others in the market by the 1960s, Onitsha booksellers confronted a problem described by Margaret Katzin:

> At Onitsha, a common complaint of traders who formerly carried on a profitable business in a particular line is that so many others have taken it up that the margin of profit has been reduced. The search for new ways of earning a profit is unremitting.[6]

Besides facing heavy competition, the booksellers were engaged in a seasonal trade. Their profit came chiefly from the sale of schoolbooks at the start of the school year in January and February. Noticing the popularity of such forerunners as *Money Hard*, *Veronica My Daughter*, and Okenwa Olisah's publications, some booksellers decided they could increase their profits by publishing their own pamphlets to sell throughout the year. 'If I stop publishing pamphlets, after three months I will have nothing to sell,' says bookseller Michael Ohaejesi. 'So I keep publishing these pamphlets for the little money they will bring in.'

When Ohaejesi published *Teach Yourself Hausa, Ibo, Yoruba and English* in 1962, he was one of the last booksellers to jump on the bandwagon without falling off in the lurch of competition. Most of the major publishers started in 1960. It was in that year or earlier that Maxwell Obi published *The Gentle Giant 'Alakuku'*, *Our Modern Ladies Characters Towards Boys*, and *Guides for Engagement* under the pseudonym Highbred Maxwell. Appolos Oguwike came out with *Alice in the Romance of Love* and *Life Story of Zik*. A. N. Onwudiwe entered the fray with *The Labour of Man*. N. O. Njoku produced *Man Suffers, Beware of Women*, and *Half-Educated Court Messenger*. J. C. Anorue followed with *The Unnatural Death of Chief Mambo* and *Never Trust All That Love You* in 1960 or 1961. Gordian Orjiako, popularly known as Gebo, started with *Learn to Speak English, Hausa, Ibo and Yoruba Languages* in 1963.

These seven booksellers, who accounted for a large proportion of the pamphlets produced before the war, are the only major chapbook publishers who have resumed trade in Onitsha. (Their addresses are listed in Appendix I.) The others died, embarked on other projects, or could not recoup from the war. Bookseller J. O. Nnadozie sold his copyrights (including the famous *Money Hard to Get But Easy to Spend, Beware of Harlots and Many Friends: The World Is Hard*, and *What Women Are Thinking About Men: No. I Bomb to Women*) to J. C. Anorue after the war and became a medicine trader in Lagos; Okenwa Olisah, who operated a stenographic institute, died before the war; bookseller C. N. Aririguzo died under suspicious circumstances during a legal suit against a competitor; B. A. Ezuma, the proprietor of Chinyelu Printing Press, was wiped out by the war and is now selling mirrors and holy pictures next to his damaged shop.

Although the seven major pamphlet publishers face new competition from several younger entrepreneurs, they still produce most of the pamphlets. Each buys manuscripts from authors for £3 to £20. Assuming complete ownership of the manuscript, he makes any changes he wants: he can alter the title, revise the content, or put his own name as the author. Next he takes the manuscript to a printer and 'beats price' or haggles over terms. For £225, he might order 6,000 copies. Selling these to vendors at a fixed rate of eighteen shillings per dozen, he stands to make a profit of more than £200 on each impression. The vendors take the pamphlets to markets. motor parks and thoroughfares in small villages and big cities all over Nigeria. While most pamphlets are now marked to sell at five shillings, the normal price is two shillings or two-and-six unless the purchaser is unusually meek or aggressive as a bargainer.

Thus the publishers are the central figures in pamphleteering. The system can be described more fully by elaborating on the relations of publishers with one another and with other key figures.

Relations with one another

The publishers are able to operate as a kind of guild, as Obiechina puts it, because they share close ties transcending the rifts of competition. Most of the scores of booksellers in Onitsha are from the town of Urualla in Nkwerre Division southeast of Onitsha. Just as the sale of motor parts is dominated by traders from Nnewi, bicycle parts by traders from Awka-Etiti, and used clothing by traders from Abiriba, so the sale of books is dominated by Urualla traders.

The typical way to enter trade is to become an apprentice to an established trader who is a townsman or a kinsman. The apprentice (called 'boy') is both a ward and a servant who helps his master at home as well as in trade. Usually unpaid throughout his service, the apprentice is 'settled' by his master when he has the maturity and skill to go into business on his own. The settlement may be cash, credit on goods, support for education, or some other reward.

All the pamphlet publishers have 'boys' and all of them except J. C. Anorue, who began as J. O. Nnadozie's partner, started that way themselves. Michael Ohaejesi describes the process:

> Really first year I was just doing some domestic works. Washing clothes, keeping the house clean, cooking – and at times I go to the market to help in selling. That was the first year. Then as for the second year I started staying in the market, went and travelled to Lagos to collect books, and then I continued although by then I was under somebody in the market. We are all serving one person but there is one somebody who is the senior servant. Then the third year I was left with a full shed. And I started managing one... That wasn't my shed but still I am serving the man.

Finally he got his own shed. Ohaejesi will not say what he received when he was settled, but other publishers mention a variety of practices. N. O. Njoku was able to enter school after he had served his master for five years. Appolos Oguwike started business with £60 from his master and his father. A. N. Onwudiwe's master gave him £30, They all started business between 1954 and 1963.

It is through the apprentice system that the dominance of Urualla booksellers persists. Such prominent businessmen as Alaka, Anebere, Ugoji, Ibetu, Mogu and Dike (none of them pamphleteers) are among the many booksellers from Urualla. Three of the seven publishers are also from Urualla: Highbred Maxwell, Michael Ohaejesi, and Gebo. Maxwell and Ohaejesi both served under T. A. Obi, a pioneer in the book trade, who came to Onitsha in the 1940s. When Maxwell earned his independence, he trained Gebo. After Gebo got his own shed, he brought Peter Udoji from Urualla to be his apprentice. Udoji started publishing pamphlets in 1971. The system continues.

The other four publishers are not from Urualla – J. C. Anorue is from nearby Ihioma, Appolos Oguwike and N. O. Njoku are both from Ogwa in Owerri Division to the south, and A. N. Onwudiwe is from Ogbunka to the north – but they share close ties with one another and with the Urualla group. (These ties are schematized in Figure 1.) Ohaejesi and Anorue are partners in the Do-Well Press. Anorue has also teamed up with Appolos to produce 10,000 register books. Appolos and Njoku are kindred: a wife of Njoku's father is the sister of Oguwike's father, and Njoku's senior brother married Oguwike's sister. Onwudiwe, whose Trinity Printing Press produced several pamphlets for Highbred Maxwell, used to share a market shed with him. Maxwell lives in the same compound as Gebo. Maxwell, Gebo, and Ohaejesi meet monthly for the Urualla Progressive Union and for a singing club called the Urualla Choral Party. Gebo and Ohaejesi belong to another social club called the National Social Board Movement. Besides the formal connections, friendships – some close, some casual – tie the publishers together. Anorue and Ohaejesi are 'tight' friends who are frequent companions. 'We are all friends. We are very friendly,' affirms Njoku. 'Oh yes, sometimes we argue and fight, but we are friends. You know, birds of a feather flock together.'

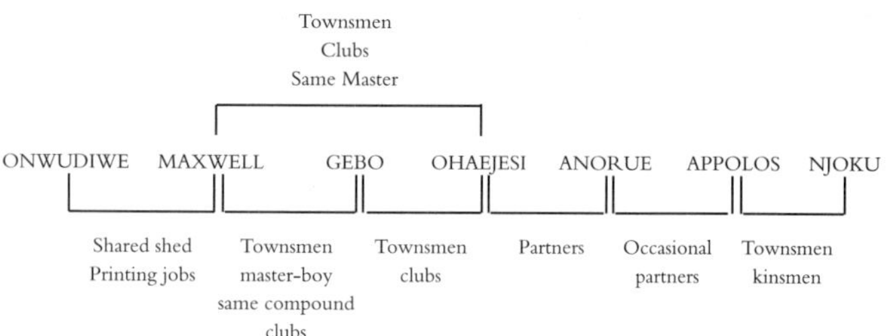

Fig. 1. Relationships among publishers

The arguments rarely get as bitter as the one that ended with the death of C. N. Aririguzo. Although squabbles about underselling or plagiarism sometimes erupt, the publishers enjoy remarkably amicable relations. Grievances can be aired at meetings of the grandly named Pamphlet and Novel Publishers Association of Nigeria. The aim of the association is to set fair trade practices (such as the rate of eighteen shillings per dozen pamphlets for vendors) and to plan joint projects. Founded in August 1971, the group met with uneasy camaraderie every other week until the fifth meeting was postponed and then disbanded for lack of a quorum. Appolos is chairman, Anorue secretary, and Njoku financial secretary. The other members by early 1970 were Ohaejesi, Maxwell, Gebo, and Udoji. The only major holdout was Onwudiwe. This stirred the resentment of the others, who interpreted his obstinacy in different ways. While one thought Onwudiwe did not have to join because he 'is very wealthy,' another muttered with the didacticism that pervades the pamphlets:

> I think he's a little soft in the head. He doesn't keep up his shop He is more interested in showing that he has a car than in staying in his shop and working. But if he rides around in his car all day and doesn't keep it in repair, then one day he won't have it anymore, will he?

Onwudiwe, naturally, offered different reasons:

> I don't have the money now... You see, we are all from different areas, so we don't think alike. We have different kind of view, different kinds of ideas. We have different responsibilities ... They told me they was going to open a meeting, but many a time I wasn't in ... The position is this: It is very difficult to control books or prices.

His real reason seemed to be suspicion of the others. Onwudiwe admitted to underselling them. For a 'large quantity' of pamphlets he sometimes charged vendors seventeen shillings instead of the usual eighteen shillings. Such independence annoyed his competitors, who wanted to bolster the guild aspects of pamphlet publishing. 'There are some publishers who refuse to join and we are going to hit them,' vowed one member of the association in 1971. 'The printers won't print their books again.'

Relations with printers

The printers used to have their own association that set uniform prices and salaries. Efforts to revive it since the war have floundered. With inflation and the generally chaotic state of business after the war, publishers must 'beat price' with the printers. Estimates for printing 6,000 copies of a 72-page pamphlet in 1971 ranged from ninepence to one-and-ten per copy. Ninepence to a shilling was the usual response. The more copies, the lower the rate. Although 6,000 copies is the typical print run today, it is often as low as 2,000 or as high as 20,000. Printers, who used to be willing to print impressions of 1,000 to 2,000, will not print less than 2,000 today.

All presses do jobbing: printing handbills, business cards, labels, wedding announcements, and the like. Only a few still specialize in pamphlets. Many of the pamphlet printers (including Popular Printing Press, New Era Printing Press, Eastern Niger Printing Press, Chinyelu Printing Press, and Onwadiwe's Trinity Printing Press) were either destroyed in the war or so enfeebled that they are struggling to revive. Oguwike's Appolos Brothers Press and the Do-Well Press of Anorue and Ohaejesi are operating again. But even Anorue and Ohaejesi farm out many of their jobs to the two biggest pamphlet printers: Providence Printing Press, which has moved to Awo-Idemili, and All Star Printers, which nas moved to Nnewi.

Providence owner G. O. Onyenwe and All Star owner C. C. Obiaga say they are good friends with the publishers. 'When they come to me,' says Onyenwe, 'it's like doing business with one of your friends.' Obiaga concurs: 'They are very good friends to us. We used to go to their home town when they need us to go.' Most of the publishers reciprocate the warm words, but the friendship does not run as deep as it does among the publishers themselves. Although one publisher says 'Providence' and 'All Star' are his good friends, he does not know their real names. J. C. Anorue says of the printers: 'They don't know much of the publishers. They only print what we send to them.'

Printers find the publishers hard bargainers. Says Onyenwe:

> Publishers will get lower rates ... because they will resell their product, so they have to get their costs down... It is difficult to get profit from these type of publishers because bargaining is the thing they do day and night.

Transactions, however, are informal. Obiaga asks for a third of the bill in advance, the rest payable at any time. He explains:

> They used to pay gradually. Some of them don't even pay this advance. One man now hasn't given anything on two pamphlets. If he have, he pay us. If he have not, we have to give him some copies until he can pay us gradually.

Onyenwe asks for a fifty per cent deposit with the rest payable on delivery, but he too is flexible: 'We can let him take and then pay out of his profits.' Like most of the pamphlet printers, he finds J. C. Anorue the most reliable customer. But he describes another regular customer this way:

> He's not a first class gentleman, but he's somehow good. If he owes you £100, he will pay £90. When he comes to pick up the order he can ask how many extras you gave him. You can tell him that you used all the papers and there is only one or more extra. Then he will say, 'Ahh! Take £10 from it.'

And Onyenwe took one publisher to traditional court for default of payment. Such open conflict between publishers and printers is uncommon.

Relations with writers

Relations between publishers and writers are more strained. There are few personal friendships to ease the natural tensions. 'Many of these authors are hungry writers.... I can say that the authors who write pamphlets are much more after making money than making name,' asserts a publisher. One of his writers, screwing up his face in distaste, counters: 'He is a cheat. Why? He pays a few pounds for your labor and he becomes rich off it.'

While a publisher can expect to make at least £200 off of each large printing, the author rarely sees more than £15. The payment varies widely depending on market appeal and the author's bargaining skill. Gebo says he paid 15 shillings for *Chains of Love*; Appolos says he paid £100 for *Veronica My Daughter* after it had proved itself as a best seller; two of the most popular writers, Thomas Iguh and Wilfred Onwuka, say they usually receive between £15 and £20 for a manuscript; lesser writers can expect between £3 and £10; some have never received any payment beyond promises.

Publishers usually buy manuscripts outright. There are two ways this is done. Sometimes the author seeks out the publisher. Both Iguh and Onwuka sold their first manuscripts this way. Iguh recalls:

> I wasn't really sure who to approach with my manuscript initially. I simply walked into the market, found the book section, confronted one man [Appolos] with my manuscript and he agreed to print it. Later, traders became interested in me and started coming to me to scout for these manuscripts.

The publisher just as often seeks out the writer and commissions him to write a pamphlet to his specifications. Although many authors like Iguh or Ogali Ogali or Ahanotu Umeasiegbu write primarily for self-expression, some who accept commissions feel they are doing hack work. Armand Odogwu, assistant editor of the *Nigerian Mirror*, says he sold a manuscript to Appolos for £10 so he could finance the typing of another story, *Anger Behind the Trigger*, which he took more seriously. He recalls:

> I met Appolos just surprisingly – he was introduced by somebody – and he said, 'You are Armand Odogwu!' I said, 'Yes.'
>
> 'Why don't you do me some pamphlet? I would like it.'
>
> I said, 'Okay, I'm in need of cash. I could give it to you in a few days time.'
>
> This is my own approach; If I want to imitate trash, and you say give me a pamphlet and I need £5, as soon as I make sure that you are serious about publishing it sometime I'll put it out, give it to you, you pay me £3 out of the £5, I leave the manuscript with you – and that's exactly what happened.

While his motivation for *Anger Behind the Trigger* was 'the irresistible urge to write,' his motivation for the Appolos job was 'purely for the money.'

Occasionally publishers give royalties. Peter Udoji offered the author of *Ideal Friendship Between Boys and Girls*, Ahanotu Umeasiegbu, a royalty of twopence on every copy sold. Thomas

Iguh sometimes asks for royalties as well as a lump sum. 'But there,' he chuckles, 'you see the Nigerian businessman is a subtle character: He will never tell you how much he has printed.'

Many authors can point to such abuses. Some of them are never paid the full amount promised. Others have been victims of plagiarism. Iguh says he submitted *Dr. Okpara (The Power) in Political Storm* to a bookseller who could not pay the price he demanded. The bookseller paid another writer to make some changes and published it under a different name without paying Iguh. Iguh then sold the manuscript to Highbred Maxwell, who published the legitimate version. Plagiarism is fairly common. Publishers blame writers; writers blame publishers. The attitude of most is aggrieved tolerance. Claiming that several of his pamphlets have been copied, Wilfred Onwuka says he doesn't care

> because I have sold the manuscript to a publisher... If they want to take action they must do it themselves. But they will not take action because they do the same thing themselves. When I copy your book, you will know that you have done the same thing worse, so you will be embarrassed to take action. They are after money, that's all.

Publishers, on the other hand, complain about 'hungry' writers. One author admits accepting £7 for three manuscripts from a bookseller, then printing one of them on his own. He justifies his action by asserting that he never signed a final agreement.

A few publishers sign contracts only if the author demands it. Gebo says he signs contracts only occasionally. 'We are all Igbos,' he remarks. 'You can sell a land without even a receipt according to Igbo customs.' Other publishers always sign contracts with authors. Appolos, for example, insists on contracts specifying that 'the author has given up all rights and benefits in the book to the publisher.' This is the usual understanding even if it is not certified on paper. When an author sells his manuscript to an Onitsha publisher, he relinquishes control over it. The publisher can do whatever he wants with it.

While Gebo and Highbred Maxwell make minimal changes in manuscripts, others make extensive changes. There are three kinds of changes: title, attribution, and content.

Publishers almost always change titles to underscore the themes of romance or success.

Publishers sometimes use their own name or a pseudonym in place of the real author's. Highbred Maxwell acknowledges he has never written a pamphlet even though his name appears under such titles as *Our Modern Ladies Characters Towards Boys*, *Wonders Shall Never End*, and *The Gentle Giant 'Alakuku'*, which was copied from *The Sunday Times*. Several of his pamphlets were written by his junior brother Charles. Most of the pamphlets published by J. C. Brothers Bookshop are attributed to J. C. Anorue, J. Abiakam, or R. Okonkwo. Asserting that Abiakam and Okonkwo are his own pseudonyms, Anorue swears he has written everything published under those names. Some of his acquaintances scoff at this claim. It is clear that at least a few of his pamphlets, including *The Complete Story and Trial of Adolf Hitler* by J. C. Anorue and *The Complete Life Story and Death of Dr. Nkrumah* by J. C. Abiakam, were actually written by Wilfred Onwuka. But Onwuka, like almost everyone else who has dealt with Anorue, is unstinting in his praise: 'J. C.'s an honest man. He's very kind.... He wouldn't mind paying higher. He's a man of justice.'

Although some authors resent such changes, others have asked their publisher to use his own name. Okwudili Orizu did so because 'I considered the stuff very low.' N. O. Njoku, who published *A Guide to Marriage* with his own name in place of the real author's, has turned down similar requests. He says he refused to take credit for John Uzoh's *Love Shall Never End* 'because of the grammar there. The book contains some Latin words and I don't know how to speak Latin. If I am questioned as the author, how can I answer?' Felix N. Stephen wanted him to take credit for *How to Behave and Get a Lady in Love*, Njoku recalls, 'But the grammar there! In fact it's above my own.'

It is difficult to ascertain authorship because of such practices and because all of the publishers except Highbred Maxwell have done some writing themselves. As Onwudiwe says, 'You know, I write a bit, I write small.' The writing of the publishers generally consists of revising the manuscripts they buy.

Few authors complain about changes because they recognize that their work has become the property of the publisher. 'They have the right to take away what they doesn't like and put their own,' Onwuka says of the publishers. 'They never say anything about it after they have sold it,' says Appolos of writers, 'because you ask him to write this thing. It's not his own sense. It's not his own creation.' The pamphlet is viewed as a commodity in which the creator has no inherent rights. It is manufactured for the market.

The publisher standardizes the product by adhering to successful conventions. If he has solicited the manuscript in the first place, he may not make any changes. Explains Appolos: 'I usually get a title, jot down the contents, give you the key notes and then say "Write on this".' If he is not satisfied with the result, he may ask the author to make changes: 'You've got to sit down and say, "Look, this thing you have written is not appealing to the public. You've got to make more valuable points, more appealing points."' Or he may make the changes himself: 'Sometimes the author will write something that won't interest the public. I will like to change it. I will substitute more interesting amendments... If one writes with very academic English, we can bring it to normal English.'

N. O. Njoku often makes alterations for new editions of a pamphlet. He says he expanded Okenwa Olisah's *No Condition Is Permanent* by adding everything from '24 Charges Against Wives' on page 25 to the end of page 48. Changing the title of Felix N. Stephen's *How to Get a Lady in Love* to *How to Behave and Get a Lady in Love*, Njoku added the first ten pages and made some other alterations:

> I only arranged it in a way that will suit the public. Seeing that the ending is not attractive or is not so good, I added some pages to conclude the whole show. Now what matters in a pamphlet is the beginning and end, and the title.

Juggling content does not bring publishers into conflict with authors like Onwuka who are happy to write on demand. But sometimes there is conflict with writers who see their work as a calling rather than a business. Okwudili Orizu, who has dropped pamphleteering, comments: 'My ideas are in conflict with the requests of the publishers. That is because the publishers, as businessmen, are trying to make money while I, as a writer, am interested in changing things in society.' Armand Odogwu, a dedicated member of the Scripture Union, declares:

> When you start talking about morals in what you write, as soon as they buy off the copyright the booksellers may decide to remove it. Because these pamphlets published locally are for a certain grade of people. In *Man Must Work* and *Love in the Bunker*

I was forced to bring in pidgin English by the booksellers, and a lot of rotten romantics because one, it is the taste of the majority of their customers.

So you wouldn't be surprised if you see the final thing, they have removed the moral aspect of it. They publish what they want to publish.

What they want to publish is what they think readers want.

Relations with readers

What the publishers think readers want are love stories and letter writing handbooks. The great majority of pamphlets are in these categories. Pamphlets on money or politics are also popular.

A few publishers perceive changing tastes. Onwudiwe says the main criterion of popularity is topicality:

> One, if it is a story that connects the present wave, the immediate wave, which connects the country, like this Nigeria civil war now, you know this connects the country now. If it's anything on the civil war, it will sell. If the book is published during that period, it will sell like hotcake – as I published that book on Lumumba during his death – it sells.

Njoku finds that readers are not as interested in love as they used to be: 'I don't put more importance to that yet. After the war, what they want now is only money – how to rehabilitate themselves.' Gebo articulates the variety of public taste most sharply. 'You know, minds are not steady,' he remarks. 'Perhaps you like eating foofoo today, tomorrow you like rice.' In 1965, says Gebo, the public was interested in letter writing; in 1966, political dramas; after the war, 'nothing yet, they aren't interested in anything.' Gebo thinks tastes also vary from area to area: Onitsha buyers like pamphlets about business, Northerners like love, Westerners have more general tastes. But love and letter writing remain the dominant themes of Onitsha pamphlets.

Closely mirroring the responses of readers who were questioned, the publishers seem to perceive public taste accurately. How do they know what the public likes?

The most important clue is sales. If something 'moves' well, it will be reprinted and imitated until all profit is drained from it.

Another basis is contact with readers. There is little direct contact because the readers generally buy from vendors. Although Njoku maintains that 'I don't have any association with readers, I don't have anything in common with them,' he suggests that public tastes can be sensed by a kind of osmosis: 'Psychologically, I'm a social man. So when we go to functions and gathering, from there you know the opinion of people.' This ambivalence toward the public is typical of the publishers. When asked to describe their contact with readers, most mention correspondence. They used to receive many fan letters and requests for advice. Ohaejesi recalls: 'Some want to know how one will operate a lover after quarrelling – how he or she should contact the opponent for reconciliation.' Njoku received this letter after the war:

> Dear Sir,
> I am indeed very happy to congratulate you about what you have wrote about 'NO CONDITION IS PERMANATE.' I am very happy about it and it shows a good thing in my future life because I am very young and I also praised the author of the book. The author is the Master of Life exactly because you wrote many things which shows you are a good man.
>
> I want you to send me one of your best catalogue in which important things are written.
>
> Please I beg you not to fail me. May God be with you where ever you go and as far you are good man. You are among the chosen people and Jesus explaining this said, 'For many are call but few are chosen.'
>
> With love from …

The flow of letters has subsided since the war and now consists largely of orders.

The third way publishers gauge public taste is to assume that their own taste approximates the average. Appolos explains: 'Myself, I know what I like. And through myself I know what I like and other people may like it, you see.' Feeling that their writers tend to get lost in ivory towers, the publishers think they can speak to their 'semiliterate' audience more effectively. This attitude has some justification. Although they are wealthier and older than the average reader, the publishers share his level of literacy and education. All of them stopped schooling after Standard VI. They are common men who have succeeded in the hurly-burly of trade – as their readers hope to do – rather than in the halls of learning. They are men of the world whose advice on *How to Get a Lady In Love and Romance with Her* or *How to Start Life and End it Well* is earthy and pointed. The publishers emphasize both education and entertainment in the pamphlets. J. C. Brothers pamphlets sometimes carry this blurb:

> Read J. C. books for the following reasons:
> 1. It will teach you many things which you do not know,
> 2. Constant reading will improve your knowledge in education,
> 3. Interesting novels will inspire happiness in you.

Echoing the claims of the publishers, many readers praise the pamphlets for their educational value. Some cite pamphlets as moral authorities. 'Since I read *Money Hard*,' says Albert Mbadugha, a cosmetics trader, 'I have learnt to beware of women with stricted measure. Women are generally after money. One must know this in order to succeed in business.' Some read them to improve their English. Michael Olumide, a Yoruba soldier, says: 'I read them mostly to gain a good conduct of English language. It has given me help.' Others utilize the pamphlets more directly. When asked whether *How to Write Love Letters* is useful, army clerk Ezekiel Onanoga replies, 'Yes yes yes … yes yes yes. I have copied the letter.' An Onitsha trader says he read *How to Write Love Letters* because 'I just got a new girlfriend. There are some good letters in it which are exactly what I wanted to write.' Sometimes two rivals unwittingly copy the same love letter to send to the same girlfriend.

This may be the most embarrassing but least important way readers are led astray. Wavering fact and fractured English make the pamphlets shaky guideposts. They are guideposts nonetheless. Even their exploitation of romance answers real problems of sexual conduct created when marriage is postponed by the collusion of poverty and brideprice. While *How to Behave and Get a Lady in Love* is not the most urgent social issue in Nigeria, it is a pressing personal problem. The commercial basis of Onitsha market literature forces the pamphleteers to focus on the stuff of common dreams: success in love and money.

Conclusion

Onitsha market literature, as the term implies, is a commercial as well as a cultural phenomenon. Commercial constraints mold the cultural conventions. The pivotal figure in the commercial system is the publisher. He takes the risks and makes the profits. He minimizes risks by standardizing the product. What has sold before is what is published again. Like other traders, the publisher is more concerned with saleability than quality.

A few publishers who control most of the pamphlet trade are interlocked in a kind of guild with common practices for buying and selling their product. While the links between them smooth some of the competitive ruffles, their pursuit of profit has been complicated by new competitors in a tight postwar market. Some of the older publishers are seeking new ways to make a profit. Appolos Oguwike, for example, wants to concentrate on printing and selling stationery:

> I don't expect to invest much more on pamphlets. It absorbs your money and fluctuates it too much. It takes a long time to realize your gain. If I am going to invest £1,000 to print four pamphlets it is better to put it into something that will bring immediate liquid cash. I will continue printing pamphlets, but just on a small scale. I will concentrate on postal orders because there you get the full price for the pamphlets.

Appolos says he made £2,000 producing Christmas cards in both 1968 and 1969. Many booksellers were producing Christmas cards in 1971. Michael Ohaejesi alone printed 44,000 in his first effort to carve out a niche in the Christmas market. The unremitting search for profit continues as each innovation is threatened by imitation.

Appolos sums up the driving motive of all traders, whether they sell pamphlets or cosmetics or bicycle parts, when he muses:

> I like business. All I want is to chop one fowl a day, to get a nice car, to build a nice house in town, and at home a nice country house, and to educate my children to whatever level they want. Publishing pamphlets is a means to those magnetic but elusive goals.

Notes

[1] See, for example, Nancy J. Schmidt, 'Nigeria: Fiction for the Average Man,' *Africa Report*. 10 (August 1965), p. 39, and Emmanuel Obiechina, *Literature for the Masses: An Analytical Study of Popular Pamphleteering in Nigeria* (Enugu: Nwankwo-lfejika & Co., 1971), p. 3.

[2] Emmanuel Obiechina, *Onitsha Market Literature* (New York: Africana Publishing Corporation, 1972), pp. 9–19.

[3] 'Onitsha Market Literature,' *Transition*, 19 (1965), p. 29.

[4] The research was supported in part by the National Science Foundation, and the African Studies Committee and the Center for International Communication Studies at the University of Wisconsin. An earlier version of this paper was presented at the Fifteenth Annual Meeting of the African Studies Association in 1972. When the research was conducted, Nigeria had not yet converted to a decimal currency. For the sake of simplicity, therefore, pounds and shillings are used in this paper.

[5] Obiechina, p. 4.

[6] 'The Role of the Small Entrepreneur' in *Economic Transition in Africa*, ed. Melville J. Herskovits and Mitchell Harwitz (London: Routledge & Kegan Paul Ltd., 1964), p. 189.

Appendix I

Established Pamphlet Publishers

Appolos Oguwike	Academy (Nig.) Bookshops 75 Upper New Market Road Onitsha
	Appolos Brothers Press 18 Modebe Avenue Onitsha
Maxwell Obi (Highbred Maxwell)	Students Own Bookshop 58 Venn Road South Onitsha
Gordian Orjiako (Gebo)	Same mailing address as Highbred Maxwell
A. N. Onwudiwe	Membership Bookshop 87 Upper New Market Road Onitsha
N. O. Njoku	Survival Bookshop 81 Upper New Market Road Onitsha
J. C. Anorue	J. C. Brothers Bookshop 26 New Market Road Onitsha
	Do-Well Press 29 Francis Street Onitsha
Michael Ohaejesi	Minaco Bookshops 13 Iweka Road Onitsha
	Do-Well Press

New Pamphlet Publishers

Peter Udoji	Udoji and Brothers Bookshop 54 Moore Street Onitsha
Shakespeare C. N. Nwachukwu	Nwachukwu Africana Books P. O. Box 585 Onitsha
Donatus Adikaibe	Dona Brothers Bookshop 8 Yahaya Street Onitsha
G. C. Osakwe	Pacific Correspondence College 71 Old Market Road Onitsha

Primary Text 2

Reproduction of J. C. Anorue *How to Become Rich & Avoid Poverty*

Reference

J. C. Anorue, *How to Become Rich and Avoid Poverty*
Onitsha: J. C. Brothers Bookshop, 1962?

HOW TO BECOME RICH
AND
AVOID POVERTY

READ AND BECOME WISE.

If you have no money, you are talking for nothing. Everyday when you get up in the morning kneel down and ask God to help you O! God help me. Give me good health, best luck and long life, direct me to the work which I will do to become rich and also give me a good wife and children.

P.P.P

HOW TO BECOME RICH
AND
AVOID POVERTY

Experience in Life is a Key to Success

Copies Obtainable from:–

J. C. BROTHERS BOOKSHOP,
No. 26 New Market Road,
ONITSHA.

Net Price 5/-

PRINTED BY

P. P. P.

PROVIDENCE PRINTING PRESS.
AWO—IDEMILI, P. M. B. 9,
ORLU.

INTRODUCTION

This booklet is written in order to advice men and women who have started or are trying to start life. It is a dictionary of life since it touches many things that happens in this world.

There are many troubles in the world today and if you are not wise you become useless. Remember the proverbs which says that "Mr. trust died because bad friends killed him".

Since many people cannot tell the truth, it is difficult to know whom to trust. No money and lack of sense makes a man common, but enemies and bad companies kill a man.

Do you know why some people are rich while others are poor? If you want to get money and know how to save it, Read: How to become rich and avoid poverty.

J. C. ANORUE
(The Author)

CONTENTS

BUY

HOW TO BECOME

RICH

AND AVOID POVERTY

READ IT VERY WELL

YOU MUST LEARN SOMETHING VERY NEW

WHICH WILL HELP YOU

IN YOUR LIFE.

5

HOW TO BECOME RICH

No efforts, no progress. You cannot win a raffle when you don't sign it, or to become a carpenter without tools.

If you want to become rich, your must be sensible and hardworking, you must work under sun and rain, you must think for yourself and plan for tomorrow. You must not spend your money in a careless way. You must be truthful, honest, clever, and careful. You must respect the laws. You must avoid enemies and bad companies. You must plan your business and know how to save money. You must know your monthly income and expenses. You must avoid troubles and quick temper. You must think well before you decide. You must look neat and must have respect. You must not think of women and forget your business. You must pray everyday and ask God to help you. You must not talk against others, so that they may not talk against you. You must trust in God but fear your enemies.

MONEY AND WOMEN

This is the picture of the Boy *Ghanna* giving money to a hotel girl. Harlots gave him this big name because he can spend. Please do not be like this foolish boy, who does not think of himself. He must suffer at last.

Women like money too much. A woman's love for a man is money. When you get plenty of money you get plenty of women and by then you become Mr. Somebody. But where there is no money, you become Mr. Nobody. A woman cannot love you if you cannot spend. And when you do not spend for them, they will hate you and begin to call you money miss road.

When a woman answers you sir and calls you master, know that she wants your money.

Women like sweet things and talk too much. They are like empty gallons that make the greatest noise.

7

BE A MAN OF YOUR WORDS

Be a man of your words because good name is greater than money. Let your yes be yes and let your no be no. Never talk lies in order to win a favour. Remember the Proverb which says "Ill got, ill spent.

Do not think of things that have past. Remember the proverb which says that "It is a waste of time to cry for a spoilt milk.

Think very well before you say and once you say stand on it.

Do not talk bad of any person remember the words of God which says "Do to others as you would like them to do to you"

8

DO NOT PRAISE YOURSELF

Do not praise yourself even though you have done the best. Let the mouth of people prove your worth. Self advertisement and boast of wisdom are the signs of a foolish man.

Do not call yourself a good man. God knows the best. Experience, good manners, honesty, cleverness and truthfulness are the steps to wisdom.

Never condemn the ideas of other people but you can correct them.

Mr. Jack who claims too much know was unable to answer questions when the right John Goodman challenged him.

9

DO NOT TALK TOO MUCH

It is not wise to talk too much, because a talkative has no respect. During a quarrel, just strike on the points and leave the other person to talk like a mad person.

People will judge you by the way you talk, behave and act.

A talkative is a great liar and can never keep secrets. A sensible man do not like to discuss with a talkative because as he tells you of others, so he will one day tell others about you.

10

READ AND BECOME WISE

Money maketh a man!

Dresses Maketh a woman!

A woman's pride is her husband!

A man of straw is worth a woman of Gold.

A man who doesn't die of a woman must live long life!

Life is money and money is life!

Trust but not too much!

All that glitters is not Gold!

No Smoke without fire!

Avoid enemies and bad companies.

A woman cannot love you without money.

Love all but be to them as oil on the surface of water.

A talkative can never keep secrets.

Read and think twice: A word is enough for the wise.

11

LOVE YOUR BROTHERS AND SISTERS

Love your brothers and sisters and remember your last day. Death comes as a surprise and does not give notice.

No one is above death in this world.

Whatever your are, whatever you do, whether handsome, beautiful or ugly, whether tall or short, whether rich or poor, whether educated or illitrate you must one day die.

Avoid quarrels and become free from troubles. Do not hate your enemies but fear them.

12

LAGOS LIFE

This man loves women too much. He has lived for 12 years in Lagos, but has no bank account. He banks his money on public women and women call him a tough man, pocket never dry.

There is a big dance in the central Hotel and he is matching to the dancing hall with his woman friend.

All his mates in his home town has married and many have erected buildings.

But he never thinks of that. He is educated and receives reasonable salary every month but he spends all on women.

Please dear friends, do not be like this foolish man who never know that the world is hard. Think twice before you do anything

13

DO NOT TRUST IN TIME

My dear readers, Do not trust all you see in the world. Many friends are dangerous enemies I have told you A word is enough for the wise.

Do not lend money to your friend without a strong agreement received and do not tell all your secrets or planes to your friends.

When you look left and right you understand better. Be careful the world is hard and full of lies and changes.

Since brother does not trust his brother, father does not trust his son, sister does not trust her sister, mother does not trust her daughter and master dose not trust his servant. I cannot tell you whom you can trust.

Read and become wise, good advice is the best medicine of life.

THINK WELL BEFORE YOU DO ANYTHING

The World is hard. It is full of of sufferings and temptations It is too competitive, that people have no time to rest.

It is good to hope for success in any good thing you are planing to do. Every one has two educations:- One which he receives from others and one more important, which he gives himself A person who doesn't think for himself does not think at all

HOW TO RUN AWAY FROM TROUBLES

You should be patient, careful, sensible and wise in order to escape from certain troubles, in this world. There are so many troubles, and temptation in the world today, if you are not wise enough, you will be taken by these things.

You should have foresight to see evil plans against you, know when a person comes to attempt you or get you deceived. It is not simple to know when a clever and tricky man comes to deceive you. There are so many words and cunning ways used to deceive somebody, or get some thing from him.

HOW TO GET HELP FROM PEOPLE

If you want to get help from people, you must be clever, honest, truthful and sensible.

Let me here assume that your name is Joseph. Now if I want to get something from you, I will not call you that Joseph, but Joe. This is more lovely and it can make you give me the thing which I may request from you. One can also get help from people by giving them respect which are rather above their merit (worth).

SOME PEOPLE ARE VERY WICKED AND UNGRATEFUL

A person you help may even begin to call you a bush man. Therefore when one embraces you or befriends you suddenly, give a thought to it. Perhaps, he seeks favour from you or wants to get an important information from you. Be very careful and wise. The world is deep, know how you associate with people. They are very clever, cunning, envious, poisonous, harmful, wicked and dangerous. They are difficult to deal with. Some of them are wizards and tigers in the uniform of sheep.

HOW TO THINK AND LIVE

If you can think and study this world as book, things will happen to you less, but if you have no sense, people will handle you as they like. To be too wicked, quick temper and retaliative is not good, and at the same time, to be too simple and quite, is not good. A person can insult you to know what you can do, if you fail to warn him, no more you have killed your respect before him.

From that day upwards, he will no longer fear or respect you. He will think that you are afraid of him. But if you warn him in respect of the insult, he becomes afraid of you, and makes you friend. Wisdom starts from the fear of God. To acquire wisdom, one should mingle with people, study them, find out what they generally like and hate, their tricks, how to follow them and win them. You should develope certain important qualities. You should be observant, watchful, and take notice of things and talk less.

Question: Is it wise that man should tell his friend, brother, sister, his parents, or his relative, all his secrets and other things in his mind?

Answer: This is not wise. There are certain secrets and things in your mind which you will never let anybody to know, however you may be in love with the person. It may be that if you disclose those secrets or

things, that person will never regard you as somebody because you have naked yourself before him. I myself, there are certain things in my mind which I will never make any body to know, not that those things are bad, but they are my "Personal secrets", if I venture to say them out, it means that, I have naked myself, and thereby reduce my regard and respect. Therefore it is not all things that you will tell your friend and not all things you will hide in your mind.

HOW WAYORISTS DECEIVE SOME PEOPLE

Sometimes, if not all the time, some people deceive others by "first impression". A person may come to you and borrow you the sum of £2 and you give him. On the scheduled day of repayment, he can bring the £2 for first impression. Next time, he borrows you £2 and you lend him, he repays it again on the scheduled day. Then next time, perhaps the last you might see him, he borrows you £50, and you lend him. No more, he leaves the town or the country. You will not see him any more. The things you will hear is that he had left the town to unknown place.

What are you going to do when you hear this? You cannot do any thing. You do not know where he is. If you meet his people to give you information where he is, they will not tell you anything. Next time, when another person comes to borrow from you and you drive him away, some people may say that you are wicked, not knowing why you did so. That is why one book says "man makes man to be wicked."

ALWAYS GUIDE YOURSELF WITH EXPERIENCE

Do not wait until somebody tells you: "Do not come to my house again", if you are going to some one's house, always take notice of things and be very observant to know when he or she no longer wants you in his or her house.

EXAMPLE: In order to know when he no longer wants your visits, he will not be giving you face again. When you come in, he will not give you chair, you have to sit down by yourself. There will be other unusual things he will begin to do. If you are a wise man, you say good-bye to his quack house otherwise he insults you one day.

QUESTIONS How can you approach a hard or wicked somebody whom you are badly in need of his favour or wants to obtain some important information from?

Answer: If I know that somebody is difficult or wicked to deal with and I am badly in need to get favour from him or obtain some important information from him, what I shall do is this; I will try to find out what he likes best. If he is a man who does not want anybody to oppose whatever he says, I should not do so. I shall not bother whether he gives me face or not, because I know my mission. I shall be going to his house very frequently and each time I reach, I shall dash things to his children, I shall never dash anything to his wives otherwise he suspects me.

Only to his children I shall be presenting gifts. The man is not a satan, he is a human being, therefore the gifts I am giving his children shall make him develope interest in me.

As time goes on, I shall get him. No man is rather impossible. At the first time, he will be very tough to you, but after sometime, if you know the line, and if you are wise enough, "you win him". People like gifts too much, therefore if you are pursuin anything, be generous in your gift. Do not look money on face.

Let me tell you a short lesson story. In 1959, there was one young man who passed West School Certificate (formerly called African Cambridge).

20

The young man wrote an application to certain Company, for employment, but he got no reply. A friend of his told him that his application would not be replied, unless he meets the Manager at home and "Bribe" him £30. The young man has no money for bribery.

He had only ten shillings with him. What he did was that he put the 10s in his pocket went to the Manager at home. When he reached, he saw that the Manager's wife delivered a baby boy. He put hand in his pocket and brought out the 10s and presented it to the baby boy. "This is a soap-money" he said.

This surprised every body in the house and they all gave him thanks. "Who are you asked the manager. "Sir allow me to tell you whom I am latter", replied the poor wise young man seeking free employment with sense. A bottle of beer was presented to him by the Manager.

After tak.ng the beer he saluted "Thank Sirs, Thank "Madam", "Thank God", replied all. He further said: Master I am now willing to introduce myself. I am by name, Bernard Chukwuma, who forwarded the application dated 4-4-59, to your Office, but up till now I have not got any reply".

"Sorry" said the Manager. The Manager did not know what to do. He saw no way to ask the young man to bribe him, before he could be

21

employed, because the boy had greatly impressed him by the 10/- he dashed his baby-boy. He told the young man to meet him "Tomorrow" in his office by 8.30 a.m. with all his credentials.

In the "night" the Manager and his happy wife discussed this young man's coming, and the wife urged the Manager to offer the man an appointment. "He is a good man. He will not forget you", said the wife to her husband. He agreed. In the morning, the young sensible man, met the Manager in his Office with all his certificates and Testimonial. He was employed. You have now read how this sensible and wise young man secured an appointment free of charge. It is now very important that one should always make use of his sense. When one has no money, he should deeply think what to do. We are given senses to make use of them when we are in difficulty.

HOW TO KEEP A SECRET

Anything which two ears hear, must spread. Therefore if you want to keep something secret, do not tell any body. If you tell somebody and advice him, not to tell another person, the man will tell his friend and tell him, not to tell any person, it is secret. From there it licks and spread to your surprise like wireless.

22

We have many types of people in the world. People who cannot talk, people who can talk, people who are born lawyers, whenever something falls between you and them, they begin argument.

HOW TO KNOW WHO HATES YOU OR LOVES YOU

Sometimes man does not know who hates him or loves him. It is not simple to know certainly who hates you or loves you. A man who hates you will always support you, at anytime when you think out bad thing to do. He cannot give you good advice. Only bad advice he can offer you. Do not wait until one openly makes you to know that he hates you, some people when they hate you, they would not make you realise in their manners. They will laugh with you, play with you, eat with you but you know not that they hate your life. These types of people are called "DANGEROUS PEOPLE"

They laugh always even when they are annoyed, but if they see poison they give it to you.

What is life? Life is nothing but an empty dream. One can make hell or paradise out of life. Man must live according to his good works.

23

LAW KNOWS NO KING

Question: Is it true that law know no king?.
Answer: Yes.

Question: Why do many people choose to pay heavy fines rather than to go to jails? Is it because harder works are done there?
Answer: It is not.

There are some road-labourers who do harder works than some prisoners. So many people choose to pay heavy fine rather than to go to pirson because they don't want their previleges to be arrested, and do not want their photographs to be presented in the Police Charge Office.

Another reason is this: If you are serving under Government department and happens to go to jail, after serving the sentence, you loose your job. If you are due for pension or gratuity you loose them. You are not going to get employment under any Government Department again. The most reason is that so many people do not like their names to be spoiled.

A prisoner may have what he likes. His previleges are arrested. He has no right to go out and please himself. If he is a smoker, he will never try to smoke it. If he is a drunkard, he shall never be allowed to taste any wine. A prisoner has no respect. It is good to respect the law and become free from troubles. Law knows no King.

24

MR. JACK IS FIGHTING HIS WIFE.

This is the picture of Mr. Jack fighting his wife. Mr. Jack says, "My wife did not give me food last night and his wife says that Mr. Jack did not give her money yesterday. This was the cause of their fighting.

It is a bad habbit for a man to beat his wife and it is also bad for a wife to neglect her husband. A husband can not stay with a wife if he cannot endure certain things and a woman cannot stay with a husband if she cannot respect him. It is only a bad wife that fights her husband.

25

A STORY ABOUT A MAN WHO MARRIED SO MANY WIVES.

This is the picture of a man who married many bad wives. This man does not rest in his house. Everyday his wives will fight him. Look at the man running and the wives pursue him with sticks and knife.

One wife means one trouble and two wives mean two troubles. This man bought troubles with his money. He thinks that he is very wise and rich. I am very sorry for him.

26

SHORT STORY ABOUT ROSE MARY

This Harlot is Rose-Mary and she is popularly known as "The one in town" She is beautiful and educated, but she refused to marry a man. She can marry twenty husbands a day and you can always see her in a private car, along the roads. She has many tricks and she has liquideted so many men.

Please my dear young men, If you want to become rich and live long life. Beware of Harlots. Things are not what they are and there are many changes in the world today.

27

HOW TO GET MONEY

If you want to get money, you must work hard. Do not say that rain or sun is too much. You must be gentle, trustworthy and sensible. This man pushing truck is a strong man. He works very hard everyday but he dose not know how to save mony.

He can get £2 a day but he spends all on public women. He does not know how to save money because he is not sensible. Not only to get money is hard but also to save it, you cannot cash a bird without a net, and you cannot therefore become rich if you don't work hard. Read and become wise.

28

ABOUT A COURT MESSENGER

The name of this man is Ben. He is a court messenger, he is not educated but he is very wise. People call him, "No leave No transfer". He became a court messenger since 1929, but no promotion.

29

NO CONDITION IS PERMANENT IN THIS WORLD

Why do you blame your God because you are not yet very rich? Think of the people who cannot see or those who conrot walk yet they are happy. Good healthy is greater than money. When you are healthy you think of money but when sickness comes, you forget all your wealth and think of life. God is very wonderful. He knows all our troubles. The above picture is the picture of a blind man, he cannot see but yet he is very happy. Please when you see these type of people, do not neglet them. Anything you give to a begger is not a waste. "Blessed are the merciful for they shall obtain mercy,,

30

A GOOD MAN WHO WINS ELECTION

This is the picture of a good man who wins election. He said I am happy because, My people love me. For many years this man struggled and contributed much to the development of his town.

During the time of election, his people voted him in.

I have been to East, West, North and South, but there is no place like home.

31

EVERYDAY IS NOT CHRISTMAS

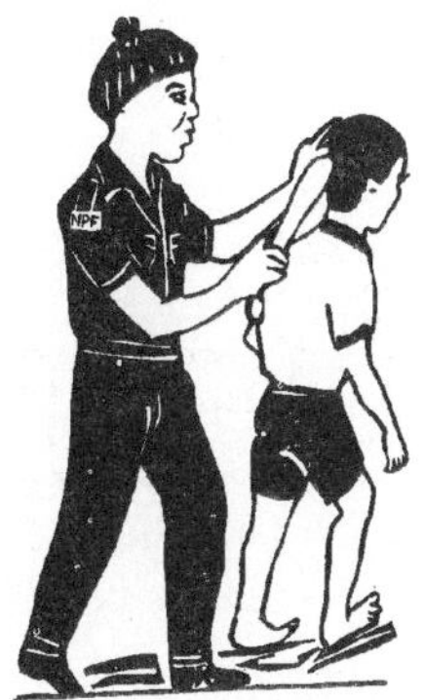

Today is a bad day for Benbella He is popularly known as "Tomorrow is another day". Benbella is a thief of no comparison. He is very strong and clever. He is the master of harlots. As soon as he gets money, he spends it hopping to get more money tomorrow.

Everyday has been a lucky day for Benbella but today is a very bad day for him. Look at this picture, you will see a police man heating him on the head. Many days are for a thief but one day is for the owner of the house.

32

MONEY MISS ROAD

Look at this man pointing at his houses. He is a rich man but he dosen't know how to enjoy his money. He eats two times in a day and he has never tasted a bottle of beer since his life.

If you neglect your life and seek for money, you will die. When you get money, enjoy your self, and help people who need your help.

What you eat is what you gain. Nobody knows tomorrow.

33

A WICKED MAN WHO FAILED ELECTION

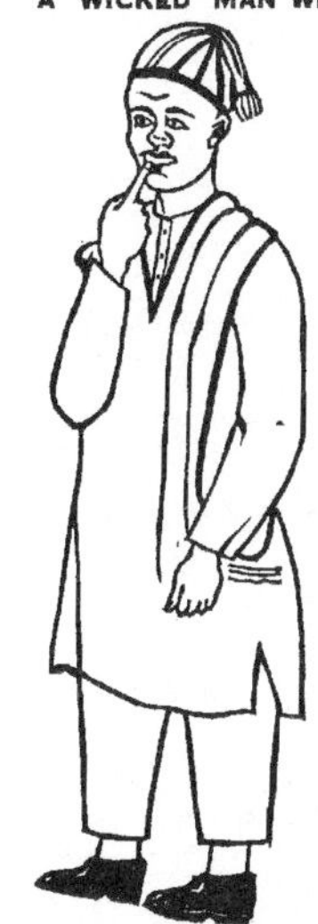

This is the picture of a wicked man who failed election. He is a rich man but he neglects to associate with his people. He does not like the progress of any other person in his town except himself. He does not attend the meetings of his town and does not contribute towards development of his town. He often said that once he is rich, if any body talks against him, that he will sue the person to court and jail him.

During the time of election he started to bribe his people and spent big sum of money in order to vote him in.

What happened? When the result came out, he failed.

He remembered the money he spent and started to cry. My people had disappointed me.

So my good friends, whatever you do, home is the best. Remember the proverb which says "Charity begins at home" and the wicked can never go unpunished.

34

A BAD TRAFFIC POLICE MAN

This is a bad Traffic police man. He likes bribe too much. He is very trikish. He has agents who receive bribe for him while he pretends to do his work. He does not mind whether you drive with particulars or not provided you give him bribe. If you commit any traffic offence and bribe him, he will tell you to go. But if you don't bribe him, he will seize your particulars and ask you to see him after work in the office. He has a big pocket note book where he pretends to keep records.

He does not always like to do his work on the popular roads, He likes to stay at the corner roads where he will get chance of receiving bribe. He is very big and clever, he is black in completion with big head and red eyes.

He works from morning till night without getting tired.

This type of Traffic Police man is very dangerous to the Government.

35

WHY MEN NEVER TRUST MONEY MONGER LADIES

Beware of those girls who ask you to buy them many things. Please give me 10/-, I have no good shoes to wear, I have no powder and pomade to rub. My leather box is becoming old, I want a new gown and I have not taken photograph for a long time. Ladies hand watch fits better and the modern Italian shoes are out for sale.

That bush teacher and one boy living in that new house with glass windows have been worrying me to stop coming to your place. The teacher gave me £1 yesterday but I refused. Do not trust this type of girl. She is after your money. If you continue to spend for her, you become useless. Money is hard to get but easy to spend.

Question: Why do men never trust ladies of the present time?

Answer: Because they are money mongers and cannot tell the truth.

Question: Can a money monger lady love you if you do not spend money for her.?

Answer: No.

Question: Why do ladies love some ugly men?

Answer: Because they can get money from them.

Question: Is it good to forget your business and think of your lady friend?

Answer: It is not. No money no ladies.

36

Question: Is it bad to trust your friend?

Answer: It is not, but money monger Ladies have made it difficult to trust them.

Question How do you know that Ladies are not trust worthy?

Answer: Because I have seen many men whom they have disappointed.

Question: If you spend all your money for your friends, whom are you to blame?

Answer: I will blame myself for that.

Question: Who is that beautiful lady walking in that corner road.

Answer: She is the wife of Johnson.

Question: Why is she dressing so, is she a harlot?

Answer: I cannot tell.

Question: Is she an illiterate or an educated lady?

Answer: She is educated.

Question: No wonder, educated women are the worst harlots. They are very clever to get money from men easily. They do not obey the commands of their husbands. They want their husbands to be under them.

MONEY MONGER MEN

Some men are great money mongers. They can pretend to be honest people but immediately they get your money, they seize and deny it. Do not trust those men who are ready to speak lies because of money. They are clever, wicked and dangerous rogues.

When they come to you, they would tell you, give me £2 there, I will return it just now. I see something to buy now but my money here is not complete I keep money at home, but can not

37

go now to take it. Immediately he gets the money, He will say, Let me go, I am coming back just now to refund it. But he will not come as he promised. He only said so to get the money from you. Do not trust them, Don't allow them to deceive you. Be wise and know yourself.

Wise Sayings For The Public:

1. One sensible word is enough for the wise.
2. Whatever you do, remember your last day.
3. Death knows no King and does not recieve bribe.
4. Good health is the honour of life.
5. Good manners and respect is the crown of a good citizen.
6. Do not neglect a man, so that he may not surprise you.
7. Never boast of your wisdom, but let others boast of you.
8. A person who respects the law is the wisest man
9. If you think you are above me, do you think that you are above the law?
10. If you say there is no God, where were you when you were not born?
11. If you say you know everything, do you know when the world shall end?
12. Do not trust all friends, because many people are dangerous.
13. Do not pity a man because of his poverty, but pity him because of his ignorance.
14. A person who loves court loves case and must spend.
15. A person who likes to fight must be prepared for the prison.

38

16 I am strong, I am rich, I am beautiful, I am educated end in this world.
17 Men be careful, salutation is not love.
18 Poverty makes a man to be quiet.
19 When you get money, you get enemies and many friends.
20 Money is not evil but the way you get it.
21 Money makes a man and dress maketh a woman.
12 High life without enough money is dangerous as devil.
23 Do not be too much after new styles for the ones of to-morrow is greater.
24 My boy, come to me and tell me where you are going, so that I may tell you what to say.
25 Do not discuss with talkatives so that they may not tell your enemies of your plans.
26 Tell a fool where he is wrong so that he may correct himself.
27 Life is like a motor but heart is the engine, and when the engine fails to start the motor stops.
28 Happiness of one day covers twenty years past sufferings.
29 When some people laugh some will cry and when some cry others will laugh.
30 Your progress in business may be a loss to other people and your loss in business may be gain to others.
31 When some people are dead some are born (Soldier go, Soldier come.)
32 Nothing comes out of nothing. Whenever something happened something caused it. No smoke without fire and no

39

history without event.

33 Check yourself well before spending so that you may not be jack of all trade master of none.

34 It is better to prove you have a shilling when you have two shillings than to prove you have pound when you have ten shillings.

35 Do not say more when you have less to do.

It is better to say less and do more.

36 The land of people is the land of devils,

PROVERBS

1 A gentleman without policy is like a motor without brake.
2 Wickedness is not a crown to human life.
3 Gold and Silver is important to a person who knows the value.
4 High standard is not high education
5 No telephone to heaven
6 Whatever that breaths must die.
7 A boaster is a great liar.
8 A man in the day but a devil in the night.
9 Half bread is better than none.
10 An angry man is the devil's messanger.
11 Good brother is better than a bad father.
12 A drunkard is a law breaker.
13 Love of God is the true love of man.
14 A person who wants to buy a motor car must first check his pocket.
15 Never trust a debtor.

40

16 A person who travels by the power of engine must never be too sure of his life.

17 Good luck is the gift of nature.

18 A person who eats with the devil must have a long spoon.

19 Whatever that eats must grow.

20 Your way of movement shows what you are

21 Not how far but how well

22 Love for money is love for evil

23 Animals in the bush know their ways

24 A talkative is not a great thinker

25 Men who chase their neighbour's wives always pretend before the husband.

26 Good English is important to a person who understands the language.

27 When the cat is away the mouse Governs the house.

28 If you want to drink with a Queen, you must have a golden cup.

29 A person who does not care for his way, does not care for his life.

30 Ill-health is not a new thing on earth.

41

A WORD IS ENOUGH FOR THE WISE

(1) If you really mean to be wise, you should learn from both wise and unwise people.

(2) Never trust all that call you friend for as all faces differ, so the minds differ.

(3) I like you is not I love you for it is said that all that glitters is not gold.

(4) When somebody befriends you suddenly, guide yourself with experience in order to find out whether he or she has some secrets.

(5) Good advice is the second mother of a child

(6) Do not trust people by the words of mouth, trust them by their manners and behaviours.

(7) If you want to become rich, you must work hard and learn how to save money for it is said that not only to get money is hard but also how to save it,

42

(8) If you want to be gentle, respect yourself, keep yourself clean whether rich or poor for nobody will come to check you to know how you are.

(9) When a person comes to you at the first time and tells you, I love you, pretend to love the person as well but be very careful and study his or her ways in order to find out the type of lover that comes to you.

(10) Do not say I am a wise man in public gathering, only people and the words of your mouth will prove your wisdom.

(11) I study everyday and read big books from all corners does not matter a lot, what really matters is whether you understand what you read and be able to make use of them.

Thank you.

THE END.

MISTY BASTIAN

Irregular Visitors

Narratives About Ogbaanje *(Spirit Children) in Southern Nigerian Popular Writing*

'So she has at last decided to stay with us, this regular visitor who has been visiting for a long time.'
Ogbanje Ojebeta's father, in *The Slave Girl* (Emecheta 1977: 19)

Abiku l'o so oloogun di eke (which literally means that the Babalawo is rendered ineffectual by the antics of the Ogbanje).
Yoruba proverb quoted and translated by Ife Babalola (1997)

Irregular visitors: spirit children in Southern Nigeria

Spirit children in contemporary, urban life

When Ben Okri's critically acclaimed novel, *The Famished Road*, won the Booker Prize in 1991, many readers were taken by the author's African form of magical realism. What has received less notice in international literary circles is that Okri's protagonist is one of a growing number of Nigerian fictional creations who are what is known in Igbo as *ogbaanje* (called *emere* or *abiku* in other Nigerian languages, as Okri notes in the novel).[1] Although a comprehensive survey of all Nigerian fiction would demonstrate that the importance of spirit children is nothing new to this country's writers,[2] it appears that there has been an escalation of published narratives that center on not-quite-human creatures like *ogbaanje* in the past two decades. However, before considering why Nigerian writers and the Nigerian reading public might be so intrigued by the *ogbaanje* phenomenon, or in what guises *ogbaanje* make their appearance in Nigerian writing, we must first consider how these beings are represented in popular discourse and as part of larger socio-religious systems.

Ogbaanje are, first and foremost, what my Igbo friends would call (when feeling charitable) 'returning children'. Such a returning child embodies, in the human world, a mischievous, spiritual person – one who is interested in human life, who could almost be said to experiment with the idea of being human, but who is not him/herself human and who has little interest in committing to a human lineage. Victor Manfredi (personal communication; see also his discussion in Manfredi, 1993:16) glosses the very term *ogbaanje* as 'one (a visitor) who hits the road', a wanderer, peripatetic in his/her inclinations and, indeed, in his/her very nature. Literally, a lineage is said to be afflicted with an *ogbaanje* when a woman bears a number of children, all of whom die before they reach an age of maturity. Maturity, among peoples in the Nigerian south, can be measured by marriageability and even by the prospect of having one's own child, so these putative *ogbaanje* deaths may take place as early as just after birth or as late as when people have passed their teens and moved into their twenties.

Child deaths need not occur sequentially to constitute 'ogbaanjism', as some urban Igbo call the affliction, but may take place at intervals interspersed with normal births and lives, especially among wives of a polygynous household. Several of my Igbo informants in the late 1980s suggested that an *ogbaanje* would 'come' only to one wife in a household, disrupting her childbearing again and again, while leaving other wives alone. Nonetheless, few Igbo-speaking people I asked about this condition would agree that the spirit child wanted to torment only his/her human mother. This was perceived as an affliction of the entire patrilineage, particularly of the child's father and mother, but with negative ramifications for everyone in the kin group. As northern Igbo ideologies of female personhood (Amadiume, 1987) imply that no woman is 'complete' without children, however – that is, that no woman can truly enjoy the status of womanhood while without offspring – the *ogbaanje*'s propensity to keep his/her mother from bearing any other human children is seen as a personal tragedy for his/her mother.

Ogbaanjism is not gendered in some everyday sense: both male and female children are said to be *ogbaanje* if they afflict their would-be parents and lineage by dying repeatedly. However, to be an *ogbaanje* is to be categorized other – and to bring alterity home in a way that transcends the more ordinary, bifurcated 'otherness' of gender. We could even speculate that *ogbaanje* children fall under a third gender category, that of human-looking spirit. This other gender is marked from birth – as male and female statuses are marked – by special behaviors towards and physical adornment of the child. The sexual appearance of the *ogbaanje* may, indeed, be seen as a sham – yet another promise that the *ogbaanje* is likely to break in its refusal to act according to human norms. Because of this as well as in an attempt to convince the *ogbaanje* to 'stay', *ogbaanje* who appear female are often catered to as precious commodities, more like the general experience of male children than that of their human sisters.

Male and female *ogbaanje* who grow up and can speak for themselves tell me that their childhoods, even while marred by illness and odd sensations, felt relatively privileged. As one young woman from Onitsha described her youth to me in 1988, 'All the adults were afraid of me. I did what I pleased, and they said, "Yes".' Such extraordinary permission, coupled with unsuppressed adult anxiety over children's actions, is antithetical to most Igbo childhoods, and this gives *ogbaanje* (or former *ogbaanje*) people a somewhat skewed understanding of their place in southeastern society.[3] Their socially constructed difference can lead to difficulty when *ogbaanje* are called upon in later life to take on the serious responsibilities of marriage, perform servile tasks for elders or demonstrate their commitment to lineage or community in some other fashion. As Chinwe Achebe (1986: 30) notes:

> Some [*ogbaanje*] are extremely honest, bold, courageous and of impeccable character. In other words they tend to have an excess of every good attribute. However such qualities do not last long. For this group experiences a meteoric rise to success [which] peaks then fades out almost as rapidly and dramatically as they started. This is why in the final analysis an '*ogbanje*' is never credited with anything really positive.

Acquaintances in southeastern Nigeria who were identified to me as *ogbaanje* either were younger and very timid children or were extremely confident young adults with a good deal of physical beauty and personal charm. The younger children were said to be afraid of people outside their known kin group – especially of me, as *onye ocha* (a white person) – and to suffer from visitations from *ndi otu*, their spirit companions. These spirit companions supposedly call out to the *ogbaanje*, reminding him/her of oaths sworn before birth that tie the *ogbaanje* child to the world of spiritual forces.

Returning to that world, of course, entails the death of the *ogbaanje* in this one, and the subsequent bereavement of his/her family.

Most older *ogbaanje* declared to me that they did not believe in *ndi otu* any more, but that they found it difficult to 'rest' and act like ordinary people. Almost all older *ogbaanje* I spoke with reported having vivid dreams which could be very disturbing but which they could not, quite, recall the next morning. Some of these older *ogbaanje* also hinted that they 'knew things' before others, and that their special insights could cause them problems. The young woman already quoted above was concerned that she could not bring herself to marry any of the several eligible young men who were courting her. Whenever she was close to agreement about marriage, something would occur that would give her a distaste for the man in question. Even her most determined suitor confided in me that he did not believe his *ogbaanje* love would ever wear the white wedding dress she spent a good deal of time in designing for herself.[4] Although a beautiful woman with many social connections, her friends routinely referred to her as moody and complained that she was hard to spend time with. When I queried whether this melancholy was thought to be part of her ogbaanjism, even the young woman herself agreed it was. Before I left the field in mid-1988, she was considering a trip to Elele in order to see Father Edeh, a charismatic Catholic priest who had a reputation for 'cutting *ogbaanje*' through prayer, as well as for other mystical feats. (Removing the affliction of ogbaanjism is a mainstay of many Nigerian evangelical ministries, both Protestant and Catholic.)

The 'tough' emere*: a tabloid account of spirit children*

Whether tormented by spirit companions or expressing an angst about personal relationships that seems quite familiar to those of us who live outside the continent but under similar pressures of modernity, the *ogbaanje* was a figure of deep interest to my friends and acquaintances in southeastern Nigeria during the late 1980s. Not only were known *ogbaanje* the locus of gossip and rumors in the houses and markets of Onitsha, where I lived during my fieldwork, but *ogbaanje* as a category of (inhuman) beings figured largely in the sensationalist print media of that period.[5] Many of these tabloid stories focused on healers/diviners who could help people afflicted with ogbaanjism, and most included case histories of *ogbaanje* who had come, looking for help, to the healer being interviewed. These case histories were generally in the form of a confession, as here, in a 1987 *Lagos Weekend* interview (or English, paraphrased interview) with a very young emere boy:

> I became an 'emere' when I was in my mother's womb. I will briefly explain how this happened. At one O'clock [sic] one sunny day, my mother was going to a function in company of three women. When they got to a junction near the house the function was taking place. I entered her womb and sent out the child that was there before. My mother did not know that anything like that happened. When that happened, she only felt a pang in her stomach.
>
> We, 'Emere,' meet on some occasions at junctions. This is why junctions are associated with evil by some people. [...] It is not good to sell in a junction, especially, if you are pregnant. If we are in our meeting, and a pregnant woman is sighted, our mother in the world of 'emere' will tell any of us to go into the womb of the woman. [...]
>
> [On why he gave the menstrual problem to his mother, the boy said,] when I was two years old, my mother bought shoes, different ones, for my siblings during an Ileya Festival and failed to buy mine, in spite of the fact that my father gave her money to do so. She thought I would not know what was happening. I knew all that happened. To punish her for the offence she committed against me, I created menstrual problems for her and these have been preventing her from becoming pregnant. (Tokode, 1987)

Such an elaborate story of the birth and revenge of an *emere* may not have emerged fully developed from the mouth of a six-year-old boy, as reported in the tabloid, but is completely in keeping with other, oral narratives I heard during my 1987–8 fieldwork. In this instance, the *emere* was taken to Chief M. A. Olowo's clinic in Isolo, southwestern Nigeria. The healer – who declares in the interview/advertisement for his clinic that he is 'a herbalist, but a modern one' – cautions *Lagos Weekend*'s readers that *emere* 'do evil. When they behave, you will be surprised by their actions. They are just tough.' Spirit children, in their tabloid guise, are almost invariably cunning, manipulative and demanding. Like the *emere* above, they 'know all that happened' and exact punishment for any perceived slight. Very rarely do they conform to the real life *ogbaanje* children I met while living in southern Nigeria, but seem more like young adult *ogbaanje* – and are even credited with greater verbal skills, as we can see in Tokode's 'interview', and spiritual knowledge than any of the *ogbaanje* with whom I actually spoke.

However, these narratives do resonate very strongly with the sense that my informants had of the *ogbaanje*'s selfish, individualistic nature while in the world of human beings. Almost everyone characterized to me as *ogbaanje*, including babies, was said to require his/her parents and siblings, if any, to sacrifice their own material desires for the *ogbaanje*'s beautification or entertainment. At the same time such children are seen as inherently ungrateful. As the crafty emere above would have it, his mother purposefully denied him his special, festival shoes, thereby acting more like a thief (in southern Nigerian terms) than a mother. He had no recourse but to punish her severely for her transgression – ignoring the fact that his very birth, in the narrative, is itself a theft and displacement of a 'real', human baby whose shoes these should have been.

Instead of promoting intimate relations of reciprocity and affection, then, the tabloid *emere/ogbaanje* represents a breach within the lineage and uterine family structures, causing all members of the family to act aggressively and selfishly towards one another. Chief Olowo even later accuses the *emere* boy of killing his own father because of a fight that took place between the boy's parents just before he was born. In a patriarchal society like that of Yoruba-speakers in the Nigerian southwest, a son killing his father is a terrible transgression, one of the most abominated. Using the example of the power of a spirit child who had, at least according to Olowo, 'spoiled' his father's family before the age of six, the healer advised *Lagos Weekend* readers to be vigilant about children in their own homes: 'It is good for parents to be observant. They should observe the ways their children behave in order to know whether they have certain evil forces controlling them.' Here the *ogbaanje* is represented as an anti-child: a source of horror rather than joy, observed not for the anxiety bred of affection but in order to detect any signs of moral taint and perceived as a being meant to destroy the social life of a lineage rather than to continue it.

Exposed to the possibilities of modern life (as we will see below in our discussion of *Dizzy Angel* and as symbolized here by the missing festival shoes), the cunning, media *ogbaanje* becomes the ultimate consumer; taking his revenge out in fertility and blood when his acquisition of the good things of the human world is thwarted. In a society like that of contemporary Nigeria, where the paradigm of wealth-in-people is still actively contesting with the paradigms of wealth-in-money and wealth-in-things, popular representations of *ogbaanje* as conspicuous consumers seem to posit that these irregular visitors are more than spiritual or emotional drains on those who must 'host' them. They are also represented as financial and material drains, beings who pervert important social relations and desiccate the already thin family purse. Such representations of *ogbaanje*, however, are only a part of the popular discourse on spirit children. In the next section we will consider some fictional accounts of ogbaanjism which are more sympathetic to the spirit child and which try to develop a more complex picture of life within the *ogbaanje* skin, perhaps seeking to advocate for these young people who feel themselves to be 'betwixt and between' worlds in modern Nigeria.

The *ogbaanje's* surprise: 'Running,' *Dizzy Angel, The Slave Girl* and *Date with Destiny*

> *Ogbanje* refers to the iconoclast, the one who runs back and forth from one realm of existence to another, always longing for a place other than where s/he is. It also refers to the mystical, unsettled condition of simultaneously existing in several spheres. (Ogunyemi, 1996: 62)

> 'Which of us will last forever on this earth, anyway? Are we not all here to buy and sell for awhile?'
>
> 'Yes, yes, we know that,' the first man replied impatiently, 'but the problem is that these Ogbanjes hardly step into the market before they run back.' (Osifo, 1985: 279)

'Running' away: ogbaanje *and problematic mobility*

Movement, notably running back and forth, is a theme of both quotations about *ndi ogbaanje* (*ogbaanje* persons) above, and it may well be that the mobile, boundary-transgressing quality of ogbaanjism is one reason why *ogbaanje* seem such an integral part of the modern Nigerian scene. For a graphic example of this concern with mobility, we might take a recently published Nigerian short story entitled 'Running' (Njoku 1998), which considers the transience of modern, urban friendships. The story focuses on the circle of friends of an *ogbaanje*, John, who thrives in the city but lives in fear of 'the ritual', an ominous event associated with his parents' home village and what sounds almost like the parents' desire for revenge against their son's *ogbaanje* nature.[6] The ritual in question is the 'cutting' of his *ogbaanje*, an event that is meant to signal his decision to become fully human, that he means to 'stay' with his human lineage and take part in building those social relations.

As John's ultimate fate proves, however, the stasis required by his village-based patrilineage is too much for a mobile, urban *ogbaanje* to bear. Bereft of their *ogbaanje* companion, who returns to *ndi otu* (his spirit companions) rather than be 'cut', John's three childhood friends drift apart. Their ultimate alienation within contemporary Nigerian society and from one another manifests itself in the separate lifestyles they affect: the narrator as disenfranchised, shell-shocked intellectual, Dele as well-to-do, moralistic, born-again Christian and Janet as shadowy 'damsel in distress', a prostitute glimpsed briefly during a melee at a hotel bar. It is as if John's *ogbaanje* spirit has entered the very milieu where it once was incarnate and has made all the denizens of urban Nigeria into unstable, 'unsettled' spirits who can never be at home in this world.[7] The conflicted, nostalgic and deeply modern narrator describes just this condition for us at the end of the story, when his younger self learns of John's death in the village: '"Leave Me Alone!" I screamed and I ran. I've never stopped running.' Uprooted from the stable, intimate relations they shared as children and cast into a world that offers few alternatives to those early neighborhood friendships, the former friends of John seek connectedness through writing, religion and commodified sex. However, they are all too much in motion even to see one another clearly, as lost to the ogbaanjism of contemporary Nigeria as John was to that of the spirit world.

David Njoku's reading of the nation as *ogbaanje* is a much more pessimistic one than that given to us by Gracy Nma Osifo in her 1985 novel *Dizzy Angel*; although here again an *ogbaanje* confronts the temptations of modernity and mobility away from the familiar rhythms of village life. *Dizzy Angel* is the tale of Ogbanje, a spirit child born as a daughter to Obiagele, the third wife of a prosperous western Igbo farmer, Dolise. Before the novel begins Obiagele has borne three such daughters (Angelina, Ezinwa and Gold), none of whom has consented to 'stay' with their mother and father more than year or two. Ogbanje's birth is therefore not taken very seriously; her mother rests after the travail and waits for her to cease breathing. When the infant shows signs of stirring and even hunger, the new mother is swift to run to *onye dibia* (a healer/diviner) and discover if this *ogbaanje* might be convinced to remain with her parents.[8]

From the 'oracle-man' Obiagele learns that Ogbanje, too, is fated to die in two years' time, because she is not only an *ogbaanje* but also an 'Olokun's daughter' (Osifo, 1985: 44). I have written elsewhere (Bastian, 1997) about northern Igbo connections between *ndi ogbaanje* (*ogbaanje* people) and *ndi mmili* (water spirits). In this case, Ogbanje is said to be one of the daughters of Olokun, the premier Edo (Benin) water deity. The importance of such an Edo deity to Osifo's story tells us something about the hybrid religious practice of Igbo-speakers living on the western side of the River Niger, the complex political history of western Igbo and its close association with the great West African kingdom of Benin – as well as that western Igbo believe, along with Igbo to the east, that ogbaanjism can be complicated by kinship with other spiritual forces beyond *ndi otu*, the spirit companions.[9]

Here we can compare Ogbanje's spiritual connection to Olokun/Benin with that of another fictional western Igbo *ogbaanje*, Ogbanje Ojebeta in Buchi Emecheta's *The Slave Girl* (1977). In Emecheta's well-known novel, Ogbanje Ojebeta is also the product of an extended period of ogbaanjism, again associated with girl children. When Ogbanje Ojebeta is finally born and demonstrates a willingness to 'stay' with her parents, a diviner informs her mother that Ogbanje Ojebeta can be kept on earth long enough to make her own decisions about life if she is hung about with potent charms. As the diviner describes the *ogbaanje* charms and their effects to Ogbanje Ojebeta's mother, we can almost reconstruct three centuries of Igbo contact with the great kingdom to the west:

> When she moves the bells will ring, the tin metal will rattle, the cowries will rumble, and then her friends from the other world will run away, for they will never have seen anything like that

> before. If you want this casual visitor to stay and be a permanent member of your household, to be your daughter, you will see to it that your husband gets someone to go to Idu for him to get this copper metal which the Potokis give the king of Idu in exchange for the human slaves they buy. (Emecheta, 1977: 18)

These charms must come from Idu, the local Igbo name for the kingdom of Benin, and the sounds they make are the sounds of wealth and war, the rough music of the slave trade. If we think of *ogbaanje* children, at least here in Anioma (the western Igbo region), as missing children – much like children pawned to or stolen by distant and arbitrary powers such as Olokun or the Oba of Benin – then we also begin to historicise the entire *ogbaanje* religious phenomenon, situating it in a deeply temporal, southern Nigerian experience of fear, loss and mourning.[10]

In *The Slave Girl*, Ogbanje Ojebeta suffers a twist in the classic *ogbaanje*'s fate. She does not 'stay' with her people, but she is not taken away through the agency of *ndi otu*. Although her Idu charms and facial tattooing might ward away her spirit companions and their temptations to death, those same charms have no efficacy against the machinations of greedy kin. Ogbanje Ojebeta, orphaned by the influenza pandemic of 1918, is sold as a domestic slave by her brother – who rationalises the deed to himself, saying that she will have a better future away from Ibuza village, across the Niger in the large market town of Onitsha. Here the connection between the *ogbaanje* and the historical betrayal of slavery is made explicit. In Gracy Osifo's novel, the sale/betrayal is represented, as we shall see, as another form of slavery within the transforming world of her village: that of an educated, modern girl tied to an old, 'traditional' man without her consent.

The theme of the *ogbaanje* being sold and sent away by his/her intimates is also present in Njoku's story, above. The nameless narrator of 'Running' is given thirty kobo, a tiny sum, and one that echoes Judas's thirty pieces of silver, to reveal the whereabouts of John, so that John's parents can take him to the village for 'the ritual'. But again in this tale set in a more contemporary Nigeria, the movement is reversed from more historical modes of capture. Instead of kin selling a child into permanent exile or helplessly letting it disappear into the land of the spirits, John's parents try to ransom their son, carrying him away from the dangerous city streets to what is often encoded in popular Nigerian discourse as the safety of the natal village. But there is no safety in the village for a modern spirit like John. The only people who return to the city after 'the ritual' are his parents, who wear black and grieve bitterly beside his obituary photograph. John's human *otu* (companions) are left by this loss without their moral compass, spinning out in every direction, running from their friend's absence.

Mami Wata, evangelical Christianity and the Devil in Osifo's Dizzy Angel

Having looked, in two *ogbaanje* novels, at the past of religious practice in Igbo-speaking southwestern Nigeria, David Njoku's short story reminds us that human experience as represented in fiction is necessarily Janus faced. It also looks forward into contemporary life, drawing its characters and situations from the author's own direct engagement with the world. Olokun, in *Dizzy Angel*, might therefore as readily be considered the ancestor and present kin of Mami Wata, the water deity who most northern Igbo now suggest is involved with *ogbaanje* births.[11] From textual evidence, we learn that Mami Wata worship has penetrated, by the 1940s, into the western Igbo village where Ogbanje is born. Although she does not hear of 'the Mermaid ... Mami-Water' (Osifo 1985: 153) until she leaves home to travel to secondary school in the northern part of the country, Uloji the Olokun priest scarifies her cheek in order to discourage the attention of the water deity:[12]

> The mark was necessary, Uloji said, so as to make her less charming to her riverine mother – the Mermaid – who, it was said, preferred spotless beauties to any other, she herself being the paragon of all beauty. The Mermaid, or Mami-Water, was also said to be the wife of Olokun, the sea god. (Osifo 1985: 46)

Nonetheless, Ogbanje has the looks and some of the manners of a classic 'Mami Wata daughter': she is tall, extremely attractive and has fair skin as well as large, compelling eyes; she also is intelligent, somewhat impulsive and headstrong. As we discover when her father takes her to witness a witchfinding, she possesses flashes of psychic ability, is able to detect witchcraft from a distance and even can identify witches by name. (This last proves to be a dangerous gift, since Ogbanje's greatest enemy in the novel is the witch she correctly identifies to Dolise; a witch who maintains her anonymity in the poison ordeal through her use of powerful 'medicines.') Later in the narrative we learn that Ogbanje has premonitions of future events and can see into mundane human motives long before others. The fact that she is the spiritual daughter of Olokun and Mami Wata, and manifests these other, nonhuman accomplishments seals her fate at birth: if she is to be convinced to 'stay', Ogbanje must be married to the Olokun priest or to his son before she is fifteen years old. Otherwise, according to the diviner, she would return to the spirit world like all the other *ogbaanje* born to Obiagele and Dolise.

Ogbanje's infant betrothal and proposed marriage to Uloji, the local priest of Olokun, directs her life long before she is aware of the arrangement. Because her mother Obiagele has been informed that she will never conceive another child until Ogbanje marries and leaves her father's household, Obiagele is both over-protective and takes little pleasure in her daughter's accomplishments. Obiagele is especially ambivalent about Ogbanje's interest in school and the village's Anglican mission. The politics of being a wife in a large, polygynous compound like that of Dolise are difficult for a woman who has only one child, a sickly girl, known to be *ogbaanje* and hence unlikely to live to maturity. This situation is made no better by Dolise, the *di* (husband/master) of the household, who demonstrates an unusual interest in Ogbanje – his only girl child.

The senior wife, Adorie, has no children of her own but is a successful trader; she is also extremely fond of Ogbanje and helps her as much as she can. In this she represents a model for womanly behavior within a polygynous marriage, even though she is pronounced *agan*, or barren, by the community at large. It is the second wife, Adafor, who has borne the male children necessary for the continuation of Dolise's patrilineage, and who is jealous of the attention given to Ogbanje and Obiagele by other members of the household. Adafor loses no time in reminding anyone who will listen that it is a waste of resources to send such a girl as Ogbanje to school or to church – when she is not only a spirit child and liable to die but already engaged to a 'pagan' priest and unlikely to use her learning within her husband's household. Dolise nonetheless persists in his sponsorship of Ogbanje and is proud of her examination results and other, modern accomplishments. To please Obiagele and her persuasive mother, Dolise agrees to accept Uloji as his son-in-law, but he forbids the consummation of Ogbanje's marriage until she is almost fifteen. In the intervening years, he manages to convince Uloji to allow Ogbanje to continue in her education – and not to keep the girl from learning about Christianity – by suggesting how these activities enhance Ogbanje's value as a wife. Entranced by Ogbanje's growing beauty as well as by the portrait painted for him of the advantages of having an educated, young wife, Uloji agrees to countenance Ogbanje's scholarship to a northern boarding school on the condition that she will return before completing her course, just before she is fifteen.

While in the throes of her first infatuation for Peter, a well-educated boy from a neighboring town, Ogbanje learns that not only can she never marry an urban Christian, but she must leave school before taking her final qualifying examinations – to become the wife of the Olokun priest.[13] Ogbanje acquiesces, under pressure from Obiagele and Dolise to agree to this match so that she will be assured of a full life, even though she is unsure whether she is indeed the *ogbaanje* everyone assures her that she is, and so that her mother will be able to be a 'complete woman' and bear more children. She undergoes the wine-carrying ('traditional' marriage ceremony) and becomes Uloji's girl-wife before leaving for school in Ghenero. Once away from the village, Ogbanje flourishes and finds many new interests. Her studies are difficult, but she continues to excel in them.

Ogbanje is especially taken with one of the European teachers at the school, Miss Bricks. Miss Bricks is the sponsor of a 'born-again' Christian fellowship for the girls, and Ogbanje is soon a devoted, evangelical Christian. In her new faith Ogbanje feels completely free from ogbaanjism but is increasingly anxious about becoming what she calls 'Mrs. Juju Priest' (Osifo, 1985: 171). She also is conflicted by Peter's determined pursuit of her, coupled with written protests of love and expensive gifts, as well as by her growing affection for Moses, Uloji's son – who has run away from his father and his place as the Olokun priest's apprentice to become a Catholic catechist. Nonetheless, when the last term before her fifteenth birthday is over, Ogbanje packs her bags and returns to the village to fulfill her obligations.

Ogbanje's desire for a Christian, 'modern' life outside the confines of her home village along with her personal distaste for Uloji send her into crisis, forcing her to flee the village and make her way into a nearby motorpark where she can find transport back to the north and the sanctuary of her school. At the motorpark, one of the most liminal and transgressive of Nigerian urban spaces (see Bastian, 1998), Ogbanje discovers Miss Bricks, who has come to rescue her from this 'pagan' marriage and who brings news of a scholarship which will enable Ogbanje to finish her education without the support of her family. Although it pains Ogbanje to go against her father's and mother's wishes, she hopes that this fortuitous set of events is evidence of divine providence. Knowing that she might be triggering her *ogbaanje* destiny, she resolves to finish her course and use her success to demonstrate the power of her faith. Miss Bricks, at this point, exercises her own, born-again Christian prophetic gifts:

> 'You are doing the right thing', Miss Bricks consoled [Ogbanje]. 'In the near future your father and mother will praise and thank you for your courage in doing what you have done today. All we need do is to continue praying that God will grant them the understanding that they need.' (Osifo, 1985: 233)

The Christian God, however, still has to contend with the powers of western Igbo witches and Olokun priests before *Dizzy Angel* can be brought to the conclusion required of its subgenre (what we might call the Nigerian 'born-again' romance novel). Uloji's sister, Atiti, is the same witch identified by Ogbanje when a child. Atiti has been against Ogbanje's education and christianization from the moment that Ogbanje became betrothed to Uloji, and the fact that her sister-in-law runs away to an unknown destination and humiliates the Olokun priest before the marriage can be consummated offers Atiti the opportunity to take revenge.[14] First the witch asks her brother to distribute powerful medicines at Dolise's compound, ensuring that its occupants will take ill and possibly die.[15] After sending a veritable set of plagues to all of Dolise's wives and children, finally frightening Adaor and her sons away from the village altogether, Atiti turns her attention to Ogbanje herself. The witch's revenge cannot take effect until Ogbanje is over fifteen years old, the date set out by the original 'oracle-man' for her death if she did not marry the Olokun priest.

Since she does not immediately suffer after running away from the village and her marriage, Ogbanje is moved to write Dolise an inspiring letter, declaring her independence from Olokun, oracles and her purported ogbaanjism:

> I know you have a large mind, father. I am relying on you to back me up in my fight against ignorance and superstition. It's all superstition, father – everything about the oracle and my being an Ogbanje. God helping me, I shall prove to the world, especially to our villagers, that God is stronger than the Devil. (Osifo 1985: 246)

Dolise feels much heartened by this correspondence and takes Ogbanje's part in the face of village disapproval, even standing up to Atiti and Uloji and admitting to Obiagele that he never liked the marriage between his daughter and the Olokun priest. (One reason Dolise sent Ogbanje to school was that he always felt drawn to mission education and the 'modern' life offered to educated men under colonialism, but he was not allowed to go to school when young.) Unfortunately, though, Atiti has only just begun her sorcerous campaign against Ogbanje, who falls seriously ill and has to be hospitalised.

Burning with an undiagnosed fever and in the throes of visions that include Atiti boiling her in a pot, Ogbanje's sufferings almost bring her to the point of death.[16] Finally when she hears the witch's voice calling her name – just as *ogbaanje* supposedly hear *ndi otu* calling them towards the spirit world – she rises from her bed and attempts to leave the clinic. Ogbanje is stopped by a born-again friend, who calls her by her baptismal name (Hannah) and places the Bible in her path, transforming the evil witch's voice and pot into a vision of the crucifixion. Arrested in her *ogbaanje* movement toward death by this privileged viewing of Christ's passion, Hannah/Ogbanje recovers her senses, joins her friend in prayer and begins her journey back to health. Not only this, but she induces her entire prayer group to develop a special prayer for her mother, Obiagele: that Jesus grant Hannah's mother her long-looked for pregnancy, making God's triumph over witchcraft and the Devil complete.

Having secured the first rank in her class, Ogbanje graduates from school and returns home to see her parents and to confront those who wish her ill. Pleased to see her happy and in the best health of her short life, Dolise tries to return Uloji's bridewealth. If Uloji accepted the return of the money, this would free Ogbanje from any obligation towards him or other members of his lineage. Uloji, who is even more in love with his schoolgirl wife than ever, becomes enraged at the thought that he will never have Ogbanje and attacks her father. Dolise defends himself and fatally wounds the man who would be his son-in-law. Uloji dies, admitting to Atiti that he had not used all of her evil medicines against Ogbanje and her parents and giving his blessing to a marriage between his first son, Moses and Ogbanje. A short time later, significantly on Christmas Eve, Atiti herself is killed while trying to do mischief in Dolise's compound. Having taken the form of an owl (a common disguise of Igbo witches; see Metuh, 1981 and Bastian, 1993), she is captured and beaten to death. The way is thus clear for Hannah/Ogbanje's real Christmas present: betrothal to the born-again Moses, whose devotion to her is finally appreciated and rewarded.

Dolise is extremely pleased with the match, giving his blessing to it and saying that he hoped Moses's 'dead father's spirit will be appeased. Ogbanje will still be married to him, as it were, being married to his son' (Osifo, 1985: 273). Dolise and Obiagele also discover another benefit of their daughter's triumph over 'superstition': Obiagele is at last pregnant and feels secure – in that Moses is the son of the Olokun priest – that Ogbanje has fulfilled the oracle after all. Ogbanje and Moses continue their education; Ogbanje becoming a teacher for her village and Moses studying medicine. Three years after Atiti's death, on Christmas Eve, 1962, Hannah Ogbanje and Moses Nkechi celebrate one of the town's first 'white weddings,' appearing in western bridal dress sent, thanks to the ever-helpful Miss Bricks, all the way from England.

The novel ends not with the wedding itself but with a set of comments (quoted above, p. 61) made by some of the villagers about *ogbaanje* and their flightiness. The author thus reproduces the concerns still felt about ogbaanjism, even as she gives the reader a homily about evangelical Christianity's power over such evil beings as witches, 'juju priests', and *ndi otu*. We might say, indeed, that the tension underlying this popular piece of Nigerian fiction is one still felt by urban Nigerians in the late 1990s: How to reconcile indigenous powers and spiritual forces like *ogbaanje* with the growing importance of born-again Christian experience? It is certainly possible to read *Dizzy Angel* as a meditation both on the persistence of local experiences of spirit and the development of a newer, evangelical consciousness that demands this experience be left behind or reconstructed in a completely negative fashion.[17]

Writing in the mid-1980s, however, Gracy Osifo's novel skirts the starker choices facing pentecostalist Nigerian Christians today. She is no Emmanuel Eni, whose immensely popular 1987 tract on the spirit world and the necessity of being born again, *Delivered from the Powers of Darkness*, has become a template for evangelical fiction and video. Eni (1987: 5) states categorically: 'A child when left alone in the world is controlled by one of two powers: good or bad, right or wrong, God or the Devil.' Although we hear an echo of this position – which places all indigenous religion in the camp of the Devil – in Ogbanje's letter to her father above, in practice the author enables her heroine to have it both ways. Ogbanje is properly born again, marries a fellow evangelical Christian (although he is a Catholic and she is a Protestant, again a compromise that would be more difficult to defend in the late 1990s) and enjoys all the benefits of Christian modernity. Yet her marriage is the one ordained by the oracle at her birth and technically releases her from her obligations to Olokun. The marriage, as Dolise's prayer makes clear, is even properly leviritic; Moses Nkechi has inherited his father's wife in the old western Igbo style. It is also unclear from the text whether Hannah's prayer group or Ogbanje fulfilling the ritual prescriptions for breaking her ogbaanjism is responsible for Obiagele's pregnancy and subsequent birth of a son. As Osifo's use of the baptismal name Hannah and the birth name Ogbanje in the latter chapters of the novel suggests, evangelical Christianity is still seen here as somewhat situational or even transitional. Moses calls his bride 'Hanny', a lover's nickname based on her Christian name, but Ogbanje herself calls her new husband Nkechi (which means a 'thing of the spirit'), the name given to him by his lineage. God and the Devil seem more at peace in Osifo's early 1960s Igbo village, although the lines of future conflict are certainly being demarcated. Perhaps the author declines, in the end, to make such sharp distinctions, because she herself is unsure of what ogbaanjism means. As the townspeople who are evaluating Ogbanje/Hannah's situation go on to suggest, she has surprised them before by living and becoming one of the town's most successful and famous citizens. Who knows what she may do next?

Some conclusions: a date with destiny?

Even in the slightly more tolerant world of 1960s evangelical romance, as we have seen, Osifo's novel remains ambivalent about the nature of the *ogbaanje*. Ogbanje is not portrayed as a complete victim of her condition, and in this we may perceive similarities to the characters (to a lesser degree) of John in 'Running' and Ogbanje Ojebeta in *The Slave Girl*. Although Ogbanje is continuously marked for death, she manages to survive – with the help of her family, her prayer group and her future husband. John, who is betrayed by a member of his human *otu* and by his parents, is not so fortunate. Ogbanje Ojebeta does become a slave and is lost to her lineage mates during her girlhood, but she eventually leaves her owner's household in Onitsha to return to Ibuza. Then she meets a local, Christian man who eventually marries her. Emecheta is more conflicted than Osifo, however, on the question of whether her *ogbaanje* heroine has escaped a destiny of servitude:

> One does not ask whether they loved and cared for each other ever after; those words made no sense in a situation like this. There was certainly a kind of eternal bond between husband and wife, a bond produced by centuries of traditions, taboos, and, latterly, Christian dogma. Slave, obey your master. Wife, honour your husband, who is your father, your head, your heart, your soul. So there was little room for Ojebeta to exercise her own individuality, her own feelings, for these were entwined with Jacob's. (Emecheta, 1977: 173)

The difference between Emecheta's and Osifo's views of Christianity – and marriage – may give us as good a reason why Emecheta's work has never been popular in Nigeria as the fact that she was first published in the west.[18] There is much less room for Ogbanje Ojebeta to move; her enslaved, *ogbaanje* character is perceived by the author as endemic to her human gender. What Osifo's Ogbanje embraces as freedom and equality under Christ becomes another link in the chain created by Ogbanje Ojebeta's *chi* (personal spirit). John, the *ogbaanje* hero of 'Running', is exempt from this problem of gendered victimhood by reason of his early death – although even that could be seen as a masculine refusal to be ensnared by the stability of marriage. John and Janet, who later becomes the rootless prostitute, are said by the narrator of the story to have a special bond. John saves Janet from her own foolishness again and again while they are children. The narrator cannot do the same for her when he tries to reach her during a battle at a juju concert. He may have been her lover in university, but he has not been able to protect her from the urban world they both inhabit, and he notes sadly, 'I'm not John' (Njoku, 1997).

Besides Ben Okri's *The Famished Road*, which probably does not qualify for an extended treatment in this chapter because of its strictly European publication, there is only one other, recent Nigerian novel I know of in which the protagonist is a male *ogbaanje*. Uchegbulem Okorie's *Date with Destiny* (1992) offers us a view of ogbaanjism that is both comparable to and strikingly different from that given to us by Emecheta, Njoku and Osifo. Okorie's *ogbaanje* hero Agu is not really aware of his status as a spirit child. His father, an early adherent of the Christian missions in the southern Igbo town of Ebomzi, claimed not to be interested in such superstition, even changing his son's name from one that signaled his ogbaanjism to the more neutral Agu. It is only after Agu – who, though young as the novel opens, has already been successful in both education and business – returns to Ebomzi and decides to take part in village politics that his 'weakness' as a returning child is discussed.

A paternal aunt, *Nene* Nwaeruru, comes to pay a visit to her 'son' Agu and to warn him that his desire to build a secondary school in Ebomzi has attracted the negative attention of several local big men. She is concerned that Agu does not know his true nature, is over-educated in Western terms and therefore is vulnerable to mystic attacks:

> Nene warned Agu to keep indoors, reminding him that he was the first son of his parents – a son that arrived after four males and a female had been born and lost... 'Forget your later name Agu. At your birth I named you 'may worries over beggeting [sic] and retaining children male and female not kill me'...The spirit that reincarnated in you was tough in coming. I spent hens, cocks, eggs, alligator pepper, kegs of cam-wood dye, to name a few, to attract you into my brother's compound. You must therefore keep away from this your Ebomzi college if you want to continue to call me *Nene*. Onu, Oso, and all the rest – visible and invisible – are after your head. Of course they will land their hands on the red earth not on your body! Our ancestors will forbid their evil plans.' (Okorie, 1992: 24)

Nene Nwaeruru is also concerned that Agu and his family have rejected every *dibia* (healer/diviner) she sends to them, and that Agu has never been 'medicated' against the envy and hatred of others. The young man listens to his father's sister politely, but seems to forget her injunctions as soon as she leaves the house. The rest of the novel chronicles the many ups and downs experienced by Agu on his 'date with destiny:' a glorious destiny for both the young man and for his townspeople. Ogbaanjism is never again directly mentioned, and Nene Nwaeruru never again appears as a major character.

I would like to argue, nonetheless, that it would be improper to discount the importance of Agu's *ogbaanje* nature while reading the remaining 155 pages of the text. Not only does the backcover blurb include the fact that Agu is an *ogbaanje*, but it questions in relation to his unusual birth: 'Could it be that Destiny had a duty for Agu to perform?' (Okorie, 1992). In *Date with Destiny*, the *ogbaanje* protagonist must transcend his impermanent nature, as well as his attraction to material wealth and overt power, in order to help his town 'get up'. As Igbo ethnographer Victor Uchendu noted wearily about his own 1960s village social position, such 'leadership is a trying as well as thankless experience' for many young men in southeastern Nigeria (Uchendu, 1965: 9). Agu learns, first-hand, how much villagers will depend on him and how little credit he may expect along the way towards making Ebomzi one of the premier towns of the region.

The plot is full of twists and turns, as Agu and his few allies are thwarted at every turn by wily elders who wish to see the college built in the town but who do not wish Agu to be the one to bring transformation to the village. Each of these trials enables Agu to prove that an *ogbaanje* may indeed surprise his agnates. In what may seem like tedious detail to a reader from outside Nigeria, we learn of one committee after another constructed by Agu only to have leadership and effectiveness wrested away by Oso and his colleagues. Through each instance, though, Ebomzi is brought a step closer to the building of the college. Finally the administrative work is done, the school is built, and the teachers and students flock to Ebomzi's and Agu's 'triumph of reason' (Okorie, 1992: 177). The town becomes justly well known as a center for learning and modernity, and Agu feels contentment in having proved that he – and young men in Ebomzi more generally – can accomplish what they set out to do. Even if they seem to have *ogbaanje*-like natures, always moving between worlds and rarely 'staying' in one, Agu's achievement demonstrates that there is virtue in such movement. It does not have to be pointless mobility (upward or otherwise); it may be useful for friends, enemies and lineage-mates alike.

This is an optimism that – even if somewhat tempered – is shared by Gracy Osifo. Her Ogbanje does not aspire to build a school for her western Igbo village, only to excel and teach in one. Okorie's *ogbaanje* hero, Agu, is a more secular figure than Osifo's Ogbanje as well. He believes in the rubrics of Nigerian modernity: education, development and a community-based self-help ethos. The national ogbaanjism that infects David Njoku's short story (and could be said similarly to infect Ben Okri's fiction), written in the aftermath of the horrors of the Abacha regime, is absent from Okorie's and Osifo's work. For Osifo, Christ will provide against all powerful enemies, even transforming a 'dizzy angel' (*ogbaanje*) into a successful and solid member of her village community. Okorie suggests that the solution to ogbaanjism is trust in those who are now distrusted, and in a willingness on the part of those in power to share some of their responsibilities, at least, with those who one day must inevitably be their successors.[19] Emecheta's notion that ogbaanjism is deeply inscribed into the fraught history of Nigeria would make sense to Njoku's postcolonial urban *ogbaanje*. Osifo's Ogbanje, however, might not feel the ties of her gender oppression as strongly as Emecheta because of her adherence to evangelical Christian ideologies, and Okorie's Agu is attempting to transcend the past with a dogged and cheerful progressivism.

In 1990s Nigeria, readers of popular fiction and the tabloids were exposed to various portraits of the *ogbaanje*. She or he may be 'tough', like the Yoruba *emere* child above, displaying a hatred for lineage ties and any authority, consuming family resources more quickly than they can be generated. Conversely, the *ogbaanje* of Osifo's and Okorie's novels may be modern-minded without being rapacious, people who respond sensitively to their changing environment, who desire only the best for themselves and their intimates. Such a socially and spiritually sensitive *ogbaanje*, as we see in Njoku's story, may not survive the rough and tumble of life in the urban (or rural) kleptocracy of modern Nigeria, although Okri's picaresque and changeable *abiku* narrator in *The Famished Road* or even Ogbanje Ojebeta, settling down in her slave journey to the title of Mrs. Okonji, might disagree. Whichever portrait of *ogbaanje* particular Nigerian readers prefer, however, the authors who are drawn to this theme produce stories with a general appeal for a nation that has undergone extensive transformation in this century. As Ife Babalola's *abiku* proverb that opens this chapter suggests, both Nigeria's *ogbaanje* and its *ogbaanje*-like character as a country may yet astonish and confound even those who seek to know them best.

Notes

[1] A notable exception to this lack of critical attention on the importance of *ogbaanje* can be seen in Ogunyemi (1996: 61–74).

[2] See, for example, information given to us about the attachment of Flora Nwapa's heroine Efuru to the world of the spirits. Efuru is probably more a 'Mami Wata daughter' than a classic *ogbaanje*, but as I have argued elsewhere, these categories are connected for northern Igbo-speakers. See Bastian (1997).

[3] Igbo childhood in various parts of the Nigerian southeast has been characterised as relatively permissive for all children, although here again girls may be given more domestic responsibilities than their brothers. See, for example, Henderson and Henderson (1966) and Ottenberg (1989).

[4] Eventually this young woman did marry, but hastily and not any of her old boyfriends, almost as if she did not want time to consider her decision. At last report (in the late 1990s) she was the mother of one child and seemingly not inclined to become pregnant again.

[5] This has not changed substantially in the 1990s. For example, a 1998 article entitled 'Witches Invade Nigeria – Over 4,000 Men Allegedly Destroyed', in *Conscience International* insists that 'ladies who claimed to possess familiar spirits (Ogbanje) ... have their "powers" in their private parts and also seduce men with the powers in their eyes and curse with the ones in their mouths' (Anonymous 1998: 5).

[6] This dislike of the *ogbaanje* comes across strongly in a Nigerian English exchange between John and his mother: '"Una see this John, ehn," his mother would say. "We born am six times, and six times him die go back to the spirit world, before this time him say make him stay small." And John would cry, "Na lie, na lie," and his mother would cuff him sharply: 'Who you dey call liar? We do the ritual you no go fit dey go dey come anyhow again."' (Njoku, 1998)

[7] Provocatively, a letter to the editor published in the *Post Express-Wired* online newspaper on 26 May 1997 posed the question, 'Is Nigeria a Victim of "Ogbanje" or What?' In this letter, Chukwuemeka Igwe wonders if the constant return of military rule could constitute a form of ogbaanjism on the national scale. See Igwe (1997).

[8] This beginning is so much like that of Buchi Emecheta's *The Slave Girl* (1977) that it may well have been inspired by that novel. However, *The Slave Girl* is set in the first three decades of the 1900s, and Osifo's novel begins in the late 1940s.

[9] Interestingly, Henderson and Henderson (1966: 17) note that all Onitsha neonates (*umu ofu*, 'new children') were once suspected of communicating with their spirit companions and plotting to leave their parents. In the late 1980s, when I did fieldwork in Onitsha, I mainly heard this accusation leveled towards suspected *ogbaanje* infants. The very term *otu* itself may be an Edo loan-word, since it is the same term used historically to denote the palace associations that served the Oba of Benin. See Bradbury (1967) for more information on Benin's connection to western Igbo, palace associations and the Edo conflation of the Oba with Olokun.

[10] This move towards historicising West African religious practices is hardly novel. See, for example, Rosalind Shaw's (1997) article on witchcraft, modernity and memory in Sierra Leone. Helen Henderson (personal communication, 1999) relates that one *ogbaanje* girl she heard about in Onitsha during the 1960s was constantly being pulled and moved by invisible hands. The image is evocative of capture and enforced mobility, once more like that reported in historical accounts of the slave trade. For instance, during capture some people were rendered unconscious or sensorially deprived, waking up or emerging from inside sacks or baskets to find themselves in a new, strange place and under the control of unknown persons.

[11] Ogunyemi (1996: 30) notes that Mami Wata (called by her Mammywata) may well be a hybrid representation of the colonial period: a mixture made up from indigenous observations of biracial girls, childless colonial wives and older deities of wealth and beauty like Osun.

[12] The novel is set in the late 1940s and early 1950s. From a letter Ogbanje receives from her boyfriend Peter, we know that she is in her third year of boarding school during 1957. (Osifo, 1985: 168)

[13] Emecheta's Ogbanje Ojebeta ia also torn between a duty marriage, to her owner's son, and to a Christian man. As in *Dizzy Angel*, the *ogbaanje* who marries a staunch Christian – with all his connections to colonial and mission society – seems to benefit spiritually as well as materially from the match.

[14] The jealousy and spite of their husbands' sisters is legendary among Igbo-speaking wives; as is the grasping and selfishness of brothers' wives among Igbo-speaking sisters. Atiti, as a renowned witch, carries this time-honored cultural hatred to a different level.

[15] This is not the first intimation we have that Atiti is more powerful than her brother. As Uloji himself admits, in admiration of his sister's magical schemes: 'I have always known that the creator made a mistake about your sex. You should have come as a man.' (Osifo 1985: 235) In patriarchal Igbo terms, he can pay her no higher compliment. Yet he wonders to himself later 'why my father gave her all his power and left me none.' (Osifo, 1985: 235)

[16] The covert image of cannibalism here is probably intentional. Igbo witches are said to mystically cook their victims, then devour them internally until they shrivel and die. Of course, it also has resonance with stereotypical notions of 'pagans' common to missionaries and missionised Christians during the period of the novel – notions which maintain their currency among late twentieth-century evangelical Christians.

[17] See Meyer (1998) for a discussion of 'born again' memory and post-colonial modernity in Ghana for a fascinating corollary to Osifo's literary compromises.

[18] Ogunyemi (1996: 220) makes the point that Emecheta's oeuvre could be considered the quintessence of *ogbaanje* writing: 'Her been-to fiction straddles sharply contrasting worlds, which she departs from, arrives at, revisits and longs for, yet criticizes like a restless *ogbanje/abiku*.' In an earlier, short review of Emecheta's fiction, Oladele Taiwo (1984) also noted Emecheta's importance as an African writer but saw her main contribution as publicizing Nigerian fiction for an international audience.

[19] I heard this theme often during my fieldwork in 1987–8. One of the most potent pleas for young men's importance in village-level society that I read in the Nigerian media at the time was, coincidentally, written by an Agu. I have discussed this piece extensively in Bastian (1993).

Bibliography

Achebe, Chinwe. 1986. *The World of the Ogbanje*. Enugu: Fourth Dimension Publishers.

Amadiume, Ifi. 1987. *Male Daughters, Female Husbands: Gender and Sex in an African Society*. London: Zed Books.

Anonymous. 1998. 'Witches Invade Nigeria – Over 4,000 Men Allegedly Destroyed'. *Conscience International* 2 (1): 5-7, 10.

Babalola, Ife. 1997. 'Other Things Being Equal'. *Post Express-Wired* (Lagos). Editorial published 04/03/97. http://www.postexpresswired.com/postexpress.nsf/

Bastian, Misty L. 1993. '"Bloodhounds Who Have No Friends": Witchcraft, Locality, and the Popular Press in Nigeria'. *Modernity and its Malcontents: Ritual and Power in Postcolonial Africa*, eds Jean and John L. Comaroff. Chicago: University of Chicago Press.

—— 1997. 'Married in the Water: Spirit Kin and Other Afflictions of Modernity in Southeastern Nigeria'. *The Journal of Religion in Africa* XXVII: 116-34.

—— 1998. 'Fires, Tricksters and Poisoned Medicines: Popular Cultures of Rumor in Onitsha, Nigeria and Its Markets'. *Etnofoor* XI (2): 111–32.

Bradbury, R. E. 1967. 'The Kingdom of Benin'. *West African Kingdoms in the Nineteenth Century*, eds Daryll Forde and P. M. Kaberry. Oxford: Oxford University Press: 1–35.
Emecheta, Buchi. 1977. *The Slave Girl*. London: Braziller.
Eni, Emmanuel. 1987. *Delivered from the Powers of Darkness*. Ibadan: Scripture Union (Nigeria) Press and Books, Ltd.
Henderson, Richard N. and Helen K. Henderson. 1966. *An Outline of Traditional Onitsha Ibo Socialization*. Ibadan: Institute of Education.
Igwe, Chukwuemeka. 1997. 'Is Nigeria a Victim of 'Ogbanje' or What?' *Post Express-Wired* (Lagos). Letter to the editor published 26/05/97. http://www.postexpresswired.com/postexpress.nsf/
Manfredi, Victor. 1993. 'Igbo Initiation Revisited'. Unpublished paper presented to the Social Anthropology Seminar, Harvard University.
Metuh, Emefie Ikenga. 1981. *God and Man in African Religion: A Case Study of the Igbo of Nigeria*. London: Chapman.
Meyer, Birgit. 1998. '"Make a Complete Break with the Past." Memory and Post-Colonial Modernity in Ghanaian Pentecostalist Discourse'. *Journal of Religion in Africa* XXVIII (3): 316–49.
Njoku, David. 1998. 'Running'. *Post Express-Wired* (Lagos). Short story, published in the Arts and Culture section 03/21/98. http//www.postexpresswired.com/postexpress.nsf/
Ogunyemi, Chikwenye Okonjo. 1996. *Africa Wo/Man Palava: The Nigerian Novel by Women*. Chicago: University of Chicago Press.
Okorie, Uchegbulem. 1992. *Date with Destiny*. Ibadan: University Press Limited.
Okri, Ben. 1991. *The Famished Road*. New York: Doubleday.
Osifo, Gracy Nma. 1985. *Dizzy Angel*. Ibadan: University Press Limited.
Ottenberg, Simon. 1989. *Boyhood Rituals in an African Society: An Interpretation*. Seattle: University of Washington Press.
Shaw, Rosalind. 1997. 'The Production of Witchcraft/Witchcraft as Production: Memory, Modernity, and the Slave Trade in Sierra Leone'. *American Ethnologist* 24 (4): 856–76.
Taiwo, Oladele. 1984. *Female Novelists of Modern Africa*. London: Macmillan.
Tokode, Yambo. 1987. 'Menstrual Problem that Disturbs Pregnancy'. *Lagos Weekend*. Friday 11 December: 14.
Uchendu, Victor C. 1965. *The Igbo of Southeast Nigeria*. New York: Holt, Rinehart and Winston.

ALAIN RICARD

Félix Couchoro

Pioneer of Popular Writing in West Africa?

The life of Félix Couchoro is in itself a chronicle of Togolese political history; but his main passion in life was writing and his main aim to achieve literary success. He holds the distinction of having produced twenty novels, read locally, which earned him the lasting admiration of a local audience. In this respect he was a true popular literary phenomenon, comparable to what happened in Onitsha in the 1960s in terms of communicative exchange. But unlike the Onitsha writers, Couchoro worked alone and his career started in the 1920s, culminating in the 1960s. His capacity to remodel his works in view of their prospective audience shows a functional attitude towards literature, for he considers the writing process to be, firstly, a question of textual practice, and secondly, a question of communicative exchange. This is truly the mark of the popular writer: but in a situation where these textual practices also involve the invention of literature in foreign languages, these criteria of the popular may lose their relevance.

The life of an activist

Félix Couchoro was born in the Brazilian quarter of Ouidah in Dahomey (called Bénin since 1975), one of the capitals of the slave trade in the nineteenth century; in this city a peculiar hybrid coast culture was invented, which provided the background for Bruce Chatwin's novel *The Viceroy of Ouidah* (1988). After his primary education in a Catholic school and a short period as a primary school teacher, he became the manager of a local branch of SCOA, a French trading company in Grand Popo (Dahomey) in 1924. Grand Popo was a Dahomean enclave on the Togolese side of the River Mono, which, before the First World War, marked the boundary between German Togoland and French Dahomey. According to Westermann and Bryan (1970: 83) the whole coast of Benin Gulf between the Volta River (in today's Ghana) and the Oueme (in today's Bénin) is the land of the Ewe and the consciousness of the unity of this Eweland is essential to an understanding of Couchoro's work.

At a very early date Couchoro became involved in Togolese politics. Togo, being a mandate territory, had more political freedom than the colony of Dahomey even though in the 1930s a more liberal colonial attitude prevailed in Dahomey and allowed the rise of an independent press. Couchoro was the editor of *L'Eveil Togolais/Eveil Togo-Dahoméen*, a liberal paper advocating freedom of trade between the neighbouring colonies, a theme that was to be central in his work as well as in nationalist politics.

In 1941 Couchoro left his residence in Dahomey to settle in Anecho, Togo, ten miles from Grand Popo, where he started a business as an *agent d'affaires*, combining the jobs of public letter-writer, lawyer and real estate broker, in essence being a public man of letters. The war years saw the rise of the Comité de l'Unité Togolaise, a nationalist party led by Sylvanus Olympio, from Agoué, a village near Anecho. Using the special status of Togo as a trust territory of the United Nations after 1945, the party started mobilising southern elites by asking for more trade and political freedom from the colonial powers and eventually for independence. Félix Couchoro wrote in several of the party's papers and was a dedicated activist. In 1952 after a riot in Vogan, a village near Anecho, he had to flee the colonialist police and went into exile to avoid being jailed. He settled in Aflao, the border town on the Gold Coast side, near Lomé, where he could retain some of his Togolese clients. Life became more difficult, and money was scarce with the collapse of his Anecho business. In 1958 with the granting of internal autonomy he took a job in Lomé while still living in Aflao. In 1960 the nationalists won the elections and Togo became independent. Couchoro was appointed at the age of sixty as an editor at the Togolese information service. Three years later the nationalists were overthrown and President Olympio was killed in the first military coup in Black Africa; the man behind the coup was Sergeant Eyadema, who is now a general and still rules over Togo. In 1965 Couchoro retired; he died in Lomé three years later.

A colonial novelist

Couchoro's first book *l'Esclave* (*The Slave*) was published in Paris in 1929, but for many years it was a well-kept secret.[1] It was the second novel published by an African in French (the first being *Force Bonté*, by Bakary Diallo, in 1926). In 1965 *The Bibliography of Neo-*

African Literature by Jahnheinz Jahn mentions *l'Esclave* as a serial published in 1962. In 1968 Robert Cornevin also mentions the novel as a serial, but says that it was published in 1930. Shortly before his death, Couchoro wrote to Albert Gérard, to confirm that the book had indeed been published in book form but that he did not have a copy of it. Curiously the book is not in the National Library in Paris, and escaped the Legal Deposit, compulsory for books published or printed in France.

In fact, *l'Esclave* appeared in 1929 as a book, published by the *Dépêche Africaine*, which was a newspaper that also acted as a publishing house. The novel has now been reprinted several times in Togo and it deserves a place in the literature in French from Africa. The novel reappeared in 1962 in serial form in *Togo-Presse*, the only Togolese daily, and was introduced thus: 'As a first serial, *Togo-Presse* is happy to present to its readers a novel written by a Togolese writer and whose setting is the Togolese countryside' (27 April 1962:1). However, we know – and some of his readers must have known – that the same novel had been published earlier in Paris, in 1929, by Félix Couchoro, who was at that time a Dahomean; obviously, there would have been no reference to Togo and its countryside in this earlier edition of *l'Esclave*. It is certainly true that Couchoro settled in Togo and became a Togolese citizen, and that there is nothing specifically Dahomean in the novel, but neither is there anything recognisably Togolese!

Togo-Presse's representation of the novelist as 'Togolese' is not a minor detail if we consider what Cornevin called the 'regionalism' of Félix Couchoro (1968: 35). This is an extremely interesting text for the history of francophone literature in West Africa. Couchoro proclaims himself to be the novelist of an area, of a 'region': the Mono region. Thus as early as 1929 the novel is associated with none of the colonial entities, but has a point of view that can only be called 'nationalist' from an African perspective, or 'regionalist' from a French colonial perspective. Couchoro advocates the unity – especially the economic unity – of the area along the Volta River. Beyond artificial divisions, expressed by tax differences, Couchoro defends the unity of the people of the river area. It is not a coincidence that the boundaries of his novelistic universe coincide with the limits of the Eweland promoted by the nationalist party. At the same time in his preface to the first edition in 1929, Couchoro delivers an anti-racist message: he claims that the equality of men is proved by their common capacity to suffer a love passion. *L'Esclave* clearly belongs to the category of colonial novel with its northern savage (see below) and its dark seductress, especially since Couchoro wrote it to imitate a master of the genre, J. Francis-Boeuf, author of *La Soudanaise et son amant* (1924), but as Couchoro was to write later, he had a competitive advantage over French colonial writers: being himself an African he writes from an inside knowledge of the African experience.

The most obvious difference between the two editions of *l'Esclave* is the omission of the preface of 1929. In 1962, when Couchoro recycled his novel to suit the new Togolese daily, anti-racist proclamations were no longer necessary since the nationalists were in power. Another chapter was deleted: the 1929 version ends on a chapter called 'renewal' in which the slave's son celebrates his marriage in a Catholic church. This ending, consistent with colonial missionary teachings, was probably considered superfluous in 1962.

Couchoro, the chapbook writer

Between his failed career as a Parisian colonial African novelist in 1929 and his successful comeback as a serial writer in Togo in the 1960s, Couchoro attempted another career: he invented Onitsha-style chapbooks on the Togolese coast and he partially succeeded, for he was a true 'entrepreneur'. He had two of his novels privately printed in Ouidah, and proceeded to sell them himself. His second novel, *Amour de féticheuse* (*Love of a Fetish Priestess*, 1941) was printed by the Mme d'Almeida printing shop in Ouidah. This is the first locally printed novel in francophone Africa, produced at a time when Couchoro felt very bitter, for his lack of recognition after his Parisian achievement was hard to accept. His remarkable feat had passed unnoticed in France and his nationalistic tendencies prevented him from seeking and receiving support from the local colonial authorities. Since the existing commercial distribution for books was either non-existent or controlled by trading companies, Couchoro took it upon himself to sell his book. He kept a stock in his local *agent d'affaires* office in Anecho and his sister told me years later (in 1971) that she peddled the book in the market place in Ouidah and the surrounding areas. Couchoro was thus creating literary 'colportage' in West Africa and anticipating by a decade what was to start in the 1950s in Eastern Nigeria, several hundred miles east of Lomé. This was truly the beginning of Couchoro's career as a popular writer, in contact with his audience. His book was reprinted years later, as a serial in *Togo-Presse* and the title was changed accordingly: it became *Amour de féticheuse au Togo*. Such adaptability was a key feature of Couchoro's technique.

Nine years later, in 1950, he published another novel, printed in the same shop, *Drame d'amour à Anecho* (*Love Drama in Anecho*). We located a copy of the book which, curiously, is the only one not to have been reprinted as a serial. The Anecho chieftaincy rivalry had been a cause of turmoil ever since the departure of the Germans and the manipulations by the French of the subsequent elections. The Capulet and Montagu of this Togolese *Romeo and Juliet* were the Adjigo and the Lawson, the two rival clans of which Mercy Latré and Stanley Kuanvi, the heroes, were members. Couchoro does not take sides openly in this political rivalry, although a close reading of the novel would indicate where his sympathies lie. His opinion would probably be that good nationalists should not fall prey to the divide-and-rule tactics of the colonialists. During the first decade of independence, when this novel might have appeared as a serial, it was probably deemed wiser not to resuscitate the quarrels of the past. In any case, the book did not bring fame to Couchoro and probably remained known only in nationalist circles.

Couchoro was to become well-known later, with the independence of Togo and the publication of his serials in *Togo-Presse*. First to be released, in 1962, was *l'Esclave* (dated 1950!), followed by *Max Mensah* (dated 1956), then in 1963 *Bea et Marilou* was published, and presented as a sequel to *l'Esclave*. Then in 1964 *Les Secrets d'Eléonore* (*Eléonore's Secrets*) was published in book form at the same time as *l'Héritage cette peste* (*The Plague of Inheritance*). Thus in the first few years of the new paper, Couchoro was able to dispatch most of his literary output of the preceding years. Success came at last and his texts became a selling point for the paper: in December 1962, the headline reads, 'Couchoro Returns'. From 1964 onwards, serials follow in quick succession: the recipe for success has been found!

Couchoro, the serial writer

A poll taken by the librarian at the French Cultural Centre in Lomé in 1967 showed the extraordinary thirst for reading amongst the educated fraction of the population of the city (a few thousand persons). People believed strongly in the principle that one reads to learn, but to learn one reads mystery novels! So popular was this opinion that the librarian, eager to promote a more balanced reading diet, removed the French mystery novels from the shelves, thus withdrawing precisely the type of text that Couchoro had been using as a model.

Reading habits are not yet well known in Africa, but the poll showed enduring trends: readers expressed a great desire for simple and entertaining books, especially short novels (see Ricard, 1987: 89-97). This was precisely the material that Couchoro was willing to write:

> Because of the journalistic quality of this story, the author feels it necessary to specify that all resemblance between certain characters presented here and persons living or dead, all similarity of names is due to simple coincidence. Likewise the interpretation of certain events inspired from real life is purely fictional. (*Le Passé ressurgit*, *The Past is Back*, p. 2)

By referring to 'pure fiction' and the 'work of the imagination', the writer wants to be classified outside the realm of journalism and within the realm of literature. By using these ritualised disclaimers, he certainly seeks to protect himself, but more than that, he seeks to produce the effect of being a true novelist. In a similar vein, in the preface to *Max Mensah* (1956), he writes: 'The author notes to his readers that the names of the characters in this novel have been chosen purely by chance with the aim of giving local colour and of rendering more realistic what is improbable' (p.1).

The mechanism of the serial is here revealed very clearly: to be journalistic enough to interest readers, but to fictionalise events in order to entertain them. Couchoro puts his own work into categories: *D'Aklakou à El Mina* is described as a 'romantic legend'; *Gangsters et policiers* is a 'mystery novel', while *Les Secrets d'Eléonore* is simply sold in bookstores as a novel. The eighteen serials (if we put aside the three pre-independence novels, which belong to a different literary project) can easily be classified in the categories of mystery novels and social novels or simply novels.[2]

The mystery novel takes us to Lomé, which, although far from being a tentacular metropolis such as London or Paris (the cradle of the mystery novel in the nineteenth century), is still a very appropriate setting for crimes and political investigations of all kinds. The social novel is similar to the mystery novel, but the violence is replaced by romance; additionally, the police never intervene and conflicts are settled by the interested parties. The setting of all of these novels is Lomé, Aguidah or Anecho, where the principal characters often own large estates. Thus Couchoro's entire serial production can be analysed using a simple combination of content analysis and plot devices. A still finer analysis reveals a striking similarity in their construction, which obviously has a lot to do with Couchoro's rapid outpouring of serials between 1964 and the time of his death in 1968.

His first novel, *l'Esclave* is also the longest, the first to appear as a serial and also the only one having as a hero – in fact, the Slave is an anti-hero – a character coming specifically from the north of the country. This northerner is also a monster and we have to see in this candid stereotyping the expression of prejudices of the southern elites which were hidden in the following years, in the name of nationalism. Curiously enough, the colonial stereotype, so well appropriated by the southern elites, has resurfaced in the last decade in attacks upon the northerner, Etienne Gnassingbe Eyadema, who still rules Togo.

In the mystery novel, Couchoro perfected a plot device which he uses four times. At the beginning of the novel is a romantic liaison. The man finishes the relationship and is generally presented as the guilty party who, 'twenty years after' – as in Alexandre Dumas' novel *Vingt ans après* (1845) – is jealous of the success of his former mistress and tries to blackmail her, threatening to disclose their former affair. In all of the mystery novels the woman is at the centre of a plot aimed at ruining her reputation: the victim defends herself and eventually triumphs. The possibilities of this device are quite rich, allowing Couchoro to write two novels in one: the initial episode is usually a slice of Lomé life in the 1930s, while the second part is contemporary and suits the younger readers.

In Couchoro's universe women hold the central role and this is certainly related to the part they played and continue to play in the economic life of Togo. Market women – called metonymically 'Nana Benz' – have their own organisation and can manage important economic and political resources: Couchoro is the chronicler of this original feature of Togolese life. But he cannot really choose between the well-tested devices of the colonial novel, in which the dark beauty is often a dangerous seductress, and the new social realities giving a place to Christian, well-educated ladies: his serial novels are a curious and at times incoherent mix of these two points of view.

The plots of Couchoro's social novels are even more simple. Neither the police nor supernatural forces intervene and conflicts are solved within the family circle. The moral message is very clear and motivates his entire literary activity: the moral revolves around the Togolese girl facing marriage. Couchoro is of course faced with a difficult contradiction, for his didactic purpose is rather biased: he claims to educate, but in a paternalistic way where the only hope for the girl is to conform to what men want, which is precisely the stuff of the 'romance'. There is no pornography and no crude language in these novels, just salacious hints which do not fit the part of the ethics teacher he claims to play. Couchoro is concerned with marriage but more with the conflicts it creates in a society where polygamy is prevalent, and he never condemns polygamy, in the name of man's freedom to do as he pleases.

The names of his characters are in themselves their destiny; every serial is based on the division between good guy/bad guy and on rather simplistic manicheisms. For example, in *Les Gens sont méchants* (*People are Wicked*, 1967), Couchoro writes:

> One often hears the following proverb: '*Amedome ma yi kpo*' ... It is impossible to go and look into the stomach of another. It is from this proverb that the name of our hero, the wicked office clerk of the Sototra 'Amedome' is taken. As for his victim, his name is: Homefa. Innocent. (p. 47)

In this way Couchoro is able to fictionalise newspaper reporting by using heavy stereotyping. Another technique of the serial writer which he uses successfully is the return of certain characters. But he has more trouble with this device because he rarely uses stream of consciousness narration techniques. For him characters are defined in essentialist terms: they appear under many disguises, but they never change.

Couchoro, the writer in exile

Félix Couchoro deserves a place in the history of literature in Africa. He was able to write and publish locally at least three novels, but the size of the Togolese market was too small to sustain publishing ventures and his books never sold. For complex reasons, Couchoro never had the right political support: he was too independent and too critical of the powers of the day. In Togo and Dahomey in the 1950s there was censorship and no freedom of expression. Political newspapers played a role in the struggle for independence but they were ephemeral and could not become publishing houses in the same way that Couchoro's first publisher, *La Dépêche africaine*, originally a Parisian paper in the 1930s, had done. For these reasons Couchoro, who was vaguely aware of the realities of the trade, sent his first book, *l'Esclave*, to a vanity publisher in Avignon, hoping to reprint it at his own expense. But he could not succeed in the early 1950s and he tried again in 1959, this time hoping that a prestigious publisher such as *Présence Africaine* would promote him as a nationalistic fighter. In a letter to Alioune Diop, founder and director of *Présence Africaine*, he writes: 'In 1952–53 in Togo the political climate darkened because of certain repressive measures: this forced a few patriots to take refuge in the British zone. I was one of those political refugees' (Personal letter to Diop, 6 July 1959).

Couchoro was to write few novels in the years of his exile. He needed an exchange with an audience. In the preceding thirty years he had written three novels and devoted a lot of energy to their promotion abroad – without any recognition – and at home with a limited success. Illiteracy, economic stagnation and political repression, in short, the colonial situation, inhibited his creative impulse by depriving him of an active and critical environment. He certainly was of the same calibre as the 'market literature' authors in Onitsha, Port Harcourt and Aba, but he did not have the wide audience enjoyed by his Nigerian counterparts.

Launched by political patronage, he established himself as a prolific and original serial writer. The personalisation of the serials in the headline, 'Couchoro Returns', is a witness to this popularity. He was in good company on the pages of *Togo-Presse: Dark Child*, by Camara Laye, *Cry, the Beloved Country*, by Alan Paton, *The Mysteries of Paris*, by Eugene Sue, *The Red and the Black*, by Stendhal, alternated with his own texts. Numerous statements, including letters to the editors, have confirmed to us the great popularity of Couchoro in the first decade of independence: teachers, students, office clerks, priests and shopkeepers, all knew Couchoro and read his serials.

The obituary which appeared in *Togo-Presse* gives us a precious account of the communication existing between author and audience. According to the writer of the obituary, at the time of his death Couchoro had the feeling that his novels were 'deteriorating' in popularity with his readers. Struck by their judgement, he was preparing to 'strike hard' to regain their interest. Here was an author responsive to his readers, close to them, and in this attitude lies the appeal of his work. He was also preparing to publish his serials in volume form according to a contract signed with Editogo, a local publishing firm. His death interrupted another project, a novel for CLE, at the time the largest publishing house in francophone Africa, based in Yaoundé. For the first time a publisher of international renown had accepted one of his novels: the manuscript of *Tu ne déroberas point* (*Thou Shall Not Steal*) ends on page 27. The late Janheinz Jahn, who was the first to list Couchoro as an African writer and who included his biography in the first *Who's Who of African Literature* (1972), then signed a contract with Couchoro's son to issue the serials in book form. Unfortunately the project was interrupted by the premature death of Jahn in 1973.

In a remarkably lucid article written in 1967, the Senegalese critic Mohammadou Kane lists the main themes of francophone African literature: the cult of the past, the trip abroad, the life of expatriates in Africa, the sense of the absurd. He commented that all of these novels were published in Paris and that the themes were clearly aimed at a French audience (1969: 57). He could have added that these novels were characterised by an obsessive grammatical correctness and a stylistic elegance that bore the mark of good French publishers. Félix Couchoro, who had an African audience for several decades, does not treat a single one of these themes. He shows also a boldness in experimenting with language that marks a writer eager to listen to the language of the African street.

Couchoro was one of the first African novelists, the inventor of chapbooks in francophone Africa, the master of serial writing and author of more than twenty novels in French, but he never went to France and remained committed to his local audience. His stylistic repertory, the plasticity of his plots, which are easily remodelled, the constant use of stereotype, and the willingness to educate as well as to entertain, were truly the mark of the popular writer. But given the size and the structure of the 'literary field' in francophone Africa at the time, the notion of a 'popular position' has simply no meaning: rather, we should regard Félix Couchoro as a writer with a uniquely African audience which remained loyal to his work for several decades.

Notes

[1] For a complete bibliography of Couchoro's works and manuscripts, see Alain Ricard (1987), *Félix Couchoro, Naissance du roman africain*, Paris: Présence Africaine. The most complete study of Couchoro's works is S. A. Amegleame (1998), *Metamorphoses de l'écriture dans l'oeuvre romanesque de Félix Couchoro*, unpublished doctoral thesis from the Univesity of Bordeaux.

[2] One exceptional case is *Les dix plaies de l'Afrique* (*Africa's Ten Plagues*, 1968), which is subtitled 'fictionalised documentary' although it is in fact a political essay.

Bibliography

Chatwin, Bruce. (1988) *The Viceroy of Ouidah*. London: Viking Penguin.

Cornevin, Robert. (1968) 'Félix Couchoro, premier romancier regionaliste africaine', *France-Eurafrique*, vol. 196,35–36.

Couchoro, Félix. (1929) *L'Esclave*. Paris: Dépêche Africaine.

Couchoro, Félix. (1941) *Amour de féticheuse*, Ouidah: Mme Pierre d'Almeida.

Couchoro, Félix. (1950) *Drame d'amour à Anecho*. Ouidah: Mme Pierre d'Almeida.

Couchoro, Félix. (1956) *Max Mensah*. Lomé: Togo-Presse.

Couchoro, Félix. (1966) *Le Passé'resurgit*. Lomé: Togo-Presse.

Couchoro, Félix. (1967) *Les Gens sont méchants*. Lomé: Togo-Presse.

Diallo, Bakary (1926) *Force Bonté*. Paris: Rieder.

Dumas, Alexandre (1845) *Vingt ans après* (trans. *Twenty Years After*, 1998.) Oxford: Oxford World Classics.

Francis-Boeuf, J. (1924) *La Soudanaise et son amant*, Paris: Albin Michel.

Jahn, Jahnheinz. (1965) *The Bibliography of Neo-African Literature*. New York: Praeger.

Jahn, Jahnheinz. (1972) *Who's Who of African Literature*,

Kane, Mohammadou. (1969) 'Naissance du roman africain francophone', *African Arts*, Vol.2, No.1, 54–8.

Ricard, Alain. (1987) *Félix Couchoro, Naissance du roman africain*. Paris: Présence Africaine.

Westermann, D. and M. A. Bryan (1970) *Handbook of African Languages: Part II, Languages of West Africa*, London: Dawsons for the I.A.I.

RICHARD BJORNSON

Writing & Popular Culture in Cameroon

Reference
R. Granqvist (ed.) *Signs & Signals: Popular Culture in Africa*
Umea, Sweden: Acta Universitatis Umensis, 1990: 19–33

Until the mid-1970s, Cameroonian literate culture was largely the domain of a relatively small intellectual elite. The names of the country's best known writers Mongo Beti, Ferdinand Oyono, Guillaume Oyono-Mbia, and Francis Bebey were familiar to a large segment of the population, for their works had been included on school reading lists, but despite a high rate of literacy and the establishment of francophone Africa's first major publishing house at Yaoundé in 1963, the vast majority of Cameroonians did not habitually read works of imaginative literature, even if they had attended school and learned to read. The publishing house, Editions C.L.E., had sought to create a market for such literature, but with several notable exceptions, its publications failed to attract substantial numbers of adult readers. However, the rise of modestly financed local publishing ventures and the growing awareness of a potential market for Africa-centered pulp fiction resulted in the emergence of a genuinely popular culture.

The success of this literature is instructive because it reveals the qualities that appeal to large numbers of Cameroonians who can read but do not purchase the sort of books that C.L.E. and other publishers made available to them. Many of these people have some disposable income for entertainment purposes. They attend foreign movies and consume European pulp fiction like photo-novels, detective thrillers, and romances. When a French librarian experimented with innovative selling techniques in Douala, she discovered that Cameroonians would purchase inexpensive books if they were available at readily accessible locations. She also discovered that C.L.E. books were inappropriate for this market because they cost three to four times more than most people were willing to pay.[1]

The foreign films that Cameroonians watched and the European pulp fiction that they read were often criticized by the country's intellectual elite, which viewed such forms of entertainment as corruptions of public morality and taste. In fact, these films and novels often glorify violence, romantic love, sentimental pathos, and material wealth. Stereotypical characters and melodramatic plots are common. What they offer people is a vicarious escape from the monotony of everyday life. As in Europe and America, the formulaic cliches in these forms of popular culture gradually entered the consciousness of many Cameroonians and shaped their taste in literature.

Echoes of these clichés can be found in novels published by C.L.E., but by the mid-1970s enterprising authors had already begun to explore other avenues of publication for works capable of responding more directly to the tastes of literate Cameroonians who regard novels primarily as an escapist form of entertainment. These authors translated the stereotyped patterns of European popular culture into African settings and, in the process, reinforced modern assumptions about the nature of the individual self. At the same time, their writing is characterized by an overlay of moral didacticism. Even when they focus on violence, corruption, and sexuality, they invariably establish a context of values according to which some moral lesson can be drawn from their depictions of undesirable behavior. There are several explanations for the pervasiveness of this moral sentiment: it is present in European popular fiction and in the Nigerian market literature that penetrated West Cameroon; it reflects the Christian mission schooling by means of which most Cameroonians had, until recently, acceded to literacy; and it echoes moral principles like those found in traditional oral literature. In any case, Cameroonian readers expect to extract a moral from such writing, and these authors give them every opportunity to do so, although the principal attraction of their work is its promise of a vicarious escape from everyday reality.

A good example of this form of writing is Omo Ya Eku's novel *La Prison sous le slip d'Ebela*. The title has pornographic connotations, but the 'paradise' that men seek 'beneath Ebela's underpants' is moralistically condemned from the beginning as a 'prison.' Ebela is a beautiful prostitute who beguiles the narrator's friend Zambo into giving her expensive presents to prove that he is a 'big man' worthy of enjoying her favors. However, the moral center of the novel is the narrator who demonstrates restraint by resisting Ebela's charms and repudiating the illusion that physical pleasure or material possessions can guarantee happiness. Both Zambo and Ebela are prisoners of this illusion, and their fate illustrates the folly of their blindness. Zambo is ultimately jailed for having embezzled government funds to purchase the presents he gave her, and Ebela is beaten to death by another lover who was humiliated by his inability to satisfy her sexual demands. From the narrator's perspective, this poetic justice illustrates the folly of obsessive preoccupation with wealth and sexual desire, for such obsessions produce a state of mind that is symbolically implied by the title – the prison beneath Ebela's underpants.

For Cameroonian readers, the appeal of Omo Ya Eku's melodramatic novel is at least partly contingent on their recognition that characters like Zambo and Ebela exist in real life. In fact, the common reader's propensity to identify with the major characters of popular fiction suggests that such characters reflect the public's assumptions about individual identity more accurately than do the heroes of many novels in the high culture tradition. Within this context, it is revealing that popular Cameroonian fiction focuses almost exclusively on the individual consciousness and its attempts to cope with modern life.

For example, Martin Enobo-Kosso's *Monologue d'une veuve angoissée* recounts the story of a woman who recognizes the self-destructiveness of her previous attitudes and reshapes them in such a way that she can live peacefully with her second husband. Like Ebela, the novel's principal female character, Ngon-Minlan, had been a prostitute. Troubled by the solitude to which her customers abandoned her, she married one of them, but because she never felt confident of his love, she constantly placed unreasonable demands upon him. On a subconscious level, her actions were appeals for him to demonstrate his love, although he failed to recognize this message and fled from the tensions of marriage into drunkenness and affairs with other women, thereby precipitating his own premature death. Enobo-Kosso's novel consists of a brief letter written by her first husband shortly before his death and a longer one in which Ngon-Minlan explains how she gained insight into her own blindness and atoned for the perversity of her attitude toward him.

Focusing on the individual consciousness of the woman as it reveals itself in her letter, Enobo-Kosso illustrates the necessity of love and trust in marriage. He also presents a psychologically plausible account of how the absence of these qualities can destroy a marriage and condemn people to unhappiness. The real problem for Ngon-Minlan is the self-image she brought into her first marriage. As she relates in the letter, her father withdrew her from school at an early age and then disowned her after she had been raped by four men who pretended to be his friends. Because she had been unable to prepare herself for a legitimate career, her only recourse was prostitution. Having grown vain and mistrustful as the result of her commercial dealings with men, she retained the same attitudes in her marriage with her first husband, for she wanted to harden herself against the possibility of being abandoned by him. Not until several years after his death does she realize her mistake and adopt a new self-image based on love and trust, a self-image that allows her to find happiness with a second husband. The breakdown in communication between husband and wife is a common problem in contemporary Cameroonian society, and Enobo-Kosso's solution to it reflects his belief in a modern concept of individual consciousness and its capacity for romantic love.

In anglophone Cameroon, one of the most common variations on the individualism theme involves the scoundrels who feature in the pamphlet novels that are occasionally sold in local bookstores and markets. The protagonists in these novels tend to be unsympathetic characters who are presented as examples of immoral behavior, and although the cleverness of their ruses provides a major centre of focus, they themselves are invariably unmasked and punished for their misdeeds. In John Menget's *Adventures of Tita* and Peter Akum Fomundam's *The Agony of an Early Marriage*, for example, the roguish protagonists succeed in duping other people, but they only enjoy the fruits of their dishonesty for a short time because they inhabit fictional worlds that operate according to the rules of poetic justice. However, the real tragedy of their lives derives from the hypocrisy of their relationships with other people. If Menget and Fomundam condemn the materialistic individualism of contemporary society through the depiction of such characters, they are also implying that the antidote to it is a heightened sense of individual responsibility.

The emphasis upon individual responsibility in a society permeated with ignorance and corruption is also apparent in pamphlet novels like F. C. Ngam's *Tricks of a Smuggler* and B. A. Ranndze's *The Adventures of a Mosquito*. Both present variations on the rogue theme. In *Tricks of a Smuggler*, a reformed smuggler describes the ruses he employed to avoid paying import duties and concludes that every Cameroonian has the moral obligation to cooperate with customs agents in eliminating smuggling because the government depends upon import duties for 87% of the revenues it needs to build schools, hospitals, and roads. In *The Adventures of a Mosquito*, the insect hero listens to conversations in which people divulge their corrupt activities; it then stings them as a punishment for their immoral behavior. In both books, the point is that individual Cameroonians must assume responsibility for the consequences of their actions, for this attitude is, as Ngam's reformed smuggler insists, the only way to 'build our cherished peace on a solid foundation.'[2] In this way, individual responsibility is frequently linked with national destiny in Cameroonian popular fiction.

Despite the implicit optimism in such a linkage, however, this literature frequently focuses on the unmerited suffering to which individuals are subjected in contemporary Cameroonian society. Characters like Ebela and Ngon-Minlan develop self-destructive attitudes because their society allows them to be exploited by others. Similarly, Jean-Clément Aoué-Tchany's *Du Folklore en enfer* recounts how a young student, Sam Jona, is humiliated, exploited, and ignored by many people after he suffered painful burns over most of his body in the explosion of a gas stove. Even his fiancée abandons him to pursue the material advantages of a lesbian relationship with the wife of a Dutch missionary. Yet when a kindly Swiss doctor sends Jona to a Lausanne hospital, he recovers completely and marries a young Swiss woman, who persuades him that his life is intrinsically valuable and can serve as an inspiration to others. With ironic appropriateness, Jona returns to Cameroon after the overthrow of a corrupt government and becomes a living symbol of the new president's pledge that every person in the country will be treated with compassion and respect. In contrast, his original fiancée becomes blind and deaf after swallowing poison in frustration at having wasted her life by accompanying the Dutch missionary's family to Europe.

Nearly all such novels are based on real-life experiences. However, they are elaborated according to the melodramatic conventions and popular culture stereotypes that common people have come to expect in literary works and films. None of the protagonists in these novels are particularly noteworthy for their accomplishments. They are ordinary individuals like those whom Cameroonians encounter in their daily lives. When such characters become the heroes of novels, they affirm the principle that, no matter how insignificant a life might appear to be, it is important because some lesson can be extracted from it. In addition, readers of such novels feel reassured about their own sense of themselves as they reflect from a superior vantage point on the suffering or moral blindness of fictional characters who resemble them in some ways. Within the context of nation-building, this focus on the value of common people's lives translates into the assumption that the efforts of individuals are crucial in determining the fate of their country.

This message is at the center of Pierre Epato Nzodam's *Sur les pistes d'aventure,* the story of a young man's participation in a youth camp sponsored by the government to revitalize a Cameroonian village and endow it with the modern infrastructure it needs if its inhabitants are to enjoy the higher standard of living promised by independence. Accompanied by comic-strip illustrations that reinforce the moral lessons implicit in the protagonist's experiences, Nzodam's narrative demonstrates the need for people to adopt a self-help ethic. Although widespread ignorance and corruption constitute obstacles to the realization of the volunteer project, the principal challenge is to convince individuals that they must accept responsibility for shaping their own future.

Like other examples of Cameroonian popular fiction, *Sur les pistes d'aventure* depicts an ordinary person in terms of modern assumptions about the nature of individual identity. It then uses his life to illustrate moral truths that must be respected if people desire to cope successfully with the contemporary world. The writing of such a novel reflects the influence of the Cameroonian government's nation-building ideology in the sense that the assumptions behind it are part of the modernization process, and the fact that these assumptions are linked with popular culture stereotypes indicates the extent to which they have spread through the population.

To date, the most successful author of Cameroonian popular

fiction has been Naha Désiré, a young tailor who attended school in Cotonu before wandering across Nigeria and settling in Yaoundé, where he brought out two short novels in the late 1970s and early 1980s. As a tradesman in daily contact with the unemployed and marginally employed Cameroonians who frequent the local market, he acquired a good idea of what they were interested in reading. When he published *Sur le Chemin du suicide* and *Le Destin a frappé trop fort* at his own expense, he calculated his production costs so that his modest volumes would be affordable for most people. Written in a simplified, cliche-ridden style, both books focus on a suffering victim who wallows in self-pity and fantasizes about unattainable desires while living in a world dominated by the concrete objects of everyday life.

Thousands of copies of these two novels were sold, and they proved far more popular than most of the Cameroonian novels published by C.L.E. This popularity was largely due to Naha's focus on non-heroic protagonists whose misfortunes evoke a sense of pathos with which common readers can identify. An advertising flier that he distributed to promote his first book illustrates the approach he adopted in seeking to attract their interest: 'After having lost all his relatives in an automobile accident at Cotonu, after having been defrauded and poisoned, Naha Désiré, commonly known as the Child of Misfortune, was able to tell the story of his sad and miserable life in a novel of 100 pages. In Yaoundé, the young writer is now anticipating a slow and painful death that lurks in wait for him because cancer never spares anyone. If you have ever suffered in your life or if you would like to know about the suffering of others, read *Sur le Chemin du suicide*.'[3] Naha's appeal to popular culture stereotypes is obvious. Equally obvious is the fact that such appeals were successful because they responded to the sensibility of audiences that publishing houses like C.L.E. had failed to reach with their more intellectually respectable books.

Sur le Chemin du suicide and *Le Destin a frappé trop fort* revolve around the misfortunes that befall Naha's central characters despite their good intentions. The fictional Naha in *Sur le Chemin* and Albert Goussi in *Le Destin* experience variations on the author's own journey from Cotonu to Yaoundé. Both characters experience the duplicity of fate and other people before discovering that they are suffering from incurable cancers. Yet Goussi and the fictional Naha define themselves at least partly in relation to idealistic visions of societies where peace and harmony reign. During his childhood in Dahomey, the fictional Naha is persuaded by several Jehovah's Witnesses to abandon his schooling and work toward the Kingdom of God, for he can supposedly help bring about a world where 'death will be no more, [where] there will be no more suffering, no more war, no more hatred, no more crime. Sickness and hunger will be things of the past.'[4] Similarly, Goussi frees himself from a mental illness, which had kept him confined in a Yaoundé asylum for seven years, when he dreams he is participating in the overthrow of the apartheid regime in South Africa and contributing to the unification of an Africa where 'there will be bread for anyone and everyone.'[5] Yet neither the fictional Naha nor Goussi succeed in realizing their idealistic visions because they are overwhelmed by circumstances beyond their control.

In fact, the dominant sentiment of both characters is injured innocence. Jehovah's Witnesses prove less idealistic than their rhetoric when they poison the fictional Naha and defraud him of the reweaving business he had established in Cotonu. Because the poison affects his liver in such a way that he develops a disagreeable odor, people shun him. Duped on numerous occasions as he works his way across Nigeria and reestablishes his reweaving business in Yaoundé, the poor Naha learns that he has cancer and that his sisters have been killed in an automobile accident. At this point he resolves to commit suicide, and the novel ends with the note he writes to his mother.

Although Goussi is more successful with women (he makes love to four secondary-school students at the same time, to an extremely wealthy light-skinned Igbo woman, and to a white South African woman who is a leader in the struggle against apartheid), he too succumbs to the rigors of an unjust fate. The four secondary-school students are burned to death in a gruesome train wreck, and his later mental illness results from the guilt he feels for having escaped the accident that took their lives. Within days of leaving the asylum, he learns of his cancer, and he dies shortly after seeing the son that the Igbo woman had borne him. The narrative pattern in the two novels is the same, for both central characters are self-pitying victims of undeserved suffering. They dream of contributing to a utopian future, but fate and the dishonesty of others betray them.

The success of Naha's novels reveals something about the taste of literate but socially and economically marginalized Cameroonians who are not generally interested in the sort of fiction published by C.L.E. Alluding to concrete, verifiable details, Naha encourages such readers to view his works as true accounts of individuals like themselves. Under such circumstances, they can read a book like *Sur le Chemin* or *Le Destin* as if it conveys a moral lesson relevant to their own lives. When actual readers of Naha's books were interviewed, they cited a number of lessons they had found in them: one should never be discouraged by misfortune, for there is always someone whose situation is worse than one's own; one should always be alert because others are lurking in wait for the unwary; helping those who suffer will give one courage to endure one's own suffering.[6] Such responses indicate that Cameroonian readers consciously look for a moral purpose to justify their interest in these novels.

However, the extraordinary popularity of Naha's fiction also suggests that his readers recognized a part of themselves in his portrayals of Goussi and the fictional Naha. Like these characters, many young Cameroonians fantasize about bringing peace and harmony to the world, about making love to rich and beautiful women, about living in luxury. Yet also like these characters, they usually fail to realize their dreams, and they want to believe that they are not to blame for their own misery. *Sur le Chemin* and *Le Destin* give them that assurance. In doing so, such novels capture the feelings of powerlessness and unmerited suffering that characterize large segments of the population in countries like Cameroon.

Other writers attempted to exploit the popular culture formulas that Naha had used, but none proved as successful as he had been, although Kumé Talé's *Journal d'une suicidée* and Samuel Nkamgnia's *Si Mon Mari se rend compte* did vary the pattern by introducing female protagonists. The heroine of *Journal* is a seventeen-year-old school girl who committed suicide after being abandoned by a young man who had deployed all the sentimental cliches of European movies, photo-novels, and popular music to seduce her, whereas the central character in *Si Mon Mari* is a naive young wife who feels she cannot tell her husband about her encounters with a gangster, an unsolved murder, and the police in Paris, where she has come to live with him. The former mistakes platitudes for the pure and absolute love that she desires; the latter experiences the reverse of the usual European excursion to exotic Africa when she travels from familiar Cameroonian surroundings to the mysterious chaos of Europe. One question dominates the reflections of both women: why is this happening to me? The same question lies at the center of Naha's novels, but no answer is ever given because, from the point of view of the average person, there is no answer. The question itself remains a symbol of the powerlessness that afflicts so many Cameroonians.

One way to escape this sense of powerlessness is through fantasy, and several Cameroonian writers have adapted heroic popular culture stereotypes like the James Bond character to create a vehicle for the expression of such fantasies. For example, Jean-Pierre Dikolo published four detective novels in which 'Scorpion the African' serves an African secret service agency run by a character known as 'The Old Man' in Addis Ababa. Thanks to extraordinary physical prowess and an absolute command of modern technology, the fearless Scorpion extricates himself from one difficult situation after another to defeat an assortment of enemies: white colonialists in southern Africa, representatives of the Ku Klux Klan in America, gun-runners attempting to foment coups in independent African countries.

Scorpion is not a specifically Cameroonian hero, but 'The Baron' in Evina Abossolo's *Cameroun/Gabon: Le D.A.S.S. monte à l'attaque* is, and he displays many of the same characteristics as Dikolo's hero. Serving under a man called 'The Uncle' in the Cameroonian secret service and following the well-known pattern of the Bond films, The Baron transforms an apparent triumph of evil at the beginning of the novel into a victory for the forces of good at the end. In this case, the enemy is the Soviet Union, which is establishing a clandestine communications network along the west coast of Africa to destabilize Europe-friendly nations like Cameroon and Gabon. The Baron's intelligence, lightning-like reflexes, technical expertise, and fearlessness enable him to penetrate this network and destroy it in a violent series of episodes during which he demonstrates an easy familiarity with luxury and proves irresistibly attractive to women.

Obviously modeled on the Bond stereotype, both Scorpion and The Baron are projections of an African desire to escape the sense of powerlessness that surfaces in the popular fiction of writers like Naha. Yet despite their reassertion of African manhood, the heroes of Dikolo and Abossolo reinforce an essentially conservative ideological position. Their efforts on behalf of existing African governments imply that virtue lies in defending the *status quo*, for no mention is made of the corruption that pervades these governments. Furthermore, Scorpion and The Baron are idealized embodiments of the materialistic, macho values that had fostered European colonialism in the first place. *Cameroun/Gabon* and the Scorpion novels were published in Paris, and unlike the more modest popular fiction published in Cameroon, they promoted acquisitive individualism, another facet of the modern identity concepts that are becoming commonplace in Africa.

⋆ ⋆ ⋆

In addition to the novel, a Cameroonian popular theater emerged during the late 1970s and often attracted enormous crowds. Actor-directors like Daniel Ndo, Dieudonné Afana, and Deiv Moktoï regularly performed before more than a thousand spectators at the major movie theaters in Yaoundé and Douala. They toured other parts of the country with their shows, and they made popular recordings. Moktoï even published his plays *L'Homme bien de là-bas* and *La Femme bien de là-bas* in an illustrated comic-book format. The performances of Ndo and Afana were more like extended monologues than actual plays, for having invented the colorful characters 'Uncle Otsama' and 'Jean Miché Kankan,' they merely presented them in a variety of humorous situations. However, the popular performances of Ndo, Afana, and Moktoï shared two important characteristics: they were mixed-genre entertainments that cultivated a variety-show atmosphere, and they employed deformations of the French language to situate the action in specifically Cameroonian settings.

Ndo pioneered this sort of theater in the early 1970s. After having won first prize at the 1970 national drama festival for his interpretation of Mbarga in Oyono-Mbia's *Notre Fille ne se mariera pas*, Ndo adapted a similar character for the dramatic sketches that became part of the variety-show performances he staged with his 'Théâtre Expérimental' and its successor, the 'Atelier d'Art et d'Animation.' By 1975 this group was performing large-scale productions that included jazz, dancing, mime, folktales, riddles, poems, jokes, and character sketches. According to Ndo, this mixture of genres was the most appropriate form of African drama because 'we need a complete and total theater that can embrace African life in its globality.'[7]

During the time he spent in Italy on an acting fellowship, he polished his Mbarga-like character into a stereotyped old villager whom he baptized 'Uncle Otsama' when he played him on the radio after his return to Cameroon in 1978. The character soon became well known, and when Ndo produced his first full-length dramatization of the white-bearded, bareheaded old villager, *Les Aventures de l'Oncle Otsama en ville*, more than 1,500 people attended the premiere in Yaoundé. During the next three years, Ndo developed thirteen additional Uncle Otsama sketches, always interweaving the dramatic action with musical performances, singing, dancing, mime, and humorous skits.

The textual content of these sketches is less important than Ndo's ability to sustain the credibility of a comic character who repeatedly misunderstands the significance of what is happening in the world around him. The effect of Ndo's performances depends partly on his mastery of Uncle Otsama's rustic accent and speech patterns, which echo local Ewondo usage. By exaggerating the forms of speech actually used in the Yaoundé area, Ndo developed a comic idiom that responded to the sensibility of his fellow countrymen. Although his performances often rely on slapstick techniques and one-line gags, the Uncle Otsama sketches would soon have lost their appeal if they had not touched upon problems that concern substantial numbers of Cameroonians.

Even Ndo's outrageous word plays often carry a deeper significance. In *L'Oncle Otsama à la banque*, for example, the 'sous-directeur' (deputy director) becomes the 'directeur plein des sous' (director full of money). Within the context of widespread corruption, such puns contain a veiled commentary on the venality of dishonest individuals in high places. The same is true of the action. In *La Convocation*, Uncle Otsama trembles when he receives a summons to police headquarters, and he rehearses all the possible reasons why the police might be interested in seeing him. In reality, they merely want to return his lost wallet, but it is ironic that the police commissioner should be overcome with a similar anxiety at the end of the play when he is summoned without explanation to the capital. The action and Uncle Otsama's hilariously embellished account of it produce uproarious laughter among Cameroonian audiences, but the point on which the humor turns is a serious one

– the fear of being arbitrarily arrested and having no recourse against an irrational bureaucracy.

Similarly, *Les Aventures de l'Oncle Otsama en ville* revolves around the old man's willingness to let his daughter pay an enormous bill for the round of drinks he orders at a Yaoundé bar while visiting her in the capital. The action and his account of it upon his return to the village are humorous, but the expenses incurred by city-dwellers to satisfy the demands of their rural relatives is a problem that preoccupies many Cameroonians, and Ndo's comic treatment of the issue is a form of social criticism that reached large numbers of people who do not habitually read books or attend dramatic performances.

The same is true of Afana's Jean Miché Kankan, who was originally created for Albert Mbia's popular radio programme, 'Radio Trottoir.' When Afana adopted Ndo's variety-show format and presented *Les Mésaventures de Jean Miché Kankan* at one of the large movie theaters in Yaoundé, he scored an impressive popular success that was repeated during a series of presentations in other parts of the country. Like Otsama, Kankan is a stereotyped character – a rich but miserly merchant whose fractured French and exaggerated Bamileke intonations proved hilarious to Cameroonian audiences partly because he was a caricatural distortion of what was generally regarded as a typical Bamileke mentality. Also like Otsama, Kankan often alluded to serious social problems. For example, his complaints about his difficulties with government bureaucracy or about what his son is (and is not) learning at the local school reflect concerns shared by many Cameroonians.

But Moktoï was the one who transformed the variety-show format and popular culture stereotypes into an overtly critical form of theater. His 'Uhuru Drama' began as a collective of former university students who desired to unmask 'the new contradictions of African society' and to provoke audiences into repudiating the institutions that stand in the way of 'a global and balanced development' on the continent.[8] Their first production was *Remember Soweto*, a mélange of blues music, dancing, poetry, and dramatic sketches of racial oppression. However, the group did not attract a significant popular following until it staged Moktoï's *L'Homme bien de là-bas* in 1979. During the next two years, the play drew capacity crowds to the large movie theaters in Yaoundé and Douala as well as to performances in other Cameroonian cities.

On the surface, *L'Homme bien de là-bas* is a farce. But beneath the humorous names, the one-line gags, the stereotyped characters, and the melodramatic action of the play, there is a penetrating critique of the vulgar materialism that characterizes Cameroon's privileged elites and prevents the country from evolving into a just and equitable national community. *L'Homme bien* consists of five tableaux in which Newrichard Proudlove reveals his corrupt mentality in a variety of settings. The corruption that pervades these settings and the willingness to accept it are the real source of contradictions between the government's nation-building ethos and actual conditions in countries like Cameroon. Moktoï's caricatural depiction of them makes it impossible for audiences to ignore such contradictions in real life.

The name Newrichard Proudlove suggests both the fortunes recently amassed by members of the privileged class and the arrogance with which they flaunt their wealth while treating their less fortunate countrymen with disdain. Proudlove's thick American accent evokes connotations of vulgar materialism and parodies the affectedness of the French spoken by many newly wealthy Cameroonians. The structural inequity of the situation that Proudlove exploits to acquire his six automobiles and ten villas is underscored by his willingness to give high-class prostitutes a hundred thousand CFA francs for a few hours of their time while threatening to withhold his maid's four thousand-franc monthly salary on account of her need to care for a sick child. As Professor of Social Affairism at the Higher Royal Academy in a country where the Royal Radio and the Great National Daily report the activities of government agencies like the Ministry in Charge of Improving the Situation of the People, Proudlove lectures on authentic black capitalism and on ways to describe dishonest activities so they cannot be called thievery.

The real crime exposed by Moktoï in his satirical *L'Homme bien* is society's acquiescence in the corrupt values of people like Proudlove. When Proudlove imagines that he has overheard a critical remark about his behaviour, he turns to the audience and declares piously, 'Ah gets along. Gettin' along ain't stealin'. Ah'm no crook!'[9] Behind his protestation of innocence is the implicit claim that he is merely taking care of himself and that anyone in his position would do the same. This assumption is of course widespread in Cameroonian society, but by placing it in the mouth of an exaggeratedly comic figure, Moktoï challenges audiences to laugh at it, for if they reflect on the cause of their laughter, they will recognize that such assumptions also obtain in the real world.

At the end of the play, Proudlove is arrested, and justice seems to have been served, but it soon becomes evident that Moktoï's character has come to grief not because of what he did but because he did it so brazenly. As the police inspector who charges him with the embezzlement of public funds reminds him, 'you need to embellish the facade, Mr. Newrich.'[10] In essence, he is condoning Proudlove's attitude and implying that most people share it, but he is also recognizing that, if the profiteering of the privileged class is to continue, those who benefit from it must respect a certain decorum by camouflaging their thefts. The implication is that the corrupt employees in his office will continue to be corrupt and that the new director will operate according to the same standards as he did. The justice that apparently prevails is thus undercut, suggesting that the story of Proudlove is actually an indictment of the society that bred him and others like him.

In addition to the music and poetry recitations introduced into performances of *L'Homme bien*, an offstage announcer comments on the action and invites audiences to ponder the significance of what they are witnessing. A prologist assures them that theatre is but the imitation of life. At one point, the announcer even reads René Philombe's 'Dénonciation civique,' a poem that lampoons those who demand a thousand and one meals while their fellow countrymen are starving to death. By constantly breaking the illusion of verisimilitude in this way, Moktoï prevents spectators from dismissing the play as frivolous. The farcical aspects of *L'Homme bien* are not gratuitous, for they serve to rip the veil of respectability from attitudes that people tend to regard as normal.

The performances of Ndo, Afana, and Moktoï have not been universally appreciated by Cameroonian intellectuals, who lament what they regard as a penchant for mindless laughter in comedies with no redeeming social value. One commentator referred to their drama as 'the exploitation of tribal prejudices and, at the same time, of behavior triggered by an inadaptation to rapid modernization. The most vulgar farces, misperceptions, images, and puns in the work of all three rely upon a rustic pidgin that provokes laughter among city people convinced they are above all that.'[11] Nevertheless, Ndo, Afana, and Moktoï did succeed in developing a comic style that elicited an enthusiastic response from many Cameroonians. Unlike the more conservative popular fiction of the period, their dramas contained elements of social criticism, and by late 1981 when the government began to scrutinize theatrical productions more closely, Moktoï in particular experienced difficulty in obtaining official permission to stage works like *L'Homme bien*.

The emergence of a Cameroonian popular culture during the late 1970s illustrates how writers draw upon the stereotyped expectations of common people to create literary works capable of interesting them. As in many European societies, this popular culture reached a larger segment of the population than did the high culture supported by the country's intellectual establishment. If the identity concepts implicit in Cameroonian popular fiction and drama are highly conventional, they are also modern in the sense that they place primary emphasis on individual consciousness. Although popular literature in most parts of the world exhibit similar characteristics, their presence in countries like Cameroon is significant because it suggests that people who do not belong to the intellectual elite have begun to adopt modern notions of self-definition. Such notions are often trite commonplaces, but they enter into the collective consciousness of the people and influence the way they think about themselves. Cameroonian popular literature reflects and reinforces this development in a variety of ways.

Notes

[1] Fannie Lalande Isnard, 'Vendre des livres en Afrique: Une Expérience,' *The African Book Publishing Record* 6, 3–4 (1980), pp. 205–07.

[2] F.C. Ngam, *The Tricks of a Smuggler* (Victoria: private, 1980), p. 25.

[3] Advertising flier '*Sur le Chemin du suicide*' ['Après avoir perdu tous ses parents dans un accident de circulation à Cotonu, après avoir été detourné, empoisonné, Naha Désiré dit l'Enfant Maudit, a pu raconter sa vie triste et misérable dans un roman de 100 pages. Le jeune écrivain attend actuellement a Yaoundé une mort lente et impitoyable qui le guette car le cancer ne pardonne jamais. Si vous avez souffert dans votre vie ou si vous aimez connaître la souffrance des autres, lisez *Sur le Chemin du suicide*.']

[4] Naha Désiré, *Sur le Chemin du suicide* (Yaoundé: Edition du Démi-Lettré, 1979), p. 21. ['... la mort ne sera plus, il n'y aura plus de souffrance, plus de guerre, plus de haine, ni de crime. Les maladies et les disettes seront choses du passé.']

[5] Naha, *Le Destin a frappé trop fort* (Yaoundé: Les Editions Populaires de Yaoundé, 1980), p. 26 ['... il y aura du pain pour tout un chacun.']

[6] These interviews were conducted bv Karen Keim and reported in her 'Popular Fiction Publishing in Cameroon', *The African Book Publishing Record* 9 (1983), pp. 7–11.

[7] Interview with Daniel Ndo, *Cameroon Tribune* 67 (Sept. 17, 1974), p. 4. ['Il faut un spectacle complet et total qui puisse embrasser la globalité de la vie africaine.']

[8] Interview with Deiv K. Moktoï, *Cameroon Tribune* 1271 (Sept. 14, 1978), p. 2. ['... les nouvelles contradictions des sociétés africaines ... un développement global et équilibré des peuples africains.']

[9] Deiv K. Moktoï (David Kemzeu), *L'Homme bien de là-bas* (Yaoundé: Uhuru Drama Productions, 1980), p. 37. ['Je débrouille. Débrouiller n'est pas voler. Je ne suis pas un voleur!']

[10] Moktoï, *L'Homme bien*, p. 49. ['Il faut embellir la façade, Mr. Newrich.']

[11] Antoine Ahanda, '1981: Bilan de l'année culturelle,' *Cameroon Tribune* 2275: (Jan. 14, 1982), p. 2. ['... l'exploitation à la fois de préjugés tribaux et de comportements nés de l'inadaptation au modernisme rapide. Chez les trois, les farces les plus basses, les quiproquos, les images et les calembours utilisent un langage petit nègre qui fait rire des citadins convaincus d'être au-dessous de tout cela.']

IME IKIDDEH

The Character of Popular Fiction in Ghana

Reference
C. Heywood (ed.) *Perspectives on African Literature*
London: Heinemann, 1971: 106–16

Hardly noticed, Ghanaian popular literature in English has come of age, and placed alongside similar literature in Nigeria, it reveals traits acquired during the period of character formation different from those belonging to its famous West African prototype, the 'Onitsha market literature'.[1] In Ghana most of the practitioners in popular writing have been people with considerable formal education armed with secondary school and journalists' certificates. And they have generally approached their 'art', if not their trade, with a sophistication unequalled by their Onitsha counterparts. Their books when published are not peddled at lorry stations – with all the advantages of that method – rather, they go into competition in university bookshops and leading department stores with Agatha Christie and Edgar Wallace. (I have seen them sold alongside the classics in English.) Whereas Nigerian popular literature includes a sizeable amount of experiments in drama, the Ghanaian product, except in one or two cases, has been exclusively prose fiction.[2] Nor does it exploit political and other topical issues of the day except very remotely. In one respect at least, however, it has kept to the tradition of all popular art: cooked to the taste of large numbers, finished and served out fast and consumed while it is still hot. If Ghanaian popular literature has shown nothing of the profusion of Onitsha writing – and you can almost count off the number of available titles on your fingers and toes[3] – part of the explanation must be that the bulk of this literature has a comparatively short history dating back only a few years.

Among the reasons for the late rise of popular fiction in Ghana, indeed of written literature generally, one of the most plausible is the correspondingly late rise of indigenous printing enterprise. Writing, in spite of the elusive concepts of art and inspiration, is, by and large, enterprise, and even if other forms of it are not, popular writing by its very nature is. For the pamphleteers who crowded the streets of Onitsha before the Nigerian war, setting up a small press and getting a marketable book out of it was as much a business as retail trade in cloth, the spirit that guided it, if not the methods, being that which Charles Jenner satirizes in England of the late eighteenth century:

> Why not engage with Noble or with Bell,
> To weave thin novels that are sure to sell?
> Thrice happy authors, who, with little skill,
> In two short weeks can two short volumes fill.[4]

As far as I know, nowhere in Ghana was the commercial spirit ever translated into an accumulation of indigenous printing and publishing enterprise – as one found in Onitsha, Aba and Port Harcourt – to promote literature on a popular level. Even now, although initiative in this field has risen considerably, most of the country's popular literature is printed by the public-owned State Publishing Corporation. In spite of our ideals, literary history would be inclined to the view that the economic motive in writing and the writer's well-known urge to express or communicate need not be mutually exclusive. Indeed they quite often discover art too in their company! In any case, the importance one claims for popular literature in Onitsha or Accra would be more a functional than a qualitative one.

Among the titles of popular fiction extant in Ghana, those by J. Benibengor Blay must rank among the earliest.[5] (One of the younger writers has fondly described Blay to me as 'the father of us all'.) Blay's *Emelia's Promise* first appeared in 1944 and went into three editions, followed 'at the request of several readers' by the conclusion of Emelia's story, *After the Wedding* (two editions). Recently, the two works have been combined into a neatly bound volume under the title *Emelia's Promise and Fulfilment*. *Be Content with your Lot*, 1947 and *Love in a Clinic*, 1957, are little more than short stories, each booklet being less than thirty pages long. Benibengor Blay is a versatile writer who has published works of fiction, as well as several travel books, a history, some poetry, essays and memoirs.[6] Once Junior Minister of Education in Ghana, Blay now lives in retirement, seemingly reprinting his books for a living.

If *Emelia* is representative of his work, then Blay stands for an old and past order of Ghanaian fiction. His narrative ability is considerable, his English idiom is near-perfect, yet in telling this conventional love story of an all-virtuous woman, the writer shows a lack of realism in setting, character and attitude that must shock present-day Ghanaian audiences. Everything from the lush diction to the unrelieved moral earnestness is guided by the standards of eighteenth-century England.

As a character Emelia is as implausible as the basis for her attachment to Joe Kellon is unconvincing. A kind of shallow Pamela, she is hailed in the novel as 'though human, [having] all the qualities of an angel'. Such is her virtue that in spite of all the cruelty of her husband, and humiliations from his mistresses, 'like Job she underwent those hard tests and kept her faith alive'. The setting of the novel is supposed to be a town in Ghana and the characters to be Ghanaians, but Emelia's father receives one of his daughter's suitors after dinner in 'the drawing-room', and one of the winning qualities he must display is that of 'a good conversationalist'! The names of Emelia's five suitors in themselves declare where they belong: Joe Kellon, Karl Milton, Jones Mellor, Thomas Byron and Jack Doe.

Blay stands apart from the younger writers he has helped to inspire, the pathetic example of talent warped to ruin by the facts of history. His sincerity notwithstanding, the values he holds out to his public bear little relationship to reality, least of all the reality of his own soil. If Canadians and New Zealanders have been stunned by what they now recognize as the colonial slavishness of some of their early writers, then Blay perhaps deserves more than pity.[7] Besides, his later work, for example *Love in a Clinic*, shows that his fiction is moving towards naturalization in Ghana. Perhaps political independence in the same year has something to do with this? Perhaps too, it is of significance that *Love in a Clinic* is printed by Graphic Press, publishers of a national daily, and *Emelia* is done by the Presbyterian Press?

In any case, it is in direct opposition to the puritanical morality of *Emelia* that in the fierce debate on social evils that makes up Kobina Nortey's *The Man with Two Wives*, a character can utter the conclusion:

> It's therefore a fact that the drinking of distilled alcohol is merely an artificial means of supplementing what nature had already prescribed to the well-being of the human body.

In the debate on marriage, Albert Busa, described as 'a debater capable of parliamentary behaviour', sees monogamy as 'an imported form of marriage with all its hypocritical aspects', and polygamy as

> a form of marriage native to us and as a historic institution nursed on the same cradle with the hills.[8]

And is it any surprise that in Nortey the man with two wives wins the day?

As in Western literature, the man-woman relationship inside and outside marriage is a dominant interest in Ghanaian popular fiction. But although it keeps alive the romantic tradition of wild dreams, sentimental protestations, tears and heartbreaks – and the convenience of the epistolary form is fully exploited here[9] – the positions in the man-woman tangle are often reversed. In Ghanaian fiction, the woman is almost invariably the cause of friction and disruption. The man becomes a powerless victim of her extravagance, greed, duplicity or unfaithfulness. Invariably too, it is the man's wealth or status that attracts her into any relationship. Wealth, the corrupting mammon, is condemned, and with it, the acquisitive attitude, but there is undeclared admiration for the man who has got his loot without trouble; the respect he commands, the influence he exerts, and the pleasures open to him in his community are all too lavishly emphasized. As for the woman in these novelettes, usually somewhat educated and domiciled in the town, she is condemned by standards both traditional and Christian which are contrary to her acquired urban values. In the end she ruins herself and sometimes her man as well:

> Akua Brenya's insatiable lust for easy money and expensive living had driven her ... to marry an elderly Nzima rich man...

So begins Nsiah-Bota's *Love in a Tragedy*. The story ends with the insanity of her first husband and the deaths of the second and of Akua herself. Konadu's *Shadow of Wealth*, *Don't Leave me Mercy*, *A Husband for Esi Ellua*[10] and Donkor's *Pretty Betty Sent me Crashing*[11] are all in this cycle. But by far the most corrupt woman, portrayed in her most sinister aspect, is to be found in E. K. Mickson's *Who Killed Lucy* series. It leads logically to his severest verdict on her in his latest volume.

> Truly, woman is poison. And the moment you begin to move with a woman, you must know you are moving with poison.[12]

In one instance only, in the only work in my collection designed for the stage, is an author entirely on the side of the woman. Skot, the writer of *The Tears of a Jealous Husband* protests in the preface:

> Some husbands do not permit their wives to talk to anyone – be that one a man or a woman. Is the wife to be cut off from society because she is married? No!

The action of the play takes place in court where Kwesi Maniawu is standing trial following a mistaken arrest for house-breaking during one of his spying missions on his wife. One of the play's most dramatic qualities is the hilarious rendering in pidgin English of the evidence of an illiterate policeman.

The most prominent popular fiction writers in Ghana today are Asare Konadu and E. K. Mickson. Between them they share about a dozen titles, the major part published during the last two years. Together they dominate the fiction market in Ghana. Both are young: they are in their thirties. Both started writing through journalism – Mickson is editor of the weekly *Ghana Pictorial*. Each has set up his own publishing business: Konadu, the Anowuo Educational Publications; Mickson, Micky Publications. It is to them that one must look for the trends of contemporary Ghanaian popular fiction.

By far the best known of Mickson's fiction is the *Who Killed Lucy* series. *When the Heart Decides* came out early in 1966, and following its popularity, Mickson added the main title of the series in 1967 which was easily followed by the concluding part *Now I Know* in August 1968. A month after came his latest, *The Violent Kiss* and *Woman is Poison*, and in the making is another to be called *God is Suffering*.

When the Heart Decides explains why Frank Ofosu decides to write the dramatic letter that opens this novelette to 'his own Sweetie', Lucy. Part of the letter reads:

> I have therefore been compelled to go against the very dictates of my heart to ask you to let us put an end to our love affair as from 8 p.m. this fateful Wednesday.

From this point we are led through the story of Frank and Lucy in retrospect. Over the years the innocent Frank has been the victim of Lucy's duplicity in love, 'double-crossing' (rather more than triple here!) as it is locally known. While Lucy is loudly professing love, there are in fact four other men in her life including a 'tight' friend of Frank's, and Frank's office boss. In each case Frank has discovered the trickery and his Sweetie has promised to be a good girl. But not Lucy. The instincts that drive her into unfaithfulness seem to lie outside her control. The author, however, takes little advantage of the psychological (or is it pathological?) possibilities inherent here, nor can he make Frank into anything but a weak, sentimental lover who goes on forgiving and loving the unlovable.

But Mickson's narrative technique is more complex than his characters might suggest. Frank is telling the story to confidants: his friend Seth, and Lucy's friend Lily. Seth in turn is reporting the story to us straight from Frank's mouth, with his own interjections of the shock of the Lucy story to himself and Lily. (The method reminds one of *Wuthering Heights* and some of the tales of Conrad.) The intervention of the two friends is too late, as Frank's heart has already decided. In part two the letter is delivered. Lucy, a mixture of pride, regret and more 'double-crossing' involving her other lovers, is later back with Frank – thanks to the persistent efforts of Seth and Lily. But for Frank it cannot be the same again, however good Lucy tries to be. In the end Lucy is stabbed in circumstances which tend to incriminate Frank, and she loses a leg in hospital as a result.

Part three is a mixed bag. It starts off with Lucy's great suffering, remorse and repentance, continues into a ghost story in which Frank features under an assumed name, and ends as a piece of detective exercise. But the author manages to tie them all together. Lucy dies a wretched cripple. Frank, once thought dead, reappears to be cleared of police charges. By turning the screw of suffering a little too tight on Lucy, this last part has the effect of directing the reader's sympathy towards her, for Lucy becomes a kind of Moll Flanders denied salvation. For Mickson, the strong moral purpose of the Lucy story dictates that poetic justice must work full cycle. Lucy ends up in the grave just as Janet in *Woman is Poison* walks out of court to begin a life sentence with hard labour.

The moral remains the writer's primary assignment in these stories, persistent and undisguised. And why not? In the Introduction to *Who Killed Lucy* he explains he is telling the story as 'a forewarning to many a young man desperately in love, against heartbreaks'. He goes on:

> because it will serve as a reprimand and perhaps a 'purgative' to those of our ladies who, flattered by their beauty, popularity or positions in life, make not only folly but also donkeys of themselves by remaining rolling stones in the hands of men.

Women have firmly but good-humouredly protested to Mickson against his strictures but many men have congratulated him. (A minister of religion used the Lucy story for a sermon with tremendous effect.) Was *The Violent Kiss* designed to appease the wounded women? There, Princess Serwaa deserts an eligible young man at the church door, but it is to marry her own choice even though he is a slave. The concluding sentence is significant:

> I am adding that: There is always a way where there is true love, and that in all sincerity, love knows no bounds.

In Konadu's work, responsibility for the breakdown in relationships is often more evenly shared between the man and the woman. Only Mercy comes near to being 'poison' but she is not as sinister as any of Mickson's women. Mercy tricks Owusu into marriage but only because of the man's naivety. After heartache and separation, the two are re-united.

Naivety and reconciliation come up again in *Shadow of Wealth*. Here the partners are victims of circumstance. Independent, but rural and simple, Alice arrives in Accra in search of a job and easily becomes the mistress of Frimpong, Managing Director of the big business which employs her. But Frimpong is wrong in thinking that money alone can guarantee the young woman's contentment. The novel traces Alice's naïve fascination with wealth, her subsequent disenchantment and fight to free herself; Frimpong ruins his business but gets reconciled to his wife.

A significant feature of Konadu's fiction is its abundant use of Ghanaian customs as the basis for plot – a far cry from Benibengor Blay's drawing-rooms. Konadu has personally undertaken research into certain customs of the Akan, and evidence of it is to be seen particularly in *Come Back Dora*, *Night Watchers of Korlebu* and *A Woman in her Prime*.[13] The first of these is from beginning to end an exposition of Akan customary funeral rites, but the novel unfortunately does not gain much by it. Boateng is a lifeless character who is there only to enable the author to conduct us through an episodic ritual. Neither he nor the Church is powerful enough in their opposition to the rites to effect any intended conflict in the novel. Boateng's insistence that he has 'killed' his wife and the remorse he is supposed to be living through remain unconvincing. (I am not one of those who want nothing of anthropology in our creative literature, but if the African Studies Centre of a university reprints a novel presumably for anthropological studies, then I know where it rightly belongs.)[14]

Yet Konadu is the most talented among Ghanaian writers of popular fiction and the one who, like Cyprian Ekwensi before him, could become a major figure in West African writing.[15] The fact that already he has had a novel published internationally must be seen as a recognition of his potential. Versatile and enterprising, Asare Konadu devotes all his working time to writing, publishing and allied businesses. He has successfully run an Ideal Home

Exhibition and soon he is bringing overseas publishers to a Book Fair in Accra. Part of Konadu's present ambition is to provide Ghanaians with more to read, and in this connection, his Anowuo Educational Publications is obtaining rights from foreign publishers to reproduce locally a selected number of books popular among his countrymen. In a country where prices of books are rather high and their importation has to be covered by a licence, the advantages of such an arrangement are only too obvious.

Mickson shows tremendous inventive ability. His sentimental love scenes are the type that will appeal to a great many young readers – a typical letter in *Who Killed Lucy* begins:

> My Sweet Sweetie,
> In fact life without you is lifeless ...

And ends:

> ... keep loving, till we meet, in our dreams under our usual 'forget-me-not tree'.

But he is yet to develop the creative insight and the sensitive approach to characters and situations which Konadu is capable of. Here is the opening paragraph of *Husband for Esi Ellua*:

> There had been no rain in Eshiem for some time now. The river running north of the village was dry. The bed of sand and small pebbles was dug to yield water for domestic use. Women waited several hours for the water to fill the holes and with little calabashes scooped it into long-necked earthenware waterpots. The sun came up early. The red fiery ball rose from the east, blotting up every drop of dew before it. And the tall grass which stood round the village dried up and danced with the dry winds. There were the trees too, which stood out majestically above the grass and at first seemed not to take notice of the wind and sun. Then, as the sun continued to burn everything before it and the water holes dried up, all their leaves turned brown.

That could come from the work of the most sophisticated novelist. The writer's evocation of drought is in itself excellent prose, but in this community the phenomenon described is a sign of something gone wrong, for when the evergreen 'nyamedua' tree in the goddess's grove begins to shed its leaves the villagers of Eshiem know for certain that some unusual disaster is around the corner. And that disaster which the novel goes on to describe in the life of Abaka and his village is the beginning of the Second World War. *A Husband for Esi Ellua* is far from being a great novel, though a very readable one. Like others of Konadu's works it is uneven in quality.

The question of unevenness could form a study of its own. For teachers of English the area of anxiety centres around the language of these works, as Mickson and Konadu, both with a large clientele in schools and colleges, are subject to crude journalese, cliches, grandiloquence and such-like evils, the former rather more so. And both not infrequently suffer from Tutuola-esque grammatical lapses, among the commonest in Konadu being the omission of essential pronouns:

> That is what I have been trying to get Dad to see and wouldn't (i.e. *he* wouldn't). But there is a dance at Adibo tonight and would want you to take me there (i.e. *I*).[16]

There is in addition the gamut of West African (Ghanaian) English and personal coinages – which means that lovers in Mickson write to 'themselves' not to each other, and Lucy's love affair with a certain young man ends with her 'bringing forth by him', Konadu's postal agent looks 'askantly' at customers, and Boateng is the first man to build a 'sand crete' house in his village.

No doubt a problem does exist here but it should not be exaggerated. The West African teacher of English must admit that of the factors that militate against his classroom efforts popular fiction by no means provides the greatest threat. Besides, although language is central to literature it cannot be the only consideration in it, certainly not what the great majority of young people will read popular fiction for. The will of language to change – particularly in a new home – is well known. West African coinages and other innovations which do not necessarily offend against idiomatic English will, for example, continue to press for recognition of the type accorded their more prolific American cousins.[17] A closer look at some of these writings might reveal that their untidiness is not a reflection of the writer's expressional handicap. Popular fiction by its very nature flies out of the writer's pen with supersonic speed. In Ghana, where the writer is often his own editor, publisher and distributor, a ready loaf may be only half-baked. And this is where teachers of English, critics, and experienced writers come in.

Is there any reason why the works of the more promising of these practitioners should not on publication enjoy local reviews? Surely some of the writers would benefit from comments. There are those who would appreciate help in editing. The State Publishing Corporation, no doubt with a record to be proud of in this field, cannot afford, for the sake of its own reputation, to be mere printers without the services of trained proof-readers.

For me, the most startling facts have been in the sales figures of these books, and with them, the readership. The summary is as follows:[18]

Shadow of Wealth	25,000	Has had fourth printing
Don't Leave Me Mercy	30,000	Reprint imminent
Come Back Dora	30–45,000	Still selling
Painful Road to Kadjebi	15,000	No reprint
A Husband for Esi Ellua	10,000	
Night Watchers of Korlebu	8,000	
When the Heart Decides	40,000	Has had third printing
second printing of	10,000	Sold out in 2–3 weeks
Who Killed Lucy	40,000	Fourth printing imminent
Now I Know	10,000	Sold out within a month
The Violent Kiss	10,000	Sold out within a month
Woman is Poison	10,000	Sold out within a month

Only a few hundred ever go outside Ghana. These figures are in spite of the fact that *Woman is Poison*, a pamphlet of 78 pages, sells at the equivalent of five shillings. My inquiries revealed that although the readership may be highest among people with minimal formal education, large numbers of lawyers and university people read popular fiction, even if they complain about the standard. Young women form a high proportion of readers.

After those disclosures we may have to re-state our opinions on the absence of a reading public in West Africa, and we shall be indifferent to these writings only at our own risk.

Notes

[1] Several articles have appeared on this subject. My comparisons are based on Donatus Nwoga's under this title in *Transition*, Vol. 4, 1965.
[2] I have on record only one play and a Love Letter Writer.
[3] Largely oral and in Ghanaian languages, the popular theatre of the Concert Parties is not considered here. Some of the titles in the bibliography of Ghanaian popular fiction at the end of this chapter are not available.
[4] Charles Jenner, *Town Eclogues*, 1772; quoted in J. M. S. Tompkins, *The Popular Novel in England 1770–1800*, Methuen, p. 1.
[5] The possibility exists of much earlier fiction: the blurb of Nortey's *The Man with Two Wives*, 1964, credits the writer with works 'mostly fiction ... published in the Gold Coast some thirty years ago'.
[6] For a full list of Blay's fiction, see the bibliography at the end of this chapter.
[7] Compare John Matthews, 'The Canadian Experience', and W. H. Pearson, 'The Recognition of Reality', in *Commonwealth Literature*, Heinemann, 1965, pp. 21–31; 32–47.
[8] For a similar debate on this subject, see Obi Egbuna, *Wind Versus Polygamy*, 1964.
[9] See J. M. S. Tompkins, op. cit., chapter on 'Theory and Technique'.
[10] Asare Konadu also uses the name K. A. Bediako. For convenience only the name Konadu is used in this paper.
[11] Donkor's story appears in his volume, *The Troubles of a Bachelor.*
[12] E. K. Mickson, *Woman is Poison*, last sentence.
[13] Asare Konadu, *A Woman in her Prime*, Heinemann, 1967.
[14] African Studies Centre, UCLA, is reprinting this novel. Also republished by Heinemann under the title *Ordained by the Oracle*, 1969.
[15] Cyprian Ekwensi's first novel, *When Love Whispers* was published in Onitsha in 1947.
[16] *Don't Leave Me Mercy*, p. 75; *Shadow of Wealth*, p. 121.
[17] For more of my views on this, see Ime Ikiddeh, *Drum Beats*, E. J. Arnold, 1968, p. 13.
[18] The system of sales facilitates the reckoning of figures though approximate. The writers themselves are my source.

A bibliography of Ghanaian popular fiction

BEDIAKO, K. A.
Don't Leave Me Mercy, Anowuo Educational Publications, 1966
A Husband for Esi Ellua, Anowuo Educational Publications, 1967
BLAY, J. B.
Emelia's Promise, Benibengor Book Agency, Aboso, 1944
After the Wedding, published with *Emelia's Promise* as *Emilia's Promise and Fulfilment*, Waterville Publishing House, Accra, 1967
Be Content with your Lot, Benibengor Book Agency, Aboso, 1947
Love in a Clinic, Benibengor Book Agency, Aboso, 1957
Parted Lovers, Benibengor Book Agency, Aboso, 1948
Dr Bengia Wants a Wife, Benibengor Book Agency, Aboso, 1953
Operation Witchcraft, Benibengor Book Agency, Aboso, 1956
Stubborn Girl, Benibengor Book Agency, Aboso, 1958
DARKO, D. O.
Friends Today Enemies Tomorrow, Bureau of Ghana Languages, Accra, 1959
DONKOR, WILLIE
The Troubles of a Bachelor, Liberty Press, Accra
The Weals and Woes of a Certain Scholarship
The Forbidden Taste, Facts and Fiction Agency, 1968
A Stab in my Heart
HIHETAH, R. K.
Painful Road to Kadjebi, Anowuo, Educational Publications, Accra 1966
KONADU, S. A.
The Wizard of Asamang, Anowuo Educational Publications, Accra 1963
Shadow of Wealth, Anowuo Educational Publications, Accra 1966
Come Back Dora, Anowuo Educational Publications, Accra 1966
Night Watchers of Korlebu, Anowuo Educational Publications, Accra 1967
The Lawyer who Bungled his Life, Anowuo Educational Publications, Accra 1965
MICKSON, E. K.
When the Heart Decides, Ghana Publishing Corporation, Tema 1966
Who Killed Lucy, Ghana Publishing Corporation, Tema 1967
Now I Know, Ghana Publishing Corporation, Tema 1968
Woman is Poison, Ghana Publishing Corporation, Tema 1968
The Violent Kiss, Ghana Publishing Corporation, Tema 1968
NORTEY, K.
The Man with Two Wives, Peacock Publication, Accra 1964
NSIAH-BOTA, K.
Love in a Tragedy, no date
SKOT
The Tears of a Jealous Husband, 1965
WAMEK, UNCLE
The Love Letter Writer, no date

2 Perspectives on East African Popular Fiction

RAOUL GRANQVIST

Storylines, Spellbinders & Heartbeats

Decentring the African Oral–Popular Discourse

Reference
R. Granqvist (ed.) *Major Minorities: English Literatures in Transit* Amsterdam: Rodopi, 1992: 55–70

Popular literature, it is commonly believed, is a discourse that primarily relies on broad narrative stereotypes, akin to those informing the thriller and the detective story. Other assumptions are that it is unreflective and repetitive, that the author normally disclaims originality of theme, and that the 'impersonal' voice insists on projecting a superior 'originality' and presence by mingling and compounding narrative devices to create a maximum of shock and suspense. The belief is also that this literature, the 'Spellbinders' and the 'Heartbeats,' thrives on contemporary and local issues or topics and aspires to entertain rather than explore or educate. So its success is dependent on whether, and how adequately, a contract has been negotiated between the reader and the marketplace. The oral tale or the 'Storyline' has always skirted the boundaries of the densely populated 'mainland' and also on occasion invaded it. One could put it differently, and claim that the popular story tends to be oral by origin: it is not only that its physique is largely structured by oral performance devices – the popular story, it is well known, is a mediated and 'dramatized' story that for its success has to subvert the mediatory rules of both print culture and oral culture. 'Oral-popular discourse' is therefore an appropriate designation or abstraction to qualify a cultural product that has special African connotations.

To what extent these assumptions are viable is not the subject of this essay; they only foreground what I will have to say. I will position my discussion of the African oral-popular discourse within tendencies in more recent scholarship which show that texts defined along the assumptions submitted above may best be studied as 'transgressive' and 'metonymic.'[1] They transgress the boundaries between genres, between print and voice, between 'low' and 'high,' between 'now' and 'then.' They are truly metonymic, undetermined, and continuous. This makes them also vulnerable and co-optable for hegemonic purposes. The presence or absence in them of an authoritative centre determines, then, the range of their eclectic capacity. It seems to me that an ongoing tug-of-war pervades African text productions, involving the Janus-face of 'tradition' as both preserver and liberator and the demands generated by the politics of the modern state. In the following pages I will discuss the functionality of the oral-popular discourse in four of the main text productions that I have named: the oral (-derived) tale, the manual, the pamphlet and the thriller.

The tale as nation-building device

The oral tale (or any other oral material that could be subsumed under the rubric 'folk') has always been applied to enhance group cohesion and group identity. The supposition is that oral traditions relate to the very centre of a people's founding 'authentic' culture. Of course, the crux is how to determine what or who is representative of a particular national authenticity. This is a dilemma that will always cause cultural dissension and anguish on a large scale.

Examples of such texts can be found in many parts of Africa: mine come mainly from Kenya. Its 'official' and 'sanctioned' (i.e. recommended) literature relies heavily on Kikuyu or Luo oral narratives (or translations from these) brought together because of their alleged fusion of 'authenticity' and 'popularity.' One of the many handbooks of oral literature produced for use in schools and universities describes this dichotomy in the following words:

> In the Kenyan situation, the study of oral literature offers the students and researchers ample opportunities to understand the values of the different communities. It is on these values that our nation can cultivate and enhance the creation of unity and nationhood. Once we understand these values, of the Kenyan peoples, we can use the same oral literature to negate the distorting influence that continues to adversely affect our people.[2]

The editor pursues the paradox of harmonizing the nation-building project and the notion of upholding cultural differences (Luo and Kikuyu, etc). Oral literature thus canonized would then, the editor suggests, counteract foreign or neo-colonial infiltrations. The author of Heinemann Secondary Readers' *Some Popular Ananse Stories: Ghanaian Folk Tales*, Hannah Dankwa-Smith, prefaces her book in a similar vein:

> In selecting the stories I deliberately did not include any folktales from other countries [why would she?]. The aim is to introduce young people to tales of their own land (Ghana) since they tend to read a lot of foreign stories in school libraries.[3]

Naturally, an editorial principle such as Dankwa-Smith's is legitimate insofar as its main concern is the retrieval and the familiarization of Ananse stories for readers in Ghana (and elsewhere); but if it suggests that this can only be achieved through segregation, the principle is less rewarding. A cultural ideal that is based on exclusion violates the syncretistic and 'open-ended' paradigm of the oral 'text.' The oral tale as inscribed by tradition and cultural heterogeneity will then be homogenized and particularized. Apart from the bombast, it contains a declaration such as 'we need oral literature for our self-realization and self-confidence as genuine members of an African society,' which entertains two romances: one derived from pan-African idealism, the other from Western idealism about the alleged power of literature.[4]

The cultural control which orality did exercise in its locality, it must be remembered, was always relative, as it preconditioned collaterality and communality between the individual member and the community. However, when projected through the 'recommended book list' channel, this 'controlling' principle loses its capacity to negotiate art. Oral literature has then evolved into 'conservative art,' or elite art, and excludes the 'sweet words' of the inspired tale.

> Thus it has been said that oral literature is a conservative art, educating and reinforcing in members of the society appropriate ways they should act, behave and think. It may also seem easier to pass on knowledge in a story, advice through a proverb, or suitable male/female behaviour in a dance step. Yet the 'sweet words' of oral literature are more than a form of cultural control, however honeyed they may he. Oral literature is not 'frozen' in the way the printed word becomes fixed to a page. It allows for self expression, renewal, innovation and creativity.[5]

Most African state-owned publishing companies have capitalized on the nationalistic self-presentation scheme associated with the discourse of the traditional tale. The Kenya Literature Bureau and The Literature Bureau of Zimbabwe, to name only two such companies, are extremely active in both producing and diffusing oral tale material, at costs that are acceptable to even the poorest rural village school. John Osogo's unsophisticated little anthology *The Bride Who Wanted a Special Present and Other Tales from Western Kenya*, a Kenya Literature Bureau print, first published in 1966, had by 1986 been reprinted seven times, which is quite a figure for such a publication.[6] The drive to publicize and use well-known oral tales is, we have seen, inspired by the pursuit of national homogenization. Both individual writers and publishers participate in it, even if their immediate goal may be far less altruistic or nationalistic than, say, that guiding the Kenya Literature Bureau or the Zimbabwe Literature Bureau. For many of them – in Kenya and elsewhere – publishing for schools and the state is the only means of making ends meet. A fairly recently founded independent Kenyan publishing company, Phoenix Publishers, survives on this kind of publishing. Its series 'Phoenix Young Readers Library' includes neat, handsome, cheap booklets that retell well-known stories from all over Kenya. Actually, a majority of these small books were published in 1968-1969 and earlier by the East African Publishing House. The only change in the Phoenix reprints affects the choice of colours and cover illustrations: the shift from one company to another and the intervening two decades has otherwise had no impact.

About 80 percent of the Phoenix stories are traditional, concerning animals, monsters, ugly sons and beautiful daughters. Titles such as *The Lonely Black Pig*, *The Powerful Magician*, *The Proud Ostrich*, *Beautiful Nyakio*, *The Girl Who Couldn't Keep a Secret* are typical.[7] Only a few of the 34 included in the series by 1988 deal directly with the urban vicissitudes of adolescent life or young experiences outside the narrative frame of a traditional story.[8] Naturally, the success of the series is dependent on and derives from the literary 'nationalization' strategies we have talked about, despite the Phoenix editor's urgent claims that his main interest is to make money outside and in opposition to the political infrastructure.[9]

I have so far been discussing various excluding and interventionist structures that affect the oral tale and its derivations. But the control, as we have seen, can also be inherent, encoded in the tale itself, and less exercised by an external mediator and manipulator. In the streets of Nairobi there circulated as late as 1990 copies of a cartoon series (now defunct) called *Picadithi*, which combines extremely elegantly executed pictures with well organized texts. The cartoon appeared monthly between 1984 and 1986 all over Kenya and was an immediate success, but owing to copyright problems the series was stopped. In terms of circulation, these printed stories moved between larger groups of recipients and across sequences of time and space, like the traditional oral tale. The narrative basis of the cartoons is the Kenyan popular tale; their purpose is to offer entertainment and guidance; their audience are trained listeners, if not accomplished readers. This is the way the magazine launched itself:

Fig. 1. Book selling in Tom Mboya Street, Nairobi. The year is 1994.

> An important part of our African culture is in the traditional stories which have been handed down by word of mouth over the years. The Picadithi series is based on these traditional stories. They are told in words and pictures which are easy and fun to read. *Picadithi stories are a simple way for our children, and ourselves to learn more about our rich Kenyan culture*. Each story has a message and a moral that is as relevant to modern African living as in the past. [sic]

The sentence that I have emphasized is relevant to my discussion. It was deleted somewhere half-way through the series (in no. 12 or no. 13), not only because it contravened logically the philosophy that the last sentence paraphrases. What is at stake is an attenuation of the 'nationalistic' employment of the oral tale. 'Our rich Kenyan culture,' it would seem, had become too controversial a title to describe the wealth of cultural representations that the stories address. The magazine returned via this programmatic, editorial change to the diachronic and synchronic context of the oral tale.

Ironically, in the Kenyan context, as long as the traditional material (legends, tales, etc) could be projected unabridged or unappropriated in a textbook that bore the official stamp, it was hailed as both progressive and functional; but as soon as it was co-opted for literary purposes by a novelist such as Ngugi wa Thiong'o, the same authorities rejected it and even banned the author. The retrieval of Kikuyu folktales, dances, and songs should not just be a retrieval, proudly exhibited in the government 'museums,' Rose Mwangi admonishes. It should instead be

> a challenge to the modern creative artist who has not yet been able to create a literature 'common' to all members of the society as folktales and common and comprehensible to all 'folks' young and old. It is in this communality that creative writers who wish

Fig. 2. Book selling in Tom Mboya Street, Nairobi. The year is 1994.

> to build on their traditional roots and give identity to African literature should seek inspiration and guidance in the handling of form and expression and in developing the vitality of African verbal art in their writing.[10]

But for one-party Kenya this ideal has proved to be a thorny issue. The oral tale in its 'frozen' form is an acceptable commodity for the country's literary arbiters, but the same tale when dressed up and reinterpreted is not. The inherent quality of the oral tale to invite recontextualizations and reaaffirm contiguity with other performances or/of other tales has often been suppressed. The *Picadithi* magazine – if only for a short time – managed to link with these traditions and produce a composite 'text' that combined the referentiality (listener/reader/performance [street, circulation]) of the oral tale with the requisites of print. *Picadithi* was part of the oral culture of the street.

However, Rose Mwangi's appeal for enhanced awareness of the metonymic potentiality of the oral tale in text production has not gone unheeded. Whether the writer is a Chinua Achebe, a Ngugi wa Thiong'o, an Ama Ata Aidoo or any less known (in the west) writer of children's books in the vernacular, the oral material is endlessly manipulated, transferred, or orchestrated in 'new' artistic creations. However, as my purpose is to examine the tension and usage of power inherent in the oral-popular discourse, I will limit my observations to a few texts that are tightly reader- and audience-directed.

Peggy Appiah's *The Children of Ananse* (to give an instance of this category of literature from another part of Africa) is a good example of how an oral-derived metonymic structure can be employed in the retelling of 'new' legends. The book tells about the boy Ntikumah and his life in the village and in school, but Appiah skilfully interweaves into the simple plot enactments of legends that every Ghanaian child is familiar with. So the text reverberates with echoes from an oral tradition that exploits other similar tales or story-telling sessions. The Ananse tradition constitutes a whole that is summoned by the partial contribution of Appiah's literary-cum-educational conception, which thus, as it were, surpasses itself and becomes more than the actual storyline.[11] Intended for young people (the language has been simplified in the second edition [1985]), the narrative structure and the oral tale tradition amalgamate and interact.

Longman Zimbabwe has developed a series called 'Storylines,' a title that underlines the traditional inheritance of story-telling, much as 'Phoenix Young Readers' does in Kenya by its re-printing and re-circulating business. So *Themba and the Crocodile* and *The Raintree* by Rowland Molony, two 'Storylines' books, contrast and assess value systems that are found to disorientate the young. The message they preach is: listen to the echoes from the past, follow the well-trodden paths, but also accommodate yourselves to the modernity that surrounds you.[12]

'Spellbinders,' by the College Press (Zimbabwe), is another popular series directed towards young people. One title in the series, *Tawanda, My Son*, by T. K. Tsodzo, is modelled on an old folk tale about the eagle that was possessed by a spirit.[13] In reality, however, it is a sly commentary on conflicts that haunt contemporary Zimbabwean society. Again, a well-known oral tale is appropriated to re-affirm contiguity with the past and dramatize the present. Interestingly too, the Shona story carries an official stamp of approval. On the back cover a sentence reads: 'This novel was recommended for use in schools and colleges by the Ministry of Education.'

The story as manual of instruction

As is well-known, there are a number of limitations that curb book production in Africa. First of all, there are the enormous costs entailed in local book production, which involve shortage of paper, dependence on foreign currencies, low technology, and failing distribution structures. It is today unbelievably hazardous and almost impossible for an African publisher to produce a book without state subsidies or foreign funds. It is no wonder, then, that most publishers find themselves producing books that have a select audience within the infrastructure of the state.

An additional factor hampering book production is the fact that reading for pleasure or leisure is limited to the elites and to an aspiring middle class, mostly consisting of businessmen, clerks, teachers, students and educated townspeople. Books are commodities that most people cannot afford to buy, and even if they could, reading habits are slow to develop. Novel-reading or reading of stories is in rural parts of the continent still considered an odd and alien activity. It is a preoccupation that is often ridiculed and scorned as either outlandish or colonial. For a people that have always listened to stories and learnt to re-tell and perform them with skill when the situation so required, print offers no real alternative, either by way of composition or consumption. But things are changing.

Stories that warn, recommend, emulate, or exemplify can be found all over our planet; they arise from the oral tradition; they reflect the anguish of the older generation and the natural urge to transmit collective 'memories.' Thus, to use the story to instruct, to teach various skills, and to persuade and politicize is not only a strategy – as we have seen – which oral traditions sanction and promote; it is also a matter of circumstances that originate in social and economic realities. Many African states simply cannot afford printed matter other than that directly used in education and various campaigns.

So a wealth of stories find their way into print because they have been deemed functional and instructive, or because writers have been prompted or commissioned to produce them, in the format either of school textbooks, of supplementary readings, or of simple 'manuals' for improvement of literacy and adult skills.

Normally (but not always) these texts carry the official stamp of approved literature. Many of them are also produced by publishing companies working directly under the government. The imprints of the Kenya Literature Bureau, for instance, project the image of a recently liberated African country in search of old values to combat contemporary dissonances and fractions.

Its counterpart, the Zimbabwe Literature Bureau, works under the same auspices (Zimbabwe Ministry of Education) and with more or less the same goals. It is the country's most active promoter of literature and literacy in the indigenous languages of Zimbabwe, Shona and Ndebele. Its dispatch list of November 1987 includes 115 (53) popular novels, 38 (16) story books, 13 (8) plays, 6 (2) books with proverbs and riddles, and 33 (25) comic stories, and 37 (22) 'instructionals,' all in Shona (within the parenthesis is the corresponding figure for texts in Ndebele). To these one should add 33 English titles, which span a large spectrum of works that are symptomatic of their general popularity, but also demonstrate the importance attributed to the connotations of the oral-popular discourse.

Among these relatively cheap books are titles like: *Jikinya* by C.T. Ndhala,[14] *Shumba and the He-goat* by L. Gutu, *Poultry Keeping* by D.M. Chavhunduke, and *First Visit to a School Library* by T. Makura.

The Literature Bureau normally organizes small publicity campaigns in connection with the launching of a new title. This is done, for instance, by dramatizations or readings on the radio of extracts from the works to be distributed and sold. The Literature Bureau vans then tour the country while their editors hawk the books at the entrance of the village or in the schools. The text received by such an audience is encoded with other multiple versions and extratextual implications. The structures that contain the particular story are multiform, comprising the specific story (author-specific) and the inherent oral tradition in which it is situated, the narrative itself, the Literature Bureau's dramatized radio version of it, the local oral presentation/persuasion/selling, and the interpretative act (reception) itself. This cycle of book production, book distribution, and book consumption may be the closest one can get to witnessing the oral-popular discourse in performing multiple transgressions.

The stories in these 'stories as manuals' may reflect the lives of young girls trapped and deluded, or even more frequently girls courageously combatting illusions, real or insubstantial. In each case the moral teaches the same lesson: trust yourself and accommodate to the dictates of your culture. This message may sometimes be contradictory: it celebrates woman's independence, while at the same time reminding her of her traditional roles in the African household. Such warnings may also contain the seeds of rebellion. The young woman of *Poisoned Love* gives birth to a baby whose father is a street-roamer, for which she is punished by her own death. However, it is understood that she had freed herself.[15] Nyokabi, on the other hand, in Pat Wambui Ngurukie's *I Will Be Your Substitute*, is rewarded by marriage in this life for her constancy and faithfulness to the old mores.[16] In her case, freedom implies subservience. Muthono Likimani's *What Does a Man Want?* laments in a long discursive poem the lot of woman and recommends her to 'Bluff them / That they own you too. / Tell them to walk in / Tell them to walk out / Any time – any day.'[17] Emancipation, the author is advising sardonically, can only come about through female conspiracy. Kwabena Asare Bediako (pseud. Asare Konadu) on the other hand, in his redemptive parable about separation and pain, proposes Christian marriage as an overall solution to conflict.[18] Cynthia E. Hunter has written two romance-manuals of this kind about the life of a nurse: *Truphena Student Nurse* and *Truphena City Nurse*. The parables depict a virtuous triumphant woman and a career of devotion, attachment to principles, and hard work. But it also informs the reader about work in a hospital; *Truphena Student Nurse* includes, it is worth noting, a glossary of medical and technical terms.[19]

The basic thought pattern of stories like 'Killer Drink,' 'Fixing Young Militants,' and 'Money Poisons Affection' in Henry R. Muhanika's *Killer Drink and Other Stories*, is to undermine various forms of vicious social behaviour associated with the urban life of the young; but by evoking and enlisting exemplary act of horror rather irresolutely, the authorial voice of the parables is muted.[20] *Yasin's Dilemma* by Martha Mlagata Mvungi uses a reward to preach her message.[21]

A word must be said again about the class of homiletic stories that are spun around the themes of national unity and liberation. These stories reflect the political aspiration to unite and appease, perhaps also to forget and hide. Children and students are the target, so the lessons are well-planned and no fictional space is allowed for dissent. In an earlier section I examined how these lessons incorporated the oral tale, but these aspirations transcend all literary modes. We also saw that most African countries produce a literature of this kind. Ngugi wa Thiong'o's early novels took to task Kenya's post-independence readiness to dip deep into the western purse of ideas and capital; other Kenyan writers have elaborated the same theme, if not with the same insight and skill. Tom Obondo-Okoyo's 'Heartbeat Book' (which is the name of the series), *A Thorn in the Flesh*, depicts the classic struggle of the old system of value at odds with the imported one: 'staggering under blow after blow, he [Peter Bolo, the teacher-hero] ultimately triumphs over the brash young "intellectuals" who are out to put him on place.'[22] S. Kiyeng's *Echoes of the Two Worlds* gives a nostalgic view of traditional life in Kenya, Bahadur Tejani's *Day after Tomorrow*, set in Kampala, celebrates the emergence of African independence, and Hamza Sokko, in *The Gathering Storm*, portrays the disillusionment connected with Tanzanian Uhuru.[23] In each case the stories purport to advance and discuss ideas of unity and peace. Signs of disunity, examples of political dissent, coups and tribalism are often glossed over in these early post-independence allegorical manuals. As such they are monolithic and one-dimensional; their authoritarian mode of address is not to be questioned.

The story as pan-African pamphlet

There is an expanding market for books with themes that transcend most cultural and ethnic boundaries but which are recognized as peculiar to African readers of light literature. The extremely popular *Pacesetters* books fall within this category. The series is published in Ghana, Nigeria, and Zimbabwe by Macmillan or its local representatives (in Harare by the College Press). The writers are selected from all parts of Africa, the list (there are now over 80 titles) including reputed writers such as Buchi Emecheta (Nigeria) and David Maillu (Kenya), as well as less known writers. The project of the series is to reach the generic (young) African reader, of any denomination and social and ethnic group. Thus the format of the book is small, the average page volume is about 150, the print and the style simple, and the cover picture and the blurb are delineated to catch the young (mostly male) eye. Their purpose is to entertain and to caution.

Many writers of this literature thus contrive plots that dwell on African connections with ruthless western capitalists and international crime syndicates, on gang feuds and chauvinistic politics, which impute serious failings of leadership, sometimes even accusing Africans of collaborating across frontiers (thus again stressing common concerns), on illegal border trade, on conflicts that are commonly viewed as tearing Africans apart (such as tensions between townships and rural communities, between old *mores* and new ideas, between the institution of polygamy and Christian marriage, etc). The stories often define a given evil as an alien force that has imposed itself on its naive and unprepared interlocutors with a seductive vengeance. They are fundamentally cautionary tales or freedom manifestoes. There are many *Pacesetters* that could be characterized along these lines. This is the way Hope Dube's *State Secret*, a Harare *Pacesetter*, is introduced. Its blurb reads:

> In this neatly structured and exciting story, John Talubva goes to the republic of Malambia. Briefed by the President, who fears a coup attempt, Talubva comes up against dangerous men: an ambitious vice-president; a corrupt chief of police. There is a beautiful girl who is not what she seems. And why should a South African millionaire pay a secret visit to Malambia on the eve of the coup? John Talubva finds himself the central character in a dramatic story of treason and treachery.[24]

All the well-known elements of the standard thriller romance are here: love, treachery, and violence. In addition the writer injects into her story the sociopolitical dimension of corruption, a theme which is bound to appeal to any African readership familiar, through the all-too-frequent newspaper reporting, with local representations of petty crime. But the story gets its real pan-African significance from the potentialities of action and political drama provided by the frame of the story: the destabilized zone in southern Africa.

The war against apartheid is a central subject in these discourses. The war takes on a number of appropriate metonymic functions. It can, as we saw, provide the story with a simple narrative backbone which, by definition, is uncontroversial and uncontestable; much as the dichotomy of good and bad needs no novelistic elaboration or justification. Secondly, the war against apartheid is paradigmatic, an all-embracing crusade against the evil transcending all other African skirmishes, great or small. Its figuration in these stories is thus supposed to help harmonize and unite the continent (like the politicized oral tale) against an enemy whose grip reaches deep into colonial history and encircles the future as well.

Stories about the struggle against apartheid are also deployed to subsume domestic issues. Metaphorically they may castigate injustices on a very local level. Many popular Kenyan writers choose to elaborate parallellisms of this kind. Or they are compelled to resort to allegories by the repressive situation under which they live. Finally, antiapartheid themes may stimulate visionary emblems of an Africa at racial peace, a futuristic model of harmony and cooperation that the rest of the world could emulate.[25]

Meja Mwangi's novel *Bread of Sorrow* combines the appeal and the techniques of the international bestseller with the qualitites of the African cautionary pamphlet story.[26] The argument of his novel reads like a white man's apology for his colonial arrogance and intrusion. The main protagonist of the story, a white South African, reforming miraculously in the course of the narrative, encounters an ex-settler, called the Colonel, who had colonized a small coral island off the Tanzanian coast near the Mozambique border. On his island the reformed rogue hides the diamonds he has stolen in South Africa. But when, after having served a prison sentence, he returns there to collect his treasure to hand it over to the ANC, he fails to find it and is killed by South African police. This fantastic allegory of frustrated white redemption and black liberation heroics reads like an extension of the ideological project of the pan-African pamphlet.

The story as urban thriller

Well-known to most students of African literature is the notion of the Onitsha pamphlet. This little book was made – written, produced, and distributed – at the Onitsha market place in eastern Nigeria right after the second world war. Its makers were people with a knack for local story telling and an attentive ear for imported Indian and American pulp novels and popular films. They wrote stories of an immediate interest to the people at the market: about falling in or out of love, disruption of traditional values, corruption of politicians, coercion of women, banditry. Some of these stories were peculiar intermarriages of African story telling conventions and the narrative slant of the western teenage romance; they were in most cases crudely narrated, unashamedly moralizing, and tendentiously instructive. They imbued and incorporated the talk of the day. But they were functional in the sense that they gave imprint to the frustrations, dreams, and anxieties of the people. In this period of dramatic transitions in modern African history, the withdrawal of the former colonial masters and their awkward replacement by an aspiring elite, and the rending apart of well-established institutions of thinking and decision-making, these popular stories were catalysts of no little value. Some of the narratives rose, of course, above the stereotype. In Nigerian literary history Cyprian Ekwensi's name, for instance, is often associated with the emergence of the Onitsha movement. It was through this industry that he gained his apprenticeship, fashioning his skill as a teller of stories with great popular appeal and – one could add – with minimal appeal to the western critic. And there were other writers, too, in early-1960s Nigeria who responded to the Onitsha call and started to write in similar vein.

To cater for a reading public that is present in the absolute sense of this word has always been a main impetus and a challenge in all publishing. The term 'market literature' would then describe texts that are produced and distributed within narrow social confines. They are texts that respond to the immediate needs of their readers, they intimately reflect the broad taste of the today, they are uncouth and simple in diction and style, they are repetitive and imitative, they thrive on prejudices and preconceptions, but they may also be caustic and openly critical of the very mechanisms that generate them.

The *Spear* series, produced by Heinemann Kenya, is perhaps the most reputed successor of the Onitsha pamphlets. The *Spear* books are written by Kenyans for Kenyans. Thus they normally fail to attract readers outside the country; they are not enlightened by an all-African grand subject, like the *Pacesetters*. Instead, they dwell on less sterling, but still familiar, national issues, on scandals, and on the

Figs 3 & 4. A matatu in Nairobi

Fig. 5. One picture in a series of twelve on a wall inside a coffee shop in Duruma Road, Nairobi.

lives of ill-famed Kenyan personalities, bank robbers, criminals, corrupted politicians. They rehearse the familiar, the gossip of newspapers, their topoi are just around the corner; they feed on raving bar jargon and the fast food of the American best seller. In fact the Nairobi of their fabrication could as well be the Manhattan of writers such as Ed McBain. Any one of these could have conceived the following lines that are printed on the back cover of Kenya's most widely read book, Charles Mangua's *Son of Woman*: 'My whoring ma could not figure out who my pop was... I was conceived on a quid and mother drank it. Poor mother. God rest her soul, she is dead.' These are the opening paragraphs of the novel:

> Son of woman, that's me. I am a louse, a blinking louse and I am the jigger in your toe. I am a hungry jigger and I like to bite. I like to bite women – beautiful women. women with tits that bounce. If you do not like the idea you are the type I am least interested in.
>
> Maybe you have heard about me and again maybe you haven't. Either way you have missed nothing. To you I am the crank from downstairs who is not worth knowing. So what?

The casual, devil-may-care, roguish comportment of the hero of this best-seller and the mannerisms of his expression are blank and blatant imitations – with a vengeance – of the stereotypical American thriller which since the beginning of the 1970s has been extremely popular in the urban centres of Kenya. Mangua's book appeared in 1971 and it was an immediate hit. It went through six reprints between 1972 and 1987, and his second best-seller, *A Tail in the Mouth*, from 1972 (reprinted in 1973 and 1974), also fared well.[27] It was not incorporated with the *Spear* series until 1988 (at the same time as *Son of Woman*;[28] its sequel *Son of Woman in Mombasa* appeared in the *Spear* in 1986[29]).

Story-telling can be the art of pretending to tell a scabrous lie, and to imply that it has no meaning, no purpose, no tail. Such telling may, indeed, be a provocation. Charles Mangua's books, which are filled with tongue-in-cheek claptrap, are also still banned in Tanzania (1992), along with some of David Maillu's earliest pornographic concoctions. Both Mangua's and Maillu's books provide resistance to their western models, by the very act of imitating them ad absurdum.

Interestingly, the period of Mangua's early reputation was also that of a national and cultural counter-movement in Kenya. In 1968 Ngugi wa Thiong'o and Taban lo Liyong undertook to 'decolonize' the Literature Department at Nairobi University by deciding that African literature should form the core of activity.[30] These currents, seemingly antagonistic in purpose, were no doubt part of the same tendency: recognition of the power of the written word in a society hitherto unfamiliar with its potentialities in education, politics, business, and entertainment.

The loose concurrence of these tenets can also be demonstrated by the emergence of the *Spear* series itself. It was devised by Heinemann Kenya to counter the great popularity of the American best-sellers and obviously also to expropriate a thriving marketplace. As much as English literature had to abandon its hegemony in the African institutions of learning, American pulp had to be replaced or appropriated by African pulp.

But it was not the two Mangua books that initiated the series; they were published by the now defunct East African Publishing House. The first success story was Rosemarie Owino's *Sugar Daddy's Lover*, which appeared in 1975. The caption 'A human story of a young girl's immature entry into marriage and her struggles to change the pain and problems of married life into mature fulfilment' draws attention to an ordeal that most Kenyans would have confronted in one way or another: male promiscuity and married life.[31] The *Spear* book had found a terrain where it could roam unabashedly: the topical, the particular, and the spectacular.

Its next hit proved to be even more lasting. By 1988 John Kiriamiti's *My Life in Crime* had sold 9000 copies. The Heinemann sales manager, Jimmi Makotsi, claims that what accorded this book its unprecedented success was the verisimilitude of its narration.[32] The story was known. Like an oral tale it only needed to be projected onto the expectations of a new audience for it to be rejuvenated and recycled.

This is a pattern that has been reproduced a number of times in the history of this series. Most of the very popular crime stories have a factual background: Mwangi Gicheru's *The Ivory Merchant* (1976) is based on well-known incidents of ivory smuggling and the story, the blurb claims, 'will be cherished by most readers for its topicality and matter-of-fact deftness'; Frank Saisi's *The Bhang Syndicate* (1984) combines 'the dens of petty crime and petty drug-trafficking in Nairobi'; Wamugunda Geteria's *Black Gold of Chepkube* (1985; reprinted 1987) is the story of the illegal coffee trade that rocked the border between Kenya and Uganda during the 1970s; John Kiggia Kimani's *Life and Times of a Bank Robber* (1988) is another reputed criminal's confession; and Koigi wa Wamwere's *A Woman Reborn* (1980; reprinted 1982, 1986), written on toilet paper in detention at Kamiti Maximum Security Prison, explores, in the language of the caption, the exploitation of the poor by the rich, the oppressed status of the African woman, and the dehumanizing power of money.[33]

The fascination with crime, sex and violence in these stories is always underpinned or kept back by the reformist urge to improve on a state of being. The oral-tale tradition is always active in the stories. The Kenyan situation is in turmoil, its enemies motivated by greed and sponsored by alien or neocolonial interests. David G. Maillu's *Benni Kamba 009 in Operation DXT* (1986) employs one of the myths about AIDS. He tells the story of an incurable disease that has been injected into an African people by an international conglomerate. Super-spy Benni Kamba is called in to expose this 'imperialism and exploitation.' Thomas Akare in his *Twilight Woman* (1988), in a vehement bashing of Nairobi politicians, takes us around the seedy parts of the city in the company of four prostitutes who act as insightful mediators. The sharpness of the attack is curbed by the appeasing and incredible end of the story: our main spokeswoman returns to her rural surroundings to pick up her former life as a married (and still subdued) woman. All her painful experiences seem to have gained her nothing.

The reader/protagonist is expected to see, and understand, and perhaps even act. The turnabout narrative strategy, characteristic of many of the *Spear* stories that border on regions which are politically inflammable, is ironic. This is the point. The criticism that the *Spear* book communicates to the reader is ambiguous, double-tongued. The reader is invited to read the stories in this multiform way. Any intervening authority is checked by the logo itself, which acts as the series' protective shield. 'Light' stories are not likely to embarrass a government. Some of the stories could not, in fact, have been published under any other logo.[34]

This means that for a story to be included in the Heinemann African Writers Series it has to accommodate itself to another

Figs 6 & 7. The street comedians 'Black Angels Dynamics Comedians' performing in Moi Avenue, Nairobi, 1998

aesthetic of reception. On first glance, David Maillu's *The Ayah* (1986) seems to meet the standards of the typical *Spear* book: the thriller-like narrative, the slick language and layout, the eye-catching front cover, the fusion of fact and fiction, and identifiable topical Kenyan themes.[35] It harps on the issue of the maltreated house-maid, but also attempts to provide some insight into the psychological and economic 'tribulations rampant within the *ayah* institution.' But it is this examination that distances it from the typical *Spear* book. As in Akare's book *Twilight Woman*, its victimized heroine retreats to the rural haven of long-time cherished traditions and values. But unlike Akare, Maillu's criticism is not allowed to spill over into an ironic and vehement analysis which would encourage further considerations and observations.[36]

* * *

This discussion has, I hope, shown that in the African context the oral-popular discourse – its representation, reproduction, and reception – is shaped by segregationist and interventionist powers that are either internal (genre-based) and external (ideology-specific), or a combination of these; but also that there is an ongoing antithetical process of decentering. The *oral tale*, we saw, having already been submitted to the rules of print, may be additionally narrowed through nation-building appropriations; but it may also be allowed to float freely and liberally between oral milieux and print milieux (the magazine *Picadithi* was offered as an interesting site for such dialectical transgressions). The position of the oral-popular discourse in the manual was found to be comparatively far less eclectic. Here the restrictive setting and objective of the manual were decisive factors. Impetus for the decentering of the manual was localized in the Zimbabwe Literature Bureau's literacy campaigns where the interlacing techniques of the 'two' cultures were shown to be in operation, thus undercutting the authorial voice of the manual. The pamphlet's exclusive pan-Africanism and idealism had its hegemonic counterpoint in the polemics it entertained with colonialism and internationalism; and the thriller, finally, in its *Spear* book version mainly, is a marvellous epitome of the decentering process of the oral-popular discourse: it both accepts, appropriates (the game of) power and rejects it; its underdog position in Nairobi publishing underlines this dichotomy.

So African popular story telling collects its divergent patterns and human flavour from the 'spellbinders' and the 'heartbeats,' and its modality from the 'storylines,' the indeterminacy and contextuality of the oral traditions. The festive, ritual, cultic, civic, and pedagogic activities are by definition collective, which means that the printed form that incorporates any of these usages reflects a communication pattern of great complexity. Print forms and oral forms merge and separate and come together again. The African 'storyline' has a long tail.

Notes

[1] See for instance the first two chapters in John Miles Foley, *Immanent Art: From Structure to Meaning in Traditional Oral Epic* (Bloomington: Indiana UP, 1991).

[2] Wanjiku Mukabi Kabira and Karega Mutahi, *Gikuyu Oral Literature* (Nairobi: Heinemann Kenya, 1988): 3.

[3] Hannah Dankwa-Smith, *Some Popular Ananse Stories: Ghanaian Folk Tales* (London: Heinemann International, 1990).

[4] Jane Nandwa and Austin Bukenya, *African Oral Literature for Schools* (Nairobi: Longman Kenya, 1986): 5.

[5] Asenath Bole Odaga, *Yesterday's Today: The Study of Oral Literature* (Nairobi: Lake Publishers, 1984): 9.

[6] John Osogo, *The Bride Who Wanted a Special Present and Other Tales from Western Kenya* (Nairobi: Kenya Literature Bureau) Equivalent anthologies from other parts of Africa (and there are hundreds of them) are C. Stockil and M. Dalton, *Shangani Folk Tales, Volumes I and II: A Collection of Shangani Folk Stories* (Harare: The Literature Bureau, [no year]) and C.L. Vyas, *Folk Tales from Zambia* (Lusaka: National Educational Company of Zambia, 1974).

[7] The writers of these are Anne Matindi, Daniel lrungu, J.K. Njoroge, Frederick Ndugu'u, and Clare Omanga. The books were all reprinted once or twice in 1988.

[8] Such booklets are: Fortunatso Kawegere's *Inspector Rajabu Investigates*, David Ng'osos' *Travels of a Raindrop*, and Leo Odera Omolo's *Onyango's Triumph*.

[9] In a personal communication with me in January 1989.

[10] Rose Mwangi, *Kikuyu Folktales* (Nairobi: Kenya Literature Bureau, 1983): 54.

[11] Peggy Appiah, *The Children of Ananse*, illustrations by Mora Dickson (London: Evans, 1990).

[12] Rowland Molony, *The Raintree* (Harare: Longman Zimbabwe, 1986). This book is a sequel to *Themba and the Crocodile* (1984).

[13] T.K. Tsodzo, *Tawanda, My Son* (Harare: College Press, 1986).

[14] *Jikinya* (Harare: The College Press in Association with The Literature Bureau, 1984) is a romance about racial concord, which is a genre by itself in African publishing for young people (cf J.C. Ter Laare, *A Gift of Love* Nairobi: East African Publishing House, 1984). The third volume in a series called 'Heartbeat Books.'

[15] Wilson Kaigarula, *Poisoned Love* (Dar es Salaam: Heko, 1987).

[16] Pat Wambui Ngurukie, *I Will Be Your Substitute* (Nairobi: Kenya Literature Bureau, 1984).

[17] Muthoni Gachanja Likimani, *What does a Man Want?* (Nairobi: Kenya Literature Bureau, 1981): 209.

[18] Kwabena Asare Bediako, *Don't Leave Me Mercy: Echoes from James Owusu's Marriage* (Accra: Anowuo Educational Publications, 1966). See also Joseph M. Luguya's *Payment in Kind* (Nairobi: Kenya Literature Bureau, 1985).

[19] Cynthia E. Hunter, *Truphena Student Nurse* (Nairobi: Phoenix, 1987) and *Truphena City Nurse* (Nairobi: Phoenix, 1987).

[20] Henry R. Muhanika, *Killer Drink and Other Stories* (Dar es Salaam: Publicity International, 1982). The volume is no. 1 in a series called 'Learning and Recreation'.

[21] Martha Mlagala Mwungi, *Yasin's Dilemma* (Dar es Salaam: Shudutonya, 1985).

[22] Tom Obondo Okoyo, *A Thorn in the Flesh* (Nairobi: East African Publishing House, 1975), back cover.

[23] S. Kiyeng, *Echoes of Two Worlds* (Nairobi: Kenya Literature Bureau, 1985); Bahadur Tejani, *Day after Tomorrow* (Nairobi, Kampala, Dar es Salaam: East African Literature Bureau, 1971); Hamza Sokko, *The Gathering Storm* (Dar es Salaam: Tanzania Publishing House, 1977).

[24] Hope Dube, *State Secret* (Harare: College Press, 1988).

[25] See Hilary Ng'weno, *The Men from Pretoria* (Nairobi: Longman Kenya Ltd., 1975). Other allegories that project racial concord are: David G. Maillu, *Untouchable* (Nairobi: Maillu Publishing House, 1987) (an Indian and an African); Muli wa Kyendo, *The Surface Beneath* (Nairobi: Longman Kenya, 1981) (black Kenyan and white European); Geoffrey Ndhala, *Jikinya* (white and black Zimbabweans), see footnote 14 above.

[26] Meja Mwangi, *Bread of Sorrow* (Nairobi: Longman Kenya, 1989).

[27] Charles Mangua, *A Tail in the Mouth* (Nairobi: East African Publishing House, 1974).

[28] *Son of Woman* (Nairobi: Spear Books, Heinemann Kenya,1988).

[29] See also *Son of Woman in Mombasa* (Nairobi: Heinemann Kenya, 1987).

[30] See Bernth Lindfors, *Popular Literatures in Africa* (Trenton NJ: Africa World Press, 1991): 47-60.

[31] Rosemarie Owino, *Sugar Daddy's Lover* (Nairobi: Spear Books, Heinemann Kenya, 1987).

[32] Personal interview conducted 23 January 1989.

[33] Other titles in the series include Ayub Ndii's *A Brief Assignment* (1976, repr. 1987), which professes to describe criminals who live by their wits and from what they steal from Nairobi housebreaking and 'as they flee from the police, the gang pick up women, mostly barmaids and take them to bed with regularity in the more sordid Nairobi hotels and lodging-houses. They have no morals, no conscience, no thought for their anti-social life'; Mwangi Ruheni's *Mystery Smugglers* (1975) describes a school leaver involved in an international intrigue with organized criminals, trading in uranium, and international smuggling; Yusuf K. Dawood's *No Strings Attached* (1978) is a romance about a surgeon who 'has a soft spot for children and women in tears.' 'Yet,' it is claimed, 'he maintains a clinical aloofness throughout'; Sam Kahiga's *Lover in the Sky* (1975, rep. 1987) is about young Thuo, an air force pilot in the Kenya Air Force, whose life consists of fun and frequent sex; Aubrey Kalitera's *A Taste of Business* (1976) discusses male and female viewpoints of business and pleasure, through the careers of Ralph and Della, the college boy and the air hostess.

[34] Similar in concept and style to the Nairobi *Spear* books are the following stories from Dar es Salaam: W.E. Mkufya, *The Wicked Walk* (Dar es Salaam: Tanzania Publishing House, 1977); Prince Kawema, *Chausike's Dozen* (Dar es Salaam, Three Stars, 1983); Agoro Anduru, *Temptation and Other Stories* (Dar es Salaam: Press and Publicity Centre, 1981), *This is Living and Other Stories* (Dar es Salaam: Press and Publicity Centre, 1982), *The Fugitive* (Dar es Salaam: Intercontinental, 1983).

[35] David G. Maillu, *The Ayah* (Nairobi: Heinemann, 1986).

[36] Other examples of books that are *Spear*-like, but are published under another imprint (a Heinemann Kenya Paperback), are, for instance, those by Marjorie Oludhe Macgoye, a former English missionary bookseller, *Coming to Birth* (1986), *The Present Moment* (1987), and *Street Life* (1987). The first one depicts a woman's life, within the framework of the Emergency and the murder of Tom Mboya; the second is also a portrait of Kenyan womanhood, like the former set against the history of the country; the last one describes street characters in Nairobi.

BERNTH LINDFORS

Romances for the Office Worker

Aubrey Kalitera & Malawi's White-Collar Reading Public

Reference
Bernth Lindfors *Loaded Vehicles: Studies in African Literary Media*
Trenton: Africa World Press, 1996

Modern African literature first became known to the outside world through the works of elite, university-educated writers published in Europe and America. To be sure, there had been a few exceptions such as Amos Tutuola and Cyprian Ekwensi, authors whose craftsmanship had not been molded, polished and refined by years of literary education in colonial schools and universities, but these were freaks by any standard, sports of nature whose ungainly blemishes were their chief source of interest to a Western reading public. It had been the Senghors, Diops, Layes, Betis and Oyonos, the Achebes, Soyinkas, Ngugis, Armahs and Mphahleles who had made the greatest impact on the international scene, for they had demonstrated through the force and sophistication of their art that Africa in the postwar era could speak quite eloquently for itself, interpreting its own experience in its own idiom, albeit in a European tongue. These highbrow writers produced the first permanent flowers in what was to become a lush tropical garden of literature; they were exotic hothouse plants that abruptly assumed gigantic proportions, making themselves conspicuous as much by their unexpected weight and bulk as by their dazzling variety of shapes and colours. No one had anticipated such a sudden riot of creativity.

But in the environments from which some of them had sprung there had existed prior to their efflorescence a profuse undergrowth of literary vitality expressing itself in humbier but nonetheless significant forms. This was particularly true in the anglophone territories, where writing in vernacular languages had been encouraged. Behind and beneath Soyinka, for instance, there had been a rich legacy of written literature in Yoruba, ranging from poetry and mythic narratives to episodic folkloric fantasies and detective novels. In Ngugi's formative background there had been a small anticolonial pamphlet literature in Gikuyu and a very large popular and religious literature in Kiswahili. Mphahlele had had access to a full century of school storybooks published in South African Bantu languages.

But indigenous creativity did not confine itself to mother tongues. In Nigeria the earliest Onitsha market chapbooks, produced largely in English and to a lesser extent in Igbo, antedated Achebe's first novels by more than a decade, and in Ghana a similar tradition of pamphlet romances in English prepared the ground for Armah's initial anti-romantic fictions. In South Africa, Mphahlele was stimulated a great deal by the racy township potboilers he read and edited for Drum magazine; some of the stylistic gusto of this brand of pulp fiction rubbed off on his own journalism, autobiographical memoirs, novels and short stories.

So the splendid flowering of African literature that surprised the world did not take place in a complete literary vacuum, at least not in anglophone Africa. There was already a rich compost of prior creativity out of which it emerged and defined itself. The elite writers, by reaching for the sun, may have earned the greatest glory, but the popular writers, by spreading themselves laterally rather than vertically, may have reached the widest audience.

And the populists have never been totally eclipsed or displaced by the literati. Indeed, there probably are more popular writers (i.e., authors who address themselves to the common reader in their own society rather than to intellectuals at home or abroad) in anglophone Africa today than there are elite writers, and collectively, and in a few cases individually, they may have cornered a larger share of the indigenous reading public than all but the biggest giants whose works are compulsory reading in schools and universities. The mass appeal of lowbrow scribblers such as Cyprian Ekwensi of Nigeria and David Maillu of Kenya is already well-known and well-documented. The popular writer I wish to draw attention to here comes from a much smaller country, Malawi, and has not yet attracted much attention elsewhere. But in Malawi Aubrey Kalitera is famous and in all likelihood is more widely read than any other Malawian author. His career offers some interesting insights into what it takes to survive and thrive as a writer for the masses in a small country.

I first became aware of Kalitera when I visited Malawi in 1986 and saw on the bookshelves of colleagues at Chancellor College,

University of Malawi, a number of curious paperback books of crude design and rough construction. On closer inspection I noticed that the text in these books was not set in type but appeared to be reproduced from ordinary typewriting on a rather antiquated office machine. The covers had bold, stenciled lettering and sometimes carried simple illustrations. The volumes were fairly sturdily bound and ran to about 400 pages each. Most were novels but a few were collections of short stories, all written by a single author, Aubrey Kalitera, and published by a firm that called itself Power Pen Books. I had not seen such works in any of the local bookshops, so I asked where I could obtain copies. 'Oh, you'll have to see Kalitera himself,' I was told. 'He not only writes them but also manufactures and sells them.'

Kalitera lived in Blantyre, so I made a point of contacting him when I passed through that city a few days later. We met and chatted for about an hour. Here are some of the things he told me about himself:

> One disadvantage I had in life is that I didn't have much schooling. I lost my father when I was very young – when I was ten – so I didn't have much formal schooling. When I sat down to write, it was out of frustration. I simply had nothing to do. When you are in the village, all you can do is go to your garden in the morning. Well, you toil, then you come back at about 10 or 11, and unless possibly you go out hunting, you've got nothing to do. If you've had a little education, you may want to express it. That's all. That is the way it started.
>
> Almost twenty years ago – I think I was sixteen – I thought possibly I could play with writing. Gradually I got attached to it, but it took me something like ten years to publish my first book, *A Taste of Business*, which came out in Nairobi. Then a year later I followed it up with *A Prisoner's Letter*... What I was trying to do was to write for an international publisher. When I wrote my books, I used to send them to London. I sent this book, *A Taste of Business*, to Heinemann in London and they forwarded it to their office in Kenya. That's what happened.
>
> When I started to write, there was only one man who had written a real book here: that was Aubrey Kachingwe. Most of the writers I was reading were foreign... When I thought I had the ability to write, I had a dream of being able to live on my writing. But those two books I published in Kenya sort of disillusioned me; I realized I wasn't going to be able to live on my writing if I continued to publish with someone else. I had this feeling that if I could publish my own books and sell them myself, possibly I would get a living out of them. I had no money. In fact, I had nothing, so I picked up an old duplicating machine and then bought some stencils. Somewhere along the line I had learned to type very well, so I typed my own stencils. After that, I bought a bit of paper, ran possibly one hundred and twenty copies, and then sold them by hand.
>
> Before I went into book publication, I was running a short story magazine called *Sweet Mag*. When I began, I printed a thousand copies, but then, alas, it was a new thing and was almost valueless. People were not looking at it, so I was not very careful with the copies. But then after two or three months people began wanting the copies.
>
> I wrote the stories. It was ABC. Writing then was very easy. I started by producing a thousand copies, but when they didn't all sell, I produced only five hundred the next week. Those I did manage to sell. By the following week, there was a greater demand, so I went back to a thousand, then fifteen hundred. I think I did seventeen hundred at one point...
>
> I marketed them just by selling them around here in Blantyre. I didn't go to other cities. I think the price was thirty tambala and later forty tambala. I was just taking them around to shops, around to offices. People were buying them like that. Then I'd go back home, write some more, and in the mornings take them out again for selling...
>
> So I started as a short story magazine publisher, and I was writing all the stories myself. As a matter of fact, one of my books, *She Died in My Bed*, is just a compilation of some of the short stories I had written. A few of my other books are also compilations of some of those stories in *Sweet Mag*. When I started doing these books, people came to know me as a writer and began asking, 'Why did you start?' When they heard there had been a magazine, they said, 'Now we want those stories,' so I had no choice. By then the magazines had been thrown away, so the only way I could actually reproduce them was to put them out in book form...
>
> If I remember right, I think I wrote at least one book before I started writing these stories. I didn't know how to get it published, so after some time I went ahead and published it myself. I thought I would do both the magazine and the books, but being single-handed, I found it impossible. I dropped the magazine and went ahead with the books. The magazine stopped about the time the books got started...
>
> As a matter of fact, producing books that way was very cheap because stencils are cheap; they're just about the cheapest way of printing, only the quality is very poor. But in this case, the people were glad to see something that had been done locally. Also, some people said the books were well written, so actually they were buying them very quickly...
>
> I was printing about six hundred a month at that time. First, I would produce six hundred copies of a new book; then the following month I would produce possibly three hundred of that book and three hundred of another book. There were times when the number of copies per month was running up to a thousand. Selling them wasn't a problem. The people liked the writing and were very eager to get them...
>
> I was able to survive till I made a business mistake. When I was doing my own selling – that is, when I myself was going around to offices and selling the books – I was able to generate an income of something like a thousand kwacha a month. Then I said to myself, 'Possibly I could double or triple this by employing other hands to help me.' So I had some people come in to do the cutting of the stencils. Then I brought in some more people to do the running of the duplicator and the binding, and finally I hired something like twenty people to go round and sell the books across the entire country. That was a business mistake, because when those people went out to sell the books, some of them never came back with the money. So that was a big business mistake.
>
> I was writing these books as I went along, and I would publish a book the moment it was completed. To me, writing wasn't difficult. It was comparatively easy for me to produce a book. As a matter of fact, what actually got me to stop was my awareness that I wasn't getting my money back. So I said, 'Let me reorganize the whole thing.' The last book I wrote is still not published, and it was ready about a year and a half ago. Now I've got an idea of taking my books to the conventional bookshops, but in order to do this, I've got to bring them to an acceptable

quality. There's an organization here in Malawi called SEDOM – Small Enterprise Development Organization of Malawi – which actually bought an offset printing machine for me for that purpose. I'm trying to get all my books typeset professionally now, the old ones as well as the new ones. I will have the books printed professionally, and then I will go and dump them in bookshops and see if they will sell. Obviously they will go at a much slower pace than I was able to achieve by selling them from office to office, because there is no way you can move a thousand copies of any book in this country. The market is very small. You can't sell that many copies in the bookshops.

I don't know how I can break into the outside market, but if the market is there, obviously I would be prepared to go and dump a few copies abroad. But I'm a simple man. As I said earlier on, I didn't have much formal schooling so there are a lot of things I don't know. I don't think it's going to be very easy for me to break into outside markets, but eventually possibly I'll do it. (Kalitera 3-9)

This interview was conducted in July of 1986, and since then no new books have rolled off the stencil sheets or offset printing equipment at Power Pen Books; but, according to a letter, Kalitera intended in 1989 to reprint in a more professional format his most successful earlier title, *Why Father Why*, and in the meantime had taken up an entirely new enterprise – filmmaking. In fact, in late 1988 he produced Malawi's first locally made feature film, *To Ndirande Mountain With Love*, which was based on one of the novels he wrote, published and peddled in 1983. Unfortunately, this new effort in reaching a mass audience was not commercially successful, but Kalitera gave it his best effort, investing his energy and entrepreneurial skill in attempting to make it succeed. He is a bold risk-taker, but not everything he touches turns into gold – or even copper, for that matter.

To date Kalitera has published at least eight novels and two collections of short stories. With the exception of the first two novels, *A Taste of Business* and *A Prisoner's Letter*, which were published in Nairobi in the late 1970s, all his books were brought out between September 1982 and the end of 1984 under the imprint of Power Pen Books. At that point he was producing a new book every three months. Prior to starting up *Sweet Mag* in January 1981, he had published a few of his short stories in *Malawi News* and had written at least one play and some stories for a local radio programme called 'Writer's Corner.' *Sweet Mag* appears to have ceased publication in September 1983 when Kalitera was too busy as a book publisher to continue it.

Kalitera has always chosen themes for his novels that are of great interest to his readers. Many concern unfilial behavior. He writes about men who abandon their girlfriends after getting them pregnant, about women who abandon or kill their children in order to live a life of luxury unencumbered by parental responsibilities, about sons and daughters who desert or neglect their parents, about fathers and mothers who interfere in the marriages and romances of their grown-up children. But most of all he writes about marital infidelity, focusing on complications in the love affairs of men and women who cheat on their spouses or fiancées. Nearly all his narratives deal in one way or another with the making and breaking of contracts of the heart.

In these romantic melodramas the culprit often is a man whose biological instincts draw him irresistibly to beautiful women, most of whom ultimately yield to his persuasive advances. Men are seen as amorously gregarious and polygamous by nature; they are hunters always on the lookout for fresh prey. Women, on the other hand, though capable of being stirred by passions that override their inherent predisposition toward caution, tend to be more circumspect in making liaisons, looking for evidence of steadfastness, tenderness, and economic security. But they are vulnerable to flattery and the sheer libidinous persistence of their pursuers, and once they are won, they are quite prepared to take extraordinary risks to stick with their lover, even it if means leaving forever the contentment of a former way of life. They too can abandon themselves to the urgency of heartfelt emotions, but usually they are awakened receivers, not initiators, of erotic pressures.

Although love contracts are taken very seriously on both sides of the gender divide, they frequently are entered into in an abrupt, almost heedless manner. Love at first sight is common, the magnetic attraction generated at a random encounter proving impossible to suppress. The suddenness and intensity of this current of feeling overwhelm two strangers, and before long – certainly before marriage they are strangers to one another no more, having found opportunities to sneak off to bed together to savor the sweetness of their reciprocal passion. Sometimes their quickly ignited sparks of love cool and die, for the man ordinarily cannot be depended upon to be forever constant, but more often than not the electricity of their connection holds them fast until they legitimize their union through marriage or until some tragedy finally separates them.

The marriage contract, however, is not as fixed and firm as the original love contract. Adulterous philandering is common, especially for the man, but this tends to be tolerated for the sake of maintaining the stability of the home and family. Sometimes, of course, great unhappiness ensues, culminating in divorce, murder, suicide or other desperate acts. The marriage contract, once abused, can be irrevocably shattered.

This is the stuff of romantic fiction all over the world, but Kalitera grounds his tales in a milieu that is unmistakably Malawian so his readers can easily identify with the men and women caught in these highly emotional entanglements. The landscape, the names, the material culture, the predicaments are all recognizably local, not foreign or exotic. There is also a fairly explicit message in some of the tales, giving even the most titillating of them a trace of traditional moral earnestness and the aura of a didactic parable or folktale. Kalitera, though operating in a popular medium of widespread international currency, still keeps his feet planted in his native soil.

A typical example of his moralistic manipulation of a popular romantic formula can be found in his first novella, *A Taste of Business*, which concerns the rise and fall of an adventurous small businessman. Ralph Namate, who has earned a business management diploma at a local polytechnic, is fed up with his junior executive position at an import/export firm, and wants to launch out on an entrepreneurial venture of his own in order to get 'a taste of business.' Since he lacks substantial start-up capital and marketing experience, his earliest forays into the fish business do not yield enough to satisfy his ambitions, but he is lucky enough to meet Della, a well-heeled airline stewardess who immediately falls for him and expresses her willingness to bankroll his smalltime enterprise. Though Ralph is more than willing to exploit Della sexually, he is reluctant initially to take her money, but eventually he not only borrows a small sum but also allows himself to be guided by her to better business opportunities. He sees her as a good-time girl, sugar mommy and potential spouse; she sees him as an investment for the future, telling him quite bluntly, 'I won't make you a good wife unless you are a good businessman. You wouldn't satisfy me as a husband unless you are a good businessman' (67).

However, this well-calculated bond does not require that he remain faithful to her. Ralph does not hesitate to pick up an attractive undergraduate with whom he spends a four-day weekend at a fancy hotel, squandering his first major earnings. When Della finds out about the affair through her brother, who turns out to be the manager of the hotel, she confronts Ralph but is willing to accept his explanation that he was just obeying 'the law of the three F's in action. Fool, fuck and forget' (64). However, she demands that he start to get serious about succeeding in business.

Ralph needs no further prompting. Following one of her business leads and displaying great ingenuity and courage on the job, he soon so distinguishes himself as a bigtime fish trader that the Chief Fisheries Officer at a lake research station notices him and arranges that he be offered a scholarship to go abroad to study for a B.Sc. with a major in fish handling and processing. But Della wants him to stay home and marry her; she is ready to settle down and cash in on her investment. Ralph now must choose between love and career, and when he disappoints Della again by flying off to London, she commits suicide by jumping off a bridge. Shaken, Ralph returns home and drops out of the fish business entirely. He has learnt his lesson.

The story is told by Ralph, who readily admits his weakness for beautiful women. Here is his account of his first encounter with Della:

> I will never even know what made me turn. All I can say is that I looked back down the queue and there she was. A woman so womanly, all woman – is the only way of describing her. Take it that God, by way of a demonstration to Jesus and the angels, made one model woman. Only one. That woman was Della...
>
> My reaction was purely reflex. We jump for our lives when we see a snake a foot from our feet. On the other hand, we men cannot help drawing close to a Della-ish woman. Seeing her, the feeling simply struck me that she was put in the world to be worshipped and to be given favours...(l)
>
> She was a woman who was all a man desired. Gentle and sweet. A woman, all woman. On top of that, educated. (4)

Five short, love-filled chapters later, he meets another girl whom he cannot resist:

> Well, honestly, when I left Zomba, I had fully intended to go and pick up Della for company. But on the Express, I met a Chancellor College lass called Memory. Boys will be boys! I felt I would have more fun with Memory than Della who I was beginning to take for granted now...(45)
>
> Memory and I laughed till our mouths hurt. We made love in every position in the book till our bodies felt worn. To put it all in a nutshell, I kept asking for more and more of Memory. Memory kept giving it till all self-control was over-ruled by passion, to borrow from Don Gibson's words. (46-47)

Ralph feels a bit ashamed of himself for having betrayed Della, but he justifies his conduct with the cavalier claim that 'boys will be boys!' – a statement implying that all males observe the 'law of three F's in action.' Significantly, it is not his behavior in bed but his ambition in business that ultimately brings him low.

This is not to say that Kalitera fails to preach that irresponsible fornication is morally wrong. In certain circumstances, such as when the act produces offspring, the man is expected to honor the love bond by marrying his pregnant girlfriend. This is the message underscored time and again in the first novel Kalitera published in Malawi, *Why Father Why*, which focuses on the plight of a young boy who grows up without a father. The boy struggles through life and eventually makes a success of himself as a bestselling author, but he has suffered so many torments and deprivations along the way that he resolves to track down his father and ask him why he absconded, leaving the woman he impregnated and her unborn child to fend for themselves. When the feckless father fails to offer a satisfactory answer, the young man, by now a fabulously wealthy author, turns away from him and refuses to shelter, comfort and protect him in his old age. The heartless, deserting parent thereby gets his just deserts.

George, the boy hero, unlike most of Kalitera's other male protagonists, is a model of virtue who remains completely celibate before marriage. He won't even sleep with Mag, his fiancée, for fear of getting her pregnant. When another man seduces, impregnates and marries Mag, George tries to forget her, but a few years later, after the husband drives her and her child out of the house, George comes to Mag's rescue by marrying her and acting as surrogate father to her fatherless son. A complicating factor is that by this time he is engaged to marry Sue, a woman he loves equally deeply. When he tries to shed her, Sue, distraught, is seduced and impregnated by a married man who refuses to assume any responsibility for her and the unborn child. George, touched by her plight, comes to the rescue again by taking her as his second wife. The book concludes with a lengthy argument in favor of polygamy as the best solution to an age-old problem:

> Before the white man came our people married more than one wife. No matter who'll argue to the contrary, I will stand by my word that when it came to protecting girls and children, that system was the best ever.
>
> In those communities there were no mothers without husbands. No children without fathers. If you wanted a girl you simply married her regardless of the number of wives you had already. You didn't use her then discard her. This guaranteed that there was a responsible father to every pregnancy.
>
> If a husband died, his wife or wives immediately became the wife or wives of his brother or brothers. And this guaranteed that there would never be mothers without husbands. No children without fathers...
>
> This one-husband-one-wife system we've inherited from the white man...was ill-conceived. One had to agree that the idea was beautiful. One man worrying with no more than one woman and the children by her. But which one man was so holy that he ignored every other woman the moment he got married? The idea ignored the maxim, 'Boys will be boys.' That was the reason it was a washout. Because everything which ignores human nature always failed...
>
> In a nutshell what the west told us was 'Don't bother with marrying more than one wife. What you should do is to marry one woman. Anybody. Now, if at any time you come across another woman you can't resist go ahead and have an affair with her. Use her as much as you like. And once you feel you've had enough of her, discard her...'
>
> If you look at it that way, you will see that this system of one man one wife adopted from the west is the mother of so much suffering because it says that mothers without husbands are a normal thing; so are fatherless children. Yes, they may look

> normal, but mothers without husbands and fatherless children are perpetually miserable. And in my book the polygamous system is superior to this hypocritical monogamous system. Because it eliminates the misery. (393–395)

This frank and forceful argument may have been one of the factors that led to the commercial success of *Why Father Why*. According to Kalitera, the book was very popular, selling

> possibly ten times more than any of the others. *Why Father Why* broke all the records. This is an everyday story, especially here. We've got fathers running away to the mines and leaving children unsupported. So there were many people, especially office girls, who came and said, 'I want that book. I want to send it to George in Britain.' (Kalitera 10)

Since Power Pen Books were marketed mainly in office buildings in Blantyre and other Malawian cities, Kalitera wrote about matters of immediate interest to secretaries, managers, businessmen and other white-collar workers. Many of his heroes and heroines are employed in offices of one sort or another, urban workplaces in which bureaucratic intrigues, dishonest business dealings, and behind-the-door intimacies between bosses and clerical staff are routine events.

Sometimes these office imbroglios serve merely as starting points for stories that carry the reader to rural or exotic environments: forests, farms, mines, airplanes, fishing boats. *To Ndirande Mountain with Love* begins as a fairly predictable account of an illicit love affair between a company publicity manager and his new secretary but quickly develops into a mountain adventure tale involving rape, kidnapping, attempted murder, hot pursuit, and exquisite revenge. *Why Son Why* and *Daughter Why Daughter* focus on urbanized, westernized individuals who, after a series of mishaps, become aware of the importance of establishing a family homestead on the land. Kalitera's villains ordinarily end up broken and in the red; his heroes and heroines, on the other hand, frequently wind up in the pink, having inherited vast riches, built up very solid business enterprises, married into money, or enjoyed windfalls such as winning first prize in a lottery. Virtue seldom is solely its own reward: a pot of gold usually accompanies it.

Most of Kalitera's stories are first-person narratives told in a brisk, colloquial idiom that is refreshingly direct. There are no ambiguities or purple passages, no strainings after novel or precious effects. Clear communication is the top priority. Stories often open with a gripping statement calculated to pique the reader's interest:

> Well, it is over, thank God. People, who include my friends and my wife, ask me if I could do it again. They could be teasing me and they could not be teasing me. Still they don't seem to understand that I can't be sure, and how can I be sure? Suppose my next secretary was even more beautiful than Memory? (*To Ndirande Mountain with Love* 9)

> I first suspected that Felix was fooling with Raymond's wife, Alice, almost 24 hours before I made up my mind that I was right. (*To Felix with Love* 9)

> Maybe if it wasn't for the sake of the funeral Robert Kandulu would not have met the South African suitor of his daughter that day. (*Daughter Why Daughter* 9)

> One fine afternoon some twenty-five years ago now a man was fatally stabbed by a hired assassin. (*Mother Why Mother* 9)

> If Celia Zedi had dropped the baby face down in the pit toilet, she would have managed the killing she failed. (*She Died in My Bed* 132)

Kalitera then proceeds to build up suspense by involving the reader in a mystery or problem confronting the narrator/protagonist. Often we are told right from the start what is most worrisome or vexing about the situation, but sometimes information is withheld to deepen the enigma, forcing us to empathize with a character who must take a crucial decision without being able to anticipate its eventual consequences. Kalitera is adept at putting us in a character's mind so that we can share his or her anxieties and obsessions. In one story, 'On Wedding's Eve,' he even allows us to penetrate the psychology of an angry water snake. In his best-told tales – *Why Father Why* and *To Ndirande Mountain with Love*, for instance – he succeeds in sustaining suspense to the very last chapter, thereby building to an effective climax.

Other appealing aspects of Kalitera's writing are its genial tone, lively sense of humor, and occasional flashes of what seems to be self-revelation. Kalitera evidently takes great pleasure in writing and in being known as a successful writer. Since all his narrators are presented as if writing their own story, and since several of them are said to have taken up writing as a career, it is amusing to note their remarks on the craft of writing, for one suspects that some of these may reflect Kalitera's views on his own profession. At one point in *A Taste of Business*, for instance, the narrator states:

> But how on earth did one construct sentences that would carry a listener over every step you had taken, over all the things you had heard, over every beat your heart had missed in your desperation? How? I had read somewhere that accomplished writers often had the same dread. To put into words that clear picture they had in their mind! So that in the end their words would clearly and easily draw the same picture in the minds of the reader.
>
> I am adding this piece about writers to try to slam into you the full picture of my frustration. Because if you understand that, if I had been a practised writer, my problem couldn't have been simpler, you will understand that as an ordinary man with an ordinary command of language my problem couldn't have been more difficult. (82)

And in *Why Father Why*, George, the would-be best-selling novelist, reflects:

> The first time I had made up my mind that I wanted to be nothing but a writer, I had been horrified myself. I personally knew nobody who had become a writer. On the other hand I wanted two things in life. Money and fame. Not money alone. (258)
>
> As every honest writer will admit it, what all writers want is to be applauded. So after producing my first piece of writing, I took it to Sue for criticism. I wanted to be told that I was better than Ian Fleming, Hammond Innes, James Hadley Chase, Erle Stanley Gardner, all bundled together.
>
> Instead Sue told me, 'I don't know how people become writers. But if they all begin this way, then you are a long way off. Why don't you go ahead and write to a correspondence school like you said you would?'
>
> I could not help wondering if Mag would have said the same thing. But I took Sue's advice. Despite the pain. The next day I wrote to a school whose advertisement – in a magazine – had barked at me two weeks before: WE WANT PEOPLE WHO LOVE TO WRITE. (264–265)

> When I become a writer, there are things I would like to say. And I am going to write solely for fellow Africans. (267)
>
> Now, those who know how hard it is to fill a page with valuable writing will wonder how I could take ten pages at a sitting. You know what, it is so funny. A good writer will always find if very hard to fill a single page. A bad writer will always find it easy. (288)

Also, one of the characters in *Why Son Why* makes this comment on a leading journalist:

> You see, Jack is a communicator. One of the greatest. There is very little about himself or the next man he doesn't want to lay bare. I guess that is what makes his writing stand out. Every piece of his writing is a revelation. I caught someone at one of the hotels the other day telling his friends, 'Gentlemen, we've got to admit that Jack Kathumba has a wonderful brain. Here is what I mean. On page 241 in *No Oh No*, a woman tells a man that if he came into this world to receive, then even if he lived to be a hundred, he wasn't ever going to achieve anything. Because on earth, whatever may be the case elsewhere, people only succeed when they are giving and not getting. When I read that first time I told myself that Kathumba was mad. Then I read it a second and third time. That was when I realised that the man has something upstairs.'*

Kalitera adds the asterisk to draw our attention to a footnote at the bottom of the page that reads:

> *Something about giving, but not in these words was said in *Mother Why Mother* by Aubrey Kalitera. Published by Power Pen Books. (139-140)

In addition, there is a blurb on the back cover of this book where Kalitera quotes himself even more overtly:

> Aubrey Kalitera himself says, 'I have got my problems on earth. But none of them is on how to write well.'

After reading a good sample of the fiction produced by this prolific, self-taught author, publisher, salesman and promoter of Malawian popular literature, the average reader is likely to agree with this boastful statement. And for those who might feel inclined to dispute it, Aubrey Kalitera, businessman *par excellence*, has the cold, hard sales figures to prove it true.

BODIL FOLKE FREDERIKSEN

Joe, the Sweetest Reading in Africa

Documentation & Discussion of a Popular Magazine in Kenya

Reference
African Languages & Cultures 4 (2), 1991: 135–55

For urban Africans an ordinary, comfortable everyday life, free of misery and harassment is the adventure. The opposite is the norm. The implications of this state of affairs for popular literature are that what is regarded and dismissed as fairly drab descriptive realism in Europe and the US is fantastic in an African context. Many popular novels from Kenya, Tanzania and Nigeria may best be seen as realistic fantasies, meticulously describing the lives of the fabulously rich. Or the lives of the not-so-rich in terms of their efforts to grab and enjoy a modern lifestyle, closely associated with consumer goods, amenities and leisure, but also with regular work and ability to afford school fees.

The ordinary is the utopia. But in a dynamic situation the ordinary has to be imagined and constructed. In this creative process popular arts and popular culture more broadly play a key role. In areas of popular culture issues central to the everyday life of the majority of population are being articulated and debated, and new modes of life are made visible, audible, thinkable.

In Africa cities are the locus of what is modern. They are hotbeds of social and cultural change, and the turmoil characteristic of all levels of African urban life finds expression in a multitude of popular culture genres which are themselves changeable and evanescent – in tune with the pulse of urban life. In her discussion of popular arts in Africa, Barber (1987) points out that this diversity and the accompanying stress on innovation is of the essence of popular art. I wish to suggest that this quest for novelty which often takes fantastic forms may be in the service of the ordinary.

Popular literature, written by participants in the urban milieu, is interesting from two perspectives. From the perspective of the researcher wanting to do urban ethnography or qualitative sociology it is a source of insight into the way meanings are created and identities are formed and discussed. It is raw material. In a popular novel, characters inhabit and embody social dimensions like ethnicity, gender and generation, and negotiate them between the city and the countryside. The important characters are types, e.g., the prostitute, the gangster, the rural wife newly arrived in the city, the big man – individual incarnations and illustrations of clusters of social configurations and problems. At the same time they are realistic figures, rooted in everyday life by their language, mundane concerns and problems in even fulfilling the most basic of needs.

From the perspective of the researcher interested in the creation and influence of particular discourses the focus will be slightly different. Ideally the whole process of cultural change should be followed, from the presence of the modernising cultural institutions and practices to the way they influence vocabulary and meanings in the novels, to the reception by the readers and possible impacts. Popular literature in this case is not so much raw material as a part of a discursive process. It is from this latter perspective that I want to examine the role of popular writing.

I want to trace the didactic and socialising nature of popular writing – didactic from the point of view of the producers, socialising from the point of view of the recipients. Historically, oral and written narratives have been important socialising agencies, closely connected to social and religious institutions. Popular writing has continued to articulate areas of concern and contest, now de-linked from traditional social events and institutions, but available in the market and in modern institutions.

Joe magazine and urban culture

What follows examines the role of a popular magazine in the creation of the ordinary. Why is a popular magazine interesting? In it an urban discourse unfolds, more richly, perhaps, than in narrower cultural genres such as fiction, painting and music.

In popular magazines we find a motley of genres and formats. As regards written material there are editorials, feature articles, pastiches, spoofs, reviews, competitions, short stories, advertisements, jokes, genuine and faked letters from readers. The graphic work also appears in many sub-genres. The full-page political, satirical drawing, cartoons, traditional comic strips with talk bubbles, illustrated narratives, illustrated jokes with a punch line, and once again advertisements. The ensemble represents a variety in form which contributes to the creation of the ordinary. It throws a multi-faceted light on the fairly limited number of issues, thus mimicking everyday life – also a mixture of impulses and modes of communication centering around a cluster of key concerns.

What I hope to demonstrate is that the magazine, *Joe*, emerged as a mouthpiece for the new African middle and lower middle classes, as a socializing agent, educating people in how to be urban, and as a contribution to a fairly democratic public sphere in which issues of importance to the urban population of Kenya could be voiced and discussed. If this is so, a popular magazine like *Joe*, printed and accessible, close to the grassroots as it is or tries to be, is of great interest to an examination of the contents and forms of urban culture in Kenya.

Joe came out fairly regularly in Nairobi between 1973 and 1979 (see Primary Text 3, p. 103) at different times called *Africa's Humour or Entertainment Fortnightly* or *Monthly* and by 1979 *Joe Homestead*. It took its name from a character called Joe who had grown popular in a satirical column in the *Daily Nation* – 'With a Light Touch' written by Hilary Ng'weno, illustrated by Terry Hirst.

This is the way the magazine presents itself in an early number: 'Karibuni, it's where you belong. Where? Well, here with us at *Joe Magazine*, Kenya's, East Africa's, even Africa's first humour monthly magazine. Become a part of it, share it with us, and let it become part of you, because it's about you.' Right from the beginning the voice of *Joe*/Joe was relaxed but insistent, inviting dialogue.

Joe was one of many popular magazines in Kenya during this period. The mid-1970s was the heyday of Kenyan publishing. According to Henry Chakava, the doyen of Heinemann Kenya, thirty-six periodicals came out regularly in 1976 (*Kenya Times*, 15.1.1989). The most well-known was *Drum* which still exists, an offspring of the South African *Drum*, but in the 1970s, according to Terry Hirst, experiencing an ebb, partly because it was edited from London, and thus not really in touch with Kenyan reality.[1] That was what *Joe* hoped to be. Other magazines were *True Love*, *Trust*, *Viva*, and *Men Only*.

To varying extents these and other magazines were similar forums to *Joe* magazine, and had similar functions in this period in Nairobi, particularly *Viva*. My reason for choosing *Joe* is, to put it briefly, its excellence. Three features were central in reaching its high quality: the mixture of writing and graphic work; the thematic organization of the issues; and something less easy to pinpoint, the tone of voice including the innovative use of language. Finally *Joe* carried an original short story in every issue which makes it particularly interesting for an examination of the role of popular literature in the wider context of popular culture. (See Primary Text 3, pp. 104-5)

Joe circles round its chosen theme, throws light on it from various angles, with varying degrees of seriousness, in different genres, in words and pictures, advising readers and making fun of them. The magazine creates the possibility of conversation, which in spite of being written down, is relaxed enough for readers to join in with editorial suggestions in letters such as: 'Joe, why don't you introduce or allow the wananchi to write articles in the form of conversations, fiction or nonfiction, to you for publication with picture illustrations like the ones of Gitau E. on the City? Joe, the person, is the one who is addressed, and he is also the one who solicits letters from the readers: 'Why don't you drop me a letter expressing your feelings about things – even about me? I might print it and then I might not. Joe.'

Joe, the common man

Joe, the common man, 'a survivor who has to laugh to keep from crying'(Terry Hirst), is the pivot around which the concerns of the magazine revolve. Wittily put across in the June 1973 issue, in which he sets up 'Joe's Election Advisory Service', he muses over the problem that the politicians have 'lost touch with the average man ... I figure I am an average man. For a small fee I will allow the MPs to pay me a visit ... And for an additional fee I could show one or two fellows more like me in Nairobi: average fellows with average aspirations and concerns.'

In a marginally more serious vein in the December 1973 issue, which celebrates ten years of Independence under the theme, *Uhuru and the Common Man*, Joe counts the blessings of Uhuru. In order of importance they are, 'bottled beer, land redistribution, African owners in River Rd.' It happens in 'My Friend Joe', the regular column which features Joe in conversation with his friends, most often in a bar.

Drawn by Terry Hirst, Joe is on the front cover of most of the magazines, now dressed up as a tourist Masai, now on the operating table in an issue dealing with the medical services, now in a derelict and empty shop, reading *How to Succeed in Business* in one dealing with the small businessman. Always slightly disreputable, Joe is balding with a stubbled chin and accompanied by his faithful dog. In January 1976, relieved that the Women's Year is over, but not untouched by it, Joe suggests that 1976 be named The International Common Man's ... er ... Person's Year.'

The death of *Joe*, and reasons why

Just before the magazine folded in late 1979 it had after a pause been relaunched as *Joe Homestead*. The amount of comic strips and cartoons was quadrupled and a whole new section to do with family, health and nutrition was introduced – knitting, cooking, and gardening ideas. The change reflects an attempt by Terry Hirst to move from an urban bias towards a rural one, in the face of what to him seemed the insoluble problems of African urban life.[2] But the last two issues of the magazine did not attract new advertisers, a problem all along, and *Joe* closed after the August issue.

In an interview with Bernth Lindfors, Terry Hirst, one of the two founding editors of *Joe*, indicates the kind of problem which a magazine aimed at an African rather than Asian or European readership had to battle with: 'In Nairobi, where there is a certain amount of social imbalance in the importance that minority communities have, advertisers think of *Joe* as an African magazine and assume there's not much of a market there for their consumer products' (Lindfors, 1979: 91). In other words, Africans were not regarded as a group of the population which might develop into middle-class consumers, although, as Terry Hirst points out, 'Kenya is a country that is ninety-five percent African.'

So from the beginning, in May 1973, when the first issue on the informal sector was brought out in 10,000 copies, and sold out in two days, the idea was to base the magazine mainly on sales and subscription, not so much in order to be independent, but rather from a realistic assessment of the market in terms of readers and potential advertising. According to Terry Hirst things went well until 1976 when inflation set in. Circulation dropped to 22,000 from the record 30,000 the year before, and printing costs doubled. At the same time it was decided to bring out *Joe* twice a month instead of once – 'a crazy commercial decision' according to Hirst. This decision coincided with the collapse of the East African Community which stopped sales in neighbouring countries.[3] But in terms of both quantity and quality 1976 was a vintage year all the same.

Founders of *Joe*

The first serious crisis hit *Joe* when the other founding editor, Hilary Ng'weno, decided to leave the magazine at the end of 1974, in order to launch the still successful *Weekly Review*. This step upset the balance between art work and written work. Terry Hirst, who was a former lecturer in Fine Arts at the University and at Kenyatta College, was in charge of the graphic work, using not only his own work, but that of other artists as well, some young, some more experienced.

Hilary Ng'weno had been chief editor at the *Daily Nation* for several years, but decided that he 'didn't like being employed', and quit in order to freelance, and later set up *Joe* with Terry Hirst. Most of the writing in the early issues came from his hand. But towards the end of 1974 he left – 'I felt it was really important to tell people what was happening before making fun of what was happening'[4] – and the first issue of *Weekly Review* came out in the beginning of 1975. But *Joe* survived and even improved in quality. Ng'weno went on contributing and new writers appeared. According to one of them, Sam Kahiga, the whole concept of *Joe* was Terry Hirst's, which was why it was possible to carry on even after Ng'weno had left.[5]

Facts and figures

Before going on to characterise in more depth the particular mix which made *Joe* so unique, and so appealing, some background information is in order: every number of *Joe* contained thirty-two pages (except the *Homestead* issues in 1979 which were longer), and started out costing one Kenyan shilling, rising to five towards the end. Until 1975 the staff was: Editor Hilary Ng'weno, art editor Terry Hirst, business and production manager Nereas Gicoru, plus an advertising sales manager and a secretary. In February 1975 Terry Hirst became the new editor, with Nereas Gicoru as the business manager, a construction which was kept more or less through the years, with the addition in 1976 of an assistant art editor, Oscar Festus, and an assistant editor, Nick Ayub who had been writing a new music column. In the following sections I describe the main blocks which made up the magazine, and the themes around which it was organised.

Advertisements

In a typical 1976 issue advertisements will take up between seven and nine pages, two or three pages of book ads, the same for electrical household appliances – fridges, gramophones, radios etc. – and the rest a mixture of beauty products, soap powder and cigarette ads, and advertisments for various institutions, e.g., insurance companies, banks, correspondence schools and beauty salons. In the September 1974 issue there is only half the amount of advertising, and in *Joe Homestead* July 1979 not even one ad, although the whole slant of the magazine had moved towards family and consumption, thus addressing the problem of the lacking African middle class, as discussed by Hirst.

Some of the advertisements carry illustrations, drawings by Terry Hirst or other *Joe* artists, or functional photographs of the goods advertised, e.g., an open fridge, full of bottles of *Tusker* beer. Only the cover of *Joe* is glossy and in colour, and the inside of the covers is most often used for full-page ads in the life-style genre. One for 'US – the anti-perspirant that keeps you fresh', shows a happy looking man dancing in a multi-racial disco, and brings testimonies to the effectiveness of US from two Africans and a blonde model who may well be from the USA, all in colour photos.

The book ads in this period are full of self-confidence: 'Laugh with Longman! Weep with Longman!'; 'Spear Books, ideal reading for your leisure hours. Ideal gifts'; 'Buy your own local paperbacks. Read a Spear Book today!'; 'Afromance is a moving series of sincere novels about love ... about life. Make sure you don't miss this month's heartwarming story'. An advertisement for *Joe* itself in November 1976, nicely illustrated, matches this spirit: '*The New Yorker* and *Punch* are fine, but in Kenya you really need *Joe* if you are serious!'.

Jokes and competitions

Popular throughout was a two-page spread with illustrations – *Joe's Bar Jokes* – in which readers are invited to send in their best jokes and are paid ten shillings for each one. According to Terry Hirst there was a massive response, people making up jokes themselves, or sending in jokes taken from old copies of *Reader's Digest*. (Lindfors 1979: 89). A quarter-page *Facts from History* which appeared during most of 1976 was in practice facts from African or black history in the form of beautiful drawings and brief information about, for instance, Great Zimbabwe, or 'Who were the Rastafarians?'. Even the Crossword tended to be didactic. In the 15 April 1976 issue it aimed to exercise the reader's knowledge of Nairobi geography, 'You go down Government Road ...'.

Joe also contained various competitions such as, 'How many titles of African novels do you know?', or 'Con-Men Observed: In 250 words readers are asked to describe a "con-trick" of their own'. The prize was a hundred shillings. In general *Joe* upheld the importance of quick exchanges with readers, as well as a quick response to small and big events in the everyday life of Kenyans. In January 1977 *Joe* announced the granting of the OBE (Only Bosses Eat) award to *Nation* columnist Virginia, 'who can't imagine why food kiosks keep springing up in the Industrial Area after the Keep the City Clean cleaners have pulled them down.'

Comic strips, cartoons and illustrations

Cartoons, comic strips and illustrations take up approximately the same amount of space as advertisements. One of *Joe*'s chief attractions was undoubtedly the amount of high quality, purpose made graphic work, spread liberally all over the magazine – even to the extent of spilling over into the advertisements, as we have seen. All short stories and many feature articles were illustrated, usually in very eye-catching styles. The front cover was a masterpiece of Hirst art work, featuring a number of very human human-beings, Joe usually among them, engaged in activities connected with the theme of each particular issue.

Comic strips play a prominent role, many of them reflecting the urban slant of the magazine, representing the pleasures and the dangers of big city life. The most striking and original comic strip, or rather drawn narrative, is *Gitau E. on City Life*. Taking up a full page, and consisting of six or seven carefully filled out frames, depicting incidents and settings in the city, *City Life* tells typical tales of what happens when the ignorant person from up-country comes to Nairobi. It was drawn by the well-established artist Edward Gitau who is better known as the creator of Kalulu in *Taifa Leo* and *Taifa Weekly*. The strip is without direct speech, subtitles tell in words what the pictures illustrate.

Each narrative has a title. 'Crooks from Shanty Village' is the story of the deception of an innocent farmer who comes to the city to sell his goods; 'Every Thing Artificial' portrays the transformation of a seemingly beautiful prostitute when she removes her wig, her false teeth, her left eye, her bra and breasts; 'Robbery Under a New Cover' deals with fake educational institutions which swindle gullible parents out of fees. 'Drowning Their Troubles' is set in a bar in which 'Mr Kimere ... drinks every night after office hours because he has no friends and no transport home', until his wife comes along and drags him out by the feet. 'The Wolf Under Sheep's Skin' deals with another urban phenomenon, 'a very popular preacher who attracts big crowds of followers through the city's streets.' The special followers pay him two shillings, 'follow him to a pavement', and are given a roll of bhang each. (See Primary Text 3, p. 106)

The companion piece to *City Life* is *Kunde Farm* by Njuguna Wainaina (story) and Ivanson Kaiyai (drawings), a continuous narrative rather than separate episodes, set in a village, but emphasizing the inroads which the money economy has made into a subsistence based social structure. A young couple, Komo and Njoki, run away to Nairobi after the elders of the village have failed to reach an agreement on bride price. The plot of the story takes us in turn to a town house – 'life does seem a bit empty in the city,' Njoki muses, left alone in her new home, while Komo is out, looking for food – and to the village where the elders fume and plot to get the young couple back.

Kunde Farm is as meticulously and elaborately drawn as *City Life*, not quite as professionally, which probably reflects Terry Hirst's policy of creating an East African tradition of graphic art, by taking in talented, but formally untrained people and putting them in the studio.

'*O.K, Sue!'A City-Girl's View* – a plainer, more traditional half-page, six-panel comic strip by Kimani Gathigiri – appeared not so regularly, but is noteworthy for putting a woman's point of view, equality of women being an important strand in the over-all egalitarian thrust of *Joe* magazine. Sue's counterpart may be *Tom Mandazi and Co.* created by Hirst, featuring another common man as a young child, Tom, an optimist and his friend Kioko the eternal pessimist, both equally powerless and playing up to the fickle girl friend, Agnes.

In June/July 1977 a new, full-page Terry Hirst strip is launched, *Daddy Wasiwasi & Co, Ltd.* It portrays a modern nuclear family, headed by a slightly more than middle-aged, perplexed (wasiwasi) executive. The other members of the household are his wife and two grown-up children, blasting away on the stereo set, his wife's brother who moves in 'temporarily', and the old family cook Tumbo, who refuses to change his out of date ways, and serves ugali and tea for breakfast instead of Wheatablocks and coffee.

The most peculiar comic strip is *The Good, the Bed and the Ugali*, also by Hirst, which started its relatively short run in the October 1974 issue, a slightly crazy spoof on a western, set in East Africa. The hero is 'East Africa's first cow person', the Shadow, 'bootless and free', and his gold are his two trusted feet, Kung and Phew. They take him everywhere and in the Kung Fu street fighting manner outkick his enemies in a matter of seconds. In one instalment a lady in distress is maltreated by her husband who prevents her from going to *Maendeleo ya Wanawake* (the Kenyan Women's organisation) meetings, and the Shadow gallantly kicks him around and makes him surrender all his money to his wife, who decides to become a Sugar Mummy.

Kung Fu

Kung Fu was very much in the air in Nairobi at this time. In letters from readers Joe is asked about his view on Kung Fu, and whether that martial philosophy is part of his personal make-up: 'I am inviting you to Mombasa so that you can teach some of us Kung-Fu to enable us to protect ourselves from the gangsters in this town.' In *Joe* August 1973 the film reviewer of *The Killer* and *Bloody Fists* suggests that one reason for the popularity of Kung Fu and karate films is that they represent low-cost violence, basically relying on each person's physical skill – more appealing because more applicable than the contemporary high-tech, high-cost super violence associated with for instance James Bond films. 'What the Africans need is the equivalent of the Karate Western (Ugali Westerns?). For this they will need a set of good guys and bad guys. They will also need the equivalent of the karate chop, the donkey kick or the Colt 38. Perhaps some spears and a lot of tomato ketchup will do.'

The pervasiveness of Kung Fu discourse – in a short story describing an evening out, 'the band was belting out a Kung Foo number with great violence' – may have to do with its Third World origins. Bruce Lee, the cult figure and possible object of identification, was born and grew up in Hong Kong, but worked in and became a citizen of the USA, and was in his way a man of revolt.[6]

Features

Signs of The Times appeared on the same page as the colophon and was witty gossip and tart comments on news items from the world press, or the latest news in Nairobi. *Firingline* was a topical and semi-serious article, most often reflections on the theme. *My friend Joe*, written mostly by Hilary Ng'weno, featured Joe in conversation with friends in the bar: 'Wait a minute. Drinking is the most African thing God ever created after creating the African race. Look around you. What do you see? Drunks. African drunks. I tell you that's the most African thing on this earth, drinking' (November 1974). Other features occurred irregularly, sometimes diagnosing the current political scene in the form of an allegory, e.g., Horace Awori's 'Domestic Crisis' around election time in September 1974.

Two recurring special features were unique to *Joe*: One was called *Ask a Stupid Question* and would show Joe being approached by naivety in one or the other guise. In the *Joe* issue devoted to witchcraft he is seen with an optimistic looking (American) tourist who is grabbing a Makonde wood carving, asking, 'Is this a magic carving?' Joe would then provide some 'snappy answers', e.g., 'No, its actually a stick-insect trying to emigrate', or 'Certainly! If you buy this carving, a meal will miraculously appear on my table!'

The other one was *Reporter Roving Mike* (microphone), interviewing a selection of 'typical' Kenyans on the particular monthly theme, all invented and drawn by Terry Hirst. In the witchcraft issue, the question is, 'Do you believe in Witchcraft, and does it make a positive contribution to modern life?' The interviewees are: Sheik Mganga, Consultant, Eastleigh (most likely a reference to the consultants which football teams had, and have, to use to deal with the issue) – 'Of course I believe in it! It's what I do for a living ...'; Mike Mpira, Soccer Player, Nairobi; V. Kijanna, D.O. (District Officer) with a topee; Mary Ann O. from Homa Bay, who thinks her lover has cast a love spell on her; the modernising A. Theist, Manufacturer, Nairobi, who ends his condemnation of superstition with Touch wood!', to be on the safe side. Finally there is Omar Kiyam, Mombasa, who warns the too investigative reporter off from areas which he does not understand anyway, and which are better left alone.

Joe themes

The thematic organisation of Joe was upheld all through the years. Each issue had a particular theme which coloured pretty much every written and graphic item in the magazine. The themes were presented as subheadings on the cover of each issue, and also provided the subject matter of the cover illustration. An issue called *Before the Law* shows a very humble Joe, cringing and looking up at a formidable wigged and robed, irate judge. An illustration of the perspective favoured by *Joe* magazine: bottom up. The themes were social rather than political and many verged on life-style or 'Quality of Life' issues, as *Joe* itself described it.[7] In the following section I shall mention and briefly discuss most of the themes.

Women and marriage

Five numbers dealt with women and gender relations. The theme of the first – *Women's War: Uganda vs. Kenya* – was the reaction of Kenyan women (and men) to the Idi Amin-induced influx of Ugandan women, many of whom were, or were seen as, prostitutes. The general trend of the (humorous) articles is that in fact the Ugandan women are welcome to take over the Kenyan men, who are 'either too drunk or too stupid'. The other four were: *Love and Marriage*; *Secretaries*: *Myth and Realities*; *The Great Debate* (on a proposed new marriage bill); and *Women for a Change*. Marriage is one of the changing institutions to be taken up by *Joe* and dealt with fairly thoroughly. Others are the Medical Services, the Civil Service – in an issue called *How Civil is the Service* – and the Church in *Where do Christians Stand*?

Three *Joe* issues dealt with youth, education and employment: *On the Tarmac, a Guide for School-Leavers*, 29 February 1976; *Starting the New Term?*, January 1977 and the last-but-one *Joe* to appear in July 1979, *Educated for Unemployment?* In other issues such as *Rolling Joe* on rock and pop music, the creation of a youth audience is a hidden agenda. The emphasis on youth is particularly noticable after Nick Ayub, who wrote on popular music, joined the editorial staff in the beginning of 1977.

Transport, holidays and housing

An informal institution of great importance in the world of ordinary Kenyans is dealt with in *Transports of Delight*, the fairly scandalous institution of the *matatu* which *faute de mieux* carries millions of people to and from work and pleasure every day. Sam Kahiga, a regular contributor of fiction and satirical colums, describes getting to work in Nairobi in 'With a Little Help from a Matatu': From around the corner, like a little busy bee comes a matatu rushing into the bus stage at a hundred KPH. A little happy road pirate with worn-out brakes, tyres as smooth as oranges, a 1973 road licence, a forged log book, a driver with three hangovers piled up together, and a conductor who was once nuts. It rushes in, its radiator boiling with enthusiasm. Its motto: TRUST IN GOD.'

A page of Terry Hirst cartoons, 'Close to the Tarmac' illustrates traffic-related incidents in the life of Kenyans, and the stupid question of *Ask a Stupid Question* for this issue is, 'Do Buses Stop Here?' The snappy answers, 'Possibly, if you are brave enough to lie down in the road!', 'I'm not sure, I've only been waiting here for three hours!', etc.

In the November 1974 number *Joe* introduces the concept of holidays. Again the treatment of the theme is humorous, 'the trouble with holidays are that they're un-African,' Joe muses in *My Friend Joe* and decides that holidays are not really for him anyway as they presuppose a job.

Two issues deal with housing. In the August 1973 issue on *The Housing Scene* Joe is worried that he 'may have to move out to Mathare Valley', and is warned by his friend: 'Once in a while the City Council will come tearing down your home ... And there will be the *chang'aa* drinkers and the criminal types ... Man, Mathare Valley is just not the place for you, Joe' (in *My friend Joe*). The June 1976 issue on *Habitat and Shelter* coincided with a conference on that theme at the Kenyatta Conference Centre. An article points out that while from a great height slum houses are an eye-sore, for the people who have built them and live in them they represent 'a tremendous investment in terms of labour and capital'.

How to make money

In *The Small Businessman* (11 March 1976), which appeared at the time of the ILO interest in the Kenya Informal Sector, business section, 'Business Joe', reports on the fluctuations at the Mathare Stock Exchange, and the merger between Pius Mbitiri, waste paper collector, and the 'doyen of the recycled bottle trade, Mama Njeri'. The number also contains down-to-earth advice, both in a serious and jocular manner on how to set up a business: 'avoid middlemen!' Some of the issues raised here, are carried forward into the October 1976 number *Money, Money, Money*, which in spite of the promising title deals more with the lack than the presence of money. *Beating Armed Robbers* (June 1974) reflects the increasing urban violence which citizens of Nairobi experienced.

Is witchcraft necessary?

The two issues on witchcraft, *Who Needs Witchcraft?* (August 1975) and on con-men, *The Confidence Tricksters* (29 April 1976) are related not only because many *ngangas* are con-men, but also because they both explicitly deal with anxieties and ambitions of modernity, particularly in their urban version: 'Urbanites have wisened up to cardsharks on the pavements, the weak tea, peddled as whisky, the classic con of the dropped envelope', but may not be prepared for swindle in areas that are at the same time the most vital and the most remote from experience such as education. Joe himself, who is not exactly a babe in arms, in *My Friend Joe* is bewildered enough by his problems to take, as he calls it, 'informal sector medical advice', which persuades him that he has been bewitched. On the front page we see him, very worried, entering the sinister house of a 'consultant'.

In *Firing Line*, the column which is most consistently serious and straightforward, the editorial position is made clear on operators in the area of witchcraft. True to *Joe* ideals it happens in the form of a question rather than as a statement: 'Isn't it time we sorted out the legitimate, traditional wisdom from the contemporary nonsense, before everything is obscured by these new con-men?' In the same issue appears Gitau E.'s *City Life* strip on fake educational institutions, 'Robbery under a new Cover', a graphic illustration of what to beware of. Another strip, 'Joys of the Promised Land', equally didactic, shows a fake estate agent at work, selling land titles to non-existent land to naive Nairobi citizens, affected by the 'Back to the Land' fever.

Fiction

In an interesting paper on 'Popular Literature in Tanzania', Richard Mabala writes: 'Popular literature reflects and speaks to the rising urban classes. The writers themselves are of and for these classes ... their works express ... the preoccupations and contradictions of those classes.'Mabala suggests that the popular writers are not simply 'an urban phenomenon but in fact ... are representative of the classes of the future' (Mabala, 1990: 30).

Almost every issue of *Joe* carried a new, original short story, illustrated by different artists.[8] Some were by writers who were already well known, or have since become so. Ngugi wa Thiong'o's 'A Mercedes Funeral' appeared in two parts in early numbers. Meja Mwangi published 'Like Manna from Heaven' in the November 1974 issue; in June 1976 there is a story by him about the universal Ben and a prostitute, 'No Credit, Terms Strictly Cash', and his Incident in the Park' appeared in November 1976.

In many ways the stories by Mwangi are typical of the style and themes of the *Joe* short story. The opening lines of 'Like Manna from Heaven' run like this: 'The evening blows cold, rather windy. Ben pulls his coat tight round his chest as he makes his way through the parking lot.' Ben is moneyless, looking for a job and meets a prospective employer in a bar. They quarrel over the bill and Ben's job chances evaporate in a drunken brawl.

All the short stories have urban settings and urban themes: money, alchohol, unemployment, corruption, prostitution, unfaithfulness. Bars occur as the setting in about half of them, the people who work are in private business. Men are protagonists in most stories, but in one, 'The Light', by Ngumi Kibera (15 April 1976), a hard-working and long-suffering women tells the story of her life which was spoiled by an alchoholic husband. 'The Whore', by Maude Olimba (15 January 1976), is the autobiography of a highly successful prostitute who ends up by marrying a white man and inheriting his property when he dies, but who in reality prefers women. In most stories women are present, but mostly as a problem.

Here are some more samples: 'Brave New Dimensions' by Mugambi Karanja (December 1974) deals with a bank robbery: 'Hot, stuffy, crowded. The banking hall was packed with desperate, penniless wage earners all fidgeting and anxious for their money.' 'Double-Cross' by Jolimba (August 1975) is about a young man who comes to the city to look for work, and is finally successful after having been double-crossed by a prostitute who is in fact a man: 'Lawrence was a newcomer to the throbbing metropolis of Nairobi ... With school behind him, he thought paradise must lie ahead. He soon discovered that a little palm-greasing could be of more assistance in getting employment, than his precious School Certificate.' In 'End of the Month' by Chege Mbitiru (11 March 1976), Marete, an old man in search of free drink, is spotted in a bar by his daughter Mumbi, prosperous, contemptuous and unforgiving – he had abandoned mother and children earlier. He addresses her: 'These ... these ... these streets are poison, my child,' but is thrown out of the bar: 'There was a roar of laughter as Marete ... stumbled to the door. He watched Mumbi across the street and called. She spat on the ground, as a man put his arm around her waist and then started caressing her buttocks.' Marete is knocked down and killed by a car amidst 'squealing of tyres, screams and shouts.' Death on the tarmac. Tarmac plays a big role in *Joe*: 'Five months I trekked the streets of Nairobi. / Five months on tarmac'.[9] A short-lived cartoon was called *Song of the Tarmac.*

Language style and life style

Some writers are much influenced by the tough-guy style of American thrillers of the James Hadley Chase type, although they keep an authentic, or perhaps mock-Kenyan flavour, using 'Holy Ngai!' instead of 'Holy God!' Or this description from a story called 'Pubic Relations' by Johnie Olimba (29 April 1976): Larry Nyita walks down Kimathi Street 'in flat heeled shoes. The highly polished tops belied the worn out soles, which he replaced daily with layers of cardboard.' He is down on his luck and meets Nick, his old school mate, 'in swinging bellbottom black and white check trousers ... a black silk shirt that clung to him like a rainy day in the Aberdares, and Man ... those platform boots, black with silver tasselled zippers.'

To say that life-style is of the utmost importance in these stories is not to exaggerate. When down-and-out Larry comes to see Nick at home in the evening, this is the setting: 'centre of town, modern bedsitter, slick and classy, shining bathroom all white tiles, flush choo, big veranda overlooking the main drag, from where you can see it all ... T.V., Radio and Record player all built into the wall.' Nick is there 'stretched out on his bed-cum-sofa', and with him his secretary, 'the cutest chick'. The writing here is clearly carrying the reader out of this world into the realm of fantasy in spite of the faithfully rendered specifications of interior design.[10] The story goes on: 'She had a note book in one hand, and I hate to think what was in the other.' The secretary gets up and adjusts her clothes, and 'Nick gave her a slap on the bottom and told her to beat it! and be back in an hour.' Larry is set up as a successful public relations man, hence the elegant word play of the title. The most important part of the setting up is again style – the new outfit he gets for himself. He discards his old life in his 'four-in-a-bed cube', and his old clothes on which 'even the stains had stains'. Fantasy here, as in most of the *Joe* stories, reflects urban preoccupations and does not as a mode necessarily detract from the basic realism of the narratives.

Marriage and infidelity

'Don't Trust the Playgirls who Live in the Cities' is the title of one of the Swahili stories from *Baraza* listed by Lepine (1990) in his examination of Swahili newspaper fiction; another is called 'Love Affairs with Playgirls Poison for Executives'.[11] These stories and countless more in the same vein, indicate the preoccupation with modern marriage, prostitution and the unequal situation of men and women in the cities which is a central theme in popular culture, and also present in *Joe*.

The five stories in the magazine which deal with marriage also deal with infidelity. In 'The Elected Ones' by David Maillu (August 1973) the husband is a successful executive, fairly happily married: 'When he married her she was slim; now she was nicely round. But now things had, sort of, changed. Sleeping with her was like one of his duties. After it was over he hardly thought about it. He began thinking about money, politics, new girls and himself.'

In 'A Day in your Life' by Njuguna Wainaina (November 1973) the theme is similar, but there are two points of view. Both the husband, the executive, and his wife have affairs – he contracts a venereal disease, she becomes pregnant. The same symmetry is characteristic of 'The Coincidence' by Omondi wa Radoli (December 1973) in which two couples plan to be unfaithful with each other's spouses, but pick the same place to be it in. The wives faint and the husbands in the last line of the story 'looked seriously at each other, not knowing what to do or say.' It is fairly clear that the writer does not know what to say either, so the rest is up to the reader.

Urban realism

In a review Meja Mwangi's *Carcase for Hounds* is called 'satisfying realism', and in a letter in the April 1975 issue his short story, 'Like Manna from Heaven' is praised: '*Joe* is really proving to be a stimulus to creativity in East Africa and will prove to have a lasting place in the history of African communicators.' But the letter writer, K. Musyoki, Nairobi, has a suggestion: 'What about some stories like "Manna from Heaven" where the central character is a woman?' In a review of David Maillu's *After 4.30*, by Chris Wanjala (January 1975) from the Department of Literature at the University, the woman question is again linked with literature: 'The women represented in the book-length poem are voices of disillusion in and criticism of married life in a modern African city.'

So, finding a voice in literature, and a forum in *Joe* is, according to Professor Wanjala, 'square social commentary on the nascent urban communities in East Africa.' And he goes on to specify that Maillu's book deals with 'urban lifestyles', particularly to do with the uneven development of the two sexes: 'All the book shows is men are ashamed of their wives, and wives do not seem to reflect the positions their husbands have acquired in the civil service probably after Africanisation.'[12] Wanjala reminds the readers that Okot p'Bitek has also dealt with this issue, and recommends his superior treatment in *Song of Lawino* and *Song of Malaya*. Not only social issues, but also quality and aesthetics can be discussed in *Joe*.

Terry Hirst is modest about the role *Joe* played on the literary scene: 'I wouldn't say that we were a launching pad, but I think we've been a supporting hand with writers who are going to make it anyway' (Lindfors, 1979: 90). He mentions Meja Mwangi as one of them, and his stories together with those of Ngugi and Sam Kahiga set the standard of high quality which most stories at least approach. Sam Kahiga's touch is lighter than Ngugi's or Mwangi's, and in many ways he is *the* representative *Joe* writer. So I shall take a closer look at his work.

Sam Kahiga, a professional writer

Apparently he walked into the *Joe* office some time in 1973 and decided that he liked it there and stayed on as a regular freelance writer until the magazine folded.[13] In a short autobiographical piece in *Joe* (May 1976) one can read that he had tried to make a career earlier as a singer and a guitar player. First he made a duo with Kenneth Watene, who later became a well known playwright and novelist. They called themselves *The Twilighters* and wanted to sound like *The Everly Brothers*. Later he joined up with David Maillu and a third person in a group called *The Cousins* 'because we felt that close. We composed lots of Swahili, Kamba, Kikuyu and Embu songs. But the records were not paying because the middle-men were getting everything.'

Sam Kahiga, born in 1947, is the second out of nine children of an African colonial civil servant. His parents were divorced, the father authoritarian: 'If you'd asked me if there is a reason why I write, I'd say: my father'.[14] Kahiga graduated from art school where he probably met Terry Hirst. As a writer he first made his reputation with *Potent Ash* (1972), a collection of short stories, which he wrote with his elder brother, Leonard Kibera who before his early death published the novel *Voices in the Dark*, and became highly regarded as an experimental writer. Most of the stories in *Potent Ash* are set in the 'Emergency Period' and atmosphere of the 1950s, and deal with the disruption of links and loyalties between Africans, which was one of the most destructive consequences of the colonial counter-insurgency strategy. Stories by the two brothers alternate: Kahiga's are linear, direct and to the point, whereas Kibera's are broken, indirect and full of atmosphere. *Potent Ash* is dedicated 'To Mother and Father'.

In Kahiga's career as a writer for *Joe*, his eye for a story was important. He wrote quite a few regular short stories, 'The Ivory Princess', 'The Return of the Ivory Princess', 'The Ambulance', 'The Sorcerer's Apprentice', but perhaps more importantly for *Joe* could turn any topic into a pointed, humourous narrative, with a human angle.[15] Often he would use an autobiographical form, making available his own fictive experience with *matatus*, secretaries or the law, and in brief sketches and descriptions bring to life the quick and hard qualities of urban existence. The following example is taken from a feature called Who needs Strippers?' (August 1977):

> Warimu Rufus looks like a ghost and is in fact a ghost of her former self. After failing her CPE and mislaying her virginity in some dark maize field, she got fed up with the countryside and its cheap tricks and joined the bright people. She bought some cream and applied it on her face until she was as bright as a Chinese. She bought a European wig – auburn colour, slipped into platforms and sought the neon lights. Forgot all about goats, maize, the shamba and the dreadful countryside darkness. Light is her element.

The other side of Kahiga's preoccupation with the life of the city is his dreamy interest in astrology and the significance of the stars (many *Joe* numbers carried horoscopes), documented for instance in the January 1978 issue in a humorous article 'Astrologers in My Life ... A Confessional Report'. In it Kahiga claims that in 1954 the famous Mau Mau leader, Dedan Kimathi, had his horoscope made on the basis of finger prints which he sent from the forest. The story documents Kahiga's great interest in Kimathi which has born fruit in a documentary novel *Dedan Kimathi* (1990).

The story deals with the various competing factions, fighting from the forests during the Mau Mau rising and particularly with the personalities of the leaders and their relations to women. The novel, which is of high quality, is built on historical sources and will undoubtedly be important in the continuing discussion about the character and significance of the Mau Mau and its leadership. Interest in the life and career of Dedan Kimathi was kept alive at the time, also in *Joe*, by two plays centering on his character – Micere Mugo and Ngugi wa Thiong'o's *The Trial of Dedan Kimathi*, showing heroism, betrayal and revolutionary ardour, and *Dedan Kimathi* by Kenneth Watene, Kahiga's friend, presenting a revisionist version of the story.[16]

Sam Kahiga has brought out several books; another collection of short stories, *Flight to Juba* (1979); three novels, *The Girl from Abroad* (1974a in the prestigious Heinemann African Writers' Series), *The Stars are Scattered* (Longman Nairobi 1974b, now out of print), *Lover in the Sky* (1975, one of the first batch of Spear Books). Since *Joe* folded, Kahiga has tried to continue his life as a professional writer, against heavy financial odds. He has written pieces for the *Standard* newspaper, and for *Signature*, Diner's Club's Nairobi magazine.

Three claims on behalf of *Joe* magazine

I wish in conclusion to return to the three claims which I made for *Joe* at the outset of the article, and to see whether in fact the magazine lived up to the claims. I suggested that *Joe* served as a mouthpiece for aspirations and issues of concern to middle and lower middle-class Africans, that *Joe* functioned as a socialising agent, educating people (the readers) in how to be urban, and that it constituted a fairly open and democratic public sphere, perhaps one of the few which was accessible.

Joe *as a mouthpiece*

Terry Hirst stated that *Joe* was aimed at an African readership. Indirect evidence points in the same direction: Hirst himself was an expatriate, but otherwise only few non-Africans make an appearance in the magazine (Bernth Lindfors was one of them, in a very disapproving review [September 1976] of the Nigerian writer Dilibe Onyeama's novel, *Sex is a Nigger's Game*). So the magazine was written and drawn by Africans, and advertisements were also directed at the African majority of the population. The readers who wrote letters and sent in jokes were almost all African, judging from their names.

This may be worth noting in a general way, but is of particular interest only if the issues and themes voiced in the magazine were of central concern to emerging and modernizing sections of the African population. This can be confirmed or not, as the case may be, by interviewing readers, by consulting newspapers, novels and popular music of the same period, and by the findings of urban ethnography. Apart from that, common sense and knowledge of what urbanisation in a Third World country involves make it likely that themes like housing, transport, marriage and sex, jobs and education, witchcraft, and the law constitute areas of concern.[17] The magazine, filled up with variations on these themes, sold well. So I wish to suggest that it is fair to say that *Joe* magazine functioned as a mouthpiece for pressing concerns of the African middle and lower middle classes.

Joe *and socialisation to city life*

I claim that there was in *Joe* a preoccupation with *urban* life, not modern life in general, but its versions in cities. The evidence for this takes several forms. First of all the language, including the coining of new expressions, which are repeated almost to the point of incantation: 'On the tarmac', 'Urban Nomads', 'A City Girl's View', 'On City Life' (Gitau E.'s cartoon), 'A Nairobi Tale' (Crossword), 'Five months I trekked the streets of Nairobi. Five months on tarmac!' (short story by Ngure Mwaniki). Many writers were, as we have seen, influenced by the urban tough-guy type thriller from the USA, particularly those written by James Hadley Chase. The settings and topics of the short stories, described earlier, are also evidence of the urban preoccupation of writers for the magazine, as are the themes around which each issue was organised.

The knitting together of language and themes was brought about by the particular didactic stance of *Joe*. Into its make-up went a will to educate – hence the claim for *Joe* as a conscious socializing agent. In spite of the magazine's irreverence it also has a flavour of the classroom, for instance in straightforward features like *Facts from History*, but also, more or less tongue in cheek, in unlikely places, e.g., the crossword puzzle, Gitau E.'s *On City Life* – *Lehrstücke* of the slums, a competition on the coining of contemporary proverbs, 'relevant to our times' (August 1975). Emphasizing the centrality of urban life. the inevitable move from the countryside to the city, was in tune with 1970s thinking on modernisation.

Joe *and a public sphere*

The third claim, that *Joe* functioned as a fairly open and democratic public sphere, is more problematic. In the first place it certainly only worked as such for the limited part of the population who spoke English and at the same time spent money (one to five shillings) on the magazine. If the average number of copies published was 20,000, and each was read by about ten people, which was *Joe*'s own estimate, that public sphere was relevant to about 200,000 people in Kenya plus their immediate communities.

Secondly the direction of communication, particularly on controversial issues, was naturally mostly from the magazine to the readers. In early issues of *Joe* some of the letters to the editor dealt with serious issues, like the need for allowing Oginga Odinga to stand for Parliament, but as time went on contributions from readers became increasingly light-hearted. A tendency which brings Hilary Ng'weno's stated reason to leave *Joe* to mind: it is important to inform about what's going on it before making fun of it. What *Joe* encouraged was more the habit of communicating than the taking of political positions. A conversational ease was the ideal, and that ideal may have made it the 'sweetest reading in Africa', as one reader suggested.

So the conclusion relating to *Joe* magazine as a significant forum for democratic debate is more hesitant. In its form it encouraged the habit of discussion and dialogue, but when it came to bringing serious issues into play in that discussion, it was less successful, at least as far as one can see from its pages. Whether it did help to feed discussions in other settings must be looked into in different ways.

Joe *as a contributor to and a source of knowledge on urban culture*

If *Joe* lives up to the three claims to the extent I have suggested, it follows that it is of interest to an examination of the urban culture of Nairobi in the period it covers. One great advantage for research into urban culture is that *Joe* is materially, solidly there. Many articulations of the evanescent, modern urban culture are difficult to recall, let alone recover. Who remembers the urban dressing styles of the seventies, enormous platform shoes, jaunty cap, bell bottom trousers and shirts which clung to the body 'like a rainy day in the Aberdares'? In *Joe* we find the style photographed, caricatured in drawings, written about, advertised. We circle round its expression and understand it in the context in which it was located.

Notes

[1] *The African Book Publishing Record* 5 (2), p. 91. I wish to thank Bernth Lindfors for drawing my attention to the very informative interviews in this periodical. Lindfors (1976) refers to interviews in this volume.
[2] Personal communication (p.c.), Nairobi, October 1990.
[3] Lindfors (1976: 91) and personal communication from Terry Hirst, Nairobi, October 1990. According to Richard Mabala *Joe* magazine gave rise to a monthly Tanzanian cartoon magazine, *Sani*. 'Closely based originally on Ng'weno's *Joe* magazine, it has developed its own style of humour and produced a series of classic comic characters which appeal both to children and adults. Several of the cartoonists have developed to producing their own extended comic stories in book form' (Mabala, 1990: 9).
[4] Interview with Hilary Ng'weno (Lindfors, 1976: 159, 160).
[5] Personal communication, Nairobi, April 1990.
[6] In a similar way the possibilities of identification seem to have made American or European films in which the hero was black immensely popular in Nairobi, regardless of their quality. In the interview with Lindfors, Hilary Ng'weno mentions two: *Shaft in Africa* and *The Wilby Conspiracy* (Lindfors, 1976: 159).
[7] In a *Joe* three years' Birthday Message, April 1972–1976.
[8] *Joe* was not the only publication to feature short fiction regularly. On the large body of Swahili fiction, published in *Taifa Weekly*, *Baraza* and *Fahari*, see Richard Marshall Lepine's fascinating study, *Swahili Newspaper Fiction in Kenya: the Stories of James I. Mwagojo*. PhD, University of Wisconsin, Madison, 1988.
[9] Ngure Mwaniki, 'No Chance at All, I Think', August 1976.
[10] Yusuf K. Dawood, a popular Kenyan writer, makes this point on the very last page of his novel, *The Price of Living*, calling the setting and the characters of the novel 'this make-believe world' (Dawood, 1989: 168). *The Price of Living* was serialised in *The Standard* in September 1989.
[11] *Usiamini Vipusa Waishio Mijini*, by F. Mubezi and *Mapenzi ya Vidosho Sumu kwa Wenye Madaraka* by F. Dumila.
[12] One short story in *Baraza* by T. Pella was called, 'I Can't Get Married to You Because You're Uneducated' (*Siwezi Kuolewa Nawe Kwani Huna Eliu*) (Lepine, 1976).
[13] Personal communication, Nairobi, April 1990.
[14] Personal communication, Nairobi, April 1990.
[15] Lepine during his fieldwork in 1977-78 asked writers of Swahili fiction which were their favourite authors. One writer, Azizi Mchangamwe singles out Sam Kahiga: 'This writer seems to spell out my deep sense of humour and understanding whenever I read him' (Lepine,1988: 567).
[16] Watene's play was reviewed in *Joe*, February 1975, and in the following issues there was a lively debate about the character of the protagonist, on whether Watene had been influenced by 'white' stereotypes in his view of Kimathi. In November 1976 Terry Hirst reviewed the National Theatre performance of *The Trial of Dedan Kimathi* in a manner which reflected *Joe* ideals: he stressed the play as an act of communication, talked of the 'communication magic' of the play, and pointed out that in the play issues were raised and debated which rarely get a popular airing in Kenyan art' – in this case whether there is 'anything worth having in between winning and losing in the freedom struggle?'
[17] Some writers were very conscious of what might interest the reading public. David Maillu, a very successful writer of popular literature, says that he has systematically studied the psychology of the African reader and the African storyteller. He 'tried to find out' what they liked talking about and hearing' (Lindfors, 1976: 86).

Works cited

Barber, Karin. 1987. 'Popular Arts in Africa', *African Studies Review* 30 (3): 1–78.

Bardolph, Jacqueline. 1983. 'Naissance d'une littérature populaire à Nairobi', *L'Afrique Litteraire*, 67: 160–74.

Dawood, Yusuf K. 1983. *The Price of Living*. Nairobi: Longman.

Frederiksen, Bodil Folke. 1991. 'City life and city texts. Popular knowledge and articulation in the slums of Nairobi' in *Culture and Development in Southern Africa*, edited by Preben Kaarsholm. London: James Currey, 227–37.

Kahiga, Sam. 1974a. *The Girl from Abroad*. London: Heinemann.

—— 1974b. *The Stars are Scattered*. Nairobi: Longman.

—— 1975. *Lover in the Sky*. Nairobi: Spear Books.

—— 1979. *Flight to Juba*. Nairobi: Longman.

—— 1990. *Dedan Kimathi*. Nairobi: Longman.

Kahiga, Sam and Leonard Kibera. 1972. *Potent Ash*. Nairobi: East African Publishing House.

Kibera, Leonard. 1970. *Voices in the Dark*. Nairobi: East African Publishing House.

Lepine, Richard Marshall. 1988. *Swahili Newspaper Fiction in Kenya: The stories of James I. Mwagojo*. PhD dissertation University of Wisconsin-Madison.

Lindfors, Bernth. 1979. 'Interview with David Maillu', *The African Book Publishing Record* (APBR) 5(2): 85–88.

—— Interview with Terry Hirst. *The African Book Publishing Record* 5(2) 88-91.

—— Interview with Hilary Ng'weno. *The African Book Publishing Record* 5(3): 157–61.

Mabala, Richard. 1990. 'Popular Literature in Tanzania'. Paper presented to AATOLL, Botswana.

Mugo, Micere and Ngugi wa Thiong'o. 1976. *The Trial of Dedan Kimathi*. London: Heinemann (African Writers Series: 191).

Mwangi, Meja. 1974. *Carcase for Hounds*. London: Heinemann (African Writers Series: 145).

Watene, Kenneth. 1974. *Dedan Kimathi*. Nairobi: East African Publishing House.

Primary Text 3

Facsimiles of Cartoons, Stories & Covers from *Joe* Magazine

This page: From January 15, 1976, advertisements, p.30; cartoon strips from February 29, 1976, pp. 22, 20
Overleaf: 'The Farmhands: a tragic short story by Mithano Ngungute', p. 18 (illust.), p 19.

ANSWERS

How well did you do? The rather surprising results of 'Intelligent Guessing?' are as follows;

1.	19 days	7.	150 days
2.	22 days	8.	165 days
3.	31 days	9.	280 days
4.	60 days	10.	336 days
5.	107 days	11.	400 days
6.	113 days	12.	700 days

The new-style JOE Crossword was, we know, a little tough. But after you have checked your results, please drop us a line to tell us how you enjoyed it, and to offer any suggestions that you may have.

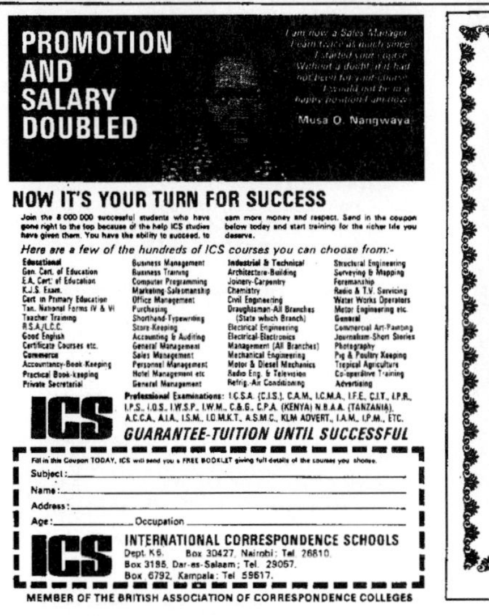

30 JOE Magazine, January 15, 1976

MULLA Nassir

22 JOE Magazine, February 29, 1976

TOM MANDAZI and Co. by *Hirst*

THE WISDOM OF TUMBO *Githinji*

20 JOE Magazine, February 29, 1976

THE FARMHANDS

IF one saw Kairu going to work that morning, one would have got the impression that he was fully conscious of what he was doing. However, such an impression of Kairu, the farmhand, proved wrong. For fifty years of Kairu's working life, he had been walking to and fro this path. On each and every day that he could remember. Consequently, he had come to know all the geography of that path that there was to master. He knew where the path bended, or where of late a small pebble had decided to occupy the path. All these details were in his being and his feet did the walking and seeing, for his mind had long agō stopped to function with regard to his immediate surroundings.

Behind him walked his elder son, Njuguna. Both of them were going to Idyll Fruits Limited, where they were employed as farmhands, like generations had done before them. In actual fact, three weeks after Njuguna was concieved, his unwilling mother took him to the farm. She placed the baby under a shade while she worked and alternatively, hammocked him in her back when he cried. For no minute could be lost following the manager's directive that work had to continue from sunrise to sunset. Managers meant what they said and disobedience meant a throttle to one's life.

Njuguna was brought up on that farm and now on the 21st January, after thirty years, he was still working there. When he dies his body will be crushed to "Idyll fertilizers" which his childrenwill apply to the fruit trees. As a result of which the fruits shall yield both quantitively and qualitatively but the "jembe-man", as the Kairus are called, shall never as much as touch the fruits: let alone eat them.

On this morning, the Kairus were going to a site where a new "Idyll Fruit Factory" was being constructed. At this time of year, there was little work on the farm, therefore all labour had been turned over to the building site, because the building had to be constructed before the following harvesting season — at all costs.

They reached the site at 6.09 a.m. and found work already underway. A large menacing hunk of flesh, which everybody referred to as the "supervisor," approached them.

"Where have you been, you beasts?" asked the big man.

Like his superiors, the supervisor, had learned the language of administration.

"Excuse me, Sir!" Trembled Kairu as he lowered his eyes.

"We are sorry to be late," added Njuguna.

"Sorry, indeed!" sneered the worthy supervisor. "Listen, today you are working with no pay! Go away, you morons! No wonder you have been sharing Njuguna's mother."

"Thank you very much sir!" chorused the Kairus as they scuttered away, happy to move from their supervisor.

Njuguna ran to the section where a

A tragic short story by Mithano Ngungute

group of people surrounded a concrete mixer, seemingly very much at home with the clouds of blue smoke that the machine exhaled. He went directly to where a heap of cement bags lay and without noticing the white clouds of cement which issued from the fifty-kilogram bag, he started feeding the machine with cement.

Meanwhile, Kairu had reached the back of the building where a gang of workers were involved in transporting nine-by-nine stones to the third storey. They had arranged themselves on a series of drum-supported planks of timber which served as a ladder to the upper storey. The man on the ground heaved a stone, handed it to the person above and the stones passed from hand to hand until they reached Kairu, who accompanied by a break of wind and a cough, handed it to the mason.

"Look here, oldman," said the mason, "you stop breaking the wind, otherwise I shall shove you down."

"I know you will," replied Kairu, "Because you never even excrete!" Upon which, the mason and those who were around, bust into fits of laughter.

"Say, Kairu, how do you like your work here?" asked the mason.

"A change is as good as a rest. Naturally I feel honoured to have broken the monotonous routine of my life."

"I heard that you wanted to quit the fruit work?" enquired the same mason.

All of them now had abandoned their work and were looking at the old man.

"Yes," replied the old man.

"What had driven you into such unprecedented adventure?" persisted the mason.

"For the simple reason that I am a human being."
reasoned the old man. "Most of my ancestors were here, did the same good old job and died here. I wanted to change the routine and face a new life. I wanted to diverge from the path no matter how dangerous it was — so I thought."

"No wonder you were not allowed to go." Put in an extremely thin labourer who was reputed to be an extra ear for the manager.

"I was there with him," said the gallant voice, directly below Kairu on the ladder. "The manger asked him, "where else could you get such conditions of work, if you left the Idyll Fruit Ltd?' Kairu with a firm voice said, All I want is to quit, if the conditions in the next palce will be worse, then I will keep on the road until I get a better place or until you fellows recognize that we are human beings".

By this time Kairu was crying softly to himself, and when the rest realised this, they turned back to their work without consoling him. He felt bitter towards himself for having cried, but he consoled himself by arguing that he did not want to, but the tears had streamed down on their own accord on remembering how the manager had slapped him on the face and spat in his mouth. Afterwards he had been forced into the farm truck and taken to a local police station and by the word of the manager, he was caned on his bare buttocks until they turned into blood and exposed flesh.

"Hey! get hold of this stone!" shouted a stone lifter who was below Kairu.

"Yes, sir," said Kairu as he accepted the stone.

The individual whom Kairu had addressed as "sir" did not feel in any way honoured. Kairu had that word on his lip always. He even applied it to his children and more annoyingly so to his wives. It had cost him a lot to have the word always at the ready.

Now it was around eleven o'clock and the work was progressing at the rate which was to be expected from the farmhands. The click-click of the hammers, the response of chisels, the cry of the shovels, the coughing of the concrete mixer, the noise of the birds was mingled with the soft murmurs of the old men and the sighs of the youngsters.

However, this melody of ill-assortment was short lived for soon it was replaced by a tragedy. Prior to this, Kairu had assumed his usual role of an automaton and was picking stones and passing them over without thinking. So when a particularly slippery one was handed to him, he did not take extra precautions and the stone slipped from his fingers and hurtled towards the ground. For a split second he did nothing but that time was enough to revive his decayed humanity. He realised what was nappening. Fearing that the stone might harm one of his dear comrades, he gave a high pitched yell and jumped down in an endevour to retrieve the stone. But too late!

There followed an ominous silence during which they all watched the chase of the stone across the air. All people held their breath as they saw the stone crash on a wheelburrow in motion. The unfortunate driver of the wheelburrow was thrown on top of the stone and it was on him Kairu landed — with a terrific thud.

Everybody left their places of work and hurried to the scene of the tragedy. All people began shouting and asking questions to no one in particular while they cautiously removed the unfortunate people from the wheelburrow and placed them under a shade. A systematic examination of the casualties revealed that although the wheelburrow pusher was unconscious he was not hurt much but Kairu had broken his right leg — slightly above the shank, and the jagged wound was bleeding profusely.

Njuguna was among the last arrivals and he flung himself on his father, crying like a small boy.

"Father, you are not hurt much," he said, "this is only a scratch which will heal overnight. You must be well tomorrow because we must earn overselves money to buy ourselves some maize."

"Sure, sure," replied Kairu with an effort. "Tomorrow is the polling day. Maize or no maize we must go to vote. The leg will not hinder me. After that you and I shall attend the party's rally at Njoro."

"One of us shall have to remain behind to look for money," Njuguna said.

"You don't understand, my son," said Kairu. "tomorrow will be a very busy day for us. Together with what I have outlined, I will also go to look whether the fruits need weeding after which I shall go to your in-laws to negotiate about the return of your wife."

"Oh! father not that woman again!" protested Njuguna.

"You shall have her whether you like it or not," was the final verdict of Kairu in that moment of his life when all consciousness was drawn away from him and was speaking the things which occupied his mind.

At this point there was commotion around the Kairus as the spectators gave way for the advancing supervisor.

"I knew you are bone lazy, Kairu," belowed the supervisor. "Stand up before I skin you alive."

"Yes, sir," said Kairu as he struggled to rise.

"No father, please, your leg is broken." implored Njuguna.

"Please sir, for the love of mankind, let my father be. Give him a lift to hospital!"

The supervisor lifted a big stick and struck Njuguna on his back as he shouted "Move boy, work is the key word here. We will soon have you dead if you decline to work."

While Njuguna was too stunned to do anything the big stick was seen to land with a crash on Kairu's arm. Kairu remained unmoved — no contempt, no pain. Even if he felt pain, it was the metallic part of him which did otherwise his face was as indifferent as it was ignorant of the happenings around him...

Gitau E. on CITY LIFE

THE WOLF UNDER SHEEP'S SKIN

JOE Magazine, January 15, 1976 23

Dear Joe

WHERE IS YOUR WIFE?

The past year has been a year of women but your wife (Mrs. Joe) didn't appear on the magazine cover. Does it mean that your wife is not there or was she busy with her matatu? If she needs Service, I have a 'credit' in Mechanics and you can ask me to come with my box full of spanners. I know she will soon be on the way. If she doesn't have an outfit, I have with me two spare sacks to make her an overall or maybe a maxi would suit her better!

Onesimo Kiten'ge, Kangundo

Stop these filthy rumours! My wife appeared on the cover of the first issue in Women's Year. Having satisfied her desire for extravagant publicity I then relegated her to her proper station — 'Machakos Airport' Bus Station. But I warn you she's not to be tinkered with.

STRICTLY FOR JOE!

I read your magazine and I respect you. Ask me why? The reason is it follows a pattern that all bald-headed men are rich. I respect the rich including you. But it is only when I bought your December issue that I discovered you are all ambitions, aren't you Joe? Since 1975 was the Women's Year I expected to see the picture of your wife on the front page acting as MOTHER CHRISTMAS! But there you were with two dwarfs and the long-eared mongrel of your — whatever breed is that!

Mbugua P. G., Nairobi

You've guessed our secret! All bald men are rich because we have sold our hair to make super-soft mattresses for export. Join us! Shave off all your hair today, and mail it to the Curly Stuffed Silent Mattress Co., Private Bag Tinderet. A fortune awaits you!

AN OUTCAST

This is serious — really — so none of your cheek. . . I am a girl of 23, reasonably attractive, building a good job. So all should be best in the best of all possible worlds. .. . . This is far from the truth however, I simply feel like an 'outcast' you see, I am a virgin. All my friends spend their time swallowing pills and discussing problems of that nature. To tell you frankly, I am sick and tired of my virginity but the process of putting an end to it gives me nightmares. What do you suggest I do Joe or better still what are you going to do about it?

Lucy, Nairobi

Yes, I agree, better still. . . You are clearly in need of my Private Consulting Service. Think of me like a trusted teacher or friendly doctor. No, on second thoughts, don't think of me like that. Don't think anything. Just wait where you are, and I'll be right over.

THE GIRL NEEDS HELP

She is 18 and I am 21, I love her very dearly and she professes to love me. We have been in the same school for the whole of 1974. But now I am employed and she is in Form Two now, I also left in Form Two. What bothers me is, I have heard from a friend in the same school that the girl is occupied with some two teachers from that school, and he proved the girl has another boyfriend at a different school. But in her letter she tells me we still are on good terms. Joe should I continue with this girl? Help me Joe I really need it.

Charles K. II, Elwak

If I were you I would investigate your informant a little. He could be very imaginative, with a plan of his own in operation. The English have an old French saying 'Honi soit qui maly pense' or 'Evil to him who evil thinks'. I am sure there's a simple explanation for your girlfriend going out with all these men at the same time. She's probably a nymphomaniac!

INFLATION

Would you kindly give a thought to the chaotic state of my finances. I believe, and all concerned agree, that this can't go on. I earn 1,000/- per month and out of this I am supposed to pay 600/- for rent, 150/- for electricity and water, 42/50 for transport. . . On top of all this I have to buy a dress each month (if I am to keep my boyfriend), not to mention that I do have to eat and also to send money for my brother's school fees. Is there no way of improving this situation Joe, apart from loitering with intent?

Desperate lady, Nairobi

Whatever you do, do not loiter within any tents, no matter how desperate you are, lady. Clearly you need a manager, and I could help you there for a small management fee. For example, what kind of violent boyfriend do you love, if you have to buy a new dress every month? My first duty would be to move you in with a gentler guy.

A LET DOWN

What the hell have you done, Bwana! I've been a good and faithful customer to you, though you don't know that. And I've never complained of anything you've done, never, not even when you rode on a donkey the other day complaining bitterly that you had no money to buy some fuel. Now then during the recent Nairobi Show you attended on a cow, a real cow with a capital 'C', wasn't that a let down to K.B.S. officials who offered so many buses to serve the show attendants? To what extent do you claim to be fit in the skull?

Annoyed Alex the K'sang

Healthy competition never hurt anyone, and my cow was certainly more healthy than most Kenya Buses. I never claimed to be 'fit in the skull'! as you put it. I leave such extravagant claims to be made by others is more need of them than me.

UNFAITHFUL WIFE

Hey Joe, the best of all you do, is just when you give free advice to people. To me your help is very much needed. Three months ago, I was a happy family man taking care of a wife and my two-year-old daughter. In May last year, I discovered the unfaithful connection between my wife and a drunken bachelor who was then our neighbour. I had good reasons to believe it, and when I asked her she agreed she had been unfaithful to me and asked for forgiveness. But I sent her away from me, and now she is at her parents' home. Did I do the right thing?

P. M. Henry, Mombasa

How can I tell until I see your bank balance? It sounds as if you came away from her parents' home empty-handed! If you must play these silly games, why don't you stick to the rules. You could undermine us all.

WHY not drop me a letter expressing your feelings about things — even about me? I might print it — and then I might not!

JOE magazine,
P.O. Box 30362,
Nairobi, Kenya.

Joe.

32 JOE Magazine, January 15, 1976

PARTY JOKES

An executive friend of ours is so dedicated to his work that he keeps his secretary near his bed in case he gets an idea during the night.

S. Mutungi,
c/o S. Hindiya,
P.O. Box 30011,
NRB.

*

At a party, a man commented, "Women cannot keep secrets!"
A woman who was in the group said, "Rubbish! I can. I've kept my age secret since I was 21!"
"Oh, but you will one day slip it out," the man insisted, but the woman, who was now getting worked up said, "What non-sense! I have managed to keep it for 17 years and I should be able to keep it much longer!"

John B. Mwangi,
P.O. Box 77121,
NAIROBI.

*

A notice in the rooms of a large hotel frequented chiefly by international businessmen read: "If you can't sleep, don't start by blaming the bed. First examine your conscience!"

Simon Muchui,
c/o J. Solomon,
P.O. Box 117,
KIAMBU.

A man found his wife in bed with another man. He pulled out his gun, shot his wife and yelled at the man to get the hell out of the house. Later, when asked why he shot his wife and not the man, he said, "Better shoot her once rather than one man every week!"

John B. Mwangi,
P.O. Box 77121, NAIROBI.

*

A policeman was trying to stop a man from jumping off a bridge one very cold night.
"If you do jump," reasoned the policeman, "I'll have to go in after you. After I pull you out, we'll probably have to sit in the bitter cold until an ambulance arrives. We'll probably both get pneumonia and die. Why don't you be a good chap and go home and hang yourself?"

R. A. Nurmoh'd,
P.O. Box 80239,
MOMBASA.

The doctors at a busy clinic often had too little time to write full reports on each patient. On one occasion, when the patient was an expectant mother, the doctor spent some time with her and then filled in her report, "Pregnancy persists."

Simon G. Muchui,
c/o J. G. Solomon,
P.O. Box 117,
KIAMBU.

*

Interviewer: Have you ever worked for the Government?
Applicant: Nearly did Sir, on one occasion.
Interviewer: What exactly do you mean?
Applicant: There wasn't enough evidence for conviction with hard labour!

Jacinta Wairimu,
P.O. Box 21048,
NAIROBI.

*

A wise old man was once asked to settle a dispute between two brothers about the fair division of a large estate left to them, by their father. The old man said, "Let one brother divide the estate and let the other brother have the first choice."

Paterson Chuchu,
P.O. Box 35,
GITHUNGURI.

JOE Magazine, February 29, 1976 21

Above left: Comic strip, Gitau E. On City Life, 'The Wolf under Sheep's Skin', 15 January 1976, p.23.
Above Right: Letters page – 'Dear Joe', 15 January 1976.
Below Left: 'Party Jokes', from 29 February 1976.

Above: From February 29, 1976, Front Cover, 'On the Tarmac: a guide for school-leavers'.
Right, above and below: Miscellaneous front covers: November 1974, 'Did You Ever Have a Holiday'; January 1975, 'New Year Resolution'.

NICI NELSON

Representations of Men & Women, City & Town in Kenyan Novels of the 1970s and 1980s

Reference
Adapted from *African Languages & Cultures* 9 (2) 1996: 145–68

I have always loved reading imaginative literature. Long before cultural studies and the postmodernists' emphasis on texts and multiple voices gave social scientists permission to look beyond the conventional sources of 'data' for inspirations and understandings, I encouraged my East African ethnography students to read East African novels in addition to ethnographies. Convinced that good novelists produce social descriptions of interest and authenticity to students of society, I felt that novels would give the students' imaginations wings and bring to life anthropological models and generalizations of societies they were unfamiliar with. Recently, my encounters with post-modern re-analyses of anthropology have made me realize that even bad novelists can give the reader insights into the novelist's culture. If authors inevitably write out of local discourses, they are all involved in a process of constructing and reconstructing representations of aspects of interest and/or importance to their societies.

Until recently anthropologists have all too rarely used literature as a text through which to explore a culture. Obviously anthropologists have traditionally dealt with non-literate societies. Ethnographers have recognized the impact of globilization by expanding their original research concentration on kinship, religion, ritual and subsistence agriculture to include issues such as urbanization, migration, development, and industrialization. However, the methodology of the discipline has not responded as quickly. In addition fiction, being imaginative, has been considered problematical as a research resource. Post-modern textual analysis points the way for how anthropology could deal with works of fiction to further understanding of complex societies. 'Expressive forms' can give us insights into indigenous representations of culture and social structure (Shore 1995).

The 18 novels I selected were written between 1965 and 1983, with one follow-up novel written in 1986. Eleven authors are represented, two of which are women (see Figure 1).

Figuring prominently in all of novels are two sets of representations, one which opposes the categories of men and women and another which opposes those of city and countryside. These representations arose from discourses of gender power and the impacts of rapid urbanisation on post-independence Kenyan life.

I settled on these two discourses not only because they were rich and well developed themes in these novels but also because they resonated with my own interests in issues of gender and urbanization, important elements in the urban research I have carried out for the last 25 years in and on Nairobi. I was intrigued by the similarities and differences between these two discourses, developed both in English-language novels written by university-educated men for the educated elite and in the day-to-day preoccupations of the men and women I worked with during the 1970s. I had spent 4 years working with people in Mathare Valley, a large and thriving 'shanty town' as it was termed then ('spontaneous settlement' as it would be characterized now). What was striking was the ways in which discourses on men/women and city/country used by the novelists and Mathare residents coincided and conflicted.

In the 20 year period after Kenyan Independence, major novelists were men, with the exception of Grace Ogot, though she mainly wrote short stories. I selected 18 novels by the 10 major novelists of that period (8 male, 2 female). This is not by any means an exhaustive list of Kenyan novels of this period. The novels I have chosen, with a couple of exceptions, were published (or in the case of *The River Between*, by Ngũgĩ, written) in the 1960s and 1970s. I have included two novels published after the mid-eighties because they seem to be continuations of earlier writing by the same author (e.g., Mangua's *Son of Woman*). I have not included short story writers such as Miriam Were and have only considered one poet, Okot p'Bitek, whose *Song of Lawino* is almost a novel in verse. Most of the novelists were central Highland Bantu (Gikuyu, Meru, Embu) with the exceptions of Okot, Dawood and Ogot. Okot was born a Ugandan but the majority of his professional career was spent in Kenya. (See Figure 1 for list of novelists and titles and dates. I will not use dates in the text, except for quotations.)

I will first examine representations of two opposed categories, men/women and city/country in these novels as evidence of discourses on gender power and urbanization. I will then demonstrate where these representations from the University literary sector coincide or connect with representations being developed from a poor urban Gikuyu perspective.

Fig. 1. Kenyan novels read for this article

Okot p'Bitek	1969	*Song of Lawino*
Okello Oculi	1968	*Orphan*
Yusuf Dawood	1983	*The Price of Living*
Mwangi Gicheru	1979	*Across the Bridge*
Charles Mangua	1971	*Son of Woman*
	1972	*A Tail in the Mouth*
	1986	*Son of Woman in Mombasa*
Meja Mwangi	1973	*Kill Me Quick*
	1976	*Going Down River Road*
	1990	*Striving for the Wind*
Mwangi Ruheni	1972	*What a Life*
	1973	*Future Leaders*
	1975	*Minister's Daughter*
Mike Mwaura	1972	*The Renegade*
Rebecca Njau	1978	*Ripples in the Pool*
Grace Ogot	1966	*The Promised Land*
Ngũgĩ wa Thiong'o	1965	*The River Between*
	1967	*A Grain of Wheat*
	1977	*Petals of Blood*

Representations of men and women

The wicked city women

The most powerful and pervasive stereotype in many of these novels is that of the wicked urban women. Prostitutes, often referred to as 'whores', are not distinguished clearly from 'good-time girls', who just love the high life of town and drink and dance in bars.

Sex and drink are entwined in the representation of the wicked urban women. There is a great deal of meeting and interaction in bars. Ruheni's male protagonist (*What a Life*) can't leave Ada, the barmaid, alone. Each meeting with her at the bar where she works brings a disaster in train (arrest for drunkenness, theft of his wallet, his wife leaving him, potential loss of his job). Helplessly he moans that Ada gives him too much to drink and makes his life a mess (1972: 108). The protagonist Ben in *Going Down River Road* (by Mwangi) meets Win, the woman who directly and indirectly shapes his life for the duration of the novel, in a bar. She is studying for her secretarial exams in order to better herself, but he cynically assumes that this is a ploy. Subsequent events bear out his cynical assessment of her as being a sex worker. Time and again female characters tempt men to drink ... and then to sex, usually for money. Either such city women get men to buy them drinks and then pay them back with sex or they get money for sex and drink it. Dodge, a self-styled 'son of a whore' (in Mangua's *Son of Woman*) says 'I was conceived on a quid and then my mother drank it!' (1971: 2). In the opening lines of this novel, he calls himself 'son of woman, that's me' and then goes on to describe his mother (the archetypal woman?) as 'my whoring mother'. The connection cannot be avoided: women are whores – at least, urban women.

Women are often represented in these novels (with exceptions to be discussed) manipulating their sexual attractiveness to men to entice, tantalize and entrap male characters. Either that or they are represented as sexual objects with nothing to offer a man but sex. In Mangua's *A Tail in the Mouth* a minor character refers to his girlfriend as 'a problem with tits' to the general approbation of his listeners. In another place in the narrative, Sam claims to be unable to stand women in any context except in bed (1972: 13). All the female characters in Mwangi's *Kill Me Quick* are nothing more than 'screws' of the male characters. Women in bars deserve the most violent and degrading of treatment; their persona as women who exploit their sex means that they do not deserve sympathetic or understanding treatment. Ben in a drunken rage rips the clothes off a prostitute who tries to seduce him in a bar. Without a qualm (from him or the male author) he leaves her nude and vomiting on the floor commenting that she looks like nothing so much as a nude hippo (Mwangi's *Going Down River Road*). Later, the same Ben treats a young girl prostitute (with a month-old baby) who has brought him to her room for sex, with appalling insensitivity and viciousness. In principle he objects to the fact that her practically newborn child is sleeping in a cardboard box in the room they are having sex in. But he does not manifest a shred of understanding that she might be forced into this situation to support herself and her fatherless child.

An interesting variant of this representation is the one which Ruheni develops in *Minister's Daughter*. Here the wicked Eunice withholds sex to 'catch' Lewes (by pretending to be a virgin) while the initially innocent, rural girl, the minister's daughter of the title, Jane, yields to Lewes' sexual advances because she loves him and assumes he is going to marry her. When he impregnates her, he kicks her out, branding her a 'whore' and 'spoiled goods', and tells her not to mix her boyfriends up when she is trying to claim him as the father. No urban woman deserves respectful treatment and anyone who succumbs to male advances merely proves the assumption. Yet ironically, in the narrative, it is Eunice, the truly wicked woman, who pretends to be a virgin, playing on this representation to confuse the male protagonist.

Not only are urban women irrevocably connected with drink and sex, they are represented as corrupt; they are by nature liars and cheats who will either suck a man dry or emasculate him. Samson (in Mangua's *A Tail in the Mouth*) says that whenever he remembers what that whore, Delilah, did to his namesake, he wants to spit at any woman in sight. In Mangua's *Son of Woman*, one of Dodge's major problems is that all the women in his life lie to him and deceive him. His foster mother constantly lies to him and steals the possessions left by his dead mother, and Tonia, his 'foster sister', gets him kicked out of the house by falsely claiming that he tried to rape her when in actuality it was she who insisted on their sexual experimentation. Various girl-friends lie to and deceive him in the course of the narrative. Later in the book Dodge and Tonia meet again; she lies about being married to someone else while pretending to be sexually attracted to him in order to steal a large haul of money he has just stolen from someone else. Dodge's indignation against Tonia's perfidity ironically ignores the fact that the money she steals is already stolen. One does not feel the irony is deliberate on the part of the author.

When the protagonist of *The Renegade* dances with a girl, she steals his money. A friend counsels him that he has been foolish. 'You don't know what you are thinking about. They [meaning women] are blood suckers. They'd suck your blood. They'll suck you to the bone' (Mwaura 1972: 33). Gikere in Njau's *Ripples in the Pool* marries Selina, a wicked city woman par excellence. She sells his mother's plot, drives him to drink, ruins his dream of having a clinic and ultimately kills his sister.

The theme of urban women's corruption and untrustworthiness is often worked out in terms of women's treatment of their children (cruelty, neglect, abandonment, abortion). In Mwangi's *Going Down River Road*, Ben is deceived by Win, the woman whose flat he lives in. She runs off with her white employer, leaving him instructions to put her unnamed boy child, referred to as Baby (not Ben's child) in a charity home. (This is a way of presenting the child, Baby, as uncared for and neglected.) Thus at a stroke, she deceives both Ben and the baby. Ben's friend Ocholla sympathizes with him saying 'Women are bitches, Ben. All of them.' (1976: 159). Win is damned out of hand because she abandons her child to an orphanage. The 16-year-old prostitute Ben abuses later in the same book is the object of his anger because she is entertaining customers in her room with a one-month-old child in a cardboard box next to the bed. (This despite the fact that seen from another point of view, one might assume that this pitiable young woman is trying in the face of unbearable odds to support her young child.) Jane Njeri, the main character in Ruheni's *Minister's Daughter*, starts her long journey into degradation, depravity and corruption when she give up her illegitimate child to adoption (abandons him, in other words). She only achieves redemption when she regrets this abandonment and tries to find him again. Women who abort their children are vilified by Oculi. The rural wife in Oculi's *The Orphan* speaks to her husband: 'I am not like the woman of town ... the woman of emancipation ... I am not the woman of town, who celebrates the latest abortion, with the alcohol of machines from chemists, on the laps of the abortion's father' (1968: 69). This combines many of the negative elements of the representation of the wicked urban woman: emancipation, corruption as symbolized by the fact that she aborts the foetus and then celebrates it, while drinking, with the foetus's father. Tonia, the perfidious woman, in *Son of Woman* had an abortion early in life and has no uterus. She therefore lacks a 'real' woman's capacity to reproduce. This makes her no longer a woman, but a 'whore'. In the second book she is found in Mombasa working for a family planning clinic, a fact which Dodge attributes to her hatred of women and children because she could never bear children. The implied equation here is that 'unborn' women try to control and limit conception which makes them less than women, motivated by hate.

Sometimes the vilification of urban women as wicked and corrupt reaches such a pitch that it almost seems as if a magical power to destroy men is being attributed to urban women. The mother of the male protagonist of Ruheni's *What a Life* (1972) tells him that if men go to prostitutes their minds turn into the minds of small children, attributing to the urban woman the power to work a destructive witchcraft on men. An old woman in Mwaura's *The Renegade* preaches to the protagonist 'Beware of women, especially those from town. Women, my child, can divert your aim in life. They have a dangerous way of sapping one's determination' (1972: 97). In other words, urban women are dangerous!

The least negative representation of urban women in these novels is that they are pleasure-loving and trivial. Grace in *Minister's Daughter* by Ruheni, is gutsy, fun-loving and keen on clothes and dancing. While she is recognized as religious (therefore good) it is a trivial and thoughtless kind of religion she is committed to. A character describes her as 'religious as all women are religious. It changes with the weather' (1977: 3). In Ruheni's *Future Leaders* a character confides that he does not want a girl who talks too much academic stuff. All he wants from a woman is 'the basic commodity' (e.g., sex). Ocholla explains to Ben in *Going Down River Road* that his wives are stupid and do not understand friendship. 'They don't understand things the way we [men] do. They are different, Ben. They are stupid' (1976: 213).

Other representations of urban women

There are, of course, other representations of women in these novels which are more understanding, more nuanced and even positive. Women are practical and well organized, they can be seen (rarely) as men's redeemers, and are sometimes portrayed as betrayed innocents.

One prevailing stereotype of women, whether rural or urban, is that they are competent – sometimes frighteningly so. The protagonist of *Oh What a Life* admits to being an appalling manager of his money compared to his wife. Dodge, who married the perfidious Tonia in *Son of Woman in Mombasa*, calls Tonia 'his better half' partly because she manages to hold down a job and support them, and partly because she does all the housework and manages their money. All in all, Mangua demonstrates a certain inconsistency in the drawing of Tonia's character between these two novels (published 17 years apart), while that of Dodge is remarkably consistent. Tonia evolves into a much more sympathetic character in the second book, a hard-working woman more sinned against than sinning. It is impossible to tell whether this is a shift in the author's attitude or in the gaze of Dodge, through whose eyes we see the world in these first-person narratives.

In Gicheru's *Across the Bridge* there is another representation of women as practical and accepting of the reality of things. Chuma works as a houseboy for a rich Kenyan elite family. He seduces, impregnates and subsequently runs away with the daughter of the family. The father refuses to recognize the union. In the end it is the mother who manages to send the young couple money and who eventually persuades the father to accept the inevitable.

This same novel presents a rather more unusual representation of urban women, that is, woman as the redeemer of a man who has lost his way. The beautiful daughter tries, as it happens in vain, to convince her lover (the family's houseboy) to turn to education to better himself. In fact it is in the tutoring sessions she gives him that they fall in love. He prefers to turn to crime to 'get rich quick'. Ultimately, after a long saga of mistreatment and wickedness, during which the reader is at a loss to understand why she does not give up on this cruel and stupid man, Chuma is redeemed and brought to understand the error of his criminal and violent ways. This highly unlikely turn of events makes *Across the Bridge* the Kenyan equivalent of those sentimental English novels like *Pamela* or *Clarissa* by Richardson, where the love of a good woman redeems a hardened rake ... surely one of the most pernicious myths in the history of gender relations to be promulgated by literature!

The last way in which urban women are represented in these novels is as a betrayed woman, whose descent into sex-work is a result of betrayal by men. Again this more sympathetic, if patronizing, representation is relatively rare. As one would expect from Ngũgĩ, a novelist of the first rank, his is the most sympathetic, nuanced and unstereotypical representation of an urban prostitute in this group of novels. Wanja, in *Petals of Blood*, tells her story – a sadly familiar one in post-independence Kenya – a tale of seduction by a family friend and then by her own teacher, the inevitable premarital pregnancy, the failure in her exams followed by rejection by her parents. She had had to run away to town to make her living any way she could, which, without any educational qualifications, meant sex work. While she enjoys her power over men, titillating them with her beauty, she comes in the course of the novel to realize that 'in the long run, it was men who triumphed and walked over her body' (1977: 56). She leaves the city and moves back to the rural area where she gets a job managing a store for a local entrepreneur. In the narrative structure of the novel, she is a character who brings harmony and order wherever she is.

In Mwangi's *Going Down River Road*, Ben abuses and rages at the 16 year-old sex-worker who takes him to her room where a 3-month-old baby sleeps in a cardboard box. Ben, through whose eyes the action of the book is seen, is outraged at what he sees at her mistreatment of the child. The sensitive reader wonders why he does not chose to save some of his anger for the unknown father who impregnated and abandoned a schoolgirl. It is difficult to tell whether Mwangi actually intends us to wonder this. Palmer maintains that Mwangi displays a convincing sympathy for 'prostitutes dogged by basic insecurity and the fear of hunger' to be vulnerable to the sadistic whims of the drunkards, thugs and addicts which people the urban underworld (1979: 316). I myself remain less than convinced. Ben dominates the narrative and it is through his selectively-moral gaze that we see the young sex-worker. (I say 'selectively-moral' because Ben obviously does not consider his own behaviour immoral. The men who tempt the sex-workers with money are not judged.) How ironic is Mwangi in presenting the amoral Ben as a moralizer about women?

Representations of urban men

Most of the novelists in this period were men and many of the novels are either written in the first person or focused on a male protagonist. The exceptions are the three novels by Ngũgĩ wa Thiong'o and that by Grace Ogot which are multi-focused narratives. One thing that is very clear is that urban men are not represented as judgementally as women are. For example, men drink constantly and drink to excess. However, this is not glossed as negative. Either it is just the inevitable behaviour of men or it is the fault of women that men drink.

In addition men are often the criminals, thieves or con-men. In the urban-based novels *What a Life*, *Going Down River Road*, both *Son of Woman* novels, *Tail in the Mouth* and *Across the Bridge*, the main male protagonists are involved in lives of crime in some way. Even where the context of the novel is a more middle-class milieu (as in *What a Life* and *The Price of Living*), the male protagonists are involved in bribery and corruption in various guises. The one exception to this rule is *Minister's Daughter* where two of the main female protagonists (Eunice, the truly wicked *femme fatale*, and Jane, the betrayed innocent gone wrong) join their men in theft and con tricks. The interesting aspect of this representation is that it is either presented neutrally (it just is – it is not commented on negatively) or it is explained, justified, and/or rationalized. These characters are forced into prostitution by circumstances. In *Kill Me Quick* no one will give the two male protagonists jobs and they have to eat from dustbins and turn to mugging and thieving. Anyway, their crimes pale into insignificance compared to the cruel and corrupt behaviour of the police, businessmen and property owners who exploit them. Class inequality explains and justifies their immoral behaviour. In *Across the Bridge*, the houseboy turns to increasingly violent crime because he cannot support his upper-class lover. The fact that he cannot wait and do it gradually through education and hard work is seen as unworthy of comment. Why? Because it is men's true nature and must be accepted. It is true that ultimately Gicheru the houseboy is weaned from his criminal life when he is reconciled with his wife.

That leads me to another interesting assumption which seems to lie behind representations of urban men, namely, that men deserve the love of women. Beatings, rapes, abuse, desertion, infidelity hardly seem to matter a jot in the eyes of the authors. Women should and often do stick to their men. In fact in *Across the Bridge* one is totally baffled as to why the gentle intelligent girl who married her father's houseboy should continue to love Gicheru. He beats her up when she does not stand by him in his trial for mugging tourists on a Mombasa beach. At various times be beats her, rapes her, goes to jail and ultimately throws her downstairs causing her to break her back. Yet the author allows her to see the true man under the façade of all this violence and crime, and continue supporting him. This is neither questioned nor seen as surprising.

Some women do fight back against the bad behaviour of their men, as in *Son of Woman in Mombasa* where Tonia and Ben are described as at war. In *What a Life*, the protagonist's wife leaves him when he continues to be unfaithful to her with the barmaid Ada. In both cases this spirit of defiance is greeted with outrage by the male protagonists.

Men bond together and care for each other. This is a very pervasive stereotype of men in these novels. At the same time women constantly try to divide men. In *Going Down River Road*, there is a well developed example of male bonding. First Ben reluctantly learns to care for and ultimately to love his son Baby abandoned by Win. Ben then falls in with Ocholla and the three males live happily together in a shanty hut. Later in the novel, Ocholla's wives come into town from the rural area and try to force Ben and Ocholla apart. It seems until almost the last line of the novel that they will succeed, but at the very end, instead of parting sadly on River Road, Ocholla turns back. The reader is left to speculate whether or not male friendship will win out over wives' intervention.

The head of the gang in *Kill Me Quick* who welcomes the desperate and impecunious pair, Meja and Maina, runs his gang to take care of its members against a hostile world. This male bonding occurs in the male companions involved in political activity in *Petals of Blood*.

Conversely, women are rarely portrayed as friends, the exception being Grace and Jane in the *Minister's Daughter*. Most women are in competition for men, as Tonia and Dodge's girlfriends in *Son of Woman in Mombasa*, the wife and the barmaid-lover in *What a Life*, and Eunice and Jane in *Minister's Daughter*. In addition, there are no examples of men and women being friends. On the contrary, women are represented as being incapable of interesting conversation or real friendship. Women are good for sex and conceiving children. Remember Ocholla's comment to Ben from *Going Down River Road*, quoted above, to the effect that women do not understand friendship and are stupid. In another place he says that women oppress their husbands with constant demands for sick children, school fees and new dresses!

Representations of rural women and men

Rural women are represented only as wives and mothers. There were, in these novels few striking representations of rural men.

The representation of the rural mother is the polar opposite of the wicked urban woman. In none of these novels is there a negative description of a rural mother. She is a bridge to a pure past, a talisman which the beleaguered urban man holds up before him to ward off the temptations and obstacles of town. Stratton refers to it as the 'Mother Africa trope' (1994: 39). The rural woman warns her son of evil that will befall him if he doesn't beware of the temptations of town. In *What a Life* the hero muses sadly on the unheeded advice of his rural mother:

> Long ago my mother told me many stories in the evening by the fireside while waiting for food in the pot to cook up. She told me stories of people who live in towns. She said some of them drink gin and go mad. Others smoke Bhang [marijuana] and their brains go soft. Still others go with prostitutes and their minds change into the minds of small children (1972: 120).

This passage also reveals the nostalgia for evenings spent as a child around the cooking fire, protected and cared for by a loving mother, the combination of intimacy engendered by the firelight, the pleasure of listening to stories, and the comfort of the cooking food. Such women are represented by Okot p'Bitek as the guardians of 'culture'. 'Listen Ocol my old friend, the ways of your ancestors are good. Their customs are solid and not hollow. They cannot be blown away by the winds because their roots reach deep into the soil' (1969: 29). The one who keeps these roots watered is the wife in the old, rural homestead.

Mothers are also seen as protecting her offspring even after death. In Ogot's *Promised Land*, the male protagonist Ocholla was orphaned young but continues to communicate with his mother over her grave. After he migrates with his wife to supposedly undeveloped lands in northern Tanzania, her spirit intervenes twice to help him when he falls ill from the powerful magic of his witchdoctor neighbour, angry and jealous at the invasion of hard-working Luo foreigners. First the mother's spirit calls his brother to leave Kenya and cross the lake to look for him when he has been lost in the thorn forest; later she appears to Ocholla to cool his fever at a crisis in his illness.

The rural mother is independent, strong, supportive and holds the rural home together. She is both productive and reproductive. In Ruheni's *Future Leaders*, Monica Watitu is described as a woman who was born to bear children. She is a rural woman who had fully accepted the fact that if the father abdicates responsibility it is only right for the mother to take over. Mama Pesa in Mwangi's *Striving for the Wind* spends her time in their village trying to compensate for her greedy and anti-social husband's rudeness and meanness. She is always soothing angry neighbours and secretly helping those in the community less fortunate than themselves. Absolom, the minister, in the *Minister's Daughter* is a religious fanatic and his wife is the one who not only keeps the family together but creates a family in the first place. In the face of her husband's absurd refusal to have sexual relations with her (on the grounds that it would be sinful for a minister to do so) she 'gets a child' outside the marital bond. Subsequently she adopts a baby boy and inadvertently in the process is instrumental in saving her daughter's illegitimate child for the family after it has been put up for adoption.

Rural wives are strong and, in general, uncomplaining in the face of their husbands' financial meanness or even, in Monica Watitu's family, their abandonment. She does not panic when the man of the house is not seen for years on end. In the end her faith is rewarded and he returns. It is men's role to travel and do what a 'man's gotta do' in the urban area and it is women's role to wait patiently and keep the cooking-fires burning.

The one example of a negative description of rural wives is in *Going Down River Road* when Ocholla's wives keep getting pregnant, even though he does not go home, and then unreasonably expect him to provide money for these children's upkeep. They visit town at one point to find their absent husband and to extract money from him. The impression Ocholla gives is that their desire for new dresses motivates them more than the need for medical care and school fees for the children.

Rural women are the one steady point for members of their ethnic groups who make journeys away (whether these are journeys into new cultures or literal physical journeys away from the rural home). Ocholla in *The Promised Land* regrets only one thing when he migrates to Tanzania: his separation from his mother's grave. The true marker of Maina's (one of the two male protagonists of *Kill Me Quick*) inability to extract himself from his life of crime and to return home to the rural area is when he goes back to find his mother and finds his parents had sold their farm and left for an unknown address.

Rural women are also represented in another way by Ngũgĩ wa Thiong'o, that is, as the 'bearers of culture'. Cochrane maintains that 'It is in Gikuyu women that Ngũgĩ sees the greatest strength of the Gikuyu tribe residing ... that it is they, rather than their menfolk who seem to have a better understanding of the needs of their own people and the new Kenya and who seem better able to reconcile these needs with traditional values and customs' (1985: 190).

Muthoni in *The River Between* states that she wants to be a woman who is totally situated and 'made beautiful in the tribe', that is, circumcised fully in the rites and ceremonies of the tribe (1985: 51). She 'had the courage to attempt a reconciliation of the many forces which wanted to control her' (*ibid.*: 163). She returned to the tribe, opposing her father's, her Christian religion's, and her school's opposition to female circumcision, in a personal act of courage which strikes at the conscience of other characters in the novels.

There are several strong women in Ngũgĩ's *A Grain of Wheat* which contribute to this representation. Njeri reveals a great strength and determination of a true Gikuyu woman when she makes a vow to devote herself to Kihika when he leaves home to become a guerrilla fighter in the forest. In the same novel, Wambui is a respected elder who has long been a source of strength for the tribe, in early labour strikes, during the Mau Mau and after. She always acted on the premise that women had to act to influence events, especially where men had failed to act or seemed indecisive.

Another character, Mumbi, aspires to lofty visions 'which take her beyond the confines of village life' who also learns 'the necessity of compromising her vision in order to live'. 'Depicted with hard lines of suffering on her face and big with child, Mumbi stands, along with the other Gikuyu women in Ngũgĩ's novels, for the suffering, endurance and pain of the past, and for the traditional values of tribal customs and life' (Cochrane 1995: 98).

In *Petals of Blood* the hero is inspired by the sight and sound of a truckload of relocated Gikuyu women singing 'traditional' songs, strong fatalistic and defiant. (During the Mau Mau period scattered homesteads were consolidated into stockaded villages as part of the British military strategy.)

Ngũgĩ is more ambivalent about men. Frequently they are vulnerable, treacherous, lacking in heroism and the resilience and resourcefulness of women. They often put too much emphasis on the religion, culture or education of the colonizers.

The only other rural male character who is well developed in these novels is Baba Pesa in Mwangi's *Striving for the Wind*. Baba Pesa (*lit.* Father Money) is a grasping, greedy, money-minded character. He is described as being infected by the money ethic of the city.

Representations of rural and urban life

The rural area, the countryside, is represented in much the same way as it frequently is in European novels. It is a place where the environment is clean and the air is pure. This becomes a metaphor for the moral cleanliness of the rural society as opposed to the moral corruption of urban life. Mangua, on the last page of *Tail in the Mouth*, has Samson return full circle to his rural roots while saying that from now on he is 'for the fresh air, the green grass and open fields'. He is, in other words, giving up the life of crime and corruption he had been living in the city.

Not only is the rural area an idyll of purity, it is also represented as a source of identity or tradition. Ngũgĩ's entire corpus has explored the ways in which Gikuyu land is the source of Gikuyu identity, its past, its cradle and its future. He equates the rural life with Gikuyu custom and identity. In the opening line of *The River Between*, Ngũgĩ hyperbolically describes Gikuyu-land in this way: 'These ancient hills were the heart and soul of the tribe.'

Sometimes this representation of the rural area as the place from where individuals derive their identity is demonstrated in its absence. Dodge in *Son of Woman* is born in the city, to a sex worker who claimed not to know who his father is. In fact he goes so far as to say he was conceived on a quid. He therefore is a person without place or identity. He is only the 'son of woman'. According to the rules of pre-colonial Kenyan societies, he would be defined as a man without land, without clan, without family in other words, without ethnic identity. The City is his father, and what kind of a heritage is that? Only a struggle to survive, degradation and corruption, says Mangua. At the end of the first of the two linked novels, Dodge meets his father (purely by accident) while they are both in prison. Sadly, his father dies before Dodge can get to know him. But at least he has learned what his identity is or could be. At the conclusion of the second novel, *Son of Woman in Mombasa*, Dodge, the confirmed urbanite born and bred, deserts the urban area for his father's land, intending to build a timber (rural as opposed to urban) house and to run for parliament. He will achieve his identity in the rural area and then be its representative in this focus on state power.

The city then is set in opposition to the countryside. It is a bad place. In only one of the novels is the city described in terms that might even be considered positive (at least faintly so). In *Tail in the Mouth* Samson, fleeing a murder charge from his rural village, rejoices that '... town is good. People don't care about what others do. They're only there when you want them' (1972: 251). He also feels that he has come to where the action is, that he has left 'the stupid country'. Sadly this initial excitement or enthusiasm proves illusory. One feels that Mangua was being ironic at the reader's expense. What Samson soon discovers is that the city is a sink of depravity and crime. He is sucked into it all. The city corrupts or cheats those who move there. In Mwangi's *Kill Me Quick*, Meja arrives in town, a gentle, polite ambitious youngster wishing to get a job commensurate with his education. His career in town is a downward spiral of degradation (such as eating from dustbins), crime and prison. Maina, his companion in the struggle for survival, arrived in the city earlier than he did. At one point, desperate and seeking sanctuary, he returns home to the rural area. He is met by his young sister who throws her arm around him and carols happily that he must have come to give her the blue necklace he promised her and to fulfil his promise to his parents to provide money for his younger siblings' school fees (including hers). Mortified with shame, Meja realizes that he has forgotten his promise to bring her a necklace and his entire worldly wealth consists of a shilling. He flees, unable to face his parents, leaving his name written in the dust. Maina too goes to his home village as a last resort, only to find that his parents have disappeared. He is told by the new owner of their farm that '[t]hey squandered all their money sending a son [Maina] to school. He went to the city and *became spoilt*. He never came back' (1973: 134, emphasis mine).

The *Minister's Daughter*, Jane Njeri, is as pure and innocent as could be imagined. She goes to town and is introduced to beer-drinking, dancing, good times and sex. These seem to lead almost inevitably to illegitimate pregnancy, crime and even murder. Samson's rural friend, Kamau, in *Tail in the Mouth* tells him that the city has cheated him, that he is an exploited man.

That seems to be the key. There is in the representation of the city the germ of a class analysis. Money, or the lack of it, is the major problem in the urban area. Everything in urban areas is based on money. As everywhere, those poor migrants entering the system are either reduced to begging or badly exploited in low-paid jobs. Those that have nothing will do anything (beg, scavenge, mug people, steal and even murder) to obtain the wherewithal to live. Those who already have a job find it very hard to manage their money. This inability to budget their money is a major corrupting force for the upper echelons of urban society. Mangua's conman, Dodge, in the two *Son of Woman* novels, makes a living because businessmen and civil servants are constantly looking for ways (legal and illegal) to increase their incomes. The demands of an elite lifestyle, inflation and the high cost of imported goods (such as cars etc.) are a constant concern for such people.

This distrust of the cash economy expresses the angst of the rural peasant who has always owned the means of production (land) and therefore the capacity to be, partly at least, independent in a self-sufficient subsistence economy. With the cash economy, the expansion of a modern economy, rural-urban migration and industrialization – all of which reach their zenith in the urban area – the in-migrating peasant loses his independence and self-sufficiency. At the same time socio-economic inequalities emerge and begin to solidify into a class structure.

Just as it is inevitable that poor migrants to the city (like Meja and Maina in Mangua's *Kill Me Quick* or Kamau in Mangua's *Tail in the Mouth*) will find it difficult, if not impossible, to support themselves, it is also represented as inevitable that the elite urban dwellers will lose their roots and their identity. They will be swallowed up by the city. In a delightful passage in Ruheni's *What a Life*, the hero questions his son about 'where he comes from' and the son insists he comes from a suburb of Nairobi. His father questions him further in a futile effort to make him accept that they actually came from Limuru, a rural district. Pensively, the boy describes his grandmother's Limuru farmhouse as a place full of smoke, with no toilet and where they were served a football-sized piece of 'African meat'.

The elite protagonist of Dawood's *The Price of Living* is very isolated by his wealth. He speaks English to his children, who attend both school and university in the United Kingdom. His life-style would not be out of place in New York or London. While he has an extended family somewhere in the rural area, his children barely know or relate to them. The extent of their separation from their rural and ethnic roots is illustrated by the fact that at the end of the novel Karanja, the widower businessman, and both his children have married Europeans. This is the way Dawood represents the new Kenyan elite, which is by definition urban. So distanced are they from their ethnic or even Kenyan identities that they would become European if they could; faced with an inability to change the colour of their skins, they do the next best thing. They marry white in an attempt to merge with the hegemonic culture of the ex-colonial power.

Class exploitation, divisions and prejudice are at the heart of *Across the Bridge*. The objection of the top civil servant to his daughter marrying his houseboy is rooted in class prejudice, nothing more or less. The houseboy, Chuma, runs away with Caroline, the daughter, to his rural home. The rural people do not recognize the class division and see nothing wrong in the couple marrying if they wish to. In fact a delegation of elders from Chuma's village visit the civil servant to reconcile him with the young couple. In their oversized, shabby coats and unfitting shoes, they cut very comic figures, overawed by the beautiful mansion in Nairobi and facing the arrogant senior civil servant. Incidentally, Caroline's stay in the rural area illustrates the way she has 'lost' her Kenyan culture. Her 'soft stomach could not eat a plate of grain and call it a meal' (1983: 77). She cannot greet Chuma's mother in the traditional Gikuyu fashion. Gicheru's description of her father's life-style explains why:

> Kahuthu [the Minister] was a progressive Native in this corps of New Africans. A top civil servant, lived among the dignified, owned a large bungalow and uncountable property. Like most people in his social bracket, he lived the Western way, talked western, laughed and coughed western, dinner jackets and all.

> His children hardly spoke their mother tongue or used their native names. His son Peter did not know the difference between a dog and a goat (1979: 3).

Sadly the money ethic does not just stay in the urban area. In the latest of novels included in this selection, Mwangi's *Striving for the Wind*, published in 1990, it is clear that the city is corrupting the countryside. Baba Pesa is drunk with making money. He no longer thinks communally but only individually. His only motive is the profit motive. In Ngũgĩ wa Thiong'o's *Petals of Blood*, a number of local men are infected by the capitalist ethic and are 'developing' the isolated area of Ilmorog, bringing insensitivity, callousness, ambition in the place of a previous more communal life.

The final representation of the rural area is that it is the last bastion of redemption from urban values and corruption. In several of the novels this theme is developed. Jane Njeri in Ruheni's *Minister's Daughter* becomes disgusted with her life of fast living and crime. She takes a teaching qualification and returns to the rural area to teach in her father's village. It is at this point of return to her roots, her innocent beginnings, that her redemption is complete. She discovers her child has been adopted by her own mother. Her sins are forgiven, she is welcomed back into the family. She is a whole woman again, reunited with her baby. The return to the rural area has been a return to morality and justice.

In Mangua's *Tail in the Mouth* Samson makes a complicated circular journey from the purity and innocence of a rural boyhood to urban corruption and back again (the circle an animal would make if it takes its own tail in its mouth). Samson rejects tradition and his own 'pagan' parents and joins the Catholic church with a view to becoming a priest. As a boy, he rejects religion and joins the Mau Mau (which Mangua depicts more as lawless banditry than a noble freedom movement). After that he returns home to find his father dead and his land taken by someone else. He flees to the city to seek anonymity after an accidental killing. There he is dragged into indulgence, drunkenness and crime by bad companions. Ultimately sick at heart with his depravity he returns to a church intent on making his confession. The priest throws him out. Fortuitously he discovers at this time that a friend has fought to have his land returned. The end of the novel finds him returning to his village, intent on becoming a farmer there. He expresses his desire to get married and have a son and to name it after his father (a reference to the 'traditional' Gikuyu naming custom, thus signalling a return to his ethnic roots). A return to the country and purity (the fresh air spoken of above) is a journey of redemption for Samson. The same thing happens in Ngũgĩ's *Petals of Blood* when the sex worker, Wanja, returns to the rural area to 'escape' her life of 'whoring' and to be redeemed.

In *Striving for the Wind* (by Mwangi), the land quite literally counters the negative effects of westernization and the cash economy, the corruption of the countryside by the city, spoken of above. Here Baba Pesa is let down by modernization. Just before the planting rains, supplies of diesel fuel are unobtainable to run his tractor. He is forced to cooperate with his old-fashioned neighbour (with whom he has been quarrelling throughout the novel). Together they hitch up his neighbour's old ox plough to Baba Pesa's landrover and plough both holdings. In his haste to get the ploughing done in order to plant and take advantage of the coming rain, he forgets to put on his wellingtons (a marker of his status and success throughout the book). Instead he is out in the fields in his bare feet helping his neighbour. He revels in the mud oozing between his toes, which starts a process of increasing humanization and growth of neighbourly feelings. One almost gets the feeling at the end of the book that Baba Pesa might be a human being after all. Contact with the soil has redeemed his humanity which has lain dormant under an increasing weight of balance sheets and worries over profits and losses.

Congruence of novelistic discourses with day to day discourses of Mathare residents in the 1970s

In the first half of the 1970s, I conducted research in a large spontaneous settlement in Nairobi known as Mathare Valley. It was truly an 'informal sector' suburb. Most of the housing had been built by owner-occupiers with mud and wattle on land they did not own but had merely occupied. At the time I worked there, 60,000 people occupied this valley along the Mathare River. The inhabitants were largely involved in informal sector activities, that is to say, they were self-employed in small-scale, low skill, low capital investment forms of production of goods or services usually conducted in the open air or their own homes. Men were hawkers, recyclers of urban rubbish, shoe makers, barbers, tailors, leather workers, carpenters, furniture makers. etc. Women were hawkers, street cleaners, barmaids, house servants, sex-workers or beer-brewers (Nelson 1995). In Mathare of this period an inordinately large percentage of the women (compared to other parts of Nairobi) were single heads of household, most of whom were engaged in sex work and beer-brewing. The two discourses, opposing men and women and rural and urban, were not just the construction of the university writers. In ways which overlapped and differed, the low-income, relatively uneducated residents of the shanty towns of Nairobi shared similar discourses.

In this last section I will discuss the representation of urban men and women, rural men and women, and the urban and rural context. In this section I will show how these representations were created in different ways in Mathare at the same time that these novels were being written out of the academy.

The most interesting and dramatic difference was the rejection of the 'wicked urban woman' representation. This was a very common representation of urban women in Kenya in this period. The letters to the editors of newspapers, the pronouncements of politicians and the discourses of ordinary so-called respectable people all created and recreated this stereotype. In Mathare where so many women are engaged in sex-work, it is only to be expected that they would reject this stereotype. Both Mathare men and women rejected this stereotype in all its guises. In fact they turned it on its head and created a representation of the 'wicked urban man'. The true seducers and corrupters are the men who offer women money for sex. I cannot remember how many women explained to me that the word *malaya* (translated as prostitute) did not define women who sold sex but the men who paid for it. Men were defined as being incapable of faithfulness, neglectful of their children, violent and prone to crime. By contrast, Mathare women would definitely have related to the more positive representations of urban women recounted above – women as good managers and women as betrayed. I am not sure they would have accepted the role of redeemers because their views of men were so jaundiced that they would not have seen any possibility of redemption. 'A man rescued from sin by the love of a good woman' was a discourse on gender relations that would have elicited sardonic laughter from these women. They certainly defined urban women as hard-working, reliable, independent and strong. Sex-work was cleared of all immoral connotations. It was referred to as 'selling from one's kiosk', a reference to owning a small shop. Selling sex was defined simply as a service like selling milk. Women justified their sex-work on the purely pragmatic grounds that, first they had no education, second they had children to support, and third it was a service no different from cooking food. To put it another way, they were defining sex-work as the commercialization of one of the reproductive roles of wives, a slant on the oldest profession developed in an historical overview of sex-work in Nairobi by Luise White (1990). This was at best a positive and at worst a neutral definition of sex-work, and one which was shared by many of the men and women living in Mathare. Even married women (who did not themselves practise sex work, and might be expected to take a moralistic stance on it as an activity) participated in the same discourse. It was a sort-of 'a woman's got to do what a woman's got to do' discourse, and if men are unreliable and roving, then women are forced to care for themselves and their children in the only way which the cash economy permits them to do.

In addition, all women (rural or urban) were represented in local discourses as warm, loving and understanding of the troubles of other people because they had experienced 'the pains of childbirth.' Men, on the other hand, were cruel, unreliable, uncaring of their children, obsessed with sex and prone to use women badly. Many of these women had played the role of the rural wife effectively abandoned by a migrant husband (who ironically enough was usually in town spending the money he was supposed to send home to wife and children on urban women, like those in Mathare). Many others had been rural schoolgirls impregnated and betrayed by the fathers of their children, whether those fathers were teachers, older men or fellow schoolboys. They had good reasons in their personal history to define men as unloving and unreliable. In a fascinating reversal of the novelistic representation of women by the male protagonists as 'good only for one thing: sex', Mathare women defined men as 'good for only two things: sex and payment in cash for same'.

Sadly my field data is insufficient to speak with any authority about how Mathare men constructed their models of urban men. Those few for which I can speak represented women in Mathare and others like them in the same callous and stereotyped way as 'wicked whores'. On the other hand they probably would have agreed with the novelists in feeling that men bonded well together and that women were not really fit for friendship. They were more consistent than the novelists because they thought that *both* men and women engaged in illegal and immoral activities only because the urban system was unequal and unfair, and prevented people from obtaining reasonable jobs to support themselves. The novelists are guilty of a definite double-standard in this regard because they justified or excused only men whose economic activities were illegal. Mathare men, often the customers of the women typified as 'wicked urban women' (discussed above), often agreed with Mathare women's representation of men as sexually promiscuous and unreliable, in a partly proud and partly shamefaced manner. The justification to explain away any possible imputations of immorality went this way. *Zamani* (long ago) men were polygamous, therefore it is in the nature of 'African men' to have many sexual partners. The economic situation (lack of land, lack of steady employment) prevented men from having many legitimate wives, and so they had to resort to lovers or sex workers to fulfil their 'natural' desires.

Both Mathare men and women shared the novelists' discourse on the rural mother. This figure loomed large in the nostalgic reminiscences of both men and women. She was a talisman of caring and lost innocence. This was reinforced by the fact that for many women, raising children alone, the rural mother also provided the intense mothering that women in Mathare, attempting to survive in a harsh urban economy, did not have the time to give. Women assumed that their rural mothers would provide the good food and close supervision they did not have the time to do. When asked to explain why they were fostering their children with rural mothers, the answers resonated with the representations in the novels discussed above. More than that, the rural mother was definitely represented as the 'bearer of culture' in local discourses. This rural mother will produce good, hard-working, well-mannered children. She will teach the customs and language of the home area. Children raised without their cultural identity were seen as lacking a moral centre and low in self-esteem (Nelson 1987).

Mathare men and women were in Nairobi through necessity and not through desire. They were landless and seeking work in town. Some received a certain level of education which educated them out of agriculture. They were only able to find jobs commensurate with their education levels in the urban environs. To a large degree Mathare men and women would have recognized and reproduced many aspects of the discourse on the pure and redeeming countryside contrasted with the wicked corrupting city developed in the novels discussed above. The rural area is a place of cleanliness, physical and moral. (The former was an obvious point of nostalgic discussion for these people living amongst the uncollected rubbish and open, stinking drains of a shanty town.) The countryside is a place of peace and order – a representation made up of dreams, nostalgia and unrealistic comparisons. Almost all the people I knew who had been born in the rural area dreamed of 'going home' when they had earned enough money. Barring that, they all wished to be buried at home. One of the major foci of communal activity in Mathare at this time, were the collections of money to send a corpse 'home' (to the rural area) to be buried. Only true urbanites, those few residents of Mathare who had been born and raised in town, had no other home to return to. As with Dodge in Mangua's *Son of Woman*, the city was for them mother and father.

Mathare men and women reacted to the cash economy dominant in the urban system with ambivalence. On the one hand, both men and women, but especially women, regarded the economic opportunities of town as a blessing, a resource, and something to be grateful for. Women, who at this time were excluded from access to land for farming unless they were married to a man with land, called the informal sector activities they engaged in (for most, beer-brewing) their *shamba* (fields), in other words their source of income. On the other hand, many wished to translate the products of their urban *shamba* into a literal *shamba* somewhere in the rural area. Few have afforded to do so, over the years. Only the lucky ones have managed to save enough to buy land.

Mathare women added a positive gloss to representations of the city not found in the novels, that the city is an easier place for women to live and work. They spoke often of the back-breaking work of hoeing, of carrying water for miles in large containers strapped by tump lines around their foreheads or balanced on their heads, and the constant search for wood fuel. Working in town was more psychologically stressful, but much less physically arduous.

Both men and women appreciated the 'bright lights' of town. They expressed positive feelings about the *raha* (luxuries) of town. Many of the younger ones complained that the rural area was boring and lacking in variety of activity. The city was not just where the jobs are located in Kenya. It was the source of political power, the centre of fashion and 'what was happening!' Mathare men and women felt better informed and superior to those from the rural area because they were urbanities participating in national events at the centre. There was an age dimension too in these representations. Older men and women smiled indulgently and said that they would prefer to trade the excitement of town for the peace, or boredom, of the country in their old age. In fact, in the course of 25 years of fieldwork, I have observed a few successful middle-aged women disengage themselves from the excitement and *raha* of town by purchasing small plots of land to retire to the peace of the country or retire to stay with a rural relative. A young person's boredom is an older person's peace.

Finally, Mathare men and women would have agreed with the representation of the city as a place which swallows up the elite. At the time, one of the local phrases for the elite and politicians was *waBenzi* (people who drive Mercedes Benzes). This says it all. The elite mimic the departing colonialists and take on their ways. I once came on a group of young men in the 1980s in Mathare listening to Bob Marley's music in a cafe. They were wearing dreadlocks and sporting the green, yellow and black of the Rastas. In discussion with them, I asked who they saw as the white enemy of the songs, thinking that the lyrics of the reggae might not be consonant with their experience. Not at all. It was earnestly explained that Kenya had its 'white men', admittedly ones with black faces. Fanon would have felt at home in the discussion of black faces and white lifestyles.

To a certain extent, Mathare people might have also extended this representation to say that in the end the city swallows all her sons and daughters. Few migrants ever really go home again – especially from a place like Mathare, where almost nobody had land awaiting them in the rural area. Only the most successful entrepreneurs could afford to purchase fields in the rural areas.

In the 1970s Kenyan novelists were exploring themes which concerned them deeply. In the period after Independence, Kenya had embarked on a period of very rapid change. Trends which had only just begun in the colonial period escalated. The loss of clear ethnic roots or identity, the growth of towns, the dissolution of the rural family and increasing loss of control by the patriarchal kinship organizations of women and younger men. All of these trends struck deep at the heart of all that was considered 'traditional' Kenya. The ones who felt most threatened were men. Women were determined to seize the new opportunities many men had already benefited from. The problem was that as women took these opportunities, men lost their privileged position in the domestic sphere, the rural farms, the urban economy and urban sexual realms. It is no accident that most of the novelists on the list were men because, in this period, many fewer women than men had achieved university-level education. Since the premise of this paper is that novelists manipulate the discourse of their times in the creation of their works of art, inevitably they were expressing the concerns and the fears of men. Grace Ogot, the one substantive female novelist of this early period, did not write about urbanization and industrialized change in *The Promised Land*. But even in her discussion of post-war rural Luo society it was clearly apparent that she was describing changing domestic power relations. The patriarchal husband asserts his authority and ignores the wishes of his wife by leaving Kenya and going to Tanzania. In the end he suffers dreadfully for his hubris and her fears and apprehensions are realized.

After Independence, women were seeking their day in the sun usually in the city and Kenyan men did not like it (and, I might add, still do not). Hence the representations developed in these novels. City women are wicked. Rural women are (as women should be) hard-working and productive as well as loving and supportive of their men. The city (the place of change) corrupts the sons and daughters of the country. Conversely, the rural area – a rural idyll – is where one can be safe and where true Kenyan identity is forged and maintained.

The times move on and many things have changed in the last 25 years. For one thing, more and more Kenyans are urbanites, born and bred in town. Tensions and competitions for national resources have changed the parameters of ethnic identity construction and interrelations. Women have forged ahead in education and participation in the economy. The increasing number of single parent families has altered the discourses on 'the wicked urban woman' (in ways both positive and negative). And, in the realm of novel writing, there are more women represented on the shelves since the late 1980s. In 1995 a national novel prize was won by a woman, Margaret Ogola with her *River and Her Source*. This novel celebrates women both rural and urban, their strengths and determination. An historical novel which traces a line of daughters in Luoland from the late nineteenth century till the present day, its representation of women is established by quoting a saying, 'a house without daughters is a spring without a source.' Throughout the novel, women fight, strive and work to keep the family together in the face of the weakness, venality and stupidity of the husbands, sons and brothers of the story. Women novelists' voices are now being heard. They are renegotiating the representations of men and women in their writings in much the same way as real-life women in the Mathare I knew of the 1970s and 80s were already challenging both the structural realities and discourses of gender relations in their day-to-day lives.

Works cited

Cochrane, J. 1989. 'Women as Guardians of the Tribe in Ngũgĩ's Novels' in *Critical Perspectives on Ngũgĩ wa Thiong'o*, edited by A. Killam. Washington DC: Three Continents Press, 90-100.

Nelson, Nici. 1987. 'Rural-Urban Child Fostering in Kenya: migration, kinship, ideology and class' in *Migrants, Workers and the Social Order*, edited by J. Eades. London: Tavistock (ASA monograph 26), 181-98.

Nelson, Nici. 1988. 'Marital Options and Gender Power in Mathare Valley, Nairobi' in *Culture and Contradictions: Dialectics, Power and Symbol*, edited by M. de Soto. San Francisco: E.M. Texts, 5-32.

Nelson, Nici. 1995. 'The Kiambu Group: A Successful Women's ROSCA in Mathare Valley, Nairobi (1971–1990)' in S. Ardener and S. Burman (eds), *Money-Go-Rounds: The Importance of Rotating Savings and Credit Associations for Women*. Oxford/Washington DC: Berg Press.

Palmer, E. 1979. *The Growth of the African Novel*. London: Heinemann.

Shore, C. 1995. 'Anthropology, Literature and the Problem of Mediterranean Identity', *Journal of Mediterranean Studies* 5 (1): 1-13.

Stratton, Florence. 1994. *Contemporary African Literature and the Politics of Gender*. London and NY: Routledge.

White, L. 1990. *Comforts of Home: Prostitution in Colonial Nairobi*. Chicago: University of Chicago Press.

Primary Text 4
Excerpts from Charles Mangua *Son of Woman*

Reference
Charles Mangua *Son of Woman*
Nairobi East African Educational Publishers
[1971] 1994: 7–32

1

Son of woman, that's me. I am a louse, a blinking louse and I am the jigger in your toe. I am a hungry jigger and I like to bite. I like to bite women — beautiful women. Women with tits that bounce. If you do not like the idea you are the type I am least interested in.

Maybe you have heard about me and again maybe you haven't. Either way yqu have missed nothing. To you I am the crank from downstairs who is not worth knowing. So what?

I am the son of woman and I'll repeat it till your elephant ears ache. Never had a dad in my blinking life. My whoring ma could never figure out who my pop was. A very short memory — that's what she had. It was one of the scores of men who took her for a bed-ride but she wasn't bothered to remember who among them I resembled. That's my mother. Nothing bothered her. Didn't bother to get married either. All she did was collect a quid from the punks who came for a tumble. That's me. I was conceived on a quid and mother drank it. Poor mother. God rest her soul, she is dead.

Yes, I am the son of woman. I ain't no brother to the son of man and I ain't no brother to nobody either. If I had a brother probably the punk wouldn't like me. Maybe you wouldn't like me either if I told you a few things about myself. So what? Nobody asked you to like me. If you don't like me take a short-cut to bed and snore your silly head off, but if you like me, I'd advise you to take the first opportunity to consult a psychiatrist. You are sick.

"Damn you and damn you again, you onion-eating pale-faced son of a coolie. Who the hell do you think you are?" I am not thinking about you, my friend. I wouldn't say such a thing about you. I am thinking about this Indian magistrate who put me in jail. Merciless bastard, that's what he is. God! I can still see him. He is sitting on his ass and chewing some leaves. Damn him again.

I am the son of woman and I've said it before. If you are bored,

7

plug your ears. Don't get any funny ideas that there was something between my mother and the holy ghost because she never saw a ghost in her life. She never saw the inside of a church either. The only time she saw a ghost was when the cops picked her up from a ditch and put her in the can because she was dead drunk. She confused the cops for ghosts on account of the hooch and the poor lighting in the cell.

I have inherited a few of her qualities and that is why I am cursing this magistrate. She was always cursing some man who'd taken her personal goods and refused to pay the bill at the specified time.

"Horrid, that's what they are. All men are horrid," she used to say to Miriam, the whore next door. "They smile when they take you and at the end of the month they run to avoid you. They go to fish in fresh waters. Laughing, cheating bastards, that's what men are. They want everything for free." She'd curse men and then go looking for them.

I remember this vividly. I was just a lad at the time and very green at that. I had a little back room but I always heard them when they came in. They came roaring drunk and singing drunken tunes but I didn't know what they came for. There was always the talk of money, but all I knew about money was that it could be used to buy sweets. I liked sweets. I've always liked sweet things. Perhaps you do.

One day, when I was still too young to understand, it happened. My mother died. She was run over by a car when she jumped off a moving bus to confront a fellow who owed her some dough. She was dead drunk again. Miriam, our next door neighbour, took me to her house. She was a prostitute too. God! Even as a kid I had to go through hell.

There was this little girl Tonia in the house. She was the daughter of this Miriam and she was my age. We were both eleven. When there was nobody in the house Tonia used to ask me to do to her what the men did to her mother. When I confessed that I didn't have the vaguest idea what the men did to her mother Tonia gave me a wallop. She used to wallop me just for kicks. I hate being walloped by girls — even little ones. Later on I found out. I had to, otherwise Tonia would get fresh on me. It wasn't so bad once I learned. Tonia stopped beating me after that.

Skip the years, mate. I am now thirty but there are times when I feel twenty-one. Me, I don't believe in one woman. Inheritance again. I like to have a bird here and another there just in case one of them happens to lay an egg when I am in the tumbling mood. If you are the type that sticks to one woman, you should have your apparatus examined. You are blind, my friend. You are probably blind to the

8

fact that the beautiful frill you possess only sticks to you because you furnish a contrast. This explains why cute dames more often fall for ugly mugs. If you are this type of mug we all join hands in sympathy. If I were you I'd be nice and faithful but don't get me wrong. I am not like you.

I am one hell of a fellow. My name is Kiunyu. Dodge Kiunyu, known to my friends as Dod. If you don't like my name, just don't. I don't blame you because I don't like it myself. The priest who baptised me must have been nuts. Most priests are nuts anyway. I can never figure out how this crank invented this name for me. He must have been thinking about the bishop's car instead of the holy waters he was pouring right into my eyes instead of my forehead. Very devoted priest, this fellow was. At least he didn't have a one-track mind. One priest among many, I must say.

Everybody in this goddam place is clamouring for education. Me, I am not. Take it away. I have had some but I don't want it. I am a rebel. It has done me no good. Maybe I'll end up becoming a thief, so what? Damn exciting life until you are caught. Most thieves are caught anyway and I'd hate to think myself one. I have gone for two days without food and by God I'll have to pinch some from somewhere tonight or tomorrow. I simply can't survive on my bitter saliva while mugs are feeding meat to dogs. It ain't fair. I've got to eat something and I don't care how I get it. If you know how, you are wiser than I am.

As I walk, I am counting my old friends. Friends who are not friends any more. They were friends at university. During my five years at Makerere I made plenty of friends. Then we came out. I had a B.A. Honours in Geography. Lousy subject this Geography. Jack of all trades and master of none.

I took this job with the Ministry of Labour and Social Services. I was a Labour Officer, and a good one at that. I was doing fine but got no promotion. I didn't humour my boss and I believe I was supposed to. Anyway I didn't humour him and consequently I didn't get a promotion. Fellows who I knew to be mugs were getting ahead. Not me. A fellow I'd always detested on account of his stupidity, lack of guts and lack of bodily cleanliness became my boss. He was the type that thought that his hat was more important than his head. A punk. They must have been nuts to promote him. I just couldn't get over it. The fellow didn't brush his teeth and he insisted on summoning me to his office just to infect me with some of his foul breath. It was real Chinese torture listening to this fellow telling you what to do and what not to do. That was the beginning of the end. My end. I couldn't

9

stomach the blighter and I didn't beat about the bush in letting him know it.

In my dingy office the most intelligent companions were evil smelling cheating bums bothering me for jobs. I sympathized with them but there were no jobs going. All they had to do was register.

I was getting bored. Bored stiff. I started applying for jobs. I wrote at least two applications a week. Nothing doing. I always got regrets. I was called for three interviews but again I flopped. In whatever I tried I flopped. My friends were pinching my girlfriends. My fianceé left me high and dry and got married to a butcher. A butcher! My ass! Fancy that. A blinking butcher. Whenever I imagined him acting husband in bed I'd go to the john and leak.

The devil take his soul. The bitch was pretending to be mine and mine alone while secretly letting the bloody butcher work some overtime on what I considered my goods. The thought that I was having a tumble with a woman who'd allowed the butcher to put his dirt in her made me puke. I mean it really. I did it in the bathroom. Yellow stuff that left my mouth bitter and dry.

I started feeling sorry for myself. I was really sorry for poor me. Folks were laughing at me. Others were sorry for me. I hated them and hated myself. The only company I enjoyed was my own. I'd brood and muse and curse and spit. There was something wrong with me. I tried to figure out what, but two and two always made five. I couldn't get four. I noticed some change in my countenance. In case you haven't seen me I am a handsome cuss. I mean it. I've got what it takes if you know what I mean.

I decided to see a psychiatrist but changed my mind. He would merely bother me. Loneliness was the best thing for me. One by one my friends dropped me like a hot cake and I was not invited to the usual weekend goat eating, beer drinking parties. I had this depressing feeling of inadequacy and my office became dingier than before. Job seekers grew fewer and fewer on account of my bad temper. I had to do something.

I started to hit the bottle. When I say hit the bottle, I mean hit the bottle. No half measures. I simply drank myself silly every evening and went to the office late with my constant friend, Mr. Hangover. He bothered me but I couldn't get rid of him. I realized the stupidity of it all and to punish myself, I hit the bottle harder. Funny enough I made friends again; drinking friends. Different friends. People who'd forget you as soon as you were out of their sight. Friends who would cut your throat if by so doing they'd gain something.

Then there were the women. I had plenty at my disposal. I was

10

dishing out money and drinks right and left and naturally running down my savings. It was during this time that I met Doris and others. I was just carefree but rather unhappy at heart. Somehow I knew I was going downhill but I wasn't bothered. I even caught V.D. but instead of pulling the girl's ears I gave her money to go and see a doctor. Being charitable pleased me. It pleased me to see women pleased when I bought them drinks — and I bought plenty. There is no bar in Nairobi I have not set my foot in and if there is then it is not worth a visit.

After six months I was broke. I had only my salary to drink on and that was that. My savings were completely finished. Gone. I had somewhat recovered my composure. I was thinking seriously about life. The job did not look so dismal and I was going to marry Doris. She was my blessing. Together we would set up a home and breed brown kids. Brown like myself and as beautiful as Doris. God be praised.

I remember that fatal day very vividly. I was driving to Limuru and some cops who stopped me pointed out that my road licence had expired. They were damn right and they were prepared to let me go if I bribed them. That was how I became a jailbird. It was the first day of my present life. I didn't bribe them though. I merely got fresh and we had a fight. It's seven months ago but the memory is dew-fresh. I was tipsy as hell and I can still hear myself addressing the cops.

"The devil take your soul, you foul-faced ill-smelling bow-legged cop. I ain't going to give you no bribe. Why don't you ask your dumb superiors to redesign your uniforms for you? You wouldn't be sweating like pigs. Gosh! You'll soon sweat blood if your ass doesn't burst out of your pants." I was real fresh but I got the surprise of my life. Cops are not that dumb. The bastard hit me. He hit me real hard. I reeled backwards and then lashed out. I clouted him bang on top of his silly mouth and hurt my knuckles against his teeth. You should have seen the poor devil. Never saw a cop look so murderous. He came at me and gave it to me hard and proper. Nearly broke my arm, the stupid fool. Twisted it till I saw the innocent clouds turn pink. With one final effort he hurled me to the ground. He felt his lips. He licked them and spat blood. He called me something nasty.

I rolled on the ground to ease the pain in my arm till his companion gave me a kick in the ribs and asked me to raise my arms. He slipped on the bracelets in spite of my curses and yanked me to my feet. He searched my pockets and came out with my car keys. Locked all doors, checked them and then rechecked them. Gave me a kick on the ass and shoved me forward.

11

"Move on, bull fighter," he says to me. "We leave your bus here. We shall feed you for a while at the police station. Good meals we provide. See how you manage on fried water. Move!" Fancy that! A cop promising to feed me. I'd rather be fed by a snake. They both feed you on poison. Not much difference — between cops and snakes. Both can be very vicious. In their protection I didn't feel so good.

I take a look at the bow-legged cop who gave me the wallop and I smile inwardly. I understand why the bastard lost his goat. He's got a tooth missing. He doesn't look beautiful with this big tooth missing. Hasn't improved his appearance any. I smile again because I can see his tongue sneaking between the gap and licking the bleeding gum. I reckon that this fellow had a right to wallop me. Maybe I'll get even one day.

That was seven months ago. I remember the incident vividly. They prosecuted me and found me guilty of assault and causing actual bodily harm. Put me in the cooler for six months and the damn magistrate would not accept a fine. Six months, no fine. Six good months in the can among stinking criminals, lechers, sodomites, burglars and lots of other filth. God!

It's a month since I left the cooler. I have been hanging around for a whole month without a job. My friends are scared of me. They don't like my looks. Behind my back they refer to me as a jailbird. Jailbird! Me! Gosh! I am a jailbird — so what? My old girlfriends don't want me. Fancy that. They actually sympathize with me. My foot! They make me laugh. A pain in the neck — that's what they are.

I am thinking about this girl I was going to get married to. This Doris girl is a receptionist at the New Stanley Hotel. I met her through this tutor of mine at Makerere. He came to the New Stanley, met Doris and got amorous. I met her in his room when I paid him a courtesy call and I liked her ass. When he left I took over.

Doris gave me a few tumbles and I liked the tumbling. I have had tumbles with all sorts of women in all sorts of places and believe you me, I know the difference between a good so-and-so and a hollow ass. This Doris is different. She sort of doesn't let you have all of it. You are left with a feeling that there is some secret hidden depth where you have not been allowed to reach. Some sweetness further down the street which you have not been allowed to taste. It doesn't matter how hard you try, you don't get there. If you are an explorer like me, you want to keep trying. You must discover what is in darkest Africa and so did I.

It was all very funny. First it was greed. Greed for a tumble. I got it all right but I couldn't help begging for another. I got that one too

12

and I became a slave. I couldn't help myself. Doris was my master and mistress. Then she told me a fib. She told me that she was going to have a baby. She was merely testing my feelings but I believed her. I believed her because I am allergic to rubbers and I don't use them anyway. They make me droopy, that is what they do. I hate them. Doris hated pills and I don't blame her. Nothing exciting in them, if you see what I mean.

We were going to get married. She had to provide the money of course but then I got fresh to the cops. I'll never forgive them on account of Doris. She was married after I'd been wallowing in the cooler for four months God have mercy on her. She had no baby in that little tummy of hers. She'd told me a fib. Women are always telling me fibs.

It was four weeks ago that I went to see her — the day they opened hell's gates and let me out. I'd bathed myself and had my beard barbered twice but I reckon I still looked like a jailbird. I had my arms open and I was striding like the King of Siam when I saw her at the old reception counter and was I beaming? Gosh, man! My heart was beating like a ram and the look on my face was the real personification of joy. Happiness unbound. I was grinning like the cat that swallowed the bird.

This Doris catches a glimpse of me approaching like a batman and her mouth pops open. Her bosom sags and she looks around as if she wants to run. I check my stride and approach slowly but deliberately. I am all excited. I want to fly at her but I dare not.

"Hi, kid, guess who. This is Dodge. I've dodged my way out of Satan's jaws. Mighty glad to see you again, my human doll. You look like the flowers in heaven." I extend my hand and she responds in a feverish manner. I feel something ooze out of me. I am getting confused and embarrassed. To save my face I grab her and administer one quick kiss on the cheek. That did it. She rubbed her cheek where my lips had touched as if I'd put some prison dirt there and faced me.

"No, no, Dod." She always called me Dod and I liked it. Sometimes it sounded like Dad. She extended her left arm and spread the fingers in front of me. Sure as hell it was there. A gold wedding ring on her finger. A wedding ring — my foot! I couldn't get my silly eyes off the ring. I stood there dumbfounded and dazed.

"So?" I enquired, shrugging my shoulders slightly and feeling very unsure of myself.

"I know it's a shock, Dod, but I got married. I am married, Dod. I have been married two months. I — I had to. Do you understand? I had to. I had to restore faith in myself. Friends deserted me when they

13

put you in. They referred to me as a criminal's girlfriend. I couldn't bear it, Dod. I simply couldn't. At times I prayed for you and hoped that some miracle would open prison doors and bring you to my arms. Other times I wished I'd never met you. I could have waited, Dod. I could have waited but I felt that it would never be the same. I kept telling myself that I was wrong but I couldn't believe myself. It was terrible. I was lonely and sad. My life was hollow. I didn't know where I was going or where I was coming from. Then it happened, Dod. It happened. Don't look at me like that because it can't be undone. It has already happened. I am married now. It's all different, Dod. Yes, Dod. I am sorry but you must understand. It happens to people you know."

"Who is the fellow?" I asked. Her face furrowed and her complexion changed. She said seriously.

"He is my husband. Let that suffice. Please."

"Do I know him?"

"Yes. You know him, Dod. He is your friend. He was your tutor at Makerere. He's the one that led you to me. That same man is my husband."

"God Almighty! You mean Dugan! That short stout bald headed bad tempered fellow is your husband? Jeez! You must be out of your mind. Of all the news that falls on passing ears, what could have possessed you to choose a middle-aged pink-faced Englishman instead of me, jailbird though I be? Gosh, Dory, I'll murder him for you. By Jingo I will. I wouldn't let you. I wouldn't let you be ruined. No, no. No, thank you. Where is he?"

Then I had it. I am always having it even from women. Unlucky fellow, that's me. She called me a poor conceited worthless opinionated blackguard who spent my beggarly life smearing other people with dirt while I was dirt itself.

"How dare you breathe such words about my husband? I'll have none. Not from you. Please leave me now. I have work to do. Don't try to see me again even when you've learnt to have respect for others. Please go," she hissed.

There and then I spat. I spat on the floor and walked out. That's me. I simply can't stand women hissing at me. Women should not hiss at all. At least not at men. I couldn't be bothered if they spent their whole goddam life hissing at each other — but at me! Oh no. For that I shake my head. That's why I spat.

My shoes are number ten. They are long, broad and brown. I notice with disgust the red familiar dust on them as I walk towards Eastleigh. They are always dusty, my shoes. I can't afford shoe polish

14

and the shoe-shine boys wouldn't even lend me their brush. I am slouching at a slow unsteady pace because I have lost the nail of my big toe. The thick bandage does not help. The blinking toe is beating drums. Wet pus is making the inside slippery. God! I hate myself at times. I hate pus. Ruins my appetite, it does. Gosh, my toe hurts. I must see a doctor soon. I am all confused.

I have walked and cursed for a mile and a half. I have fathoms to go. I mean furlongs. I wish I was sinking fathoms instead of walking furlongs. I am hungry but that is nothing compared to my toe. I never realized that it was such a long walk from the centre of Nairobi to the Eastleigh slums. My old car has grown a beard. The damn thing wouldn't start and it is growing moss and lichens at Tigoni Police Station, where they dumped it after dumping me in jail. It is the only real friend I had — my car I mean — and it is the only thing I own that has a roof. The road licence expired a couple of million years ago and I can't get a friendly soul to buy the damn car even as scrap metal. That's me. Plain broke. Broke as a dry twig. Broke as hell. Not a thing. Nothing. Damn it. And I am a graduate. That's what I am. A graduate. University of London Geography Honours at Makerere and I can't get a job. That's how helpful education is. Very helpful. Gosh! I am hungry.

I am there now. I mean I have arrived at Eastleigh. It's two-thirty and the sun is melting my head. I have little hair on my dome because the first thing they do when you are received in the cooler is unhair your head. Tin roofs are shimmering everywhere and the smell of dust, dirt and prostitutes is offending my nostrils. A plane is taking off at the airport and it is raising a sandstorm along the murram runway. It sounds like ten thunders. What a place? Gosh! I am hungry.

There is a prostitute standing there and there is a prostitute standing here. There are prostitutes standing everywhere. Maybe some are not, but they all look alike. They are hungry for money. It's written on their faces. Can't help them. Not me. I don't have a cent. Not one thin cent.

As I pass this respectable-looking house a Johnnie emerges from inside buttoning his trousers. A middle aged Somali woman is at his heels angrily demanding the tumbling fee. She is talking in Swahili and English at the same time.

"*Toa pesa* Johnnie. *Lipa*. Twenty shillings. *Mzungu* pay. Twenty shillings you pay. Not *bure*. Not free. Give." She got hold of his collar and yanked him — an ill advised move. He whirled round and slapped her hard with the back of his hand. She kissed the ground and started screaming — "Thief! *Mwivi!* Johnnie thief!" and the

15

Johnnie took to his heels.

I don't know where the people came from. It's hard to believe that those small houses sheltered so many people. They came out like hordes of desert locusts and the poor English soldier was cornered like a rabbit. The cruelty — God! They kicked him and kicked him and kicked him. He lay lifeless on the ground and yet they kicked him. Everybody wanted to kick him. Another half-dressed Johnnie burst out of a house and fled barefoot towards the army barracks. Everybody shouted something or other but nobody pursued him. The prostitute he was having a tumble with came out of the house and started pissing behind the house. Horrid. She didn't mind whether you were staring at her or not. Gosh. These women have no respect for their asses. Makes me wonder whether this is the type of woman God designed for man.

As sure as hell there is going to be trouble here. The beaten up Johnnie is not stirring. He is a bleeding mess. The English soldiers will sure take some revenge. They'll beat up men and rape women. I must get the hell out of here. Might get raped by a homosexual. You never know English soldiers.

I walk past several blocks and turn to the left. The house I am looking for is on the far side, one row from the airport barrier. I have never been here before but I got very precise instructions of how to get there. Judy is always like that. She makes sure that you find her.

As I look to the right, the number is staring at me, 1564, written neatly in charcoal with "welcome to my den" scribbled below.

I am now approaching the den. I don't feel so good on account of my toe. It will be the second tumble in a month. I have come all this way for it, heat or no heat, toe or no toe and now I want to turn back. I don't like this den. I am holding a brief discourse with myself but I am still slowly walking towards the den. I am in two minds but I can't stop walking. Something is pulling me. I hear a scream somewhere behind me and I walk fast and knock at the door. Nothing happens. Not a sound. I can hear more screams and I knock frantically at the door. Then I hear it. I hear the bed creak. Light footsteps are approaching the door. I control my breathing. Sometimes my lungs are very stupid. They just don't control my breathing.

The door opens. I have prepared a smile for Judy but I get a surprise. Women are always surprising me. This one is not Judy. She is a halfcaste. A cross between a Chinese and an African. A real dish. She is as different from Judy as I am different from you. The smile dies on me and my brain is not working very fast. This is

16

unusual. I am a quick thinker.

"Yes?" she blurts out, raising her eyebrows and inspecting my anatomy. All the time I am looking at her tits. Real medium rare her tits are, and I make a mental calculation that they are better than Judy's. I like tits. I like to put them in my mouth and think of babyhood.

"My name is Dodge — Dodge Kiunyu and I like your tits. I am looking for Judy — Judy Waira. Does she live here?" She eyes me with disgust and is just about to bang the door shut when we hear another scream from the direction of the fighting place I'd just scrammed from. She hesitates.

"She is not here," the Chinawoman says. I say Chinawoman because she is more Chinese than African. Never saw an African with bulging oblique eyes.

"Does she live here?" I ask politely.

"Yes, she does but she is not here now." I notice that she is not as hard boiled as she makes out to be. This Kimono-like nightdress she is wearing is thin and vaguely transparent. It doesn't show much but I can see all that I want to see. She is wearing pants all right and I can see they are blue. I go for pink but blue is tolerable especially when the woman wearing them is this woman in front of me. I am secretly praying but don't ask me for what. You should know.

"Forgive my disturbing your mid-day nap but would you know where I can find her? I had an appointment for three o'clock." She looks at me queerly.

"A business appointment?"

"Yes, and no," I tell her. "Friendly business if you like." She smiles archly and then sneers.

"Free trade eh?"

"Again yes and no. Simply business without trade."

"You broke?" God! Her white teeth are killing me and she is showing them tits of hers to advantage. The light afternoon breeze is blowing her nightdress against her thighs and I start seeing shapes. Blast! And she is asking me — what the hell was she asking me?

"You are, aren't you?" she asks again.

"Oh, sure. I am. Oh—wait. You asked me whether I was broke?"

"Uh."

"Sorry. I am not. I mean yes and no. We are all broke in a way. We can't have all we want. We are all broke and yet we are not. Hey, can I come in for a while? I don't like this screaming from over yonder. Gets on my nerves, it does." She thought for a while and then smiled. This really gets my goat. Prostitutes are always thinking or letting on

17

to be. They don't want you to take them for granted. The only time they don't think is when you show them a brand new currency bill. The bill does the thinking.

"Eh, O.K. You may come in for a while. I am not sure that Judy will be back today."

"And where the hell is she?" I ask her as I pass through the door. The interior of the den is dark even at three — reason being that the only window has these carton slabs to serve as curtains. She moves over and removes one of the slabs and immediately some light filters through. I like to see myself during daylight, besides, this dame here is an eyeful. If you have any imagination you'll agree with me that a cross between a Chinaman and an African is bound to be an eyeful. And they are so rare.

She sits down on the bed as if she's not heard my question. There are no stools or chairs and when she says have a seat I don't know whether she is offering me the floor to sit on or the bed. I hesitate and she motions the bed. I am feeling uncomfortable, the reason being that the perfume she is wearing starts to drift to my nostrils and it sure dilutes my blood. My heart doesn't beat steadily either. Very stupid, this heart of mine. I sit huddled up for fear that some part of me might start trembling and repeat the question.

"She went to a movie with her boyfriend," she answers.

"At this hour?"

"They left at eleven o'clock. Movie is one thing. There are other things."

"You are telling me," I echo, pretending to be disappointed. I am not. I am looking at this dame's tits through the corner of my eye and smiling the crocodile smile. If I could make this dame, Judy could go nut-cracking for all I care.

This Judy promised me a tumble. One for free. I used to know her when I had the dough and she must have unloaded a thick wad off me. I met her three days ago and I told her I was broke and flat out. She gave me a quid out of kindness and actually persuaded me to come to this den of hers for a free so and so in memory of old times instead of which she gallivants away with this other mug, and leaves a cute Chinawoman in her place. The fellow who said that life is nuts knew his words although he was nuts himself. It takes a nut to say life is nuts. It ain't nuts.

"Do you also live here?" I ask. She shakes her head.

"I only came here this morning because I have a friend at my house. She has her boyfriend with her and they want some privacy. They haven't met for a long time. I had to leave my room to them."

18

"And will they wash the sheets?"

"That's a silly question. What did you say your name was — George or Gorge?"

"Dodge, my dear girl. Dodge not Gorge. What do they call you? Honeypot I suppose."

"Something similar."

"And that is not telling me."

"Annie. It sounds like honey, doesn't it?"

"It sure does. Now that you mention it, I remember that I haven't tasted honey for centuries." I teased. "It's a beautiful name. Almost as beautiful as you."

"And your name is gorgeous. I'd have preferred Gorge though. You'd better go home now. Nobody's screaming."

"I'll start screaming," I tell her. She gives me a look that would open the mouth of a meditating Yoga King. I give her a shy close look.

It was difficult and it was easy. I used delaying tactics and something in heaven came to my aid. There was this roar of thunder and yet another. Annie is the type that get scared when the heavens clash. Thunder gets into her stomach. I was licking my lips as she unconsciously drew closer to me. Then the rain. Some women simply go soft when it rains. The rhythm of the falling rain brings music to their ears. The humidity makes them sleepy and lax and they want you to sing them a lullaby as they snuggle and cuddle close to you. The stage is set. No resistance. Softly please. Gently my friend. You have a free ticket to Hongkong. So did I with my Annie. A trip to Hong-Kong and back.

It is night and I am walking back to town. Back to the centre of Nairobi. I am not sure where I am going. I have nowhere to go. I have no house, no friends. I am a jailbird. Thrice I have slept at the railway station and on several occasions I have kept various watchmen company throughout the night and the stones near the fire are as good a place as any to rest one's wearied bones. When I remember what I used to be, I curse this big star above me because it looks like the star under which I was born. It blinks at me and my toe starts up all over again. I hate toes.

I am thinking but I don't know what the hell I am thinking about. Painful process, thinking. Some part of me is happy. Real happy. I close my eyes and I see Annie peeling off this subtle Kimono-like nightie and my heart kisses my lungs. Gosh. The softest miracle ever to come into contact with a male — and the works? Boy oh boy! If you haven't screwed Annie you've never had a screw. You're going through life with blinkers on. Gosh! I am hungry.

19

2

It's eight o'clock and it's bitter cold. Very unusual for January. My fingers are frozen, absolutely frozen. Rubbing them together doesn't help. It never does. Tonia is by my side and we are going to school. It's about one mile away from home and we have to walk it. We are always walking, Tonia and I. We don't have much else to do.

There is a hole in my khaki pants and there is a white patch on the hole. The patch is getting worn out too. Miriam fixed it for me the second time two months ago so that I can use the pants for going to school but there's something wrong with my ass. Keeps wearing away patches. Perhaps there is something wrong with my sitting posture. There are lots of things wrong with me.

Today is Friday and it's our fifth day in school. Tonia's mother has been trying to hammer into our silly heads, the importance of education and the comforts she has to deny herself in order to send us to school. How depressing. Miriam never denied herself anything in her whole blinking life. The only thing she denied herself was our presence while we were at school. Our presence was a real headache to her. Sent us out she did, every time some fellow paid her a visit for an hour or two during which the door would be locked and the curtains drawn and then the fellow would walk out looking somewhat weaker and ashamed. A damn nuisance men are really. Some would come when it was raining and Miriam wouldn't know what to do with us. At such times we were a real pain in the neck to her. One day when I was reluctant to go out on account of the heat outside which wasn't conducive to curing my aching head, she poured a flagon of God's drink on my head and asked me to go dry myself. Very clever this Miriam. Knows how to temper heat and cure headaches. Damn her.

The only thing we learnt at school yesterday was the importance of having our nails clean and not to have foul breath. The teacher's breath was most foul. Hadn't cleaned them damned teeth of his after

20

his last encounter with onions. He must have taken dry smoked fish for dessert and later tried to eliminate the gaps between his teeth by smearing avocados. Very remarkable he is — this teacher of ours. He's even got an artificial plastic carnation in the buttonhole of his coat and laughs at his own jokes which we are too stupid to understand.

His name is Jack, this teacher of ours. Whenever he says Jack you always hear Jock which is what some people call their draught oxen. Looking at him, he reminds you of an ox. No horns, tails or humps but all the same, an ox. Fat like an ox, our Jack is, but only slightly more stupid. A remarkable fellow.

On Wednesday we spent half the morning pouring water in the classroom to drown the dust. Very dusty our classroom is. You blow your nose and the mess that comes out is half dust. Perhaps there won't be much dust today on account of the cold. Dust is better than cold anyway. You can wash it off or blow it off your nose but you can't wash cold. Chills your blood, the blinking cold does, and when there is a hole in your pants directly under the ass it doesn't help to ease the situation. No part of your body wants to get chilled, not even your ass.

Tonia is wearing a nice new little light blue dress on account of being daughter of her mother which I am not. My mother is dead. This Tonia keeps asking me whether I like her dress and I grunt something to that effect. She thinks she is a perfect lady at eleven and a half — we are both eleven and a half but she looks down on me as if I was six. Looks down on me she does, on account of this hole in my only pair of pants.

Miriam cannot afford to buy me clothes. I am not her son. Don't get me wrong though. I would not like to be her son. No, sir. Not by a long chalk. Oh no. Miriam should not mother anybody. My mother should not have mothered me either. This I'll swear and you can go to hell if you don't agree with me.

Miriam took possession of everything we owned. She wears my mother's clothes and cooks in her pots. She sold a few of the things that she didn't need, got drunk on the proceeds and then rented the house — our house. That is why she is so kind to me which accounts for the hole in my pants and Tonia's new dresses. Gosh! Women can be kind. Miriam's kindness is very remarkable. A gold-digging, oversexed, fat-assed whore, that's what she is. No kidding. She's real bad, this Miriam who is also my guardian.

I was telling you about Wednesday. After drowning the dust Jack started teaching us a, e, i, o, u. We sang a, e, i, o, u, the rest of the morning so that by lunchtime I was so bored that it would have been

21

a relief to play with green snakes. The most boring half morning in my eleven and a half years' lifetime. A very interesting teacher, our Jack. I am hoping and praying that I'll never have to repeat a, e, i, o, u. God! I wish my prayers would be answered — I really do.

On getting to the school compound we find that there are only a few kids around. We join this group leaning against the mud church wall and I start chatting with a girl on my left. She is real cute but she talks too much. When I tell her that I am cold she rubs my cheeks and they glow. Me, I like little girls with warm hands. They make your cheeks glow, they do. Tonia does not like this little girl I am talking to.She grabs my hand and says "Come!"

I don't feel like going so I ask: "Go where?" Tonia pulls harder and repeats more loudly, "Come". I am not feeling so good. I don't like to take orders from little girls. Tonia wallops me once in a while but I ain't no dog and she ain't my master. All the same I decide to obey Tonia but I ask her again, "Where are we going? It's cold you know."

"Never mind," says little Tonia.

"But I mind," says little me.

"Do you want to go back?" Tonia asks.

"Not particularly but where are we going?"

Tonia pushes me back and yells in her little cooing voice, "Go back then. Go. I'll tell mother." Fancy that. She'll tell Miriam.
I don't know what she'll tell about but whenever she tells something about me Miriam gives me a hiding. It doesn't matter what. Whenever she accuses me of something, I get a beating. These beatings are becoming too frequent for my liking. Sometimes she pinches me with those coarse hands of hers and it doesn't improve my cheeks. Very coarse, those hands of hers. Worse than sandpaper, I am not kidding. They are real bad, especially when they pinch your cheeks.

I ease back and start talking to my cute little girl. Her name is Lucy and her mother works for the City Council. She sweeps drains and what-have-you. Respectable, though filthy as a profession. Earns a living, Lucy's mother does. Better than whoring with charcoal sellers.

Little Tonia follows me and stands behind me. I don't see her because I am whispering something to Lucy and I am not aware of her presence till she grabs me by the collar.

"What shit are you cheating now?" Tonia asks me and I turn to face her. I am so annoyed that tears are almost welling up in my eyes. I am struck dumb and I am shaking all over. My knees are knocking. Stupid knees, my knees. They are always knocking. Murderous rage, that's what I am in.

22

I look at Tonia and spit at her. I spit right on top of her flat nose and she lets go my collar. I am thinking that it would be unseemly to have a showdown with Tonia so early in the morning but she doesn't. Slaps me she does, this little Tonia, and slaps me again. She pins me against the wall and spits right in my right eye. The great worm in my brain turns on his back and I lash out. I go slap, slap, slap, slap, kick, and my little Tonia takes to her heels. Lucy is thanking me for the good performance when this boy with a round head comes along. A real bully, this boy, and he is wearing the devil's smile.

"Come and fight me," the roundhead says. I don't say a thing because I don't like his fists. They are too big.

"Are you coming or shall I drag you by the hair, you girl-fighting lousy lily-livered mongrel?" I am thinking that this roundhead is the devil himself and I don't like devils. And he is smiling, this roundhead. Teeth like maize grains he has.

"Go to," I say to the roundhead instead of which he darts at me and smashes his dome against the wall because this stomach of mine he was aiming at had already moved. I moved to the left swift as a lover's wink and unwittingly occasioned the ramming act that the roundhead's dome was performing on the wall. A good smash it was, woe to the harmless wall. Damn stupid to start a war on the wall.

The roundhead doesn't feel so good. He shakes his head and focuses his hippo eyes and sees me.

"Rat!" the roundhead cries and springs at me like a cat. This time he gets me but he is too annoyed to use his fists. He squeezes me between his hands, intent on squeezing the life out of me. All the time his foul breath is offending my nostrils. I get one hand free and as I try to raise it to grab his hair, one of my fingers goes "poke" right into his right eye.

"Aao!" the roundhead yells and lets go. I go smack, smack, smack, push, and the roundhead starts kissing the ground. Lucy is congratulating me again when the teacher comes around — this Jock, I mean Jack. Our Jack. We all hurry into this big dusty hall which is both a church and a gymnasium and as we are walking, whimpering roundhead edges his way close to me and gives me a dig in the ribs with his elbow.

"Another round at lunchtime, what say you?" he asks.

"What?" I ask him.

"A boxing session and God have mercy on your teeth." He winks maliciously at me.

"Thank you very much and may your maize teeth fall out," I

23

retort as we get in this big dusty hall. I make sure that I don't sit anywhere near master roundhead. When he moves to the benches on the right, I move to the left just to keep away the germs. Real infectious our roundhead is. Poor roundhead. The following morning he was run over by a fire brigade's vehicle while on his way to school.

We all felt sorry for him. All except me. He'd given me a wallop on the way home and promised me another the following day. I was scared to the white patch of my pants and spent the whole night praying. I was praying that master roundhead be run over by something the following morning and by Jingo my prayers were answered. The fire brigade did it for me. I felt that the Almighty God loved me. At least He had listened to my prayers and I was glad. Later I was very sad. I knew that I was responsible for this catastrophe but I didn't tell anybody. Not even Tonia. Tonia was too self-important. Carried her neck high she did, and shouted "shut up!" whenever I opened my sweet mouth to speak to her. Fancy that. A girl my age shouting "shut up!" at me.

Me, I don't like Tonia. I don't like her one little bit. I don't like her hair, her ears, her eyes, her mouth, the mucus on her nose, her teeth, her neck, her tummy, her legs, her feet and I don't like her blinking ass. I don't like her dresses, her shoes, her pencils, her books and I don't even like her whoring mother. I don't like Tonia. Gosh! I hate her.

Our Jack is teaching us A B C D. He has invented a tune for singing the alphabet and that's all we have done for the past two days. We have just sung the alphabet. Of course, we can't write it but we can sing it. Today is the third day that we have been singing this song and Jack reckons that we know it well. To make sure that we know he now wants us to sing the alphabet backwards starting with Z. He asks us whether there is anybody who can do it satisfactorily and the tall boy who raises his hand starts: "Z Y X V S T," and Jack tells him to sit down. He adjusts the false carnation in his button hole and calls out: "Anybody else want to try?" Nobody volunteers so our Jack points at Lucy.

"Give it a try, will you?" Lucy merely giggles and hides her face between her hands. Very shy this little Lucy. She goes on giggling and Jack is still pointing at her. Reminds you of a tired ox, our Jack does. When Lucy continues to giggle he wags his tail — I mean he scratches his head — and points at me. He points at me because I am sitting next to Lucy and my hand is halfway up because I want to help her.

"Z Y X W V U S T R P Q," my mouth is saying and Jack

24

asks me to shut it up and I do. He is always asking you to shut up this Jack. He is like Tonia.

I am wondering where I went wrong when Lucy tickles me. I am very ticklish so I let out a loud "Wao!" and Jack looks at me in surprise and finally tells me that the alphabet does not start with a Y anytime even if you are saying it backwards. Lucy laughs aloud and Jack throws a piece of chalk at her. Then he goes to the board and writes the alphabet backwards. We all sing after him.

The house is locked when we get home. It is locked from the inside because there is no padlock on the outside. Tonia knocks but there is no answer.

"Mummy! Mummy!" she calls out. There is no answer. Miriam must be sleeping like the python that swallowed a goat. She is always sleeping during the day. She sleeps more during the night. "Don't disturb her," I say to Tonia but she does not listen to me. She knocks harder, all the time calling, "Mummy, Mummy, Mummy, open up." The door is opened a crack and Miriam is wearing her night things. She also wears a frown that would have scared the devil himself. We have seen the frown before.

"You are lice and I hate lice. Go away," she says and bangs the door shut again. She is a very loving mother, this Miriam. She loves us, she does. God loves her and that's why she is very kind. Very kind.

We saunter away speechless because we are not very stupid. This is not the first time that this has happened. One time it was raining but we had to stay out. We understand. Tonia is very bitter about this but I don't care a fig. I am not Miriam's daughter. My happiness is my tummy. Once my tummy is full, which is rare, my heart is full. I am a simple fellow, that's me. Too simple. Fill my tummy and I'll give you all the treasures in my kingdom. They are plenty, my treasures. They include my khaki pants with the white patch. I love them, my pants.

We are sitting under this jacaranda tree and it does not give enough shade. Its little leaves are gone. Gone with the wind. The sun has baked them and when they are this ripe yellow colour, the wind picks them. Most of them have of course dropped right under the tree and we are sitting on them. Tonia is very clever. She had pulled up her little pink dress and is sitting on her little green panties because she does not want to soil this little dress. Very ladylike our little Tonia. Very much like her mother.

We are staring at the row of shanty houses in front of us. I am wondering why we must always have dust and flies. Dust and flies, smoke and evil smells, that's what we've got. Nude hungry children

and dirty whoring mothers — that is the order of the day. This is Eastleigh. Most famous place in Nairobi for advanced prostitution. Ninety per cent of the kids are fatherless. They are bastards. I hate the word. I hate the word bastard. Jack calls us poor little bastards and the damn fool is right. That's what we are. Bastards. God! I hate myself.

We have our eyes focused on the door of our shanty mudhouse when this burly-looking smiling gentleman comes out. He is combing his hair with his fingers and his eyes are blinking on account of the strong sunlight. He looks round like a thief and starts to walk away. He notices our keen eyes on him and walks in our direction. I have a good mind to run but before my mind is made up he is standing in front of us. He looks at us as if we were vermin but doesn't say a word. He just stands there scaring the pants off me. He puts his hand in his pocket and comes out with a shilling. He looks at it and then drops it without a word and walks away.

When he has gone a few steps we look at each other, at the man and then at the shilling. As if by a signal we both jump. We jump for the shilling. Tonia rolls me over and the shilling gets buried by these dry jacaranda leaves. We are both chasing frantically for the burly man's shilling but it's no longer there. Tonia is calling me bad names and blaming me for the precious loss but I am not listening. She is always calling me names but I never listen. I don't care a fig.

Then I see it. I catch a glimpse of it under the leaves near Tonia's right foot. She is almost stepping on it. By God she'll see it! I am hoping she won't. I am praying very hard. I go in front of her and pretend that I have seen it. She dashes at me and I roll back. I keep rolling till I have the shilling in my hand. She doesn't see me pick it. She is still looking for it. Poor Tonia.

I start walking towards the house and she suspects something.

"Have you got it?" she asks. I shake my head because I don't like telling lies but Tonia is not satisfied.

"You've got it," she says. Again I shake my head and Tonia does not know what to believe. She makes a final search and decides to give it up as a bad job. She comes to join me and we walk to the house together. I am smiling like the cat which swallowed the canary. I am absolutely satisfied with myself and am even starting to like myself. Tonia smells a rat but so what? Tonia is always smelling a rat. She's always calling me a rat. It's a hell of a good name when you have a shilling in your pocket.

Miriam has dressed in a hurry and she is now making the bed. There is no smell of food. No food has been cooked in this place. It's

not the first time either. It has happened many times before. When Miriam has a male guest she doesn't bother to soil her nails with pots and pans. She takes us to the little tea kiosk near the charcoal seller's dump and buys some tea and dry bread for us. We like this because it is not always that we have bread but we never have enough of it. Two dry slices and a mug of tea each is all that Miriam can afford for our meal. Thereafter she goes away and comes home at midnight drunk and buzzing like a bee, tagging a man at her heels. Very thrifty, this Miriam. Knows how to save her money, she does.

We are walking towards this kiosk and I am licking my lips. We are going to have tea and bread. This tea kiosk would be a nice place if there weren't so many flies hovering all over the place and sometimes dropping into your tea. They are always dropping into your tea, these flies, and you've got to fish them out with your finger. Real dogs in the manger these flies.

Miriam is looking beautiful in spite of herself. She has these long earrings that are dangling to her shoulders and is wearing some lipstick which is too red for her black skin. She is wearing a light blue blouse that shows her breasts to advantage and a tight brown skirt that has a big chocolate heart in front. Seeing her from far off one would think that she had cut a heart shaped hole in her skirt. Her skin is shining and fresh on account of the soap lather that she smeared on herself just before we left. She is also wearing this cheap Sudanese perfume that speaks out to men. If she wasn't fat, she would be a beauty. A real beauty.

She orders tea and bread for us and tells us to go home when we have finished. There are some men who are winking at her but she pretends not to notice. She looks straight ahead and pays the bill. Very modest, this Miriam is. Real modest. Modesty is her name.

She collects the change and scrams. She doesn't even bother to look back at the winking gentlemen. She walks haughtily like a new-born queen in the direction of the bus stop. I look at Tonia but she is too busy gulping her tea. I take mine slowly and feel the shilling in my pocket. I am grinning to myself.

We finish the tea and the dry bread and Tonia rises to go. I can see that she hasn't had enough but I let her walk out. When she is out I ask this thin-faced kiosk keeper to give me four buttered slices and two mugs of tea. I give him the shilling and I almost kiss it as it leaves my fingers. He supplies the order quickly and I pocket the change. Twenty cents, my change was. Enough to buy twelve sweets. Twelve round ginger sweets.

Tonia comes back to find out what I am doing and I smile at her.

"Fall to," I say. "This time the wheat stuff has some butter on it."

"Who bought it?" she asks.

"Father Christmas, my dear girl. Long beard and all. Came down my chimney he did. You'd better start or the flies will eat all of it."

"Did Father Christmas drop a shilling?" she asks.

"Go and ask him. When you find him say I said thank you. Eat, Tonia. Aren't you afraid of earthquakes?"

"No, but I'll eat. I saw Father Christmas coming out of our house. Dropped a shilling he did. Oh! you hypocrite, we should have shared that shilling."

"That is what we are doing," I tell her. "You are eating your share."

"Not all of it. You are real mean. Most boys are."

"I've got to be like other boys, haven't I?"

"They don't all talk with lots of bread in their mouths, or do they?"

"Next time they buy you tea and bread, have a close look at their mouths. If they are unlike me, they'll let you have all of it. I am happy today."

"Get wings and fly. How I would thank God."

"Is that a prayer for me?" I ask. Didn't know what she meant. No kidding. Talks in parables sometimes, Tonia does.

"Yes it's a prayer for you. For you to fly away. Away never to return and good riddance it would be surely."

"You are stupidity itself," I tell her. "What would you do without me to buy you buttered bread and sweets later?"

"I'd be glad to be rid of you, sweets or no sweets. I give you sweets more often than you give me. You are gloating because of a mere shilling while you are feeding on us. Mother could afford more things for me with you out of the way."

I am starting to get annoyed, which is rare. Tonia keeps reminding me that I don't belong there and that I am feeding out of her mother's hand. She's a real pain in the neck. One of these days I'll go from here and find refuge on Mt. Kenya where the old gods are supposed to live. I can't stand Tonia's tongue. I have tried but by jingo I have failed. I have failed miserably but I can't help but be in her company. Her company is the worst torture. Continual torture to my young immature brain. God! She hates me, little Tonia does. She thinks that I am standing between her and nice things. She thinks that Miriam would be able to afford four slices for her at the kiosk if I didn't exist. She hates me.

We finish our meal but instead of going home to quarrel we walk towards the shops because I have promised Tonia some sweets. She really wants her share of the shilling. We get there in less than no time on account of our full stomachs and I ask this fat Indian shopkeeper to give me sweets for twenty cents. I point at the glass jar containing round ginger sweets and he gives me twelve. On second thoughts he gives me an extra sweet and says "Merry Christmas!" I accept the sweet with a smile although of course it is nowhere near Christmas. It's April now.

"Thank you very much," I say to him and we walk away. Tonia extends her little hand and I count six sweets into it.

"What about the thirteenth sweet?" she asks still extending her hand. I have a good mind to kick her hand and send her six sweets to the four winds but I control my temper. I am always controlling my temper.

"It's my Christmas gift from a kind friend," I tell her.

"No," says Tonia. "It was given to both of us. Split it into two."

"How?"

"Use your teeth," she says.

"All right," I tell her. "Have all of it. The Christmas gift was meant for you." She has no shame, this Tonia. She actually grabs it from my hand. I look at her and make a mental note that her name should have been "Gluttony." I put a sweet in my mouth and try to whistle. I can't on account of the sweet so I challenge Tonia to race me to the house. She scowls at me and tells me that she is not the dead roundhead to go competing with me. I decide that she is horrid company and I race myself all the way to the house. When I get there I look and notice that Tonia is also racing herself and I burst into laughter.

We go inside and Tonia goes to her bed. She lies on her back and says "Come."

"What for?" I ask her.

"Come. Let us play."

"Let's go outside then," I tell her. She shakes her head and looks at me playfully.

"Right here on the bed. Let's play our old game. My mother does it with the men."

"Oh! no. Not for the love of God. No. It's stupid and I'll not play it. It's shameful. No. I wouldn't. Let's go out and hop. God, Tonia, you must be out of your mind."

"It's too hot for that. Come over." I protest like mad but I don't know how it happens. In spite of myself we are playing this old game when the door bursts open. Miriam rushes in and stands looking at us

with her mouth open and her eyes flying out of their sockets. She doesn't say a thing. She is too shocked for words. She just stands there and stares like a cow. Looks like a cow she does. All she needs is a tail and she'd start eating grass.

We scramble off the bed and dash into the other room because Miriam is blocking the door. We know we are due for a king size wallop. I open the window and I am squeezing myself through when Miriam dashes into the room to squeeze the caloric out of us. I just manage to slip through as she tries to grab my feet and I fall to the ground. A mad dive it was. Hit the ground head first and lay down there stunned. Then I feel my limbs go limp and there is this funny darkness and bees are buzzing all over the place, then out. I pass out there below the window and I don't even know it. I am dead to the world.

When I come to, Miriam has this wet cloth on my face and it's already night. The lamp is burning feebly where it hangs on the wall casting dubious shadows that look like walking ghosts. There is no sign of Tonia.

I shake myself and try to focus my eyes instead of which bees start buzzing again. I relax and stare at the hurricane lamp and the blinking lamp stares back at me. No kidding. Miriam lets go my head and I reckon I go to sleep again because when I wake up, there is no one in the room. I yawn and try to sit up. As I do so I let out a loud fart and I feel better. I sit up in bed. I can't hear a single sound. The lamp still burns dimly and depresses my spirits. I get out of bed and start prowling but I am afraid to make a noise. I am wondering what happened to everybody else when the door to Miriam's bedroom opens and she stands arms akimbo looking at me.

"Are you all right now?" she asks.

"Yes," I stammer.

"Go to bed then. There is no dinner for you." I ease back to my little bed and cover myself from head to toe. I can't stand the sight of Miriam standing there arms akimbo staring at me. I hear feet approaching and the lamp is taken off the hook. My heart is in my mouth and I am just about to piss on myself because Miriam hasn't moved away. The blankets are pulled off my head and I find myself staring at the lamp again.

"What were you doing when I came in?" she asks. My throat is dry and my saliva glands have gone dead. I can't speak unless I croak.

"What were you doing?" Miriam demands fiercely.

"Playing," I tell her.

"Playing what?"

"A game. A new game we learnt in school. It's called "Press ups."

"And how is this presses or whatever you call it played?" she demands.

"One pushes up the other pushes down."

"In that posture?"

"Posture?" I am feeling very stupid.

"Yes, posture. Is the game played like that in school?"

"Almost similar with minor modifications. We don't like it," I say.

"You are lying. That is not what Tonia told me. Games like that are not played anywhere. There are no such games. That is vice. You have brought vice to my house and infected innocent Tonia with your filth. You are like your mother. Always filth and more filth. It's in your blood. You will leave this house tomorrow. Tomorrow morning you must go. You can go and live with your grandmother back in Nyeri if she is not dead. Go you must." She walks away and bangs the door of her bedroom shut. I am left to the night and my poor little head to bother me. Poor me.

It all happened a long time ago but my memory is as fresh as a fresh shave. Those were the days indeed. When I reflect, as I have been doing, I laugh and cry. Sometimes I do both simultaneously. So what? You can laugh and cry if you damn well please. Nobody is stopping you. Go ahead and yell your head off.

This old watchman I am sleeping next to keeps poking his fire and telling me a lot of filthy nonsense about his youth. He waits till I am just starting to snore and then starts talking. He keeps on repeating the same words if I don't say "uh" and his voice is starting to give me the creeps. I wish I had somewhere else to sleep but I haven't. Since I had that wonderful time with Annie this afternoon, I have had no rest. I have been chasing for food and a place to sleep and I haven't succeeded either way. I turn to the watchman.

"Hey friend. Do you know of a place where one can safely grab some grub? I am famished."

"It is never safe to pinch," the blighter tells me. "If you are a thief walk from here this minute before I clout you on the head with my club."

"Easy mate," I tell him. "I was merely joking." The blinking watchman is not satisfied. He has decided that he doesn't like my company any more. He stands up, adjusts his heavy overcoat and holds his club firmly.

"Walk from here this minute," he says fiercely. I can see that he is not kidding. He means to clout me. I get to my feet slowly and look

pleadingly at the fellow.

"You are making a mistake, friend. I merely ——

"I don't make no mistakes and I ain't your friend." He cuts me short. "Walk from here this minute." Blimey! Just fancy that. A watchman sending me away from his fire to brace the solitary cold of the night in the streets of Nairobi. Gosh! Is my company so low that even an old watchman won't accept it? Damn it. There is something wrong somewhere. I simply can't live like this.

I am walking away in all directions because I have no fixed direction. I am wondering why I left Judy's den. I could have pleaded with Annie and she might have agreed to take me to her place because her friends were leaving at eight. I could have spent the night there. Damn fool. That's what I am. I am getting foolish in my old age.

I limp away and I am cursing mankind. I am also cursing my big toe because it's throbbing again. A damn nuisance, this big toe of mine.

The cold is penetrating right to my belly. It's very empty, this belly of mine, and a damn nuisance too. I can't get a thing to put into it. Haven't done so for days. I am thinking about Annie licking my lips and pitying you. I am pitying you with all my heart. Poor you. How very sad.

I can't walk any more. My limbs are failing. I must rest awhile. I am out of breath. God! I am hungry. I lean against a dustbin and close my eyes. God's sleep says hello and I smile.

J. ROGER KURTZ
& ROBERT M. KURTZ

Language & Ideology in Postcolonial Kenyan Literature

The Case of David Maillu's Macaronic Fiction

Reference
Adapted from *Journal of Commonwealth Literature* 33 (1), 1998: 63–73

Until recently, serious scholarly discussions of African language, culture and literature rarely included the work of the popular Kenyan writer David G. Maillu, unless to dismiss it in passing. Local and international critics alike have vilified Maillu on moral and aesthetic grounds. A typical example appears in an early collection of East African literary criticism, *The Season of Harvest*, in which Chris Wanjala targets Maillu – along with Charles Mangua and George Kamau Muruah – in his attack on popular novels, which were at the time a relatively new phenomenon in the region. Wanjala terms these a 'trashy and scabrous imitation of brothel and low life, especially yarned for the low-brow reader in this country.'[1] Sounding a similar note, Bernth Lindfors once classified Maillu's writing among the more noxious of the 'harvest of weeds' springing up in East Africa's literary landscape during the mid-1970s.[2]

David Maillu makes a handy target because of his status as *primus inter pares* on that long list of Kenyan popular writers who have produced the racy romances and titillating thrillers that have dominated the region's literary output since the early 1970s. He did not originate the popular genre in Kenya, but he has been its most famous, or at least infamous, practitioner; in the volume of his output and the nature of his subject matter, Maillu is Kenya's answer to Nigeria's Cyprian Ekwensi. Shortly after Charles Mangua's surprise bestseller *Son of Woman*[3] demonstrated the potential local market for such writing, Maillu did a little market research of his own, discovering in an informal survey that readers were interested in half a dozen rather fundamental topics: sex, politics, human relations, religion, death and money. He tailored his writing accordingly, quickly producing bestsellers with titles that speak for themselves: *Unfit for Human Consumption*, *My Dear Bottle*, *After 4:30* (about what happens between bosses and secretaries at the end of the workday), *The Kommon Man*, and the like.[4] These works, all from the 1970s, put Maillu on the literary map, but in the stigmatized category of 'popular' writer. Stories of Kenyan schoolgirls reading his scandalous *After 4:30* under their desks abounded, and for a time his books were banned in Tanzania.[5]

These days Maillu's reputation appears to be on the mend, for three main reasons. In the first place his sheer tenacity, the unmatched volume of his production and his willingness to innovate have earned him the grudging respect of his erstwhile detractors as well as a significant place in Kenyan literary history. Someone who has published as much as Maillu has (almost 50 titles over 25 years) simply cannot be ignored. The second reason for Maillu's rehabilitation, in academic circles at least, is the relatively recent respect accorded to popular culture as an acceptable object of study in addition to elite culture and folk culture. Popular literature is being taken seriously, in part because it is perceived to offer insight into 'the reality experienced by a majority of East Africans,' presenting a 'true mirror of the hidden reality of the region's social experiences.'[6] Finally, Maillu's reputation is slowly changing since much that he has written since the 1970s has surpassed his initial repertoire of popular themes. As Francis Imbuga notes in his retrospective review of East African literature in the 1980s, 'there is reason to believe that Maillu will gradually settle down to address more serious themes of East African experience.'[7]

The more recent references to Maillu and his work are consequently less excoriating than earlier accounts, with some critics revising their earlier stands. Henry Indangasi has offered the first serious and comprehensive overview of Maillu's work by a Kenyan critic,[8] while Lindfors has proclaimed, in a favorable retrospective essay, that there is a 'new David Maillu' afoot:

> Maillu cannot be ignored in any systematic effort to understand the evolution of an East African literature, for he has extended the frontiers of that literature farther than any other single writer.[9]

Innovation and the extension of literary frontiers are indeed Maillu hallmarks; the sheer variety of his work makes him difficult to pigeonhole. In capitalizing on the new market for popular writing in the 1970s, he took the song style developed by Okot p'Bitek and turned it to his own purposes, attaching the trappings of indigenous cultural form to his sensational (and very contemporary) subject matter. He has turned his hand to polemical non-fiction treatises on African religion, philosophy and cultural practices such as polygamy. He was the first Kenyan to make extensive use of the epistolary form. He has produced pithy pamphlets on success in love and marriage. With *Kadosa*, he has written what must qualify as the only Kenyan science fiction novel to date. His memorable character, Benni Kamba ('Agent 009'), has more than once saved the entire African continent from foreign menaces. Most recently, he has produced the longest East African novel yet, the epic *Broken Drum*, which weighs in at more than 1100 pages.[10]

In attempting the daunting task of categorizing Maillu's works, one might divide them into two broad groups: his popular pieces, most of which are set in Nairobi and feature urban conflicts; and his moralistic or didactic works, which tend to center on rural values and settings. Most of the works Maillu produced under his Comb Books label before it folded would fall in the former category, as would the Benni Kamba adventures. The later, didactic works have been more readily taken up by mainstream publishing houses, and include moralistic lessons about growing up (as in *The Ayah* or *For Mbatha and Rabeka*) as well as treatises on African tradition (such as *Our Kind of Polygamy* or *The Black Adam and Eve*).[11]

It is within this context that we wish to discuss Maillu's little-known linguistic innovation, the macaronic novella *Without Kiinua Mgongo*,[12] which he composed entirely in a mixture of Swahili and English. If nothing else, *Without Kiinua Mgongo* is remarkable as an historic artifact in Kenya's literary history, and it offers credence to the claims that Maillu deserves credit for testing the boundaries of literary expression in East Africa. The language of the novella is unprecedented in the region's literature, featuring what we are defining as a version of linguistic code-mixing in a manner that is reminiscent of (although it does not precisely match) the code-mixing and code-switching of Nairobi speech. But *Without Kiinua Mgongo* is also a fascinating sociological artifact because of the way that the linguistic form that Maillu has selected matches the work's ideological subtext – a decidedly conservative and hegemonic subtext – in particularly close ways. Linguistic form and ideological content forge a remarkably harmonic marriage in *Without Kiinua Mgongo*.

The novella's storyline is largely forgettable and primarily didactic. When Katherine Mbuta, the spoiled daughter of a Nairobi millionaire, becomes pregnant, she blames it on Nzuki, the son of an unusually loyal family servant. Nzuki's promising scholarly career is ruined, and he is sadistically tortured by the police until he agrees to sign a confession. Nzuki, innocent and idealistic, comes to the bitter realization that without *kiinua mgongo* (literally, a 'back straightener', i.e., money), it is impossible to get ahead in today's Nairobi. In order to avoid family shame, Katherine's parents contrive to reunite her with Nzuki, to the great surprise of both youngsters. In the end, Katherine and Nzuki fall in love and are married in Nairobi's historic All Saints Cathedral. Katherine's father is pleased since Nzuki, who is far more clever than his own inept sons, can run the family business and, as he notes, adopted children can be more devoted and responsible than biological offspring.

What is not so forgettable, indeed what makes the work a delight to read, is the macaronic language that Maillu employs. Throughout the novella he joins English vocabulary to Swahili syntax in a manner reminiscent of common Nairobi speech. Here, for example, is the description of Katherine's overweight mother, who contrasts with her scrawny husband:

> Lakini what Bwana Mbuta had lost in weight, alicompensatiwa na bibiye, Hilda. Hilda, extravagantly fleshy, alikuwa mnene, mwili wote macurve matupu, commonly referred to hapa nyumbani as Mummy; mwenye silaha matiti na behind kubwa. Hivi iwe akikuangukia, you're finished. Wriggling about nyumbani kwake convincingly kwamba alikuwa a well-eaten mke wa millionea, alipendelea kutoboka huku na huko akiwacommand ama kuwa-abuse wafanyi kazi. Mwenye kupenda kuvaa ki-expensively kabisa. Ngozi yake ember yang'ara; kwani mali ilimkwaruza na kumsugua vyema sana. A woman of ma-neclaces na ma-earrings ya kila aina na gharama.[13]
>
> [But what Bwana Mbuta had lost in weight was compensated for by his wife, Hilda. Hilda, extravagantly fleshy, was stout, her whole body sheer curves, commonly referred to here at home as Mummy; a formidable bosom and a large behind. Thus, if she were to fall down on top of you, you're finished. Wriggling convincingly about her home like a well-eaten millionaire's wife, she loved to force her way here and there, commanding or abusing the workers. She was a person who loved to dress very expensively. Her clothes gleamed like amber; for riches scrub and polish them very well. A woman of necklaces and earrings of every kind and cost.]

Although Maillu had previously published in his mother tongue Kamba and in English (at one point even providing a side-by-side version of each in the didactic epistolary work, *My Dear Mariana/Kumya Ivu*),[14] his *Without Kiinua Mgongo* represents a unique linguistic experiment in East African literary history, since it is written entirely in this macaronic combination of English and Swahili.

Mixing languages is this manner, while not exactly commonplace in literature, is certainly not unheard of either. The linguist Braj Kachru notes that the use of two or more languages within a literary work is an established technique in Indian literature, dating back at least to the twelfth century.[15] Charlotte Bronte's English novel *Villette* contains a great deal of dialogue in French which the author does not translate in the original edition. There is also a well established tradition of mixing Spanish and English in recent Puerto Rican poetry. However, this technique has no precedent in postcolonial Kenyan fiction, which has always featured languages in their separate and standardized forms.

We have so far described this mixture as macaronic, a fairly generic term for combining languages within a single text. A closer look at *Without Kiinua Mgongo* reveals a very specific and consistent type of macaronic language, whose formal linguistic features have much in common with Maillu's underlying ideological agenda.

Generally, the alteration of linguistic codes takes one of two forms: code-switching or code-mixing. While they seem to be related, and while the line between them sometimes appears quite fuzzy, these are in fact distinct phenomena. Code-switching generally involves a speaker staying with the same code for a somewhat extended period. When it does occur, the sentence is the basic unit of code-switching, with switches occurring only at sentence boundaries or at clause boundaries within complex sentences.[16] Switching often occurs due to some environmental factor. Four such factors are: (1) a topic shift, especially to a topic which the speaker is more comfortable discussing in a given language; (2) an aside comment made for a listener other than the primary addressee; (3) the arrival of a participant whom the speaker wants to include or exclude; or (4) shifting attention to a new listener (in effect, beginning a new conversation). There are abundant examples of this phenomenon of code-switching in anglophone African literature, particularly in West African works where characters speak pidgin or their mother tongue in addition to the language of the text.

Code-mixing also involves moving back and forth among two or more codes, but two features distinguish it from code-switching. The basic unit is the morpheme rather than the sentence, and the switches are much more frequent, often coming within a sentence or clause. Furthermore, whereas in a code-switching situation the speaker and hearer do not necessarily share the same code repertoire (the speaker may be bilingual and the listener(s) monolingual), code-mixing occurs in a context where the speaker and the listener(s) have more than one language in common and can draw heavily from both or all of these, being reasonably assured that they will be understood.[17]

Code-mixing thus seems an accurate description for Maillu's technique in *Without Kiinua Mgongo*, which we can illuminate with the following excerpts. The first, from the beginning of the book, introduces Mwangangi, the family cook. The others are from the middle of the book. In excerpt 2, Mwangangi's son Nzuki, although innocent, has confessed to raping Bwana Mbuta's daughter after being tortured. Excerpt 3 shows Bwana Mbuta beginning to have second thoughts about Nzuki's guilt:

1) Mwangangi, being a Mkamba, mwana wa Kulatya, was in his forties. Mtu shortish, large-chested labda because of pondaring chakula kizuri. Kwani commander wa jikoni huji-do atakavyo. Mwangangi alikuwa mweupe; mwenye macho sharp sharp, mwenye kupenda kusema jokes. Alikuwa a very good-hearted binadamu. U'youth ulimkaa usoni mwake handsome daima.[18]

[Mwangangi, being a Kamba, a son of Kulatya, was in his forties. A shortish man, large-chested perhaps because of pounding down good food. For the commander of the kitchen tends to do well for himself. Mwangangi was black; a man of sharp-sharp eyes, one who loved to tell jokes. He was a very good-hearted human. A youthful face kept him perpetually handsome.]

2) 'Nyamaza!' roared the policeman.
Nzuki hakunyamaza. Alilia kama amepigwa in another torture. Lakini Slim-Slim alimwangalia in readiness to strike Nzuki into silence mkubwa akimwamrisha. Police nao watu heartless, having been hardened by seeing too many people crying. Duty yao hiyo kuona machozi wa watu. Lia, ulie wanakuangalia tu. Huyu mwenye rusty teeth watched Nzuki with some amount of pride; labda akibudget the incoming bonus.
Polisi akaswallow tena.
In a way, Bwana Mbuta alikuwa touched by the tears of this boy. Hivyo, alismoke nervously, thinking. Finally, alimwuliza Nzuki, 'Are you crying sababu you're sorry, or ...?'[19]

['Shut up!' roared the policeman.
Nzuki didn't shut up. He cried as if he were in another torture. But Slim-Slim watched him in readiness to strike Nzuki into silence if the big man would order it. Police are heartless people, having been hardened by seeing too many people crying. It's their duty to watch people's tears. Cry, cry stones; they just watch you. This one with the rusty teeth watched Nzuki with some amount of pride; perhaps he was budgeting the incoming bonus.
The police swallowed again.
In a way, Bwana Mbuta was touched by the tears of this boy. Thus, he smoked nervously, thinking. Finally he asked Nzuki, 'Are you crying because you're sorry, or ...?']

3) Bwana Mbuta hakupursue the matter with Nzuki any further. Angetaka kumwuliza some serious questions, but he didn't know how to do it. Angeweza kumwinterrogate Nzuki namna gani and with which words concerning the rape and mimba yenyewe? He could not ask him adescribe vile ilivyohappen. A civilised father anajirestrain from details za sexual affairs za bintiye ...
Nzuki was praying in his thoughts wakati huo huo when yule Katherine alipoingia nyumbani from some shughulis of hers outside.[20]

[Bwana Mbuta did not pursue the matter with Nzuki any further. He wanted to ask him some serious questions, but he didn't know how to do it. How could he interrogate Nzuki and with which words concerning the rape and conception? He could not ask him to describe how it had happened. A civilized father restrains himself from the details of the sexual affairs of his daughter ...
Nzuki was praying in his thoughts at the very moment when Katherine entered the house from some errands of hers outside.]

In these excerpts, and throughout the entire novella, there are frequent switches within each sentence, and even within each word. Word-internal switches include the words 'pondaring', 'huji-do', and 'U'youth' (excerpt 1); 'akibudget', 'akaswallow', and 'alismoke' (excerpt 2); 'hakupursue', 'kumwinterrogate', 'adescribe', 'ilivyohappen', and 'anajirestrain' (excerpt 3). Furthermore, these passages require that both narrator and reader be relatively conversant in English and Swahili.

So this is certainly code-mixing, but of what type? There are three main ways to account for cases of mixing: pidginisation, borrowing, and the creation of a new code. In our opinion, none of these adequately describe what Maillu is doing.

Pidginisation entails a simplified grammatical structure, usually not conforming closely to standard forms of the lexifier language(s). In Maillu's case, the grammar of both the English and Swahili used in this book is quite standard, with no simplification – this is not, for instance, *ki-settla* (the pejorative term for pidginised, 'settler' Swahili). Furthermore, the common domain of a pidgin is as a *lingua franca*, used among speakers who do not share a common language. Maillu's audience would have been able to understand had he chosen to write in either standard English or standard Swahili. We thus cannot describe the language of *Without Kiinua Mgongo* as a pidgin. By the same token, the novella's language is clearly not a version of *sheng*, the Nairobi street slang. *Sheng* features the characteristics of a pidgin: its grammar is simplified and it serves as a common language for a diverse population, borrowing from English, Swahili and various Kenyan vernaculars. Like any argot, much of the purpose of *sheng* is to exclude certain listeners, often those who are older or of a different social class. Like any argot it is ephemeral, with the vocabulary shifting as soon as it is understood by the 'wrong' group.

It is tempting to dismiss the second type of code-mixing – borrowing – out of hand, because most examples of borrowing involve isolated lexical items that fill a functional gap in the debtor language (such as Greek and Latin words in English for scientific terms). Maillu uses whole phrases in both languages that could readily be expressed in either: the entire book could be expressed wholly in Swahili or wholly in English. A person with limited proficiency in either language might produce this sort of mixture, but Maillu's prior works show that this is not what he is doing. Thus, neither the English nor the Swahili in *Without Kiinua Mgongo* is being borrowed to fill a lexical gap.

One might make a case for labelling this work Swahili with heavy English borrowing, since where mixing occurs within words, Swahili morphology dominates (as in alismoke, hakupursue, kumwinterrogate, ilivyohappen or anajirestrain). English inflections for tense, case, number, and gender are used on English words but generally not on Swahili words: being but not 'kuwaing,' jokes but not 'mchezos', touched but not 'gusaed'. Two exceptions to this pattern of borrowing are the word pondaring (excerpt 1; the Swahili word *ponda* plus English -ing; the intervocalic 'r' is a phonological feature reflecting British pronunciation) and the word 'shughulis' (excerpt 3; the Swahili word *shughuli* plus the English plural -s).

In general, the usual pattern of borrowing from one language to another is such that the morphology of the donor language is replaced with that of the borrower language. Exceptions are usually limited to 'learned terms' such as one occasionally finds in English terms from Latin (alumni, not 'alumnuses'), or Greek (phenomena, not 'phenomenons'). This pattern does occur in this novella, but not nearly as often as it might if Maillu were truly in a Swahili mode while writing. For example, he writes Mtu shortish, not 'Mtu mshortish', which would agree in number and gender as is required between Swahili nouns and their modifiers. Such untaken opportunities abound throughout the text. Thus, borrowing is not an adequate label to explain what is happening.

Should we then credit Maillu with deploying the third type of mixing, a new code entirely, one that might be dubbed 'Swinglish'? We suggest not. Inasmuch as there is more structural similarity than difference between a monolingual's code repertoire and that of a multilingual, one can expect a multilingual to do the same sort of switching and mixing of languages as the monolingual does with registers, so as to adapt to the context of the speech event.

Thus, rather than using a new code, we might say that Maillu is simply exercising more of his multilingual code repertoire than he would be if he wrote entirely in English or Swahili (though still not the full range: he does not use Kamba, for example). Kachru notes that a multilingual writer's code repertoire, particularly the ability to mix and switch codes, at once *limits* the text and *extends* it.[21] While the multilingual's repertoire is presumably wider than a monolingual's, thereby expanding opportunities for creative expression (the multilingual still controls registers and other variations within one or more of his or her languages), the multilingual writer must choose between restricting the text to include less than his or her full code repertoire on the one hand, or restricting the readership of the text to those who share the writer's multilingual code repertoire on the other.

In other words, by mixing English and Swahili, Maillu has undoubtedly given himself an opportunity for creative expression beyond linguistic boundaries to which he had previously conformed. *Without Kiinua Mgongo* illustrates a creative use of code repertoire available to members of a multilingual speech community such as one finds in Kenya, where a significant percentage of the population speaks both English and Swahili fluently. But he has at the same time restricted the readership of the book to a much narrower speech community – those who understand both English and Swahili – than if he had written monolingually.

This formal linguistic framework, interesting enough on its own terms, becomes additionally noteworthy because it is closely analogous to the work's ideological framework. Despite the apparent variety of Maillu's writing, of which *Without Kiinua Mgongo* is a recent example, a closer analysis reveals that in both his popular and his moralistic works, in his fiction and non-fiction alike, Maillu's writing is ideologically consistent. This ideology posits a restoration of wholeness, both individually and communally, on a return to a rather loosely defined indigenous cultural tradition. That tradition, by this account, has been fragmented and disrupted by external forces that are most evident in two developments: the growth of the modern African city and changing gender relations. Maillu's ideology, manifested repeatedly in his various writings, suggests that wholeness can only come through a return to traditional, rural ways of life and to traditional, patriarchal family structures.

For Maillu, the evils of Kenyan society are concentrated in the cities, while their antidote is in the countryside. All problems and pathologies in *Without Kiinua Mgongo*, as in Maillu's other works, are located in Nairobi, which is represented as fundamentally alien and un-African. The millionaire Mbuta is corrupted because he is alienated from his roots. By contrast the good characters, Nzuki and his father Mwangangi, are closely tied to their home in Machakos. It is to his credit (for instance) that even in his darkest hour, Mwangangi refuses to sell his plot of land in the country.

A key turning point in the story occurs when Mbuta hunts down Nzuki near Koola, just before the desperate Nzuki can flee to Mombasa. When Mbuta shows up and asks, 'Did you think I would never find your home?' Nzuki assumes that he is going to be punished further. In fact we see that Mbuta, despite his corruption in the city, has managed to return to his rural roots (his true home and, by extension, his proper cultural framework) and from this point on things are likely to be different. Indeed they are, since this is the point at which Mbuta realizes that Nzuki is in fact much smarter and more hard working than his own urbanized children, and he begins the process of adopting Nzuki into his family.

Maillu's writing also highlights patriarchy as a key traditional value. Initially, the gender relations in Mbuta's family are all 'wrong'. Mbuta is weak, thin, and suffers from hypertension, while his family (especially his wife and daughter) are combative; when they fight, Mbuta gets the worst of it. The language Maillu uses describes Mbuta in the diminutive case (kamtu kembamba) while his wife is compared to a tractor (tingatinga):

> Bila shaka, Mbuta mwenyewe alimwogopa Hilda kummeet chest to chest. Mummy alikuwa kama tingatinga, asichezewe na kamtu kembamba na frail kama Mbuta.[22]
>
> [Without a doubt, Mbuta himself feared to meet Hilda chest to chest. Mummy was like a tractor, not to be messed with by a thin and frail little fellow like Mbuta.]

Things return to their rightful place only when the men are restored to authority and control. In the rather contrived ending, the once combative Katherine becomes a properly docile wife, clean-spirited and faithful, all thanks to the influence of Nzuki: 'Akamchange Katherine completely akawa mwanamke mwenye roho safi kabisa, then mke faithful kamili.'[23] [He changed Katherine completely and she became a woman with a pure heart, then a completely faithful wife.] In a David Maillu story, this is what constitutes a happy ending: rural values and male authority are restored and unquestioned. Whatever concessions are made to foreign influence (such as a church wedding) should only occur within the framework and syntax of this tradition.

This prescriptive ideology closely matches the linguistic structure that Maillu employs throughout *Without Kiinua Mgongo*. Maillu's multilingual repertoire makes use of a particular variety of code-mixing dominated by a Swahili base and inflectional framework to which English borrowings are appended; in the same way the thematic content of the work assumes that, in a society such as Kenya's, proper cultural mixing occurs by way of selected foreign graftings onto indigenous stock, and not the other way around. One may draw on a broad cultural code repertoire, in other words, but there is by this account an 'appropriate', canonical way of doing so, in which the indigenous elements (however they are construed) have precedence.

Borrowing from Abdul JanMohamed's terminology, we note that this type of ideological subtext results in hegemonic literature – that is, a literature that 'justifies the established ascendancy'.[24] Unlike nonhegemonic texts, which call social structures into question either by attacking the dominant group or by raising questions about the status of the subjugated group, hegemonic texts like Maillu's offer solutions to conflicts in ways that do not challenge the social *status quo*. *Without Kiinua Mgongo* does not ask us to consider, for instance, how Bwana Mbuta came by or maintains his riches or whether it is right for him to have so much control over his servants' lives.

We conclude with three general observations regarding the congruence of ideology and linguistic form in *Without Kiinua Mgongo*. First, it should be noted that the model of authentic indigenous culture on which Maillu's works rely is based on a very specific interpretation of African traditional culture whose accuracy is open to question. Certainly, the literature shows, not all Kenyan writers would concur either with Maillu's account of how traditional society functions or with his prescription for the way a culturally mixed society should be; the depictions of rural society in Grace Ogot's *The Promised Land* or Ngugi's *The River Between*, to name only two important works from Kenya, offer radically different perspectives.[25] Maillu's vision of an idyllic (and static) African tradition seems highly debatable.

Secondly, even though ideology and linguistic form complement each other so readily in *Without Kiinua Mgongo*, there seems no necessary or inevitable correlation between the two. The use of a particular linguistic form does not necessarily lead to a specific ideology, and neither is the inverse true – a writer's ideology need not necessarily lead to the use of a particular form, such as code-mixing. While covert, emotive structures may indeed help to shape a work's overt ideological discourse, as JanMohamed would argue,[26] linguistic patterns like code-mixing are surely separable from those structures. In another salient example from Kenya, Ngugi's use of Gikuyu and oral forms in his recent novels is certainly ideologically motivated, but there are significant differences between the perspectives of Maillu's work and, say, *Devil on the Cross*,[27] particularly in relation to gender issues. While it is logically and intuitively satisfying that Maillu's version of code-mixing should reflect his ideology, that connection is not due to any organic relationship between ideology and linguistic form.

Finally, it seems surprising that the type of linguistic experiment represented by this novella has not caught on more in East Africa. To our knowledge, this is the only such published prose work from Kenya, apart from a second title by Maillu that is currently out of print.[28] It is hard to imagine that any stigma associated with reading nonstandard language would be any more significant than the stigma attached to reading popular writing in general. Code-mixing is, after all, a common phenomenon in East African speech. As we have suggested, however, one result of code-mixing is to limit one's audience, so this may account for the general reluctance to emulate Maillu's example. *Without Kiinua Mgongo* was a Maillu Publishing House production, which suggests that other publishers were reluctant to gamble on this experiment, which would have a limited readership outside of East Africa. That the book has not been reprinted since 1989 implies that those publishers may have been prudent from a financial point of view. A final reason might again relate to form. *Sheng* and other types of code-mixing are often seen as part of an oral cultural tradition, appearing frequently in drama as well as in some poetry, rather than in prose. But while this association of code-mixing with oral forms seems logical, it is not necessarily inevitable, and there should be no reason why more works featuring code-mixing of various types should not be forthcoming in East African writing.

Notes

[1] Chris Wanjala, *The Season of Harvest*, Nairobi: Kenya Literature Bureau, 1978: 135.

[2] Bernth Lindfors, *Popular Literatures in Africa*, Trenton, NJ: Africa World Press, 1991: 58.

[3] Charles Mangua, *Son of Woman*, Nairobi: East African Publishing House, 1971.

[4] *Unfit for Human Consumption*, Nairobi: Comb Books, 1973; *My Dear Bottle*, Nairobi: Comb Books, 1973; *After 4:30*, Nairobi: Comb Books, 1974; *The Kommon Man*, Nairobi: Comb Books, 1975.

[5] See 'Unfit for Tanzanian Consumption', *Afriscope*, 6, 9 (1976), 9-10.

[6] Francis Imbuga, 'East African literature in the 1980s', *Matatu*, 10 (1993): 127.

[7] Ibid.: 128.

[8] Henry Indangasi, 'David Maillu', in *Twentieth Century Caribbean and Black African Writers*, ed. Bernth Lindfors, Detroit: Gale Research, 1996: 150–8.

[9] Lindfors, *Popular Literatures in Africa*: 98.

[10] David Maillu, *Kadosa*, Nairobi: David Maillu Publishers, 1975; *Broken Drum*, Nairobi: Jomo Kenyatta Foundation and Maillu Publishing House, 1991.

[11] David Maillu, *The Ayah*, Nairobi: Heinemann, 1986; *For Mbatha and Rabeka*, London: Macmillan, 1980; *Our Kind of Polygamy*, Nairobi: Heinemann Kenya, 1988; *The Black Adam and Eve*, Nairobi: Maillu Publishing House, 1989.

[12] David Maillu, *Without Kiinua Mgongo*, Nairobi: Maillu Publishing House, 1989.

[13] Ibid.: 3-4.

[14] David Maillu, *My Dear Mariana/Kumya Ivu*, Nairobi: Maillu Publishing House, 1989.

[15] Braj Kachru, *The Alchemy of English*, Urbana IL: University of Illinois Press, 1986.

[16] Ibid.: 63.

[17] Ibid.: 65.

[18] Maillu, *Without Kiinua Mgongo*: 1–2.

[19] Ibid.: 33–34.

[20] Ibid.: 34–35.

[21] Ibid.: 164, Kachru's emphasis.

[22] Maillu, *Without Kiinua Mgongo*: 5–6.

[23] Ibid.: 75.

[24] Abdul JanMohamed, *Manichean Aesthetics: The Politics of Literature in Colonial Africa*, Amherst: University of Massachusetts Press, 1983: 267.

[25] Grace Ogot, *The Promised Land*, Nairobi: East African Publishing House, 1966; Ngugi wa Thiong'o, *The River Between*, Nairobi: Heinemann, 1965.

[26] Abdul JanMohamed, *Manichean Aesthetics*: 267.

[27] Ngugi wa Thiong'o, *Devil on the Cross*, Nairobi and London: Heinemann, 1982.

[28] David Maillu, *Anayekukeep*, Nairobi: Maillu Publishing House, 1990.

Primary Text 5
Excerpts from Ben R. Mtobwa *Dar es Salaam Usiku* (*Dar es Salaam by Night*)
translated from Swahili & with a short introduction by Felicitas Becker

Reference
Charles Mangua *Son of Woman*
Nairobi East African Educational Publishers
[1971] 1994: 7–32

Introductory comment

The main character of the novel is Rukia, a street prostitute, who is attracted to two men. One of them is Peterson, a rich, but awkward and lonesome businessman. The other is Hasara, a young man with no money or connections, but a conviction for murder, albeit committed in self-defence. At first Rukia's interest in Peterson is only pecuniary. While her heart warms to his clumsy, but increasingly dedicated attentions, she meets Hasara and falls hopelessly in love with him. She does not know that Hasara is being used by a gangster with the intention of murdering Peterson. After numerous turns of the plot, it comes to a showdown in which it is revealed that Rukia and Peterson are siblings, and Hasara their step-brother.

The cover description states that the novel gives 'a true picture of the actual state of the city of Dar es Salaam'. The claim of realism affords the author the opportunity to include salacious sex scenes, a novelty in Swahili literature. *Dar es Salaam Usiku* is a very unashamed piece of pulp fiction, voyeuristic, sensationalist and saturated with cliche. It is telling that in the first scene translated here, the author actually invites the reader to visualise the scene as if in a film, and to imagine Rukia as an actress. A lot of Swahili 'market literature' is lifted off films or even television series. Video shops and television stations provide an ample supply of mostly western-made films, as well as some Hong Kong and 'Bollywood' (Indian) ones. Both violent action and romance are popular. Nevertheless, Mtobwa pays great attention to portraying the different social settings and contrasts that characterise Dar es Salaam.

The description of night in Dar translated here begins with a reference to the darkness and quiet of night in the villages, and includes the misery of beggars in the back streets. On the other hand, the author vividly expresses poor peoples' fascination with wealth. When Hasara first spots Rukia's 'sugar daddy' Peterson, he sizes him up with the sharp eyes of the have-not: Peterson smells of money, his whole appearance exudes the air of comfortable living. Throughout the novel, Mtobwa takes pains to point out the trappings of wealth, giving details of dress worn and of cars driven, evoking plushy suburbs and fancy hotels. Sensitivity to such things is great in Tanzania, where even simple western commodities still have an air of novelty, and continue to be beyond the reach of many. Still, the author's attitude is ambiguous, for while wealth is attractive, the wealthy often are not: Peterson with his refined manners (Mtobwa does not fail to mention that he swallows his sputum after coughing, rather than spitting it out like a peasant) is a hapless creature. Hasara's friend Hasira has been corrupted by the quest for wealth to the point where he is ready to kill. On the other hand, it is Rukia, the most debased, socially marginal figure on the scene, who is also portrayed as the most independent and resourceful, as full of initiative and capable of compassion. When it turns out that the street prostitute Rukia and her man Peterson are siblings, the reader is left to contemplate how random and devoid of reason is the distribution of wealth in the city.

There is a very moral side to Mtobwa's story. In his account, the freedom of manners and the quest for happiness in the city lead people to make fools of themselves. He recounts the resulting grotesquerie carefully and sardonically, as in the description of the revellers at Tausi. Desperation is close to the surface in their efforts to enjoy themselves, exemplified in the incessant dancing of the drunk who 'only gets round to sitting down when he falls over'. He uses his characters' inner monologues to develop ideas about what the city, or contemporary life, does to people: it is full of ambiguity, and insecurity, and plays havoc with preconceived social roles and expectations. This is especially true for relations between the sexes. But Mtobwa does not suggest a clear judgement. The attraction of Rukia's character lies partly in the fact that she is an outcast and therefore beyond the constraints of women's domestic roles. In some ways she is a male reader's dream: although she is African, we are told her hair is naturally straight, something considered highly attractive in Tanzania. Needless to say, she is great in bed. Moreover, she beats up an Arab customer who tries to get away cheaply, taking a symbolic revenge for past days when, as popular stereotype has it, Arabs treated African women as easy to get and easy to dispose of. Also, it takes her only a few days to learn how to drive. Freedom from social constraint, it seems, can free unforeseen capacities in a woman.

Rukia's thoughts and emotions reflect upon the incertitude of city life in a very fundamental, personal way. She is unsure of her own motives, mistrustful of romance, and sharply aware of the material underpinnings of even the most (supposedly) authentic and unquestioning emotion, love. She veers between sheer cynicism and the desire to live by her better motives, her gratitude towards Peterson and her devotion to Hasara. Rukia's encounter with Hasara, in the almost-ideal love story, seems to suggest that there is a right state of relations between men and women. In his arms, Rukia, who routinely takes her customers apart in bed, is meek, overpowered by emotion, and ready to believe in romance. But their relationship is tainted by scheming and ulterior motives on both sides. The regular state of affairs, where men lead households and women are domestic and accommodating, may well be beyond their reach. The realisation that they are siblings, even if not biologically, puts a question mark over the future of their relationship.

Little is known about Ben R. Mtobwa, the author of the novel. The publisher's blurb states his date of birth and, with characteristic lack of modesty, accords him an international reputation. The novel is written in Swahili, yet not in the language of the venerable literary tradition of the Swahili coast. Mtobwa uses 'upcountry' expressions common in Dar es Salaam, where many inhabitants are migrants from the provinces. He also has no qualms about using words of English extraction. His style is colloquial, not at all far from the language spoken in the streets of Dar. All the same, the novel contains elements that have precedents in the work of well-known academic Tanzanian writers. For example, Hasara resembles a figure in one of the best-known 'serious' Swahili novels, May Matteru's *Shida* (1975). As with the main female character in *Shida*, his name is not the one given at birth, but a symbolic one chosen later: it means 'damage'. Also like *Shida*, where the main male character goes to jail, Hasara comes to town to escape rural penury and ends up in prison. Rukia is not only, as 'the prostitute with a golden heart', a stock-in-trade character of newspaper novelettes, but also resembles the sophisticated girl that ruins a simple-minded young man – a figure that appears in traditional Swahili stories. Also, the portrayal of the hardship of rural life, which here takes the form of flashbacks to Hasara's childhood, and attention to the plight of the poor, are recurrent features of post-independence Tanzanian prose fiction.

Still, the closest affinity the novel has is to popular fiction. Since the late 1970s, small publishing houses have been coming into and out of existence in Tanzania, publishing crime and love stories often with little regard to quality. Newspapers, too, regularly publish stories, often readers' submissions, which are of vastly varying quality. Figures on numbers printed and sold are hard to come by, but the fact that the novel went into repeat editions suggests that it was a success. It also managed to raise a few eyebrows, and not always in disgust, in the academic community concerned with Swahili literature. It has been called 'the first erotic novel' in the Swahili language.

Dar es Salaam by Night

Ben R. Mtobwa

Another night has fallen. A city night. A night that does not know it is night, for it is filled with comfort and good living. Even the darkness which rules the night of the villages and the outskirts of the city has no might nor power here. From the lampposts along the roads, many shades of light mock the darkness, making of the night another kind of day.

The lovers of the good times anywhere in Dar es Salaam, old and young, were bustling in their quest for amusement (*walikuwa katika pilikapilika za kujistarehesha*). The drinkers were many in the bars without number, which are scattered across the city and its suburbs. The lovers of music were soaking it up in many venues. The lovers of cinema were crying and laughing in the various cinema halls. Also, the whores were selling themselves here and there in the streets and bars, rubbing shoulders with no-gooders and professional thieves, who in turn were also at work, looking out where and what to pinch next. Only the beggars have gone to rest with their sorrows, in their back streets. They are trying to coax sleep into taking them away, to allow them to forget the cruelty of the mosquitoes or fleas and the pain of hunger, even just for a few hours.

We are at the Embassy, one of those big modern hotels, built with only the tourists in mind. We are in the Roof Garden Bar, on the top of the building. Today the city of Dar es Salaam is at your feet. If you let your eyes wander here and there, you can observe its streets and houses. Cars speed by below. The sound of music just about reaches you from various buildings. You turn your eyes away from the scene and direct them towards the bar. You look at the beautiful, healthy flowers in this bar, so dense you have no good view of your fellow patrons at the other tables. In the middle of this space is a swimming pool, filled with blue water so quiet as if it wants to entice you to undress and get in. Your eyes leave the pool and contemplate in detail the other guests. There is only one European, who seems to be very flattered by two African girls who are placing orders with the waiter while he pays for them; they are laughing at him. They play with his thighs. He laughs. He finds it agreeable. There are people at the other tables who don't have to be persuaded to look on. That one over there looks like a man with his wife. This one here is obviously with his recently acquired love interest. Those three are professionals (*wahudumu*) who are planning their moves in low voices.

Hasara's eyes are drawn to a table where a girl is sitting, alone like himself, drinking her beer without haste. Hasara finds it hard to take his eyes off her. He cannot remember when he has last seen a girl as beautiful as this one. Sure, the city of Dar es Salaam is full of very beautiful girls, beauty queens even. Still, there isn't one among them who has attracted Hasara like this one. The beauty of the others often vexed Hasara, the way it was made up and put on with incomprehensible cosmetics and alluring dresses, so that it made the girls look like angels or devils rather than beautiful daughters of the family of man. This girl's beauty was genuine. Her hair did not need strange chemicals to appear straight and shiny: she was born like this. Her body did not need cleansing oils to make it soft and light in colour: she was born like this. She did not need to wear intimidating dresses or go half-naked like the others in order to attract the gaze; she wore a heavy green skirt which covered her from feet to waist, a little blouse not quite buttoned up. Her belly and arms were perfect enough to make anyone notice that these garments covered an angel.

With great effort Hasara took his eyes off this girl and turned them to the waiter, who was opening him a second beer and asking what he would like to eat. 'I will order later. I am waiting for someone', he said while looking at his watch. What was going on with Hasira? he wondered. 'Does he have to make sure every day that I wait for him for hours before he shows up? And what sort of news is it that he needs to tell me, which he wanted me to wait for here at the Embassy?' He decided to take his mind off these questions by turning his eyes back to the girl. She was still on her own; she had lowered her head as if she was looking at something in her glass. Then she raised her face slowly, in a lovely manner, as if performing for the pleasure of the onlookers. If she were acting in a film, the result would bring the film-maker praise. Suddenly their eyes met. For half a minute their eyes rested on each other; they were looking at each other as if reading each other's thoughts. Then the girl smiled.

Hasara felt as if a knife had suddenly entered his chest and cut his heart. The smile of this girl caused him pain! He could hardly bear it. He stooped over his table and began to pour the beer into his glass. The glass filled with beer and began to overflow without him noticing. Before he knew it, his trousers were getting wet. Avoiding the eyes of the girl, he called the waiter and asked him to wipe up the table. Then he quietly continued to drink his beer.

When he lifted up his eyes again to have a look, he saw that the girl was now with a man. A man who had had his fill. From where he was sitting Hasara could note the smell of that man, the smell of money. It was evident in the way his dark face was quiet, like that of someone free of troubles, who has anything he might want in this world. Also, his clothes showed clearly that they had been imported into the country at high price. The girl was saying something to the man, and she was smiling, the same smile that had hurt Hasara. Now it was directed at another man! Hasara felt as if hit on a sore spot. He poured himself some more beer, after looking at his watch and reproaching Hasira for his delay.

This time he did not look up until he felt another man's hand resting on his shoulder. He raised his head and met the gaze of his friend Hasira. A face where, although it had tasted pleasure, all the signs of hardship were still visible in the eyes, so that he appeared to be crying every time he smiled.

'Am I very late?' he said, laughing. 'Don't take notice. I was at work.' Suddenly he took Hasara's hand and said, 'Get up, let's go, otherwise we will lose them.'

'Let's go where?'

'Follow me!'

They left in a hurry. Hasara glanced at the table of the beautiful girl and found it empty. They had left unnoticed! He felt angry. He did not know what upset him. But he was not enough of a hypocrite to deny that he had begun to dream a wonderful dream about himself and that girl. How lovely it would be to be with her, in the streets, in the gardens, in bed! A waking dream. For as large as the city was, with millions of people in it, it would be amazing to meet her again, and a miracle to get her. Especially having seen the sort of men she went around with. But don't miracles occur here in Dar? What sort of miracle? He could meet with this girl and they could love each other and get married. What sort of miracle? Look at Hasira, just the other day he was poorer than him. Now he is much richer. And not only he. There are many people here with pitiful wages but owning cars worth millions. In Dar it is commonplace to find a manager who has sorted himself out in such a manner that even his home servant has four houses. What sort of miracles...

'Speed up, Hasara', Hasira ordered.

When they arrived downstairs they saw a 505 car leaving slowly. Hasira smiled, saying, 'Good job we caught them', while he directed Hasara to where he had left his car. It was a black pick-up double cabin. They entered, started the engine and proceeded to follow the 505.

'I think, Hasira, you've got to the point where you should tell me what you are doing. I am very grateful for your help with money and clothing. But do you think I like to follow you like a flag, one day waiting in the Coffee Bar, one in the Embassy, one time going somewhere without knowing what is happening? I ask you to explain to me, please,' Hasara explained.

Hasira smiled a bit. 'What's the haste, Hasara? We have the whole night today. As soon as we get the time I will explain it to you in detail. It is a job which I am sure you will find easy.' (...)

It is night, yes. But here at *Tausi*[1] it has just dawned. Everyone is on their feet, everyone is celebrating being alive. They please the eye with the elegant clothing on their bodies, with the broad smiles on their faces, and with the happiness that fills their souls. Here, hunger is forgotten, and so is death. Everyone has come to enjoy, and enjoy they do. This is really what the fame of this dance hall rests on, *Tausi* here in Kinondoni.[2] Liveliness. This hall is alive all night long. And it makes every customer feel alive, and happy to be alive.

Over there those two youths, a man and his lover. The young lady realised that her gentleman was not feeling comfortable on his sloping iron chair. So she has decided to cradle him in her lap. Now the man is having a good time sitting on his girl's thighs, while one cigarette after another burns up in his mouth. The beer he was brought has been all but forgotten, the glass sits half empty on the table.

The table over there is occupied by five people: four men, one woman. The woman appears to be more drunk than her companions. Or maybe she is kinder than they are. Look how she takes care of every one of them by turns: she grabs this one by the beard and plays with it...she tickles the other one...this one she strokes on the thighs...kisses yet another one...now she has returned to the first one and embraces him. Everyone is laughing.

And that one over there! Ever since he came in here, even before the music began, he has been dancing. He still is, now that the music is playing. But he dances with more force than the music itself. Look how he is dripping with sweat! Look how he wears himself out in restless jumping! A trace of blood is trickling from a wound he obtained on the head in one of his wild leaps. But he does not feel any pain. He is dancing powerfully and happily, as if trying to prove to the world that he is a happier man than everyone else. Look!

All this Rukia had been observing ever since she had entered the hall with her man. She had been lucky to find two seats in a corner. Drinks were standing before them, a well-fried chicken was resting in their stomachs. This was their third beer each. Rukia was beginning to feel livened up like her fellow guests. As usual, when she had sat down here and waited for their drinks to be brought, she had felt debased, and the other, already tipsy drinkers had appeared not just stupid, but complete fools. Now, she began to see them as normal people who were having a good time and knew how to have a good time.

'What do you think, darling', she said smiling. 'How do you like it here? Don't you think it is livelier than the Embassy that you're so fond of? If someone decides to have fun, they need to have it. What fun is there at the Embassy? Firstly there are hardly any people, then the way they sit around makes you think they are in a church or mosque. But here people are laid back (*barabara*).' She finished speaking and placed her free hand on a particular spot on this man's body, letting her fingers play in a manner that slowly woke up a certain creature inside it.

He coughed a bit and swallowed what he had in his mouth, then he said, 'Eh...yes, it's nice. But...'

'But what, Peterson?' retorted the girl. 'I know that you don't like places like this one. But just wait a bit, and you will like it. This music is still only to attract the crowd. In a little while you will see a live show by those youths of *Mlimani*.[3] I tell you, you will like it.'

'You know why I object?' Peterson said defensively. 'What I complain about is things like that man: look how he hurts himself. That is no fun. He can die or kill someone any time. It is dangerous to have fun this way!'

Rukia laughed. 'But it is also fun to watch a disgrace such as this. A grown up man, maybe he has got a wife and children at home, who chooses to behave this way, and in public. It's like watching the cinema for free.'

'Maybe...but–'

Rukia looked carefully at Peterson. She noticed every sign that he was hating it here, and that he was feeling trapped, in his eyes as well as his voice. He seemed a complete stranger here. Like an angel who has missed the door to heaven and finds himself in hell. His habit was to lock himself into an air-conditioned room, with European music playing at low volume, while a few people with lots of money drank quietly as if praying, while their talk would be about new plans to make even more money. Somehow Rukia felt pity for this subdued young man. Then she reminded herself that her mission tonight was not to pity, but to corrupt him.

There was no way she could forget that aim. This man had already ruined three days for her, and had left her alone in bed without any gift. To leave her like that, alone in bed and empty-handed, was not the behaviour of a freeborn man.[4] He had to pay for it dearly. First she would take him apart like a doll, then she would put him together as she liked him!

Now the music had become lively. A great mass of people was in motion on the dance-floor, dancing happily. In front of the crowd, the untiring musicians sang and danced happily. Three musicians were singing and dancing together, a pleasure to watch. Rukia observed them for a while. Also she looked at the other dancers, her eyes drawn to one little boy who was dancing on his own without restraint, moving his hips and thighs suggestively. Many people were drawn to him. Some of them threw money his way which he didn't even bother to pick up. When Rukia's eyes left him they moved over to the other drinkers who were sitting in their chairs consuming their drinks. The table where a girl had been holding her man on her lap was now surrounded by five men. Rukia knew one of them. Isn't that Sam Kitogo? Yes ... the stout guy who always has his hands in every pie, and writes books. And that one? Is that not Hammie Rajabu? Rukia had not met him. But she didn't have to be told. His appearance was exactly like the pictures she had seen in the books and newspapers. Undoubtedly Kajubi Mukajanga had not yet arrived. For he and Hammie were seen everywhere together. And those others ... One looked like Nico Mbajo ... and that one had to be John Rutayisingwa. Rukia saw a waitress going over to them and listening to them. Kitogo said something which made the girl smile. Hammie added some words, and she fell over laughing. Now she was scratching Kitogo's beard. And when she left to get them their beer her gait had changed: she moved her behind with more dedication. The writers laughed and slapped each others' shoulders. Rukia found herself laughing with them without them knowing, while taking her eyes off the table and directing them to another one.

She spotted two young men sitting more quietly than the rest. They were looking at her and her companion. Their eyes clashed. Rukia knew one of them. Wasn't that the man who had been at the Embassy a short while ago? The one who had been staring at her, with every sign of desiring her trumpeting from his eyes? When had he arrived? And what was he following? Had they been planning to come here anyway, or was it possible they were following her? Why were they looking at her like that? Rukia tried to avert her eyes. It didn't work. As had happened at the Embassy she found that her heart was softening without reason, and involuntarily a smile appeared and lit up her face. Something in the eyes of this young man caused or forced her to do so. Rukia extinguished the smile with a little cough, turned away her eyes and looked at Peterson.

The beer had begun to do its work in Peterson's head. His eyes had become more awake, his body livelier. It was obvious now that the taste of this night was entering his spirit, that he felt it in his blood. Even his hands were no longer resting quietly. Every so often they broke away from his body and slipped into the enticing hills and valleys of Rukia's body. His mind too was refreshed by the sweetness of the singers' voices and their untiring play.

Another lovely night
Darkness has spread all over
Covering the world
But I am dancing here and there
My heart full of joy.

Rukia looked at him for a while. Then she grabbed his hand which was making its way towards her thighs, seeking to stroke them. She took it into both her hands and played with his fingers to raise his desire, and said softly 'get up, let's dance'. When Peterson hesitated she pulled at his hand and said, 'let's go, my man.'

Peterson was no dancer. Ever since his childhood dancing to music had been one of those 'jobs' that he found particularly hard. It was also true that when at secondary school, he had taken special lessons in dancing, although if he had been made to take an exam in this subject, he would have ended up at the bottom of the table. As he realised that his classmates began to laugh at him every time he tried to dance, he had decided in his childhood not to concern himself with dancing at all. As an adult, other than buying an expensive radio and all the tapes of famous musicians, he had not taken an interest either. He danced with the eyes only, by watching others dance.

But Rukia does not bother taking advice or information on this. She has already got up, and now she is pulling Peterson energetically. He cannot refuse. He walks towards the dance floor feebly. Rukia has already begun to dance.

Yes...the heart full of joy,
For the figure of this companion
Is like the light of the moon
And her soft skin
Like sweet water in the desert.

Peterson looked at Rukia. Then he looked at the other dancers. Slowly he raised one leg to follow their movements. Then he lifted the second leg. He tried to shake his waist. As usual, he suddenly felt heavy. His legs were as if bound by a rope, the waist as if held by an anchor. He did not give up hope and picked himself up carefully, making every effort to follow the beat of the music while watching Rukia's legs. In his mind he was amazed at Rukia's skill. He knew that she was of a very beautiful build that would serve her well for all performing arts, including music. But he had not thought she would be so good at dancing. Look at her slender legs ... look at her waist ... look! Peterson cannot remember ever having seen another girl dancing like this. Yes, there is one, one only. He saw her on a video. This girl from Zaire. What was her name again? Mbilia Bell? Ledi Issa? Faye Tess? Or is she in the stage show of one of those bands?

Look...!

Rukia was observing the amazement in Peterson's eyes. She too was amazed in her way. She had not yet seen a rich man, an educated man, advanced like this one, being so sheepish (*mbu mbu mbu*) when it came to dancing. Look how he patters about like a camel brought to town.

Really her eagerness to bring him here and to compel him to dance was part of her scheme to corrupt him. She had wanted to get him to dance like mad, so that this gentleman with his money and his suits would feel at one with the brutish crowd. After that a second punishment would follow. But now Rukia felt as if she had already bullied and punished him beyond measure. A respectable man, now he was in a state, he was miserable, he could begin to cry any minute. People were even beginning to look at them with their eyes openly laughing.

Yes ... a night that instills fear
But it brings joy
Every time my girl
Fragrant like incense, laughs

Rukia slowed down her gyrations. Dancing slowly, she helped Peterson with his heavy legs. At the end of the song she embraced him and kissed him on both cheeks, murmuring 'thank you, love'. They took each other's hands and returned to their seats.

The night continued to be sweet, the beer continued to flow. The next song was even sweeter. Peterson, with lots of beer in his head, thought the music more alluring after he had found that he danced 'like anyone else' with Rukia, and wanted to dance again. But Rukia refused, saying they should rest a bit.

'Pardon me, Sir,' a voice struck them. The speaker was a rather tall, rather lanky young man, with shining eyes and a pleasant appearance. He was wearing good, up to date clothing that fitted him perfectly. It was the man whom Rukia had noticed at the Embassy. He was talking to Peterson. 'I ask for a dance with this lady, please. If you will let her.'

Peterson looked at Rukia. 'Will you dance?'

'Wait, I will go for a dance with him. Just one.'

They entered the floor and began to make their steps. At first shyly, as they did not know each other at all. The music wiped their embarrassment away. Soon they were like hand and glove (*chanda na mpete*) in their dancing, their steps and moves were all in line. For a while they danced quietly. Their moves absorbed their minds, and those of others. Many of those who were not dancing were looking at them carefully. In every way they were pleasing to the eye, like twins that had been born together on the dance-floor.

The next song was a European one, and slow. They danced embracing each other.

Rukia had forgotten that her man, Peterson, was sitting nearby, that he was undoubtedly looking at her with anger and surprise. She had forgotten, too, that she was supposed to dance for one song only. In short, she had forgotten everyone and everything. Her feelings were running free, she was refreshing body and soul. In her mind she felt as if she had arrived in the shadow after a long journey in the desert, plagued by hunger and thirst. Her head rested quietly on the wide, warm and life-filled chest of this young man. She closed her eyes and began to dream of things that she had never dreamed of before in her life. A dream of Adam and Eve in the big garden of love. Even the song she heard as if from far away.

'What is your name then, love?' the young man asked. His hands were wandering over the hills and valleys of the girl's back and waist.

'Rukia' she murmured.

'Rukia?'

'Just call me Rukia,' she said. 'And you?'

'They call me Hasara.'

'Why Hasara?'

'They know.'

'Who are they?'

'It's a long story.' He hesitated a bit and added, 'I don't know if I can live the next twenty-four hours without seeing you again. Where can I find you tomorrow at lunchtime?'

'Why this haste?'

In the silence that followed they realised that the music had stopped. Only they remained on the dance floor. Yes, they and that drunkard who never got round to sitting down unless he fell. Embarrassed, they ended their embrace and left the dance-floor.

Hiding his anger and jealousy behind a phoney smile, Peterson looked at them as they approached him. He had all reason to be jealous. They looked like a man and his loved one who just got married. Their eyes too showed shame and guilt, as if their marriage was illegitimate.

'Thank you, Sir', Hasara said while he handed him Rukia. Then he returned to his table.

Peterson finished his beer slowly. When Rukia had finished hers as well, he stood up and took her hand. 'Let's go home.'

'Right now?'

'It's enough. There is tomorrow and the day after that. Why should we stay overnight here?' Rukia got up and followed. She tried to make an effort not to throw a glance at Hasara. but she could not keep it up. Their eyes clashed. A smile of farewell passed secretly between them.

Notes

1 *Tausi* means peacock.
2 A district of Dar es Salaam that includes a variety of neighbourhoods.
3 'Mlimani Park' is a popular dance band in Dar es Salaam.
4 '*muungwana*', referring originally to the patrician families in Swahili coastal towns, is the term for 'freeborn man'.

3 Perspectives on Southern African Popular Fiction

NJABULO NDEBELE

Rediscovery of the Ordinary

Reference
Njabulo Ndebele *Rediscovery of the Ordinary: Essays on South African Literature & Culture*, Johannesburg: COSAW, 1991
Reprinted in Njabulo Ndebele *South African Literature & Culture: Rediscovery of the Ordinary*
Manchester: Manchester University Press, 1994: 41–59

The history of black South African literature has largely been the history of the representation of spectacle. The visible symbols of the overwhelmingly oppressive South African social formation appear to have prompted over the years the development of a highly dramatic, highly demonstrative form of literary representation. One is reminded here of Roland Barthes' essay on wrestling.[1] Some of Barthes' observations on the wrestling match seem particularly apposite. 'The virtue of all-in wrestling,' Barthes opens his essay, 'is that it is the spectacle of excess.'[2] It is the manifest display of violence and brutality that captures the imaginations of the spectators. Indeed, we have seen the highly organised spectacle of the political wrestling match of the South African social formation. Everything in South Africa has been mind-bogglingly spectacular: the monstrous war machine developed over the years; the random massive pass raids; mass shootings and killings; mass economic exploitation, the ultimate symbol of which is the mining industry; the mass removals of people; the spate of draconian laws passed with the spectacle of parliamentary promulgations; the luxurious life-style of whites: servants, all encompassing privilege, swimming pools, and high commodity consumption; the sprawling monotony of architecture in African locations, which are the very picture of poverty and oppression. The symbols are all over: the quintessence of obscene social exhibitionism. And at the centre of it all, are the main actors: the aggressive Boer who has taken three centuries to develop the characteristics of the massive wrestler. It could be said, therefore, that the most outstanding feature of South African oppression is its brazen, exhibitionist openness.

It is no wonder then, that the black writer, sometimes a direct victim, sometimes a spectator, should have his imagination almost totally engaged by the spectacle before him.

T. T. Moyana must have had this situation in mind when he pointed to the problematic relationship between art and objective reality in South Africa:

> An additional difficulty for the creative artist in South Africa, especially the black writer, is that life itself is too fantastic to be outstripped by the creative imagination. Nkosi calls the theme of the absurd the theme of daily living in South Africa. Indeed, many writers of the absurd school would find their plots too realistic to startle anybody into serious questioning of their deeper meaning. How would the quarrel over a bench in Edward Albee's *Zoo Story* startle anybody in a country where thousands of people have been daily quarrelling over who should sit on a particular park bench, and the country's parliament has had legislation on the matter? That's much more startling than Albee's little quarrel between two men. And Kafka himself would not have bettered the case told by Lewis Nkosi. He was arrested by a policeman who then phoned his superior to ask, 'What shall I charge him with?' Or the incident of a white man and a coloured woman who were tried for being caught kissing. The court got bogged down over the question of whether the kiss was 'platonic or passionate'. One reporter who covered the case for a local newspaper wrote: 'Lawyers and laymen are certain that the Minister of Justice will now have to consider an amendment to the law which will define the various degrees of kissing from the platonic to the passionate.'[3]

What is on display here is the spectacle of social absurdity. The necessary ingredients of this display are precisely the triteness and barrenness of thought, the almost deliberate waste of intellectual energy on trivialities. It is, in fact, the 'emptying out of interiority to the benefit of its exterior signs, [the] exhaustion of the content by the form'.[4] The overwhelming form is the method of displaying the culture of oppression to the utmost in bewilderment.

A very brief review of black South African writing in English will reveal the glaring history of spectacular representation. The stories of R. R. R. Dhlomo, for example, are characterised by tightness of plot, emphasis on the most essential items of plot, the predominance of dialogue, and sudden, almost unexpected shocking endings, all of which are the ingredients of dramatic writing.[5] Dhlomo is interested only in the outward, obvious signs of individual or social behaviour. Causality is a manner of making simple connections in order to produce the most startling and shocking results. There is very little attempt to delve into intricacies of motive or social process. People and situations are either very good or very bad. Those who are bad invariably abandon their evil ways overnight. And so, Dhlomo takes us, in this highly dramatic manner, through the working conditions in the mines, through the physical and moral squalor of Prospect Township, and through the sophisticated domestic life of young African couples playing with the game of love.

In *Drum* magazine, we see a similar penchant for the spectacular, although the symbols are slightly different. It is not so much the symbols of oppression that we see in most of the stories in *Drum*, as those showing the growth of sophisticated urban working and petty-bourgeois classes. The literary ingredients for the dramatic in these stories are: pacey style, suspenseful plots with the unexpected ending, characters speaking like Americans, dressed like them, and driving American cars. Perhaps the detective story serials of Arthur Mogale typify this kind of writing. Detective Morena is a self-made man, confident, fast talking, and quick thinking, playing the game of wits with his adversaries. He wins. Clearly, it is the spectacle of phenomenal social change and the growing confidence of the urban African population that we see being dramatised here.

It might be asked why the vast majority of these stories in *Drum* show an almost total lack of interest in the directly political issues of the time. After all, the Nationalists had just acquired power in 1948 and were busy 'putting the Kaffirs in their place'. The writers of these stories seemed keen only to tell fantastic stories so that readers could enjoy themselves as much as possible. They were pushed forward in their writings in order to indulge the lively imagination of the urban population. They reflected the tremendous energy that was generated in the urban areas of South Africa. But going hand-in-hand with these stories was a very lively journalism: the investigative journalism of Henry Nxumalo, for example, revealed much of the gross ugliness of economic exploitation in South Africa. The covering of strikes and political meetings was done in a highly spectacular journalistic fashion. There seemed no confusion at this time between the language of exposition on the one hand, and the language of creative writing on the other. Creative writers simply titillated the readers with good stories, and the journalists concentrated on their work, writing about politics, sports, fashion, etc. What was common though, was the penchant for spectacular representation or reporting. The thick lines of spectacle were drawn with obvious relish.

At the end of the fifties, and following the banning of the ANC and the PAC, we begin to see the emergence of what has been called protest literature. This kind of writing follows the disillusionment that came in the wake of the bannings of the major political organisations. Here we see the return to the concerns of Dhlomo. We see the dramatic politicisation of creative writing in which there is a movement away from the entertaining stories of *Drum*, towards stories revealing the spectacular ugliness of the South African situation in all its forms: the brutality of the Boer, the terrible farm conditions, the phenomenal hypocrisy of the English-speaking liberal, the disillusionment of educated Africans, the poverty of African life, crime, and a host of other things. The bulk of the stories of James Matthews, Ezekiel Mphahlele, Alex La Guma, Can Themba, Webster Makaza, and others falls into this category.

Picking out a story at random, we shall find the firm outlines of this kind of writing. 'Coffee for the Road', a story by Alex La Guma, is about an Indian woman and her children driving through the Karroo on a long tiring journey to Cape Town. The strain of driving, and the lack of social amenities for blacks to provide rest along the way, are described vividly by La Guma:

> The mother had been driving all night and she was fatigued, her eyes red, with the feeling of sand under the lids irritating the eyeballs. They had stopped for a short while along the road, the night before; parked in a gap off the road outside a small town. There had been nowhere to put up for the night: the hotels were for Whites only. In fact, only Whites lived in these towns and everybody else, except for servants, lived in tumbledown mud houses in the locations beyond. Besides, they did not know anybody in this part of the country.[6]

The glaring contrasts are put there before us together with the very *obvious* explanation for their existence. The similarity to another dramatic story is evident here: the heavily pregnant Mary being turned away from every inn until the baby Jesus was born in a simple manger. The difference is that in La Guma's story there is no relief for the woman and her children. But it is the ritualistic enactment and the drawing of significant meaning that is at the aesthetic centre of these two stories:

> The landscape ripped by, like a film being run backwards, red-brown, yellow-red, pink-red, all studded with sparse bushes and broken boulders. To the east a huge outcrop of rock strata rose abruptly from the arid earth, like a titanic wedge of purple-and-lavender-layered cake topped with chocolate-coloured boulders. The car passed over a stretch of gravel road and the red dust boiled behind it, skimmed the brush beyond the edge of the road, flitting along as fast as the car.

The symbolic barrenness of the landscape cannot be missed. The travellers pass a 'group of crumbling huts, like scattered, broken cubes'; and 'in a hollow near the road' they see 'a bank of naked, dusty, brown children'. They see three black men trudging 'in single file along the roadside, looking ahead into some unknown future, wrapped in tattered dusty blankets, oblivious of the heat, their heads shaded by the ruins of felt hats'.

But finally, they have to stop at a white town 'Just some place in the Karroo' in order to refill their coffee flask. Ignoring a 'foot-square hole where non-whites were served', the Indian mother simply walks into a cafe on the white side. The description of the white woman behind the counter is done with spectacular relish:

> Behind the glass counter and a trio of soda fountains a broad, heavy woman in a green smock thumbed through a little stack of accounts, ignoring the group of dark faces pressing around the square hole in the side wall. She had a round shouldered, thick body and reddish-complexioned face that looked as if it had been sand-blasted into its component parts: hard plains of cheeks and knobbly cheek-bones and a bony ridge of nose that separated twin pools of dull grey; and the mouth a bitter gash, cold and malevolent as a lizard's chapped and serrated pink crack.

The very picture of a female ogre! Her response to the Indian woman's request for coffee is equally dramatic:

> The crack opened and a screech came from it, harsh as the sound of metal rubbed against stone. 'Coffee? My Lord Jesus Christ!' the voice screeched. 'A bedamned coolie girl in here!' The eyes started in horror at the brown, tired, handsome Indian face with its smart sun-glasses, and the city cut of the tan suit. 'Coolies, Kaffirs and Hottentots outside,' she screamed. 'Don't you bloody well know? And you talk English, too, hey?'

The response of the Indian woman is heroically sudden, unpremeditated and spectacularly proper in its justice:

> The mother stared at her, startled, and then somewhere inside her something went off, snapped like a tight-wound spring suddenly loose, jangling shrilly into action, and she cried out with disgust as her arm came up and the thermos flask hurled at the white woman.

At this point, it might be best to leave to the imagination of the reader what damage was inflicted on the white woman by the flask. But La Guma will not leave anything to imagination:

> The flask spun through the air and, before the woman behind the counter could ward it off, it struck her forehead above an eyebrow, bounced away, tinkling as the thin glass inside the metal cover shattered. The woman behind the counter screeched and clapped a hand to the bleeding gash over her eye, staggering back... The dark faces at the square hatch gasped. The dark woman turned and stalked from the cafe in a rage.

Victory or retribution? It is bound to be one of the two, spectacularly drawn. Indeed, retribution follows. The Indian woman does not get far for there is a road-block ahead:

> A small riot-van, a Land Rover, its windows and spot light screened with thick wire mesh, had been pulled up half-way across the road, and a dusty automobile parked opposite to it, forming a barrier with just a car-wide space between them. A policeman in khaki shirt, trousers and flat cap leaned against the front fender of the automobile and held a Sten-gun across his

thighs. Another man in khaki sat at the wheel of the car, and a third policeman stood by the gap, directing the traffic through after examining the drivers.

We see the travellers for the last time as they are escorted back to town, a police car in front and behind, for whatever retribution is to follow: 'You make trouble here then you got to pay for it'.

Everything in La Guma's story points to spectacle: the complete exteriority of everything: the dramatic contrasts all over the story, the lack of specificity of place and character so that we have spectacular ritual instantly turned into symbol, with instant meaning (no interpretation here is necessary: seeing is meaning), and the intensifying device of hyphenated adjectives. Is it germane to ask whether there ever can be such unaccountably terrible people as the white woman in the story, such unaccountably dignified women as the Indian woman, such barren landscape, such utter desolation? Where is causality? Such questions are irrelevant. Subtlety is avoided: what is intended is spectacular demonstration at all costs. What matters is what is seen. Thinking is secondary to seeing. Subtlety is secondary to obviousness. What is finally left and what is deeply etched in our minds is the spectacular contest between the powerless and the powerful. Most of the time the contest ends in horror and tragedy for the powerless. Sometimes there are victories, but they are always proportionally secondary to the massively demonstrated horror that has gone before.

It needs only be stated briefly that spectacular representation is not confined to fiction; it is there in painting and sculpture where we are most likely to see grotesque figures in all kinds of contortions indicative of agony. In poetry, it will suffice to quote some lines from Dennis Brutus's famous untitled poem:

The sounds begin again;
the siren in the night
the thunder at the door
the shriek of nerves in pain.

Then the keening crescendo
of faces split by pain
the wordless, endless wail
only the unfree know.[7]

Beyond that, we can find the culture of the spectacular in *mbaqanga* music, in free-style township dance and even in football, where spectacular display of individual talent is often more memorable, more enjoyable, and ultimately, even more desirable than the final score.

Much of this writing has been denounced as unartistic, crude, and too political. There was more politics in it than art. In defence of the writing, it was asserted that there was nothing wrong with politics in literature because everything in South Africa, anyway, is political.[8] Both positions, it seems to me, miss the mark. As far as the former position is concerned, Chinweizu, Jemie, and Madubuike have comprehensively documented how a powerful Eurocentric school of criticism of African literature has imposed on the literature evaluations based on false assumptions.[9] Such assumptions never enabled the critics using them to understand the real nature of much of what African literature was doing and what its methods were. The same goes for the criticism of what has come to be known as Protest Literature in South Africa.

Once we begin to see an artistic convention emerging, once we see a body of writing exhibiting similar characteristics, we must attempt to identify its origins, its methods of operation, and its *effective* audience. Such factors will establish the validity of the writing. The writing will validate itself in terms of its own primary conventions; in terms of its own emergent, complex system of aesthetics. The whole plane of aesthetics here involves the transformation of objective reality into conventional tropes which become the predominant means by which that objective reality is artistically ritualised. The aesthetic validity of this literature to its own readership lies precisely in the readers' recognition of the spectacular rendering of a familiar oppressive reality. We have seen the South African origins of this literature, we have also had a glimpse of its methods in La Guma's story, but what of its audience?

The question of the audience for this 'protest literature' is a problematic one. Conventional wisdom proclaims that the literature was premised on its supposed appeal to the conscience of the white oppressor: 'If the oppressor sees himself as evil, he will be revolted by his negative image, and will try to change'. Indeed, the class position of most of the writers, the publications in which their writings appeared, the levels of literacy in English among the African population would *objectively* point towards a white audience: an English-speaking liberal one at that. But that audience, schooled under a Eurocentric literary tradition, was in turn, schooled to reject this literature 'meant' for them. They rejected both the methods of representation as well as the content. Where they yielded to accept the validity of the content, they emphasised the crudeness of the method. But what of the audience for whom this literature was not 'objectively' meant? What about the *effective* audience?

We are familiar with how in the days when South Africa still participated in world soccer international teams visited the country for games. We are familiar with the spectacle of how African fans always cheered the visiting team against the white South African side. It happened in rugby too. It seems reasonable to assume that, at least at the populist level, if all black South Africans could read this 'protest literature', they would naturally take sides much to their aesthetic delight. The Indian woman in La Guma's story would be cheered, while the white woman and the white policeman would be detested. The black audience in the story itself is described as having 'gasped', probably in shock. But I am also certain that this was the response of having witnessed the unexpected. Inwardly, they must have experienced a delightful thrill at this 'great spectacle of Suffering, Defeat, and Justice'.[10] To evoke this response, the literature works in this way: the more the brutality of the system is dramatised, the better; the more exploitation is revealed and starkly dramatised, the better. The more the hypocrisy of liberals is revealed, the better. Anyone whose sensibility has not been fashioned by such conditions will find such spectacular dramatisation somewhat jarring. In the same way that western dancers of the waltz found African dancing 'primitive', the aesthetics of reading this literature, for the black reader, is the aesthetics of recognition, understanding, historical documentation, and indictment. All these go together. For the white audience, on the other hand, what has been called protest literature' can, to borrow from Brecht, be considered a spectacular 'alienation effect'; a literature that refuses to be enjoyed precisely because it challenges 'conventional' methods of literary representation, and that painfully shows up the ogre to himself.

Why the misnomer 'protest'? The misnomer devalues the literature as art since 'protest' carries the implications of political and specifically expository declaration of dissent. The misnomer is obviously taken from the concept of 'politics of protest'. But this literature, while definitely labouring under the pressure of the expository intention, deliberately sets out to use conventions of fiction, not of exposition. To call it 'protest literature' is to deny it any literary and artistic value: and those values are to be found in the phenomenon of the spectacle. On this basis, it should be clear why I said above that even those who have come in defence of this literature have fallen into the same trap. They defiantly said: if you accuse us of being political, hard luck, that's what our writing is going to be because that is what the conditions dictate. The fault is not so much in the statement itself as in the assumption that the statement reinforces. It reinforces the expository intention without establishing its own evaluative literary grounds.

We can now summarise the characteristics of the spectacular in this context. The spectacular documents; it indicts implicitly; it is demonstrative, preferring exteriority to interiority; it keeps the larger issues of society in our minds, obliterating the details; it provokes identification through recognition and feeling rather than through observation and analytical thought; it calls for emotion rather than conviction; it establishes a vast sense of presence without offering intimate knowledge; it confirms without necessarily offering a challenge. It is the literature of the powerless identifying the key factor responsible for their powerlessness. Nothing beyond this can be expected of it.

Every convention will outlive its validity. Judging from some of the new writing that has emerged recently from the South African townships, one can come to the conclusion that the convention of the spectacular has run its course. Its tendency either to devalue or to ignore interiority has placed it firmly in that aspect of South African society that constitutes its fundamental weakness. South African society, as we have seen, is a very public society. It is public precisely in the sense that its greatest aberrations are fully exhibited. One effect of this is the suppression of deep-rooted individual as well as social fears. But not only fears are suppressed: the deepest dreams for love, hope, compassion, newness and justice, are also sacrificed to the spectacle of group survival. Rationality is never used for the refinement of sensibility, even for the group itself, but for the spectacular consolidation of power at all costs. Ultimately, South African culture, in the hands of whites, the dominant force, is incapable of nurturing a civilisation based on the perfection of the individual in order to permit maximum social creativity. Consequently, we have a society of posturing and sloganeering; one that frowns upon subtlety of thought and feeling, and never permits the sobering power of contemplation, of close analysis, and the mature acceptance of failure, weakness, and limitations. It is totally heroic. Even the progressive side has been domesticated by the hegemony of spectacle. For example, it will lambast interiority in character portrayal as bourgeois subjectivity. The entire ethos permits neither inner dialogue with the self, nor a social public dialogue. It breeds insensitivity, insincerity and delusion. We all know how, at least in the last twenty-five years of our fully conscious life, South Africa was always going to be free in the next five years: a prediction that is the very essence of the culture of spectacle. The powerful, on the other hand, have been convinced that they will rule forever. Clearly, the culture of the spectacular, in not permitting itself the growth of complexity, has run its course.

I now want to introduce some of the new work that seems to me to break with this tradition of spectacle. It is as if these writers have said the spectacular ethos has been well documented and is indelibly a deep aspect of our literary and national history. There should be no anxiety that its legitimate political springs are about to run dry. The water will continue to flow, only it is destined to become sweeter, if only because more life-sustaining minerals, the minute essences, will have been added to it. The three stories to be used as examples of this new trend significantly emerge out of the tense and bitter aftermath of the mass uprising and mass killings of June 16, 1976, another spectacle among spectacles. I want to look at 'The Conversion' by Michael Siluma,[11] 'Man Against Himself' by Joël Matlou,[12] and 'Mamlambo' by Bheki Maseko.'[13]

Siluma, to begin with, consciously participates in the spectacle tradition as he opens his story:

> A heavily bandaged head: a puffed-up shin: black face with swollen black eyes reduced to mere slits; a mouth with swollen and broken front teeth. This was the picture in Mxolisi's mind when he entered the bedroom, trying to imagine what his cousin John looked like after what had reportedly befallen him three days before.

There are several other conventional symbols of oppression: John has lost his pass and since he is Xhosa speaking, he is referred to his Bantustan in order to fix his papers. But more immediately, John, a Bachelor of Science graduate working as a computer programmer for an American company, has been short-changed by an unscrupulous 'Portuguese or Greek' cafe owner, patronised at lunch time by 'labourers from a nearby construction site'. When John demands his correct change he is urged on by the workers to fight for his rights. He does so, and is severely beaten up by the cafe owner. A clear case of injustice drawn with all the customary details! The disillusioned figure of an educated African in South African fiction has long become a trope for the illustration of injustice. But there, Siluma parts with tradition.

As John recounts to his visiting cousin, Mxolisi, what took place, we note the tone of self-pity in him. He refers to what happens to him as 'strange things'. But Mxolisi is impatient with this self-pity. There is nothing 'strange' really about what happened to John. It is the experience of African people all the time in South Africa. Bitter with remorse and self-pity, John wants to avenge himself:

> 'You know, I feel like going back to that bloody white man's cafe and smashing all the windows. Then he could do his damnedest,' John thundered, for a moment forgetting the pain in his body.

Traditionally this would be the moment for cheering him for he will have fulfilled the demands of spectacular justice. But as the following passage illustrates, Mxolisi is not impressed:

> 'You argue like a child, John. Look man. There are thousands and thousands of white people with mentalities like that cafe owner's. Smashing his windows might, according to you, serve the purpose of teaching him a lesson. But others like him might still do the same thing he did to you, perhaps even killing you this time. Apart from satisfying your desire for revenge I still insist that your smashing his windows cannot solve the problem.'

The problem, Mxolisi argues, can only be solved by the unity of the 'discriminated against' through organised struggle. John must join the struggle:

> 'Unity, my cousin. Only when we are united as people who are discriminated against can we manage to solve the problem. we must never think that because we are B.Sc. or B.A. graduates

> and can earn lots of money that we are immune from the sufferings other black people are forced to endure. We must remember that it is only a matter of when we shall come face to face with these problems, just as you have now.
>
> Only a few months ago I invited you to a Hero's Day commemoration service and you told me you were not a politician. I hope what has happened to you knocks some common sense into your so-called educated head.'

We notice immediately that Siluma has moved away from merely reflecting the situation of oppression, from merely documenting it, to offering methods for its redemptive transformation. His story combats, among other things, the tendency to resort to self-pity by the powerless when their situation seems hopeless. His approach is dispassionately analytical. He de-romanticises the spectacular notion of struggle by adopting an analytical approach to the reality before him.

For example, the system is seen to use words to validate falsehood: 'The people at the office of Plural Relations, formerly Bantu Affairs Commissioner, formerly Native Affairs Commissioner ...' The same institution is given the false impression of having changed by the mere changing of its name. We have an example here of the manipulation of reality with language. The effect of this realisation is also to reveal that *rationality can be detected behind the brutality of the system.*

Previously, it was easy and falsely comforting to portray the enemy as being irrational.[14] Also, John's self-delusion is shattered. Just because he has a good job at an American company, he thinks he has made it, and is free from the problems of his own people. In reality, he has been bought, and turned into a false symbol of legitimation. Thirdly, we learn that knowledge of the existence of oppression does not necessarily enable one to fight it. For example, the fellow Africans at the cafe, having urged John to fight on, do not help him when he is being severely beaten up in their presence by the cafe owner. People, without being actually organised, will not necessarily go out to fight for their rights.

The story, then, can be seen to work at various levels of analysis. Siluma has gone beyond spectacle in order to reveal the necessary knowledge of actual reality so that we can purposefully deal with it. The manner in which the story is told reflects its own intentions. The analytical ability of Mxolisi is reflected in the manner in which the story is told so that the story itself is a demonstration of its own intentions. It is an analytical story; a story designed to deliberately break down the barriers of the obvious in order to reveal new possibilities of understanding and action. In other words, Siluma has *rediscovered the ordinary*. In this case, the ordinary is defined as the opposite of the spectacular. The ordinary is sobering rationality; it is the forcing of attention on necessary detail. Paying attention to the ordinary and its methods will result in a significant growth of consciousness. Mongane Serote typifies this attitude in the following words

> child
> if you stop weeping, you may see
> because that is how knowledge begins.[15]

Where before the South African reality was a symbol of spectacular moral wrong, it is now a direct object of change.

'Man Against Himself' by Joël Matlou forces onto us a terrible problem. If there is a sense of the ordinary that is the very antithesis of spectacle, it is to be found in this story. It displays a sense of the ordinary that may be frustrating and even exasperating. This is a kind of initiation story in which a young man in search of work is advised to go and look for work at a mine, and there he grows suddenly into a man. His journey to the mine is a long odyssey of suffering. When he gets to the mine, he undergoes further suffering and humiliation. The terrible working conditions at the mine are amply revealed. The problem we have to deal with in this story is how a man who has undergone such brazen and humiliating exploitation should emerge from the entire experience feeling triumphant.

When he receives his pay, he remarks: 'The money was ninety-six rands. It was for my own work. I risked my life and reason for it.' And as he is leaving the mine, returning home, his money in his pockets, he thinks:

> I just thrust it [the money] into my empty pocket and walked out of the main gate towards the bush to free myself. That time life was not endless but everlasting. The earth was once supposed to be flat. Well, so it is, from Hlatini to Northam. That fact does not prevent science from proving that the earth as a whole is spherical. We are still at the stage that life is flat – the distance from birth to death. Yet the probability is that life, too, is spherical and much more extensive and capacious than the hemisphere we know.

Here is deeply philosophical contemplation. Here is the discovery of complexity in a seemingly ordinary and faceless worker. For this faceless worker, life is complex. There is a lot more to it than the inherent simplification of spectacle. Even under oppression, there are certain fundamental lessons:

> Suffering taught me many things ... Suffering takes a man from known places to unknown places. Without suffering you are not a man. You will never suffer a second time because you have learned to suffer.

And what powerful writing Matlou can unleash! Listen to him when he sees beautiful girls on his return home:

> When I saw the beautiful girls I thought of my own beautiful sweetheart, my bird of Africa, sea water, razor: green-coloured eyes like a snake, high wooden shoes like a cripple; with soft and beautiful skin, smelling of powder under her armpits like a small child, with black boots for winter like a soldier, and a beautiful figure like she does not eat, sleep, speak or become hungry. And she looks like an artificial girl or electric girl. But she was born of her parents, as I was.

A reader schooled in the tradition of spectacle may very well ask himself anxious questions: is the narrator a man labouring under a form of 'false consciousness'? Is this a man who has succumbed to the pressures of oppression and agreed to become a willing agent of the system? It is easy to disregard this story if the answer to these questions is 'yes'. Yet, would it be wise to do so? Can we easily dismiss the honesty, the piling up of detail, those brilliant flashes of philosophical revelation? Why is it that this man is not our proverbial miner (perhaps a figment of our bourgeois imagination?) who is supposed to present the image of a helpless, exploited victim? How do we account for this apparent ambiguity?

The Oral History Project at the National University of Lesotho has conducted numerous interviews with migrant workers, and has come up with a preliminary study of the group of Basotho who called themselves Russians. One particularly interesting informant named Rantoa declared:

> I did not study. I just see blackness on these things, I can leave my letter at the post office not knowing that it is mine because I did not study. What I have is a natural sense that God gave me – and gifts – as for them they are many.[16]

His has been a life of jail, escape, fights, securing lawyers for the best defence, and a variety of jobs. Rantoa, comment the authors, 'is a man who has consciously developed a philosophy, a set of ideas, drawn from his own experience and which integrates his life and his understandings of it... His philosophy is not an abstract one, but emerges from concrete situations. He sees life as a struggle, a fight, in which one must always be consolidating one's forces, undermining the opposition, and developing a strategy which avoids the obvious, frontal attack and strikes where it is not expected'. The remarkable convergence and similarity of philosophy between Matlou's character and this real-life informant is too striking to be ignored.

The school of criticism which favours explicit political themes will be exasperated by the seeming lack of direct political consciousness on the part of Matlou's character. But we must contend with the fact that even under the most oppressive of conditions, people are always trying and struggling to maintain a semblance of normal social order. They will attempt to apply tradition and custom to manage their day-to-day family problems: they will resort to socially acquired behaviour patterns to eke out a means of subsistence. They apply systems of values that they know. Often those values will undergo changes under certain pressing conditions. The transformation of those values constitutes the essential drama in the lives of ordinary people.

The range of problems is ordinary enough but constitutes the active social consciousness of most people: will I like my daughter's boyfriends or prospective husband? how do I deal with my attraction to my friend's wife? what will my child become? Relatives can be a nuisance; someone I despise has bought a better car than mine; the principal is messing up the school, I'm going to try to be the next principal. The list is endless. We are confronted here with the honesty of the self in confrontation with itself. Literature cannot give us lessons, but it can only provide a very compelling context to examine an infinite number of ethical issues which have a bearing on the sensitisation of people towards the development of the entire range of culture.

So how do we deal with Matlou's character? The experience of working in the mines has a human dimension to it that is seldom accepted; a personal testimony that shatters the liberal image of pathetic sufferers. We are faced with the validity of his experience against the problematic nature of the method of presenting experience. This is the kind of tension that is the very substance of narrative complexity. That the writer did not explore the ultimate implications of his materials is no doubt connected to his inexperience both as a writer and in the inadequacy of his education. But the significance of the story is that the writer has given us an honest rendering of the subjective experience of his character. There is no unearned heroism here; instead there is the unproclaimed heroism of the ordinary person.

Finally, the crux of the matter is that it is natural for us to want to condemn the obvious exploitative conditions of work in the mines. But we should be careful that condemnation does not extend to condemning the necessity for work and the satisfaction that can result from it. Indeed, that aspect of Matlou's story which celebrates the values of work and experience should be rescued and separated from the conditions of exploitation in which that work is done. The necessary political vilification of exploitation should be separated from the human triumph associated with work, a triumph which constitutes a positive value for the future. Matlou confronts us with the painful dialectic of suffering and the sense of redemption that can result from it.

We shall spend less space on the next story because I think the point has been made already. 'Mamlambo' is a story that participates in that aspect of the folk tradition that concerns luck. How does one come across the luck to push one towards success and the achievement of goals? One can turn to an *inyanga*, or *isangoma*, to a faith healer or to other similar people who are believed to have control over the forces of nature. In this case, a woman, living in the backyards of posh white suburbs in Johannesburg, has had no luck getting a regular partner. She turns to an *inyanga* who seems to live somewhere in the city too. The *inyanga* gives the woman, Umamlambo, the mythical snake that brings luck to anyone who possesses it. Indeed, the woman gets a Malawian lover who marries her. But she has to pass on the snake. This she does in a most amusing manner. As the story ends, she sees below her Johannesburg getting smaller and smaller as the plane takes to the sky with her on her way to Malawi.

Of the three stories, this is probably the most thematically ordinary. A woman simply wants to get a man. She desires the security of a lover, a husband. Yet what vibrancy of imagination is displayed by the writer! African folk culture has an independent life of its own right bang in the middle of 'civilisation', of western 'rationality'. The surrounding 'superior' civilisation is rendered of no consequence whatsoever. It is as good as not there. The experience is accorded a validity that does not have to justify itself at all. Bheki Maseko's stories always remind me of Haitian paintings: vibrant with colour, a combination of naturalistic and fantastic elements. Indeed, as Soyinka asserts,[17] the rational and non-rational constitute a single sphere of reality in African lore. Bheki Maseko's stories represent this living continuity between the past and the present. What we have here is a story of escape and fulfilment, but it is the imaginative cultural context evoked that, in the final analysis, is most memorable.

It now remains for us to draw some theoretical conclusions from the phenomenon before us. It should be stated from the outset that the overwhelming injustice inherent in the South African social formation is something that cannot be ignored under any circumstances. For this reason, it is natural to expect that people engaged in every human endeavour ought to make a contribution towards the eradication of injustice. The problem, as we have seen, is that it now appears as if the means of combating the situation have become too narrow and constricting. This weakness has been premised on the demand that everything must make a spectacular political statement. According to this attitude, Maseko's and Matlou's stories could very easily be dismissed as irrelevant since they offer no obvious political insight. Even if Siluma's story could qualify, its message could easily be embraced at the expense of the sobering details such as given above. The habit of looking at the spectacle has forced us to gloss over the nooks and crannies.

The significance of these stories for me is that they point the way in which South African literature might possibly develop. By rediscovering the ordinary, the stories remind us necessarily that the problems of the South African social formation are complex and all-embracing; that they cannot be reduced to a single, simple formulation. In fact, one novel has already attempted an infusion of the ordinary into the spectacle. Serote's *To Every Birth Its Blood*[18] attempts to deal with the ordinary concerns of people while placing those problems within the broad political situation in the country. In the end, though, the spectacle takes over and the novel throws away the vitality of the tension generated by the dialectic between the personal and public.

These three stories remind us that the ordinary daily lives of people should be the direct focus of political interest because they constitute the very content of the struggle, for the struggle involves people not abstractions. If it is a new society we seek to bring about in South Africa then that newness will be based on a direct concern with the way people actually live. That means a range of complex ethical issues involving man–man, man–woman, woman–woman, man–nature, man–society relationships. These kinds of concerns are destined to find their way into our literature, making it more complex and richer. As the struggle intensifies, for example, there will be accidental deaths, missing children, loss of property, disruption of the general social fabric resulting in tremendous inconvenience. Every individual will be forced, in a most personal manner. to take a position with regard to the entire situation. The majority will be riddled with doubts. Yet there will be those marked by fate to experience the tragedy of carrying their certitudes to the level of seeming fanaticism. It will be the task of literature to provide an occasion within which vistas of inner capacity are opened up. The revolution, as Lenin pointed out, will not necessarily take place out of every 'revolutionary situation'. Also essential is the subjective 'capacity of the revolutionary class to take the mass revolutionary actions that are strong enough to smash (or break up) the old government, which, not even in times of crisis, will "fall" unless it is "dropped"'.[19] The new literature can contribute to the development of this subjective capacity of the people to be committed, but only on the basis of as complete a knowledge of themselves and the objective situation as possible. The growth of consciousness is a necessary ingredient of this subjective capacity.

It is germane at this point to point out that there are some serious weaknesses in the three stories discussed above. In 'Mamlambo' for example, the flight to Malawi does not really go together with the growth of consciousness on the part of the protagonist on the very question of matrimony, on the question of luck, on the question of leaving to start a new life in Malawi. Matlou's character also sees no social implications of his triumph beyond himself. Some of these literary deficiencies can be attributed to the intellectually stunting effects of apartheid and Bantu education. These writers have however made superhuman efforts to explore life beyond the narrow focus of an oppressive education.

The more serious problem, because it is self-inflicted, is the fact that the intellectual tradition governing either politics or literature has not broadened the scope of its social interest. Political visions of the future have not reached art with sufficient, let alone committed, theoretical clarity.

Perhaps it was this realisation that prompted Soyinka to observe that South African writers might yet be envied for their invidious position by their brothers up north.[20] Young writers appear to have taken up the challenge, albeit unwittingly. They seemed prepared to confront the human tragedy together with the immense challenging responsibility to create a new society. This demands an uncompromisingly tough-minded creative will to build a new civilisation. And no civilisation worth the name will emerge without the payment of disciplined and rigorous attention to detail.

Notes

This paper was presented as the keynote address at the conference on New Writing in Africa: Continuity and Changes held at the Commonwealth Institute, London, November 1984.

1 Roland Barthes, *Mythologies*, Annette Lavers (trans.), (London: Jonathan Cape, 1972), pp. 15–25.

2 Barthes, p. 15.

3 T. T. Moyana, 'Problems of a Creative Writer in South Africa', in *Aspects of South African Literature*, C. Heywood (ed.), (London: Heinemann, 1976), pp. 95–6.

4 Barthes, p. 18.

5 See *English in Africa*, March 1975, Vol. 12, No. 1.

6 Alex La Guma 'Coffee for the Road', in *Modern African Stories*, Ellis Ayitey Komey and Ezekiel Mphahlele (eds) (London: Faber and Faber, 1964), pp. 85–94.

7 Dennis Brutus, *A Simple Lust* (London: Heinemann AWS, 1973), p. 19.

8 See, for example, Mbulelo Mzamane, 'Politics and Literature in Africa: A Review', *Staffrider* Vol. 3, No. 4, December/January, 1980, pp. 43–5.

9 Chinweizu *et al.*, *Towards the Decolonisation of African Literature* Vol.1 (Nigeria: Fourth Dimension, 1980).

10 Barthes, p. 19.

11 *Staffrider*, Vol. 2, No. 4 November/December 1979, pp. 6–8.

12 *Staffrider*, Vol. 2, No. 4 November/December 1979, pp. 24–8.

13 *Staffrider*, Vol. 5, No. 1, 1982, pp. 22–7.

14 See, for example, Heribert Adam, *Modernising Racial Domination* (Los Angeles: University of California Press, 1971).

15 Mongane Serote, *Tsetlo* (Johannesburg: Ad. Donker, 1974), p. 10.

16 Jeff Guy and Motlatsi Thabane, 'The Ma-Rashea: A Participant's Perspective', in Belinda Bozzoli (ed.), *Class, Community and Conflict* (Johannesburg: Ravan Press, 1987), p. 441.

17 Wole Soyinka, *Myth, Literature and the African World* (Cambridge: CUP, 1978), p. 65.

18 Mongane Serote, *To Every Birth Its Blood* (Johannesburg: Ravan Press, 1981).

19 V. I. Lenin, 'The Symptoms of a Revolutionary Situation', in *The Lenin Anthology*, Robert C. Tucker (ed.), (New York: Norton, 1975), p. 276.

20 Wole Soyinka, 'The Writer in a Modern African State', in *The Writer in Modern Africa*, Per Wastberg (ed.) (Uppsala: Scandinavian Institute of African Studies), p. 15.

MICHAEL CHAPMAN
African Popular Fiction
Consideration of a Category

Reference
Adapted from 'Matshoba: The Storyteller as Teacher' in Michael Chapman, *Southern African Literatures* London & New York: Longman, 1996: 372–6

The difficulty in writing on African popular fiction is the difficulty of the category itself. To begin with, we might ask what in contrast is Western popular fiction? I suppose – dismissively from the academic point of view – the bestseller and, more positively, forms of prose writing that address proletarian oppositions to bourgeois values. The style may be classified popular when it returns the syntax of literariness to the expressiveness of oral speech; when the vocabulary rejects the art allusion for the detail of the street. Let us focus on the 'seriously' popular by distinguishing between mass fiction (usually 'rightish', upwardly mobile boardroom dramas of sex and power) and the fiction of community or working-class concerns: for example, *Trainspotting*.

Clearly, transpositions from Western to African popular fiction require adjustments beyond substituting black for white. Yet race remains important. I doubt whether anyone turning to a book on African popular fiction would expect to encounter white Africans like the novelist Wilbur Smith, whose romances (in the Rider Haggard tradition) grace the airport book-stalls of the world. Yet in Africa more people probably read Smith – the escapist is part of the 'popular' category – than read Ngugi or Achebe. What we mean by 'more people', however, approaches a fundamental difficulty: people's literacy in the ex-colonial languages English and French tends to be thin. Material conditions ensure a very small audience for fiction of any kind. In the countries of southern Africa – I suspect in all of sub-Saharan Africa – the readership for fiction in African languages, outside the glossy magazine, is confined to the captive school market. The result has been a trivialisation of serious fiction for variations of Sunday school tracts: the innocence of rural life encounters the evil of the city and – unconsciously endorsing apartheid – the hero, sadder and wiser, returns to the supposedly regenerative tribal land. At least Alan Paton's *Cry, the Beloved Country* (1948), popular by virtue of continuing sales, complicated this formula: his country priest realised that the future lay in Johannesburg.

Given the power of the written European language to 'silence' majority speech, the temptation has been to resurrect oral tradition as popular while simultaneously applying the term to 'modern' thematic issues. Ancient tales – as they have reached us via missionary records and anti-Cartesian Westerners like Laurens van der Post – are seen to comprise a living tradition of popular folk lore. We are reminded that the ancient society, though it did not recognise our categories 'poetry' and 'fiction', had recognizable equivalents: the chant or prayer or praises encouraged elevated expression by the specially selected shaman or *imbongi* (praiser in Zulu); in the folk tale – a story of character, plot and setting – the grandmother conveyed to the children the entertainment and instruction of the community. May the tale be regarded, accordingly, as African popular fiction?

Whatever one's response, one is reminded that the learned Western allusions and influences in Achebe and Ngugi are actually directed against the domination of the West. The purpose is to recover African continuities: the existentialist drama of *Things Fall Apart* (1958) is tied to the need for 'proverbial' wisdom, while in Ngugi Western hubris is countered by the bulwark of traditional community. We are returned, in allegory, to the contemporary value of African humanism (Achebe) or, in the case of Ngugi, to the challenge to Western racial-capitalism of Marxist proletarianism. Despite his desire to write in Kikuyu, Ngugi in order to remain 'popular' (in sales) to an adult as opposed to a school readership is compelled to 'translate' his fiction into English. Yet by adopting serviceable English rather than the obscure modernism of Soyinka, Achebe and Ngugi lend popular communication to their popular concern. Unlike Wilbur Smith whose distortion of Africa is popular in the sense of 'consumed', we have in Achebe and Ngugi the serious side of the popular. As Achebe put it in distinguishing his own fiction from that of the great Western tradition, the novelist in Africa remains a teacher; the art of the novel an applied art (1965; 1988).

One should not hold Achebe too strictly to his pronouncement. A case could be made for *Anthills of the Savannah* (1987) as postmodern, or postcolonial, or magical realism. Magical realism, of course, could be re-connected to the shifts between domestic realism and fantasy that characterise so many folk tales. The categories are slippery, and perhaps that is how it should be. Why should African fiction not continue to redefine itself in a changing world? There remains, nonetheless, a useful anchor in Achebe's identification of the novelist as a teacher, the novel as applied art. The anchor is the 'poor' rather than the 'elite' condition, whether social or literary. Such a condition in South Africa, in the gathering momentum of Black Consciousness rebellion against the white state, produced the voice of Mtutuzeli Matshoba. His collection *Call Me Not a Man* (1979) may assist us in attempting to delineate African popular fiction.

Matshoba's stories did not arise spontaneously from the township streets. A cultural infrastructure – 'popular' in its challenge to any separation of art and politics – had since the rise of the Black Consciousness movement in the late 1960s formed a crucial element of the Africanist challenge. Influenced by US Black Power, the writings of Fanon and others, at home by the charismatic leadership of Steve Biko, BC did not separate the psychology of oppression from the economics of oppression. In fact, the movement was closer to the university campus than the factory floor, its members comprising not so much workers as students, journalists, teachers and clerics. BC regarded as crucial to any social revolution a revolution of consciousness, in which the mind, the imagination, would cast off negative (Eurocentric) images of blackness and find identity, pride and power in the black perspective (see Biko 1978). In short, BC cultural programmes provided a fertile ground for literary/cultural expression: the tenor and temper of the times saw the poetry of the new black poets, or Soweto poets, and in 1978 the monthly magazine *Staffrider*, in which Matshoba's stories first began to appear in published form.

Under the auspices of Ravan Press, which had emerged from the Christian Institute Programmes against Apartheid (SPROCAS), an editorial 'collective' launched *Staffrider* with the idea of creating a forum for a people's community-view of literature. The editor Mike Kirkwood, an ex-English lecturer from Natal University, had absorbed what became known as the Durban 'moment': the radicalism of the 1970s in Durban saw Steve Biko begin the South African Students Organization (SASO) while he was a student at the Natal University Medical School, and the political philosopher Rick Turner – assassinated in 1978 by a state hit squad – become involved in the massive strikes that in 1973 crippled the port of Durban and presaged the shift, during the Seventies, from BC to trade union militancy. Providing the intellectual input – a revisionist Marxism from the underside of Empire – Kirkwood articulated the views of the *Staffrider* editorial collective that Literature had a small 'l' (1978). The base was popular rather than elite; the strength would derive from township communities rather than mainstream culture; the 'autobiography' of experience in its witness of daily black life rather than its solitary contemplation would be the yardstick of value.

The *Staffrider* figure was emblematic (the daring black youth who defied authority by riding free, like staff, on the runner boards of the township trains), and the magazine sought to celebrate the spirit of defiance that in the Soweto marches of 1976 had exploded the myth of the invincible white state. Combining individuality and collectivity, the *Staffrider* figure captured the mood of the many stories, poems, interviews and illustrations (lino-cuts and black-and-white photographs) that filled the pages of the magazine. One is reminded here of Karin Barber's useful definition of the category popular, in which she distinguishes popular from traditional and elite in its hybrid form of city opportunity (1987). While the ideological 'impurity' of mingling individual daring and collective action worried radical critics, writers snatched at the 'felt' experience. In its attractive format *Staffrider* looked like an art journal and was probably read more widely among literary people than in the communities it purported to serve; like Achebe nontheless it was consistent in defining its art as applied art. It saw its contributors as having responsibility as teachers. Popular was thus conceived as emanating from the people: *vox populi* stuff. At least, that is how *Staffrider* was received by the middle-class literary establishment, by exiles and foreigners; paradoxically, perhaps, less so by township people for many of whom the magazine could have seemed somewhat 'artistic', or 'educated,' in its visual and literary style. Despite this the exigencies of the *Staffrider* moment were important to the emergence of a seriously popular voice. One of its deepest insults to literature was to imply that the artist was not as valuable to society as the community person who, in subscribing to attitudes of sharing, accessibility and accountability, probably had a worthwhile tale to tell. Matshoba was one such storyteller.

By the time his stories were collected as *Call Me Not a Man* Matshoba in his several contributions to the magazine had begun to define the characteristics of the *Staffrider* story. The literary inheritance was often the earlier generation of *Drum* stories: the stories of the 1950s by Can Themba, Es'kia Mphahlele and others linked to *Drum* magazine (see Chapman 1989). The similarities of the black urban experience, however, were offset against significant dissimilarities. It was not only that the flamboyance of Sophiatown – the world of gangsters, jazz musicians and shebeens – had given way to a different 'tyranny of place': the structural violence of the government-regulated township, Soweto. It was that unlike *Drum* writers *Staffrider* writers often revealed the effects of Bantu Education, a system that had eroded linguistic facility among both educated and under-educated African speakers of English. In line with BC imperatives (and, as I mentioned earlier on, publishing realities), *Staffrider* used English as a 'non-ethnic' mode of communication. Educated in the relatively elite mission-school system, Themba had earlier challenged the stodginess of serviceable English by coining new and unusual turns of phrase. Most *Staffrider* stories, in contrast, push their way through rather than leap over the barriers of language. It is not always easy to decide whether the dead metaphors and formulaic utterance characteristic of a great deal of the writing succeed in evoking an effective 'imitation' of oral speech, or simply confirm a flattened inter-language dependency on lists of idioms and proverbs drilled into the head at school. Yet something of an oral style emerges as appropriate. Ignoring or not knowing the conventions of the economical story of implication and epiphany, the writers built up details in amalgamations of oral recurrence as, literally, the untutored residue of close township living. Similarly, gestures to the oral culture had the characters' dialogue sprinkled with African-language phrases. Out of this unpromising situation Matshoba found his own road forward in shouldering the large subject of the black story.

In reflecting life on his 'side of the fence' so that 'whatever may happen in the future, I may not be seen as a "bloodthirsty" terrorist' (1979: x), Matshoba who dropped out of Fort Hare University and worked for many years in low-key clerical and translation jobs, *writes himself* into a central debate as the observer, the counsellor, the storyteller, of his Soweto community. The question implicit in his stories, or long testimonies, is: at what point does the sectionalism of BC cease to be affirmative in its reconstruction of the self and become racist in its negation of *ubuntu*, the sharing humanity that Matshoba's stories see as having informed the long view of the black person's struggle? In 'Three Days in the Land of a Dying Illusion' the corruption and nepotism of the modern Transkei bantustan, which in 1976 had been set up under apartheid decree for Xhosa people, is contrasted to key moments in Xhosa history:

> The baggage of the *godukas*, all *godukas*, consist of their sweat and blood in the migrant labour-system. They work hard for meagre incomes with which to buy little gifts and useful implements in an attempt to make their folks' lives a little more bearable in the wildernesses that are said to be their homelands. (1979:144)
>
> My mind was thrust back into the dubious past. Only one thing was I certain of: Nongqause had been a daughter of those parts.... In order to understand my interpretation of past and present events in relation to each other, I think it necessary to review the tale I heard from my instructional voices. (1979:164)

In 1856 the young girl Nongqause – supposedly touched by the ancestors – had urged her people to kill their cattle after which the sun would rise in the west and food would be aplenty. This millenarian action signalled Xhosa desperation in the face of advancing colonialism and ensured their utter defeat: the Cape Colony government under Sir George Grey incorporated the Xhosa into white farms as a poor labouring class. Circling his stories within other stories Matshoba's narrator, who is not really distinguishable from Matshoba himself, interprets what came to be known as the 'national suicide' not as Xhosa defeat, but as a severe reaction to the loss of dignity attendant upon colonisation. The lesson for his contemporaries, who according to Matshoba have sold their heritage for the crumbs of a farcical independence, is to take the radical stand: to recover the consciousness of their own story as prerequisite for seeing beyond current setbacks and reclaiming their pride.

In 'A Glimpse of Slavery' the famous, or notorious, *Drum* exposé of prison-farm conditions in 1952 (Nxumalo 1952), or the actuality of a repeated scandal, forms the subject of Matshoba's lesson in sharing and solidarity as the 'educated' storyteller finds comradeship among the humble prisoners on the boer's farm. As in Matshoba' s other stories, the dramatic incident, in this case the storyteller's escape from the farm, is not the key to the action; rather, the prisoners' talking through the experience shapes the narrative as a process of understanding. Similarly, 'A Pilgrimage to the Isle of Makana' converts storytelling time (brief and paradigmatic) into historical time (syntagmatic in the journey across a landscape of learning) as Matshoba sets off by train from Soweto to Robben Island to visit his brother, who is a political prisoner. With Makana, the warrior-prophet of the amaXhosa providing the inspirational myth that in BC iconography saw the political prison re-named the Isle of Makana, and with the '76 school buildings still smouldering, Matshoba charts the country as a map of rejuvenated black history. At the same time, he tries in lengthy, contemplative passages to connect his own BC predispositions to the ideals of a broader non-racialism. Like the oral teller, he 'pads' his narrative with digressions and exemplary incidents while, as in folk-tale mode, immediately recognisable types – in this story, boorish officials and resilient Mother Africas – act out their roles in sharp racial confrontation. At the end, Matshoba underplays his close links to his brother so as to shift the human story away from the personal to the historical perception:

> 'Hi son,' I said into the mouthpiece.
> 'Hey't,' the service crackled back inaudibly.
> ...
> Where could Nelson Mandela be staying on the Island?
> ...
> *A luta continua*, I thought.
>
> (1979:139; 141; 142)

The language is direct, easily accessible, even restricted in its vocabulary and literary range. Yet the style of the journey signals Matshoba's confident occupation of the cultural ground. In terms of a Manichean aesthetic, the black other has become the subject, and the story suggests that value is determined not so much by the created properties of art as by relations embodied in social communication. The thin text has the advantage, paradoxically, of putting us in touch with the author behind the tale. While we might recognise Matshoba as a product of Bantu education, we may want to appreciate his authority in a particular time and place. As in the traditional tale, the demand is ethical. In responding to Matshoba's democratic intent, critics trained to revere the brilliant artifact might find that they themselves need to undergo a kind of radical revisionism and perceive themselves as the European 'others' in relation to the community storyteller. A reading of Matshoba involves us, accordingly, not only in lessons about the black experience. For the (white) academic critic, there is a lesson to be learnt about the need for humility in the poor conditions of South African educational, cultural and literary life.

Many stories in *Staffrider* were 'thinner' than Matshoba's in their considerations of moral purpose; many were 'richer' in their presentations of ironies, subtleties and nuances. Yet Matshoba has retained the unsettling quality of attracting debates that have sharpened understanding of writing in a contested field. The debates also help sharpen distinctions between 'elite' and 'popular' expectations of the short story. According to Western, written precept Matshoba has been branded as ideologically 'incorrect': his stories do not entirely encapsulate either a race-conscious or a labour-conscious vision (see Vaughan 1981). His stories, further, have been attacked by the academic critic/writer Njabulo S. Ndebele as relying on spectacular presentations of black life thus diminishing the intricacies of black humanity (1984; 1986). Matshoba has also been accused by feminist criticism of endorsing a male 'public' narrative of struggle, in which men are fighters and women home-makers (see Driver 1990).

But the popular, as has been suggested, is by character and convention somewhat traditional, or (in modern parlance) conservative: the community – mythic in its imagination – retains its coherent entity. At the same time, the popular is modern in that Matshoba's traveller ventures beyond the community (a rudimentary community in Soweto) into the present and future possibilities of South Africa. What the black perspective requires as the storyteller guides us through the mental landscape is not so much interior gradation as the 'surface' of action and resolve. Yet despite Ndebele, Matshoba's landscape does not evince spectacle. If Matshoba employs symbols of national struggle, little is certain about his own journeys of experience. On his journeys – to turn to the point about male/female representation – Matshoba's women mouth-piece figures are treated neither more nor less sympathetically than their male counterparts. In 'Three Days' it is the woman on the bus, the Mother Africa, who asks the question that causes the men to squirm: why were they so foolish as to have accepted the hollow independence of the bantustan? If the woman is a stock figure – the wise, resilient grandmother of folk tale – she is also the symbol of a necessary attempt to re-establish continuities with a usable past. She may not mount a sustained attack on the patriarchal hierarchies of traditional African society, in which men speak from the platform while women give practical advice. Neither however does she simply bolster the men's image of their own masculinity: 'You enjoy being referred to as family heads. Father, father, all the time, but you forget the very tummies of the reasons for your fatherhood status' (1979: 154).

Matshoba is neither an Achebe nor a Ngugi, both of whom are able to make conscious decisions as to how to turn their Western education to African demands. But neither is Matshoba an ancient storyteller who is un-urbanised or un-industrialised. He lives, or survives, in the mix of urban degradation and internet communication that characterises modern South Africa. The discrepancy may be illustrated by way of comparison with other fiction of the 'post Soweto' years. Several of Nadine Gordimer's stories, for example, focused a cold, sardonic eye on brittle suburbanites whose 'conviction' could seem passé: sex in the suburbs – with (white) political mavericks – in a state of emergency (see Gordimer 1991). While the generalisation might not be altogether fair to Gordimer's achievement, it serves a purpose. Somewhere in Matshoba is a need to be progressive beyond gender relations about a humanity that has had to learn to struggle back from the edges of disempowerment: a humanity that has had to make the idea of writing one's life an actual possibility. Whereas Gordimer works by implication, Matshoba works by exposition; whereas Gordimer's stories are ideologically coherent (progressive, anti-apartheid) self-justifying literary acts, Matshoba operates at the ragged edges of ideology: his difficulties in resolving the twin demands of black commitment and human commitment speak of immediate experience. We the readers are involved in a sharing of the experience: an accessible, applicable touching of hands and thoughts.

In her continual worrying about the artist in a political domain,

Gordimer sometimes gives the impression of being more concerned about her own credentials than about communicating with people. Matshoba does not understand such an act of parsimony; rather, his is a culture of generosity which, while it charts the contemporary terrain, returns as to the purpose of early storytelling. As the Bushman ||Kabbo recognised in his recollections to W.H.I. Bleek of an ancient past, the demise of our cultural story signals the demise of our human and social personality (Bleek and Lloyd 1911). A useful way of understanding Matshoba's story of community is to locate its importance in its very lack of art pretensions. As 'minor art' the story of community – the most resilient tradition in southern Africa, probably in Africa as a whole – has permitted people who are less than artists to give expression to voices that in the realm of elite art would in all likelihood have been silenced. These include the teacher, the counsellor, the proselytiser, and teller of the apparently unexceptional tale. Perhaps we begin to give substance here to the category of African popular fiction.

Or, perhaps we further complicate the category. Unlike the 'people' of Matshoba's revolutionary (post-Soweto) milieu – the qualificatory quotation marks are almost obligatory – the people today may no longer be able to imagine themselves symbolically united to a revolutionary ideal or action. For yesterday's revolutionary group is now the governing group which, in many policy decisions, might have to deny a people's voice its legitimacy. The underclass still exists, however, and needs to make known its condition. Whether this allows for the emergence of another form of popular expression is a question. Could such expression be in English given that English is the language of state? Afrikaans for its part continues to struggle with its compromised inheritance. African languages – despite the language 'equity' clauses in the Constitution – are in danger of political, economic, certainly technological, marginalisation. Freedom might mean the popular deprived of the pressure of *vox populi*. Or, freedom might see the popular settling into 'local colour' derivations of the American soap. Perhaps the print medium of fiction has itself been superseded by the audio and visual media, in which case television productions like the gritty, violent drama of township school life, *Yizo Yizo* (Gibson and Mahlatsi 1999), will have to accept responsibilities unusual to the early evening TV mini-series. In countries in Africa with severely curtailed human resource development, including wide-spread illiteracy, or at least semi-literacy, African popular fiction could not expect to be anything but a problematic category. A consideration of Matshoba's stories is not invalid. Rather, the consideration remains appropriately open-ended.

Works cited

Achebe, Chinua (1958) 1996. *Things Fall Apart*. London: Heinemann.

Achebe, Chinua (1965) 1988. 'The Novelist as Teacher', *Hopes and Impediments: Selected Essays 1965–1987*. London: Heinemann: 27–31.

Achebe, Chinua. 1987. *Anthills of the Savannah*. London: Heinemann.

Barber, Karin. 1987. 'Popular Arts in Africa.' *African Studies Review* 30.3 (September): 1–78.

Biko, Steve B. 1978. *I Write What I Like*. London: Heinemann.

Bleek, W.H.I. & L.C. Lloyd. 1911. *Specimens of Bushman Folklore*. London: George Allen & Co.

Chapman, Michael, ed. 1989. *The Drum Decade: Stories from the 1950s*. Pietermaritzburg: University of Natal Press.

Driver, Dorothy. 1990. 'M'a-Ngoana O tsoare thipa ka Bohaleng – The Child's Mother Grabs the Sharp End of the Knife: Women as Mothers, Women as Writers.' *Rendering Things Visible: Essays on South African Literary Culture*. Ed. Martin Trump. Johannesburg: Ravan Press.

Gibson, Angus and Tebeho Mahlatsi. 1999. *Yizo Yizo*. South African Television (Channel 2).

Gordimer, Nadine. 1991. *Jump and Other Stories*. Cape Town: David Philip.

Kirkwood, Mike. 1978. 'About *Staffrider*'. *Staffrider* 1. 1:1.

Matshoba, Mtutuzeli. 1979. *Call Me Not a Man*. Johannesburg: Ravan Press.

Ndebele, Njabulo S. (1984) 1991. 'Turkish Tales and Some Thoughts on South African Fiction.' *Rediscovery of the Ordinary: Essays on South African Literature and Culture*. Johannesburg: COSAW: 11–36.

——(1986) 1991. 'The Rediscovery of the Ordinary: Some New Writings in South Africa.' *Rediscovery of the Ordinary: Essays on South African Literature and Culture*. Johannesburg: COSAW: 35–37.

Nxumalo, Henry. 1952. 'Bethal Today: *Drum*'s Fearless Exposure of Human Exploitation.' *Drum* (March).

Paton, Alan (1948) 1987. *Cry, the Beloved Country*. London: Penguin.

Vaughan, Mike. 1981. 'Can the Writer Become a Storyteller?: A Critique of the Stories of Mtutuzeli Matshoba.' *Staffrider* 4.3:45–47.

PAUL GREADY

The Sophiatown Writers of the Fifties

The Unreal Reality of their World

Reference

Journal of Southern African Studies 16 (1), 1990: 139–64

Attempts to capture the zest for life and what Geertz called 'a thick description'[1] of Sophiatown's gargantuan reality have eluded even its most faithful disciples. Mattera has claimed that 'nobody can write the real story of Sophiatown'.[2] Sophiatown was a juvenile delinquent in a city also of tender years. The mineral explosion on the Witwatersrand from 1886 hurled it into an era of industrial capitalism and the world economy. From nothing Johannesburg sprang from the near desert, 6,000 feet above sea level, with gold as its sole rationale, and a texture of life like that of an overgrown mining camp. In this context Sophiatown in the Fifties offered unprecedented possibilities for blacks to choose and invent their society from the novel distractions of urban life, and was what Raban calls 'soft' and open to a variety of interpretations, dreams, commitments, and methods of survival.[3] The Sophiatown of this era was a pressure cooker of societal potential and contradictions, and provided a 'moment' in which a collective dream emerged of a black urban culture that might have been. However, the essence of Sophiatown as place and community was a solid element in an otherwise 'soft' city, and lives on as a symbol in South African history. The co-existence of an emergent black urban culture and the National Party's intent to destroy such a phenomenon, moulded both the significance and tragedy of Sophiatown. The literature that surrounds it is less a series of individual works than a composite picture of a world, in which both Sophiatown and the writers symbolised the vitality, novelty, and precariousness of the new black urban generation.

Johannesburg is an example of what Berman, in the context of St

Petersburg's role in nineteenth-century Russia, describes as 'the modernism of underdevelopment'.[4] The modernism of St Petersburg and Johannesburg was twisted, gnarled, and surreal. As Abrahams decried in Johannesburg, 'everywhere, behind the glittering facade of the Golden City, I found bucket lavatories'.[5] Such dreams and fantasies of modernity in otherwise largely backward countries have inspired distinctive modes of literature, in both cases. Sampson has drawn parallels between South African literature (particularly of the Fifties) and that of pre-revolutionary Russia in that racked intellectuals, scenes of wild squalor, a looming sense of 'The Problem', and a powerful sense of place, pervade both.[6]

This sense of place can be even more precisely located. Berman claims that in much nineteenth-century Russian literature, Nevsky Prospect in St Petersburg was mythologised as a dazzling new cosmopolitan world, relatively free of state control where all classes mixed.[7] Sophiatown served much the same function for black South African literature in the Fifties. The contradiction between Sophiatown and its surrounds, particularly poignant after the former's demolition when its 'trips' were no longer available, was not only a constant theme in the Fifties literature but was also the downfall of many of its proponents. For both Nevsky Prospect in St Petersburg and Sophiatown in Johannesburg a juxtaposition of dream and myth with reality has inspired a literary generation to use them as a symbolic reference point. However this juxtaposition is one fraught with ambiguities.

Sophiatown was an area of many faces. It was, 'a black heaven glowing with sparks of hell',[8] in which the best and worst of black urban life were bedfellows, and a vibrant urban subculture co-existed with a profound spirit of crisis. It had 'a charged atmosphere, mouldering, smothering and sour ... of a vast energy turned in upon itself'.[9] Themba stated that only Dickens or Hugo could have understood the contrasts and pungent flavours of life in Sophiatown. He went on to encapsulate the essence of the era as follows:

> It was the best of times, it was the worst of times; it was the age of wisdom, it was the age of foolishness; – it was the spring of hope, it was the winter of despair; we had everything before us, we had nothing before us.[10]

By 1950 Sophiatown had a population of 40,000 people and a history which extended back almost 50 years.[11] Before analysing Sophiatown's 'unreal reality' as portrayed in the literary imagination it is important to outline the backdrop to this which was formed by the real reality of Sophiatown. In 1899, Tobiansky who owned the 237 acres of land that Sophiatown was to occupy, signed a lease with the govemment for the land to be used as a 'Coloured' location. However after the South African war the lease was cancelled and by 1905 freehold rights had become available. Newclare and Martindale (which along with Sophiatown became known as the 'Western Areas') were made freehold areas soon afterwards and, because of the proximity of all three to a sewage works (where Western Native Township was later to stand), they became predominantly inhabited by Africans. Although only 2,643 people occupied these areas in 1921, they were designated as exempt from the prohibition of Africans' holding freehold tenure contained in the 1923 Native (Urban Areas) Act. In 1933 when Johannesburg was finally proclaimed under the act, freehold tenure was preserved in Sophiatown, Newclare, and Martindale as a concession to both the black *petit* bourgeoisie and the labour demands of manufacturing industry. The proclamation of Johannesburg and the 1934 Slum Act combined with the growing influx of Africans to the city resulted in rapid population growth of tenants and sub-tenants in the freehold areas, which provided a kind of stage post in the move from the slum yards to the locations. The 'Western Areas' were steadily encroached upon and surrounded by white residential suburbs. The threat of removal hung over Sophiatown from 1939 and, as the noose tightened, the tensions grew within this unique reality centred around such issues as the right to freehold tenure, its race-class composition, and the co-existence of community and slum.

Although Mattera talks of, 'a colourful fabric that ignored race or class structures', Sophiatown was predominantly African, working class, and inhabited by tenants and sub-tenants.[12] However an important characteristic of Sophiatown's social structure was its fluidity. Many property owners (including over half the African standholders) had working-class jobs, while the petit-bourgeoisie ranged from Dr Xuma a wealthy doctor and president of the ANC between 1940 and 1949, who owned an eight-roomed house in Toby street, to traders and craftsmen who often earned less than industrial workers. Most property owners differed from tenants more in their social aspirations than their objective situation. Sophiatown also lacked a geography of class. One could not choose one's neighbours, and the wealthy Mabuzas, Xumas, and Rathebes lived alongside the poor and wretched. It was possible to live, or create the illusion of living, in all layers of society at once. This tendency was accentuated by the many white visitors who were lured to Sophiatown and bewitched, 'by the unfathomable magic of the condemned township and the madness that throbbed in its restless brain'.[13] The propinquity of diverse material and social conditions created the potential for both resentment and a dream world of inflated aspirations.

It was in such a race-class nexus that the co-existence of slum and community evolved. Sophiatown's complex reality encompassed a maelstrom of characteristics (illustrated here by freehold tenure and a threatened existence) which simultaneously produced attraction and repulsion, uncertainty and relative security, as well as community and slum. As a freehold 'suburb' four miles west of the city centre' Sophiatown was attractive because of its geographical situation, tenure, and freedom from the regimentation of state-owned locations (fencing, location superintendent, sterile geometry). In short, it was possible to believe that the state owned a little less of your soul. The allure of Sophiatown was allowed to gain physical expression because permit regulations, and the bylaw which stated that there should be one shack per stand were only partially enforced, and therefore largely ignored. Sophiatown's elastic housing capacity expanded to accommodate tenants and sub-tenants in backyard shacks, to the extent that by 1950 there were on average over eight families per stand.[14] Thus the magnetism of Sophiatown produced a situation of potentially explosive over-crowding accentuated by poverty which condemned over 80% of African families to living on incomes below the poverty datum line. However the relative security of freehold tenure also encouraged an investment in, and commitment to the area, by its inhabitants. This was financial, in terms of length of residence (in 1951 three quarters of Sophiatown's population had lived in Johannesburg for over ten years, and a third had been born in the 'Western Areas'), and in time, emotional. What had been mere 'space' became stained with the sentiments of its inhabitants to become intensely personal 'place'.

Sophiatown was surrounded by a surface of uncertainty and hostility, epitomised by the threat of removal which hung over it from 1939. The area was the antithesis of racial segregation but in the era before 1948 was tolerated because it in effect subsidised housing and transport costs for manufacturing industry and the state. However an uncertainty prevailed which Xuma claimed encouraged people to let their houses deteriorate, or build houses of uncertainty.[15] The threat of dispossession and a general external hostility also produced a cultural and psychological stockade in community as self-defence, in which identity was on occasion oversimplified as an homogeneous 'togetherness-apart-from'.[16] Thus in Sophiatown a mutuality amongst the oppressed and a huge generosity of spirit coexisted with conditions that made it a 'deplorable, sickening slum'.

This then was, in part, the reality of Sophiatown as it entered the Fifties. It provides the context that the literary 'unreal reality' must be situated in and contrasted with, so that an insight can be gained into the real and the unreal in perceptions of Sophiatown.

It was here in Sophiatown that a generation of writers came to maturity soon after the National Party gained power in 1948. They shared certain elements of common experience: education at St Peter's school and Fort Hare University, living in Sophiatown, working for *Drum*, exile, banning under the Suppression of Communism Act, and for many the writing of an autobiography. Most of the writers had some or all of these formative experiences. However, this overlap of experience should not be exaggerated. Modisane was born and raised in Sophiatown, but Nxumalo, Nakasa, and Nkosi all came from Durban while Themba and Mphahlele originated from Marabastad, Pretoria. If Modisane had the greatest claim to Sophiatown as his home, it was Nxumalo who became synonymous with *Drum* through his Mr. Drum features.[17] At the other extreme Mphahlele whose first collection of short stories, *Man Must Live*, was published as early as 1946, and who was later to become a major African literary figure, owed much less to formative involvement with either Sophiatown or *Drum*. Numerous other differences between these writers could be highlighted: Motsisi rejected exile to remain in South Africa until his death in 1977, Matshikiza was a talented musician and composer, Nakasa founded *The Classic* in the early Sixties which functioned as a literary 'finishing school' for many ex-*Drum* writers, and so on.

Nevertheless Mphahlele, Maimane, Matshikiza, Modisane, Themba, Nakasa, Motsisi and Nkosi all lived in Sophiatown at various stages during the Fifties, 'talking the world to tatters', and living almost as a community. It is these authors who will be referred to as the Sophiatown writers or 'set', because although their experiences before and after this period varied considerably and not all of their writing is about or originating from Sophiatown or the Fifties, it was an era and place that was influential for all of them as people and writers.

The diversity of literary knowledge within the wider community in Sophiatown was quite extraordinary. Modisane describes how a member of his child gang used Edgar Allan Poe's 'Annabel Lee' to woo passing girls, while intellectuals were often asked or forced by *tsotsis* to recite a piece of prose; for example, Caiaphas Sedumo in Modisane's story 'The Situation' is forced by *tsotsis* to recite the funeral oration of Mark Antony, and is amazed by their familiarity with the piece.[18] Instances such as this no doubt contributed to the claims that Sophiatown resembled in atmosphere the rough and tumble of Shakespeare's Elizabethan London.[19] Gordimer believes that the Fifties black writers themselves were much more widely read than black authors of today.[20] One major difference is that the Sophiatown group do not acknowledge reading very much South African fiction (although authors such as Alan Paton and Peter Abrahams were important exceptions). Many were influenced by black American fiction, particularly people like Baldwin, Hughes, Ellison, and Wright who evoked the life of Harlem.[21] The preoccupation of Modisane's *Blame Me On History* with the problems of identity and impression management necessary in the 'handling' of whites owes a considerable debt to Ellison's *The Invisible Man*. In addition, this generation of writers were familiar with realist authors such as Dickens and some of the nineteenth-century Russian novelists. There were also obviously individual idiosyncrasies such as Themba's love for the works of Oscar Wilde. The content and style of the literature that these writers were reading and the literary atmosphere of the surrounding community are important contributors to the range of variables affecting the nature of their writing.

The black Fifties writers were distinguished from their predecessors in that they were given a more consistent voice.[22] In March 1951 *Drum* was first published under the editorship of Bob Crisp as a magazine for Africans. It soon became clear that a magazine containing features such as 'Music of the African Tribes' and 'African Folklore' simply would not sell. A complaint made to Sampson illustrated the problem:

> 'Ag, why do you dish out that stuff man?' said a man ... at the B.M.S.C. 'Tribal Music! Tribal History! Chiefs! ... Give us jazz and film stars, man! ... Yes brother, anything American. You can cut out this junk about kraals and folk tales and Basutos in blankets.'[23]

Drum rapidly became 'Johannesburged' after Sampson took over as editor in December 1951. By the time Sampson left in March 1955 the Sophiatown 'set' virtually wrote the entire magazine, and the content had changed to include crime, jazz, gangs, speak-easies, pin-ups, and celebrities; which vied for space with human interest stories and exposures of the injustices of apartheid. In short, there was something for everyone. The flashy muck-raking journalistic style attempted to capture the vivid life of the townships. *Drum* became a symbol of a new urban South Africa, centred on and epitomised by Sophiatown. It was a mixture of genuine quality writing and the most ephemeral trash imaginable. It was assumed that for journalists to deal with African urban life they had to descend to its very depths as well as climb to its heights; many achieved both extremes with some aplomb.

The line between hack journalist, sensitive reporter, and creative artist was blurred on *Drum*. Many of the Sophiatown writers served their fictional apprenticeships with the magazine as well. Barnett has gone so far as to say that for almost a decade Drum represented black literature in English in South Africa.[24] Its major contribution was through the promotion of the short story, over 80 of which it published in the Fifties, often in conjunction with the six short story competitions it ran from 1952. The content of many of the stories reflected both the *Drum* style of journalism and a Sophiatown based image of township ferment. Stories were predominantly a mixture of 'fantasies of ferocity' (gangsters, boxing), and 'saccharine tenderness'. Although this fictional style was encouraged by *Drum*'s white management and protected its authors from censorship for some time, it is also undoubtedly the case that it intentionally enhanced a myth surrounding the unreality of the writers' projected urban world. With Mphahlele as fiction editor for two and a half years from November 1954, the standard of short stories improved considerably. However by 1958 fiction had been labelled a 'hard sell', and soon ceased to be a regular feature in *Drum*. The journalism and fiction of *Drum* in the Fifties drew on the same societal raw material to reflect and help create a black urban culture. One of the most important ways in which it symbolised the 'new Africa' was in the sphere of language.

Drum's aim was 'to have an African style, and to capture some of the vigour of African speech'.[25] The writers felt that by 'doing violence to standard English' and wrestling it into new forms saturated with the imagery and rhythm of *tsotsitaal* and everyday speech which provided a vivid articulation of street culture, it could carry the weight of the new African urban experience in a way that vernacular languages and 'pure' English could not. A style of tough, racy, and vital prose evolved to reflect the organic and fragile urban sub-culture and 'gain the fullest expression of the bubbling life around them and the restless spirit within them'.[26] On occasion it degenerated into sensationalism or a 'brassy' style indicative of the cracks and tensions of a new transitional language working under strain. The prose style of Matshikiza 'transformed *Drum*', and his use of language illustrates well the potential and the pitfalls of using such a dynamic hybrid of English.[27] At best, as in the example below, he appropriated the jazz language of Johannesburg's musicians and extended its vocabulary to cover a variety of emotions:

> They've written songs of thanks an' tribute askin' him to hang on. They've hung epithets of slime on him an jes 'bout skinned him an' ate him up raw ... They've had heart attacks an' headaches an' toothaches an' bellyfuls of this Huddleston bloke.[28]

However, Nkosi claimed that Matshikiza's hybrid of English was often insufficiently versatile to capture the complexities of life, and that to hide the limitations of his dialect he sometimes resorted to an invented gibberish which became a kind of private soliloquy, unintelligible to others.[29]

It has been argued by Lindfors that *Drum*'s use of English served as a unifying force amongst blacks against the multiplicity of African languages and white oppressors, and that the magazine began a substantial black popular literary movement in English in South Africa.[30] However even *Drum*'s creative English served its main unifying function among the middle class, and still estranged large numbers of rural, migrant, and working class blacks who were literate in different vernacular languages, if at all. Mattera claims that some *Drum* writers could switch into the Sophiatown patois when necessary, but that the more orthodox English which they spoke amongst themselves created a feeling of distance between them and the street culture.[31] It is also likely that the balance of linguistic influences and the dialectic between the spoken and written word in Sophiatown were to some extent place specific, and its hybrid languages were therefore not widely spoken or understood elsewhere. For the writers and to some extent the broader community, English was the language in which the outside world was introduced and made available and which opened up new horizons. Nkosi admits to using foreign literature as a form of escapism to shield himself from the harshness of his immediate surrounds.[32] English language and literature therefore was used both to capture the texture of township life in new and imaginative ways, and to cushion writers from it as they sought a haven from its uncompromising reality.

The Fifties Sophiatown writers' use of English carried and communicated a new culture and set of values as language became both a dynamic contributor to an emergent culture, and one manifestation of a more general disregard for their inherited tradition. They were the vanguard of a new, completely urbanised population, dislocated from 'tribal' social structures, for whom the city had become an often extremely patronising and intolerant state of mind. An intensive living for the moment meant the writers were trapped by their own present, and failed to see themselves as writers within a literary tradition. The Sophiatown 'set' often appeared to operate blindly in a vacuum, thereby rejecting the rich textures of vernacular literature and rural custom. Mphahlele for example has described vernacular writing as 'anaemic ... (and) meant for juveniles'.[33] The literary renaissance of the Fifties was perhaps so effectively extinguished because of the dangerously precarious nature of a literature that lacks mass roots and is confined to the printed page. The lack of reference to, or sustenance from, the content and form of traditional and oral literature was precipitated by a reluctance to analyse the processes by which rural and traditional cultures were being adapted to an urban context.

Sampson recorded attitudes that ranged from Maimane's 'disgust' to Matshikiza's 'pride', towards traditional/'tribal' practices that remained strong in urban areas.[34] Rural practices were often frivolously dismissed. Motsisi in 'Lobola? It's a Racket!' derides the practice as archaic, unfair, and financially ruinous, and concludes: 'Ah, there's the rob—oops, rub! ... catch me paying lobola!'[35] Such criticism of residual tradition in an urban context was partly because the concept of 'tribalism' smacked of cultural apartheid, but also because it diluted their self-made image of the city as a brave new world. While many of their criticisms may have had some foundation, they tended to be superficial and to communicate a profound alienation. As Themba confessed: 'those of us who have been detribalised and caught in the characterless world of belonging nowhere, have a bitter sense of loss'.[36] *Drum* and its writers also focused almost exclusively on urban areas and issues, with coverage of rural areas appearing only occasionally and usually in the form of a critique of rural labour conditions.[37]

Nkosi has dismissed pre-Fifties South African literature in English as, 'purposefully Christian and aggressively crusading; the rest was simply eccentric or unacceptably romantic'.[38] Both Nkosi and Nakasa, somewhat simplistically, saw Paton's Kumalo as the epitome of a liberalism that spanned previous black and white literature in English, and rejected his apologetic naivety and conservatism as representative of a literary generation who believed in the good faith of white society and religion.[39] The Sophiatown 'set' contrasted with this literary generation in that they were openly critical of certain forms of liberalism,[40] and did not romanticise rural areas or condemn the moral degradation of the cities; because theirs was not a myth of a rural 'Paradise Lost' but of a confused and unreal new urban world gained. The operation of the Sophiatown 'set' in a vacuum both opened up new horizons and produced a profound sense of isolation. Their break with the past was too self-conscious to succeed completely, but as with their use of language it had positive and negative repercussions, and reflected the ambiguity of their position as the vanguard of a new urban generation. Although they failed to supply a coherent alternative to the frame of reference of tradition or Kumalo, the Sophiatown writers made an important contribution to a new tradition; of black experience in the South African city.

Part of this new tradition was the 'shadow' life that many writers lived in the social circles of white liberals and radicals. Sophiatown as the centre of an inter-racial frontier provided a bohemia that authors drew upon for their fiction. The fiction that attempts to capture the atmosphere of this world portrays the predicament of the 'situation'; a black who differs in aspiration and interest from fellow blacks and yet is refused entry into the white intelligentsia. As Themba claimed, he and his fellow writers were, 'sensitive might-have-beens who had knocked on the door of white "civilisation" ... and had heard a gruff "No" or a "Yes" so shaky and insincere that we withdrew our snail horns at once'.[41] The inter-racial frontier was fraught with contradictions and anguish, but while some like Themba later turned their back on it, others made their fictional and actual home in the quagmire of its tensions.

Modisane lived between two fantasy worlds in which he sought an identity; that of defiance of, and that of acceptance into, white society. Some of his early stories explore the theme of defiance towards white authority, while in *Blame Me On History* Modisane admits to a burning desire to be accepted into white society and his mania for white friends and culture.[42] His room in Sophiatown became a flyover between two worlds and he mourns that when whites became reticent about contacts with blacks due to a frostier political climate, South Africa began to die for him. The early writing of Nkosi also looks in part at acceptance into white society, but focuses more on inter-racial sexual experience. Three of his earliest stories – 'As For Living', 'Holiday Story', and 'Musi' – use the sexual act between black and white as a metaphor for the transcendence of apartheid, but he later confessed that inter-racial love affairs often became a nightmare of worry and effort.[43] Societal barriers to inter-racial liaisons were not purely based upon sexual apartheid, but also upon the general attitudes of black and white communities. Modisane complained that he was resented as a 'native' who shared the 'rapeutation' with which black males were labelled, while Themba in 'Crepuscule' describes the sense of admiration mingled with betrayal that the black community felt at his love affairs with whites.[44]

Both Modisane and Nkosi misunderstood, or could not communicate, the contradictions of the interracial bohemia to which they aspired, and of which they wrote. Many writers became frustrated by the stereotype to which an educated African was supposed to conform, a feeling of being on display as a 'piece of rare Africana', and the continuing polarisation of material conditions and structures of personal liberty across the colour line. Gordimer in her early fiction illustrates some of the problems felt by whites in this inter-racial frontier.[45] The ambiguities of the frontier were structurally of society and personal, felt by blacks and whites, and individuals used the frontier for different purposes and either bulldozed or dodged its complexities with varying skill.

There was a belief prevalent in the Fifties among blacks and whites who mixed on the periphery of white liberal circles, that culture could be used as a weapon to crack the wall of apartheid.[46] One example of such an inter-racial cultural exercise was the 'African Theatre Workshop' formed in 1958, which included Nakasa, Modisane, Nkosi, and Fugard, and in the late Fifties performed the workshop plays 'No-Good Friday' and 'Nongogo'. However it was the musical *King Kong*, sponsored by the Union of Southern African Artists, that Coplan describes as the 'ultimate achievement and final flowering' of Sophiatown's multi-racial cultural exploits in the Fifties.[47] King Kong was a Sophiatown legend, who gained popularity as a 'famous boxer, notorious extrovert, spectacular bum ... (and) a merciless beater-upper'.[48] During his short period of stardom in the Fifties King Kong won and lost the black heavyweight boxing championship of South Africa, became a bouncer in the gang-infested dance halls, was acquitted of one murder, and then in 1956 was found guilty of killing his unfaithful girlfriend Maria Miya. He drowned himself in April 1957 believing that after serving his fifteen-year sentence he would no longer be able to fight. Bloom, who wrote the musical, believed that in his glamorous image, refusal to compromise, determination to make his own rules, and his wasted talent, King Kong personified Sophiatown.[49]

The musical *King Kong* which told the fighter's story, and the work of the 'African Theatre Workshop', appropriated their subject matter and musical/acting talent mainly from Sophiatown, while exhibiting the weakness that Luther later highlighted as generally pervading South African collaborative fringe theatre; despite often progressive intentions the racial hierarchy of society is mirrored in such theatre in terms of control over production, ideological emphasis, and content.[50] For example in *King Kong* while the cast and musicians were black, Matshikiza was the only black member of the production team. Both *No-Good Friday* and *King Kong* were in some ways critical of apartheid, but failed to suggest any culpability on behalf of their mainly white audiences. King Kong is merely led from the stage after murdering his girlfriend, whereas Nakasa reported that the police shot him three times first.[51] Both productions lack a political protagonist, and by emphasising gangs as the enemy and a social problem, they conceal the real political issues. Thus, white liberal dominated inter-racial cultural exploits, then as now, reflect the contradictions of the social circles they represent, and subconsciously mirror apartheid's racial hierarchy which they seek to transcend. Sophiatown as the focus of the inter-racial frontier and its varying black, white, and collaborative literary outputs, inspired a genre of writing that was as ambiguous as the world it represented, and as such captured the atmosphere of a specific group at this time.

What Matshikiza described as the 'white claw' in the context of white capital's increasing hold over commercial black urban theatre and music, Kavanagh has claimed was also dictating the message and orientation of *Drum*.[52] *Drum* was largely owned by English-speaking mining capital, and its proprietor Jim Bailey was the son of Sir Abe Bailey the mining magnate, and a member of the board of directors of the Argus newspaper group. However *Drum* differed from other white-controlled inter-racial experiments in that it was intended mainly to serve a black audience. Yet despite the nature of its ownership and the variety of its content, *Drum* under the editorship of Sampson, Stein, and Hopkinson, made an important contribution to political journalism in the Fifties. It provided a coverage of events and a critique of apartheid, thereby supplying a comment upon the political context that directly affected and was the backdrop to, Sophiatown, in what was an electric political period.[53]

In fact, it was in their journalistic writings that many of the Sophiatown writers formulated their most penetrating and coherent attacks on apartheid.[54] The contrast between politically relevant journalism and often politically light-weight fiction written by the same authors for *Drum* may perhaps be explained by a desire to nurture complementary (or contradictory?) writing styles, resulting in a division of labour within their mastery of form and content between different written genres. The texture of *Drum*'s political coverage varied and was somewhat idiosyncratic due to the lack of political consistency between writers and within the writings of individual authors; changing editorial policy (for example Sampson was the least politically radical of the Fifties editors); and different modes of presentation (Mr Drum exposés, opinion pieces, the delegation of the role of political reporter to Mphahlele in the mid-Fifties). While by no means revolutionary or even radical, *Drum* revealed what Sampson called its 'black hand' to forge a link with a black readership' and several authors argue that a major reason for *Drum*'s sustained commercial success in the Fifties was its accessible and humanitarian analysis of South Africa's political situation.[55]

However, political tensions remained. A racial wage hierarchy soured the internal political relations within *Drum*, with what Modisane described as a 'monthly mockery' of a salary paid to African journalists in effect subsidising the magazine.[56] But political friction was not simplistically racial in nature; Stein and Hopkinson both resigned after disagreements with Bailey which were at least partly fuelled by differences over the political seriousness and direction of the magazine.[57] It is also interesting, while looking at the degree and nature of Bailey's control as proprietor, to question whether the major omission in *Drum*'s political coverage, the mines and migrant labour system, can be explained by Bailey's association with the Chamber of Mines. Modisane's claim that the white-owned black press was more 'yellow than black' is too categorical,[58] because *Drum* did reduce (but not eliminate) the ambiguities and contradictions of liberally motivated inter-racial cultural experiments. Ultimately however, the social and cultural worlds of the Sophiatown centred inter-racial frontier contributed to the anguished inner lives of the aspirant black writers, who were offered what Berman calls a 'shadow passport' to an unreal reality and the frustration of a world that they could taste but not make their own.[59] Ideological confusion however was not isolated to a collective interracial frontier; the writings of the black authors both commissioned for, and independent of, *Drum* lack a political consistency and focus which indicates that the black writers were anything but politically coherent as individuals.

The Sophiatown writers are often criticised for a lack of commitment, as none of them gave expression to or joined (with the exceptions of Mphahlele and Modisane) the liberation movements, and neither did they ground their criticisms of apartheid in the bed-rock of an ideological system. The few non-white political activist authors of the decade were mainly 'Coloured' (Brutus, La Guma, Hutchinson). In South Africa, where even the most private events are set within the fabric of apartheid laws, it is nearly impossible not to be in some way committed. As Modisane stated, 'a non-committed African is the same black as a committed Native'.[60] Commitment in South African literature is gauged less by one's choice of subject than how one deals or aligns oneself with it, because while 'black writers choose their plots, characters, and literary styles; their themes choose them'.[61] Despite the Sophiatown authors' criticisms of certain forms of liberalism, many like their literary predecessors couched their protest in liberal terrns; for example by perceiving Afrikaners as the main enemy, and advocating the benefits of missionary vis-a-vis 'Bantu Education' without fully acknowledging the psychological and social tensions caused by the former, which they personified.

Mphahlele is a good example of the tendency for Sophiatown writers to take a political stance only on specific issues and/or state attacks on their privileges. Mphahlele strongly opposed 'Bantu Education' as secretary of the Transvaal African Teachers Association (a post which lost him his teaching job in 1952), and after joining the ANC in 1955. He condemned the syllabus as one which would place the quality of black education and literature on the 'threshold of a dark age'.[62] And yet on other issues he remained reticent and indecisive, stating that he could not see himself 'finding fulfilment from engaging in political acts whose immediate public value could not be grasped'.[63]

Modisane's political universe was one fraught with confusion. He was a member of the Youth League in the early Fifties, but suspected the ganging up of racial minorities against the Africans in the 'Congress Alliance'; he feared a manifestation of the white claw even here. There followed a retreat into the political wilderness until the end of the Fifties when Modisane felt a growing mental affiliation with the PAC. He describes the Fifties in black politics as a series of misadventures in a political game played by amateurs in which politics remained at the level of, 'mouthy resolutions, sing songs, petty quarrels for leadership, and pathetic slogans like "freedom in our lifetime"'.[64] This, as will be discussed below, is a grossly inadequate summary. The contradictions of his philosophy included an abhorrence of white racism and praise for the multi-racial nature of Sophiatown, and yet he practiced his own narrow form of African nationalism; he advocated revolution but detested violence; and claimed a huge intensity of political feeling and yet by his own admission was dismissed by politicians as an uncommitted playboy.

Many of the remaining Sophiatown writers claimed to be apolitical. According, to Motjuwadi, Themba was 'as political as his ever-torn sock ... a political virgin', while Themba himself confessed to his 'insouciant attitude to matters of weight'.[65] His desire to appear apolitical and his self-corrosive cynicism in a sense became his ideology. There was a 'cosiness' about the writing of Nakasa, which enabled him to write a weekly column for the white *Rand Daily Mail* without causing offence. A final example is Motsisi, whose 'booze and boodle' humour was an ineffective medium for political comment. Themba likened him to 'Puck', claiming he had not known a shred of serious thought in him.[66] Many writers, torn between the desire to be objective and the inevitable frustration of their daily lives, adopted variations on a political confusion characterised by individualism, cynicism, and a lack of direction.

The Fifties was a decade in which the viability of black extra-parliamentary opposition was steadily eroded.[67] Interestingly the fictional book which most effectively plots this process is *Second Class Taxi*, which was written by a white (Sylvester Stein). The ANC-led resistance was conditioned by the fact that sections of the black population were in the process of feeling their way into and through socialism. As Slovo states, in the context of the Fifties resistance efforts, 'failure' was the companion of political endeavour by a dominated group which was not yet capable of assuming power.[68] However a heritage of such 'failures' is important in perpetuating and reinforcing the tradition of resistance. If blacks were not yet sufficiently politically equipped, it was partly because of the distractions and novelty of city life. In the townships (and especially Sophiatown), 'the cycle of living made a continuous and simultaneous assault on your senses',[69] and the resident was barraged with images of what s/he might become as the boundary between fantasy and reality became eroded. The brashness of Sophiatown made it 'soft', and the multitude of people's dreams, identities, and methods of escapism/survival became diffuse.

The gangster, as cultural hero and villain, is a product of the imaginary city. During its life Sophiatown was the home of such notorious gangs as 'the Cowboys', 'the Black Cops', 'the Orange and Blacks', 'the Berliners', 'the Gestapo', and in the early Fifties the legendary 'Americans'. The 'Americans' engaged in large-scale crime, stealing from city shops and railway delivery trailers, and selling their goods by the 'back door' by undercutting shop prices. The most important thing about being an 'American' was the image. They drove Chevrolets and Buicks, and dressed from *Esquire* magazine. Mattera states that from food to fashion most gangs in fact followed styles from America.[70] Actors like Richard Widmark, Bogart, and Bolansky became imitated heroes through the cinema, and many gangs and individuals took their names from films. For example. Mattera's 'Vultures' took their name from the film *Where No Vultures Fly*.

The context for gangsterism and crime was created by a variety of circumstances including unemployment, poverty, social frustration, and a legal system that was widely held in contempt by blacks and which often ignored black-on-black crime. Sophiatown in particular in the Fifties was the major incubator for gangs in Johannesburg because 'there were more *tsotsis* than people at work', it was close to white suburbs, relatively free from administrative control and had a volatile social composition. The combination of a 'hands-off' policing policy and a network of gangs willing to fiercely defend their 'turf' meant that Sophiatown became something of a state within a state,[71] in which conditions were rife for crime and very high levels of violence. In the words of Modisane, violence 'was a piece of the noise that was Sophiatown, of the feverish intensity of Sophiatown life', while violence provided for the young Mattera, 'the only language I knew and understood'.[72]

The ways in which gangs were perceived varied enormously. Gangsters provide an interesting example of Sophiatown's social fluidity, being largely composed of the unemployed, while in terms of social esteem being viewed as both thugs and a kind of 'African aristocracy'. Gangs provided a sense of identity, belonging, and a peer group for their members. More generally, in the community gangsters were admired for their style and those such as the 'Americans' who preyed mainly upon whites acquired at least in part, a 'Robin Hood' type image. However this romantic picture of the gangster is largely a self-image and needs to be contrasted with a less flattering reality. Modisane states that gangs secured their reign in Sophiatown through both admiration and fear, while Mattera claims that the gangs' main aim was, 'to be noticed, to be spoken of, and to be feared'.[73] In 1950 on the Reef two murders were committed every day and 1 in 30 Africans were killed prematurely. Sophiatown was a 'slum jungle of here today and dead tomorrow'[74] which was obviously in part a societal creation and responsibility, but which also highlighted the violent and ruthless competition and parasitism amongst the oppressed. At their worst, as when the 'Russians' fought the 'Civic Guard' in Newclare, gangs were the instigators of virtual community civil war. Thus black attitudes to gangs were an ambiguous mix of admiration of an image, some approval for their defiance of and attacks upon white society, and fear of their violence when it was turned upon the black community.

Drum carried an article about gangs and/or crime nearly every month. This coverage both flattered and infuriated the *tsotsis*. For example the 'Clean Up The Reef' challenge to the police caused considerable consternation, while after 'Mr. Drum Goes To Jail' the Orlando *tsotsis* threw a party for Nxumalo.[75] *Drum* covered numerous gangster 'conversion' stories and generally ended articles with a 'crime does not pay' type conclusion. Interestingly, some of the Sophiatown writers as individuals admired and expressed an affiliation with the *tsotsis*. The writers in a sense had more in common with *tsotsis* than black professionals; they drank together, spoke a similar language, and so on. Themba claimed that the *tsotsis* saw the *Drum* writers as cousins, while he perceived the gangs along with the township as a symbol of African resistance and creativity in the face of white power.[76] However Nxumalo was brutally murdered by gangsters at the age of 39, and Maimane cites as his main reason for going into exile in 1958 fear for his life in the face of gang threats.[77] Themba tried to ally himself to a private conception of the *tsotsi*, and thereby to the people. He was the supreme 'intellectual *tsotsi*', who eventually romantically compared the violence of the gangs to that of the possessed, self-destructive artist, that is, himself. On to the romantic myth of the gangster Themba super-imposed his own myth of the artist.

Gangs, although representing an illusive current of resistance and often in the vanguard of violence against the police, were always only on the threshold of resistance. They were constrained by their lack of social vision and ideology. Mattera records how in the 1957 bus boycott the 'Vultures' were offered money by the ANC to dissuade people from using the buses, and by PUTCO to use them, and profited from both.[78] Gangs therefore were forces of social organisation and disorganisation, who sought an identity in the 'trips' of a confused world of cultural resistance and self-destructive violence, and political ambiguity and wish-fulfilment.

Gangs provide a useful example of the way in which American culture was appropriated both to deal with the realities of oppression and to sustain a world of fantasy. As Sampson described in the context of *Drum*, blacks wanted 'anything American'. The American influence pervaded many dynamic aspects of black urban culture such as cinema, dance, music, language, dress, and literature.[79] For example the cinema for many became a 'sanctuary'. Its role in moulding perceptions and values in a culture so in need of, and pliable to, identities, should not be underestimated. Modisane has stated: 'if Hollywood had intended to influence the development of a particular type of person, I am that product; the tinsel morality, the repressed violence, the Technicolor dreams'.[80] Several Sophiatown writers used American comic magazine, detective story, and better prose styles to a greater extent than their own oral and written traditions. This imported culture gave blacks in Sophiatown and other urban areas, who were to varying degrees cut off from their tradition, a sense of stability, their own importance, and a further language in which to dream.

Berman has claimed that the city comes alive when animated by such needs as money, sex, and drink; but that the depth and intensity of these desires tends to distort perceptions.[81] Many of the Sophiatown writers alleviated their frenzied quest for emotional release in sex and drink. Sophiatown was the shebeeniest of them all, and this 'beloved institution' became a cult for some writers. Sophiatown's shebeens such as the Church, the Classic, the 39 Steps, the Falling Leaves, the White House, and the Back o' the Moon represented the distilled essence of Sophiatown's image of a black urban culture. The role of these institutions was to provide an atmosphere in which one could maintain 'a trance-like existence ... a break from reality, with time frozen at the moment of the nice time'.[82] Of the writers, Motsisi in particular created a fictional world in his *Drum* column 'On the Beat' based on Sophiatown's shebeens, and through the creation of Aunt Peggy, the double-fisted shebeen queen with a heart of gold, made a major contribution to the black urban literary pantheon.

However, accompanying the vibrant cultural role that shebeens played was the destructive effect of excess alcohol consumption. Alcohol was an enormous problem for the staff of *Drum* who Hopkinson described as having, 'about as much discipline as a crew of pirates'.[83] It basically destroyed the lives of Matshikiza, Nakasa, Motsisi, and Themba, who all drank copiously to deaden the pain of their lives. Themba captured the ambiguity of this process:

> I was really fighting something inside that nibbled at my soaked soul. Yet, what the hell! We were cavaliers of the evanescent, romantics who turned the revolt inwards upon our own bruised spirits. It was flight now, no more just self-erasure.[84]

In the same article he expresses an awareness that his talent was being drowned in alcohol, and remained filled with despair that the most potent brandy could not wash away.

Modisane in particular sought sanctuary and forgetfulness in sex. He was a playboy who surrounded himself with beauty in an attempt to purge the ugliness of his life, and claimed, 'through sex I proved myself to myself. I am a man'.[85] The writing of the Sophiatown authors was frequently sexist (Motsisi refers to women as 'girlos', 'cherries', 'sizzlers', 'sheilas' and so on), as is their functional attitude to sex in which they pursued both escapism and identity. The writers and others failed to survive or find a coherent identity in the plastic totality of Sophiatown because their 'trips' in such worlds as its fluid social structure, inter-racial frontier, gangsters, American culture, the shebeen, alcohol, and sex distorted their perceptions of, and ability to deal effectively with, the oppressed reality of their existence. Yet their failure was the result of the juxtaposition between the vibrant and distractive quality of Sophiatown's life and the political structures of apartheid South Africa. A major political act which contributed to the decline of this literary generation, and proved to be the ultimate real reality of Sophiatown, was the destruction of the community.

Sophiatown was one of the first communities on the Group Areas Act's death row. There had been Johannesburg City Council resolutions concerning the removal of the 'Western Areas' (Sophiatown, Newclare, and Martindale) as early as the Thirties; however the removals only became central government policy in 1949 after the National Party came to power. By 1953 the government had bought the land upon which Meadowlands was to stand, and created a new local authority, the Western Areas Resettlement Board, to circumvent an increasingly reluctant city council. The official reasons for the removals were to establish residential apartheid, and slum clearance. However removals were really an attack on freehold tenancy and an attempt to extinguish what had become politically troublesome areas. The 58,000 residents under threat in the 'Western Areas' faced the prospect of a tightening of administrative control, greater insecurity of tenure, increased rent and transport costs, the undermining of the informal sector, and illegal residents faced being forced out of Johannesburg altogether. In addition they were to lose their homes and communities and all the meaning that Sophiatown in particular had taken on in symbolic terms.

Resistance was surprisingly slow to respond to this threat. It was not until residents were informed that they were not to receive freehold rights elsewhere, that a private meeting took place at the Odin cinema, Sophiatown on 28 June 1953. The main participants were the Transvaal branches of the ANC and Indian Congress, plus important individuals like Huddleston. Opposition to the removals soon gained momentum largely through the ANC and the Western Areas Protest Committee under Huddleston. In April 1954 the ANC's National Executive took over the co-ordination of the resistance campaign from the factionally divided Transvaal branch. Differences emerged between national level and ground roots rhetoric concerning opposition to the removals. While Tambo for example stated that the ANC was not in the position of gladiator, Resha the Volunteer in Chief of resistance in Sophiatown who co-ordinated 500 local freedom volunteers, used fierce rhetoric calling upon the volunteers to lay down their lives and 'murder' if necessary.[86] The official ANC line was that opposition should be non-violent and people were urged not to fill in Resettlement Board forms, not to sell property, and not to get into removal lorries willingly. As it was announced that the first 159 families would be moved on the 12 February 1955, the ANC began to plan a stay away from work in an attempt to dilute the government's forces. Luthuli had called the 'Western Areas' campaign the 'Waterloo of Apartheid' while Mattera claims that many, especially the youth, felt that resistance to the removal of Sophiatown would be the spark to ignite the revolution.[87]

Perhaps the only anti-climactical thing about Sophiatown was its end. On 8 February the government banned all meetings in the area for 20 days and changed the date of the first removals to 9 February. On 9 February, 80 lorries and 2,000 armed police moved into Sophiatown. Although freedom volunteers helped a few families move to alternative premises in Sophiatown, the stay-away was stillborn and resistance almost negligible. The ANC apart from being outmanoeuvred underestimated the fact that many tenants welcomed the chance to rent their own house and escape Sophiatown's overcrowding and exploitative landlords. In addition they could not sustain opposition to removals that were staged over almost five years to dissipate resistance, were internally divided, overwhelmed by force, and failed to adequately communicate the form resistance was to take.[88]

In September and October 1959 the final residents of Sophiatown were evicted. Modisane begins his autobiography, and returns periodically during it, to a walk through the ruins of Sophiatown which has become a ghost town of faded dreams and rousing memories, and where the slogans of defiance like 'We Won't Move' and 'Hands Off Sophiatown', read like a dusty mockery of a boast. Many of the writers stayed in Sophiatown as it was pulled down around them, and their sense of loss, tragedy, and hopelessness is perhaps best summed up by Boetie on his return after release from prison:

> I was crying shamelessly ... Sophiatown was flat! A ghost town of grass and rubble ... I felt defeated. Like a king returned from war to find his kingdom smashed to dust.[89]

When this literary generation was faced with a choice between the torment of a life in South Africa without Sophiatown's 'trips', and exile, almost all chose exile.

Motsisi in his article 'We Remember You All ...' looks at the landslide of exiles that took place from the late Fifties and proclaims that, 'Sophiatown must've been the busiest, brightest ant heap ever when the government spade turned it over. and now all the king and queen ants have gone to other heaps'.[90] By 1966 Mphahlele, Nkosi, Matshikiza, Modisane, Nakasa, Themba and Maimane had all left the country. Many left South Africa as a result of acute frustration rather than absolute necessity or personal danger, and Sole finds disturbing the alacrity with which some chose the option of exile.[91] While for example Nakasa's collection of writings, 'From Johannesburg to New York', sometimes suggests an escapist flight to a 'place in the sun', his and others' experiences of exile were painful (and in the case of Nakasa, fatal). More realistic and usual is the anguish of separation from one's home experienced by Mphahlele and Modisane. During the course of *Down Second Avenue* the comfort of community and family recede into the background as bitterness and frustration take root. In the end Mphahlele claimed, 'conditions were crushing me and I was shrivelling in the acid of my bitterness: I was suffocating'.[92] Most importantly he was forbidden to teach, and the oppressive atmosphere had become a 'paralysing spur' to his writing. In South Africa Mphahlele was living in exile with himself, and he hoped that a geographical exile would enable him to re-acquire a greater ontological stability; but it was not a decision lightly taken. Modisane claimed to have mutated in South Africa into a hollow man, devoid of human feelings. He left South Africa in search of an easier political climate in which to humanise himself, but his emotions on leaving were shared by many:

> South Africa and everything I had known, loved and hated remained behind me. I was out of South Africa. But it was no victory or solution, and the compulsive agony was still with me, the problem was still with me; only its immediacy was removed.[93]

The complexity of feelings on leaving South Africa was matched by their experience in exile.

Most writers maintained a commitment to the situation in South Africa, feeling as Baldwin had felt about the 'Negro problem', 'the need to unlock it before I could hope to write about anything else'.[94] For several exile became the keystone event allowing them to take stock and structure their preceding experiences, and as time restraints fell away and political tension eased, greater depth and reflection enabled the autobiography to be the flowering literary achievement of many of the Sophiatown writers.[95] However, important to the creative tensions within these autobiographies, which operate as both social documents and psychological mirrors, was a sense of alienation and rootlessness in exile. This marginalised state later manifested itself in the form of a creative drought, as many of the authors proved unable to re-create the dialect between writer and surrounding context and were forced to live on second hand experience, or write as if South African history froze after Sharpeville. Writers whose reputation has survived or even been enhanced in exile, such as Brutus and La Guma, were more talented writers and more coherent people than the majority of the Sophiatown 'set'. Exiled authors have been isolated further by censorship laws within South Africa. The 1963 Publications and Entertainment Act and 1966 Amendment of the Suppression of Communism Act (which banned Themba, Matshikiza, Modisane, Nkosi, and Mphahlele) led to the loss of the nucleus of emergent black writers, who ceased to exist on the printed page in South Africa. The tragedy of exile lies not only in its sapping of literary talent, but also in its toll on life itself. Freedom has been an uneasy, and for some even an intolerable, burden. Themba, Modisane, and Matshikiza all died, disillusioned, in exile. Nakasa committed suicide in 1965 in New York. The exile condition has proved to be as ambiguous as life in South Africa, as has its literary output.

The importance of Sophiatown in the lives of the writers varied, as did its importance in their motivations for, and sense of loss in, exile. The autobiographies of Modisane and Mattera in particular attempt to capture the magic of the Sophiatown that was. Theirs is an attempt to preserve what has disappeared, describe a culture, evoke a community, and re-affirm a sense of belonging. Sophiatown functions in these two books as what Olney refers to as a 'metaphor of the self'.[96] Both Modisane and Mattera recall that something inside them died with the death of Sophiatown.[97] According to Modisane the inhabitants of Sophiatown did not live in it, but *were* Sophiatown through their celebration of a kind of wish-fulfilment. He draws parallels between its desperate plight during its demolition and his own; having resigned from *Drum*, been left by his wife and child, and his feeling of being buried alive in his own confusion and hatred. The destruction of his soul is montaged against that of Sophiatown: 'I could not tell us apart, both of us had spent ourselves'.[98] Modisane stayed in Sophiatown until the last minute, caught between its dying gasps and his lack of desire to commit himself to any future.

It is interesting that as it was for the 'marabi' era, whose texture was not adequately captured in literature until Dikobe's *Marabi Dance* published in 1973, so time, distance, and reflection were needed for the most complete picture of Sophiatown's kaleidoscope of moods so far achieved: Mattera's *Gone With The Twilight*. Mattera differs from the other Sophiatown writers in that he was not part of the Fifties literary generation, has done most of his writing since this decade as a poet, and has remained in South Africa. However he was from Sophiatown and claimed that, 'she was in me, and I was in the warmth and comfort of her dirty blood'.[99] The cosmopolitan complexion of his family and their ability to combine solidarity and hostility, was symbolic of Sophiatown. Mattera was a gangster who began to come of age as the removals started in 1955, and who eventually transcended Sophiatown's decadence to reflect what was 'solid' in the concentrated essence of its lasting importance. He finally situated his dreams more solidly in the reality of South Africa, as writer and political activist.

The Sophiatown 'set' made an important contribution to South Africa's heritage of short story writing and autobiography. These literary forms flourished because of the ways in which the writers' style interacted with their South African context. Given the absorbing, immediate, and dangerously insecure nature of experience in Sophiatown, the short story provided the writers with a short-cut to get things off their chests and could reflect a reality best illustrated by pin-point incidents or the explosive registry of the moment. Exile allowed the writers a breathing space in which to organise their mental and emotional faculties, and the necessary reflection required to write an autobiography. Most of the writers were first and foremost journalists (the main exceptions being Mphahlele and Modisane) and their skills lay in the description and documentation of events, personal experience, and Sophiatown's complex chemistry, rather than in their ability to analyse or interpret interiors and the structures and processes which underlay these surface patterns. Thus the literary forms used were by no means compartmentalised;[100] they utilised and were suited to the authors' style of writing and the raw material of Sophiatown.

Nkosi claims that the fiction writers of the Fifties were robbed of their vocation because many lacked the imagination to create anything more real or fantastic than the reality of literal experience. Writers were often reduced to just trying to document the elusive magic of Sophiatown's unreal reality through an almost cinematic reconstruction of the ready-made plots and characters of racial violence, social apartheid, inter-racial love affairs and so on.[101] Mphahlele has criticised this tendency for sensationalising sex, crime, and violence; the style also provided one manifestation of a more general temptation for writers to use Sophiatown as a yardstick of all things to which non-white South Africans wished to aspire.[102] For Nkosi the Sophiatown 'set' lacked a significant enough talent to respond with the vigour of imagination and technical resources necessary to the complexities of life in South Africa, and at its worst produced literature in which, 'journalistic fact (was) parading outrageously as imaginative literature'.[103] However, although the interaction between journalism and more creative writing is clear, the imaginative and literary achievement of these writers should not be so readily dismissed because the unrealness of Sophiatown was both their creation and a reflection of its often unlikely actual reality.

Some South African writers, such as La Guma, have written excellent fiction in an oppressive and colour-bar society, but these burdens became a 'paralysing spur' to the human spirit and creative imagination of the Sophiatown writers. While it is important to appreciate the difficulties involved in writing anything at all in South Africa, the Sophiatown 'set' were unable or unwilling to fully accept the didactic and educational responsibility of the writer within a broader culture of resistance. Mphahlele condemned 'escapist pot-boilers' such as Themba's 'Mob Passion' and Maimane's 'Chief' stories, and felt that the writers individually, and *Drum*, should have shaped and created a taste and readership rather than merely reflecting a narrowly defined popular culture.[104] Finally, there was a tendency to portray blacks as passive victims, thereby concealing mechanisms of survival and resistance. These included victims of poverty (Themba's 'Kwashiorkor'), drunkenness (Themba's 'Will To Die'), humiliation (Modisane's 'The Situation'), and thuggery (Motsisi's 'Mita').[105] Mphahlele and Modisane, in particular, did explore the themes of survival, defiance, and the conservation of human dignity under oppression. However, elsewhere the defiance of characters like Dugmore Boetie is largely overlooked.[106] As a vanguard within the vanguard of newly urbanised blacks, the authors in their lives and writing provided an example full of contradictions. Sharpeville heralded a new tougher political era for blacks, and a general change of emphasis within literature from social to more overtly political concerns. However, Sophiatown had contributed to the context of expression within which later literature, culture, and resistance would come to light.

Sophiatown attained literary significance because the literary imagination is incurably local and also because Sophiatown's ambiguous reality conditioned, inspired, and was partly the creation of, a school of writers. Sense of place was no longer merely a geographical condition but was located at the heart of the writers' society, culture, and very being. This is evident for example in the way in which Sophiatown functions as a 'metaphor of the self' in some of the fiction already mentioned. However, people produce and are produced by history and places not in conditions of their own choice but in the context of existing political and social structures. Sophiatown's political importance (and a further source of literary significance) was generated by the juxtaposition of it as culture, community, and new urban generation with a hostile external environment, and the implicit and explicit confrontation between the two, which ended with its destruction.

Sophiatown, while providing a crucial stimulant, was by no means the only inspiration for black literature in the Fifties. District Six for example was another place which harboured an important literary group including such writers as Rive, La Guma. and James Matthews. While these writers were not cut off from their Sophiatown counterparts (as indicated by their contributions to *Drum* [107]) their concerns were on the whole more overtly political and they were chiefly responsible in the Fifties for sustaining the protest tradition in black South African fiction. District Six has similarities with Sophiatown, through, for example, its considerable heritage and eventual removal, and also differences, such as its largely 'coloured' composition. However, both have taken on symbolic meaning in literature and politics, and they both supplied writers (such as Matthews, Rive, and Motsisi) who provided a crucial link between the Fifties and the Black Consciousness cultures within South Africa. They serve as examples of places whose stories have been given a voice and a prominence while others made/make their contribution to literature, resistance, and/or history under their shadow.

The strength and weakness of the Sophiatown literature and its authors is that they provide a concentrated reflection and personification of the vitality and contradictions of an era and a world. The writers made the maelstrom of 'the swarming, cacophonous, strutting, brawling, vibrating life of the Sophiatown that was'[108] their own. From the co-existence of a brash new city and 'suburb' within an otherwise largely backward country, and an air of excitement and potential with poverty and oppression, came the distractions and feverish babble of Sophiatown's influenza. The 'soft' city both liberated and swamped identity in its elusive and slippery reality, the contradictions within which created the unreal reality of Sophiatown's 'trips'. It was in the interactions between these ambiguous worlds of reality and unreality that the writers found their literary, and actual, home.

Despite its destruction the importance of Sophiatown as a community and a culture has lived beyond its death, because not all that was solid melted into air. Sophiatown operated on a vast and complex scale, comprising innumerable fronts, some of which appear to have been in desperate competition with each other. The residue from and counterpart to an urban culture that at one level can be seen as a collection of 'trips', fantasy worlds, and modes of escapism, is a process of self-discovery, the assertion and creation of an urban reality and identity not imposed from outside, and ultimately a form of resistance to apartheid. Sophiatown is one of the Fifties political 'failures' that perpetuates and reinforces the tradition of resistance The solid essence of the Sophiatown collective dream remains because its inhabitants as they were driven from their homes took up the cry of Evgeny in Pushkin's *Bronze Horseman* as he was driven from the city, and the cry has retained its echo: 'You'll reckon with me yet'.[109]

Notes

This paper is a revised version of an MA dissertation submitted to the Institute of Commonwealth Studies for the Area Studies (Africa) course in September 1988. I would like to thank for their comments and general encouragement Shula Marks, Liz Gunner, Arthur Maimane, Sylvester Stein, Anthony Sampson. Mafika Gwala, Richard Rathbone, and Meg Wiggins.

1 C. Geertz, *The Interpretation of Cultures* (New York, 1973), p. 6.

2 D, Mattera, *Gone With The Twilight – A Story of Sophiatown* (London, 1987), p. 49.

3 J. Raban, *Soft City* (London, 1974), pp. 1–9.

4 M. Berman, *All That is Solid Melts into Air – The Experience of Modernity* (New York, 1982), pp. 174–76.

5 P. Abrahams, *Return To Goli* (London, 1953), p. 55.

6 A. Sampson. 'Introduction', in N. Gordimer and L. Abrahams (eds), *South African Writing Today* (London, 1967), p. 11.

7 M. Berman, *All That is Solid*, pp. 194–95.

8 D. Boetie, *Familiarity is the Kingdom of the Lost* (London, 1969), p. 19.

9 N. Gordimer, *A World of Strangers* (London, 1958), p. 194.

10 C. Themba, *The Will To Die* (London, 1972), p. 5.

11 See A. Proctor, 'Class Struggle, Segregation, and the City: A History of Sophiatown, 1905–1940', in B. Bozzoli (ed.), *Labour, Township, and Protest – Studies in the Social History of the Witwatersrand* (Johannesburg, 1979), pp. 49–89.

[12] D. Mattera, *Gone With The Twilight*, p. 74; details of Sophiatown's social composition are given in extracts from the 'Survey of the "Western Areas"' undertaken in 1950 by the Non-European Affairs Department of the Johannesburg City Council in SAIRR (ed.), *The 'Western Areas' Removal Scheme* (Johannesburg, 1953), pp. 6–8.
[13] D. Mattera, *Gone With The Twilight*, p. 80.
[14] According to the extracts from the 'Survey of the "Western Areas"', Sophiatown contained 1694 stands most of which were 50 by 100 feet in size.
[15] The 'Survey of the "Western Areas"' found that 401 of Sophiatown's stands were in need of no repair or only minor repair, 103 were vacant, 982 were 'major/minor' slums (in need of reconstruction or demolition), and 208 were 'major' slums (in need of immediate demolition). See A. Xuma, 'African Reactions', in SAIRR (ed.), *The 'Western Areas' Removal Scheme* (Johannesburg, 1953), pp. 23–28.
[16] See D. Ley, *The Black Inner City as Frontier Outpost* (Washington, 1974), especially pp. 93–118.
[17] The Mr Drum exposés which appeared every March for the years 1952–1957, provided an engaging and very popular treatment of specific grievances. These were in order of appearance: 'Bethal Today' which criticised the contract labour system in rural areas, a condemnation of conditions on the Natal sugar plantations; 'Mr Drum Goes To Jail' which highlighted the maltreatment of prisoners in Johannesburg's main black prison; 'Number Four', a further damnation of rural labour conditions in 'I Worked At Snyman's Farm', 'Brothers In Christ,' which looked at the treatment of blacks in 'white' churches; and finally an investigation into child labour on the Natal sugar farms. These articles were mainly researched and written by Henry Nxumalo.
[18] B. Modisane, *Blame Me On History* (London, 1965), p. 70; 'The Situation' in U. Beier (ed.), *Black Orpheus* (London, 1964), pp. 68–69.
[19] For example see A. Sampson, *Drum – A Venture into the New Africa* (London, 1956), p. 80.
[20] N. Gordimer, 'An Interview', in P. Stein and J. Jacobson (eds), *Sophiatown Speaks* (Johannesburg, 1986), p. 29.
[21] *Drum* published fiction by such American authors as L. Hughes, G. Davis, O. Stewart, and R. Fisher.
[22] Previously the main outlet for creative writing in English by blacks had been papers such as *Umteteli wa Bantu*, *Bantu World*, and *Ilanga*, all of which usually printed poems.
[23] A. Sampson, *Drum – A Venture*, p. 20.
[24] U. Barnett, *A Vision of Order – A Study of Black South African Literature in English, 1914–1980* (London, 1983), p. 18.
[25] A. Sampson, *Drum – A Venture*, p. 27.
[26] This is a remark by Themba quoted in U. Barnett, E. Mphahlele (Boston, 1976), p. 31.
[27] See A. Sampson, *Drum – A Venture*, pp. 28–29, for a description of Matshikiza's English. While one can make certain generalisations about the ways in which the *Drum* writers used English, they obviously did not all experiment with language to the same degree, nor did the nature of their experimentation take on precisely identical forms. For example Nkosi, *Home and Exile*, p. 131, identifies 'a certain dullness of phrase' in Mphahlele's prose. Another writer with a great reputation for innovation with language was Motsisi, whose slang and ludicrous metaphor are discussed in D. Dodson, 'Four Modes Of *Drum* – Popular Fiction and Social Control in South Africa', *African Studies Review*, 17, (1974).
[28] This passage is from T. Matshikiza's tribute to Father T. Huddleston in *Drum*, February 1956.
[29] L. Nkosi, 'South Africa: Protest', *Africa Report*, 7 (1962), p. 5.
[30] B. Lindfors, 'Popular Literature in English in Black South Africa', *Journal of Southern African Affairs*, 11 (1977), pp. 121–122.
[31] D. Mattera, 'An Interview' in P. Stein and R. Jacobson (eds), *Sophiatown Speaks* (Johannesburg, 1986), p. 13.
[32] L. Nkosi, *Home and Exile, and Other Selections* (London, 2nd ed. 1983), pp. 7–8.
[33] E. Mphahlele, in *Staffrider*, 6 (1986) p. 40.
[34] A. Sampson, *Drum – A Venture*, pp. 32, 88.
[35] C. Motsisi's article 'Lobola? It's a Racket!' appeared in *Drum*, December 1956.
[36] C. Themba, *The Will To Die*, p. 8.
[37] *Drum*'s exposés in the first half of the Fifties were often critiques of rural labour conditions, as were the following stories; L. Nkosi, 'Potgieter's Castle', in H. Shore and M. Shore-Bos (ed.), *Come Back Africa* (Berlin, 1968), pp. 129–141; E. Mphahlele, 'Master of Doornvlei' in E. Mphahlele, *In Corner B* (Nairobi, 1967), pp. 96–107.
[38] L. Nkosi, *Home and Exile*, p. 4.
[39] See ibid., pp. 4–7; N. Nakasa, 'Writing In South Africa', *Classic* 1 (1963), pp. 56–63.
[40] The best critique of liberalism is in E. Mphahlele, 'Mrs Plum', in E. Mphahlele, *In Corner B* (Nairobi, 1967), pp. 164–208.
[41] C. Themba, *The Will To Die*, p. 110.
[42] B. Modisane's early fiction, 'The Dignity of Begging', 'The Fighter Who Wore Skirts' and 'The Respectable Pickpocket', all appeared in *Drum* (September, 1951; January, 1952; and February, 1954). B. Modisane, *Blame Me On History*, pp. 260–261.
[43] For an analysis of the early Nkosi stories see D. Rabkin, 'Drum Magazine (1951–61) and The Works Of Black South African Writers Associated With It', unpublished Ph.D, Leeds University, 1975, p. 127. The problems of inter-racial love affairs are discussed in L. Nkosi, *Home and Exile*, p. 22; B. Modisane, *Blame Me On History*, pp. 212–235; C. Themba, *The Will To Die*, pp. 2–11.
[44] B. Modisane, *Blame Me On History*, p. 220; C. Themba, *The Will To Die*, pp. 2-11.
[45] See N. Gordimer, *The World of Strangers*; 'Which New Era Would That Be', in N. Gordimer, *Selected Stories* (London, 1978), pp. 85–97.
[46] T. Huddleston, *Naught For Your Comfort*, pp. 195–210; L. Nkosi, *Home and Exile*, pp. 16–17.
[47] D. Coplan, *In Township Tonight* (London, 1985), p. 175.
[48] T. Matshikiza, *Chocolates For My Wife* (Cape Town, 1961), p. 111.
[49] H. Bloom, *King Kong – An African Jazz Opera* (London, 1961), pp. 1–20.
[50] See C. Luther, 'South African Theatre: Aspects of the Collaborative Fringe', unpublished Ph.D, Leeds University, 1987.
[51] N. Nakasa, 'The Life and Death of King Kong' in *Drum*, February 1959.
[52] R. Kavanagh, *Theatre and Culrural Struggle in South Africa* (London, 1985), p. 59.
[53] The Fifties included such political events as the Defiance Campaign, introduction of 'Bantu' Education, Sophiatown removals, the 'Congress of the People' organised by the Congress Alliance which ratified the 'Freedom Charter', the Evanton bus boycott, introduction of passes for women, Treason Trial, and the launch of the Pan-African Congress. The Sharpeville massacres in 1960 in a sense closed the door on one political era in South Africa and heralded another. For an analysis of the Fifties as a political decade see such sources as T. Karis and G Carter (eds), *From Protest To Challenge – A Documentary History of African Politics in South Africa, 1882–1964; Vols. 2 and 3* (Stanford, 1977), T. Lodge, *Black Politics in South Africa Since 1945* (London, 1983).
[54] See note 17. Other examples of pertinent political journalism include Themba's 'Banned to the Bush' (*Drum*, August 1956), which condemns the treatment of political prisoners in a 'concentration camp' at Frenchdale, Mafeking, and the particularly sharp criticism that *Drum* gave 'Bantu' education in such articles as 'The Shut Down on African Education' (June 1955) and Modisane's 'Education Shebeens' (November 1955). This last article looked at the ANC attempts to provide an alternative education in 'cultural clubs', and the efforts of the authorities to suppress them.
[55] A. Sampson, *Drum – A Venture*, pp. 24–36. Sampson has claimed that the 'Bethal Today' feature in March 1952 which launched the career of Mr Drum, and the eight page article about the Defiance Campaign in October 1952, transformed the commercial fortunes of *Drum*. See A. Sampson, *Drum – A Venture*, pp. 37–54, and 134–35. Similarly under Hopkinson's editorship two of the best selling editions were those of April 1960 which contained the article, 'Africanists: Fireworks or Falsealarm?' and went on sale just after Sharpeville by pure coincidence' and the issue that covered the Pondoland uprisings. See T. Hopkinson, *In the Fiery Continent* (London, 1962), pp. 352–353.
[56] B Modisane, *Blame Me On History*, p. 285.
[57] Stein claims to have been more politically radical than *Drum*'s black

editorial staff in a discussion with E. Mphahlele recorded in N. Manganyi, *Exiles and Homecomings: A Biography of E. Mphahlele* (London, 1983), p. 123; he also goes on to describe the political disagreement with Bailey which led to his departure from the magazine (pp. 129–130). For Hopkinson's views on his reasons for leaving *Drum* see, *In the Fiery Continent*, pp. 350–358.

[58] B. Modisane, *Blame Me On History*, p. 153.

[59] M. Berman, *All That is Solid*, pp. 284–86.

[60] B.Modisane, *Blame Me On History*, p. 145.

[61] N. Gordimer, *The Black Interpreters* (Johannesburg, 1973), p. 11.

[62] E. Mphahlele, *Down Second Avenue* (London, 1959), pp. 167–169, and E. Mphahlele, 'Black and White', *New Statesman*, 10 September 1960, p. 346.

[63] E. Mphahlele in N. Manganyi, *Exiles and Homecomings*, p. 162.

[64] B. Modisane, *Blame Me On History*, pp. 157, 170.

[65] S. Motjuwadi. 'Obituary', *Classic* 2 (1968), p. 13; C. Themba, *The Will To Die*, p. 115.

[66] C. Themba in E. Patel. *The World of Can Themba* (Johannesburg. 1985), p. 208.

[67] The Suppression of Communism Act (1950), Criminal Law Amendment Act (1953), Public Safety Act (1953) and others were specifically designed to frustrate organised resistance.

[68] J. Slovo, in J. Slovo, B. Davidson, A. Wilkinson, *Southern Africa. The New Politics of Revolution* (London. 1976), p. 167.

[69] N. Gordimer, *A World of Strangers*, p. 152.

[70] D. Mattera, *Gone With the Twilight*, pp. 96–109.

[71] The 'Berliners' for example played an important role in clashes with the police during the 1949 Sophiatown tram boycott. For details about this and further outbreaks of popular violence directed largely at the police in 1949 and 1950, which contributed to Sophiatown having a reputation as a hotbed of resistance entering the Fifties, see T. Lodge, 'The Destruction of Sophiatown', in B. Bozzoli (ed.), *Town and Countryside in Transvaal* (Johannesburg, 1983). pp. 345–351.

[72] B. Modisane, *Blame Me On History*, p. 57; D. Mattera, *Gone With the Twilight*, p. 72.

[73] B. Modisane, *Blame Me On History*, pp. 61-68: D. Mattera, *Gone With the Twilight*, p. 61.

[74] D. Boetie, *Familiarity is the Kingdom*, p. 19.

[75] 'Clean Up the Reef' was in *Drum*, March 1953; 'Mr. Drum Goes To Jail' was printed in March 1954.

[76] C. Themba. *The Will To Die*, pp. viii and 110.

[77] A. Maimane, 'An Interview', in P. Stein and R. Jacobson (eds), *Sophiatown Speaks* (Johannesburg. 1986). p. 53.

[78] D. Mattera, 'An Interview', pp. 14–16.

[79] See D. Coplan, *In Township Tonight*, pp. 143–182.

[80] B. Modisane, *Blame Me On History*, p 177.

[81] M. Berman, *All That is Solid*, p. 198.

[82] B. Modisane, 'The Situation', p. 68.

[83] T. Hopkinson, *In the Fiery Continent*, p. 116.

[84] C. Themba, *The Will To Die*, p. 111.

[85] B. Modisane. *Blame Me On History*, p. 218.

[86] Resha made a speech in November 1956 at the ANC's offices on West Street in which he said, 'If you are a true volunteer and you are called upon to be violent, you must be absolutely violent, you must murder! Murder!' The rhetoric of grass-roots activists in the 'Western Areas' campaign was extensively used in the Treason Trial, because of its fiery and angry tone. See T. Karis and G. Carter. *From Protest To Challenge*, Vol. 3, Document 53. p. 588.

[87] D. Mattera. *Gone With the Twilight*, p. 138.

[88] For an evaluation of the ANC's resistance to the Sophiatown removals see T. Lodge, *The Destruction of Sophiatown*, pp. 352–360.

[89] D. Boetie. *Familiarity is the Kingdom*, p. 118.

[90] C. Motsisi in M. Mutloatse, *Casey and Co. – Selected writings of Casey 'Kid' Motsisi* (Johannesburg. 1980) p. 129.

[91] K. Sole, 'Class, Continuity, and Change in Black South African Literature, 1948-1960' in B Bozzoli (ed.), *Labour, Township, and Protest – Studies in the Social History of the Witwatersrand* (Johannesburg. 1979), p. 164.

[92] E. Mphahlele, *Down Second Avenue*, p. 200.

[93] B. Modisane, *Blame Me On History*, p. 318.

[94] J. Baldwin, *Notes of a Native Son* (London, 1949). p. 15.

[93] Examples of autobiographical writing include E. Mphahlele, *Down Second Avenue*, T. Matshikiza, *Chocolates For My Wife*, L. Nkosi, *Home and Exile*, B. Modisane. *Blame Me On History*, C. Themba's 'The Will To Die'. 'Requiem For Sophiatown', and 'The Bottom of the Bottle', in C. Themba, *The Will To Die*, and N. Nakasa's 'From Johannesburg To New York' pieces in E. Patel (ed.), *The World of Nat Nakasa* (Johannesburg, 1975).

[96] See J. Olney, *Metaphors of the Self – The Meaning of Autobiography* (Princeton, 1972).

[97] B. Modisane, *Blame Me On History*, p. 7; D. Mattera, *Gone With the Twilight*, p. 145.

[98] B. Modisane, *Blame Me On History*, p. 291.

[99] D. Mattera, *Gone With the Twilight*, p. 47.

[100] For example E. Mphahlele's 'The Woman' and 'The Woman Walks Out' from *The Living and the Dead and Other Stories* (Ibadan, 1961). pp. 35–46, 55–60, are incorporated into *Down Second Avenue*, pp. 59–67. Also see the similarities between A. Maimane's short story, 'Hungry Flames', in M. Mzamane (ed.), *Hungry Flames and Other Black South African Short Stories* (London, 1986), pp. 85–94, and C. Motsisi's journalistic piece 'The Flame Throwers' which appeared in *Drum*, January 1957.

[101] L. Nkosi, *Home and Exile*, pp. 12–13 and 131–132.

[102] E. Mphahlele, *The African Image* (London, 1962). p. 224. The dominance of Sophiatown in the writers' perceptions is illustrated by remarks such as the one below from A. Maimane, *Victims* (London, 1976), p. 31, which describes Sophiatown and its inhabitants as 'the arbiters of fashion mores, and jargon in black Johannesburg, and therefore in all black South Africa'.

[103] L. Nkosi, *Home and Exile*, pp. 131–32.

[104] C. Themba, 'Mob Passion', in E. Patel *The World of Can Themba*, pp. 9–20; A. Maimane's 'Chief' stories appeared in *Drum* between January 1953 and January 1954. For a general critique of the black Fifties literature, see E. Mphahlele, *The African Image*, pp. 223–237.

[105] C. Themba, 'Kwashiorkor', 'The Will To Die', in C. Themba, *The Will To Die*, pp. 14–26, 62–66, B. Modisane, 'The Situation', in U. Beier (ed.), *Black Orpheus*, pp. 58–70; C. Motsisi, 'Mita', in M. Mutloatse (ed.), *Casey and Co*, pp. 72–77.

[106] See E. Mphahlele, 'The Woman', in E. Mphahlele, *The Living and the Dead*, pp. 38–46; 'Man Must Live', and 'Grieg On A Stolen Piano', in E. Mphahlele, *In Corner B*, pp. 22–36, 37–61; and B. Modisane's 'The Dignity Of Begging' and 'The Respectable Pickpocket' in *Drum*, September 1951 and February 1954. Also see D. Boetie, *Familiarity is the Kingdom*.

[107] Several stories by Cape writers appeared in *Drum*. These included 'Penny For The Guy' (November 1956) by James Matthews, 'Black and Brown Song' (May, 1955) by Richard Rive, and 'Battle For Honour' (November, 1958) by Alex La Guma. In addition in April 1956 Rive, Matthews, and Clarke all contributed to a piece about a young 'coloured' delinquent, called Willie-Boy.

[108] C. Themba, *The Will To Die*, p. 104.

[109] M. Berman, *All That is Said*, p. 188.

DOROTHY DRIVER

Drum Magazine (1951–9) & the Spatial Configurations of Gender

Reference
K. Darian-Smith, L. Gunner & Sarah Nuttall (eds)
Text, Theory, Space: Land, Literature & History in South Africa & Australia
London: Routledge, 1996: 231–42

Drum magazine is crucial in South African literary and cultural history.[1] Its short stories are frequently reprinted, and its political exposés remain models of investigative journalism. Embracing a modernity apparently yearned for by the rapidly growing black urban population of the time, *Drum*'s circulation rose steadily through the 1950s, letters poured in from readers, and its journalists were emulated and adored. Although both Lewis Nkosi and Ezekiel Mphahlele have stressed the constraint the magazine placed on writers because of its 'ready-made plots',[2] *Drum* ran regular short story competitions and in other ways gave space to a group of writers, who made up what has since been called a South African literary renaissance:[3] Alex la Guma, Can Themba, Nat Nakasa, Richard Rive, Bloke Modisane, Casey Motsisi, Todd Matshikiza, Arthur Maimane and Peter Clarke, besides Mphahlele and Nkosi themselves. For these black writers, the magazine offered a vehicle that was part training ground and part enabling community. It offered quite the reverse for women. Only two black South African women published books written in English in the 1960s – Noni Jabavu and Bessie Head – and both did so from outside the country. Moreover, as the threatening manifestations of the 'nice-time girl' in Head's *A Question of Power* tell us and as her recently resurrected early work, *The Cardinals*, suggests, Head survived as a writer in spite of *Drum*.

Besides the short stories, literary competitions and investigative journalism, *Drum*'s monthly issues included essays on boxing, jazz, gangsters, businessmen, beauty queens, and housewives. It also ran beauty contests, beauty columns and advice columns, and published advertisements for skin-lightening creams, hair-straightening treatments, blood-purifying tablets, correspondence colleges, and the plethora of domestic items that were meant to make up urban life. Gender was deeply implicated in the modernizing process. As part of its general promulgation of a black middle-class within the context of the massive urbanization of the time, the magazine had an interest in constructing consumer desires and forging an ideology of domesticity through the aggressive demarcation of masculine and feminine spheres. *Drum* engaged in a process of psychic resettlement, from country to city, from 'Africa' to 'Europe', across the threshold into a nuclear family and 'home'. Some of the implications of this resettlement, for both women and men, provide the focal point for this essay.

Among the numerous analyses and reminiscences of *Drum* magazine,[4] none see it in relation to black South African literature written by women, and very few even refer to gender.[5] Yet *Drum* gives invaluable insight into the ways in which rural patriarchal structures were giving way to urban forms, as well as into the ways in which women's voices were silenced and a set of 'feminine' voices constructed in their place. It also shows, more generally, how gender was being reshaped as part of the rapid and large-scale processes of urbanization in the mid-twentieth century. Not only was *Drum*'s so-called 'vibrancy' constructed at women's expense, but the magazine's shift from rural 'past' to urban 'present' was negotiated largely by means of belittling and damaging misrepresentations of women.

Drum's domestic ideal bore virtually no relation to material reality. For instance, its demarcation of a certain kind of home as the 'proper place' for modern black South African women and as economically accessible to the men who wished to marry them, ignored the crippling conditions of apartheid, which forced both women and men to work long hours for very little pay. Moreover, *Drum* reshaped and in other ways adjusted women's bodies in order to confirm, in the eye of the beholder, the modern 'male gaze'. Femininity was being made to fit a certain space, but it was always also threatening to exceed that space; contradictorily, then, in a state of 'nervous condition',[6] *Drum* writers sometimes celebrated femininity as a force that might work *against* the very ideology of domesticity that the magazine was using to contain it.

For many black South Africans during the first half of the twentieth century, gender was in a marked state of flux, mostly because of rapid urbanization. During the 1940s, and particularly during the period of post-war industrial expansion, Africans flocked to the cities, with the African population of Johannesburg and the surrounding Reef area increasing substantially by the end of the decade. Migrant labour among men had already caused a massive disproportion between the sexes, in both the rural and urban areas, but in the 1940s and 1950s increasing numbers of women left the reserves, although not enough to balance the sexes. *Drum* reported four men to one woman in the Johannesburg area, and, in the Reef's mining communities, an even higher disproportion: in Springs, for instance, it was seven to one.[7] Community and family structures were in disarray.

In the face of this social confusion, *Drum* magazine blandly reproduced European and American constructions of gender as part of an overall ideology of romantic love. This was not romantic love in the courtly tradition, but a modern form of romantic love within an ideology of domesticity, aiming for the establishment of a consumer-oriented nuclear family, headed by the husband and father and hospitable to female authority in only its most carefully controlled domestic forms. Gender constructions were both imposed *on* and negotiated *in* the magazine. The magazine was part of a signifying system whereby patriarchy manfully reasserted itself in the face of the destabilization of its traditional rural form, but it also necessarily acknowledged women's increasing power, even as it tried to exploit and contain this power.

During the 1950s, 'modern' black men and women were being positioned in a set of contradictory ways. While the South African government was busy with its policies of 'Bantu retribalization' and 'separate development', consumer interests – as evidenced in *Drum* – were promoting a 'universal' figure with 'universal' desires: shiny pots, fresh armpits, tidy houses, polished shoes. Migrant labour, the pass system, urban influx control and single-sex hostel life were destabilizing the family, while Christian and humanist groups were preaching its cohesion. Although the extended family had become all the more important in the absence of other forms of social security for black South Africans, Western influences were promoting the nuclear family instead.

Moreover, as already suggested, black urban women were inevitably working women, yet the developing ideology of domesticity forged an ideal distinction between the public and social as a masculine sphere and the private and domestic as the feminine sphere. These contradictory social prescriptions were written into *Drum* magazine in fascinating ways. What is of particular concern to me is the way *Drum*'s move from rural 'past' to urban 'present', from 'tradition' to 'modernity', was negotiated by means of the representation of women: woman as 'sign'.[8]

Drum's shift of focus from the 'traditional' rural to urban modernity took place very suddenly, with a change of editors at the end of 1951. Among its more blatant modernizing gestures were the replacement of features on the value of mother's milk with advertisements for milk substitutes, and the use of the 'cover-girl', a figure passively positioned by the male gaze. Most importantly, 'Dolly Drum' made her entrance, nominally in the form of a monthly column, 'Ask Dolly', and imagistically in the form of the single woman out to have – and to offer – a 'nice-time' in the city. The very first features on 'cover-girl' women gave background sociological and biographical detail. These very quickly disappeared, however, and features began to withhold the kind of information which – for female readers – might work against the idea of a dream life being lived. Similarly, for its male readers, features withheld material which might undercut the idea that women would only achieve fulfilment in the presence of male desire.

In the advertisements, the beauty pages, the 'agony' columns and letters, the feature articles, and the short stories, *Drum* established gender in its Western configuration. In April 1952, after *Drum*'s circulation soared following a courageous piece of investigative journalism by Henry Nxumalo, this newly authorized 'Mr Drum' moved through Johannesburg streets in quest of 'the ideal of African glamour'. *Drum*'s first beauty competition, in March 1952, had been for 'Miss (or Mr) Africa', since a number of male readers had clamoured to enter. But in the beauty competition advertised the following year, *Drum* took care to say, 'So, ladies – and not you gentlemen – send in your photos now!' Thus was gender being defined. Advertisements for skin-lightening creams, hair-straightening lotions and competitions around the three 'vital statistics' defined the modern African woman's body as an idealized European or American look-alike. Pond's Vanishing Cream promised that blackness itself, like dirt, would vanish.

After the photograph of the 'most popular pin-up girl', Priscilla Mtimkulu, first appeared in *Drum*, she was said to have received thirty proposals of marriage within a fortnight. And so it is that one of *Drum*'s women readers sends in the following letter:

> Greetings to you, MR DRUM,
> I am one of the girls who read DRUM every month and I am not satisfied to see other girl on the covers. And please MR DRUM help me to be a cover girl too and one thing is this MR DRUM I am the Kit who does not have her father and Mother, and I am suffering about Mr Wrong. I can't get Mr Right, and please MR DRUM I wish one of our readers can help me to get Mr Right, because I don't want to be Miss M – for ever, no marriage.
> So now we pray
> Our father and mother who are in town hallowed be thy name C–M–
> Amen.[9]

If town had become heaven, *Drum* was now God-the-father who took the place of customary patriarchal structures.

As 'the director of desire' (Rene Girard's term), *Drum* presented itself as if it owned its models, made jokes about the journalists 'beauty editing' all night, teased readers about their possible (sexual) possession of *Drum*'s women, and liked to broadcast the fact that its models, besides being continually 'proposed to', were fought over and even abducted by gang members for days at a time. *Drum* also suggested that domestic commodities were the features of the new 'bride price'. A famous jazz singer and model posed in the kitchen: 'I'm just crazy about cooking … I guess the guy who'll marry me will be satisfied if he can find me a kitchen.'[10]

Although the rules for 'getting' a woman were in fact quite different – economic success, and in its absence, rape – men who wished to be worthy partners of the new woman were told to obey the precepts of a romantic tradition propagated largely by the columnist 'Dolly Drum', who was, in fact, 'a worried syndicate of men'. Anthony Sampson, *Drum*'s first major editor, reports the following conversation between the male journalists on one of the days the column was being written:

> 'Here's someone in Orlando who wants a second wife.'
> 'Tell him he can't love two women at once.'
> 'Why not? I can.'[11]

Despite the name, 'Dolly Drum' was in fact a contrapuntal 'feminine' voice, a voice produced partially or even largely by male journalists in the name of the ideology of domesticity and romantic love. Similarly, the South African short stories *Drum* published in the 1950s under women's signatures, under the names Rita Sefora, Joan Mokwena, and Doris Sello, were in fact not written by women.[12]

Thus the place of the 'feminine' in the magazine was particularly complex. 'Dolly Drum' delivered to the public a set of modern urban precepts which the men did not themselves believe but which represented the world they felt should be passed on through *Drum*. Promiscuous, rural and 'uncivilized' male attitudes were thus deflected through the male-constructed 'feminine' voice of modern, 'civilized' urban Africans – men and women. Reminders of a wilder sexuality ('Why not? I can') were retained: a virile masculine force which received its confirmation not from the columnist 'Dolly Drum' but from her alter ego: the 'other' women placed outside the modern, civilized, nuclear home. Yet for the purposes of *Drum*'s domesticating theme, sexual desire in women (as opposed to 'love') was evil, a 'poison' that might seep into the family, as in Joan Mokwena's 'My Husband was a Flirt'. Women's uncontrolled passion was even associated with tribalism in Can Themba's 'Mob Passion'.[13]

Drum's representation of housewives, sportswomen, and political women always emphasized their femininity, and involved a characteristic mixture of idealization, anxiety and contempt. Writing about Lilian Ngoyi when she was president of the African National Congress Women's League, Ezekiel Mphahlele described her as 'tough granite on the outside, but soft and compassionate deep down in her' in a trope which smoothly reproduced the woman's body in terms of conventional space–gender dichotomies. Ngoyi's voice was less easily managed. Quoting a member of the audience – 'She almost rocks men out of their pants when she speaks' – Mphahlele added: 'She can toss an audience on her little finger, [and] get men grunting with shame and a feeling of smallness.'[14] In an essay on women's hockey in 1957, the little finger became a 'big stick', wielded with energy and strength by the women players, who were also said to wear out the male referees by the end of the game, as if the real contest were between them and the women.

The author Casey Motsisi referred twice in a short space of time to the fact that the women could play a game once reserved for men, and do all 'their womanly chores at home'. He also took care to feminize their bodies: 'I asked one cutie whether they padded themselves as a precaution against injury. "No," she panted at me. "Everything we've got is our own".'[15] During the game the women, or 'girls' as Motsisi generally called them, still behaved with 'masculinity', as on a 'battlefield', or were 'tigerish hellcats', mad women neither masculine nor feminine. But after the game the women became, in Motsisi's words, 'well, FEMALES! Combs, lipstick, powder puffs, feeding bottles, babies, husbands, boy-friends'; a 'magical' transformation, as Motsisi let slip, for this change happened 'as they walked *towards* the dressing room' (my emphasis), as if Motsisi's litany, and not the actual use of 'powder puffs', was all that was required to transform these unnatural beings into the most natural of things, 'wisp[s] of cloud'.[16] Writing – 'the big stick' – remained in male hands after all. Similarly, in an essay on women playing softball, Motsisi had the male coaches 'put their arms round an otherwise reluctant belle as they show the curvaceous Miss how to hold a bat'.[17]

In *Drum*'s representation of jazz singers, however, a different spatial gender configuration opened up. Here, the process of eroticization sometimes seemed to allow desire to pass back and forth between 'subject' and 'object', threatening to disturb the hierarchy maintained so carefully at other times. Dorothy Masuka, as described by Todd Matshikiza, had a dress whose wide stripes seemed to run 'down her whole body, neck to hem. Round her curves. Under the belt round her cute waist. Into the men's eyes. Yes, man!'[18] She too had eyes, 'bedroom eyes' and 'goo-goo eyes' used so successfully that you would think she wanted every man around (this is 'most exciting'). Of course, in *Drum*'s standard pattern of promise and denial, the essay went on as follows: But 'those eyes gents ... those eyes are as fully booked as the December train': not to a large number of passengers, as one might expect from the simile and the context it is given, but to one man in particular: 'Mister Simon Petto', who had two shops, two butchers, two cars and 'lots of dough'.[19]

According to *Drum*'s representation, authority in the urban world was invested, nominally, in the male head of the family, rather than in the patriarch whose power was linked to that of the chief in a mutually reinforcing relationship. But at the same time this modern male authority was under continual threat. It promoted a false ideology of separate male and female spheres despite the reality that urban African wives were not confined to the domestic realm but were economically and politically active. *Drum* was also misleading in its (male) reproduction of domestic, female authority regarding courtship, monogamy and family life – urging men to be home for mealtimes, to help in hanging out the washing, having tea. Yet at the same time, women's domestic authority was seen as a threat.

How did *Drum* manage this double contestation? By means of the discursive abuse of powerful women, on the one hand, and an abiding contempt for the norms of romantic love and domesticity, on the other hand. Thus, even while being glorified in terms of the domestic ideal, housewives were said to do nothing but 'yak, yak, yak' all day.[20] Through a set of gestures ranging from domestication to eroticization, intelligent, active and energetic women were returned to subjection: put back in the narrowness of domesticity or physically recast as self-conscious and sometimes even slightly ludicrous feminine bodies. Yet the voices and eyes of female jazz singers kept offering something one might call subjectivity, figured in some cases as 'promiscuity', which, like male polygamy, signified the opposite of modern domestic love.

However 'exciting' it may have seemed, this untamed female sexuality was also seen as dangerous to men, for it spelled the loss not just of patriarchal authority but of any masculinity which found its power in spatial separation and sexual control. Nevertheless, in a fascinating move, it came for a moment to represent a politically useful force, as shown in Can Themba's presentation of Dolly Rathebe, top model, film star and jazz singer.[21] While Rathebe is quoted as saying that she likes men to be men, and deplores women who wear slacks, she is spoken of in terms that confuse the gender categories of the masculine and feminine. She is a tomboy, which (complicatedly) is glossed as 'fond of boys'; she sings gruffly in a voice that is also 'husky, furry', kindling dreams of 'torrid love and wanton abandon'; she uses the stage 'as if she were a boxer in a ring'. Gender is not stabilized, and a different and wilder kind of femininity is produced than the 'wisps of cloud' Motsisi managed to conjure up in his re-vision of skilful sportswomen. Rathebe is presented uncontradictorily as the desiring subject: 'She wanted men at her feet'; she stopped seeing one of her lovers because 'you can't harness a race-horse with a mule'; and, unlike so many other women represented in *Drum*, is said to have fought successfully against an attempted abduction. She would not settle down – 'marriage was utterly unnecessary' – and was particularly appreciated for her refusal to be a domestic servant or factory-worker, which is glossed as 'work ... for a white man'. As a singer of jazz, giving out 'the pounding rhythm that interpreted township jazz so well', and thus identified with 'all Africa', Rathebe gave her audience songs of township life which spoke about their own class and race positions.

In black America, jazz had become the signifier of an energy that had not been harnessed by white authority. Jazz replaced tribal music in *Drum* magazine when the magazine moved into its modern phase, but it also signified a space where a vision of Africa might persist: an Africa which refused the enforced separation between rural past and urban present and the policies of Bantu retribalization being pursued by the white government. Through jazz, 'Africa' moved to the city; 'Africa' infused the present. By the end of the 1950s, jazz became contained within a European space. *Drum* spoke sarcastically of the way it was now listened to by white South Africans, in halls where you got a 'nasty look' if you so much as tapped your foot on the floor. Dolly Rathebe took her audience back to an earlier time when jazz shows were held at the Bantu Men's Social Centre, where 'men were men in those days and did not want to dance with women'.

Jazz was an antidote to romantic love, which was first formulated in *Drum* as a means of liberation from traditional rural patriarchy and as an entry into modernity but then came to ensnare men instead. This new world of domesticated desire kept men not only in psychological thrall to the 'feminine' voice but also in financial debt as they strove to 'earn' modern women, thus intensifying the oppression experienced under apartheid. Like jazz, a quite different form of female sexuality entered *Drum*'s pages, active rather than passive, wild rather than tame, promiscuous rather than domestic, black rather than white – in dialogue (sometimes) with male sexuality rather than subordinated and owned. This femininity was associated with an 'other' world which combined the rural and urban, the 'past and the 'present'. In two ways, then, this 'other' femininity worked against European domination, for it not only reproduced Africanness but also maintained it as part of the urban present. Powerful as it was, it could not be permitted to transform itself into something 'un-African', something which might transgress the spatial separations deemed necessary for masculinity and femininity and thus go to work against black men as well: 'men were men in those days and did not want to dance with women.' Dancing with women, in couples, would bring African men into the romantic, domestic and European space, a world dominated by women and whites.

For a moment, it seems, a different space had started opening up in *Drum* magazine: a different relation between men and women, a different relation between the urban present and the rural past, and even, perhaps, a different dialogue between 'black' and 'white'. But *Drum*, mistrusting itself in its state of 'nervous condition', turned back on its own gestures of liberation from the categories of gender and race. And then, from the 1960s into the 1980s, with the development of Black Consciousness, *Drum* would be misread (Harold Bloom's term) as nothing more than a 'non-white' or 'assimilationist' gesture, and women's subjectivity would take a less interesting turn, compelled once again to take a subordinate position rather than to emerge in a voice of its own. In 1990 Christine Qunta, for instance, was able to claim, 'I take the view that we are Africans before we are women',[22] as if racial identity obliterated gender difference, as if a subjectivity specific to African femininity did not after all exist.

Notes

Note: The financial assistance of the Centre for Science Development (HSRC, South Africa) towards this research is hereby acknowledged. Opinions expressed and conclusions arrived at are those of the author and are not necessarily to be attributed to the Centre for Science Development.

[1] *Drum* was established in 1950 and is still published: this study refers to the years 1951–9.

[2] Lewis Nkosi, 'African Fiction: Part I: South Africa: Protest', *Africa Report*, no 7, Oct. 1962, p. 3; see also Ezekiel Mphahlele, *Down Second Avenue*, London, Faber & Faber, 1959, p. 188.

[3] See N. W. Visser, 'South Africa: The Renaissance that Failed', *Journal of Commonwealth Literature*, vol. 9, no. 1, 1976, pp. 42–57.

[4] For published accounts of *Drum*, see Anthony Sampson, *Drum: A Venture into the New Africa*, London, Collins, 1956; Tom Hopkinson, *In the Fiery Continent*, London, Victor Gollancz, 1972; Michael Chapman, 'More Than Telling a Story: *Drum* and its Significance in Black South African Writing', in M. Chapman (ed.), *The Drum Decade: Stories From the 1950s*, Pietermaritzburg, University of Natal Press, 1989; Mike Nicol, *A Good-Looking Corpse*, London, Secker and Warburg, 1991; Rob Nixon, 'Harlem, Hollywood, and the Sophiatown Renaissance', in *Homelands, Harlem and Hollywood: South African Culture and the World Beyond,* New York and London, Routledge, 1994.

[5] Nicol, *A Good-Looking Corpse*, has a chapter entitled 'Love and Hot Dames', pp. 143–5; See Dorothy Driver, 'Woman and Nature, Women as Objects of Exchange: Towards a Feminist Analysis of South African Literature,' in Michael Chapman, Colin Gardner, and Es'kia Mphahlele (eds) *Perspectives on South African English Literature*, Johannesburg, Donker, 1992, pp. 454–74.

[6] See Tsitsi Dangarembga, *Nervous Conditions*, London, The Women's Press, 1988.

[7] For population figures, see Tom Lodge, *Black Politics in South Africa since 1915*, London, Longman, 1983, pp. 11–12; and Deborah Posel, *The Making of Apartheid 1948–1961: Conflict and Compromise*, Oxford, Clarendon Press, 1991.

[8] See Elizabeth Cowie, 'Woman as Sign', *m/f*, vol. 1, no. 1, 1978.

[9] Reprinted in Hopkinson, *Into the Fiery Continent*, p. 359.

[10] *Drum*, Dec. 1954, p. 26.

[11] Sampson, *Drum: A Venture*, p. 122.

[12] Although the stories sometimes read like Can Themba's, Arthur Maimane has told me that he himself wrote at least two and perhaps all three of them. Ironically, the story by Doris Sello was reprinted in Annemarie van Niekerk's recent anthology of women writers: *Raising the Blinds: A Century of South African Women's Stories*, Johannesburg, Ad Donker, 1990.

[13] *Drum*, Apr. 1953.

[14] *Drum*, Mar. 1956, pp. 63–5.

[15] *Drum*, Oct. 1957, p. 31.

[16] *Drum*, Oct. 1957, pp.29–31

[17] *Drum*, Sept. 1955, p. 73.

[18] *Drum*, Jan. 1955, p. 35.

[19] *Drum*, Jan. 1955, p. 39.

[20] See, for instance, *Drum*, Mar., 1953, pp. 17–19; Oct. 1956, p. 63.

[21] The essays are reprinted in Essop Patel (ed.), *The World of Can Themba*, Johannesburg, Ravan, 1985.

[22] Christine Qunta, *Tribute*, Aug. 1990, p. 44.

Bibliography

Brown, D. M., 'The Anthology as Reliquary: *Ten Years of Staffrider* and *The Drum Decade*', *Current Writing,* vol. 1, no. 1, 1989, pp. 3–21.

Chapman, M., 'More Than Telling a Story: *Drum* and its Significance in Black South African Writing', in M. Chapman (ed.), *The Drum Decade: Stories from the 1950s*, Pietermaritzburg, University of Natal Press, 1989, pp. 183–232.

Coplan, D., *In Township Tonight: South Africa's Black City Music and Theatre*, Johannesburg, Ravan, 1985.

Cowie, E., 'Woman as Sign', *m/f*, vol. 1, no. 1, 1978.

Dangarembga, T., *Nervous Conditions*, London, The Women's Press, 1988.

Driver, D., 'Woman and Nature, Women as Objects of Exchange: Towards a Feminist Analysis of South African Literature', in M. Chapman, C. Gardner, and E. Mphahlele (eds), *Perspectives on South African English Literature*, Johannesburg, Donker, 1992, pp. 454–74.

Lodge, T., *Black Politics in South Africa since 1945*, London, Longman, 1983.

Mphahlele, E., *Down Second Avenue*, London, Faber & Faber, 1959.

Ndebele, N., 'The Ethics of Intellectual Combat', *Current Writing*, vol. I, no. 1, 1989, pp. 21–35.

Nicol, M., *A Good-Looking Corpse*, London, Secker and Warburg, 1991.

Nixon, R., *Homelands, Harlem and Hollywood: South African Culture and the World Beyond*, New York and London, Routledge, 1994.

Nkosi, L., 'The Fabulous Decade: The Fifties', in *Home and Exile and Other Selections* (2nd edn), London, Longman, 1983, pp. 3–24.

Patel, E. (ed.). *The World of Can Themba*, Johannesburg, Ravan, 1985.

Posel, D., *The Making of Apartheid 1948–1961: Conflict and Compromise*, Oxford, Clarendon Press, 1991.

Sampson, A., *Drum: A Venture into the New Africa*, London, Collins, 1956.

Sole, Kelvin. 'Class, Continuity and Change in Black South African Literature, 1948–1960', in B. Bozzoli (ed.), *Labour, Townships and Protest: Studies in the Social History of the Witwatersrand*, Johannesburg, Ravan, 1979.

Visser, N.W. 'South Africa: The Renaissance that Failed', *Journal of Commonwealth Literature*, 1976, vol. 9, no. 1, pp. 42–57.

Primary Text 6
Facsimiles of Front Covers, Articles, Letters & Advertisements from *Drum* Magazine 1952–5

(Top) *January 1952, front cover*
(Bottom) *March 1952 front cover*
p. 161 *March 1952 advertisements*
pp. 162-3 *March 1952 Short Story, 'Ntomo Gets a Job' by Douglas Sidayiya, pp. 23, 29*
p. 164 *September 1952, front cover*
pp. 165-7 *September 1952, Short Story, 'Blood Between Us', by Sam Mokgalendi, pp. 26-28*
pp. 168-9 *April 1954, Short Story, 'His Only Home', by Kenneth Mtetwa*
pp. 170 *April 1955, Dolly Drum advice column, and advertisement*

12 DRUM, MARCH, 1952

For YOU a skirt tailored in Britain

Gor-Ray offer you every-day skirts—with a future! Beautifully cut and beautifully finished, in British-loomed pure woollens—they keep good-looking through many years of wear. When you shop—look for the Gor-Ray label—there's a Gor-Ray skirt in a cloth, a style and a size to suit you.

GOR-RAY REGD.
Skirts one better!

Obtainable at all leading stores.

GOR-RAY LTD., 107 NEW BOND STREET, LONDON W.1. ENGLAND
General Agents: K. N. Derrington 528-9 C.T.C. Building, Plein Street, Cape Town. Harolds Industrial Agencies Ltd. P.O. Box 626. Port Elizabeth.

LEARN TO DRIVE AND DOUBLE YOUR WAGES!

THE
ANGLO-AMERICAN DRIVING SCHOOL

offers you:

(1) Expert instructors;
(2) Latest model cars, fitted with dual safety controls;
(3) Lessons at all times (including Sundays);
(4) Each lesson **ONE FULL HOUR**

ENQUIRIES: 12a Moseley Building, Cor. President and Rissik Streets, or Phone 22-8625
PLEASE NOTE: We are open all day on Saturdays

SANDAWANE,
The Great Prophet

If you are ill or in trouble and unhappy, this great friend of the African people awaits you

at

113 MOOI STREET (Corner Bree Street), JOHANNESBURG
Phone 23-4606 P.O. Box 6047
9 a.m. until 6 p.m. daily

She has to use up her strength. Her body will get tired. This is a sign that she must look after herself. For a woman's body is not as strong as a man's. So she should take FELUNA PILLS. They will give her strength, and make her body healthy for the work she has to do. Her blood will be clear and pure. Even during her bad days she will feel able to work without trouble. FELUNA PILLS are a special medicine for women and girls. They fight pains and tiredness, and give health and happiness to women.

40 Feluna Pills cost 3/3
20 Feluna Pills cost 1/9

You can buy them at any store.

4172-5

Ntombo Gets A Job

"He went stealthily and cautiously toward the verandah."

by Douglas Sidayiya

NTOMBO was worried. Everything seemed to be staring at him. Unseen fingers seemed to be pointing at his face from the corners of his small room. Even the rustling of the leaves on the trees outside gave him an eery feeling. Listening silently, he could hear the ticking of the small watch on his wrist, beating more loudly than usual. Even worse, his heart was beating as if he had just run a mile in record time. In plain words, Ntombo was unhappy and very frightened.

And why not? Who wouldn't be unhappy when he knew that, sooner or later, he would find himself behind bars? Who could be happy when he knew that nearly everyone thought of him as nothing but a crook, connected with every kind of crooked deed short of murder?

And today Ntombo viewed his own methods and found them to be very much the same as those of any killer in the eyes of the law, and he didn't like the thought. And that was what was worrying him now. Could he break away from his old life, for he did not want to be a criminal, hiding from the police, any more. And now he had a chance. That morning he had heard of a job as a waiter in a modern hotel. He had no money to leave Johannesburg and return to his home in the "colony," so he must either get the job or fall deeper and deeper into the life of a criminal. If only he could be successful, then everything would be all right.

Early next morning Ntombo eagerly boarded a bus which whisked him into the town. He was happy and full of confidence when he set out, but when he came to the big, modern hotel he began to feel nervous; began to wonder if he would ever be any good as a waiter even if he did get the job. He hesitated outside in the street and then he took the plunge.

A few minutes later he was ushered into the manager's office, and what a shock awaited him inside. For there in front of him sat the very man who had chased him for almost an hour the night he had stolen his bicycle.

For a moment Ntombo was speechless, then, "Good morning, sir," he said politely, his hands behind his back, hat in one, his fingers twitching nervously. "I have come to look for a job, as I understand you are in need of a waiter."

"That is so," replied the manager, looking him over from head to foot. "Yes, we are short of a waiter here. Now tell me, where have you been working before and have you any testimonials?"

Now these were just the kind of questions Ntombo had been dreading.

"I'm sorry, sir, but I haven't got any references with me. My room was broken into by 'tsotsis' two weeks ago, and they took most of my things with them, including my papers, which were in a pocket of one of my jackets."

"Oh, I see," said the manager. "That is difficult. But, anyway," he went on kindly, "you look a decent man and capable for the job."

Then he looked at Ntombo more closely. "Somehow," he went on, "you look very familiar to me. I've seen you somewhere before, I'm sure I have, but I can't think where it was."

★

FOR a while the manager went on staring at Ntombo. "No, I can't remember where it was," he said at last. "But I will trust you. When can you start work?"

Ntombo thought for a second. "I can start tomorrow morning, sir."

"Very well, then. Be here at seven o'clock."

Outside in the street Ntombo couldn't decide what to do. One question was burning in his mind: supposing the manager did remember during the day where he had seen him before, what then? Would he, in the morning, find himself once more in the hands of the police? "Well," mused Ntombo, at last, "job or no job, they're not going to get me as easily as all that. I know now just what I'm going to do. And the idea of a job went out of his mind, at least it had gone for the time being, for in his heart Ntombo really wanted to work as a waiter in the hotel.

Thinking about the situation all day, Ntombo decided at last that the best thing he could do would be to pull off one more big job that evening and then quit for the "colony" the following day when he had the money for his fare. During the day he had even picked out his would-be victim, and now he must wait until late that night to proceed with his plan.

★

IT was after 10 o'clock when he alighted from the bus in one of the fashionable suburbs of the city and proceeded towards his destination on foot. Although the streets were brilliantly lit, the spot he had chosen for his plot was far away from the sparkling lights, and this suited his plans well. He knew that at a certain time the place would be safe to enter and would, therefore, be at his mercy.

It was quiet and dark in the house as he approached it. Coming to the gate at the back, he saw that the big yard was empty. Carefully he opened the gate and went inside, leaving it open for any emergency which might arise. The place was in complete darkness. Nothing moved as he went stealthily and cautiously toward the verandah. Mounting the steps, he came to the door and turned the handle. No, nothing doing here. He went to a window next to the door. It was locked inside. Well, there was only one thing to do. Pushing his hand under his trouser belt,

(Continued on Page 29)

My First Experience of England

by Dr. J. M. Nhlapo

AS one who had been born in the Orange Free State, Union of South Africa, and had never been outside the Union bounds except to Basutoland, I looked forward to my visit to England with a fast throbbing heart. All who had to do with the matter of my transport—and practically all were Afrikaans-speaking—were most courteous and helpful to me.

When we left Cape Town on September 14, 1951, by the Pretoria Castle, a veritable floating palace, I experienced a foretaste of the reception awaiting me in England. The voyage was not many days old when English men and women who were returning home from the Union and the Rhodesias began to show us genuine kindness.

Dr. Nhlapo is seen here on his voyage out to England.

KINDNESS AND RESPECT

On setting my foot on English soil, for the first few days I could not obliterate the thought of a "location," a non-European cafe, buses and tram-cars "reserved for coloureds only." I am almost fully acclimatised now to the ways of England, where everything is for everybody. The kindness and respect with which I am treated are so genuine and unaffected that I have found a warm place in my heart for the people here. My colour makes me conspicuous. This immediately arouses the interest of those around in me.

English people are great travellers, readers and thinkers. I have since coming here found an ocean of reading matter. In this country of fine libraries to which I also, with my black skin, have free access, I have come across literature on my country in particular and the rest of Africa in general which I have never seen in South Africa. This, in addition to thinking in a freer atmosphere, has helped me to think and speak more clearly and convincingly than I remember having done before.

CORRECTING WRONG IMPRESSIONS

After a week or two of my work here I discovered it was providential that I should have come to Birmingham with so little material and so little preparation, for I would have had to throw away or generously supplement the scanty fare from South Africa on arrival at a place where there is no end of literature with which I am gorging myself as much as I can. It was also providential, because I can now make my lectures incorporate some of the material which both the library, the English Press and my contact with folk here is daily pouring into my mind. Incidentally this enables me not only to dish out fresh and hot food in place of canned and cold stuff for my eager hearers, but also to correct wrong impressions that some of our countrymen make in this country. I find my lectures an excellent means of serving my people and my country. The task is, of course, a stupendous one, and I would have to live in this country more than just a year to make an appreciable impression. Still, "al die bietjies help."

LECTURING ON AFRICA

SPEAKING of my lectures makes me remember to shed a bit of light on my mission here in Great Britain and the colleges I am serving. I am a William Paton lecturer whose subject is "Africa." My syllabus, though arranged before I left South Africa, is the most flexible one. I am not going to write it down here, but I have to mention that it is so planned that I first had to give the students, who are not English-speaking only, but represent various nationalities from the Continent of Europe, a picture of old Africa. On this old background I have to deal with Africa as it is today. The influence of Western civilisation, the impact of Christianity, education, health, problems of a multi-racial society, etc., are part of the syllabus.

I also hear a couple of lectures regularly and I am free to have a taste of as many of them as I like. At the Council of the Colleges, one of whose members is the Vice-Chancellor of the University of Birmingham, Sir Raymond Priestly, M.A., D.Sc., LL.D., a great scholar and scientist, who went with Scott to the Antarctic, I was asked to speak. The fact that after the meeting the Vice-Chancellor and I immediately became friends and another member seriously and sincerely flatters me with the words, "You speak English extremely well, and you think in English," should indicate to you that the speech was, after all, not so very poor.

NTOMBO (Continued from Page 23)

he pulled out a piece of iron about six inches long. A light tap on one of the window panes proved that the glass was thick. Then, tapping harder, he sent the glass shattering on to the floor inside.

Then he heard it. A big, coarse voice came from somewhere inside the house. "Hey—y," it bellowed very loudly.

Ntombo took fright. How he came down the steps he didn't know, but he found himself running for the gate. He saw it wide open in front of him and he went straight for it.

Smack! He was nearly thrown on his back. He had missed the gate and knocked himself against the post. When he recovered from the blow he made for safety. The only thing that mattered now was to get out of that dangerous vicinity.

When he reached his room that night he couldn't sleep. He was thinking hard of what he could do next, for he didn't want to remain in this town any more. He wanted to go home and start a new life. If he remained here he would for certain be tempted to continue with what he was desperately trying to avoid.

Thus he remained for hours, awake on his bed, meditating without reaching any conclusions. At last he got up to get a cigarette and went back to bed. Reaching for the matches on the soap-box which served him as a bedside table, he struck a match to light his cigarette, and, while still holding the light, his eyes wandered across the room to the opposite wall and came to rest on the calendar. He remained staring at a certain date until the match went out. He didn't bother to light another one. He only thought about the date on the calendar, for it was today's date; and today it was Friday, Friday the thirteenth. So that was it! Friday the thirteenth. Well, tomorrow might be a lucky day. And with this singing in his brains, he fell asleep.

The following morning a neatly dressed young fellow, with a piece of plaster smoothly pasted on his left eyebrow, reported at a hotel for duty. The manager looked at him smilingly and remarked: "Now I recognise you. You used to serve me with drinks at the Lion Hotel. All right, you can start your work. I know you are a good man."

Ntombo smiled, donned his white jacket, and started his duties and a new life.

MY FAVOURITE TEXT

For what is a man profited if he shall gain the whole world and lose his own soul?

—St. Matthew, V., 16-26.

Durban. *MARY FRANCES NLOTHA.*

Nigerian Christening in London. Water from the River Niger was used to christen the son of Lapido Solanke, Chief of the Yoruba tribe. The baby is held by his godmother, Mrs. Gladys Smith, while his father (right) and godfather, Oladigbolu-Coker, look on admiringly.

Adontenhene of Akim Abuakwa State, Gold Coast, who is second in rank to the Paramount Chief, is the only living ruler of the Gold Coast with a University degree. Although he is a Bachelor of Arts of London University, he has never been to Britain. He studies privately in his palace.

DRUM

BIG SPORTS NUMBER

"Secrets of FAH FEE"

£120 MUST BE WON!

DAGGA

MURDERS AFRICA

Africa's Leading Magazine

4d

SEPTEMBER 1952

Blood Between Us!

By Sam Mokgalendi

It was one afternoon in May when the break came—bitter, angry words, and then the parting.

At 45 Mr. Thulare Modiba was a stern, though thoughtful, husband. But to his pretty 22-year-old wife, who loved gaiety and laughter, smart dresses and the company of lively people, he had grown dull and often appeared harsh and unloving. No passing cloud had caused this quarrel—it was one of a dozen others, the growth of week upon week, month upon month of disharmony between them. To have looked into the room of their house in Sixth Avenue, Marabastad, Pretoria, on that May afternoon, one could see that everything that lavish wealth could buy was there. But one thing was absent, and that was happiness.

They had been married four years when their one child was born. A year of uninterrupted happiness followed; the happiness of love and understanding. Then the clouds came. I do not know what brought them—perhaps something very simple—a harsh word or an angry look; but I do know what caused them to settle and deepen. It was a worthless scamp who came into their lives with his good looks and his soft words; words to charm and turn the head of any pretty young wife. And, indeed, pretty and foolish Mrs. Modiba was no different. She was bewitched by this smiling, handsome intruder and, in fact, utterly blinded to the foul intention that lay beneath his smiles and flattery. It was not long before she began to find her husband's quiet and unassuming ways more dull than ever, his faithful patience irritating, and soon the rift between them grew too wide for mending. And now, inflamed with jealousy, Mr. Modiba turned furiously on his wife.

"Woman," he burst out, "unfaithful woman. If you're unhappy in the home I've given you, if you feel chained to a man without a soul as you say you are, why not leave me—go to your lover—he seems to make you happier than I do."

"Why—because I'm a mother. Because I love my child and no misery you can bring me would drive me from her." She hid her face in her hands and began to cry bitterly. "Oh, why couldn't I have died before she was born?"

"Why, indeed?" echoed her husband, trembling with anger and humiliation. "Or before my eyes were cursed with your prettiness—before I picked you up from the gutter and gave you a fortune and a love, which alike you have thrown to the winds. A mother, you say! Cruel, worthless woman. Lost to shame and all feeling of honour, you disgrace the name of mother. I could kill you with my own hands if it weren't for our child." And he hurled the book in his hand straight in her face.

She let out a cry of pain as the book caught her on the mouth and cut deeply into her lip. "Brute, murderer," she shrieked at him as the blood flowed down her chin and splashed on to her dress. "Now you have cut the last tie—now there is blood between us: there will be death itself if I stay in this house." Her voice was high-pitched and hysterical.

She ran from the room, slammed the door, and was gone, leaving him shaken and petrified.

Scarcely knowing what she was doing, Mrs. Modiba ran upstairs, blood still smearing her face. Panic-stricken, she threw all her belongings into a suitcase and swept down the stairs again, as swiftly as if hell itself were behind her. Only once did she pause. A run of tiny footsteps caught her ear and a cry of "Mamma" from the nursery. For a second she hesitated, distraught and fearful, and then, before the nursery door could open, she had torn herself away, and was gone into the street. She hailed a nearby taxi. "Away! Drive me away!" she cried hoarsely, not daring to look back at the house she had left for fear of glimpsing a tiny form which might overturn all and break her resolve.

"Quick, or it may be too late!" she added as she jumped into the taxi.

"Where to, madam?"

"Anywhere—out of the city—away from this house of murder! But wait. Take me first to the market. I must see him before I go." The last words were whispered as if to herself.

In a moment they were gone, and a husband and wife were separated—perhaps for ever.

★

A few nights later there was a knock at my door, and a stranger stood there.

"Are you Mr. Ngwenya?" he asked, and handed me a card that told me that this was Mr. J. B. Modiba.

"Have you read this," he inquired, unfolding a local African newspaper and pointing to a column headed "Scandal."

"I have," I replied, somewhat surprised. "Is your business with me in any way connected with this sad affair?"

"It is, Mr. Thulare Modiba is my brother. I have come to put myself in your hands, for I believe you can help my brother."

The service required of me was both curious and interesting, and at once showed the noble heart and deep affection that dwelt beneath the husband's stern appearance.

"There is no doubt that there has been an elopement," Mr. Modiba went on, "for the taxi duly arrived at this other man's house and then together they went to the railway station and

You MUST read this thrilling tale of passion and hatred!

there took a train to Johannesburg. And now my brother fears that it will not be long before her money runs out and then she will be cast off—deserted, to be scorned by all the world. Now this is what my brother wishes to be done. Although he still loves her deeply, he can never see her again, but in spite of this he cannot bear the thought of her being starved and despised. He wants a watch to be kept on her, and the moment the break comes he wants sufficient money placed at her disposal."

"He is very good, and I would like to help him," I replied, "but what you ask is more the work of a private detective."

"That is very true. But you may, perhaps, be able to recommend such a man?"

After I had given him the address of a friend, we parted, and I saw him no more for months. During those months I could not help watching the deserted husband. I met him often, always in the company of his little girl—always smiling, stately and cool. The world pronounced him happy—well rid of a bad bargain, but the world, as usual, was completely deceived. It saw the smiles, but failed to note the wasting form, stooping gait and pallid cheeks. And then it came to my ears that Modiba was confined to bed.

Early in December the long-looked-for break came. Mr. Modiba, the younger brother, appeared one day in great dismay, and placed in my hands the following telegrams, from the detective: **MRS. MODIBA DESERTED. LEFT WITHOUT MONEY AND THREE MONTHS' RENT TO PAY. TELEGRAPH ORDERS.**

The second ran thus: **MRS. MODIBA DISAPPEARED. UNABLE TRACE HER.**

I stared at the two flimsies.

"Well, what is to be done?"

I thought for a moment. "There are two things we can do," I said at last. "Firstly, we could advertise in all the local papers she is likely to read, and the second matter applies to the second telegram. The detective says he does not know where to look for her. I do. What magnet was it that made her hesitate to leave her husband and home? It was her child, and it is her child who will draw her back to Pretoria, though mountains stand between."

"But she has no money—no friends—nothing!"

"Money?" I echoed. "She is a mother—that is enough!"

There was emotion in his voice as he cried, "Mr. Ngwenya, I believe in what you have said, but there is one other possibility, and the idea of it is killing my brother. She may commit suicide."

I was astounded by such a suggestion. "Surely not," I said at last, "not until she has seen her child. But still I shall do all I can to help you."

Next day the local papers contained the following announcement: **IF MATSIDISO MODIBA, WHO LEFT HER HOME IN SIXTH AVENUE, MARABASTAD, IN JUNE LAST, WILL COMMUNICATE WITH HER HUSBAND, SHE WILL HEAR SOMETHING TO HER ADVANTAGE.**

I need scarcely say that this advertisement, vague and meaningless though it might appear to the general reader, was looked through and through by the inquisitive eyes of the Marabastad gentry. And then there was such a lifting of hands and screwing of faces, a perking and sniffing of noses and such pity for "the poor misguided man, who could ever dream of making provision for such a worthless woman." The wonder is that the noses ever came back to shape again.

But the advertisement brought no response. Others appeared with a like result.

★

AND then one night it happened. It was late and I was on my way home from the Empire Theatre. The streets were empty and quiet. I paused to light a cigarette and the match sizzled and went out as I dropped it into the wet gutter. I started to cross the road. Then suddenly I caught sight of a strange figure, hesitating in the shadows that edged the great circle of light that spread out from the theatre front.

"Murderer!" she shrieked.

Then as she crept as if ashamed into the harsh light, I saw that it was a woman. She was dressed in the meanest rags and over her head she clutched a tawdry black shawl. At every step she limped painfully, and it seemed that she was afraid of being seen. I stopped to watch her, my curiosity aroused. Slowly she dragged herself across the street and disappeared into First Avenue. I crossed, too, wondering if she were just one of the usual "drunks." There was something so strange in her whole appearance that I resolved to follow her. The bitter wind was blasting full in her face as she went on up the street. Soon I was close behind her, and it was then that I saw that this poor woman was walking barefoot.

"God help the poor girl!" I thought. "What fearful errand can bring her here on such a night, and so late?"

By now she had turned into Sixth Avenue. I paused, and as I did so I saw her start back, her hands clasped tight over her breast. Then I realised that she was standing in front of Mr. Modiba's house. The front door was open, and close to the gate a taxi was drawn up. The poor woman gazed sadly at the brightly lit bay window of the dining-room. I could see but one person in the room—Mr. Modiba himself, lying on a sofa, propped up with pillows. There was a dreadful change in his appearance. His face was a mere shadow, worn and gaunt. It was then that the door flew open and a little girl of about three or four years old, dressed in the nicest clothes, ran in with outstretched arms and made straight for the sofa. A cry broke from the poor woman clinging to the rails outside. The sick man, with every look of pain and sadness chased from his face, half-raised himself, lifted the child in his arms and kissed her bright face. The poor woman looked on. The next moment a nurse appeared and the little girl was lifted in her arms and carried from the room. In a minute the nurse hurried out, cowering before the driving wind, but, short as was the distance to the shelter of the taxi, she did not reach it. A wild shriek of delight burst from the watching woman. With one bound she had the child in her arms and was kissing her passionately. "My child, my child!" she cried. "My own little darling!"

"Woman, how dare you!" the nurse shrieked as she snatched the child from her.

"How dare I?" was the impassioned reply, and the woman's shawl dropped to the ground, her dark and beautiful hair revealed. "How dare I? I am her mother!"

There was a rush from within the house and Mr. Modiba appeared in the doorway. He had heard the outcry and found strength to get to the door. As he turned round full in the light, the woman shrank back with a cry and straightaway she was gone into the dark night.

I ran across the street and reached the spot just as the child was sobbing, "That horrid woman—she squeezed me tight and said she was my mamma."

Mr. Modiba staggered, gripping the door for support. I caught him in my arms and, with the help of the taxi-driver, carried him into the house. There I told him what I had seen.

"Thank you, thank you," he gasped faintly. "Follow her . . see where she goes."

★

THE next morning the following advertisement appeared in all the morning papers:—

MRS. MODIBA—RETURN, IF ONLY FOR AN HOUR. YOUR HUSBAND IS DYING.

I was out the whole day on the hunt, but it was night before I came on my clue. A lady, a perfect stranger, had found her fainting in the street, had taken her to her own home, and then, like a good Samaritan, bound up her cuts and bruises, fed her like a child and with motherly tenderness tucked her into the first bed she had slept in for more than a week. She was still weak and feverish when I was introduced to her, but at last she consented to accompany me to her husband's bedside. We half-carried her down into the cab. She sobbed quietly till we reached her husband's house. When we arrived Mr. Modiba was propped upon a sofa and lying so still that I thought at first he was dead. But no, he opened his eyes and raised himself to look into our faces.

"She has come at last. Bring her closer to me."

There was a low wail, a weary cry of delight, and then they were clasped in each other's arms, the woman crying bitterly.

"Don't—don't, Matsidiso!" he gasped out. "The past—bury it. I am dying and perhaps it is best this way. Matsidiso, I left all to you. Swear to remain pure and I will leave you my child."

"Heaven is my witness!"

Continued on page 28

Blood Between Us

Continued from page 27

cried the poor mother in a wild burst of grief, raising her eyes to heaven. "I swear it."

"Now I can die—so happy!" murmured the dying man, resting wearily on her breast. "And you will forgive—forgive all my . . .?"

"I did months ago. That is past. I will be at peace, where there is no sin."

There was a long pause, broken only by the stifled sobs of those present, and then the dying man, with a great effort, pointed to the window.

"Let me—let me—see outside," he gasped with painful slowness. And then his couch was moved gently close to the window.

A brightness came into his eyes as he looked out on the sloping housetops of the sleeping city, gleaming white and pure in the clear moonlight, with their yellow lights shining in clusters, like earthly stars trying to rival the clear sparkle of those in the dark heaven above.

"Ah, Pretoria! Beautiful, cruel, cold-hearted city!" he murmured. "It has killed me, torn out my heart and trampled on it. But I still love it . . . darker! . . . darker. Pray—oh, God, protect my child and my wife." And with this whisper lingering on his lips, he sank back and lay still.

Mr. Modiba was dead.

It was only by force that we could tear the mother and child from the room.

FOR two years a lady, always dressed in mourning and deeply veiled, went to and fro blessing the dark places of our city with her presence, her advice and her fortune. Always she was alone; and always she left a ray of sunshine behind her which still brightens many a poor home. I can say no more without revealing the identity of the lady.

She died two years after her husband and was buried, at her own request, without name or mark, down in the Atteridgeville Cemetery. But the story is not quite at an end, for lately I have come to know that a brilliant young lady, just returned from being educated in the Cape, went down to the cemetery, searched out the spot, and on the grave she placed a wreath of the loveliest flowers.

Disc-ussing . . . .

TOMMY TURNS TO JIVE!

Tommy Ramokgopa

TWO months back I promised you a treat when I made mention of a brilliant young team of vocalists, LO SIX. This month they introduce themselves with an excellent arrangement by Tommy Ramokgopa, which the Harlem Swingsters made famous — they give you MAJUBA *under the title of* LERIBE. Tommy doesn't smoke, doesn't drink and it's truly a sober piece of work he has produced. This number, originally a purely instrumental work, is not deprived of its colourful rhythms and accents in its vocal re-adaptation by these still very young fellows. Then again you might think Tommy wears his hair long because he is the serious writer of Matsiliso, but when you hear his LERIBE on the backside, an essentially jivy affair, you meet a different man. Hear them on HMV JP 119. Both the vocals and the accompaniment are in perfect tune. A rare achievement for African combos.

TRAGEDY TO TRIUMPH

FROM the Columbia stable, James Chili makes a very welcome comeback. James' life is linked with sadness. He moved his family from Natal to Johannesburg where a dashing city slicker grabbed his wife from him. Recently his cousin M. Chili was thrown off a fast-moving train by hooligans, breaking his leg in the fall. But tragedy does not show in James' music. His latest releases on Columbia YE 71 (Balekani and Kukona Indaba) reflect an uncrushable soul and prove his BRAVE LIONS among the best known male voice choirs in this class.

Then there's the chappie who decided to set out on his own because his mate did him out of a handsome sum of money. Job Dlangalala of the former Play Singers now records as a solo artist and works as a milkman by day. There must be something in his milk bottles for he is even greater by himself. Accompanying himself on guitar he tells the sad tale of his girl friend Josephine, who never seems to come home on time. Watch out for Job, recording as the Play Singer on YE 70.

SPANKING THE CAT!

I'M bursting to tell you of Al Debbo. Ever heard of him? Why, of course, he's the fellow who is that shy in private life but a very comedian on stage and platter. You'll rip your sides with laughter when he tells you how he spanked a stray cat in the street. I tell you, what happened to that cat is nobody's business! Al is accompanied by Nico Carstens's "Boereorkes," and need I say more than that his is the best of its kind in the country? Most people couldn't care two hoots about Afrikaans records because they loathe the concertina. Well, you won't hear a *concertina on this platter*, brother. You'll enjoy the lyrics and the rhythm of "Ricksha Booi," you laugh at "Stoppie,"

James Chili

the skollie boy, on HMV, HS 32 and HS 33, and you will meet yet another great guitarist, Neels Steyn, who does some great work on the G string with Carstens's orchestra on Columbia, DE 244. The titles are "Outa in die Lang Pad" and "Mossie se Moses."

JAZZ UP THE PARTY

YOU remember the pretty American thrush, Doris Day, who gave you "A Guy is a Guy" and virile Frankie Lane, They've teamed up in a refreshingly good arrangement of "Sulker Bossie," renamed "Sugar Bush." It's on Columbia DS 61.

They certainly make up for the losses in "Sugar Bush." It's selling as only hot cakes do.

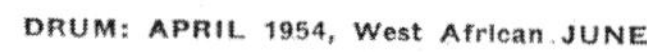
DRUM: APRIL 1954, West African JUNE

HIS ONLY

By Kenneth Mtetwa

HURRICANE sat huddled in his seat in the bus that was carrying him to Alexandra Township. His mind was in a whirl. He was thinking of the last few days at school — the exciting days before end of term. He had been eager enough to go on holiday, and yet, as soon as the college walls were out of sight, he had been left with a queer empty feeling in his stomach. Just then he noticed that the bus was approaching his destination.

He saw the township spread before his eyes as one who has been climbing a hill suddenly comes to the summit and sees the valley stretch out before his eyes. His heart missed a beat as he had remembered that he had come to this location to see his girl friend.

He conjured up a picture of what she would look like, and how she would be dressed. Had she changed her dress style? Probably not! Would she be wearing her lovely sea-green frock with Cuban shoes to match? Would it be her navy-blue costume? Possibly, because she loved navy-blue as much as he did.

His thoughts were cut short by the swerve of the bus as the driver endeavoured to reduce speed, and, with a sudden jerk, the bus came to a standstill. Hurricane, like many others, was thrown half out of his seat.

ALIGHTING, he looked at his watch and found that he had a lot of time in which he could keep his appointment. For one thing he was too much of a dandy and a gentleman to arrive at a place sweating like a pig, nor did it pay to arrive at a place half an hour late. He had a full hour before meeting Emerald, and so he decided to stroll down to the African Star Restaurant, the most modern of its kind in the township, where he could spend a few sixpences at the juke-box. Moreover, he had still to revive his memories of the old times with Emerald at the familiar haunts they usually frequented when he was with her during one of his visits—he wanted to see if the township had changed much.

Alexandra lay lazily under a blazing sun. Dust and smoke had turned the extensive township into a miniature factory town. It seemed like the hub of an industrial area. Spirals of smoke rose vertically from hundreds of house chimneys and braziers. The latter could be seen in front of countless houses which were crammed shockingly together on small plots of land owned by miserly and inconsiderate landlords. Adults and children alike sat huddled together near the braziers, shouting and screaming at each other at the top of their voices.

Sunday was no excuse for peacefulness and rest. Everywhere there was noise and shouting. African religious sects mingled freely with pedlars and youngsters out for a spree. Streets were crammed alarmingly with a milling crowd of aimlessly wandering humans; drunkards staggered to and fro with unsteady gait, and now and then one of these unsteady persons would fall prostrate. Nobody cared.

Neither were the South African Police, in their tight-fitting uniforms, concerned. Some stood uninterestedly by while others lolled in their vans wearing smiles of contentment on their faces. A burly, half-naked man who was very drunk and seemed to have collided with a steam engine was dragged unceremoniously into one of the vans nearby; while a European sergeant with five African constables were rounding up skokiaan queens and their now senseless customers. In the next street the noise of a gun duel was heard. Nobody took notice of any of these things—if they did, they did not show.

Nor was Hurricane interested. He had seen a lot of these things in his short span of life. These incidents made life pleasant, he ruminated. What would Africa be if some of her ruthless children were not killed? And why should these hounds of the law—the police—have to arrest a drunkard? After all, he was drowning his sorrows! Perhaps it was better so, provided the Government would feed the poor underpaid fish—the scum of the earth.

THESE thoughts whirled through Hurricane's mind as he half-ran, half-walked across the busy street, passing women and boys who drew attention to their various wares in the loudest voices they could manage. Life was certainly fast in this place, he thought to himself; but

He saw her walking hand-in-hand

DRUM: APRIL 1954, West African JUNE

LOVE!

then life was fast in the whole of Johannesburg. People did not have time to stand and stare. With these thoughts in his mind he turned into First Avenue and made his way to the African Star Restaurant.

He was approaching the door of the restaurant when he saw someone who looked like his Emerald, hand in hand with someone else. He stood petrified, not knowing what to do, and a sudden pang of jealousy shot through his heart. But he was not sure yet: he had to be certain because he did not want to be rash. If he acted on the spur of the moment, he might find that he was confronting a couple totally unknown to himself, and the consequences might be unpleasant considering the way in which boys guarded their girl friends. And so, resisting the impulse to follow the couple who had caused his faith in Emerald to receive such a sudden jolt, he turned into the restaurant. He drank two milk-shakes, played a few of Louis Armstrong's and Duke Ellington's numbers on the juke-box, but all the time he was like one in a trance. Eventually he decided to go to Emerald's home.

On arriving he found the girl wreathed in the best smile she could muster, awaiting his arrival. Hurricane cursed within himself. These girls! Only a short while ago she was hanging on someone else's arm, but now here she was beaming with delight! "Oh, God," he muttered within himself, "can deceit in a woman never end?"

He held out his hand formally to her, though his arms were straining to embrace her. She took a step forward to take his hand, but before she could reach him, the young man Hurricane had seen leaving the restaurant came out of the sitting-room. Hurricane recoiled as if he had been stung. His hidden anger and the fear of losing Emerald now came out to show clearly on his clouded face, mingled with a pained expression. How could Emerald do this to him? he thought with a feeling of helplessness.

SUDDENLY Emerald laughed gaily. She had seen the pained expression on his face.

"I want you to meet my cousin."

Her words were directed to Hurricane. Hurricane stretched out his hand to him and gripped the other's warmly in his relief. It was only then that he remembered that she had told him about her cousin Patrick, who stayed in Evaton. He felt ashamed of himself for distrusting his beloved. With a scarcely audible "How do you do?" to Patrick, he stretched out his arms to Emerald and she flew into them with delight.

He carried her into the cool recess of the capacious sitting-room and deposited her gently on to the soft comfortable divan, where they were both lost in a blissful and breath-taking kiss— a kiss that summed up the feelings of their hearts and needed no verbal explanation. They both knew that the only happiness one could find was in the arms of the beloved.

In the distance could be heard the hooting of the buses amid the tumult of a world sunk in debauchery. At last they knew what their love meant to them.

with the handsome stranger

Wanted: A Wife!

I AM *a clerk, aged 24, and want to marry a girl of sober habits who can read and write English. She mustn't be older than 19. I have seen much trouble about in-laws in the past and would prefer an orphan. Dolly, please help me find such a girl.*

● This column's function is to give advice to readers on their love problems only and not to act as a marriage bureau. I pass your request on to my readers and any replies I get will be sent to you direct.—Dolly.

Miss "Right"?

I AM 19 and in love with a girl of 17. We intend to get married. But my parents say I must not marry now until I am a little older. Please Dolly, tell me how long I should wait?

● *Why not hang on another few months and show your parents that you have really found "Miss Right"? You could invite her around to your home several times until they become as fond of her as you are! Then they will probably add their blessings to their consent to your marriage.—Dolly.*

Wife Deserted

SOME time ago my wife deserted me and I later found her living with another man. I don't know whether to take her back by force and have the man arrested or to sue for divorce without claiming her back. Please Dolly, tell me what to do.

● *This is a legal matter and you had better see a lawyer. But whatsoever you do, young man, don't use force.—Dolly.*

Marriage Bonds

I AM an old bachelor and I hate marriage because I think it is a form of bondage. I work hard and earn my living honestly. But some people envy me my single life and hate me; they're always sending me abusive letters accusing me of being snobbish, playboyish and what not. What should I do?

● *It's human nature, old bachelor, so don't worry. Jealous people will always criticise successful men and women, married or unmarried. They'll try to find fault even where they should be showering praise. And with bachelors and spinsters the position is even worse. So unless its a threat on your life, don't bother.—Dolly.*

Loves His Money!

I AM 22 and in love with an Indian boy. He is 25 and a shopkeeper, and always gives me articles from his shop free of charge; but my parents don't know about this. I have just found out that I don't love him deeply enough. Do you think if I reject him he will ask for his articles back?

● *Your problem, my dear, is a tricky one. You are old enough to know when you really love someone; and you made a mistake by encouraging this foolish man to build extravagant hopes about you and spend his money on you. Naturally he will be hurt to have to part with you after all this, but at the same time he will realise that you have been deceiving each other all along and that to carry on with an affair which is based more on material attractions than on love will do neither of you any good.—Dolly.*

Platonic Friendship

I AM friendly with a girl of my age who has the habit of inviting me to tea with her at her home from time to time. She is now so curiously interested in me that I am beginning to suspect that she wants me to make love to her and I want to discourage her. What should I do about this girl?

● *A platonic friendship provides chances for occasional friendly gestures, and there are times when such friendships have ended up at the altar. But if in your case you are convinced that this girl is building a love friendship which you want to discourage, you can do so politely either by introducing her to someone else or showing more interest in another girl.—Dolly.*

Let Him Go!

I AM 17 and have been madly in love with a teacher. He fell in love with another girl while I was away and made her pregnant. In order to keep his post he was compelled to marry her, but I understand that he is unhappy about that marriage. Should I ask him to come back to me?

● *No, my dear, don't try to win him back. He is already married to someone else. I think if he really loved you he would have waited for your return instead of getting himself involved with the other girl in such a disgraceful way!—Dolly*

Heartbreaks . . .

Ask Dolly Drum for Advice!

ROGER FIELD

La Guma's *Little Libby*: *The Adventures of Liberation Chabalala*

Reference
Rewritten for this volume from 'Art & the Man: La Guma's Comics & Paintings', *Critical Survey* 11 (2), 1999: 45–63

Better known as a South African writer and political activist, Alex La Guma's work in the area of popular culture has received very little attention to date.[1] My article seeks to correct this imbalance by examining his political comic strip, *Little Libby – The Adventures of Liberation Chabalala.* The strip appeared during 1959 in *New Age*, a Cape Town based weekly left-wing newspaper for which he worked as a journalist from 1956 until a banning order in 1962 effectively ended his public political and literary career in South Africa. Besides providing a political and aesthetic context for the comic, this article also proposes that the comic, not the acclaimed novella *A Walk in the Night,* was La Guma's first major piece of published fiction. In so doing, I suggest that exploration of La Guma's interest in and debt to aspects of popular culture provides additional perspectives on the novelist in whom most critics have found Gorky, Dostoyevsky and American Naturalism rather than Popeye, Krazy Kat, Juliet Jones and the Katzenjammer Kids as well.[2]

A number of critics have used graphic or artistic terms to describe La Guma's novels and short stories, but we should not confuse this with analysis of his graphic work.[3] At least four factors have contributed to the comic's low profile. Firstly, La Guma himself has directed attention away from it by stressing an interest dating from childhood in 'serious works, both political and literary' in which his father encouraged him. As a child, he read Robert Louis Stevenson, Alexandre Dumas, Victor Hugo; in adolescence he shifted to 'adventure stories, westerns, detective stories, and gradually began to turn towards the more serious classics such as Shakespeare, the Russian authors, Tolstoy, Gorky, and then the American writers James T. Farrell, Steinbeck, and Hemingway'.[4] However, friends and relatives have indicated other interests that do not always support this linear progression. While he was still in South Africa these interests included detective stories by James Hadley Chase and Raymond Chandler; Damon Runyon's romanticised New York underworld; newspaper comics such as the Katzenjammer Kids, Big Ben Bolt and Juliet Jones which he read in the late 1950s; local manifestations of popular culture such as the Coon Carnival; the cinema in general and Westerns in particular throughout his life.[5] During the early years of exile, he worked on a detective series.[6] This suggests that the range of representational and narrative models on which he drew was diverse and spanned his total reading and creative life, and that his models for comic strips were primarily American. It also provides confirmation for J. M. Coetzee's view that 'the popular crime and low-life story' influenced La Guma.[7]

Secondly, La Guma's prose fiction was more accessible than the comic which, until the early 1990s, could only be found in publications that had been banned in South Africa since the early 1960s. Thirdly, the critics who have acknowledged the strip have not dealt with its graphic and experimental qualities. In his seminal thesis, Gareth Cornweall notes the 'mischievous and irreverent sense of humour which can be glimpsed once or twice in the short stories, but is never allowed to disturb the severe concentration of the novels'. He adds that La Guma 'even wrote and drew a comic strip in *New Age*...which followed the picaresque adventures of one Liberation Chabalala', but does not develop this observation.[8] The general movement from 'irreverence' to 'severe concentration' is undeniable but I will provide some evidence from *The Stone Country*, La Guma's third novel, which suggests that images derived from popular culture were present in later, serious works. In an otherwise comprehensive analysis of La Guma's output, Chandramohan stresses *Little Libby's* contribution to the depiction of ethnic groups not usually found in La Guma's fiction. Here Chandramohan mentions 'African society of the 1950s' or 'the political contribution' of 'the Indian community', but he pays very little attention to *Little Libby* as a *comic.*[9] Fourthly, despite the impact of cultural studies on the analysis of literature and the steady erosion of barriers between 'high' and 'popular' culture in the analysis of images and texts, few critics have explored the numerous signs of La Guma's interest in popular culture scattered throughout his novels. Nor have they considered the possibility that a more subversive, anarchic and anti-establishment La Guma existed alongside the serious and politically correct public persona.

As a regular visitor to the La Guma household in District Six during the 1930s, Communist Party of South Africa (CPSA) and SA Congress of Trade Unions (SACTU) stalwart Ray Alexander recalled that as a child La Guma always seemed to be drawing, sketching or writing.[10] La Guma's earliest documented illustrations date from 1937 when he was 12 years old. He and the sons of several other leading figures involved in the National Liberation League of South Africa (NLL) contributed to its publication, *The Liberator: A Non-European Anti-Imperialist Magazine*, which his father edited. In the first issue Alex la Guma is credited with 'Designs and Reproductions'. The NLL's political activities such as its anti-segregation campaigns meant that he was also required to produce campaign material such as banners, placards and leaflets.[11] During this period he attended still-life drawing classes at the Hyman Liberman Centre in District Six where he was born and grew up. The 'Liberman' was closely modelled on Toynbee Hall in London's East End.[12] By the early 1940s, La Guma was also painting figures. He also produced at least one self-portrait. During the late 1940s, while working as a clerk in the Art Department of Caltex, he attended life-drawing classes. There he met the artist and writer Peter Clarke who later designed the cover for the first edition of *A Walk in the Night.*[13] Though the available information on the classes suggests that their aim was the realist representation of the body, it is also possible that La Guma was indirectly exposed to the conventions of comic strip production through John Coplans, at one time the class instructor, who later developed an interest in pop artists such as Lichtenstein and Warhol.[14]

In 1947 and 1948, La Guma joined the Young Communist League and CPSA respectively. He remained a member of the CPSA until it was banned in 1950. Between 1954 and 1956 he held a series of executive positions in the South African Coloured Peoples Organisation (SACPO). SACPO was one of the member organisations of the Congress Alliance – the others being the African

National Congress, the SA Indian Congress and the SA Congress of Democrats. By the time La Guma produced the comic strip, SACTU had also joined the Alliance.

Arrested along with 155 others in December 1956 and charged with high treason, the Treason Trial brought many changes to his life and his output. It was also the first time since infancy that he had been to Johannesburg, and there are several indications from his satirical column 'Up my alley' and *Liberation Chabalala* that he saw it as 'the big city'. This view coincides with popular perceptions of Cape Town as smaller and more laid back than brash, bustling and dangerous Johannesburg (Fig. 1, p. 177), which he compared with 'Chicago in the heyday of Al Capone, John Dillinger and the hectic days of illegal booze'.[15] In this respect, his image of Johannesburg consolidated the Americanisation of urban African experience that the magazine *Drum* had already popularised and mythologised. There were also more specific references from 'Up my alley' that found their way into the strip. Started during the Trial's preliminary stages, these references included Johannesburg's Chinatown (Fig. 2, p. 177); 'a quartet of the "Ghost squad"', a plain clothes police snatch squad that enforced the pass laws, (Fig. 3, p. 178); the ruins of Sophiatown, the site of Johannesburg's equivalent to the Harlem Renaissance and already destroyed by the Group Areas Act (Fig. 4, 178); Vrededorp, former home of the novelist Peter Abrahams, now on the eve of its destruction 'awaiting the Group Areas axe'.[16] Thus by the time *Little Libby* appeared, La Guma had a useful 'bank' of textual images with which *New Age* readers who had followed his 'Up my alley' column would already be familiar. Some, like the *Drum*-oriented images, were public property while others, based on his own writing and sense of humour, gave the strip its personal trademark.

During late 1956 and early 1957, the defendants were held in the Johannesburg Fort. The trialists tried to use the time constructively. While some turned to exercise, La Guma completed a modest portfolio of life drawings. He was not the only one to do so. Sketches by Ike Horvitch, CPSA national chairperson at the time of its banning, appeared in *New Age* during the course of the trial.[17] Fellow trialist Alfred Hutchinson had this to say about the period and some of its players:

> A fortnight of waiting. The fraternity of strong men in the 'lower house' building muscles… Joe Modise in his enthusiasm landing up in the prison hospital. Robert Resha taking longer rests than exercise spells. 'General China' Chamile whittling at his wooden spoon. Mosie Moolla constantly posing in the hope that Alex la Guma will deign to sketch him.[18]

Preliminary hearings started during 1957 in Johannesburg, and later moved to Pretoria where the trial proper began. There were frequent recesses during which La Guma returned to Cape Town, and several instances when he and other trialists were detained without trial for several months. La Guma and his colleagues continued with conventional news reporting whenever possible, but he and other journalists on *New Age* had to find discourses and forms of representation that could travel well between Cape Town, Johannesburg and Pretoria and which could adapt to unpredictable interruptions. At the beginning of 1959, he was in Cape Town, in April he was in Pretoria, and by June he was back in Cape Town.[19] From this perspective, the increasing number of reviews that La Guma wrote for *New Age*, his 'Up my alley' column and *Little Libby* were convenient and pragmatic solutions.[20]

The reviews have additional significance, however, for they provide some indications of his thinking about accessibility, representation of races and political correctness in art. They therefore offer some insight into La Guma's aesthetic at this time. His review of Emlyn Williams' recitations of Dylan Thomas' poetry before a multiracial audience at the Bantu Men's Social Centre in Johannesburg appeared on the same page as his short story 'Etude' and articulates similar concerns. Both deal with the artist who had brought 'great talent and art to an audience, the majority of whom hardly get a chance to enjoy the pleasures of fine art'.[21] Here La Guma does not argue that 'folk' art is the product of an egalitarian society, or that there is no distinction between 'popular' and 'fine' art, but that a relationship between performer and audience which is unmediated and in which they share the same outlook is important. Much the same could be said of comics – a popular graphic and narrative form immediately and directly enjoyed by many and whose conventions are widely understood. Two years later, in the midst of the comic itself, he confronted the implications of negative racial stereotypes in a production by the Cape Town based Eoan Group. The group, whose performances ranged from the 'heavy' *La Traviata* to the 'light' *Rio Rita*, faced withdrawal of state funding if it continued to perform for multiracial audiences. La Guma described the musical comedy *Rio Rita* as a 'romantic tale of Texas Rangers and bandits in Old Mexico'. He acknowledged that the 'more socially conscious members of the audience might have been jarred now and then by the reference to Mexicans as "greasers"', but felt that 'on the whole' the event was 'great fun'.[22] It would be simplistic to dismiss the Eoan Group as simply a symptom of conservative and 'respectable' coloured aspiration to white society through high culture, for La Guma saw its refusal to impose racial segregation on its audiences in exchange for state funding as a demonstration that the nature of the audience and its relationship to the performance could mitigate negative or problematic aspects of content. From La Guma's perspective, then, stereotypes in *Little Libby* were acceptable because its *New Age* audience was progressive, multiracial and 'socially conscious'.

La Guma's picaresque comic strip story appeared in *New Age* every week from 5 March to 12 November 1959. It combined features of caricature and animated film cartoon with comments on the concerns and campaigns of the Congress Alliance. It was topical in another respect, for at least four of the characters were named after people involved in the treason trial. Mustapha Moonsamy and Liberation Chabalala (aka Little Libby) were derived from Treason Trialists K. Moonsamy and 'Chubby' Tshabalala, whom La Guma had described as 'a young man with an elfish face and an indomitable spirit'. 'Sgt Shark of the Special Branch' came from Sgt Sharp, a prosecution witness whom the trialists reviled as both ugly and stupid, as La Guma's sarcastic description of him as 'matinée idol of the treason trial' suggests (Fig. 2, p. 177). In 1960, towards the end of the trial, the presiding judges described Sharp as a 'dangerous witness' and struck out his evidence.[23] Fourthly, the newspaper *New Age* also featured in the story, because as a 'legal person' it too was on trial along with at least eight of its employees.[24] The strip also enabled La Guma to develop characters such as Oom Veldskoen van der Mielieblaar (Fig. 6, p. 179), who reappeared two years later as an inhabitant of La Guma's mythical backveld Afrikaner republic of Pampoen-oner-die-bos.[25] Like 'Up my alley', *Little Libby* gave La Guma more freedom of political and narrative expression than his prose, or the times, usually permitted, and by using satire as a common denominator, he established a symbiotic relationship between his comics and journalism during this period.

In the comic the relationships between caricatures, cartoons, concerns and campaigns were articulated in three ways. Firstly, within the narrative there are several references to political events and debates during the late 1950s. SACTU's 1957 campaign for a minimum wage of £1-a-day occurred after the start of the Treason Trial and was significant in at least two respects. It demonstrated continued resistance to the apartheid state and it represented a departure from the relatively limited industrial unionism that had characterised African labour organisation since the 1930s. La Guma may also have had in mind the Congress Alliance stay-at-homes of 1957 and 1958. While the former complemented SACTU's campaign and contributed to a raise in wages, the latter occurred in the year of a general election, and on this occasion the state responded with much greater violence. Consequently, it was regarded as less successful than its predecessor.[26]

Secondly, we can understand aspects of the comic in the context of debates about the political value and significance of the boycott as a strategic or tactical intervention. One element of this was the 1958 general elections – the first election after the Separate Representation of Voters Act had come into force. This act restricted the political participation of coloureds, the majority of whom lived in the then Cape Province, to qualified indirect representation. Initally SACPO decided to boycott the election, and this saw a brief convergence of interest between SACPO and its traditional 'left' opponent the Non-European Unity Movement (NEUM) which in principle advocated a complete boycott of any institution or process associated with apartheid. However, the ANC's desire to form a united anti-Nationalist front saw SACPO reverse its decision and participate in the elections by fielding progressive white candidates. As a SACPO executive member and journalist on *New Age*, La Guma unsuccessfully tried to reverse coloured political opinion on this issue before SACPO's executive committee formally changed the organisation's policy.[27] Coupled with the failure of SACPO's candidates, this further divided coloured opposition to apartheid between the 'popular front' approach of SACPO and its 'left' opponent the Non-European Unity Movement (NEUM).

In the comic strip, this debate was played out through the Bethal farm labour scandal of 1959 to which the first five published episodes of the strip refer. White potato farmers 'bought' imprisoned pass law offenders, and forced them to work on their farms. *New Age* covered this story in detail, and the scandal led to a potato boycott, which started in June that year. Another aspect of the boycott debate can be found within the panels that contain graffiti, pamphlets and posters that publicise meetings and call on people to observe the stay-at-home, not to eat potatoes (Fig. 5, p. 179), or not to buy goods produced by firms that supported the National Party. In contrast to the NEUM's blanket boycott policy motivated by the mutually reinforcing combination of a politically marginal position and a desire for ideological purity, the Congress Alliance felt that its boycott had 'tremendous potential' because it gave 'the man [sic] in the street an immediate and effective way of hitting back against the innumerable injustices and hardships inflicted upon him by the Government'. The policy had particular significance for the Cape, La Guma's political main political constituency and the base for elements of manufacturing and finance capital that supported the Nationalist Party.[28] Simultaneously disarming and politicising, the posters within the panels add texture to the narrative's reliance on a combination of the political and the picaresque. In the comic's political context, it is therefore possible that La Guma's use of the potato boycott posters was a way of distinguishing the Congress and NEUM use of the boycott.[29]

Thirdly, there is the presence of a small mouse. Sometimes the mouse comments on events or exhorts readers to political action (Fig. 6, p. 179), or participates in the action and intervenes in events that occur in the main panels (Fig. 7, p. 180). Like Ignatz, Herriman's creation of 1910 in *Krazy Kat*, La Guma's mouse displays little respect for the idea of a stable relationship between caption and picture that comprises the primary convention of comics. Like Ignatz, La Guma's mouse also challenges the established order by enacting the empowerment of the powerless. This gives the strip an instability and unpredictability that offsets its general reliance on slapstick and mock drama.[30] Later, his semi-autobiographical prison novel *The Stone Country* marked the return of the mouse in a more serious guise, though even here its links with popular culture and cartoons were obvious. In *The Stone Country* the narrator declares that watching the contest between cat and mouse in the prison yard, again a symbol of oppressor versus oppressed, 'had been as good as going to the pictures, in a place like this' prison.[31] Similarly, in *A Walk in the Night* Willieboy encounters the corpse of Uncle doughty 'with the suddenness of a shot from a horror film', and in *And a Threefold Cord* La Guma describes a dilapidated door as 'dark and ugly as that of a haunted house in a movie picture'.[32]

In La Guma's total output there were very few exceptions to the temporary or enacted surrender of the control of narrative or argument found in the comic, and they appear to have been confined to his early work. One of these occurs in 'Ten Days in Roeland Street Jail'. Here he reports on the experiences of a first time remand prisoner who has arranged for a home-cooked Sunday dinner to be smuggled into his communal cell:

> 'The basin of food was there, but crawling with cockroaches. There were really thousands of them, rustling and clicking over the food, gorging themselves. My stomach turned, and all my appetite for Sunday dinner left me.' But not so with his fellow prisoners. What? This was real rice, roast meat and vegetables. Huis kos [literally, house food]. To hell with the cockroaches. They brushed off the vermin and got stuck in.[33]

Here a combination of rapid discursive shifts, movement between English and Afrikaans, literal translations of Afrikaans idiom into English, changes between direct speech, reported speech and authoritative narrative voice all enable La Guma to blend the perspectives of narrator and characters so that we understand each character from his own perspective (the piece is about prison conditions for coloured men) while remaining receptive to the narrator's commentary, before finally returning to the viewpoint of an omniscient narrator. La Guma did not or could not reproduce these characteristics in his longer prose fiction.

With formal art training, a background in journalism, an enjoyment of popular cultural forms and a path to novel writing via the short story, La Guma seems to have sufficiently absorbed and played with comic strip conventions to produce a recognizable though unevenly plotted work. If Eisner's advice to prospective comic strip artists and script writers, that 'a steady diet of reading, particularly in the short story form, is essential to plotting and narrative skills' holds good, then La Guma was well prepared for this medium despite a lack of formal training in comic strip illustration and scripting.[34] As a comparison between characters such as Rhumba, Little Libby and

Mustapha Moonsamy suggests, he also appears to have been influenced by developments in American newspaper comic characterisation and representation in the late 1930s. This approach facilitated the combination of characters drawn in different styles.[35] La Guma's characters fall into two broad groups, though many of them were drawn with the same stick-like simplicity. There were 'stock' characters like Kasper Katchum, Oom Veldskoen (Fig. 6, p.179), the curvaceous Rhumba (Fig. 3, p. 178), a large shebeen queen (Fig. 2, p.177), a Chinese laundry man (Fig. 2, p. 177), a pot bellied policeman speaking in broken English/Afrikaans, sharp suited tsotsis (Fig. 4, p. 178), a gang leader called Chopper (Fig. 8, p. 180) and a thick-lipped African car thief named Bongo. While most had incidental roles, others such as Rhumba or Chopper were more important and interacted with 'individual' characters like Little Libby, Mustapha Moonsamy and Sgt Shark. Their names required only slight alliterative adjustments to ensure that *New Age* readers familiar with Treason Trial proceedings would recognise the real individuals and enjoy the humour of their transformations. Simultaneously, the relationship between 'stock' and 'individual' characters in the comic also throws some light on La Guma's later novels, for as Lewis Nkosi observed of the latter, 'a formula begins to emerge: minor characters, hustlers, surly frustrated cons and self-deceivers, continuously appear and reappear, orchestrated against men of serious political commitment'.[36]

In the form of curvaceous heroines who always landed up in trouble and had to be rescued, Rhumba had several precedents. Her name also carried political implications, for the 'rhumba' or 'rumba' is a dance that supposedly originated in Cuba, and it is possible that through this name La Guma was making an indirect reference to the Cuban revolution which had seen Castro take power earlier that year.[37] It is also possible that La Guma used the name Rhumba to introduce references to working class coloured culture from the Cape, for the rhumba features in at least one Kaapse *moppie*. The latter is an often ribald or derisive coloured street song often associated with oblique attacks on authority.[38] If La Guma used Rhumba to 'import' elements of coloured working class culture into the Johannesburg-based story then it is also possible, as fellow *Quartet* contributor Alf Wannenburgh has suggested, that the name Little Libby was an oblique *homage* to *Lieberstein*, a recently launched popular cheap wine of the sort which another of La Guma's contemporaries, the poet Dennis Brutus, remembers that La Guma enjoyed.[39]

Another convention from the 1930s that La Guma drew on was the use of 'descriptive phrases and subheads' for narrative continuity, though he did not deploy these consistently. The phrases and subheads are in mechanical type below the hand drawn masthead (Fig. 2, p. 177). They correspond to the authoritative disembodied voice at the start and end of each episode of a radio and cinema serial that frames the narrative and summarises significant events from the previous episode.[40] Within the story itself there were sometimes panels through which the narrator intervened to provide additional continuity, onomatapoeiac sound effects, or instructions to readers such as 'Interval'. Again this suggests that films and the *experience* of being in a cinema were strong but parodied influences, and that La Guma used this shared experience to draw in and alienate his readers by using a trope which that was familiar yet also interrupted the narrative at unexpected points (Fig. 6, p. 179). Not all of these panels contained the mouse, and generally they were narrower than those that carried the action. Often they were reversed into white text on a black background. However there were also points in a tier when he dispensed with panels, thereby establishing a stronger contrast with its surroundings and stressing the message it communicated (Figs 1, 6, pp. 177 & 179).

By today's standards, La Guma's use of perspective and narrative compression, i.e., the tendency in comics to combine a number of events in one panel, was restrained. The pace of his story is even and sedate, with seldom more than one event per panel. In most panels, except when characters run, the observer is at eye level with the events, most of which are set in the middle distance and with three-quarters of the body depicted. However, when La Guma wanted to make a particular point he used a variety of techniques. These included rapid shifts between bird's eye and worm's eye views to communicate a sense of movement and confusion (Fig. 1, p. 177), close ups of a political leaflet to stress its importance, of a face to highlight emotions or of a butcher's cleaver to emphasise danger (Fig. 8, p. 180). In the latter case, he combined a close up with a sharp distinction between bright light and darkness that he could have copied from gangster films in black and white, for this part of the comic strip takes place in Chopper's headquarters just before a robbery.

It is difficult to determine exactly when La Guma produced each episode of the strip, though we know that by the end of the story he had no more than three instalments in advance. The first five episodes cover political events of 1959 and 1957 combined. From there onwards preparations for the 1957 and/or 1958 one-day stay-at-home provide the continuity of the narrative and its political goal, while Libby's diversion with the gangsters is a subplot. The posters advocating a potato boycott first appear in episode 16 (on 18 June 1959), three issues after the boycott started. While adding texture, they remain incidental to the narrative, and could have been added later to provide greater immediacy or to vary the source of the strip's humour. If this is the case then it is possible that La Guma first conceptualised the start at what is now around episode six when Libby arrives in Johannesburg (like La Guma himself at the start of the Treason Trial) and that the first five episodes, which combine 1959, 1958 and 1957 events, were conceptualised later but appeared first. While there is no proof for this hypothesis, the omniscient narrator effects transition between episodes five and six in a clumsy manner with the phrase 'And our hero is off on a new adventure', whereas episodes six to 37 display a far more integrated narrative and hang together more satisfactorily though they are less dramatic. In this respect, Chandramohan's desire to insert the comic into his 'trans-ethnic' reading leads him to exaggerate La Guma's use of slogans such as '"Asihamba" ["as we go along"] as a link' between episodes.[41] Whatever the sequence of production, this combination of past and present has a paradoxical effect intrinsic to satire and other forms of oblique political commentary. They give the comic political relevance *and* prevent us from making a direct connection between subject matter and the immediate political concerns of the readers. Like La Guma's use of names from the Treason Trial, he created an environment that was simultaneously 'real' and 'imaginary'.

In the order of appearance the story runs as follows: as the dawn breaks Little Libby, an African schoolboy, sets off for school; he is kidnapped by 'Kasper Katchum' and sold to an exploitative farmer, 'Oom Veldskoen van der Mielieblaar'; Libby mobilises the workers who rebel against oppressive working conditions and demand '£1-a-day'; they release the farmer's 'prize red bull', and it chases away the farmer (episodes 1–5); Libby then goes to Johannesburg where he is befriended by the curvaceous Rhumba; the 'Ghost Squad' arrest her, but she is rescued by the love-struck Mustapha Moonsamy and his *New Age* colleagues (episodes 6–15); meanwhile 'Sergeant Shark of the Special Branch' follows Libby to a shebeen where he joins in the festivities and is arrested in the subsequent police raid (episodes 16–25); Libby escapes the raid and meets up with Mustapha and Rhumba; they persuade him to 'do some work for the stay-at-home'; armed with leaflets, Libby meets members of a criminal gang who use promises of wealth to persuade him to join them in a robbery; the gangsters dump his leaflets and he meets Chopper; the police interrupt the robbery and Libby escapes; as the dawn breaks over the city he recovers his leaflets and distributes them to enthusiastic workers (episodes 26–37). The effect of the stay-at-home is not covered. Given the relative success of the 1957 stay-at-home, the abrupt and anti-climactic ending might suggest that La Guma was less than happy with the results of the 1958 stay-at-home.[42] The comic ends here without any conclusion, and while he does not appear to have been detained, he seems to have been out of circulation for a while. Perhaps La Guma needed to finish *A Walk in the Night*, for two weeks after *Little Libby* had ended, he wrote in 'Up my alley' of 'three weeks of relief from the salt mines' and complained that '[r]eturn to civilisation also entails reading back numbers of newspapers'.[43] As his first long narrative, *Little Libby* forced La Guma to confront issues of closure. This was a problem that he had not yet encountered and would not encounter again in this exact form. Without implying that La Guma conceptualised it in these terms, we can define its parameters. He had to end a story that was longer than a news article, more plot-driven than a short story, and 'symbolic' and 'real' in a different way from prose fiction. Simultaneously, as much as any progressive political or historial novelist, his references to real events in which his readers had participated obliged him to provide an ending that did not contradict what his readers already knew had happened to the stay-at-home without concluding on a pessimistic note.[44] Like 'Up my alley', whose first and last entries contained by the same quotation from Tom Paine on the need for true democrats as opposed to fair-weather ones, *Little Libby* begins with the dawn, when Liberation should arise, and ends with the dawn when the people should rise up against oppression. In their combinations of symbols drawn from the natural world and hints of political developments the endings of his first two longer prose fictions were not dissimilar.

According to Blanche La Guma, *Little Libby* was

> …a great seller. It was quite strange. It [*New Age*] was a very serious paper and to bring out a lighter side in the paper was this [comic] script on *Little Libby*. Eventually it emerged that the sales were doing quite well because people were trying to get hold of *Little Libby*…because people are human beings before they are politicians or revolutionaries…Something light just sort of lifted it [*New Age*] and gave the people a break of reading this heavy stuff.[45]

According to records held by the Audit Bureau of Circulation of South Africa, sales for the first half of 1958 were 18,844, and 21,509 for the second half. They dropped to 13,407 during the first half of 1959, but rose to 18,075 in the second half of that year. Unfortunately, no figures for 1960 were available.[46] The comic strip *did* coincide with a slight rise in registered sales, though for a paper that relied increasingly on informal distribution networks actual sales could have been larger.

While there were no published criticisms about the presence of a *comic* in *New Age*, the joint authors of one letter described *Little Libby* as 'exceptionally interesting right up to the time he wins his fight with the farmer [episodes 1–5]. One could follow a definite trend. But as he comes to the big city…[episodes 6 onwards] one is at a complete loss'. They complained that from there on the story seemed to 'lack humour and punch. Surely', they argued, 'there must be some trend in the story which should hold one's interest.' They suggested that La Guma 'should consider improving it'.[47] They may have had a point. The first five episodes appear to conform more readily to the conventions of successful comic narrative formula, with the resolution of a small crisis midway followed by a concluding 'cliff-hanger' that creates suspense for the next episode. Secondly, pre-publicity in *New Age* for the strip showed two characters, Sgt Shark who would only appear in episode 16 and Frik[k]adel, the Afrikaans word for a rissole and possibly a local version of Popeye's friend Wimpy, who never appeared at all. At a time when La Guma's prose fiction was in a state of transition from journalism and short stories to the longer novella *A Walk in the Night*, the problems that *Little Libby's* critics detected suggest that at this stage La Guma had a greater capacity for characterisation and representation than for narrative and sustained plots.

Nor were they alone in this view of La Guma's work at this stage. In an early review of *A Walk in the Night*, Wole Soyinka referred to La Guma's 'theme – I cannot call it plot in the usual sense of that word', while *New Age* editor Brian Bunting's positive assessment of La Guma's characterisation was balanced by his view of its plot as 'a mere framework on which are strung a series of brilliant sketches'.[48] Not everyone would agree with Soyinka and Bunting, but by design or default La Guma's first attempt at sustained narrative, which is also his only major surviving work of popular culture, provided him with the space to experiment with the relationships between historical and narrative time, plot and characterisation, and with various authorial voices and narrative perspectives.

This article does not argue that in *Little Libby* La Guma consciously set out to produce a 'graphic novel', but that as his first published work of extended fiction, and his only one in a popular genre in which very few South African writers have ever worked, *Little Libby* has an important place in the history of South African popular culture and in the study of La Guma's work. Simultaneously, the traffic in images and representations between his pieces on Johannesburg during the Treason Trial, the comic strip and the subsequent 'Up my alley' column' suggests that La Guma's political and aesthetic world view could shift from the serious to the quirky and the anti-authoritarian, sometimes by simply representing the same situation in different media. La Guma drew on recent and contemporary events and characters, and exploited the available conventions of cartoon and cinematic narrative and representation. Politically and graphically, therefore, *Little Libby* was very much a product of its time.

My assessment of some of the ways in which La Guma handled narrative, representation and closure in *Little Libby* could substantiate the argument for continuity between La Guma's journalism and fiction, but it also suggests that at a relatively early stage in his writing career La Guma experimented with a variety of representational media and genres, and that if he consciously chose specific narrative strategies for his first extended piece of fiction, then there were several that he did not or could not readily transfer to his longer prose works. Where there are correspondences and continuities between his comics and the novels that followed *A Walk in the Night*, these seem to have taken the form of references to, rather than use of popular cultural genres such as films, cartoons and other comics; his own journalism; formulae governing the relationship between 'stock' and 'individual' characters. The comic's links with and differences from his other works means that the comic cannot be dismissed as an intriguing detour from La Guma's self proclaimed steady progress along a route marked by the classic works of nineteenth and twentieth-century realism, naturalism and progressive political engagement. These works were extremely influential and have made a significant contribution to South African literature, but this should not blind us to another La Guma of popular culture, slapstick humour and the playful subversion of narrative and representational convention.

Endnotes

[1] This article is an amended version of an earlier piece, 'Art and the Man: La Guma's Comics and Paintings' (*Critical Survey* 11: 2 (1999)). My thanks to Nahem Yousaf for comments on that version. La Guma's major prose works are: *A Walk in the Night* (Oxford, Heinemann: 1968), *And a Threefold Cord* (London, Kliptown Books: 1988), *The Stone Country* (Oxford, Heinemann: 1978), *In the Fog of the Seasons' End* (Oxford, Heinemann: 1979), *A Soviet Journey* (Moscow, Progress Publishers: 1978), *Time of the Butcherbird* (Oxford, Heinemann: 1979).

[2] For Gorky see B. Chandramohan, *A Study in Trans-Ethnicity in Modern South Africa: The Writings of Alex la Guma 1925-1985* (Lewiston, Mellen Press: 1992) and J. Mkhize, 'Social Realism in Alex La Guma's Longer Fiction' (University of Natal, PhD thesis: 1998); for Dostoyevsky see L. Nkosi, 'Fiction by Black South Africans: Richard Rive; Bloke Modisane; Ezekiel Mphahlele; Alex La Guma', in U. Beier (ed.), *Introduction to African Literature: An anthology of critical writing* (London, Longman: 1979) p. 227; for American Naturalism see J.M. Coetzee, 'Man's Fate in the Novels of Alex La Guma', in D. Atwell (ed.), *Doubling the Point: J.M. Coetzee Essays and Interviews* (Cambridge Mass.: Harvard University Press: 1992), p. 345.

[3] W. Soyinka, 'The Fight for Human Existence', *Post* (Johannesburg) 3 June 1962; W. Carpenter, '"Ovals, Spheres, Ellipses and Sundry Bulges": Alex La Guma Imagines the Human Body', *Research in African Literatures* No. 22, Vol. 4, 1992, p. 80; B. Chandramohan, *A Study in Trans-Ethnicity in Modern South Africa: The Writings of Alex la Guma 1925-1985*, p. 20; S. Whitman, 'A Story of Resistance', *African Communist* No. 77, 1979, p. 113.

[4] C. Abrahams, *Alex la Guma* (Boston, Mass., G.K. Hall: 1985), pp. 3, 7–8.

[5] Interview Blanche la Guma/Roger Field, 17 April 1998.

[6] Correspondence George Herman/Roger Field, 19 February 1997; interview Irwin Combrinck, 5 February 1997; interview Blanche La Guma/ Roger Field, 17 April 1998; C. Abrahams, *Alex La Guma*, p. ix.

[7] J. M. Coetzee, 'Man's Fate in the Novels of Alex La Guma', p. 345.

[8] G. Cornwell, 'Protest Fiction: an approach to Alex La Guma' (Rhodes University, M.A. thesis: 1979) pp. 45–6.

[9] B. Chandramohan, *A Study in Trans-Ethnicity in Modern South Africa: The Writings of Alex La Guma*, pp. 20, 120, 173–6.

[10] Interview Ray Alexander/Roger Field, 17 June 1993.

[11] *The Liberator*, Feb 1937; A. La Guma, *Jimmy la Guma: A Biography* (Cape Town: Friends of the SA Library, 1997), p. 61.

[12] Correspondence George Herman/Roger Field, 19 February 1997; R.R. Edgar (ed.), *An African American in South Africa: The Travel Notes of Ralph J. Bunche* (Johannesburg, Witwatersrand University Press: 1992), p. 333.

[13] Correspondence Sadie Forman/Roger Field, 21 April 1993; interview Peter Clarke/Roger Field, 26 October 1996.

[14] J. Coplans, *Roy Lichtenstein* (New York, Praeger Publishers: 1972); J. Coplans et al., *Andy Warhol* (London, Weidenfeld and Nicolson: 1994).

[15] A. Odendaal and R. Field (eds) *Liberation Chabalala: The World of Alex La Guma* (Bellville, Mayibuye Press: 1993), p. 51 (*New Age*, 23 May 1957); *Liberation Chabalala* contains the complete *Little Libby* (pp. 61-98); all references to the comic strip are from this book; Figs 1-8 refer to pp. 67, 79, 68, 88, 77, 63, 78, 90.

[16] *Liberation Chabalala*, p. 59-60 (*Fighting Talk*, June 1957); *Liberation Chabalala*, p. 58 (*New Age*, 16 May 1957).

[17] B. Bunting, *Moses Kotane: South African Revolutionary* (London, Inkululeko Publications: 1975); see *New Age*, 3 January 1957, 24 January 1957, 21 February 1957.

[18] C. Abrahams, p. viii; A. Hutchinson, 'The Night Marching to the Morrow…'. In *SA's Treason Trial* (Johannesburg, Treason Trial Defence Fund: 1957?) pp. 4-5.

[19] *New Age*, 22 January 1959, 23 April 1959, 12 June 1959.

[20] *New Age*, 24 October 1957.

[21] *New Age*, 24 January 1957.

[22] *New Age*, 13 September 1959.

[23] *Liberation Chabalala*, pp. xxxiii, (*New Age*, 23 January 1958), 37 (*New Age*, 31 October 1957), *New Age*, 17 March 1960.

[24] *New Age*, 13 December 1956.

[25] *Liberation Chabalala*, p. 213 (*New Age*, 31 August 1961); for a fuller treatment of La Guma's Pampoen-onder-die-bos pieces see J. Mkhize, 'Social Realism in Alex La Guma's Longer Fiction'.

[26] T. Lodge, *Black Politics in South Africa since 1945* (Johannesburg, Ravan: 1983) pp. 193–5.

[27] *New Age*, 19 December 1957; *New Age*, 26 December 1957.

[28] M. Harmel, '"*Die Burger*" is Right … Boycott IS a Two-Edged Sword' and R. Segal, 'The Power of the Pound' in *Fighting Talk*, May 1959, pp. 3-4.

[29] A. La Guma, '"Ah, Dis Die Economic Boycott"', in *Liberation Chabalala* pp. 130–31 (*New Age*, 18 June 1959).

[30] P. McDonnell et al., *Krazy Kat: The Comic Art of George Herriman* (New York: Harry Abrams, 1986); W. Eisner, *Comics and Sequential Art* (Tamarac: Poorhouse Press, 1985), p. 8; E. Shannon, '"That we may mis-unda-stend each udda": The Rhetoric of *Krazy Kat*', *Journal of Popular Culture*, Vol. 29, No 2, 1995.

[31] A. La Guma, *The Stone Country*, p. 127.

[32] A. La Guma, *A Walk in the Night*, p. 34; *And a Threefold Cord*, p. 60.

[33] A. La Guma, 'Ten Days in Roeland Street Jail', in *Liberation Chabalala*, p.16 (*New Age* 27 September 1956).

[34] W. Eisner, *Comics and Sequential Art*, p. 148.

[35] B. Blackbeard and M. Williams (eds), *The Smithsonian Collection of Newspaper Comics* (Washington DC, Smithsonian Institute Press: 1977), pp. 132 and 53–4.

[36] L. Nkosi, 'Southern Africa: Protest and Commitment', in L. Nkosi, *Tasks and Masks: Themes and Styles of African Literature* (Harlow, Longman: 1981), p.85.

[37] R. Castledon, *World History* (London, Parragon: 1994) p. 574.

[38] J. Opland (ed.), *Words that Circle Words: A Choice of South African Oral Poetry* (Johannesburg, AD Donker: 1992) p. 102. The full text of the *moppie* is: 'Ma, where's Pa?/Pa's behind the hotel./What's Pa doing?/Pa's got a bottle./Come dance with me the skimellha,/The skimellha, the rhumba./Come dance with me the skimellha,/The skimellha, the rhumba.' See also C. Winberg, 'Satire, Slavery and the "Ghoemaliedjies" of the Cape Muslims', *New Contrast*, Vol. 19 No. 4 1991.

[39] A. Wannenburgh, 'Memories of Richard', *New Contrast*, Vol. 18, No. 3, 1990, p. 29; interview Alf Wannenburgh/Roger Field, 25 May 1998; D. Brutus, 'African Thought: A Tribute to Alex La Guma', in C. Abrahams (ed.), *Memories of Home: The Writings of Alex La Guma* (Trenton, Africa World Press: 1991) p. 4; D. Biggs, *The 1999 South African Plonk Buyer's Guide* (Cape Town, Ampersand Press: 1999) p. 50.

[40] I am grateful to Gabeba Baderoon for help in clarifying this point.

[41] B. Chandramohan, *A Study in Trans-Ethnicity in Modern South Africa: The Writings of Alex La Guma*, p. 174.

[42] T. Lodge, *Black Politics in South Africa Since 1945* (Johannesburg, Ravan Press: 1983), p. 194.

[43] *New Age*, 26 November 1959.

[44] N. Visser, 'Audience and Closure in *The Grapes of Wrath*', in *Studies in American Fiction*, Vol. 22, No. 1, 1994, pp. 30–4.

[45] B. La Guma/B. Chandramohan interview. In B. Chandramohan, *A Study in Trans-Ethnicity in Modern South Africa: The Writings of Alex La Guma*, p. 205.

[46] Audit Bureau of Circulation of South Africa, 'Certificates of Average Nett Sales' 1958, 1959 (Johannesburg?).

[47] *New Age*, 11 June 1959; F. Barker, *Comics: ideology, power and the critics* (Manchester: Manchester University Press, 1989), p. 37.

[48] *Post*, 3 June 1962; *New Age*, 9 August 1962.

Primary Text 7
Facsimiles of *Little Libby* Comic Strips by Alex La Guma

Reference
Reproduced from *New Age*, March–November 1959

Fig. 1

Fig. 2

LITTLE LIBBY - THE ADVENTURES of LIBERATION CHABALALA
by Alex La Guma
THOSE BLIKSEMS WENT THIS WAY!
HAVE WE GIVEN THEM THE SLIP?
OPSKUT! IF WE DON'T CATCH THEM WE WON'T BE PROMOTED TO THE IMMORALITY SQUAD
ACH, MAN! IT WOULD BE AWFUL IF WE MISSED THAT CHANCE!
LET'S GO THIS WAY! HURRY!
! ?
BONK!
YOU WANNA BUY A WATCH—CHEAP?

Fig. 3

LITTLE LIBBY - THE ADVENTURES of LIBERATION CHABALALA
by Alex La Guma
GEE! IF IT WEREN'T FOR THESE LEAFLETS I COULD MAKE A PILE OF CASH —
AH! THERE YOU ARE LITTLE FELLER — WHAT YOU GOT UNDER YOUR ARM?
I'M GOING TO HAND OUT LEAFLETS IN THE TOWNSHIP!
YOU DON'T SAY! WELL THAT'S JUST WHERE WE GOING, TOO — RIGHT, SCARFACE?
RIGHT!
SO WE'LL JUST STROLL ALONG WITH YOU —
AND WATCH YOU WASTING YOUR TIME!
?
YOU MEAN TO SAY YOU RATHER HAND OUT PAPERS THAN MAKE EASY MONEY?
ER-
MAYBE WE OUGHT TO MAKE UP YOUR MIND FOR YOU, PAL! GIMME THAT!
IT'S ALL FOR YOUR OWN GOOD, CHUM!
ASIHAMBA!
STAY AT HOME

Fig. 4

LITTLE LIBBY
THE ADVENTURES of LIBERATION CHABALALA
by Alex La Guma
Rhumba and the boys have escaped from the Ghost Squad.
I THINK WE'VE GIVEN THEM THE SLIP — NOW TO FIND LITTLE LIBBY!
MEANWHILE LITTLE LIBBY IS LEAVING NEW AGE OFFICE
I WONDER WHAT'S HAPPENED TO RHUMBA AND MUSTAPHA
HAIRDRESSER
BUT WHO IS THIS ON OBSERV-ATION DUTY OPPOSITE?
EAT MORE FISH AND
SERGEANT SHARK OF THE SPECIAL BRANCH
THAT'S A VERY SUSPICIOUS LOOKING CHARACTER!
WELL, I THINK I'LL TAKE A WALK AND LOOK AROUND
?
HE'S PROBABLY INVOLVED IN SOME TREASONABLE CONSPIRACY!
HEH! HEH!
SMASH POTATOES
MIGHT AS WELL GO THIS WAY

Fig. 5

LITTLE LIBBY
THE ADVENTURES of LIBERATION CHABALALA
by Alex La Guma
LITTLE LIBBY HAS BEEN SOLD TO OOM VELD-SKOEN VAN DER MEALIE-BLAAR AND....
..PUT TO WORK
THESE KAFFER BOYS ARE VERY LAZY— THEY OUGHT TO BE MADE TO WORK AT LEAST 25 HOURS A DAY
STEM
NASIONAAL
KOFFI
BACHELOR'S QUARTERS
PHEW!
BEDTIME....
INTERVAL
READ NEW AGE!
BUT THIS CAN'T GO ON!
PROTEST!
WHAT AM I DOING HERE? I SHOULD BE AT SCHOOL!
!
LISTEN, YOU! I'VE HAD ENOUGH! WHAT'S MORE, I'M QUITTING!
GRR! YOU CAN'T DO THIS TO ME! WHAT'S GOING TO HAPPEN TO MY FARM WITHOUT CHEAP LABOUR?
CALL OUT THE SKIET KOMMANDOS! WHERE'S MY SJAMBOK! BRING MY GUN AND HOSEPIPE!
AFRIKA!

Fig. 6

LITTLE LIBBY – THE ADVENTURES of LIBERATION CHABALALA
by Alex La Guma
LITTLE LIBBY IS BEING FOLLOWED BY SERGEANT SHARK
DON'T BUY NAT GOODS!
AH! READING SUBVERSIVE LITERATURE ALREADY!
BUY NEW AGE!
WHAT'S GOING ON INSIDE HERE?
ASIHAMBE
COME ON IN, YOUNG MAN, AND WATCH THE FOLKS DANCE
THANKS, AUNTIE I'VE ALWAYS WANTED TO SEE THE ROCK 'N ROLL
NO SHOOTING PLEASE!
HERE'S A YOUNG VISITUH! MAKE HIM AT HOME, BOYS 'N GALS!
WELLCOME STRANGER!
SNIFF! SNIFF! HE WENT THIS WAY I'M SURE!
SNIFF SNIFF

Fig. 7

LITTLE LIBBY – THE ADVENTURES of LIBERATION CHABALALA
by Alex La Guma
COME RIGHT INSIDE, GENTS! COME RIGHT INSIDE!
HULLO, BOSS! WE FOUND A KID FOR YOU!
GOOD! LET ME TAKE A LOOK AT HIM! HEH! HEH!
NOW LITTLE BOY, DON'T BE SCARED! BOSS CHOPPER DON'T EAT LITTLE BOYS! HE'S YOUR FRIEND—HEH! HEH! HEH!
ALL WE WANT YOU TO DO IS A LITTLE FAVOUR—AND YOU'LL GET PAID WELL, SEE?
ALL WILL GO WELL WITH YOU—YOU'LL HAVE MONEY, NICE THINGS TO EAT, AS LONG AS YOU DO WHAT ME AND THE BOYS SAY—
BUT IF YOU DONT—!
HEH! HEH!

Fig. 8

SARAH NUTTALL
Reading Lives

Reference
Adapted from 'Reading in the Lives and Writing of Black South African Women', *Journal of Southern African Studies* 20 (1), 1994: 85–98

Between 1990 and 1992 I did a series of interviews with black South African women about reading.[1] Looking back at those interviews now, they seem even more revealing than they did at the time. What I find particularly useful, returning to them, is that in the discussions the women range across all of their reading – popular fiction, including romances, 'serious' fiction, both South African and other, non-fiction, newspapers, journals and so on – as well as making references to film, music and television as stories of a different kind. This offers a productivity of readings which studies of reading seldom allow: most studies of popular fiction, say, cordon off these kinds of reading practices from others, so that we read a particular genre vertically rather than as continuous with other kinds of reading. This misses the mobility of most reading lives. It also misses the ways in which powerful desires which cohere around the act of reading are refracted via different generic conventions and the rhetorical and strategic opportunities these differences offer the reader.

During the period of the interviews I was particularly struck by the fact that at a time when an increasing number of texts were being produced by black women writers (from the mid-eighties onwards), very little was known about black women's reading. Many of the texts that were appearing, moreover, were being written with foreign audiences strongly in mind. What did black South African women read, I wondered, and did what they read meet their reasons for reading? What was it to ask such a question anyway, given that reading desires will be shaped by the texts that are being read? I was influenced by Janice Radway's 1987 study *Reading the Romance,* which focussed for the first time not so much on actual texts but on what the act of reading implied in her women interviewees' lives.[2] By showing that the activity of reception, in addition to the structure and content of texts, constituted an important dimension of literary analysis, Radway rejected formalist studies of readers and reading which based their interpretations on an inscribed, model or ideal reader. Marxist analyses drew attention to the conditions of production and transmission of texts but still conceived of reading, Radway argued, as primarily being about the differential interpretation of texts.[3]

Feminist criticism, too, had looked at the construction of the woman reader primarily as a textual phenomenon rather than seeing (women) readers as constituted by a complicated set of material, ideological and psychoanalytic forces.[4] By the mid-nineties, though, work which focused on reading as a social practice began to appear, not only in relation to popular fiction – but all kinds of reading. Kate Flint, in her study *The Woman Reader 1837–1914*, wrote about what she called 'identificatory practices' in women's reading. Flint looks at how it was assumed that the woman reader of the period would 'automatically' identify with the 'most attractive – if not the most conventional – central woman character available' – but that not only could women be consciously aware of what was happening to them when they read, but that many novels by women 'encouraged recognition between consumer and character, thus implicitly appealing to certain structures of desire' while equally stressing 'the importance of knowledge, of rationality, and of critical alertness in reading'.[5] My own work looked at how reading as a social practice was imagined through representations in South African fiction and autobiography.[6] Researchers have begun, too, to look at the formation of reading publics in Africa. Ways in which practices of reading and writing were used and institutionalised, the formation of reading circles and literary societies, aspects of 'tin-trunk' literacy and the circuits of literary dissemination established by early black elites are all now being investigated.[7]

The interviews below can now be located in the context of these new studies of reading as a social and cultural practice. They give us a sense of why and what these South African women read, and they also enable us to explore the multiple lines that individual readers draw between fantasies and what we might term sets of 'realisms'. I present the interviews here in the form which they initially took, and as I saw them then. In the conclusion, I try to open the interview material to new questions which did not necessarily occur to me then. The interviews conducted involved about thirty women from a relatively small, privileged sector of the black population who had completed their schooling, usually had some further education, and had stable jobs. The choice of whom to speak to reflected my desire to reach a range of different contexts but also related to a set of personal contacts – people who could help me to reach women I would otherwise have had difficulty reaching in such a polarised political landscape and who could not have been expected to trust me as a white interviewer during that period. Each interview lasted for an hour or more, with a group of three to five women, beginning with a discussion and ending with a questionnaire, including a reading diary which I asked them to keep. I present some of them here, and in shortened form.

Study One

The first interview took place in September 1990 at Sukuma High School in the Natal township of Imbali at a time of intense conflict between the United Democratic Front and Inkatha movement and widespread state repression. Barbed wire curled along the school's cement walls and entry was via a tall steel turnstile and a large military-type gate. Rifle-clad soldiers circled a warehouse opposite and on the other side of the school, *kitskonstabels* – members of black paramilitary units set up by the government to squash township resistance, and widely hated by their own community – trained in a courtyard. Inside the school gates there had been much conflict too. Over the past year, students had been sent home en masse several times, once over the rape of women students by male students in the hostels, another time over the stabbing of a teacher, and after that over student demands for an SRC (Students Representative Council). Staff were divided in their support for students, courses were far behind schedule, and many students were expected to fail the end of year exams.

I interviewed a group of women who were employed at the school as administrative staff and teachers. Vuyelwa ('V' for short) was a typist, Mildred and Tembu senior administrative education clerks and Lungi was a teacher. They were between the ages of twenty-nine and thirty-two, had completed their schooling and had children, although 'V' was not married; Lungi had a university degree. One of the first issues to emerge from their talk about reading was the way in which books functioned as symbols, signs of status and as a signal to others. 'V' told how she had read romances during her school years, but after school had begun buying 'bigger' novels.[8]

The more expensive books were, the more status they had in V's terms. Romances, thin, light and cheap, were low status books though she clearly liked reading them. She didn't mention them in her questionnaire, stating her favourites as *Animal Farm, Macbeth* and the Bible, instead. For many women, their school years were the time of their most prolific and varied reading and throughout the interviews a notion of what constituted 'serious reading' derived from school setworks. Books and reading were also associated with white people.[9]

'V' not only aspired to communicate with white people, and to read their books, but the books she had read were all white and Western – thrillers, romances, Shakespeare and Orwell. One of the reasons why Lungi read a lot as a child was because her mother, with whom she lived – against the law – was a domestic servant ('whenever I came home from school – I called it "home" because I lived there with her – I could get books and magazines from the house').[10]

The second pronounced feature of the interview was the women's preference for television, or other cultural forms, to reading. This was unlike other interviews I did, and may have related to the violence and disruption of these particular women's surroundings. Mildred started off by recalling Douglas Bader's *Reach For The Sky* as a book which showed 'how not to lose hope', an indication perhaps of the confinements of her own life, and a sign of the potentially encouraging role that a book could play, much as a religious belief might. Yet this role was limited for Mildred; she went on to say that she was interested in records and cassettes and not books, and added that she liked songs 'which have love stories in them'. Lungi found television 'more real' than literature (she watched more than fourteen hours a week) but she preferred reading novels to newspapers, because they had the special benefit of the story. Her attitude to fiction was equivocal:

> You read a book and you expect to find the same thing in life which you just don't find. Life is real ... to me, reading books like love stories or light thrillers is an escape from – well, it *does* help you escape from reality, from the harshness of the world. For a moment you are in that book. Everything is *sooo* nice, but eventually you've got to come out of it.

Lungi liked the escape reading could provide, but didn't want to confuse the fictional with the real. The problem with fiction was the return to the world, and its 'harshness', that came afterwards. The difficult and violent conditions under which she and the other women at Sukuma lived made the transition seem particularly stark. At the time of the interview she was reading a book called *Young, Gifted and Black* which she found relevant to her own concerns and 'the school situation'. But if this indicated a concern with black identity and with knowledge of her own context, she was equally drawn to texts like *Rich Man, Poor Man* by Irwin Shaw and *Almost Paradise* by Danielle Steel ('they relate things people experience'). As with 'V', texts like the latter were 'real' to Lungi, not simply because she could relate to the emotional concerns that were expressed but because she had been reading these kinds of texts for years, so that they had become familiar to her. An intertextual world had been set up.

For the women at Sukuma, television images – because of the visual dimension – could be imbibed with greater ease than fictional ones, and less imaginative work was required by the viewer than in reading. In Lungi's case, there was the intimation that fiction could be too absorbing so that coming back to real life was too hard, and thus television was the better option. Of the television programmes they watched, soap operas were some of their favourites – proliferating stories which, unlike books, offered the pleasure of constant return, at the same time the next day, or the next week. Yet books, too, did provide some imaginative release from an often oppressive and violent reality.

Study Two

My next discussion was with six black women students at the University of Natal in Pietermaritzburg. Thabile, Zanasizwe, Nomsa and Lee had all stayed on campus during the university vacation to work on an urbanisation project in the Economics Department to earn money. They were living in a mixed, non-racial graduate residence. We met in the home of the residence sub-warden, a friend of mine and known and well-liked by the women. The women were all twenty-one or twenty-two years old, and their families lived in the neighbouring townships of Edendale and Imbali. They had all completed a first degree and were doing a Diploma in Education. They were eager to participate in the interview and frequently all talked at once. They also functioned strongly as a group, building on one another's responses. Although they voiced differences, consensus was sometimes too easily reached, opinions were too easily moulded or compromised to fit the general direction the discussion was taking.

In the interview, they talked a lot about romance reading.[11] Reading romances involved a form of learning about emotional issues and how to deal with them, although this was also a good justification for one of their greatest pleasures. They all liked reading that was easy to deal with, process and interpret and liked to read magazines because they could 'help to solve a problem'. It was the *ease* with which they could read rather than the text's contents which was important. Certain generic codes and conventions, easily recognisable by readers, more or less ensured certain kinds of emotional responses.

Lee said Sidney Sheldon's books were the only ones she could trust and whose endings she didn't have to read first because she knew that the books would be 'good'. Zanasizwe found Sheldon 'unrealistic': 'I mean in real life they cannot happen, and then I just get discouraged'. When I asked whether that ever happened with romances she replied emphatically, 'Oh, no way!' For Zanasizwe, 'knowing the ending' was a particularly intense need. Even if she was going to watch a film on television, she would try to speak to somebody who had seen it so that she could find out the ending. Despite this urgency, she was the most discerning reader of the group; the reason she liked her favourite books was because 'they best reveal what I expect from life; that is, the characters involved play the role of what is possible in life'. Books ideally provided a heightened register of ordinary life, a picture of what life could be like, and thus an inspiration to the reader. In a discussion *of Tess of the D'Urbervilles,* one of the women said:

> This book has a message for women in the sense that you can't go on trusting everyone you meet, just like she trusted Clare. As women, we've got to be very careful of ourselves.

By producing an interpretation of Hardy's novel that bore meaning in their own context, they entered the world of the novel as their own. When I asked them to elaborate on the 'message for women' they saw in the text, however, they talked no further about the text but about the way 'guys' oppress women ('guys are liars. Maybe it doesn't apply to you, but black guys ... try to boost their egos through manipulating women ... it's maybe because they've been ill-treated at work ... through woman, he can see that he's a man'). They became involved in the text to a certain extent but this soon gave way to wider emotional concerns.

The final part of the interview involved a discussion about South African fiction, in which it was again the emotions such books evoked rather than the texts themselves that were focused upon. It was not clear whether the women had actually read any South African writing; they seemed to have begun some books and not completed them or if they had, had not gone on to further reading. Their comments were as follows (it was difficult to match voices to names in this discussion as I listened to it on tape afterwards):

> I think the books about South Africa – the thing is, once you read them you get emotional, you think of the situation and you relate yourself to the whole thing and then it becomes ... um ... you feel the bitterness and all the sourness in this country, and it becomes emotional. It makes me feel emotional, angry.
>
> We know the whole thing. We're trying to forget about the past and look forward to the future, so what's the use? It just fills us with anger.
>
> I like to read about guerillas sometimes. I had a book [about a guerilla] – it's better than taking a Sidney Sheldon book. I could finish it within the night.
>
> I think it's good to read those South African books – good, but not on an everyday basis because it sort of destroys you – many people, they get so destroyed. I think with TV and the newspaper, it's okay to read those every day, just to know what's happening, but not to stick on those books.
>
> Even the movies – it may be that there's a movie on the 1976 riots. I don't like it ... We *know* what happened.
>
> In my case, I sometimes get the feeling of hope, about reading [that] this guy has done this and that, has gone through this. I mean, we're still gonna make it.

Reading South African fiction either made them feel too emotional, too angry or too 'destroyed' or, because they had experienced life under apartheid they felt they knew these stories already. Reading these texts (or the imagined experience of reading them) involved recognition, which was not a source of pleasure but an unpleasant reminder of the system they lived under (except for the last comment above, in which reading brings identification and inspiration). Because apartheid was so real and so close, they sought escape and fantasy from their reading. At the same time they seemed to be commenting on the real and perceived polemical and realist slant of much South African fiction. But they did not always make a sharp difference between novels on the one hand and magazines and newspapers on the other. Perhaps the most important difference was the length and diversity of a novel. There was almost no sense of the purely linguistic pleasures of reading – word-play and the use of metaphor and symbol, for example.

Emotional concerns were brought to the texts, or alternatively, those features of texts which appeared continuous with their own lives were the ones that tended to be drawn out. It may be, too, that they deliberately resisted other kinds of reading: a close reading and a critical distance between reader and text would have detracted from the fantasy appeal and from the 'real' feelings they experienced through their reading. Romance fiction provided them with their most pleasurable experience: reading was not a matter of exploration and self-knowledge through getting to know various texts in detail. Rather, it was something more constrained: women 'guarded against' South African fiction and the emotional response it stirred, and romance fiction was gripping rather than expansive.

Study Three

The first interview in Johannesburg was with three women who worked in the advertising department of *The Star,* South Africa's largest selling daily newspaper. We met in an assistant editor's office just off the large open-plan floor where journalists filed stories for the evening edition. The women seemed receptive and at ease. Dorcas was thirty-eight years old, had completed her schooling and was married with two children; Mpho was twenty-one, had a university degree and was unmarried and, like Dorcas, lived in Soweto; Pinky was twenty-five, brought up in Lesotho, also single, and she lived in Hillbrow, a mixed area in central Johannesburg.[12]

The women's lives were freed from some of the constraints the Natal women had faced. Not only were they better off but their lives were less stressful: public services were more efficient, for instance, and they were not confronted with the levels of violence that the women in Edendale were. They were surrounded by a 'reading culture' more than their Natal counterparts. During their working days they had more contact with whites who tended to own and read more books; they were likely to have passed or perused the city's bookshops, of which there are many, during a lunch hour; and they would have benefited from a better education, and thus had a greater incentive to read, than those in semi-rural areas. They also had access to a library on their work premises.

At the beginning of the interview different attitudes to popular culture, especially popular fiction, emerged between Dorcas on the one hand, and Mpho and Pinky on the other. Dorcas said she had never read romances (despite her later reference to Barbara Cartland), and if she bought magazines, she only did so for the crosswords. Romance reading seemed to embarrass her, and she tended to discuss her reading of English or American classics. Mpho and Pinky by contrast talked quite comfortably and with energy and humour about the romances and magazines they read.[13] Whereas Dorcas, who was a lot older than the other two women, saw some products (texts) as 'low', and did not admit to enjoying them readily, Mpho and Pinky tended to regard them as points within a diverse reading life, or reading spectacle.

Mpho's reading reflected different, apparently contradictory dimensions of herself which coexisted comfortably with each other. She discussed her reading of Mills and Boon romances as well as Pauline Smith's fiction. She greatly enjoyed her romance reading *and* felt deceived by it ('they deceived me – I thought life really was like that. You see yourself as a romantic and who wants to be a romantic in a world like this?'). She read romances after she'd felt she'd been 'very intellectual' for a while, and although she realised their deceptions, she wanted good fantasy value from romances. When Pinky said she'd recently heard of a romance in which 'the woman was on top', and welcomed this as a sign that attitudes to women might be changing, Mpho said she was 'so upset'. Mpho liked the work of the 1920s British-South African writer Pauline Smith because of its narrative form:

> You know when people write stories they always want to start at the beginning and finish at the end – 'one sunny day in a house in the Karoo'- or whatever. Well she [Smith] starts there [Mpho taps the table], right there where its happening. She plunges you right into it and when she stops, she stops abruptly. That's the end ... I love it. You can just start and go on and never finish.

Mpho liked Smith's detailed concern with the ordinary and the lack of grand beginnings and endings. Contrary to her romance reading, it was the lack of fantasy that she appreciated in this writing. In the questionnaire, when asked to describe what made her favourite books better than others, she said 'plot' and 'the author's use of language – the interesting way in which she/he conveys his/her innermost thoughts and ideas – the way in which she/he comes closest to reality'. Mpho was one of the few women to talk about the language of texts, and this had to do with the kind of books she was reading: Smith's use of language, compared to a romance writer's, would be likely to draw the reader's attention to the precision of the words chosen. Mpho was aware, too, of her own language construction, as her use of both masculine and feminine pronouns in the comment above shows. Mpho was an eclectic reader, reading a range of texts to satisfy different desires and acknowledging her attraction to fantasy, and her desire not to have it 'tampered with' by the insertion of a 'liberated' woman character, and to more decentred, open-ended narratives.

Pinky preferred facts to fiction. She read several newspapers each day as well as *Time* and *Newsweek* each week ('reading [fiction] has ceased to be a priority for me now ... what's going on around me, *that* I must know'). She spoke of fiction reading by analogy with drinking alcohol ('you escape and escape until you get to a point where you don't want to be in ordinary life anymore'). Like Mpho, and like Lungi at Sukuma School, she was aware of the dangers of losing herself in a world without interlocutors, of losing touch with the world she must inhabit. She also used reading as a screen to shut out others: she bought a newspaper to read on the bus home because she couldn't bear 'the idea of just listening to mothers and what they cooked last night and Jimmy crying out'.

Fiction, for Pinky, was equated with indulgence and defined against 'real work'. Learning facts about her own society and the world did not apply in the same way. She also commented in the interview that she would always finish a book, no matter how much it bored her and this seemed to imply her own sense of duty, or dislike of leaving a task incomplete. Thus reading was not just a textual transaction but an *act* and an investment too. On the other hand her desire to shut out the boring concerns of the women on buses marked her (perceived) difference from them. Pinky was an upwardly mobile working-class woman. As a black in South Africa she was part of a broadly dispossessed proletariat but she was also better off than many black people, and was achieving increasing seniority in her job. Her view of fiction as indulgence rather than work or education may have derived from a working-class ethic, but her wish for privacy on the bus marked her alienation from that class. Mpho never read the endings of books first, whereas Pinky said she always did. For Mpho the power of reading was the lack of control but also the lack of responsibility the reader had in a fictional world. For Pinky, reading the ending soon after beginning the book put her in greater control of the text and prevented the risk of an unexpected outcome or an anticlimax. It was the suspension of knowledge which fully entering a fictional experience involved that most women readers I spoke to, didn't – like Pinky – feel in a position to allow. Mpho also remarked that 'every person is a book, every event is a book ... if women themselves realised the potential of reading, it would emancipate them'. Reading helped the reader to understand the world better – the world was like a text, to be read, digested and 'gone over' again. If women were able to read the world around them closely, they would see it more clearly and thus have greater control over their lives.

Study Four

At Khanya College, a teaching institution run by SACHED (South African Council for Higher Education) in central Johannesburg, I interviewed six women. The College assists black students in gaining entrance to University, and the women I spoke to had been selected from a large number of applicants and were taking courses in History, English, Maths (and other subjects).

The picture of reading in these women's lives was slightly different to those presented in earlier interviews. The women were used to talking about books and exchanging them with one another, and they also, unlike most other women I spoke to, read African writing. However, this was because they were taking a course in African literature and it was difficult to know how much of this they read and would, in future, read for pleasure. The comments of one of their teachers, whom I spoke to afterwards, suggested that their interest may have been temporary. When the women arrived for their course they had had far less access to books than men, and they had read little other than romances, the teacher said. They also differentiated between work and fun reading, and African novels were seen as 'work'. One of the most popular texts amongst the women was *The River Between* (Ngugi wa Thiong'o), because 'it drew out the love theme'.

In addition to fantasies structured around love and relationships, escape was an important dimension of reading for the women. I asked the women to try to describe the kinds of books they liked to read:

> *Magauta:* I like books that are not too fictitious or idealise the characters as if they are super-beings. Some have a moral lesson or relate what is happening in my society.
>
> *Patricia:* The kinds of books that I like are those that conscientise people about their present-day life, things that affect their everyday life. Most books available today that claim to do this are in fact propaganda, written by government sources.
>
> *Thabang:* I think books kind of include you in the scene – you are almost a part of the society in the book. You get involved there – even emotionally. You wish, together with others, you pray, etc. So they are quite special in a sense that you have 'another life'. Those are good books.
>
> *Zandile*: Books must be different from the kind of life that I live.
>
> *Thembi:* The Hadley Chases I like because they are very adventurous and I like adventures and thrillers. They are exciting and arouse emotions. Romance I read just for the fun or to see how some people relate with their loved ones, and the things they do. I do this to learn more about love life in general because as you grow you meet many problems of desires about love.

> When one reads other peoples' experiences it's more fun and sometimes educating.
>
> *Alice:* As I said earlier I like books on romance, so I find pleasure in reading them.

Magauta and Patricia valued texts for their 'relevance' ('not too fictitious', 'those that conscientise people about their present-day life'), but their questionnaires showed that equally 'relevant' to African texts were American romances and thrillers. Zandile's list of her favourite books, for example, looked like this: *The Beautyful Ones Are Not Yet Born* (Ayi Kwei Armah), *Lace* (Jackie Collins) and *The Promise* (Danielle Steel); Alice listed *Tess of the D'Urbervilles* (Thomas Hardy), *Things Fall Apart* (Chinua Achebe) and *If Tomorrow Comes* (Danielle Steel). There was little attempt to conceal apparent contradictions in order to produce a 'coherent' narrative about reading. It was difficult to gauge the extent to which the different identities which their reading implied troubled them, but they seemed to co-exist with relatively little conflict. Perhaps it was the acceptance of a composite identity that distinguished these African women from, say, the women in Radway's study. Despite this, the fact that the role models set up by the books they read were generally white and American or British must have made reading, even fantasy reading, more complex and potentially more fraught.

Thabang saw books as offering separate places in which she could live. But insofar as she could 'wish together' with fictional characters, the fictional world was not alien to the world she inhabited. It was familiar but not separate. It contained, one might say, all the 'good/familiar' and none of the 'bad/familiar'. Reading was a kind of pedestrian escapism for her: it took her away from her world and provided her with another life, but it left her on the ground rather than lifting her into a complete fantasy world. Like Alice, she preferred fictional worlds to her own.

Conclusion

In Sembene Ousmane's *God's Bits of Wood*, N'deye Touti's reading is described in the following terms:

> She lived in a kind of separate world; the reading she did ... made her part of a universe in which her own people had no place, and by the same token, she no longer had a place in theirs.[14]

For Ndeye, 'real life' is in the books she reads, where she sees 'visions of mountain chalets deep in snow, of beaches where the great of the world lay in the sun, of cities where the nights flashed with many coloured lights'. Re-entering her own world, she 'would be seized with a kind of nausea, a mixture of rage and shame'. Ousmane frames his character's engagement with the space provided by a European book in terms of a narrative of loss, alienation and estrangement from an African tradition and self. But the passage also makes us want to ask: What happens when you open a book? How far can it lead you? What happens to what others thought was your identity – even though you yourself have not said? In this passage we don't hear from N'deye about who she was or who she is now, in relation to her reading. We are shown, though, the power of fantasy that reading, extraordinarily, is.

N'deye's reading also draws us towards the shifting loci of the real and the fantastical. In the interviews above, too, both notions continually and elliptically segue into each other. Television is 'more real' than fiction – yet it offers 'more escape'. Romances can 'relate things people experience' – but can also be a narcotic which can take one to a place which threatens a loss of self. The world of fantasy has a reality to it which they value – at the same time, they insist that real life 'is not like that'. Readers want to escape – but not too far from reality. Who is it here that they do not trust – 'fantasy' worlds, or themselves? While South African fiction that they have come across presents a 'realism' they dismiss ('we *know* what happened'), magazines and for some, newspapers, offer an acceptable 'realism'. Thus readers offer personal and frequently contradictory concepts of the real and the non-real, of mimesis and fantasy.

By engaging with numerous versions of the mimetic and the fantastical in relation to the texts they read or watch, the readers above, like N'deye, tell us about *all* reading. The history of fiction is generally read as a history of mimesis, and 'fantasy' is usually situated at the margins of literary creativity – as far as both readers and writers are concerned. We see, though, that the tensions expressed in the accounts above between reality and fantasy inhabit every act of reading and writing. The question of 'fantasy' is often reduced to a notion of the formulaic and attracts the reductive concept of 'escape'. But the interviews above reveal the vividness of this question, and its attendant notions of the real, across the totality of peoples' reading lives. They show us that attempts to critically think through the place of fantasy in reading and writing will not come from trying to isolate fantasy as a genre or form. As Lucie Armitt has said, we cannot 'ghettoize fantasy by encasing it within genres'.[15] They also reveal to us that we need not read the women's responses to fantasy in reading almost entirely in terms of consolation and loss, which so often occurs when 'fantasy' is read as a separate genre of its own. We may also read them as discourses of flirtation and masquerade.

It is true that on the one hand, we are struck, in many of the interviews, with the sense of *extremity* that is being expressed. A whole new sense is brought to the phrase to be 'lost in a book': for if fiction is a soporific, a stimulant, an exhilaration, a place of hope, then it can swallow up, incorporate, draw control from, the everyday, the pedestrian self – the self that must go on existing in the world. We might read this as symptomatically bearing witness to an extremely painful and harsh reality; to a reality shaped by victimhood and an awareness of loss. On the other hand, though, the narratives above position these women readers as concerning themselves with the world of beyond, modifying their relationships to their world in a way that all readers, of all kinds of texts, constantly do. If we are struck here by the specificities of context, we are equally alive to the general questions for reading that these interviews give rise to.

It is striking that for these women, unlike the readers in Radway's study, say, or in Flint's, reading is often a question of reading texts from quite other worlds. Too little work has been done on how the reading of in this case largely Western texts feeds into the intensities of the 'real' and the 'fantastical' in reading. South African writer Vusamazulu Credo Mutwa long ago observed the following in his book *Indaba, My Children:*

> If any Black man with a little knowledge of English, French or Portuguese wants to study the White man – as I have done – all he has to do is to go into the nearest town and become a regular customer of one of the second-hand bookshops there. He must buy and read no less than twenty different kinds of books and magazines a month for a period of no less than ten years. He must read classics, philosophical works and even cheap murder mysteries and science fiction...[16]

While Mutwa offers his own book in the service of a future turning of the tables, his words enable us to examine white Western worlds as 'known' to black readers with an intimacy which has seldom been examined in cultural studies. If apartheid has increasingly been theorised in terms not only of segregation but of certain intimacies, connectivities between oppressor and oppressed, which played themselves out in the spaces of the home and the prison for instance, [17] we might equally add reading as a further site for analysis. Moreover, while Sembene and others rightfully signal the cultural alienation to which such reading practices could give rise, they leave little room for other readings of relations between African readers and European texts. While readers in these interviews may actually resist 'recognition' in their reading, or recognition as pleasure (as their responses to South African reading might suggest), they may equally be asserting a pleasurable space of the unexpected, and of the abandonment required to not know what they will meet in fictions which are not of their own worlds. Reading Western fiction is likely to produce in these African readers once again a compelling and contradictory set of narratives around familiarity or recognition and non-recognition.

It is perhaps interesting to conclude by reminding ourselves that, in addition to all of the readings above, the responses of the women interviewed will have been structured in part by what they had read – about reading. An image from A *Perfect Stranger* by Danielle Steel, one of the women's consistently favourite authors, makes this very clear. A discussion of historical romances (of the sort that Steel writes) takes place between the hero and the heroine who have just met. The mother of the hero is the best-selling author of the novels the heroine has been reading for years, although the heroine doesn't yet know this. The hero asks nonchalantly whether she reads a lot of Charlotte Brandon's books and Raphaella replies:

> 'I love her. I've read every book she ever wrote'. And then she glanced at him apologetically. 'I know, it's not very serious reading, but it's a wonderful escape. I open her books and I am instantly absorbed into the world she describes. I think that kind of reading seems silly to men, but it ... she couldn't tell him that the books had saved her sanity over the last seven years, he would think she was crazy. '... it's just very enjoyable.' He smiled more deeply. 'I know, I've read her too'.[18]

The text articulates the woman reader's position, but exclusively as one of lack (the stories 'saved her sanity') and reinscribes her position as an 'un-serious' reader. It appears initially that the hero is different to other men since he reads Charlotte Brandon's novels but the reader knows that he only does so because they are his mother's books. Although romance reading is represented, the kind of narrative in which it is presented deflects the reader from thinking (too much) about reading. Thus the repeated practice of reading these texts may inhibit women's experience of reading, their thinking about reading and their talk about it. Yet while the women interviewees sometimes reproduced the kinds of responses we see above, they were also alive to multiple losses and pleasures, realities and fantasies which infused their reading worlds. When we read them in all these registers, we may begin to see who they are – and want to be.

Notes

1 These were first published as 'Reading in the Lives and Writing of Black South African Women' in *Journal of Southern African Studies*, vol. 20, no.1, March 1994.

2 Janice Radway, *Reading the Romance*, Verso, London, 1987

3 And Stanley Fish's notion of an interpretative community, she contended, was unable to consider adequately the ways in which the reading subject engaged with the more recalcitrant features of the text, or with its power and authority. By 'interpretative communities' Fish does not mean a collective of individuals but a set of strategies or norms of interpretation that we hold in common and which regulate the way we think and perceive. See S. Fish, *Is There a Text in This Class? The Authority of Interpretative Communities*, Harvard University Press, Cambridge, Mass., 1980.

4 Mary Jacobus asked, 'What would "reading woman" mean if the object of our reading (woman as text) and the reading subject (reader as already read) were gendered only as a result of the reading process?' (Mary Jacobus, *Reading Woman: Essays in Feminist Criticism*, London, 1986, p.3) Divorcing concepts of 'woman' and 'reading' from their socio-historical context, as both Jacobus and a critic like Jonathan Culler have done, had the effect of dehistoricising them.

5 Kate Flint, *The Woman Reader 1837-1914*, The Clarendon Press, Oxford, 1993, p. 315.

6 See for instance Sarah Nuttall, 'Reading and Recognition in Three South African Women's Autobiographies' in *Current Writing*, vol.8, no.1, April 1996.

7 See 'Social Histories of Reading in Africa' project, convened by Karin Barber, Ato Quayson and Stephanie Newell.

8 'V' said: 'I didn't enjoy these books as much as romances but I thought when people see me reading these big books, they're going to say, "Oh, you are better now because you are reading those books"'.

9 As 'V' said: 'We grew up in rural areas where it is even difficult to see a white man or a white lady – you can't even know what he is saying ... if we grew up with the whites, we would be able to communicate with them, we'd be able to read their books. That's why we didn't have a lot of reading.'

10 Lungi's description recalls an image in Gcina Mhlope's story, 'The Toilet', in which the protagonist lives illegally with her sister, a domestic servant in Johannesburg. During the day she would be locked in the room where her sister brought her 'books, old magazines, and newspapers from the white people. I just read every single thing I came across: *Fair Lady*, *Woman's Weekly*, anything'. Later, waiting to go to work, she would go to a public toilet in a park and sit on the toilet seat and read; eventually she started writing stories in the toilet.

11 Romances, which they'd read at school along with photo love-comics, were valued for the 'information' they provided about real life, and because they were quick to read and easy to understand. They were also a way of trying to understand men. Living in sex-segregated hostels at boarding school, they wanted to know 'about romance, about boys' and writing letters to 'so-called boyfriends' involved copying out 'well written paragraphs' from the romances they read.

12 Dorcas and Mpho worked for 'telesales' in the advertising department. Their job description required that they, amongst other things, 'answer calls promptly and in a way that represents the company in the best light' and 'assist callers with wording of advertisements which will best benefit them'. Pinky's job required more responsibility: she had to assist her colleagues, 'provide market feedback to section head and management' and 'achieve individual and group sales target'. Their work in general was involved with creating images – the company's image but also the casting of advertisements in language, choosing the right emphasis and the right words.

13 Theorists like Chartier (1995) have noted the shift away from a hierarchy of value between 'high' and 'low' culture, 'real' and popular reading, towards a view of differing cultural configurations which crisscross and dovetail in practices, representations or cultural products.

14 Sembene Ousmane, *God's Bits of Wood*, Heinemann, London, 1970 (1983), p. 56.

15 Lucie Armitt, *Theorising the Fantastic*, Arnold, London and New York, 1996, p.3. See also Kathryn Hume, *Fantasy and Mimesis: Responses to Reality in Western Literature*, Methuen, London and New York, 1984.

16 Vusamazulu Credo Mutwa, *Indaba, My Children*, Blue Crane Books, Johannesburg, 1964, p.xv.

17 This for instance is a central argument in *Senses of Culture*, edited by Sarah Nuttall and Cheryl Ann Michael, Oxford University Press, 2000. The

editors draw on new work on Cape slave history, architecture, the city, as well as biography and memoir to show these shifting registers of analysis, not only of the present but of the past.

[18] Danielle Steel, *A Perfect Stranger*, London, 1990, p. 519.

References

Armitt, L. *Theorising The Fantastic*, Arnold, London and New York, 1996.

Chartier, Roger, 1995. 'Labourers and Voyages: from the Text to the Reader', in *Readers and Reading*, edited and introduced by Andrew Bennet, Longman, Harlow.

Fish, S. *Is There a Text in This Class? The Authority of Interpretative Communities*, Harvard University Press, Cambridge, Mass., 1980.

Flint, K. *The Woman Reader 1837-1914*, The Clarendon Press, Oxford, 1993.

Hume, K. *Fantasy and Mimesis: Responses to Reality in Western Literature*, Methuen, London and New York, 1984.

Jacobus, M. *Reading Women: Essays in Feminist Criticism*, Columbia University Press, New York, 1986

Mutwa, V.C. *Indaba, My Children*, Blue Crane Books, Johannesburg, 1964.

Nuttall, S. 'Reading in the Lives and Writing of Black South African Women' in *Journal of Southern African Studies*, vol.20, no.1, March 1994.

Nuttall, S. 'Reading and Recognition in Three South African Women's Autobiographies' in *Current Writing*, vol.8, no.1, April 1996.

Nuttall, S. and C.A. Michael, eds, *Senses of Culture*, Oxford University Press, Cape Town, 2000.

Ousmane, S. *God's Bits of Wood*, Heinemann, London, 1970 (1983).

Radway, J. *Reading the Romance*, Verso, London, 1987.

Steel, D. *A Perfect Stranger*, Sphere Books Ltd, London, 1990.

LINDY STIEBEL

Black 'Tecs

Popular Thrillers by South African Black Writers in the Nineties

> Protus wagged an angry finger. 'Look ... we don't like doing this any more than you do, but common sense dictates that we maintain law and order!' (Masemola 1993:62)

> However, at the moments of intensified political and cultural struggle the balance begins to tip the other way and common sense adopts a more Utopian outlook, so that there is an active popular demand for literature which embodies alternative values (Pawling 1984:14)

The thriller, in its various guises, is essentially a 'conservative and conventional genre' (Oates 1998), one that well suits times of social uncertainty.[1] In the turbulence of the 'new' South Africa in the Nineties, with major political restructuring and social reorganisation being inevitable and indeed sought after, a genre based on certainties will clearly appeal to both writers and readers. More so even than the romance which requires some level of personal investment in the fictional lovers and their twinned destinies, the thriller with its proffered puzzle and clearly defined rules for the solution thereof, and its movement from doubt to clarity, is 'one of the most detached and soothing of narratives' (Rubin 1999:186). Basically an urban and modern genre, the thriller has middle-class concerns at its heart: protection of property and individual life, the maintenance of law and order, justice and punishment for the trespasser. The popularity of thrillers understandably surges when these middle-class pre-occupations are threatened; for example, the spate of police thriller films in the USA in the 1960s and 1970s is linked by Rubin to:

> a growing sense of urban crisis, a foregrounding of law-and-order issues in the 1968 and 1972 presidential campaigns, and a general ... swing to the right in American politics. (1999: 137)

Though the situation in South Africa in the 1990s is not comparable to that in the USA in the 1960s and 1970s, and the thriller has developed its own hybrid form here, nevertheless it is probably true to say that high levels of political uncertainty pre-1994, and the rise in crime levels post-1994, make for a good thriller climate where detectives are sharp, the villains get caught, and thus the propertied classes sleep easy at night.

In this chapter, I will firstly examine the thriller genre as it has been developed by black writers in South Africa, and then work through a number of examples of the genre by way of illustration. That it should be black men writing thrillers in South Africa in the 1990s is interesting – despite the many women thriller writers elsewhere in the world, the thriller's 'iconically masculine' (Munt 1994:1) potential is evident in South Africa. Only one of the crime stories to be discussed is written by a woman. Though more South African women, both black and white, are drawn to writing and are finding publishers, the thriller domain remains at present a largely male and black preserve with the authors I look at being members of the professional classes – a lawyer, a medical doctor, a journalist. White popular fiction in South Africa is still entirely overshadowed by Wilbur Smith who writes what could loosely be termed adventure stories. His line of heritage stretches back to Stuart Cloete, and before him Rider Haggard with his popular tales of Empire. Smith's huge national and international commercial success has inspired similar adventure-style tales within South Africa by white writers, such as John Gordon Davis (best known for *Hold My Hand, I'm Dying*, 1967) who trained as a lawyer in South Africa.

To begin with then, how best to describe the South African thriller in the 1990s? Any definition of the thriller whether in South Africa or abroad is bound to be problematic as most commentators agree that it is a '"metagenre" that gathers several other genres under its umbrella' (Rubin 1999:4). From the seminal earlier theorists of the thriller like Cawelti (1976) and Palmer (1979), to the contemporary views of Bell and Daldry (1990), Munt (1994) and Rubin, all agree on the huge range of possibilities offered under the generic title of 'thrillers'. To name just a few of the most popular varieties, there is the British classical detective story of the nineteenth century featuring Sherlock Holmes and various imitators, the American 'hard-boiled' detective story of the early twentieth century, the Agatha Christie mysteries, spy thrillers from the Cold War era, the police procedural which lends itself to television serialisation, and so on – all of which can be marketed under the 'thriller' banner. Dissimilar as all these subgenres may be in terms of setting or process of investigation or detective, the one element they all share at a basic level according to Palmer, is a hero and a conspiracy which is resolved by the book's end (1979: 53, 82).

When looking at the South African thriller it is clear that one is dealing with a hybrid and thus a distinctive form that has evolved to suit the South African context. This hybridization, or '"creolization": the emergence of creative and fully viable new syntheses' (Fabian in

Barber 1997:19), of the thriller form can be understood as a positive process of adapting existing popular forms to suit the contemporary moment and specific geographical context:

> one of Africa's oldest arts is extraversion, the ability to draw in and creatively absorb materials from the outside in order to fuel local contests and projects. The 'hybridity' of African popular culture can be seen in this light not as a purely artistic phenomenon, and certainly not as a mere by-product of 'culture clash'; but rather as the visible face of a deep and ancient disposition that shapes the social, political and economic domains as well as the cultural. (Barber 1997: 6)

Chapman (1989) made a similar point when discussing a crime short story from *Drum* magazine. He notes the 'hybridism' (1989: 206) evident in the mixture of styles within the story and attributes this mix to the paucity and eclectic nature of literary resources for black writers of the time: popular magazines, the cinema, press and school 'classics'. The eclectic style that emerged presents a challenge to the literary critic. Lindfors encourages the literary critic to 'make its [popular literature's] reverberations more meaningful…bringing out the best and the worst in art that might otherwise be considered quite ordinary'(1991: 2), whilst Chapman speaks of the 'challenge of critical response to South African literatures' in that 'combinations of disparate influences need not always necessarily lead to a failure of tone or poise' (1989: 207).

What then are the composite strains that go into the hybrid that is the black South African thriller of the 1990s? One obvious one is the crime short story of *Drum* magazine of the 1950s mentioned above. *Drum*, with its heady mix of political exposé, crime reportage, advice column and pinup photos, marked a definitive moment in black writing in South Africa and saw the writers who were to become big names make their start: Zeke Mphahlele, Can Themba, Nat Nakasa etc. In itself, *Drum* was a hybrid when it came to the crime short stories it published, with the influence of the American hard-boiled school being prominent. But it was the hard-boiled school as seen through the medium of American B movies[2] popular at the time, rather than solely the thrillers of Dashiell Hammett in the 1920s and 1930s, and those of his successor Raymond Chandler of the 1940s and 1950s. The immediate appeal of the hard-boiled thriller and its movie versions to *Drum* is easy to understand: the modern city with its possibilities of violence, glamour and corruption is the setting for the hard-boiled thriller and also the context for *Drum* writers and readers in the early days of apartheid:

> When we step from the world of the classical detective formula into the milieu of the American hard-boiled story, the vision of the city is almost reversed. Instead of the new Arabian nights, we find empty modernity, corruption and death. A gleaming and deceptive facade hides a world of exploitation and criminality in which enchantment and significance must usually be sought elsewhere, in what remains of the natural world still unspoiled by the pervasive spread of the city. (Cawelti 1976: 141)

The harsh world of the hard-boiled thriller requires special, tough skills to negotiate – it is the world of fast cars, fast dames, hot gangs and smart private eyes who aren't afraid to get their hands dirty; it's translatable to Sophiatown in the fifties, *Drum*'s world. Being black in an increasingly white man's world meant frequently treading a tight-rope between the law and crime; thus stories which glamorised crime and criminals, together with private eyes hired to contain them, would inevitably appeal. The American origin of these tales and films was part of the glamourous appeal with 'America' being shorthand for 'the good life'. Anthony Sampson, one-time editor of *Drum*, recalls one reader's request to 'Give us jazz and film stars, man! We want Duke, Satchmo, and hot dames! Yes, brother, anything American' (quoted in Chapman 1989: 187). The *Drum* writers who wrote crime short stories gave the readers what they wanted which resulted in occasional dialogue snatches which could come straight from Hammett:

> 'a dame like that is liable to start a strike in hell!'

> and:

> 'I'm leveling a torpedo at your spine, and if you do anything funny I'm liable to pump you so full of lead they'll need twenty guys to carry your coffin' (from 'Love Comes Deadly' by Mbokotwane Manqupu, *Drum* January 1955)

The tsotsi-taal of South African townships circa 1950s was enriched by the idiom and rhythms of the American city sidewalks as portrayed in the popular gangster movies.

South Africa's contribution to the hard-boiled thriller tradition as manifested in the *Drum* crime stories – and certainly in the black thrillers of the 1990s as shall be seen – is firstly the presence of political commentary, unusual in both the American and British forms, and secondly the centrality of black characters. Peter Ludbrook on the BBC's internet crime page comments on these two aspects in contemporary thrillers but what he says is equally applicable to earlier forms of the thriller genre:

> As I began to read more and more thrillers, two things struck me forcibly about the genre. The first was the absence of black protagonists. But then along came Walter Mosley with his wonderful Easy Rawlins series…The second was the absence of politics. By this I mean political ideas and their relationship to power. This is more easily found in European writers … But British and American writers still steer clear of the political. (www.bbc.co.uk/education/bookworm/crime.html 7 September 1999)

Drum's crime stories have at their heart both: black protagonists who are also situated politically by their creators. Thus in James Matthews' 'Dead End!' (*Drum* September 1954), the squalor of the township and its byproduct of crime is seen as the result of the indifference of the white city councilors; in Manqupu's 'Love Comes Deadly', township violence is seen as a direct, inevitable result of an evil socio-political system 'where illicit liquor is sold openly, where prostitution goes on day and night without even the decency of closed doors, where one is killed for no reason at all…' (*Drum* January 1955). Arthur Maimane, writing under the pen-name Arthur Mogale, created a black South African version of Hammett's Continental Op – Chester O. Morena, Private Detective and ex-cop who moves carefully in a corrupt Johannesburg.[3] Without exception, those black thriller writers of the 1990s I analyse in this chapter continue this particularly South African twist – all feature male black protagonists and all foreground political commentary at various points in the narrative. The setting of the modern, corrupt city and parts of the street-wise dialogue in the thrillers generally owe their antecedents to the hard-boiled American genre, but the fore-grounding of race and politics in the character casting and social commentary is purely South African.

If one of the main strains of the hybrid South African thriller today is composed of *Drum*/hard-boiled thrillers/American B movies/black action films; the other derives from the classical detective story of the type that made Sherlock Holmes famous at the end of the nineteenth century. This strain, which is generally held to start with Edgar Allan Poe, extend through Wilkie Collins and find its flowering in Arthur Conan Doyle's tales of ratiocination, has as its focus the solving of a puzzling crime by a brilliant mind rather than brawn. Seen by Rubin and others as a descendant of the Gothic tradition, the classical detective story is centred on the detective and his ratiocinative powers:

> the detective's eccentricity and isolation mark him as a descendant of the Gothic villain/antihero, turned to more constructive purposes as he exercises a combination of reason and imagination to tame the chaotic ambiguity that had ruled the Gothic world. (1999: 43)

The detective is the 'controlled centre surrounded by chaos' (Munt 1994:1): his approach is totally different from the blood and violence of the later American private eyes. However, like them, he is a loner confiding to an extent with one other whom he uses as a sounding board but not as a source of ideas. It is the very control and intellectual superiority of this detective which has perhaps made him the popular choice of role model for three out of the four thrillers which I discuss, despite the difference in almost every other aspect to the classical detective thriller that contemporary South African thrillers exhibit. Set in the gritty, corrupt modern city as are most of the latter, from the centre of almost every one gleams an intellectual and moral brain: Protus Sishi in *Mixed Signals* (1993), Lentswe Makena in *The Secret in My Bosom* (1996) and Jon Zulu in *Murder by Magic* (1993). This is possibly an assertion of black affirmation as Fred Pule and Lentswe Makena both have white superiors in the detective police force to whom they are seen as racially inferior but to whom they prove intellectually superior. The old racist cliché of blackness and physical strength is overlaid by the coupling of blackness and brains.

An unexpected deviation from the homosocial world of Holmes, given the masculinist world of thrillers generally, is the strong role given to detectives' wives and female family members in the South African thrillers I shall discuss. These are not the fast dames of the hard-boiled tradition but rather support their husbands in the home and in their work. Lentswe Makena's wife, Khumo, fills the 'Watson' role intellectually; whilst Fred Pule's wife, Mapula, comes up with some of the best ideas in the book; Protus Sishi's sister, Linda, acts as moral and political barometer for her brother. Despite the presence of these strong women, a sex/love interest is notably absent as befits the Sherlock Holmes formula – there is only Mumsy Moloi from *The Secret in My Bosom* who is 'hot' in the accepted hard-boiled sense, but the detectives themselves are never tempted or even put in harm's way. The only sex scenes are the entirely legitimate (and ridiculous) conjugal ones in Chasakara's novel.

An important South African connector in this particular strain of the hybrid thriller helix would be South Africa's most successful thriller writer (outside the country, that is): James McClure whose Trekkersburg mysteries of the 1970s and 1980s featured Afrikaner Detective Tromp Kramer and Zulu Detective Michael Zondi, his subordinate. Set in apartheid South Africa, Kramer is superior to Zondi in terms of power relations but the two share a sense of humour and empathy that cuts across racial lines. Kramer and Zondi, like Holmes and Watson, use their brains to sift through clues, question witnesses and figure out whodunit. Again, unusual for the genre, but typical of South African thrillers, is the political commentary, more oblique in McClure's case than in the thrillers of the 1990s, but nevertheless there:

> Although McClure claimed to be presenting South Africa 'as it is', his novels critique apartheid. This has been common fare in South African high-culture literature, but is unusual in mass-market thrillers. Most thrillers are seen as inherently conservative, forcing us to see solely from the hero's point of view as he defends society against grave threats, but McClure bends the rules. Society is protected, but we see the rot at its core. (Peck 1994: 11)

Thabo Masemola, author of *Mixed Signals*, specifically cites McClure as an influence on his writing: 'I read one of his novels and I thought that here was a different way of portraying the situation in this country' (Coan 1991: 11). This is a fortunate connection as McClure, who left the country in 1965 and who won the prestigious Golden Dagger Award for *The Steam Pig* (1971), has been far less recognised and sold within South Africa than without (Peck 1997).The connection between Masemola and McClure has been strengthened in recent times with the two meeting during a visit back to Pietermaritzburg in 1992.

A final strain in the South African contemporary thriller hybrid is the influence of the police procedural. Here there is a reliance on painstaking detail, forensics, methodical research and interrogation to solve the crime. It is surprising, in a country where the police force during the apartheid years was considered so suspect, that most of the thrillers to be discussed feature black detectives in the employ of the South African Police (SAP), albeit in the detective section. All, however, have their differences with the police force. Police methods used on political detainees are seen as illegal and abusive: Protus Sishi reluctantly brings in a suspect for questioning in *Mixed Signals* to an interrogation room called 'the Grindstone, on account of the activities which took place within' (Masemola 1993: 85); Fred Pule, a less than eager police cooperator, describes with horror how '[p]eriodically the dim light would flicker as electric shocks were applied to the tortured' (Chasakara 1996: 7) at police headquarters; Lentswe Makena is asked by Anikie to look out for her husband whom she fears is being tortured by the Special Branch of the police. Both Pule and Makena, particularly, stand apart from these excesses and maintain the moral high ground of the police being a body entrusted with the maintenance of law and order. They combine some of the ratiocinative approach to problem solving and the loner status of Sherlock Holmes, but they have the power and resources of a big organisation behind them. The wide popularity of various television series based on the police procedural form, for example *Hill Street Blues* and *NYPD* on South African screens in the 1980s might go some way to explaining the influence this form has had on the contemporary South African black thriller.

As is by now evident, many strains have gone into the hybrid that is the South African thriller of the 1990s: among them the hard-boiled American style carried through in *Drum* magazine, the classical detective style of Sherlock Holmes which carries through in James McClure, various television series of the police procedural, and black action films. In the positive sense of hybridisation and 'borrowing' earlier discussed, South African black writers have taken what is appropriate to a local context: the urban, gritty setting, street-wise dialogue, an individual detective with superior intellect, nevertheless working as part of a flawed government organisation for the greater good; then added an innovative South African twist of political commentary and a predominantly black cast with a sense of humour. The texts I have selected to illustrate these features are *Mixed Signals* (1993) by Thabo Masemola; *Murder By Magic* (1993) by Nandi D'Lovu; *The Bank is My Shepherd I Shall Not Want* (1996) by Gordon Lesego Chasakara; and *The Secret in My Bosom* (1996) by Gomolemo Mokae.

Perhaps one should begin with D'Lovu's thriller because it captured considerable media attention on publication. The detective hero, Jon Zulu, was hailed as 'the black equivalent of Sherlock Holmes' (*The Daily News*, 29 January 1996: 6), though with James Bond overtones as the review article picked up, in echoing Bond's famous opening line, 'Zulu's the name – Jon Zulu'. The film rights, the article informed us, had been purchased by an American producer for well-known playwright Mbongeni Ngema with Danny Glover as possible lead; the Zulu translation had been presented to King Goodwill Zwelithini who lavishly praised its hero as embodying 'traditional Zulu virtues', and future plans included translation into other South African languages spurred on by its popular reception in Zulu and English. Excited by the prospect of a new black South African thriller writer and a woman at that, imagine my surprise when told by the publishers that Nandi D'Lovu is the pseudonym for a white woman who, as the dustjacket tells the reader, is a freelance journalist with extensive experience 'in Namibia and Azania'. One can only speculate that the author and publishers were hoping that a black writer would be better received as the originator of a popular crime story aimed at newly literate readers – the text is under a hundred pages and simply written.

Given, therefore, that it does not technically fall into the category of thrillers under discussion, despite its misleading author's name, *Murder By Magic* will not be fully discussed, though its marketing and reception as a 'black' text have been interesting. Though there are hints of Sherlock Holmes and James Bond in this novel, the text is actually strongly reminiscent of a Rider Haggard adventure story in setting – rural Zululand, away from the modern city – and in subject matter – a village held under thrall by a powerful witchdoctor, search for the legendary Lala treasure buried during Chaka's time all muddled in with gunrunners working 'for some stupid organisation that prefers killing to living' (D'Lovu 1993: 88). Though the book highlights black protagonists, notably Jon Zulu, the 'famous Zulu detective from America'(1) and his friend, Abel Ngubane, the sharp political commentary typical of the South African thriller is largely absent; what political critique there is, is aimed at European imperialism of a distant past.

If Nandi D'Lovu is not who she at first seems to be, Thabo Masemola, author of *Mixed Signals* (1993), which won the R10,000 Bertrams VO Award for African Literature, thankfully is. Masemola returned to South Africa in 1990 after spending seven years in the USA studying for an MA degree in English and working as a journalist. Based in Pietermaritzburg, he then worked at the University of Natal, thereafter writing as features editor at *The Natal Witness*. *Mixed Signals* is his first published novel. It is a thriller, a form deliberately chosen by Masemola as a different angle to highlight South Africa 'from my perspective' (Coan 1991: 11). At the centre is Bantu Detective Constable Protus Sishi of the South African Police, whose immediate superior and senior 'partner' is Sergeant Koos Graaf, an Afrikaner of the old school. The setting is a thinly veiled Pietermaritzburg now called Covenantsburg, with other name changes evident – Edendale Township becomes Edenvale, *The Natal Witness* is *The Libertarian* etc. – strongly reminiscent of McClure's Trekkersburg stories which Masemola has acknowledged as his inspiration. The context is probably the 1980s, certainly a time when apartheid was deeply entrenched in South Africa. Sishi is assigned the case of Roger Msimang, a young lawyer killed in the township. By dint of assiduous sleuthing, Sishi tracks down the killer, Dr Cele, whose motive was an attempt to protect his name from the scandal of his drug addiction, and wife abuse which results in her murder. Msimang was Mrs Cele's lawyer and privy to her secrets. As a detective, Sishi is modeled loosely on Sherlock Holmes: he is a meticulous piecer together of detail, a loner living with his mother and sister yet without the Holmesian arrogance and eccentricity. Here is an extract from Sishi's discussion with the forensics expert illustrating the deductive reasoning favoured in the book:

> Protus nodded enthusiastically. 'Another thing, Doctor. You say the wound was inclined towards the left. According to the report, it was not exactly horizontal, but at an angle of about thirty-five degrees from the vertical, or thereabouts? I guess what I am getting at, Doctor, is that considering the wound's location, its depth, and its angle, what does that exactly signify?'
>
> The doctor stopped his pacing and faced the policeman, the glint still in his eye. 'Good question, man. So you caught on on that, eh?...Considering the weapon, the wound was deep enough to have been inflicted by a powerful blow, meaning a strong person. The assailant, evidently, could not have been, say, a woman of ordinary strength, or a weak, frail man.'
>
> Sishi nodded, smiling admiringly. 'Very perceptive, Doctor, very perceptive,' he said. (1993:114–15)

Another influence on this thriller is the police procedural tale – Sishi gets his man by following leads, garnering information with the resources, for example, forensic experts on call, offered by a large organisation. However, given the South African context of apartheid and the problematic role of the police during this time, Sishi finds himself at odds with his organisation. After reading the newspaper report on alleged police involvement in political assassinations, Sishi's political naivety and altruism are evident:

> He felt powerless, emasculated, and betrayed. He had devoted his whole working life to the service of the police, to the pursuit of justice. Throughout his career, Protus maintained that rumours of police brutality and suspected murders were malicious rumours, leftist innuendo. (149)

A combination of his sister Linda's questioning of the role of the police in an apartheid state, and his own experience at the novel's end when his moment of triumph as crime solver is stolen by his white boss, results in Sishi emerging 'a soundly beaten but wiser man' (189).

In the Graaf/Sishi combo, the influence of McClure and his Kramer/Zondi duo is evident. Though Sishi calls Graaf 'Baas' (boss) and the lines of racially determined authority are clearly evident, the two occasionally debate politics, though the camaraderie of the McClure pair is absent. This is because of Graaf's deep belief in Afrikaner Nationalist ideology which this extract from one of their conversations reveals:

> 'What do they [blacks] consider evil? Our civilised policies, our trying to give them self determination in their own states, without outside interference?'
>
> 'Right. But some of us, especially the educated class, feel they need to have a say in the way the state is run – a fantasy, I admit; but they seem to believe in it.' (140–1)

As the serious tone of the above implies, *Mixed Signals* is dominated by political commentary and exposition to the detriment of the crime narrative. Masemola as authorial commentator is ever present – there are long conversations between Sishi and his sister on, among other things, the Indian/African split, on *kitskonstabels* (the despised 'instant cops' of the times), on traditional beliefs and on the homelands, which are incidental to the plot.

In Gomolemo Mokae's *The Secret in My Bosom* (1996), a better balance between plot and political critique is established. Mokae, author of numerous short stories, a novel in Setswana, a biography of then ANC operative Robert McBride and popular TV scriptwriter, is a far more experienced writer to which his numerous prizes attest. He is by day a medical doctor with a busy practice in Garankuwa near Pretoria and a writer by night, plus a some-time politician: he was publicity secretary for AZAPO (Azanian People's Organization) until his resignation in 1995, though he remains a loyal supporter. With *The Secret in My Bosom*, his first novel in English, Mokae has continued and enlarged on the strand of South African black crime writers but not, as Zakes Mda claims on the book cover, 'introduce[d] a new genre in black South African literature: the detective story'. That, as this essay shows, can be given an earlier date in South African writing if one considers the *Drum* writers. Nevertheless, *The Secret in My Bosom* has achieved the most success out of the contemporary thrillers here studied: it has been set at university level in a popular fiction course and a four-part TV adaptation of the book, starring his uncle Zakes Mokae, is due for screening on South African television later in 1999.

The detective of the novel is Colonel Lentswe Makena of the CID, a modern Sherlock Holmes. In Cawelti's terms, Makena has the 'Holmesian ambience' – he is 'elderly, smokes a pipe, possesses poetic intuition, is endowed with incredible psychoanalytic abilities, and has brilliant eccentricity and a scientist's inductive power of reasoning' (1976: 81). Makena is a 'legendary detective' who 'can hold his own in a discussion on anthropology, physics, archaeology, paleontology, astronomy, literature...' (Mokae 1996: 6). He drives a carefully maintained 1967 Wolsley, smokes a pipe and has to watch his arthritic hip. Mokae has commented on his creation in typical wry style:

> He's too brilliant for a local policeman, let alone a black policeman. If anything, black cops had a worse reputation than white ones for being brutal automatons. (*Sunday Times*, 14 July 1996: 13)

Sergeant Kenyana, a junior partner who hero worships his superior, and Khumo, Makena's wife, share the role of Watson. As noted earlier, Makena's wife occupies a strong advisory role quite foreign to the original Holmes stories' masculine world. South Africa has a tradition of strong black women especially during the years of apartheid; Mokae's mother had to assume responsibility for her household unexpectedly, so setting a strong role model for her son. Hence, '[h]is female characters are strong and the mothers in his stories and scripts act as catalysts' (*Sunday Times*, 6 September 1998: 10). Sherlock Holmes's appeal to Mokae as role model for Makena is his intellectual approach to crime that is used by Mokae as an endorsement of black dignity. Furthermore, Mokae shares Conan Doyle's writer-doctor credentials: 'Medicine is my wife and writing is my mistress', Mokae wisecracks (*Sunday Times,* 14 July 1996).

Set in Johannesburg in the 1970s and 1980s, the plot has a medical twist to the solution: the villain, Maxwell Lesenjane, lawyer, political activist-turned government stooge, insurance fraudster, loses two wives under suspicious circumstances. After returning from 'political' exile in the States, Lesenjane is once again investigated by his nemesis, Makena. Mokae's medical curiosity shows in the denouement which involves the inability of fire to immolate silicone breast implants. If the process of deduction shows the influence of the classical detective story; the urban setting, occasional American slang dialogue and the predatory Mumsy Moloi, Maxwell's second wife, come from the hard-boiled tradition. True to the South African twist I have described, the plot is very tightly tied to a political context, though at times the tone is too dark for the genre:

> The year is 1984. An acrid smoke of burning tyres and human flesh hangs over many black townships, generated by the intense internecine violence. (1996: 30)

At other times, this is leavened by the black humour and wry cynicism which the reader can expect from Mokae who describes himself as an outspoken loner and 'the only nigger without a natural sense of rhythm' (*Sunday Times*, 14 July 1996):

> Though Anikie herself had not been an active member of the movement, Maxwell's comrades have taken over the funeral. As far as the eye can see there are flags of the movement, placards, and people in the colours of the movement. Nowadays a funeral is a God-sent [sic] to the movement, an opportunity to fly its flags and sell its ideology. Sometimes different components of the liberation movement openly tussle to bury the deceased, claiming him as their staunch member...
>
> There is a sound of a high-powered car coming to a halt in the cemetery ... The sultry Mumsy Moloi comes in swinging her hips. She is wearing a sexy black number which seductively hugs her bedeviling contours. 'Now that's what I call being dressed to kill!' Major Lentswe Makena remarks to his revolted wife, Khumo. (1996: 42,43)

Mokae is unforgiving in his criticism of Maxwell Lesenjane, a political high-flyer who uses political struggle for personal gain and prestige. His indictment of those on the 'gravy train' is clear and still has currency, given the various corruption scandals which rocked South Africa in the late 1990s.

In contrast, Gordon Lesego Chasakara's novel *The Bank is My Shepherd I Shall Not Want* (1996), upholds the dubious message of self-enrichment at all costs even when ostensibly sending out an anti-corruption message in thriller form. The book's title is the message endorsed by the protagonist, Fred Pule, an ex-diamond dealer coerced into working for the top brass of the Kimberley police who are trying to smash a Peruvian diamond and drug ring: 'He believed strongly that man is a master of his own destiny. Above all he believed that the bank or money is the true saviour of mankind' (Chasakara 1996: 66). Pule and his wife, Mapula, together with a white friend Tom, find themselves on the run from a corrupt band of policemen who have self-profit on their minds. In a hectic and frequently disjointed plot, everyone is double-crossing everyone else: the high ranking policemen Major Bradford and Brigadier Voster, Pule who opens a Swiss bank account with his illegally taken 'cut' of the stash, General Calisto of Peru and the Nigerian drug lord Ukono Ekeana. The American ambassador grants Pule and co. asylum in the embassy grounds in Johannesburg and they are personally thanked for their services to the nation by the South African President.

Like Masemola in *Mixed Signals*, Chasakara chooses to use pseudonyms: South Africa is The New Republic, whilst then-President Mandela is Motho was Batho 'imprisoned for 50 years in a notorious prison called Setlhase' (121). The setting is mostly urban, downtown Johannesburg and Kimberley, the time frame presumably post-1994, and the idiom is distinctly American hard-boiled and riddled with grammatical and typographical errors. Chasakara, born in Kimberley, studied law in the USA for some years before returning to South Africa. His admiration for the American capitalist system shows in the American ambassador's reiteration of the book's title:

> 'Fred let me tell you one of my deepest beliefs as an American. You can preach to me as much as you want ... At the end of the day, "The bank is my shepherd I shall not want." '
> 'Oh whew! The good old American dollar,' Mapula laughed.
> 'Amen, sister,' the ambassador replied. (228)

Despite Chasakara's admiration for things American, the reader is left with the overwhelming impression of a 'xenophobic stance' (Ngoro 1996: 22) towards other foreign nationals, especially Nigerians, mirroring a broad South African xenophobia that is frequently commented upon in the local media:

> Nigerians, having failed to make their country an example of economic prosperity, have decided to export their culture of drugs and corruption to The New Republic and Hillbrow is their citadel. (Chasakara 1996: 38)

Denigration of Third World foreigners is frequent in the book, as is criticism of corruption in The New Republic. The corruption is seen as having a political basis in the apartheid years – 'The old apartheid rejects are still lingering, causing tremendous havoc' (48) – but the political critique is not as sustained as it is in Mokae and Masemola's thrillers. It is also flawed by the dubious moral position of the 'hero' Fred Pule who siphons off money illegally, as well as diamonds, 'as compensation for their hard work' (85). Fred Pule perhaps has something of the folkloric trickster figure about him, whose 'guile provides a psychic escape from convention while acting as a warning of anarchy' (Chapman 1989: 201), reminiscent of Arthur Maimane's creation Chester O. Morena in *Drum* magazine. However, unlike the trickster figure who gets some kind of punishment for his waywardness, Fred Pule is rewarded financially and praised as a 'national hero' (Chasakara 1996: 220) for his attempt 'at saving democracy and the rule of law in The New Republic' (233). Unusually for the thriller genre, therefore, the consolatory function whereby criminals are finally defeated as described at the beginning of this chapter is compromised.

In conclusion, if one accepts that generally popular fiction is part of a 'process of meaning creation' (Pawling 1984: 4) in society, part of the 'meaning' that can be deduced from the small wave of black thrillers in the 1990s in South Africa is that the crime story in the South African hybrid form can still provide escapism coupled with political critique. The changes noted in the various formulae from which the South African thriller draws, mark 'one process by which new interests and values can be assimilated into conventional imaginative structures' (Cawelti 1975: 35). Some of those 'new interests' may be a new black self-consciousness expressed in the black detectives tackling the urban wave of crime and corruption engulfing South Africa in the 1990s. However no society is homogenous and thus the black thrillers discussed may represent a small contradictory fragment within competing discourses. The fact that there has been a recent resurgence of this genre among some black writers speaks, however, of a developing pattern that is worth watching by popular fiction researchers.

Notes

[1] A version of this paper was given at the AFSAAP '99 (African Studies Association of Australasia and the Pacific) conference entitled 'New African Perspectives' held at the University of Western Australia, Perth in November, 1999. Thanks to Rob Turrell and Zoe Molver for comments on earlier drafts of this paper.

[2] The later short-lived black action films of the 1970s, for example *Shaft* starring Richard Roundtree, and police serials featuring black policemen, for example *Miami Vice*, can be seen as a continuation of the American B movies, placing however 'greater emphasis on threats posed by the corrupt establishment and large criminal organizations than by psychopaths and street criminals'(Rubin 1999: 145).

[3] Struan Douglas, in a recent assessment of the continuing popularity of *Drum* links Maimane firmly to the hard-boiled tradition: 'Maimane's columns, based on the antics of real life gangsters, read like Raymond Chandler crime thrillers' (*Cape Times*, 15 October 1999: 3). Even Sylvester Stein's new book on *Drum* called *Who killed Mr. Drum?* is written in the form of a 'racy comic thriller' (1999: 7) with the characteristic mix of black protagonists, politics and dark humour.

References

Barber, Karin (ed.). 1997. *Readings in African Popular Culture*. London: International African Institute, Oxford: James Currey and Bloomington: Indiana University Press.

Bell, Ian and Daldry, Graham (eds). 1990. *Watching the Detectives*. London: Macmillan.

Cawelti, John. 1976. *Adventure, Mystery and Romance: Formula Stories As Art and Popular Culture*. Chicago: University of Chicago Press.

Chapman, Michael (ed). 1989. *The Drum Decade: Stories From the 1950s*. Pietermaritzburg: University of Natal Press.

Chasakara, Gordon Lesego. 1996. *The Bank Is My Shepherd, I Shall Not Want*. Johannesburg: Gordon Lesego Chasakara.

Coan, Stephen. 1991. 'The winner that almost wasn't', *The Natal Witness* 8 November, p. 11.

D'Lovu, Nandi. 1993. *Murder By Magic*. Durban: Falcon Books.

Douglas, Struan. 1999. 'Why the Drum still beats', *Cape Times*, 15 October, pp. 3, 15.

Fabian, Johannes (1978), 'Popular Culture in Africa', in Barber (ed.), 1997: 18–28.

Lindfors, Bernth. 1991. *Popular Literatures in Africa*. Trenton, NJ: Africa World Press.

Masemola, Thabo. 1993. *Mixed Signals*. Braamfontein: Skotaville.

Mokae, Gomolemo. 1988. 'Renaissance Man' *Sunday Times Magazine* 6 September, pp. 10–11.

—— 1996. *The Secret in my Bosom*. Florida Hills: Vivlia.

—— 1996. 'Gumshoe in Africa' *Sunday Times*, 14 July, p. 13.

Munt, Sally. 1994. *Murder By the Book?* London and New York: Routledge.

Ngoro, Blackman. 1996. Review of *The Bank is My Shepherd, I Shall Not Want* in *The Sunday Independent*, 25 August, p. 22.

Oates, Joyce Carol. 1998. 'Inside the Locked Room', *New York Review of Books* 5 February.

Palmer, Jerry. 1979. *Thrillers: Genesis and Structure of a Popular Genre*. New York: St. Martin's Press.

Pawling, Christopher (ed.). 1984. *Popular Fiction and Social Change*. London and Basingstoke: Macmillan.

Peck, Richard. 1994. 'Kramer and Zondi', *Southern African Review of Books* March/April, p. 11.

—— 1997. *A Morbid Fascination: White Prose and Politics in Apartheid South Africa*. Westport: Greenwood.

Rubin, Martin. 1999. *Thrillers*. Cambridge: Cambridge University Press.

Stein, Sylvester. 1999. *Who Killed Mr Drum?* Bellville: Mayibuye-UWC.

Stiebel, Lindy. 1996. 'Black 'Tecs', *Southern African Review of Books* November/December, p. 21, www.bbc.co/uk/education/bookworm/crime.html

Primary Text 8
Excerpt from Gomolemo Mokae *The Secret in My Bosom*

Reference
Gomolemo Mokae *The Secret in My Bosom*
Florida Hills, SA: Vivlia, 1996: 81–86

Fig. 1. The cover of The Secret in My Bosom

Makena was stirring his cup of tea. He stops and looks at Lesejane. 'The good news is that I don't think you had anything to do with the death of your second wife Mumsy, my friend.'

He turns to Mpho. 'His first wife Anikie, most probably, but not his second.'

Sergeant Konyana sits forward in his chair. '*Banna*! Colonel, are you serious?' he asks incredulously. 'Then...Then that would make...I can say, that would make all our efforts a wildgoose...'

'...chase?' the Colonel laughs. 'Just as you had suspected at the airport?'

He returns to the guarded Lesejane: '"I ain't kidding you", as you Americans might say. I mean it: *I don't think you had anything to do with her death.*'

Maxwell becomes aware of the buzz of the air-conditioner in the background for the first time now. There is a deathly silence in the room, Mpho's eyes darting back and forth between Makena and Maxwell.

Lesejane shuffles in his chair, sighing softly. He is undergoing extreme mental torture.

Mpho is surprised that he is not meeting the good news with joy.

The returning political exile dips his right hand into his trousers' pocket. It comes out with a white handkerchief, and he uses it to mop the bead of sweat on his forehead.

That reminds Colonel Makena of his obligations to the golden statuette on the table.

He opens the top-most drawer of the mahogany table, finds a yellow dusting cloth, then begins polishing the statuette of a mineworker with it.

The well-built miner with a bare torso is holding a drill in his two hands, a helmet with a lamp on his head.

Konyana knows how much the Colonel values the statuette. By the time he received it from Rand Gold Mines the sergeant was already at John Vorster Square.

At its base it is engraved with the following words: '*To the miner who struck gold: Col. Lentswe Makena.*'

Makena had 'struck gold' by cracking a syndicate which specialised in purloining gold from the many mines of the RGM. The statuette was the company's 'thank you' to him. He had saved RGM millions of rands.

'If Mr Lesejane had nothing to do with the death of his wife who then did, Colonel?' the Sergeant asks, wondering if the Makena would be able to 'strike gold' this time.

'I can say, to me the way you explained how he had both the motive and opportunity to do that was convincing enough.'

Mpho scratches his head. 'I don't understand it. Why did we go to meet him at the airport then, Colonel?'

Makena returns the statuette to its hallowed place and then bursts out laughing. 'To welcome him back home of course!'

Neither of the two other men finds this funny. Actually, Makena seems to be worsening Maxwell's anguish with this mirth-making.

Makena balances his arthritic left leg with the help of his walking stick, heaves himself out of his chair.

He goes over to the left side of his office's wall, to a section of the book shelf with countless racks occupying the better part of his wood-panelled walls.

He browses about momentarily before finding what he is looking for: a bulky physics text-book.

He returns to his chair with it in his right armpit.

Maxwell's eyes pop out of their sockets battling to decipher the writing on the cover of the book.

'Why, it's only a physics text-book, my friend,' Makena chuckles. 'Remember what I told you about the small print, sergeant?'

Mpho Konyana was sipping his tea when Makena addressed him. '*Askhis* Colonel?' he begs his pardon.

'Do you remember what I told you about the importance of the small print at the airport?'

Mpho closes his eyes with his hand and lowers his head as he attempts to recall. As Makena's words come back he lifts it and is about to show the Colonel how good a student he is when Makena stops him. 'It's alright. Keep those words in mind.'

'*You should never take the small print for granted, sergeant ... It's often the small details which get criminals into trouble. Provided the police aren't as blind as bats not to see them*,' Mpho recollects the words.

He wonders what that has to do with Maxwell Lesejane's case. Is that small print in the physics book the Colonel is opening?

When Makena places the book on the table it automatically opens to a page where he had inserted a hard cardboard. An old, yellowing newspaper cutting is pasted on the board.

The Colonel takes out the cardboard, slides it against the table towards the bewildered Maxwell.

Mpho detects a slight tremor in Maxwell's right hand as it picks the board up to peruse it.

'Pass it over to the sergeant please,' Makena asks Maxwell after he has gone through it.

'Man! What's this supposed to mean?'

Mpho itches to impress the Colonel with his power of observation: the cutting is moist from what can only be Maxwell's wet palms. But unfortunately that has to wait. He sees that it is a cutting from *The Star*; the date scrawled in Makena's distinctive handwriting has faded out, but he is sure that in the Colonel's photographic memory it is etched indelibly.

The news story is headlined 'NO PEACE FOR MEN WHO HELP OTHERS R.I.P.' It reports on the woes of crematorium owners in America.

'That is what changed my mind my friend,' Makena tells Lesejane. 'My change of mind came about in a crematorium,' he jokes. 'Or rather, on reading about the troubles of crematorium owners where you come from, Mr Lesejane: the US of A.'

He pauses to let his junior finish reading the clipping, using the time to re-fill his pipe.

As he lights it, Mpho lifts his head to face his boss, curious to know the relevance of the article to the death of Maxwell's second wife, Mumsy.

The bead of sweat on Maxwell's brow has now got strung to many others all over his face. He is avoiding the Colonel's steely gaze.

According to the report, crematorium owners in the States are complaining about those of their female 'clients' who had had silicone breast implants when they were still alive. Silicone is reportedly highly heat resistant.

Since it is virtually indestructible by fire, it is a spot of bother to them, leaving debris which are a nuisance after cremation.

Sliding the open physics text-book towards Lesejane to corroborate what he is saying, Makena tells the two men that women had started having silicone implanted in their breasts for cosmetic purposes since around 1960.

Since then over two million women world-wide had had this semi-liquid, plastic-like substance placed in their breasts to improve their vital statistics.

He further informs them that the implants were initially known by the name of a similar toy manufactured by the same company, *Silly Putty*.

Lentswe Makena points at Maxwell with the stem of his pipe: 'Actually *you* should be telling me about the implants my friend. Just recently they were in the news after America's Food and Drug Administration (FDA) issued an injunction to medical practitioners in the States to suspend use of silicone implants on their patients as some complications have been reported in women who had had such cosmetic surgery. You know, complications like arthritis, seepage of material into body tissues, scarring of the skin etcetera.'

'*Ao*?' the sergeant exclaims at how well-informed the Colonel is.

'I often tell you: *Nothing is beyond Makena's ken*,' the Colonel says light-heartedly. Then he goes on to tell them that what he is most interested in is the fact that silicone is extremely heat resistant. So resistant crematorium owners in the States are beginning to grumble whenever they have to cremate any woman who had had silicone breast implants when she was still alive.

'Now,' the Colonel says slowly, hardly parting the lips clutching the pipe; 'my dear friend Mr Lesejane, you'll agree with me that most of what your late wife Mumsy got up to did not escape the media's attention. The press was simply fixated with her.'

Maxwell twitches his nose as the smoke from Makena's pipe wafts in his direction.

'Most of what she got up to, including her celebrated "boob job" to improve her whatchicall,' Makena cups his hands in front of his chest to denote a female bosom. 'Her "knockers", "headlights" etcetera.'

Lesejane gets out of his chair in irritation. He paces up and down the office.

'Man!' he shakes his head vigorously, 'do you believe everything you read in the press, Colonel? What kind of detective are you who relies on the yellow press to do the investigations for him?'

Makena stays mum, savouring his smoke.

'Earlier on you were quoting gossip columnists as your "evidence", now this? Ain't you ever gonna learn? All those stories about Mumsy doing a "boob job" were sucked from journalists' thumbs, man! They were damn fabrications!'

Makena removes the pipe from his mouth. 'Fabrications'? I wouldn't say that. Would you sergeant?'

Konyana lets out the trade-mark, forced cough, wringing his hands. 'No, Colonel, I wouldn't.'

Makena urges him to go on with his head, returning the pipe to its usual place.

'I can say,' Konyana fishes for words. 'I really didn't know the significance of it, Mr Lesejane, but I can say, the Colonel assigned me to go and interview the plastic surgeon who operated on your late wife in 1983. The ...'

Maxwell feels violated. He comes storming towards the table, bangs it furiously. 'Without *my* permission? Goddammit! Is there anything sacred to you, Colonel? How could you go behind my back to peep into my wife's confidential medical records without first obtaining my permission?'

Makena sucks his pipe pensively.

'And that stupid Dr Planck! How could he let you see the files without my permission? I could have the son-of-a-bitch struck off the roll by the Medical Council and sue the pants off you, Colonel!'

'My,' Makena chuckles, 'have you also taken to the favourite American past-time of suing, my friend?'

Konyana cannot fathom Makena's coolness in the face of a possible lawsuit.

'It's about time it took root over here to sort out shady coppers like you!' Maxwell rages. 'How dare you access Mumsy's medical files without my permission? You're going to pay hard for this, believe you me! You ain't seen nothing yet!'

'Seems like we hit a raw nerve there, Konyana,' Makena says to the sergeant softly. 'A very raw nerve indeed.'

He directs himself to Maxwell. 'Tell you what my friend, even if we had thought about obtaining your permission it wouldn't have helped. You were nowhere to be found.'

Urged on by the Colonel, Mpho Konyana informs the war-like Maxwell Lesejane that Dr Planck had confirmed that Mumsy had undergone cosmetic breast surgery in Johannesburg's Park Lane Clinic.

The plastic surgeon said she had requested the surgery to improve her bosom. 'To increase her shelf-life on the cat-walk,' Makena adds mischievously.

'Okay then, suppose that's so,' Maxwell relents grudgingly, 'so what's the big deal? Surely even in apartheid South Africa that ain't against the law!'

'Far from it, sir,' Makena smiles. 'Far from it. Actually, come to think of it, it's for the law.'

Having unwittingly found the appropriate expression, Colonel Lentswe Makena repeats with a flourish: 'It's *for* the law; it helps the law!'

He pauses to watch the impact of this on the two young men.

The younger, his colleague Mpho Konyana, is fidgeting with his tie as he tries to follow. Finally he loosens it to cool off in the summer day's heat.

Their reluctant guest from America is both angry and anxious.

Makena tells them the report in *The Star* heightened his curiosity about Mumsy's death. He remembered that she had had the same operation which was reportedly a bane to crematorium owners in the States.

'To cut a long story short,' Makena says, though he himself knows how long it has taken to come to this point. 'To cut a long story short, my friend, I have gone through the report of the state pathologist, Dr Sefanyetso, on her examination of your late wife's body. Know what? She doesn't report any silicone implants in Mumsy's body. None whatsoever.'

The Colonel steals a glance in the direction of his junior to see if he is following. Sergeant Mpho Konyana is captive.

'Now,' Makena tells Maxwell, 'as you Americans might say: "ain't that strange"?'

A pin falling on the ground could have drowned the low drone of the air-conditioner.

'*E-e-e*!' Mpho cannot believe what he is hearing. '*Ao* Colonel, you mean...'

'Either the lady who now lies buried in grave number 3470B in Avalon Cemetery isn't Mrs Mumsy Lesejane or our state forensic pathologist is inept nowadays.' Makena answers the sergeant's question before he can complete it. 'Welcome to the world of thinking detectives, sergeant!'

Maxwell is frozen to a spot near one of the office's windows, listlessly shaking his head.

Makena expands, telling them that given silicone's heat resistant property, the implants in Mumsy's breasts would have survived the intense fire of the 'necklace'. The pathologist would then have found them when she examined her charred body.

'My friend, you'll recall that the body was burnt beyond recognition. The only proof that that was Mumsy was your word. Dr Sefanyetso could only establish that the corpse found in your Beverly Hills house after the attack was female.'

'*Banna*!' Mpho mutters.

Maxwell exhales audibly, then puts on an unintimidated mien as he moves back into his chair. He challenges Colonel Makena: if it is not his second wife Mumsy who lies buried in that grave could 'Mr Wise-guy' kindly tell him who that person is? Better still, could he tell him what became of Mumsy?

'I asked you a question, Colonel!' Maxwell shouts as Makena takes time to come up with an answer. 'Goddammit! I don't believe you kept me this long to...'

'Watch your language, my friend,' Makena smiles.

'...come with such crap! Answer me Colonel: whatever became of my wife if she ain't the person we buried in that grave?'

The heat is getting to be overbearing to Mpho Konyana. He stands up, walks towards to Colonel's bar fridge to get himself a can of *Coke*.

He offers one to Makena, another to Lesejane.

'That's not his cup of tea either,' Makena observes when Maxwell declines '*the real thing*'.

The Colonel opens his and pours the better part of it down his parched throat at one go.

'There is a way to find out if Dr Sefanyetso is losing her touch or not,' Makena says, crushing the empty can of the soft-drink. 'To find out if the person in that grave is Mumsy or not.'

'You ain't gonna do that!' Maxwell stomps the ground, his pupils dilated. 'I've indulged you long enough, Colonel! I ain't gonna allow you to re-open my healed wounds, you hear?'

Like the inflamed Lesejane, sergeant Konyana has seen where Makena is leading to: the disinterment of Mrs Lesojane the second.

His suspicion that the Colonel might be onto something is increased by Maxwell's outburst. What does he have to hide?

Makena flings the squashed can of *Coke* into the trash bin near the door.

'That's called "a slam-dunk" in America, is it not, my friend?' Makena remarks when the can falls flush into the bin. Like a Michael Jordan shot.

He then aims for another 'hoop'.

He re-opens the top drawer of his table – where he took out a dusting cloth earlier on. This time he comes out with an inking pad, a bottle of Indian ink and a cloth to wipe hands with.

He places them on the table, then heaves himself up with his walking stick.

'I wasn't thinking about such a drastic way to find out the truth gentlemen,' the Colonel smiles wryly, applying the ink to the pad. 'I wasn't thinking about such a drastic action.'

'Man!' Maxwell puffs his cheeks to blow out the full air in the pit of his stomach. 'You really are off your mind!'

'You see, there's something which no amount of plastic surgery, no amount of elocution exercises, no amount of masquerade can hide gentlemen: one's finger print.'

Maxwell slumps into his chair.

'Now, if you'll indulge me only this much and no further: I have this feeling that your African-American wife Janet and your supposedly dead second wife Mumsy are one and the same...'

Colonel Makena cannot finish what he is saying.

A loud, deafening gun-shot rings out from outside his office, followed by the thud of a heavy object falling down and banging against the door.

'*Mogalammakapane*!' the Colonel exclaims in horror. Temporarily having forgotten about his arthritis, he rushes for the door without the aid of his stick.

Konyana and Maxwell fly past him as if he is stationary, the petrified Lesejane screaming out at the top of his voice: '*Mumsy*!'

Epilogue

'In a way you were right, sergeant?' Colonel Lentswe Makena whispers. 'I *was* on a wild-goose chase.' His lips break into a faint smile. 'Though I wasn't aware of it, of course.'

'But Colonel,' Mpho tries to protest but alas, Makena has already gone past him in the infinite queue of police men and women staging a guard of honour for the detective going on retirement.

The Commissioner, General Gert Steenkamp has tugged at him gently, wanting Makena beside him all the time so that he can bask in the super-sleuth's reflected glory. He prays that the photographers from the *Sunday Times* and *Rapport* will not focus only on the Colonel and the two women in the Colonel's life Mrs Khumo Makena and *Ausi* Gladys – and take him out of the shot.

The day is a warm Saturday afternoon, on 13 March 1993. The African sky is azure, shining like the medal which the commissioner earlier on stuck on Makena's chest.

But if you look carefully above, two or three clouds are coalescing.

Who knows, maybe after the ceremony has ended it will rain, the ancestors embellishing the honour that has been bestowed upon Makena. Among blacks rain is something not to be dreaded: it is seen as a blessing.

Lentswe Makena has now become General Lentswe Makena, catapulted into the sky to skirt ranks like 'Brigadier', 'Major-General' and 'Lieutenant General'.

But General Steenkamp's wide smile to the myriad of TV and newspaper cameras is not mere pretence: trying to put up a brave face whilst well aware that Makena is rising to challenge him for his post.

Yes, with the new South Africa in the horizon, Steenkamp's future in the force is in the balance. Sooner or later, Affirmative Action or political expediency will decree that a black replacement for him be found.

But Makena is not the sort to set his sights that high. Or, in his view, 'that low'.

He is happiest trudging the streets, the highways and byways. He is happiest walking around with his nose in the air like a sniffer-dog, seeking out extortionists, serial killers, pimps, robbers and other incorrigible souls.

Not for him the starched world of office bureaucracy.

Indeed, one of the main reasons why he consented to this ceremony was knowledge that he would never have to act as 'General'. This was mere symbolism – 'long-overdue honour' to his legion of admirers. It would ensure that he got to earn a pension commensurate with his long, selfless service to the force; a General's retirement package.

He had intimated to a few confidantes that he thought it was about time he worked on his golf handicap. Also, he wished to travel the world, seeing all its seven wonders.

This maverick cop also harbours dreams of using his retirement to investigate an age-old mystery which has remained insoluble to the brightest minds in the world. He wants to locate the exact spot where Noah's ark had landed on Mount Arafat [sic].

His retirement package will come in handy in pursuing some of these dreams.

That is if no other baffling case confronting the force entices him out of retirement.

For all their haggling at Kempton Park's World Trade Centre, by now most politicians in the country have come to accept that next year – 1994 – will be a crunch one. The country's first multiracial elections will have to be held then.

Negotiations cannot go on and on like Penelope's web.

It is thus not surprising to see some of the politicos mingle with the force's top brass on the podium. They wish to increase their chances in the coming elections by being seen in the company of the legendary General Lentswe Makena.

From where he is on the podium, sergeant Konyana thinks he can make out that Makena is not at home among the opportunistic politicians and senior policemen.

Just yesterday they would have put cyanide into one another's drinks. Now they are getting along – or pretending to get along – like a house on fire. The policemen want the politicians to remember them when they enter 'paradise' – when they assume political office. On the other hand the politicians know only too well that any political order without the support of the police force and army is doomed to collapse.

Mpho wonders what the General meant when he said 'in a way' he *was* on a wild-goose chase.

Has he not been vindicated when Maxwell Lesejane's devious scheme was exposed?

Poor Maxwell! He is now in that other 'Sun City'; Diepkloof prison. He is 'doing time' for having conspired to defraud his insurance company.

He will be out of circulation for an effective fifteen years. That is, if he cannot be in luck and have some big-wig argue that his crime was politically-motivated. In that case he would be able to benefit from the indemnification of political prisoners.

Makena's hunch that there was something odd about 'a comrade' calling Maxwell's house soon after the attack on his house had been proved right. Lesejane confessed that the caller was a co-conspirator from the movement, calling to find out if everything had gone on as planned.

On leaving the movement he had retained ties with one Vusi Ndlazi. Promising Vusi a share of the spoils. he had got him to organise a group of comrades who would attack his house and burn Mumsy's *Mercedes Benz*. They would then leave the charred body of a female necklace victim in the house to pass for Mumsy.

Vusi obtained the body from some employees of the government mortuary in town. It was at the height of internecine violence at the time, there were many such bodies. Most of them ended up being buried as paupers since their next of kin could not be located.

Mumsy did not live to face the music for her part in the scam.

By the time they got to her outside Makena's office, she had shot herself with a hand-gun from her bag and was already dead. Both she and her *alter ego*, Janet Lesejane, were now truly dead.

Ausi Gladys shed light on how it came about that Mumsy should take her life just as Makena was about to have her finger-printed to establish her true identity.

The remorseful tea-lady felt she could have stopped Mumsy's death if she had warned Makena on time. Bringing tea to them for the second time, she surprised Mumsy eavesdropping on their conversation in the office against the door.

That is what she had wanted to tell Makena in the office, but decided against that when it seemed Maxwell would go outside.

Makena comforted her, assuring her that even if she had stopped Mumsy from committing suicide then, she might have gone on to do that later on. Why had she made it a point of carrying a gun in her hand-bag on their return to South Africa?

Makena told *Ausi* Gladys he even strongly suspected Mumsy was the mastermind of the motor-vehicle accident that killed Maxwell's first wife, Anikie.

She was undoubtedly the brains behind her faked death.

Shortly after the Lesejanes' scam was exposed sergeant Konyana was transferred to the violence-torn East Rand. Thus he could not ask Mukena a few questions which were still bothering him about how he had solved the crime.

Now he cannot wait for the ceremony to end so that Makena can fill those lacunae in his mind.

It is about six in the afternoon when General Lentswe Makena comes walking unsteadily towards Mpho; supporting himself on his walking stick.

Mpho chuckles to himself; realising that the General's slightly ataxic gait has little to do with his arthritis. He has been unusually intemperate with the booze which has been overflowing at the function.

But what the heck, this was the General's occasion. He can be forgiven that over-indulgence.

In fact, now that he's this well-oiled, he'll be more inclined to relate how he foiled the Lesejanes' scheme; Mpho thinks.

The General beckons him to follow him to his vintage 1967 *Wolsely*; the cream white jalopy which has become almost as famous as its owner. He tells him Mrs Makena will take *Ausi* Gladys home in her car.

'Don't crack your skull trying to reckon what I meant by that wild-goose talk, sergeant,' Makena slurs, opening the driver's door. 'It's nothing serious really. Just proof that even experienced detectives can – *and do* – make mistakes.'

Mpho is lost.

'In my mind I was chasing "the gander" – Maxwell – but you were right, "the goose" was the main architect of this scheme,' Makena expands, then guffaws. Mpho joins in the laughter.

Lentswe leans over to open the front passenger door for Konyana from inside. As Mpho gets in the General shoves a bulky file which he has taken from the dashboard, into the sergeant's arms.

'Here, I've got something for you my boy: a baton none of my children or grand-children will accept from me.'

Makena tells him the file is full of some of the major cases he has investigated during his long career. The successes and indeed, the failures. Even great detectives sometimes fail to bring criminals to book.

Mpho is ecstatic when he hears that Makena's labour of love is among the cases: how he caught the rogues who had kidnapped his twin brother Lentswê over three decades later.

'You'll have all the time in the world to study those cases, sergeant,' Makena says, noting the dark clouds forming in the sky. 'It'll be raining quite soon. As you know, I don't like driving in the rain. Nor at night, for that matter. It's already late.'

'*Ja* Colon...' Mpho stops in mid-sentence, smiling coyly. '*Askhis*... General.'

'Titles! Titles! Who cares?' Makena asks rhetorically, filling his pipe. 'As far as I'm concerned they can keep all those titles. It's results I'm most interested in. Now,' he places the pipe between his lips. 'I imagine there are some points about the Lesejane case which are still unclear to you?'

The reluctant General lights his pipe, glancing at the starry-eyed young policeman.

Makena relates that when they went to meet Maxwell at the airport he had not even suspected Lesejane would be coming back with Mumsy masquerading as Janet, his African-American wife. All he wished to do was establish whether the state forensic pathologist had indeed missed the silicone implants in the corpse or not. If she had not, was Mumsy still alive?

He wanted to confront Maxwell with the evidence that silicone was fire resistant, thus the implants would not have been destroyed when Mumsy was 'necklaced'.

The line of questioning thereafter would be determined by Lesejane's response.

But when he heard the putative African-American Janet inadvertently exclaim in Sesotho '*Ijoo*!' his plan of action changed. He began to suspect that Mumsy and Janet might be one and the same person.

'*Ao* Colo ... I mean General? Did she really say that?'

Lentswe Makena goes off at a tangent. He tells Mpho Konyana about the days when he was working as a sergeant in the cosmopolitan, now-defunct Johannesburg township of Sophiatown. About the introduction of the Dompas, the reviled identity document for Africans.

There were many Africans who 'played coloured' to avoid the *dompas* – mulattoes were exempted from that humiliating task. Also, relative to Africans, these people of mixed blood were generally well-off.

Officialdom thus devised some mechanisms to separate real 'coloureds' from impostors. One was to pinch the offspring of parents suspected of 'playing coloured'. If the children cried out in Sesotho: '*Yo mmawe*!' they were deemed African, and coloured if they exclaimed in Afrikaans: '*Eina*!'

'I know there's an intense passion to hook up with Africa among our African-American cousins, Konyana. But I don't think that connection has come to a stage where some of them can exclaim in our mother-tongues in pain. Or disbelief,' Makena informs Mpho.

'What automatically comes to one's mouth during those times is the language sucked from your mother's bosom.'

General Makena tells Konyana that 'Janet' had yelled that way at the airport, when she heard that they wanted Maxwell to come along with them to the Square.

Konyana hazily remembers the incident: Makena staring open-mouthed with amazement at 'Janet' after she had said something that Mpho had missed. His mind had wandered off, thinking about how far Makena might have gone in the force were it not for prejudice against him.

Makena playfully twists Mpho's ears, points at his eye and wrings his nose: 'Use these, these and this!'

Konyana laughs.

'That's why I was using my eyes to confirm what I had heard on our way to the Square, Konyana,' the General owns up. 'It's not as if I didn't see you keep on glancing at me in the rear-view mirror. The bat that you are, you probably thought I wanted to turn myself into Mrs Lesejane's "sugar-daddy"!'

Konyana cups his mouth in embarrassment. That is exactly what went through his mind as he noticed Makena's fixation with Maxwell's companion.

'But I guess by the time we got to the Square and Mrs Lesejane desperately wanted to come into the office with Maxwell even a blind man of Jericho like you could see red?'

At least that Mpho had noticed. He had wondered why 'Janet' was insisting on coming in as well.

It has now begun to drizzle.

Makena extends an open right hand towards the young policeman. 'So long, my son; it's time to go now.'

Mpho does not reciprocate the gesture. 'Not if you don't want to turn me into the envy of all policemen, General,' Mpho giggles. 'I can say, you want me to arrest a whole General for drunken driving? Remember, sir, DON'T DRINK AND DRIVE!'

'Tell me about it,' Makena responds quietly. He is slightly embarrassed that he has been caught out.

'Now, General, if you'll kindly shift over to this side and I'll come over to drive you home,' Mpho alights to turn around. 'It'll be a great honour to take you home, sir!' he snaps to attention outside in the rain, saluting the General.

A lightning flashes, illuminating General Lentswe Makena's wide grin.

'I knew I wasn't making a mistake handing over that file to you, sergeant. None of my descendants will have it. The damn fools, they all think the force is only for idiots with single-digit IQs. You have the makings of a top-notch cop, sergeant.'

The fair-complexioned policeman blushes. 'Coming from you, General, that's a great compliment indeed!'

The sergeant is beginning to master the indestructable *Wolsely*, its tyres hold firmly to the wet tarmac.

'So you see, sergeant,' Makena slurs, battling to resist the inviting arms of Morpheus, 'Mrs Lesejane's nemesis was the secret in her bosom. The open secret in her bosom.'

Index